RibbonX

RibbonX

Customizing the Office 2007 Ribbon

Robert Martin
Ken Puls
Teresa Hennig

Wiley Publishing, Inc.

RibbonX: Customizing the Office 2007 Ribbon

Published by
Wiley Publishing, Inc.
10475 Crosspoint Boulevard
Indianapolis, IN 46256
www.wiley.com

Published simultaneously in Canada

ISBN: 978-0-470-19111-8

Manufactured in the United States of America

10 9 8 7 6 5 4 3 2 1

For general information on our other products and services or to obtain technical support, please contact our Customer Care Department within the U.S. at (800) 762-2974, outside the U.S. at (317) 572-3993 or fax (317) 572-4002.

Library of Congress Cataloging-in-Publication Data is available from the publisher.

To all of those who made this possible.

— Robert Martin

For my daughter, Annika.
I'm sure you'll have this mastered by next year.

— Ken Puls

I dedicate my work to the very special people in my life.

I am blessed to have such wonderful family and friends with whom I share my adventures, excitement, and joy of new challenges.

Life is full of opportunities; we should celebrate them all.

I also dedicate this book to everyone who is adventuring into the world of Ribbon customizations. I am privileged to help you on your journey.

— Teresa Hennig

About the Authors

Robert Martin holds a postgraduate degree in finance and economics from the University of London. He has worked as IT Director for FairCourt Capital in the U.K., and has done pro bono work with some African charities, such as NIDOE (Nigerians in Diaspora Organisation Europe and Africa 2000). He is the author of *Excel and VBA in Financial Modeling: A Practical Approach,* and has authored many eBooks on MS Office development. He currently works as an independent IT consultant.

Robert has also run one of the most popular Excel forums in Brazil since 2004, which led to his MVP award in 2006 for helping develop the Microsoft Office community in Brazil. He is also a moderator in the Microsoft Technet forums in Brazil.

Ken Puls has worked at Fairwinds Community & Resort on Vancouver Island, British Columbia, for over eight years. In his dual role as an accountant and the only IT support person on staff, Ken was exposed to a vast number of business systems, including point-of-sale systems, databases, and analysis tools. During his tenure with Fairwinds, Ken has led the installation of over a dozen systems conversions of various types, and become addicted to Microsoft Excel. Ken currently holds the position of controller, and continues to focus his efforts in supporting Fairwinds' property development, golfing, and sailing lifestyle. More about Fairwinds can be discovered at `www.fairwinds.ca`.

Ken has also worked as a freelance Microsoft Office developer, mainly in Excel, but also with Access, Word, and Outlook. In addition, he has taught several Excel training courses in his local area. He has been an active participant in many Web forums since 2002, and in recognition of his contributions to the online community was awarded the prestigious Microsoft Most Valuable Professional award in October 2006. He hosts a website at `www.excelguru.ca`, which provides code samples for working with Excel and other Microsoft Office applications; as well as a blog at `www.excelguru.ca/blog`. The blog holds much of his exploratory work with the Ribbon, including customizing it.

Ken has held the Certified Management Accountant (CMA) designation since 2000.

Teresa Hennig loves challenges, solving problems, and making things happen. Her company, Data Dynamics NW, reflects her dynamic personality and her innate ability to quickly grasp a situation and formulate a solution. With a strong background in both the private and public sector, covering a wide spectrum of industries, Teresa provides both consulting and database development to optimize the processing, integration, and utilization of data. Her emphasis is on designing cost-effective solutions tailored to meet current and projected needs.

In recognition of her expertise and dedication to the Access community, Teresa has again been awarded Microsoft Access MVP (Most Valuable Professional) status. She continues to serve as president of both the Pacific Northwest Access Developer Groups (PNWADG) and the Seattle Access Group. Since 2005, Teresa has served on several of INETA's national committees to provide service, information, and support to user groups around the world. Her extensive writing experience includes being the lead author for the *Access VBA Programmer's Reference* series and contributing to several other books. She also publishes two monthly Access newsletters and two Access websites, `www.DataDynamicsNW.com` and `www.SeattleAccess.org`.

Teresa is passionate about helping and empowering others, both professionally and personally. One of her most notable charitable activities was developing a paperless patient tracking database for a teen clinic in Uganda and then spending nine days at the clinic to deploy the system and train the staff. She also climbed to the summit of Mt. Rainier, raising $5,000 for the American Lung Association. In addition, in honor of her brother, she rode 220 miles on a bike to raise $10,000 for the Spinal Cord Society's research to cure paralysis.

Oliver Stohr was born in Germany, but moved permanently to the United States in 2003, where he currently lives with his wonderful wife, Bonnie, and their cat and mini-dachshund, in Maryland. At present, he is a full-time student at the University of Maryland working toward his undergraduate degree in computer science.

Oliver has been working with computers from a very young age and started using Microsoft products with the release of Windows 3.1. He has provided service to online discussion forums, answering more than 25,000 technical questions. His involvement has earned him a moderator status at UtterAccess forums as well as a prestigious Microsoft Most Valuable Professional award. Oliver was also the technical editor for *Expert Access 2007 Programming* and is the owner and webmaster of `www.access-freak.com`. Since it was launched, the site has helped thousands of users of Microsoft Access make the transition from earlier versions to the new 2007 edition.

Credits

Executive Editor
Robert Elliott

Senior Development Editor
Tom Dinse

Technical Editors
Jeff Boyce
Nick Hodge

Production Editor
William A. Barton

Copy Editor
Luann Rouff

Editorial Manager
Mary Beth Wakefield

Production Manager
Tim Tate

Vice President and Executive Group Publisher
Richard Swadley

Vice President and Executive Publisher
Joseph B. Wikert

Project Coordinator, Cover
Lynsey Stanford

Compositors
Craig Woods and Craig Thomas, Happenstance Type-O-Rama

Proofreaders
Jennifer Larsen, Amy Watson, Word One

Indexer
Robert Swanson

Anniversary Logo Design
Richard Pacifico

Contents

Acknowledgments

We'll start by thanking everyone who helped research, write, test, and refine our material. We began as a team of two Excel and one Access MVPs, and later recruited Oliver Stohr, Access MVP, to write the Access deployment section. We send a tremendous note of appreciation to Oli for stepping up and sharing his expertise. In addition, because the book covers three, not just two applications, we also enlisted the expertise of two Word MVPs. Therefore, we send a special thanks to Tony Jollans, for always responding to our inquiries and assisting whenever we asked, and to Cindy Meister, for writing the macro to update all the document fields. But writing is just the first stage in the journey. We relied on our remarkable team of technical editors, Jeff Boyce (Access MVP) and Nick Hodge (Excel MVP), to check and challenge our writing. They each added a particular expertise to the book. Jeff's incessant questions may have threatened to drive us crazy, but they ensured that we provided ample background when introducing new material so that users of any level could understand and work through the examples. Nick's contributions went far above and beyond his role. His fingerprints are all over the book, and it truly would not be what it is without him.

Nor would we have this book if it weren't for the great people at Wiley. We had the great fortune of working with Tom Dinse as our development editor. In addition to making sure that our material was consistent, properly sequenced, and fit the guidelines, Tom went out of his way to get answers and find ways to make things work. And Luann Rouff, our copy editor, was remarkably attentive formatting and our deadlines—definitely not an 8 – 5 worker! We also send a very special thanks to Bob Elliott for his expertise in shaping the proposal and working through the administrative processes. We thank Colleen Hauser for inviting us to participate in designing the cover. There are many others, even those that we haven't yet met, who deserve our appreciation and thanks for helping to take this book from a concept to reality.

Writing this book has been a challenging and incredibly rewarding experience. It was only possible with the help of dozens of people and by pulling together as a team. Thank you, all!

— The Authors

I thank my girlfriend for putting up with me during a very stressful period.

— Robert Martin

I'd like to thank my wife, Deanna, and my boss and friend, Jim Olsen, for their encouragement, support, and the latitude they have given me to pursue my quest for knowledge. Without these two people behind me, none of this would have ever been possible.

— Ken Puls

I want to say what a great privilege it has been to work with Robert and Ken. They poured out the pages and maintained wonderful humor as I tried to meld everything together into a consistent voice and style. Thank you, guys, so very much; coordinating this book and working on a truly international team is another opportunity that I shall cherish forever. In addition, I can't adequately express my appreciation for Oli. When we needed very special expertise, Oli responded and immediately set to work on the Access deployment section. I also have to send a personal thank-you to Bob Elliott and Tom Dinse. I feel incredibly fortunate that you were both guiding our way.

My family and very special friends have my heartfelt appreciation for encouraging and "being with me" through my adventures, and I send a tremendous thanks to my clients for hanging in there when it seemed that I barely had time to take their calls. Most of all, I want to thank my mom, my papa, and my dad for being the caring people and stellar citizens that they are. Three of their sayings come to mind, and I'm sure that they will ring true with you: "Your word is your honor"; "A job worth doing is worth doing right"; and "Do what you enjoy, and you'll be good at it."

— Teresa Hennig

Introduction

Welcome to the wonderful world of Ribbon customizations. With the advent of Office 2007, users and developers alike are faced with major transitions. Office applications have a whole new look, and the Ribbon is the headliner. While it may have strong appeal to new users, adapting to the Ribbon can be challenging to those of us who are accustomed to the legacy menu and toolbar system. With the advent of the Ribbon, you not only lose the drop-down menus that were always there, but the custom menus and toolbars have also departed. However, we are not stuck with Microsoft's Ribbon which can appear overwhelming with thousands of commands; and you don't need advanced training or mastery of coding languages to tailor the Ribbon to your needs.

That's where this book comes in. Driven by their passion for helping others to enjoy and maximize the experience of working with Office applications, the team of authors has created a resource that enables both users and developers to customize the Ribbon to the extent that they desire. Whether that means replacing the Ribbon with familiar toolbars from prior versions, using photos and labels to personalize commands, or merely creating custom groups of existing tools, the book provides instructions and working examples so that you have the tools and confidence to accomplish your goals. Not only that, but the task can be accomplished using XML and VBA, so there is no need to purchase expensive software or learn complicated programming languages.

You will see that customizing the Ribbon can be fun and rewarding. If you are a developer, you will be empowering users to work more efficiently and you will have new opportunities to tailor both the functionality and the look to specific solutions. Power users will appreciate creating time-saving commands that can easily be shared with associates. In addition, if you are creating customizations for your own purposes, you will enjoy the latitude to truly personalize the appearance of the commands as you structure them for your convenience.

In addition to walking you through the stages for customizing the Ribbon, we also demonstrate how to work with legacy tools. Each chapter presents various options, along with their benefits and drawbacks, so that you can make informed plans and decisions.

Overview of the Book and Technology

Programming and customizing the Ribbon requires a new set of skills, and because the Ribbon is not compatible with previous custom menus and toolbars, developers and power users will immediately begin to seek ways to customize the Ribbon. We are all faced with the choice of either working with the standard Ribbon, replacing the Office Ribbon with a custom Ribbon, or foregoing the Ribbon and installing custom menus and toolbars from previous applications.

RibbonX: Customizing the Office 2007 Ribbon has two key target audiences. The obvious one is power users and developers working in Excel, Access, and Word. However, because average users continue to expand their ability to control their environment, the examples are presented so that a typical user will also be able to work through and implement the processes in total confidence. Therefore, in addition to providing key tips and techniques that developers expect, this book also contains sufficient introductory materials to enable any user to follow the examples and begin to benefit from the efficiencies that can be obtained with a customized Ribbon.

By the time you finish this book and the demo projects, you will have both the knowledge and confidence to customize the Ribbon for the three major components in Office: Excel, Access, and Word. Although the customization process is pretty much the same for the XML code, that doesn't mean the steps are the same for each application — so we scrupulously point out the similarities and differences.

RibbonX: Customizing the Office 2007 Ribbon concentrates on the following:

- XML development for Ribbon customization
- Using VBA to add functionality to the custom UI

We are sure that readers will enjoy this book and find it extremely useful as a reference tool for UI customization. It will certainly change the way that one views the new Office UI.

How This Book Is Organized

RibbonX is sure to become the definitive guide to customizing the Ribbon for Excel, Access, and Word. The book is a major resource for power users and developers. It covers the basics in enough detail that even if this is your introduction to writing code, you will learn what you need to know, understand the concepts, and be able to develop and share custom Ribbons and Ribbon components that best suit your needs or those of the intended user.

The material and examples are created using Excel, Access, and Word. We identify when the same procedure applies to all three programs, and we point out any differences among them. The chapters are filled with real-world examples and sample code, so readers will immediately be able to apply their new skills. In many cases, a separate example is used to demonstrate how to incorporate the same feature into each application: Excel, Access, and Word.

The following is a brief summary of what each chapter covers. Although you may not recognize some of the terminology yet, be assured that comprehensive explanations are provided as material is introduced. We also leverage notes, cross-references, and other notes to guide you to reference material and points of particular interest.

To help you build a solid foundation, we start with some background material, covering essential programming processes that you'll need to be familiar with. Chapter 1 discusses the user interface and points out some of the challenges associated with transitioning from menus to the Ribbon, as well as some of the benefits gained with the new UI. Chapter 2 briefly introduces the key components for customizations and how to work with them. You'll learn about XML files, the Office Custom UI Editor, and the USysRibbon table.

In Chapter 3, we lay the foundation for working with XML and explain the various containers that we'll be using — namely, the `ribbon`, `tabs`, `tab`, and `group` containers. Because this is the first time that developers have been required to use XML with their projects, this chapter will be a handy reference to turn to as you work through subsequent chapters and exercises.

Chapter 4 covers the essentials for working with Visual Basic for Applications code (VBA). If you are an experienced developer, you may breeze right past this chapter, but readers new to programming will learn what they need to know to create successful customizations, including how to work with arrays.

Next, in Chapter 5, we introduce callbacks, which are essentially the hook between the commands on the Ribbon and the code that needs to run. We also explain the processes for invalidating commands and the Ribbon. (*Invalidation* is a frequently used term throughout the book, so it's important to understand what it is and how it works.)

After that, we start creating new controls. In Chapter 6, you will actually create custom Ribbon commands, beginning with the most common command, the `button`. We walk you through creating a `button`, `checkBox`, `editBox`, and `toggleButton`.

Then, in Chapter 7, we explain container controls and show you how to create them. Container controls, which can hold other controls, include the `splitButton`, the `item`, the `comboBox`, and the `dropDown` control.

Then the creativity really gets to flow in Chapter 8. That's where you learn how to use the icon gallery and add highly personalized touches, such as including custom images in the Ribbon commands.

From there, we move to on to the menu controls in Chapter 9. These are powerful controls, such as the Save As control, that can contain a combination of controls and labels. This means that in addition to creating the controls themselves, you'll become accomplished at formatting the controls to add groupings and clarity.

Chapter 10 provides additional formatting tools, such as the `box` element, which essentially creates an invisible box for grouping controls. After that, we demonstrate how to place a visible box around a group of controls by using the `buttonGroup`. To complement these groups, we show you how to use the `labelControl` to add a heading or a description of other controls. Of course, boxes are not always the ticket, and sometimes just a line is preferable. That's when you'd use the `Separator` element or the `menuSeparator` element to insert either a vertical line or a horizontal line, respectively.

That brings us to the last chapter of our fundamentals section. Chapter 11 covers features that provide that extra level of assistance needed to have highly intuitive user interfaces. It also shows you how to make custom help and tips available when users need them the most. This includes attributes such as the `keytip`, the `screentip`, and the `supertip`. We cap it off by showing you how to modify built-in controls.

The next portion of the book deals with advanced concepts. This starts with Chapter 12, which teaches you some advanced VBA techniques that enable you to work with multiple controls at one time. After explaining collections, we demonstrate how to use properties, methods, and events. Then, as somewhat of a bonus, we'll show you how quick and easy it is to incorporate Web services right into your UI, thereby bringing online resources to the user's fingertips.

With all this material under your belt, you are ready to get rid of the Ribbon and literally "start from scratch." That's actually the name of the attribute that removes the built-in Ribbon and commands from the UI. Of course, it isn't as drastic as it might sound, because the Office button and several other commands are still available through shortcuts. Chapter 13 covers all of that and demonstrates how to build a completely custom Ribbon.

However, that isn't the end, because the Ribbon also introduced the Quick Access Toolbar (QAT). The QAT is probably the closest thing on the Ribbon to what we fondly remember as toolbars; and the QAT was designed to do exactly what the name implies, to provide users with instant access to the tools that they most often use. Because the QAT is not context sensitive, the tools are always in the same place. Chapter 14 provides detailed steps for working with and organizing the QAT.

With the Ribbon, the QAT is just the tip of the iceberg when it comes to putting controls at the user's fingertips. We take this to the next level in Chapter 15, where you learn how to create context-sensitive tabs, groups, and controls. These powerful little tools are the best replacement for custom pop-ups. In addition to creating new contextual tabs, we also show you how to modify built-in contextual tables. With those skills, the choice is yours: either start fresh or merely tweak and add to what is provided.

After we've pretty much covered the gamut of customizations, it is time to turn our attention to sharing our solutions. Chapter 16 discusses the issues associated with preparing files and packaging them for deployment. This chapter includes detailed guidance about the reasoning behind the process and walks you through the steps for each application. In addition to deploying complete solutions, we also explore the final RibbonX attribute: The `idQ` is geared toward sharing elements across files, and it enables users to load and unload Ribbon customizations from a central source.

The final chapter in the book, Chapter 17, explains the security issues that can affect creating, using, and sharing Ribbon customizations. We explain some of the rationale for various security measures, as well as how they can impact your development work and the end user. You also learn about macro-enabled and macro-free file formats, trust centers, and trusted locations. In addition, of course, we share recommendations for providing steps to ensure that users have the appropriate security settings and are still able to enjoy the benefits provided by your customization efforts.

To cap everything off, we include appendixes of reference material so that readers have everything they need at their fingertips. Appendixes cover such topics as naming conventions, and list the correct names for groups, tabs, and other necessary objects in the Ribbon and application hierarchies.

As you can see, this book is everything that we said it would be. It provides the information that you need to immediately achieve results, and it will become an invaluable reference for future projects.

Why Read This Book

This book addresses issues that are daunting multitudes of developers and end users alike. It provides the information and examples that will prepare you to create and share intuitive custom UIs, and it demonstrates the options available for working with legacy custom menus and toolbars.

RibbonX: Customizing the Office 2007 Ribbon is a one-stop reference for anyone who wants to customize the Ribbon. With that goal in mind, it not only works through customizing the Ribbon, but also covers related material. That means the book discusses the basics for working with VBA, XML, and macros. In addition, because macros and VBA trigger Windows security settings, the book also reviews relevant aspects of security, such as trust centers and digital certificates. It also explains issues and processes associated with preparing and packaging customizations for deployment in target environments, including detailed instructions for deploying Access run-time installations.

Whether you are an end user, a seasoned Office developer, or somewhere in between, this book is the perfect reference for customizing and programming the Ribbon.

Tools You Will Need

One of the beauties of this book is that if you have Office 2007, you've already made the prerequisite purchase. That's because we leverage the XML and VBA capabilities that are intrinsic to Microsoft Office 2007, and the additional tools that are available as free downloads from Microsoft. Therefore, contrary to common perception, you can customize the Ribbon without purchasing expensive developer software, such as Visual Studio Tools for Office, and without learning complicated coding languages such as C#.

Your customizations will run on essentially all installations of Office 2007. They can be developed and deployed on both Windows Vista and Windows XP platforms, and it matters little whether these are standard installations or are on virtual machines.

In short, essentially anyone with Office 2007 will be able to work through the numerous examples for Excel, Access, and Word.

What's on the Website

In addition to the material provided in the book, the chapters are supplemented by sample files that can be downloaded from the book's website, `www.wiley.com/go/ribbonx`. We strongly encourage you to download the files and use them as you work through the exercises.

The online files are invaluable resources that not only provide working demonstrations of the material being covered, but also serve as an ultra-handy source for code snippets. In addition to studying the code in the text, you can use the downloads to view the XML and VBA in their native formats, and you can copy it directly into your own projects.

Some of the files are also nice bonuses in and of themselves. For example, in Appendix C, not only do we provide the source code and file, but our example is actually a fully functional tool that will locate, group, and display the `imageMSO` for each application. Although you may not realize the value of that yet, you soon will — when you discover that the `imageMSO` is an integral part of Ribbon customizations. Robert's tool in Appendix C is just one example of how the authoring team has taken extra steps to provide you with the information and resources that you'll need.

Congratulations

We are excited about the opportunity to help fellow developers and end users to customize the Ribbon and create solutions that are both personalized and enhance productivity. You will likely be surprised by how easy it is to create customizations, not only for your own use, but also to share with others.

An exciting bonus for end users is that in addition to customizing your work environment, you will be expanding your horizons, adding new programming skills, and building the confidence to take on bigger and more challenging projects.

We recommend that as you go through the book, you download the sample files so that you can see it in its native environment, see how a finished example will work, and experiment with changes. Working through the exercises will enable you to take ownership of the concepts and incorporate them into your customizations.

Learn, enjoy, be creative. Build solutions that work for you.

Part I

The Building Blocks for a Successful Customization

In This Part

CHAPTER

1

An Introduction to the Office User Interface

When you open Office 2007, you are welcomed by a totally new user interface (UI). Although the new UI brings immediate productivity improvements to new Office users, it can take a few days or weeks for experienced Office users to adapt to and become fluent with the new interface. But it is definitely worth the investment to get up to speed with the new UI, particularly the Ribbon. Knowing what to expect and understanding the logic behind the Ribbon will make life much easier.

This chapter is designed to familiarize you with the Ribbon so that you can understand how to work with it from the perspective of an end user as well as from the perspective of a power user and developer. There are such dramatic changes to the UI that we highly recommend that even power users and developers read through this introductory chapter. It provides an important foundation, as it explains the Ribbon's background.

As you are preparing to work through the examples, we encourage you to download the companion files. The source code and files for this chapter can be found on the book's web site at `www.wiley.com/go/ribbonx`.

What Is the Ribbon and Why Does It Exist?

Office 2007 has been given a face-lift! And what a makeover! For those who got used to the old toolbars, the new UI can be a tremendous shock. However, as you learn the new interface, you will start to appreciate its benefits and, hopefully, embrace it as we and countless of others have done.

Microsoft invested a significant amount of time and money in the creation of the new Ribbon interface. Millions of dollars were spent tracking user trends, including how people actually used the Office applications and their underlying hierarchical menus. They studied where users were going, what commands they used, and in which order. They even tracked eye movement to see where people tend to look first to find a command. The results were used to develop the Ribbon.

The introduction of hierarchical menus was a great leap from the top-level menu style. One factor prompting its development was that top-level menus were running out of space for additional commands for the new features as they were added to an application. With the introduction of hierarchical menus, more room was available for the new commands being created. What this meant, of course, was an increase in the number of features displayed from one version to another.

But just as there is no free lunch in economics, there is no free lunch with such an approach. As the number of features increased, it became more difficult to actually find them due to the increased complexity of the UI.

If you think back to the very first versions of Word, for example, there was really no hierarchy as such. It had the top-level menu, and a user could quickly scan its contents for the needed feature. By the time we reached Word 97, things had changed dramatically and problems with the UI started to appear. At this point, the future started to look bleak for the hierarchical order. A change in paradigm became necessary. It was no longer a matter of whether it would happen, but rather when it would happen.

Problems with the Old UI

As the UI moved from top-level to hierarchical menus, things started to get out of control and people were frequently searching for commands. It was often so challenging to find a command that most users had difficulty in locating desired options, or perhaps worse, they would give up on trying to find something that they knew was there.

Take for example the Insert ➪ AutoText ➪ Header/Footer hierarchy in Word 2003, shown in Figure 1-1.

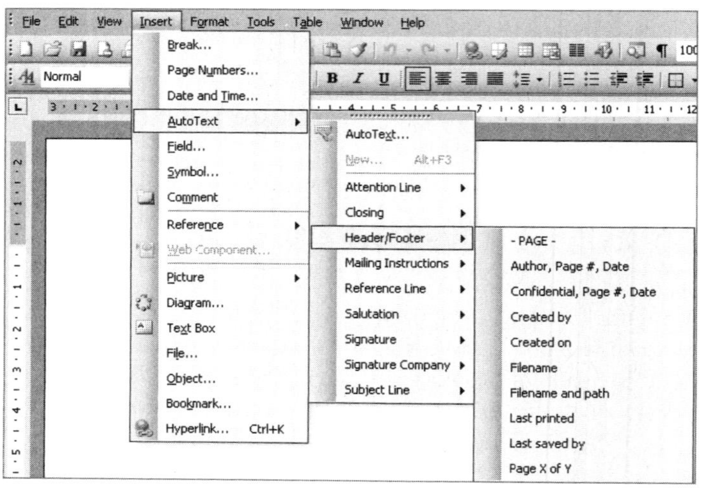

Figure 1-1: Hierarchical menu in Word 2003

Chances are good that unless you're very experienced with Word, you would have never known that this option even existed. Hence, we end up with a huge dilemma on our hands: We have a feature-rich application, but just a portion of these features are being used because they are buried under extensive branching and a burdensome hierarchy.

Thus, not only are many features unused, but it also becomes cumbersome for experienced users to keep track of things under such scenarios. Users are all too familiar with the frustration of wasting time hunting for the command to execute a needed feature.

Microsoft tried to address this issue when it became obvious back in Office 97. With Office 2000, they introduced the concept of *adaptive menus*. The idea was that the top-level menu would be shorter and only show the features that the user accessed most frequently. This selection process would translate into a UI that reflected a user's true daily needs instead of presenting dozens of commands that he never used and did not care about.

For anyone who was a bit more fluent in the UI from Office 97, this new feature actually became a hindrance. And for new users, it translated into frustration. Ultimately, a lot of users were switching off this feature and leaving the menus to show in full instead of relying on the adaptive menus technology to figure out and create a UI tailored to their actions.

To make matters worse, the introduction of full menu customization meant that users could move toolbars around, dock them in some silly place, float them on the screen, close them altogether, and perform a whole bunch of other actions such as adding and removing controls from the toolbars and menus at will. This may look great from the point of view of a power user or programmer, but the world is not made up of power users and programmers alone. Not everyone is technically savvy and this had to be taken into account too.

As anyone who has had to work the help desk for Office applications knows, many end users would close toolbars, never to find them again. In addition, users were prone to float toolbars, impairing their ability to see the document. At that point, the user would become frustrated and call the help desk with a complaint. Of course, the help desk staff and many developers might be astounded that someone would do these things — and then admit it. But we've all heard hilarious stories about the CD tray breaking under the weight of a coffee cup, so as crazy as the stories sound, they're true, and they provide valuable information to developers — one of which is that features need to be as clear and intuitive as possible.

Because of the confusion and difficulties the average user could experience, it was obvious that something had to be done. The support calls and other challenges triggered the overhaul of the UI as we knew it. A paradigm shift seemed more and more necessary.

With the release of Office 2007, the new Office Fluent UI was provided to address such issues. However, as might be anticipated with such a dramatic change, it can be met with resistance from those who are familiar and comfortable with the old ways. In addition, it has created new challenges for power users and developers who want to deliver a custom UI.

This book tackles the issues in a manner that will be comfortable for and will benefit all levels of users and developers. If you are a beginner, you will love this book because you learn the fundamentals and will be able to customize your own workspace. If you are a power user, you will love this book because you will be able to work more efficiently by customizing and sharing your Ribbon components. And if you are a developer, you will also love this book because you will be able to leverage your custom components, work across multiple applications, incorporate third-party tools, and deploy contemporary solutions.

So, it's time to discuss the old issues addressed by the new UI as well as the new issues that were created by it.

Issues Solved with the New UI

What came out of the massive budget and research on Microsoft's part when it was manifested in the Ribbon? Many painful problems in the old user interface were solved, including the following:

- **Lack of context:** Wouldn't it be nice to have the controls you need displayed when you need them? That's what contextual controls are all about. In the older versions of the applications, all commands were buried somewhere — but not necessarily where users would intuitively expect them to be. In addition, only a few features (Pivot Tables and Charts in Excel, for example,) had contextual commands that would display when the feature was being used. In the new UI format, Microsoft attempts to be much more contextual, and to present commands in a way that is consistent with what their research indicated would be the next logical step. Contextual controls are discussed in Chapter 15.
- **Command accessibility:** Microsoft seems to have put in a huge amount of effort to make the commands more "discoverable" to new and less familiar users. In fact, even power users will discover commands that they didn't know existed in prior versions. Commands have been logically grouped together, which was not always the case in the past. In addition, many features that used to be buried and difficult to find have been moved to the front lines.
- **Customizations left behind:** One of the major pain points in Office 2003 and prior versions was that a poorly designed customization could leave parts of the UI customizations exposed when a file was closed. For example, they might inadvertently change the default menu and toolbars for the user's applications, possibly hiding or removing commands and toolbars — and many users would not know how to recover them. These problems are all gone now, thanks to the new UI format. The customizations are specific to the container files. As soon as you navigate away from a file that contains customization code, the customizations disappear in the UI. Close your file or even navigate to a new one and the customizations are tossed until you return. While you can share customizations across files via add-ins, global templates, and shared workspaces, the fundamental rule still remains that when that file is closed, the custom UI is unloaded with it. Unlike prior versions, no hangovers are left behind to haunt users.
- **Corrupted toolbars:** By virtue of not having toolbars to customize, the whole problem of corrupted toolbars has disappeared. The disappearance of this feature may seem like a curse for many, but in fact many of these files were quite fragile and could cost users countless hours to rebuild. Because all customizations are now built right in to the file, they also go with the file when it is sent to a new location, eliminating any worry about how the UI will be transferred or shared. The secret to building your own custom UI for users everywhere now becomes the task of building a much more stable add-in or global template, and that is what this book will teach you how to do.

Issues Created with the New UI

While the new user interface has undoubtedly solved many of the issues that were present in previous versions of Microsoft Office, it has naturally created some new ones that we must deal with. But, hey, this is a new technology and as with any new technology it will need to be adapted and improved along the way.

One drawback (and the most immediately obvious one) about the Ribbon is that it takes up a lot of screen space, which, in itself, can defeat the purpose of giving the user a full experience of the Ribbon's potential. Therefore, the higher the resolution of your screen, the more you will enjoy and benefit from your experience with the Ribbon.

Figure 1-2 shows the Ribbon on a screen with a lower resolution. Some of the groups are collapsed; therefore, it is not possible to know what commands these groups contain until they are expanded.

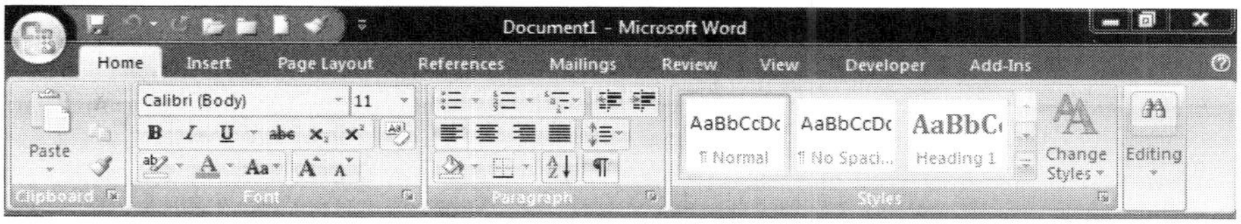

Figure 1-2: Lower resolutions or minimized windows force Ribbon groups to collapse.

> **NOTE** Resizing the window to a smaller size will cause the groups to collapse. The UI has four types of groups (large, medium, small, and collapsed) that come into play when the window is resized or when you're working in a lower-resolution environment.

A screen with a higher resolution, as shown in Figure 1-3, provides a greater visible area of the Ribbon, so the groups are all nicely displayed (compare the Styles group in Figure 1-2 and Figure 1-3).

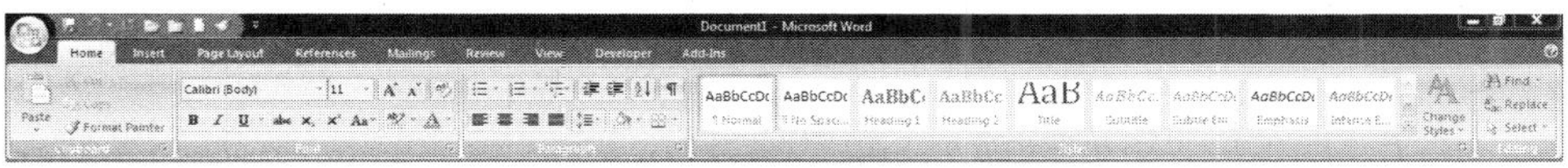

Figure 1-3: Higher resolution allows for expanded groups.

Hence, the higher your monitor's resolution, the more you will benefit from the Ribbon (the Ribbon is best visualized in a resolution of 1024 × 768 or higher). As you can see, this first issue is a visual one — that is, you do not need to know anything about the Ribbon to figure that out by yourself.

> **NOTE** Although the Ribbon occupies a lot of space, you will notice that compared to other versions, the actual document visibility is larger for out-of-the-box installations compared to older versions, as you will not have items such as horizontal scroll bars, and so on, showing up unnecessarily.

Another visual issue relates to how much is actually available under each tab. You may find yourself moving back and forth along the Ribbon to get certain tasks done. The original goal was to make commands readily available, so this seems to defeat part of the purpose. And what if the user minimizes the Ribbon? You gain visible screen space, but you end up with something akin to the old menu hierarchy. As Figure 1-4 shows, minimizing the Ribbon gives the impression that you are still under the menu hierarchy. We discuss later in this chapter the collapsing and expansion (minimization and maximization) of the Ribbon.

Figure 1-4: Minimizing the Ribbon gives the impression you are still under the menu hierarchy.

Following are some of the nonvisual issues with the new UI:

- **Less efficient for power users:** Although the Ribbon gives end users instant access to the tools they need to perform their jobs more productively and professionally, it initially causes significant frustration among power users and developers. The flexibility found in previous versions in terms of easy customization is now history. Some of the issues (such as ease of customization) are already being addressed by Microsoft, but how far they will go only time will tell. For now, we have to live with what we have and make the best use of it. Power users and programmers will be happy to know that this book provides solutions to several of the issues, and it provides full examples of how to create and incorporate customizations.
- **Fewer commands on screen:** The controls that were determined to be the most frequently used are grouped and prominently displayed. As mentioned earlier, screen resolution can play a positive or negative role here because groups will collapse to fit into a smaller display. To make matters worse, you still need to navigate between the tabs. In addition, many tasks may still require navigating between tabs, such as when you need to validate data and then format your work in Excel, and during any type of database design activities.
- **Lack of "tear away" toolbars:** This is both a blessing and a curse in disguise. It is a blessing for beginners who will no longer suffer from misplaced toolbars (the story of the disappearing toolbar). Conversely, it is a curse for power users and developers who no longer have the flexibility to dock toolbars according to a specific need, as well as for those users who want to put the tools closer to their workspace to minimize mouse travel.
- **Customization requires programming or third-party tools:** This statement is not entirely true if you could not care less about your productivity. You might sit in front of your PC, open Notepad, and type away until you create an entirely new UI. But if you are even a little concerned with productivity (as we assume you must be), you will find that without a third-party customization tool your life could quite easily become a living hell . . . and we do mean that, despite the fact that this book will give you a taste of paradise and show you how to actually get there.

- **Table-driven menus are not what they used to be:** Previously, a custom UI for an Office application could use external sources (such as tables in Access or Word, and worksheets in Excel, etc.) to lay out the UI, and then the UI could be loaded on-the-fly through a standard VBA procedure. Although this is not completely impossible to do with the Ribbon, the scope has been dramatically reduced compared to what it used to be. The reason for this limitation comes from the fact that the Ribbon UI is loaded at design-time and not at run-time. Chapter 14 includes a detailed discussion about how to do such things and what circumstances will limit the options.
- **Commands may not be in the order you need them:** It's estimated that many Excel users know about 20% of its features, but that they each use a different 20% based on their jobs and experience. Because of this, Microsoft's usage studies, despite being across many thousands of users, may not have captured your needs. Plainly put, the commands may not always be where you need them, and you may spend significant time searching through tabs to find them.
- **Only one shot to create your UI structure:** Unfortunately, there is currently no way to repopulate an entire tab, or group with controls in a dynamic manner. While you can hide or show groups (or enable/disable commands) that you've lain out at design time, you cannot dynamically add new tabs, groups, or controls to those groups on-the-fly. It's true that you can dynamically populate certain controls with content, but this is only one very small part of the new UI. The inability to build tabs and groups on-the-fly is probably the largest piece missing from the Ribbon from a developer's perspective, and it prevents us from building the truly fluent and rich UI that should be possible.

What Happened to the Toolbars from My Pre-2007 Files?

It would be a nightmare to wake up to the new UI just to find that all your previous work would be pretty much worthless. Although for some this may be partially true, it is not necessarily the end of the world.

Being forced to live with the Ribbon glued firmly in one place may not meet the unusually high standards and expectations of users who are accustomed to the docking capability. However, this "gluing" process is, in effect, quite sensible given that the majority of users (not power users and developers) have had a tendency to wreak havoc in the old UI by scattering toolbars all over the place, hiding toolbars and not being able to retrieve them, and in general creating UI mayhem.

The Ribbon eliminates all that, but in the process it creates frustrations for more powerful users, as we have to learn new habits. As you know, old habits are hard to break.

At this point you may be wondering a few things about your old customization. It is hoped that answering a few questions will dispel most of your doubts:

- Will your old customizations still work? Yes, they will, but they will certainly not look like anything you had before.

- Where do they show up? If you're planning to deploy a full-blown VBA-based customization, this new customization will be added to a new tab called AddIn. Although your project may not be an add-in, that's what the tab is named and your UI can be filled with them. This is as good as it gets, at least for now. There are exceptions to AddIns, such as pop-up menus (pop-up menus are covered in Chapter 15).

Is anything else happening to the old way of doing things? The answer is a resounding YES! Developers will be happy to know that the programming model for legacy CommandBars has been upgraded so that it contains some new methods you can use to interact with the new UI. For example, we now have the `GetImageMso` function (method), which enables you to capture the image of a control (such as HappyFace) and place it somewhere else. This method is similar to the `CopyFace` method normally used to copy the face of a button in the old UI. That may seem like Greek to a lot of you, but rest assured that this book is designed with you in mind. It covers the fundamentals, explains the scenarios, and then steps through the examples so that not only will you be able to incorporate them into your files and solutions, but you will also understand what you are doing and be able to create custom Ribbons tailored to your needs.

A Customization Example for Pre-2007 UIs

In order to give you an idea of what is going to happen to your old customization, we will work through an example. This customization has a reasonable amount of complexity so that you can have a clearer picture of what to expect. Don't worry if you don't understand how it works at this point; it will become clear as you work through the examples in the rest of the book. (This example is applicable to Excel. You can find the code on the book's website at `www.wiley.com/go/ribbonx`.)

In Figure 1-5, the menu is dynamic. When an option from the list is selected, another list is created for that particular option. In addition, if other workbooks are opened or created in the same Excel session, these custom options are no longer available (the options are disabled). They're available only for this specific workbook and adapt according to which worksheet is currently active.

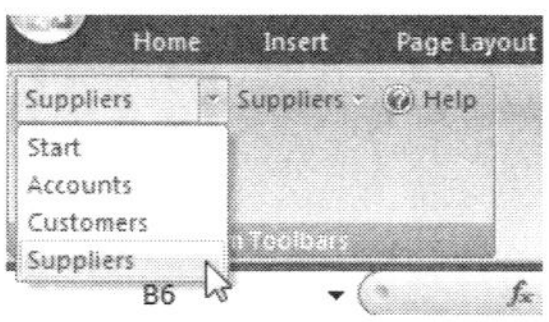

Figure 1-5: How old customization is built into the new UI

We describe the entire VBA process for this example so that you can have a look at how things would work on a relatively complex customization. If you are not fluent with VBA, there is no need to panic. Chapters 4, 5, and 12 delve into the relevant aspects of VBA and explain things in sufficient detail for you to understand and be confident in creating customizations.

For now, run this example and see how Excel 2007 handles a customization code written for Excel 2003. This will help you understand some of the key differences between the old way and the new way of doing things and it will make it easier for you to visualize what we are working with as we progress in this book.

We describe below the steps you need to follow in order to implement this solution. Keep in mind that you aren't expected to complete this exercise at this time. Rather, it is intended to give you the big picture and show you where you're headed. You might want to start by seeing what we're creating. Just download this chapter's files and open `Customization Old Style.xlsm`.

As you go through the book, you will learn about each of the steps to create custom add-ins as well as some VBA fundamentals, including how to create and work with class modules. For now, it is probably easiest to just review the code in our files. Alternatively, if you feel you want to try it yourself, you can copy the code from the referenced Excel file (or from the chapter's text file) and paste it in as instructed.

First, open `ThisWorkbook` and add the following code to the code window. (You do so by pressing Alt+F11 to open the VBE (Visual Basic Editor). From there, double-click on the `ThisWorkbook` object to open its code window.)

```
Private Sub Workbook_BeforeClose(Cancel As Boolean)
    Call wsDeleteMenus
End Sub

Private Sub Workbook_Open()
    Call wsBuildMenus
End Sub
```

Next, add a class module to your project. This is done from the Insert menu in the VBE window (Insert ➪ Class Module).

NOTE **Remember that this is just an example to give you the big picture about what we'll be covering and why. At this point, you aren't expected to understand everything or to be able to interpret all the code, but by the time you finish this book, you will be proficient with these customizations and all of their intricacies.**

CROSS-REFERENCE **Chapter 12 defines and shows you how to work with class modules.**

You can name the following class module whatever you like, but in this example we use `clsEvents`, so be sure to refer to the correct module in your own code.

```
Public WithEvents appXL As Application
Public WithEvents drop  As Office.CommandBarComboBox
```

```
Private Sub appXL_SheetActivate(ByVal Sh As Object)
    Dim ws              As Worksheet
    Dim wb              As Workbook
    Dim i               As Long

    On Error GoTo Err_Handler
    Set wb = ActiveWorkbook

    If Not wb.Name = ThisWorkbook.Name Then Exit Sub

    Set g_cmdbarcboBox = g_cmdBar.FindControl _
        (Type:=msoControlDropdown, Tag:="myList")

        g_cmdbarcboBox.Clear

    For Each ws In Sh.Parent.Sheets
        g_cmdbarcboBox.AddItem ws.Name
    Next

    For i = 1 To g_cmdbarcboBox.ListCount
        If g_cmdbarcboBox.List(i) = Sh.Name Then _
        g_cmdbarcboBox.ListIndex = i: Exit For
    Next

    Call drop_Change(g_cmdbarcboBox)
    Exit Sub
Err_Handler:
    ErrHandle Err
End Sub

Private Sub appXL_WorkbookActivate(ByVal wb As Workbook)
    Set g_cmdbarcboBox = g_cmdBar.FindControl _
        (Type:=msoControlDropdown, Tag:="myList")

    If wb.Name = ThisWorkbook.Name Then
        g_cmdbarcboBox.Enabled = True
        appXL_SheetActivate wb.ActiveSheet
    Else:
        Call deleleteControls
        g_cmdbarcboBox.Enabled = False
    End If
    Exit Sub
Err_Handler:
    ErrHandle Err
End Sub

Public Sub setDrop(box As Office.CommandBarComboBox)
    Set drop = box
End Sub

Private Sub drop_Change(ByVal Ctrl As Office.CommandBarComboBox)
```

```
    Select Case UCase(Ctrl.Text)
        Case "SUPPLIERS"
            Call setMNUSUPPLIERS
        Case "CUSTOMERS"
            Call setMNUCUSTOMERS
        Case "ACCOUNTS"
            Call setMNUACCOUNTS
        Case Else
            Call deleleteControls
    End Select
End Sub
```

Finally, add a standard module (in the VBE window select Insert ➪ Module) where we will insert the following code:

```
Public Const gcstrCMDBARNAME          As String = "DYNAMIC MENU"
Public Const gcstrMNUSUPPLIERS        As String = "Suppliers"
Public Const gcstrMNUCUSTOMERS        As String = "Customers"
Public Const gcstrMNUACCOUNTS         As String = "Accounts"

Public g_cmdBar                       As CommandBar
Public g_cmdbarMenu                   As CommandBarPopup
Public g_cmdbarBtn                    As CommandBarButton
Public g_cmdbarcboBox                 As CommandBarComboBox
Public gcls_appExcel                  As New clsEvents
Public gcls_cboBox                    As New clsEvents


Sub wsBuildMenus()
    Call wsDeleteMenus

    On Error GoTo Err_Handler

    Set g_cmdBar = CommandBars.Add(gcstrCMDBARNAME, msoBarFloating)
        g_cmdBar.Width = 150

    Set g_cmdbarcboBox = g_cmdBar.Controls.Add(Type:=msoControlDropdown)
        With g_cmdbarcboBox
            .Tag = "myList"
            .OnAction = "selectedSheet"
            .Width = 150
        End With

    Set g_cmdbarBtn = g_cmdBar.Controls.Add(Type:=msoControlButton)
        With g_cmdbarBtn
            .Caption = "Help"
            .OnAction = "runHelp"
            .Style = msoButtonIconAndCaption
            .FaceId = 984
        End With
```

```
        Set gcls_appExcel.appXL = Application

        gcls_cboBox.setDrop g_cmdbarcboBox

        With g_cmdBar
            .Visible = True
            .Protection = msoBarNoChangeDock + msoBarNoResize
        End With
        Exit Sub
    Err_Handler:
        ErrHandle Err
    End Sub

    Sub wsDeleteMenus()
        On Error Resume Next
        Application.CommandBars(gcstrCMDBARNAME).Delete

        Set g_cmdBar = Nothing
        Set g_cmdbarMenu = Nothing
        Set g_cmdbarBtn = Nothing
        Set g_cmdbarcboBox = Nothing
        Set gcls_appExcel = Nothing
        Set gcls_cboBox = Nothing
    End Sub

    Sub deleleteControls()
        On Error Resume Next
        g_cmdBar.Controls(gcstrMNUACCOUNTS).Delete
        g_cmdBar.Controls(gcstrMNUCUSTOMERS).Delete
        g_cmdBar.Controls(gcstrMNUSUPPLIERS).Delete
    End Sub

    Sub selectedSheet()
        Dim g_cmdbarcboBox As CommandBarComboBox
        On Error Resume Next
        Set g_cmdbarcboBox = _
            CommandBars.FindControl(Type:=msoControlDropdown, Tag:="myList")
            ActiveWorkbook.Sheets(g_cmdbarcboBox.Text).Activate
    End Sub

    Sub setMNUACCOUNTS()
        Call deleleteControls
        On Error GoTo Err_Handler
        Set g_cmdbarMenu = _
            g_cmdBar.Controls.Add(Type:=msoControlPopup, BEFORE:=2)
            g_cmdbarMenu.Caption = gcstrMNUACCOUNTS

        Set g_cmdbarBtn = g_cmdbarMenu.Controls.Add(Type:=msoControlButton)
            g_cmdbarBtn.Caption = "New Account"
```

```
    Set g_cmdbarBtn = g_cmdbarMenu.Controls.Add(Type:=msoControlButton)
        g_cmdbarBtn.Caption = "Delete account"
    Exit Sub
Err_Handler:
    ErrHandle Err
End Sub

Sub setMNUSUPPLIERS()
    Call deleleteControls
    On Error GoTo Err_Handler
    Set g_cmdbarMenu = _
        g_cmdBar.Controls.Add(Type:=msoControlPopup, BEFORE:=2)
        g_cmdbarMenu.Caption = gcstrMNUSUPPLIERS

    Set g_cmdbarBtn = g_cmdbarMenu.Controls.Add(Type:=msoControlButton)
        g_cmdbarBtn.Caption = "New Supplier"

    Set g_cmdbarBtn = g_cmdbarMenu.Controls.Add(Type:=msoControlButton)
        g_cmdbarBtn.Caption = "Current data"
    Exit Sub
Err_Handler:
    ErrHandle Err
End Sub

Sub setMNUCUSTOMERS()
    Call deleleteControls
    On Error GoTo Err_Handler
    Set g_cmdbarMenu = _
        g_cmdBar.Controls.Add(Type:=msoControlPopup, BEFORE:=2)
        g_cmdbarMenu.Caption = gcstrMNUCUSTOMERS

    Set g_cmdbarBtn = g_cmdbarMenu.Controls.Add(Type:=msoControlButton)
        g_cmdbarBtn.Caption = "New Customer"

    Set g_cmdbarBtn = g_cmdbarMenu.Controls.Add(Type:=msoControlButton)
        g_cmdbarBtn.Caption = "Outstanding pmts"
    Exit Sub
Err_Handler:
    ErrHandle Err
End Sub

Sub ErrHandle(ByVal objError As ErrObject)
    MsgBox objError.Description, vbCritical, objError.Number
    Call wsDeleteMenus
End Sub
```

You can now run the preceding code and see for yourself how it behaves in relation to the new UI. Start by selecting the different worksheet tabs and then open/add new workbooks to your working environment.

Ribbon Components

This section provides a guided tour of the Ribbon components. This will help you become familiar with the structure so that things will run more smoothly when you begin XML coding of the UI.

The user interface in Office 2007 is made up of a number of components (or elements, if you prefer) that determine how you interact with the application, much in the same way that the hierarchical approach had its own elements. These components are listed in Table 1-1 and Table 1-2, and illustrated in Figure 1-6. (The numbers in the tables correspond to the callout numbers in Figure 1-6.)

As previously mentioned, the idea is that this new UI will help users to get the job done quicker, which should translate into higher productivity. However, before productivity increases, you need to familiarize yourself with these elements, especially if your objective is to customize the Ribbon. The task of customizing the Ribbon will be a whole lot easier once you understand the underlying logic of the XML code.

Table 1-1: The Three Basic Ribbon Components

COMPONENT	WHAT IT IS FOR
1. Tab	Each tab brings together core tasks that you perform. Tabs bring together all these related tasks.
2. Group	In the same way that tabs bring together related tasks, groups bring together related commands.
3. Command	A command represents an action that you want to perform. It can appear packed in different forms, such as buttons, galleries, menus, edit boxes, etc.

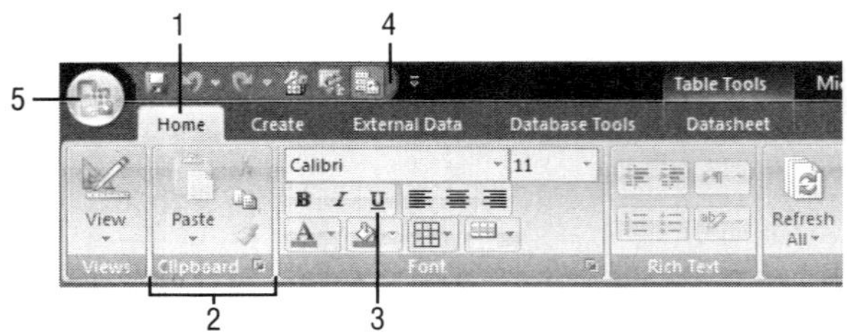

Figure 1-6: Ribbon components viewed from an Access perspective

Figure 1-6 shows a total of five components (or elements). Numbers 1, 2, and 3 are "basic" components; numbers 4 and 5 are not.

Table 1-2: The Two Non-Basic Components of the Ribbon

COMPONENT	WHAT IT IS FOR
4. Quick Access Toolbar (better known as QAT)	A toolbar for adding commands that you want just a click away. The QAT can take shared or document controls.
5. Office Menu (also known as Office Button)	A menu containing file-related tasks such as printing, file properties, saving, etc.

These elements are related in a hierarchical construct within the XML code. This construct (or concept) serves to encapsulate each control within its parent element. The way this structure works will become clear when we start to analyze the tags used to build customization.

NOTE **When adding controls to the QAT such as buttons and groups, you can choose between a document control and a shared control. A *document control,* as the name suggests, is a control that belongs to the document itself and cannot be seen or accessed by another document that might be opened in the same session. Conversely, a *shared control* is available to all documents opened in the same session or any other session.**

Tips for Navigating the Ribbon and Quick Access Toolbar (QAT)

This section discusses some tips for navigating the Ribbon and the Quick Access Toolbar. Although these tips relate to the default Ribbon, you should keep them in mind for your customization — especially the *keytips* accessible through the keyboard, as these can be changed through XML code and will work with your own customization as well as built-in tabs and controls.

Using Keyboard Shortcuts and Keytips

We start off with keyboard shortcuts and keytips. This is, simply put, the easiest, quickest, and generally most efficient way to access commands in any application. It involves pressing a combination of keys that will perform some kind of action, such as copying, cutting, pasting, or navigating through some of the Ribbon's elements.

If you have used keyboard shortcuts before, you should be happy to know that old shortcuts still work fine with the new UI (in fact, they work in exactly the same way as before). Hence, if you need to copy something, you can still use Ctrl+c; similarly, if you wish to paste, you can continue to use Ctrl+v. A shortcut requires that you press one key *plus* another.

You will remember that for previous versions of Office, you could press the Alt key to activate the top-level menu (referring to the Accelerator key). You would then use other keys (which were always underlined, indicating which key you should press next) to get to the command you wanted. Office 2007 introduces an extension of the Accelerator idea from previous versions of Office: keytips. Keytips are also accessed by pressing and releasing the Alt key (if you press and hold long enough it will show the keytips as well, as shown in Figure 1-7).

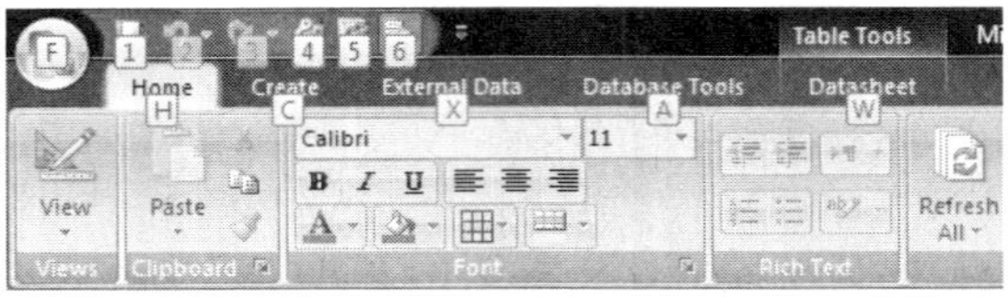

Figure 1-7: Keytips for an Access project

Next, all you have to do is press the corresponding key (or combination of keys) shown in the Ribbon. This is slightly different from the shortcut approach, because with keytips you first press one key and *then* you press another.

NOTE **Notice that some keytips are dimmed. When a keytip is dimmed it is not accessible in the current context (for example, undo will not be functional until there is something that can be undone).**

When you press the keytip key and it refers to a tab, you automatically move into that tab context. This time around, you do not need to press Alt to reveal the keytips for the controls. As shown in Figure 1-8, all the keytips are automatically revealed to you.

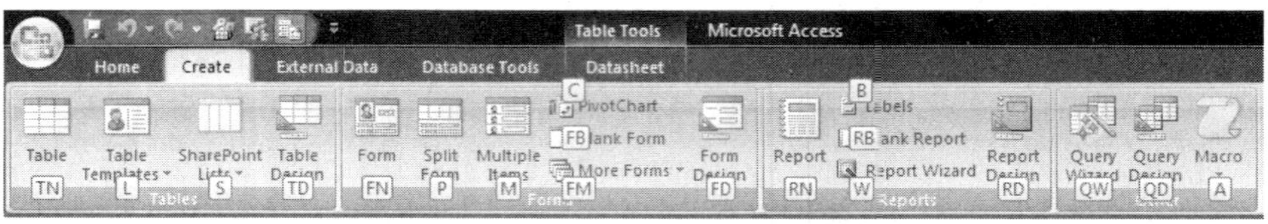

Figure 1-8: Keytips for controls under the Create tab in Access

Now, if the next keytip leads you to a drop-down or menu, these will be extended to show the keytips for any controls that may have been placed in them.

The greatest single advantage of the keytip is that it is an attribute available in almost all controls you find in the Ribbon. Compare this with the limited scope in previous versions of Office and you start to appreciate its beauty.

NOTE **Keytips are available in *almost all* controls, but some controls (such as the** `menuSeparator` **and** `labelControl`**) are not really command controls and therefore have no keytips. These are auxiliary controls and do not perform any kind of action.**

Another benefit is that you can still use the Accelerator keys in the same manner as you could in previous versions of Office. Suppose you want to open the Insert Function dialog box in Excel. Using keytips, you could press Alt+M+F. An alternative was to use the Accelerator route in Office 2003, which just entailed pressing Alt+I+F. Now, Excel 2007 keeps track of the keys you press to open the Insert Function dialog box, so it will recognize the key combinations that were used in Office 2003. Figure 1-9 shows the Accelerator sequence in Office 2007 for Alt+I+F from Office 2003.

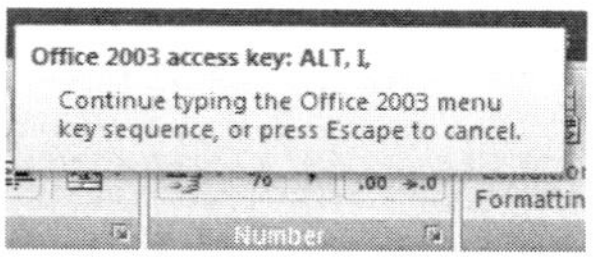

Figure 1-9: Office 2007 will recognize and respond to the Accelerator sequences used in Office 2003.

The Accelerator access mode is activated whenever you combine keys that made up the Accelerator route in Office 2003.

TIP **You can also press the F10 function key to bring up the keytips and start an Accelerator sequence.**

Using the Mouse Wheel

If you have your Ribbon maximized, you can navigate the tabs using the mouse wheel. Just place the mouse pointer on top of the Ribbon and spin the wheel.

If you scroll towards you, the Ribbon will scroll along the tabs from left to right. Conversely, if you scroll away from you, it will scroll from right to left along the tabs until it reaches the first tab on the left.

Minimizing and Maximizing the Ribbon

If you feel the Ribbon is taking up too much space at the top of your screen you can minimize it, as shown in Figure 1-10.

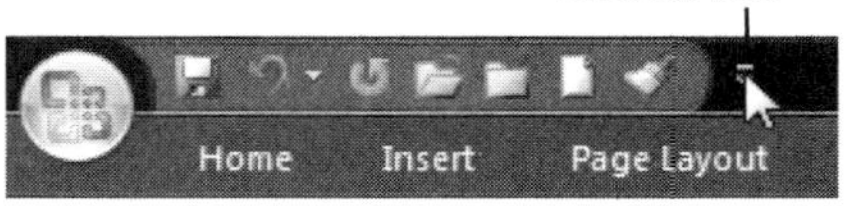

Figure 1-10: Minimized Ribbon

To minimize or maximize the Ribbon, you can do one of the following:

- Double-click on any tab.
- Click on the chevron-like icon and toggle Minimize the Ribbon button.
- Right-click anywhere on the QAT or tab strip, or on any group's description and choose Minimize Ribbon.

Once the Ribbon is minimized you will not be able to navigate the tabs using the mouse wheel, and clicking on the tabs will only temporarily expand the Ribbon content for the selected tab. However, while the Ribbon has the focus, you will still be able to choose other tabs and view the commands within any group under the chosen tab.

To expand the Ribbon back to the default display, merely follow one of the steps listed for minimizing the Ribbon. Essentially, they work like a toggle to minimize/maximize on demand.

Adding Commands to the QAT

If you use some controls more often than others (such as open/close), you can place them on the Quick Access Toolbar (QAT) so that you have just that — quick access. The QAT is the nearest you will get to toolbar-style customization. It works in pretty much the same way that toolbars did in the past, by enabling you to place controls on a specific toolbar for ease of access.

Compared to what was previously possible, the QAT's scope is rather limited, but removing unwieldy customizations, such as the docking capability, also eliminated the complexities and anxieties of managing the old toolbar.

It is remarkably easy to manually add commands to the QAT. Just use any one of the following processes:

- Click on the chevron-like icon, and then select More Commands.
- Click the Office Menu and select (Application) Options ➪ Customize.
- Right-click anywhere on the QAT or tab strip, or on any group's description, and select Customize Quick Access Toolbar. When the Customize Quick Access Toolbar options window is open, as shown in Figure 1-11, simply select the commands you want to add to the QAT and click Add.

TIP **To quickly add commands, right-click the command (Ribbon or Office Menu) and choose Add to Quick Access Toolbar.**

Note that under the Customize Quick Access Toolbar drop-down list, you will find your XLSX, DOCX, ACCDB, and so on, files. This means the command you're adding to the QAT can be specific to the file or can be shared across all other open files. By default, the customization is shared (for all files opened). If you want it to be file-specific, then the icon will change to show this subtle difference, as shown in Figure 1-12.

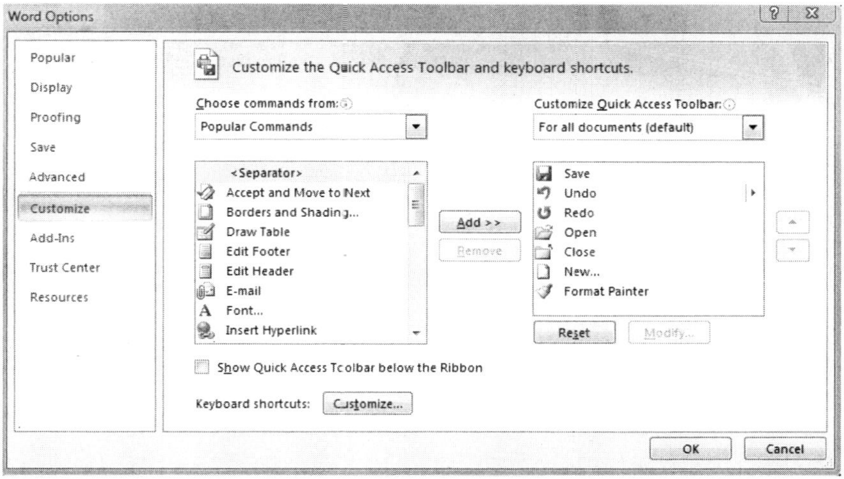

Figure 1-11: Adding commands to the QAT in Word

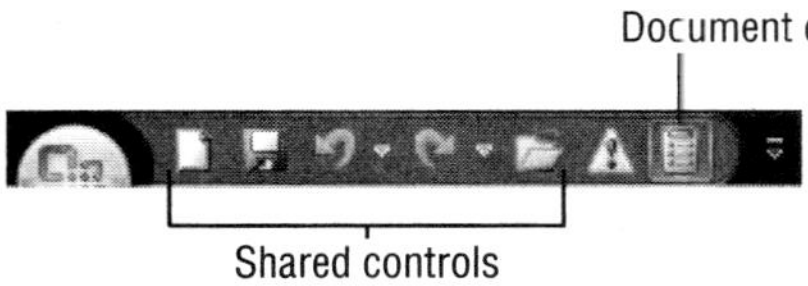

Figure 1-12: Icons with a frame refer to document controls.

The little frame around the icon indicates that it is a document control rather than a shared control. A shared control is available to all opened documents, whereas a document control is only available to the document to which it was added.

It all may look great to begin with, but as you might quickly realize, it is very easy to burden the QAT with too many buttons; and even then there will be more commands that you'd like to add.

Thankfully, the QAT is quite versatile; in addition to being able to add buttons, you can also add groups. The process is very simple and can be accomplished using one of the following approaches:

- Open the application options. Under Choose Commands From, select the tab that contains the group you are looking for. In the list, you will notice that some have an icon with an arrow pointing down. This indicates it is a group.
- Right-click on the group name tab and then click on Add to Quick Access Toolbar.

Figure 1-13 shows the QAT in an Access project. In addition to buttons, this has the Database Tools group.

Figure 1-13: Adding groups to the QAT

If you are wondering whether this applies to your custom groups, yes, it does apply to custom groups.

TIP **Notice the icons! That's right, you should look at the icons in the Customize options because they indicate what type of object is being added. An arrow pointing down indicates a group, an arrow pointing right indicates a gallery, and a vertical bar with an arrow pointing right indicates a splitButton.**

CROSS-REFERENCE **See Chapter 14 to learn more about Quick Access Toolbar customization using XML.**

Assigning a Macro to a QAT Button

If you plan to customize the Quick Access Toolbar, probably the best way is to use XML code. The problem with this, however, is that such customization can only happen if you build the entire Ribbon from scratch. This is covered in detail in Chapter 14.

If you need to add a button to the QAT for which you want to attach certain functionality, you can easily make such a customization using the following steps (see Figure 1-14 for a walk-through):

1. Go to Office Menu ➪ (Application) Options (alternatively, you can use the chevron-like QAT icon to access More Commands).
2. Click Customize to enter the Customize the Quick Access Toolbar customization window.
3. From the drop-down Choose Commands From, select Macros to show a list of available macros.
4. From the Customize Quick Access Toolbar drop-down, select the option you want (such as the Current document or For all documents (default) option).
5. Select your macro from the list and click Add.
6. Click OK when you're done.

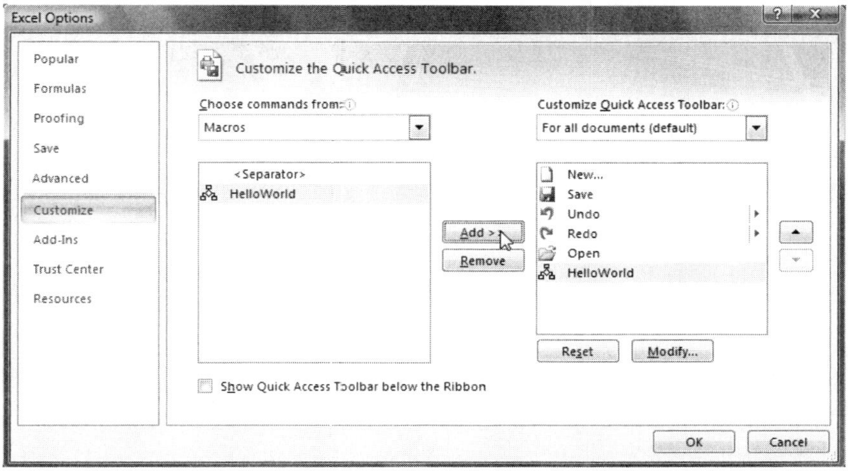

Figure 1-14: Assigning a macro to the QAT

You're probably now wondering what is up with the icon assigned to the `HelloWorld` macro. That is definitely an ugly icon and one that you would certainly want to replace, which conveniently brings us to another step in the process. To change an icon, click the Modify button to display a list of the available icons (shown in Figure 1-15).

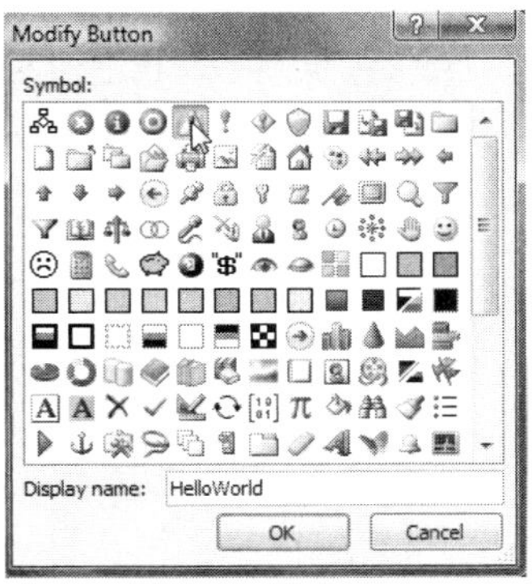

Figure 1-15: Choosing a different icon for the macro button

Look through the options and choose an icon (or symbol, if you prefer the dialog box nomenclature) and when you've made your selection, click OK to continue.

While you are at it (and before you click OK), you can also change the Display name. The Display name is the tip that will appear onscreen when the mouse pointer hovers over the button, as shown in Figure 1-16.

Figure 1-16: Display name for the macro button

Changing the QAT Location

By default the QAT is located above the Ribbon. You can change its location by either of the following methods:

- Click the chevron-like icon and select Show Below the Ribbon.
- Right-click anywhere on the QAT or tab strip, or on any group's description and select Customize Quick Access Toolbar.

Preparing for Ribbon Customization

Developing Ribbon customizations involves several steps. The first stage works mostly with structure and therefore involves XML; the second stage is functionality-related, which involves VBA code (or some other programming language such as C#). Happily, there are some fundamental components that are common to most customizations, so you can create it once and then use it as the foundation for future projects.

The following sections describe some important preparations that will save you valuable time throughout the customization process.

Showing the Developer Tab

As you work with VBA in this book, you may find it useful to have the Developer tab active. The tab itself is not critical, as the keyboard shortcuts still exist and can be used to access macro features for any work that you will do; but it will be useful to have the development tools at hand, especially if you prefer using the mouse rather than keyboard shortcuts.

We recommend having the Developer tab active because after you have finished your XML code you use VBA to add functionality to the UI, so it is convenient to have the Developer's tools at hand when you need them. Furthermore, the Developer's tools also provide an XML group, which is useful when inspecting the XML schema for the Ribbon UI.

As shown in Figure 1-17, the Developer tab appears as the last tab in the standard Ribbon.

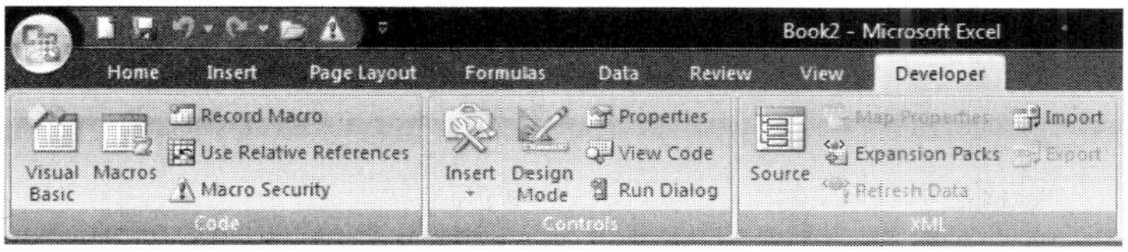

Figure 1-17: The Developer tab is useful when it's time to add VBA functionality to your customization.

To enable the Developer tab, follow these steps (as illustrated in Figure 1-18):

1. Click on the Office logo.
2. Select (Application) Options.
3. Select Popular and choose the option Show Developer tab in the Ribbon.

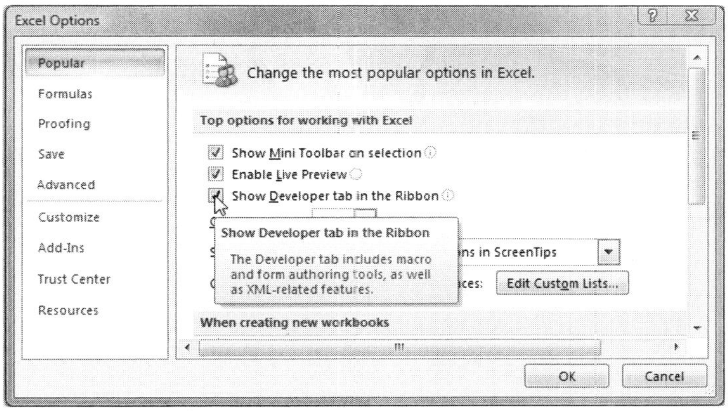

Figure 1-18: Enabling the Developer tab

These instructions and illustrations are identical for Excel and Word. In Access, however, you use the Create tab to access macro and VBA objects.

Another difference in Access is that it does not have certain features, such as macro recording. Recording macros is a very handy feature that helps us to discover important information about objects. Nevertheless, you may find that recording macros in Excel/Word can actually help you figure out information and processes that are applicable to Access.

CROSS-REFERENCE **See Chapter 4 for instructions on recording macros and for programming techniques that are used in this book and that you can apply to your daily work.**

Showing CustomUI Errors at Load Time

Before loading the UI into Excel, Access, or Word, you will always want to check your XML consistency. To help with this, a few tools are discussed in Chapter 2. Despite all good intentions, however, the UI may pass the test in these tools but fail when it loads. Therefore, it is important to be familiar with some of the factors that might cause the loading failure.

First, although each of these applications shares very similar XML code, they also contain controls that are unique to that application. Therefore, if code including an application-unique control were moved to a different application, the code would pass the test on the tool but fail on load.

Second, you may also have less obvious problems. For example, you could assign an `idMso` (we'll discuss these more in Chapter 3) to a button when it actually belongs to a `toggleButton`. Again, these may pass the first check, but will fail on load.

To ensure that consistency is also checked and that errors are displayed when the CustomUI is loaded, you can use the following process:

1. Click Office Menu ➪ (Application) Options.
2. Select the Advance option and scroll to the General group.
3. Select the Show add-in user interface errors option.

Once you've made the selection, click OK to continue. The location for this option is the same for Excel, Access, and Word.

As shown in Figure 1-19, when the document is loaded, if it contains an error it is immediately reported, indicating the line and column in which the error is located (including the file location).

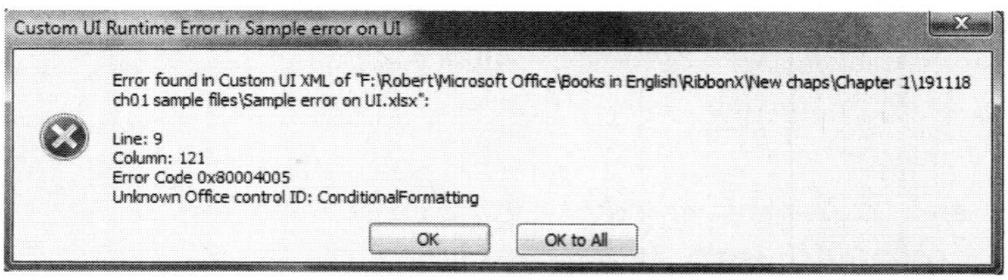

Figure 1-19: Reporting error when loading UI

In this case, an error has occurred because the UI is being loaded in Word but it contains an attribute value that is specific to Excel (`ConditionalFormatting`).

Reviewing Office 2007 Security

If this is your first time working with Office, you may want to take a few minutes to review Chapter 17. That chapter contains information about how to set up the Trust Center, macro security, and digital signatures so that you aren't constantly being harassed about potentially dangerous files while you are developing. Making these changes now will save you some time and frustration as you go through the exercises in this book.

Has Customization of the Office UI Become Easier?

Our objective throughout this book is to modify and customize the work area (user interface). Unfortunately, the task is relatively arduous with the new UI for Microsoft Office as compared to previous versions. Moreover, the challenges are compounded by the small differences between the applications, which means that we cannot rely 100% on the XML code to be exchangeable and applicable across different Office applications.

Figure 1-20 shows an example of a Ribbon customization. This has an added tab and a group containing a few command buttons. And, of course, it includes an action that will be executed when the command button is clicked.

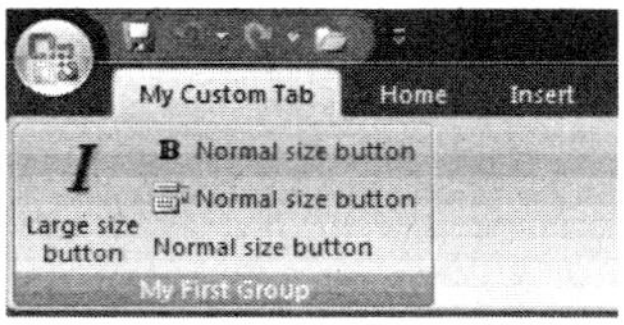

Figure 1-20: Customizing the Ribbon

If you previously created a lot of custom menus and toolbars (whether through VBA or not), you will probably have a hard time accepting the new UI. However, once you get past that first encounter and resistance to change, things should start looking a bit rosier.

The biggest challenge with respect to the new UI is the XML code it contains; and a custom UI can require more lines of code than you might currently imagine. Therefore, for now, accept the guidance that a lot of planning is required prior to writing the first line of XML for your new UI. Later, a few hundred lines into your code, you do not want to be trying to find and fix something.

Furthermore, XML is case sensitive, so writing an attribute such as `getVisible` as `getvisible` will cause a syntax error in the structure of the XML code.

In addition, now we need to create and work with *callbacks*. These take the arguments from the Ribbon objects. Fortunately, there's the Custom UI Editor that can read through your code and generate the callbacks for any attribute that requires one.

All of this might sound intimidating now, but by the time you finish this book, you will be sailing through the Ribbon customization process. Obviously, this book cannot contain everything you might possibly come across or want to know about, but it contains everything that you need to know for most common scenarios and it will help you avoid a whole lot of pain during the learning process.

Conclusion

In explaining how the Ribbon came to be, we provided a little background and history of the Microsoft Office UI. Now you can understand why it was necessary for a paradigm change after so many years of relying on hierarchical menus. As with any change this dramatic, there can be a steep learning curve, but the benefits become evident very quickly.

In this chapter you learned about the Quick Access Toolbar, shortcuts, and keytips. You learned some basic customizations that can be done without any programming and how those customizations can be incorporated into your UI as a document or as a shared customization.

Although lengthy, and maybe a bit intimidating at this stage, you also saw a sample of an old customization style so that you could try it for yourself. It is hoped that being able to contrast the new with the old has added to your appreciation for what you will soon be able to do.

In Chapter 2 we cover access to the UI customization layer, and from there on we introduce the tools you need to successfully customize the new Office user interface. Have fun.

CHAPTER

2

Accessing the UI Customization Layer

Before you can start exploring how to customize the Ribbon to get it the way you like it, you need to know how and where to place the code to do so. This chapter leads you there by discussing the file formats in Office 2007, and shows you how to crack your files open for customization.

The first section, "Accessing the Excel and Word Ribbon Customization Layers," discusses Excel and Word files, and begins by describing the fundamentals behind how the new Office 2007 files are structured. You learn how to access the Ribbon customization layer and store the required code. Once you've mastered this, you learn about a couple of handy tools you can use to make it much easier to set up, program, and debug Ribbon customizations. Rest assured that at this stage, you'll be provided with all the code you need, so don't worry about getting bogged down in learning to write it just yet.

The "Microsoft Access Customizations" section dives into storing RibbonX customizations in Microsoft Access, as this is very different from working with the other Office applications. A few different methods can be used to include Ribbon customizations in Access, and a brief introduction to each of them is covered. Again, all code is provided for you at this stage.

As you are preparing to work through the examples, we encourage you to download the companion files. The source code and files for this chapter can be found on the book's web site at `www.wiley.com/go/ribbonx`.

NOTE **This book provides processes and code for customizing the Ribbon in Excel, Access, and Word. Microsoft also introduced the Ribbon, and new file formats, for several other Office applications, including PowerPoint, Outlook forms, OneNote, Visio, and InfoPath.**

Accessing the Excel and Word Ribbon Customization Layers

This section explains how to create Ribbon modifications using only the software that ships natively with Windows. It also explains how to accomplish the customizations using some third-party tools.

What's New in Excel and Word Files?

In versions of Microsoft Office up to 2003, most documents were stored in binary files, but this changed with the arrival of Microsoft Office 2007. For the release of this version of Office, Microsoft adopted the OpenXML file format as their new standard. While it's pretty obvious that the file formats have changed, what may not be obvious is that, unlike files in previous Office versions, the new files are actually contained in a zipped XML format! This is important for a few reasons:

- We can unlock and modify the underlying XML files quite easily with Notepad. (No third-party tools are required, as Windows XP and later can work with compressed, or zipped, files.)
- We can use a similar data structure across different applications to acquire like results. From Excel to Word, and even in PowerPoint, customizing the new Office 2007 user interface follows exactly the same methods.
- Generally, files stored in the new file formats are compressed, and take up much less space than their old binary counterparts.

Creating a Ribbon Customization with Notepad

Enough talk about what can be done; it's time to actually play with a customization. For the purposes of this example, you create a very simple Ribbon customization that adds a new tab to the Ribbon and places a couple of Microsoft's built-in groups on this tab.

NOTE **While this example demonstrates the method to complete a Ribbon customization in Excel, you can use the same steps to accomplish this in Word as well. You simply open Word instead, and modify the** `docx` **file instead of the** `xlsx` **file, as demonstrated in a subsequent example.**

Creating the customUI File

The first thing to do is create the file that will hold the XML used to modify the Ribbon. To do this, create a folder on your desktop and rename it `customUI`.

TIP **Before continuing, make sure that your system is not set to hide known file extensions, as this will get in the way in the next step. Showing extensions won't cause any security issues and, in fact, it can sometimes help prevent them. To show extensions, open your folder view and choose Organize ⇨ Folder and Search Options (Tools ⇨ Folder Options in Windows XP). On the View tab, scroll down and uncheck the box that says "Hide extensions for known file types" and then click OK.**

Now open the `customUI` folder that you just made and create a new text file. When prompted for a save name, call it `customUI.xml`. Right-click it, choose Edit, place the following code inside, and save the file:

```
<customUI xmlns="http://schemas.microsoft.com/office/2006/01/customui">
   <ribbon startFromScratch="false">
      <tabs>
         <tab id="rxtabCustom"
            label="My Very Own Tab"
            insertBeforeMso="TabHome">
            <group idMso="GroupFont">
            </group>
            <group idMso="GroupZoom">
            </group>
         </tab>
      </tabs>
   </ribbon>
</customUI>
```

NOTE **This code has been validated and checked for you, so it will work as long as you type it correctly. The leading spaces on each line are to provide clarity, rather than functionality, so they do not affect code performance. However, the code is completely case sensitive, so typing the incorrect case will inevitably cause the code to fail.**

TIP **Rather than type code, you can copy the code from this chapter's companion files. The files for each chapter are available on the book's website.**

Creating the File to Use the Customized UI

Next, create the Excel file that will implement the customization. This will start out as a typical Excel file, but that won't last long because you will *attach* your `customUI.xml` file to it. Naturally, you'll need to use one of the new Office 2007 OpenXML file formats. To do this:

1. Create a folder named "Test" on your Desktop.

2. Open Excel.
3. Create a new workbook if a blank one is not already showing.
4. Save the workbook to your desktop as a 2007 Excel workbook (`.xlsx` format). As shown in Figure 2-1, for the purposes of this example the file is called `MyFirstUIModification.xlsx`.

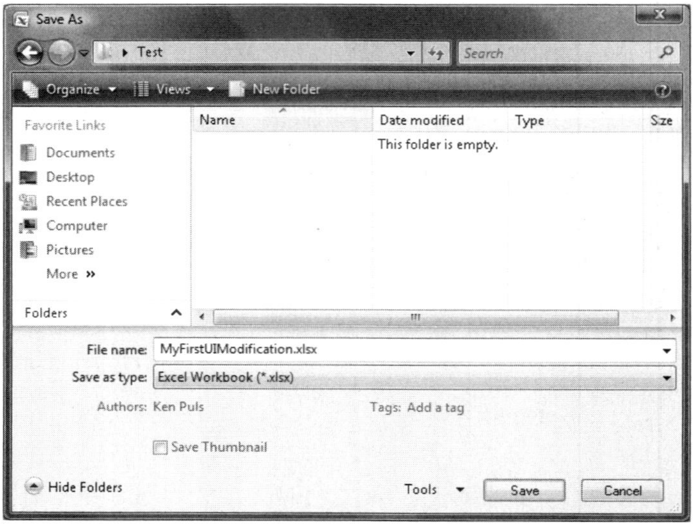

Figure 2-1: Saving an .xlsx file

Attaching the XML to the File

You are now at the stage where you can attach the XML file you created to the workbook itself. To do this, you need to jump through a couple of hoops.

As mentioned earlier in this chapter, all OpenXML files are zip containers; and in order for the RibbonX code to be read, it needs to be *inside* that zip container. Thankfully, this is easier than it sounds.

NOTE All customizations to the user interface are written in XML, which modifies the RibbonX structure within Office. These two terms are used interchangeably throughout this book.

Find the file you created (`MyFirstUIModification.xlsx`), right-click the file name, and choose Rename. Leave the entire filename, including the file type extension, intact, but add `.zip` at the end. The file should now be `MyFirstUIModification.xlsx.zip`. You are changing the filename extension, so make sure you select Yes in response to the warning about the potential consequences of your actions, as shown in Figure 2-2!

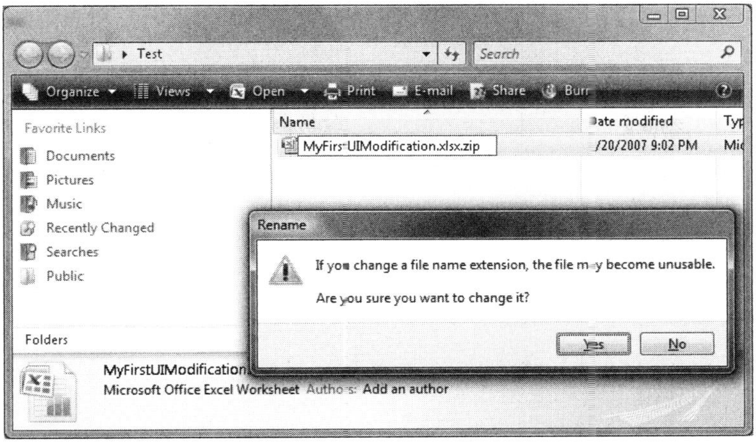

Figure 2-2: Modifying a file's extension to expose its zipped structure

Notice that the file has now changed into a zip file, instead of just a standard Office document file.

NOTE **Renaming the file causes the file to show a different icon, indicating that it is a zipped folder.**

Double-click the zipped file to open it, and you should see the result shown in Figure 2-3.

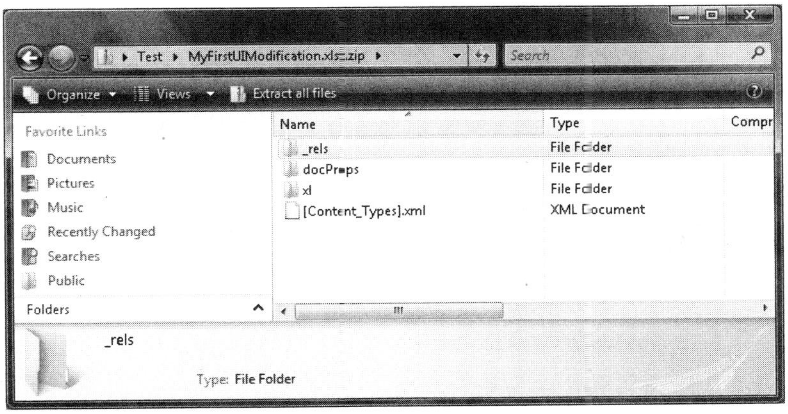

Figure 2-3: The contents of an OpenXML file

Now that you have the zipped file open, you need to move the `customUI` folder into it. The drag-and-drop approach works great for this.

Next, link the UI modifications by editing the `.rels` file to indicate a relationship between the file and the `customUI` folder. To do this, drag the `_rels` folder to your desktop (or another location of your preference). Then, open the newly created `_rels` folder and use Notepad to edit the `.rels` file.

With the `.rels` file open in Notepad, insert the new relationship immediately before the `</Relationship>` element at the end of the file. Specifically, you need to type in the following code, being very careful with punctuation, spaces, and capitalization. The code is case sensitive:

```
<Relationship
   Id="customUIRelID"
   Type="http://schemas.microsoft.com/office/2006/relationships↵
/ui/extensibility"
   Target="customUI/customUI.xml"/>
```

NOTE **The code that you will be looking at in the `.rels` file is all on a single line when you begin, but it's not at all necessary to keep it that way. To make it easier, scroll through the code and insert a hard return after every blank space and `>` character. At the end of the process, you'll end up with code that looks like what is shown in Figure 2-4.**

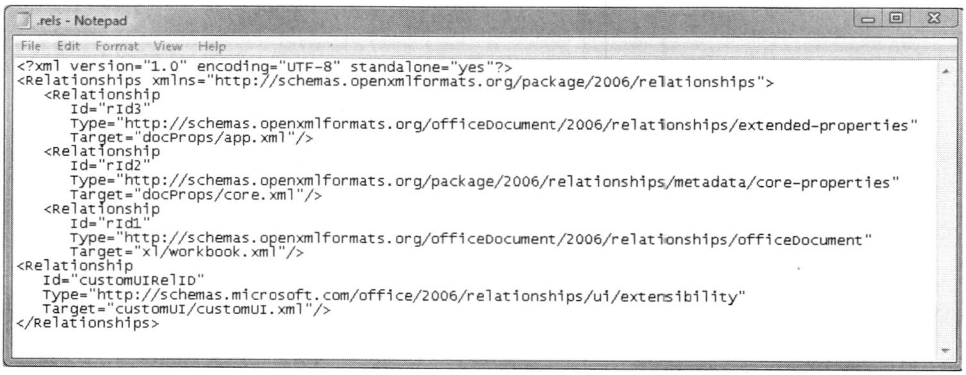

Figure 2-4: The contents of the `.rels` file

Finally, to finish the process, save your new `.rels` file and close Notepad. Return to the zip container and right-click the `_rels` folder and then delete it. You are now ready to drag your copied `_rels` folder back into the document's zip container.

Now that you've saved the `.rels` file and replaced the `_rels` folder, rename your workbook back to the `xlsx` filename that it started with. To do this, again right-click the file and choose Rename; then just knock the `.zip` off the end (so that you're left with `MyFirstUIModifcation.xlsx`). The icon should return to the familiar Excel icon. Finally, open the file in Excel and take a look at what you've accomplished.

NOTE **If you get the error shown in Figure 2-5, check your** `.rels` **and** `customUI.xml` **files. Something is written in the wrong case or spelled incorrectly! If you do see an error like the following, select OK and return to the Custom UI editor to troubleshoot the XML code.**

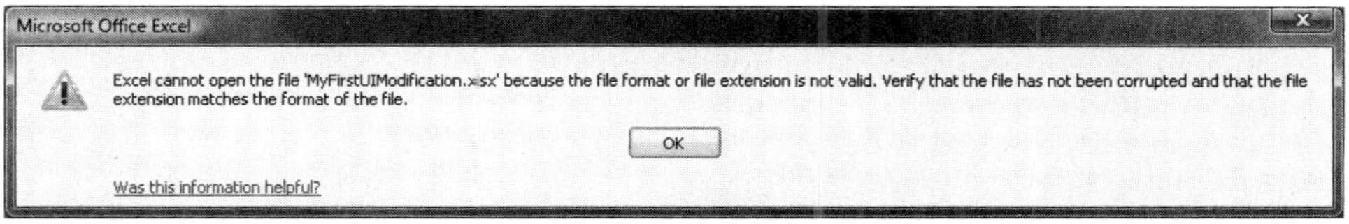

Figure 2-5: An error in the `.rels` or `customUI.xml` files

If you did everything right, a new tab called My Very Own Tab is inserted before the Home tab, which contains both the Font and Zoom groups, as show in Figure 2-6. If you try some of the commands, you'll see that they function just the same as those from Microsoft's built-in groups. Indeed they should, as they are just copies of the built-in groups placed on your new tab.

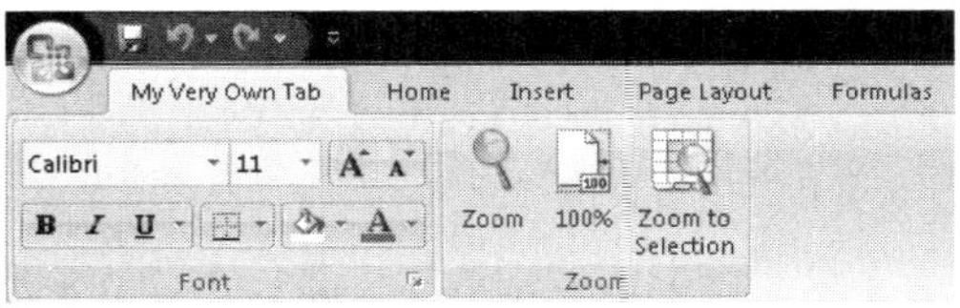

Figure 2-6: My Very Own Tab in Excel

Using the Microsoft Office 2007 Custom UI Editor to Modify Your UI

Without question, using Notepad to set up your Custom UI is a little intimidating and a lot of work. It can be especially frustrating to deal with text wrapping. Fortunately, there is an easier way: using a program called the Microsoft Office 2007 Custom UI Editor. As this is such a mouthful, we'll refer to it as the CustomUI Editor for the rest of the book.

The CustomUI Editor is a handy little utility that makes editing your OpenXML files much easier than the horribly complex route detailed earlier. In addition, it provides some validation and other tools that reduce the stresses of development. Best of all, this utility is available as a free download!

Installing Microsoft .NET Framework 2.0 for Windows XP Users

Are you one of those users who has decided to hold off on installing Windows Vista for any reason? Well, if you're still running on Windows XP, you need to know something before you can move on. We're going to be installing an application to make our jobs easier, but it requires the Microsoft .NET Framework 2.0 to run. Vista users are ready to proceed because Vista ships with version 2.0 of the .NET framework. However, it is another story for computers with Windows XP.

Therefore, before you go any further, it's a good idea to ensure that you have the Microsoft .NET Framework 2.0 installed.

The first check is to go to Start ➪ Control Panel ➪ Add or Remove Programs and check for Microsoft .NET Framework 2.0, as shown in Figure 2-7.

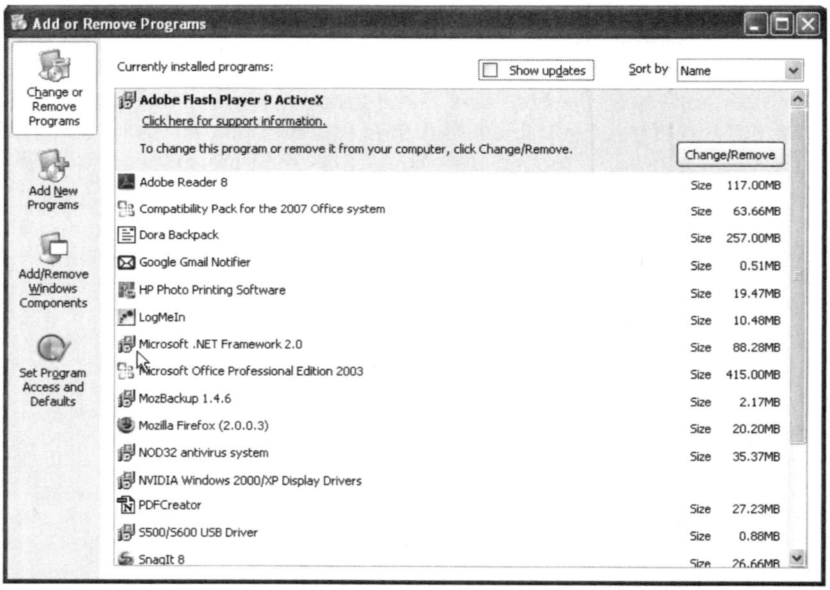

Figure 2-7: Checking for Microsoft .NET Framework 2.0 in Windows XP

If it isn't there, go to Windows Update (or Microsoft Update if you've upgraded) to get the framework. (If you know for a fact that it is not installed, you can go straight there.) The Windows Update site can be reached at `http://update.microsoft.com` (see Figure 2-8). For reference, the Microsoft .NET Framework 2.0 is included under the "Software, Optional" category.

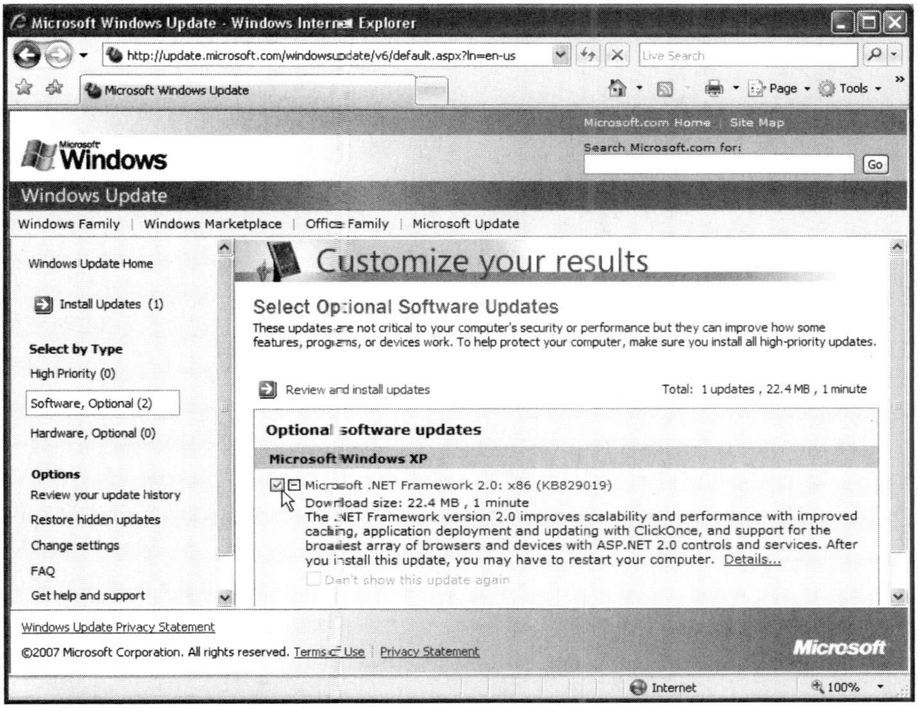

Figure 2-8: Microsoft .NET Framework 2.0 Windows Update

If Microsoft .NET Framework 2.0 isn't in the list for Optional Software updates, it means that the framework has either been installed already and you should retrace the earlier steps, or it was hidden by someone who may have been applying updates in the past. If you suspect that the update was downloaded but hidden instead of installed, click the Restore Hidden Updates link under the Options section on the left, as the update might have been flagged to not be shown.

Once you have downloaded and installed the .NET framework package, go back and check for updates. At the time of writing, there were already two High Priority updates for this product. While you're there, you may want to apply any other critical updates that may have been missed on your system as well.

Now that your Windows XP system is patched and ready, you may proceed to install the CustomUI editor.

NOTE **You could skip the step of checking for the framework and Windows updates, and take your chances that the install would be successful. If the .NET Framework is not present you will see the error shown in Figure 2-9, which will prompt you to obtain the update.**

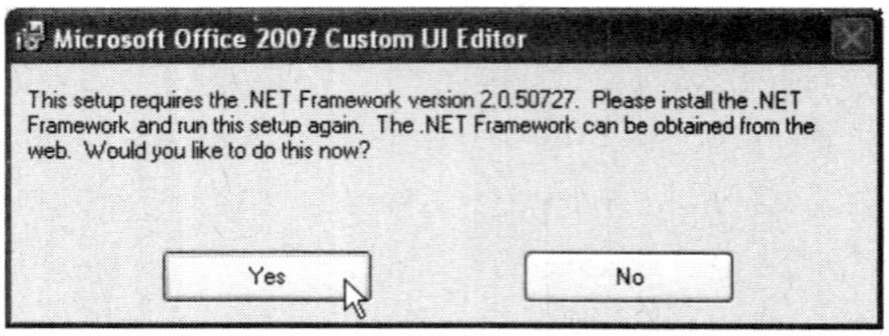

Figure 2-9: .NET Framework missing dialog

Rather than just take your chances with the CustomUI editor installation, we recommend that that you utilize the earlier process and go through Windows Update to get the Microsoft .NET Framework 2.0. This ensures that you get the latest version direct from Microsoft, and it enables you to collect all the critical updates that follow. Keeping your updates current is an important part of computer health, so using Windows Update can kill the proverbial two birds with one stone.

Installing the Microsoft Office 2007 Custom UI Editor

The CustomUI Editor can be downloaded free from `http://openxmldeveloper.org/articles/customuieditor.aspx`. Once downloaded, extract the zip file and install it on your computer.

Once the program is installed, open it. You'll be staring at a blank screen. That's not very exciting, so let's open the file that we've been working on: `MyFirstUIModification.xlsx`. Suddenly, as shown in Figure 2-10, these files are a lot more interesting.

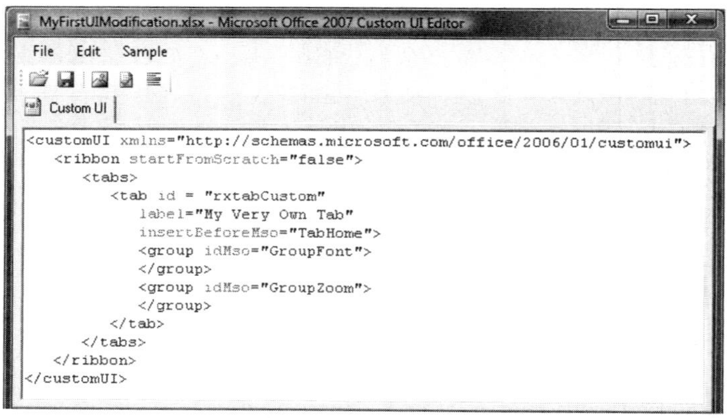

Figure 2-10: The CustomUI Editor in action

Compared to the plain bland text that we saw in Notepad, the code in the CustomUI Editor is quite colorful, rife with red, blue, and burgundy.

Sure, it's nice that it's prettier; but you aren't really interested in pretty code . . . or are you? The benefits of using this program will become much clearer as you proceed through this book; but suffice it to say that the colors help you read and interpret your code. The editor also enables you to easily package pictures, validate your code, store code snippets, and even generate the code framework required to react to callbacks. Ahh, a new term — *callbacks* are custom VBA routines that are fired when you click on your customized Ribbon controls. You'll find that this becomes an indispensable tool in your kit for working with the Ribbon.

Using the CustomUI Editor to Customize the Ribbon

Now that you have the CustomUI editor installed, it's time to try another customization. Like the Notepad method, this will work with Excel or Word files equally well, so this time you'll focus on a Word customization. To illustrate the difference in ease between using the two approaches, you'll use the exact same code, but apply it to a Word document through the CustomUI Editor interface.

To start the process, open Word, create a new document, and save it as a `.docx` file type. Close Word and open the CustomUI Editor. Open the Word file that you just saved through the Custom UI Editor.

Enter the code that we used in the previous example.

TIP **You can either meticulously type the code again or merely copy it from the workbook that you previously created or from the chapter download file.**

Once you have all of your code entered, it is a very good idea to check the validity of your XML code. This step can alert you to many issues that you might not be able to see at first glance, and it can save you a huge amount of guessing when your modifications just don't show up later. To check the validity, click the second toolbar button from the far right — the one with the check mark on it (shown in Figure 2-10). The tool will evaluate the code and report any errors that it might encounter along the way. What you are hoping to see is the message shown in Figure 2-11.

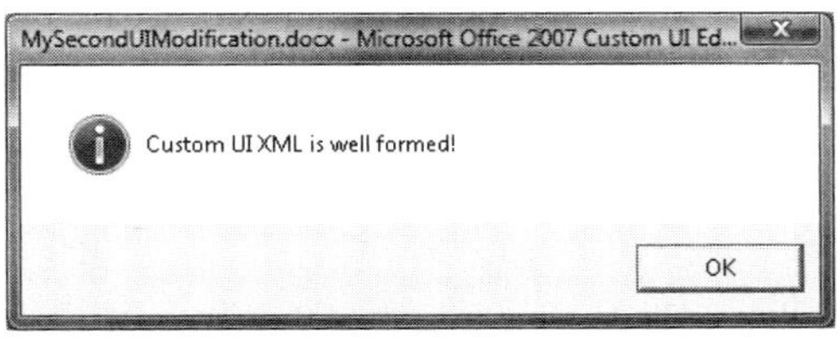

Figure 2-11: Validity check for the Custom UI XML

Ahh, isn't it nice when things are "well formed?" If, on the other hand, you get a message like the one shown in Figure 2-12, there is at least one issue in your code.

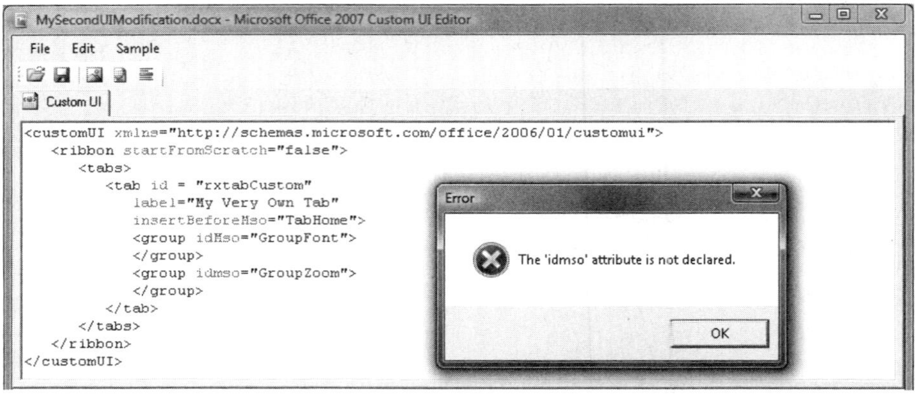

Figure 2-12: Errors in XML validation

At this point, it becomes a hunting game to track down any errors. Careful reading of the error message can help guide you toward a solution. In the case of the message shown in Figure 2-12, the `"idmso"` attribute has been spelled incorrectly; it should be `idMso`. You'll recall that we emphasized the importance of spaces, punctuation, and case. RibbonX code is indeed case sensitive, and is written in what we call CamelCase (uppercase "humps" in the middle of the terms.)

Once you have received the "well formed" message, that's it! You're good to go without making any modifications to the `.rels` file, as the editor takes care of those issues for you! Just hit the Save button and the custom UI is immediately attached to your file.

Close the file in the CustomUI Editor and open your new document in Word. Your modification should be present, as shown in Figure 2-13.

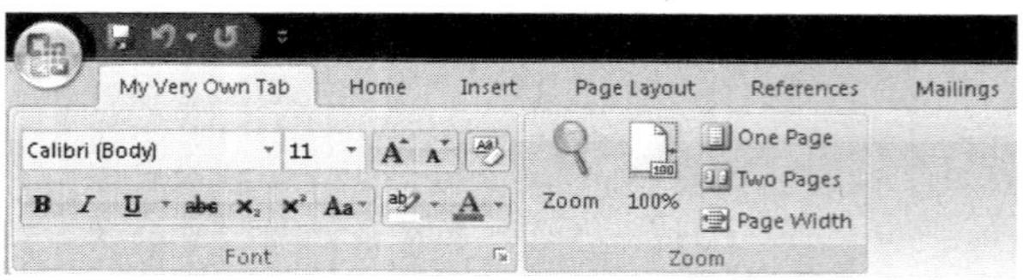

Figure 2-13: "My Very Own Tab" in Word

Note here that despite using the exact same code in both the Excel and Word files, the options on the groups are slightly different. This is because each program has its own way of setting up groups with the applicable commands, but some of the groups share common names across multiple applications.

Storing Customization Templates in the CustomUI Editor

You may encounter scenarios in which you want to refer to a custom UI that you previously developed. Again, you can use the CustomUI Editor to store and access custom templates, as shown in Figure 2-14.

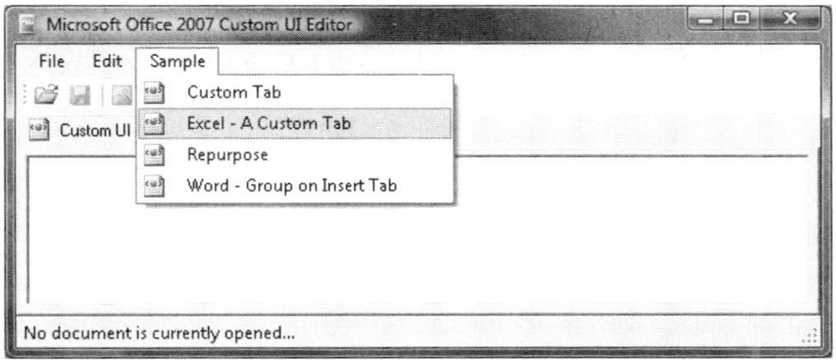

Figure 2-14: CustomUI code templates

To demonstrate the ease and benefits of setting up your own templates, use Notepad to create a new text file on your computer and enter the following code into it:

```
<customUI xmlns="http://schemas.microsoft.com/office/2006/01/customui">
   <ribbon startFromScratch="false">
      <tabs>
         <!-- Enter your first tab here -->
      </tabs>
   </ribbon>
</customUI>
```

Save the file in the folder `Program Files\CustomUI Editor\Samples` with the filename `RibbonBase.xml`.

NOTE **The `Program Files\CustomUI Editor\Samples` path assumes that you used the default installation path for the Microsoft Office 2007 Custom UI Editor. If you installed the program to a different path, you will need to modify the preceding instruction accordingly.**

TIP **If you cannot access this file in Windows Vista, it is due to the User Access Control feature restricting your permissions. You will need administrative rights in order to store these templates in the specified folder.**

Finally, open the CustomUI Editor and select the Samples menu. If your new file is in the right place, you should now see the RibbonBase entry on the list. Click it and voilà! There is your XML template, which you can use to start all future Ribbon customizations!

Now that you have this on your menu, how do you use it? It's quite simple, actually. Just create your new file, open it in the CustomUI Editor, and select your RibbonBase from the menu. It copies all of the code into your file for you, and you're good to go! What a great way to get a head start.

CAUTION **If you open a file that has customizations in place already and select your template, all of your current customizations will be overwritten with the template's code. You can, of course, close the file without saving and not lose your current work.**

Some Notes About Using the CustomUI Editor

The CustomUI Editor is a fantastic utility that makes editing XML code much easier. As with all programs, however, it is not perfect. You should be aware of some CustomUI Editor "gotchas" before you dive right in:

- The CustomUI Editor does check the form of your XML tags, as well as make sure that you only use attributes that are defined in the XML schema. What it does not do, however, is check that you have provided valid attributes within the quotes. (You'll learn about attributes later, but be aware that you can still receive errors even if your XML is well formed.)
- While writing and debugging your RibbonX code, it is very tempting to open your file in both the application and the CustomUI Editor at the same time. Trying to save the file in the CustomUI Editor while the file is open in the Office application will result in an error. In addition, even if you close the document that you are editing in the Office application and then save it in the CustomUI Editor, the editor will overwrite any changes that you made while editing your document in the application! It is much safer to close the file in each application before making changes in the other.

NOTE **If you forget and make changes in the application, you can preserve those changes by saving the file to a new filename. At least then it can be a reference if you want to incorporate the changes into the original document.**

- The CustomUI Editor does not have a Find/Replace utility, so if you're planning to do large-scale editing on your XML, you may want to copy your information to another program, edit it, and then copy it back.
- When working on files that have more lines of XML than will fit on the screen, the CustomUI Editor has an annoying habit of refreshing the screen so that your cursor is always on the last line of the screen. If you are trying to make an edit and want to read the information three lines below, this can become a major irritation. Here, again, you may want to copy your XML data into another editor to work on it and then paste the updated copy back into the CustomUI Editor.

XML Notepad

XML Notepad is another tool that you may find of interest when you are editing or writing your XML code. It is another free download from Microsoft itself. XML Notepad enables you to snap in an XML schema that will validate your code as you work. Unfortunately, as great as this is, it can be a little cumbersome to get your code into the interface. The following detailed steps walk you through linking this all together and getting your code in.

Installing XML Notepad

First, download and install the XML Notepad file. At the time of this writing, it was available at the following URL:

- `www.microsoft.com/downloads/details.aspx?familyid=72d6aa49-787d-4118-ba5f-4f30fe913628&displaylang=en`

Next, you'll also want to download and extract the Office 2007 XML schema:

- `www.microsoft.com/downloads/details.aspx?FamilyId=15805380-F2C0-4B80-9AD1-2CB0C300AEF9&displaylang=en`

NOTE The Office 2007 XML schema page makes reference to Outlook, OneNote, and Visio, but it fails to mention the more popular applications. Just ignore that little oversight and download the file anyway, because those applications are included as well.

The final step in setting up the XML Notepad program is linking the schema to the program. Open the XML Notepad program, and choose View ➪ Schemas from the menu. When you reach the XML Schemas screen, choose File ➪ Add schemas and browse to the folder to which the XML schemas were extracted. (The default location is `C:\2007 Office System Developer Resources\Office2007XMLSchema\CustomUI.xsd`). Once the schema has been added, as shown in Figure 2-15, click OK.

Figure 2-15: Adding an XML schema to XML Notepad

Using XML Notepad

The most difficult part about using XML Notepad is getting your file into it to begin with. It does not just open Excel or Word files like the CustomUI Editor; and, sadly, you can't even create a new file from within it. Instead, you need to open an existing XML file. There are two main strategies for doing this:

- You can rename your document to a zip file, as you would do when editing with Notepad, and copy the `CustomUI.xml` file out so that you can work on it. Naturally, when you've finished editing your code, you'll need to copy the updated `CustomUI.xml` file back into the zip container and again rename the .xlsx file to use the original file extension.

or

- You can create a blank text file, copy in your existing XML from the CustomUI Editor, save the file as an XML file, and then open it in XML Notepad. At this point, you could edit the code and then send it back to the CustomUI Editor, where you would save it with your file.

You're probably now wondering why you would want to go through all this pain. The answer lies in the ability to use the XML Notepad program to your advantage. Unlike the CustomUI Editor, this program offers you several features to easily create valid files without any risk of typing errors. That, as any developer knows, is a huge benefit. To demonstrate this:

1. Open the `MyFirstUIModification.xlsx` file in the CustomUI Editor.
2. Copy all of the code there and then close the CustomUI Editor.
3. Right-click your desktop and create a new text file. When prompted for a name, call the file `temp.xml`.
4. Right-click the new file and choose Edit (do not choose Edit with XML Notepad at this stage).
5. Paste the code that you copied from the CustomUI Editor.
6. Save the file and close it.
7. Right-click the file again, but this time choose Edit with XML Notepad.

NOTE **If you are working in Windows XP, the Edit with XML Notepad option will not be present on the right-click menu. You will need to choose Open With and select the XML Notepad program from there.**

Once you are in the program, click to expand all the little plus (+) icons, and you should be looking at a screen like the one shown in Figure 2-16. Talk about a graphical display. You just entered developer heaven.

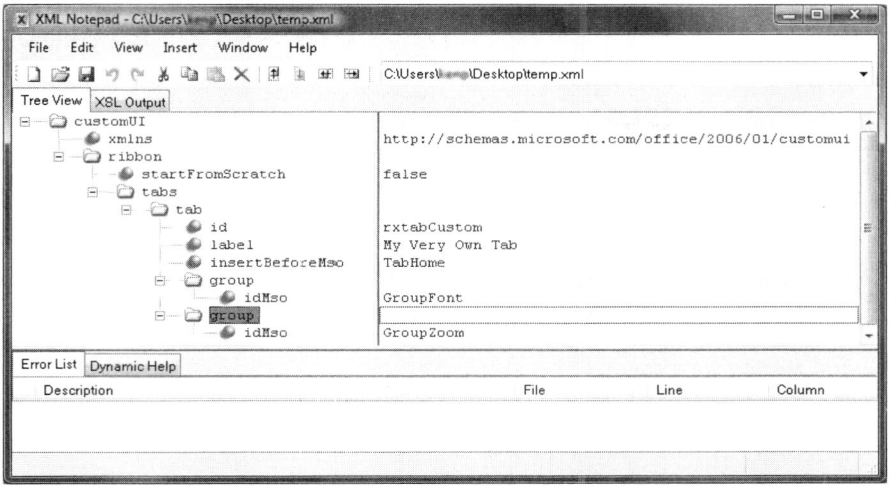

Figure 2-16: XML Notepad

Right-click the "tab" element, choose Element, and then choose Child. As shown in Figure 2-17, this will create a new element under the last group.

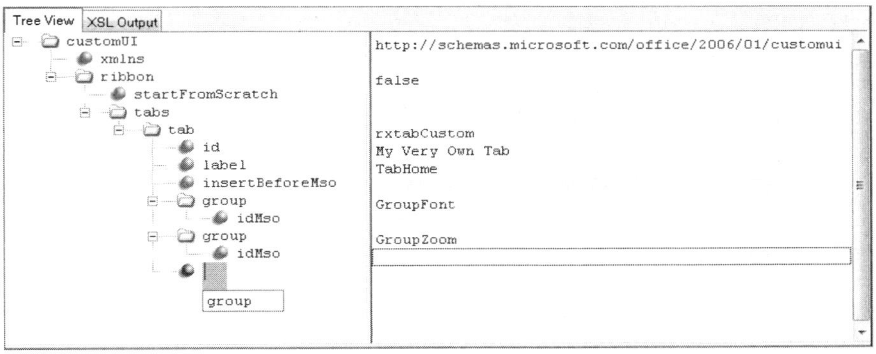

Figure 2-17: Adding an element to XML Notepad

Notice that the program provides you with a list of all the items that will fit here — in this case, the "group" element. Click it to set this element as a group in the code.

Next, right-click the group, choose Attribute, and then choose Child. This time the list will be much longer. You're after `idMso`, so scroll until you find it, and then click to select it. Once you've done this, you'll notice that your cursor appears on the right side of the screen. Click on the line corresponding to `idMso`, and type in the following case-sensitive text: **GroupStyles** (see Figure 2-18).

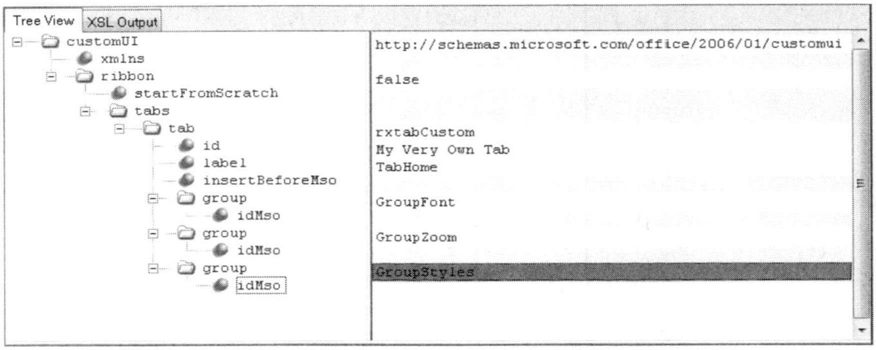

Figure 2-18: Adding an attribute to XML Notepad

Now that you have some newly modified code, you'll want to try it out. From the View menu, choose Source, and select Yes when prompted to save your code. You'll then see a screen like the one shown in Figure 2-19, which shows your new markup.

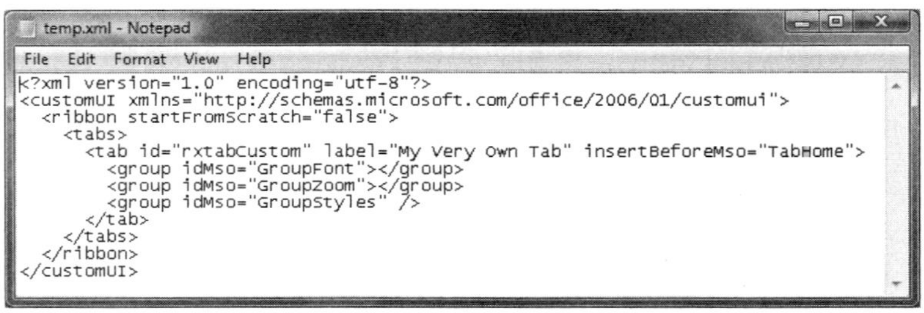

Figure 2-19: Viewing XML source code in XML Notepad

Notice that the code is in a slightly different format than what was previously written, and that there are some extra elements that you might not have seen before. That is to be expected, as the XML Notepad editor adds markup that is valid but not required. Don't worry if the code that you create manually does not have all of these tags.

Now that you've had a good look at the view shown in Figure 2-19, you'll want to do the following:

1. Copy the entire set of code and close the window.
2. Open your `MyFirstUIModification.xlsx` file in the CustomUI Editor.
3. Press Ctrl+A to select all the existing code.
4. Paste the code that you copied from the XML Notepad program.
5. Run a validity check (just to be sure), and then save and close the file.

Finally, open the `MyFirstUIModification.xlsx` file and check the appearance of the My Very Own Tab tab. It should look similar to what is shown in Figure 2-20.

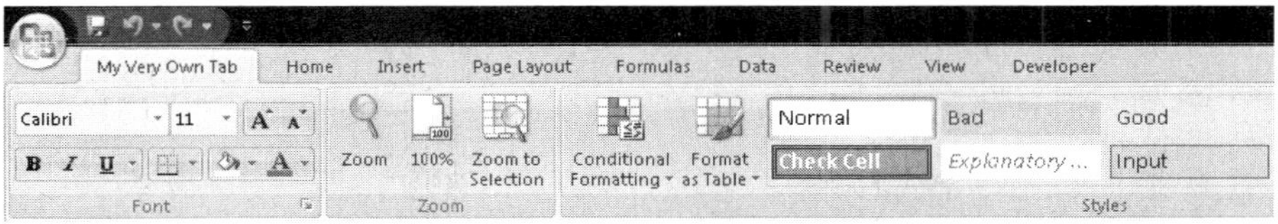

Figure 2-20: The updated My Very Own Tab tab in Excel

If you chose to apply this customization in Word instead, it would look like what is shown in Figure 2-21.

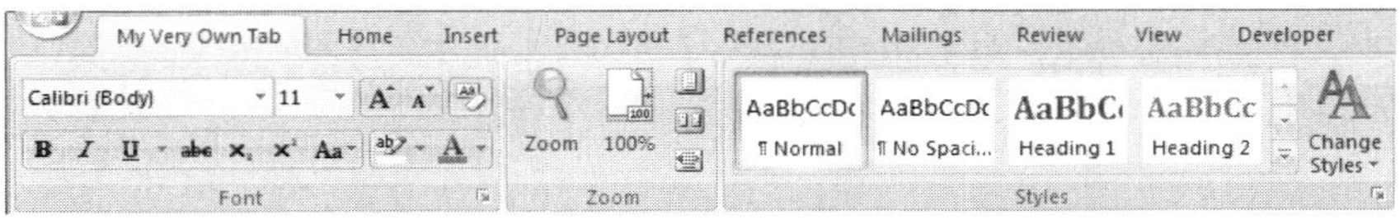

Figure 2-21: The updated My Very Own Tab tab in Word

The Benefits of XML Notepad

XML Notepad offers many benefits that are not available in the CustomUI Editor or standard Notepad, including the following:

- XML Notepad can make development easier because, with the relevant schema installed, valid elements and attributes are available from the drop-down lists, similar in function to the IntelliSense features available in most Microsoft coding tools.
- XML Notepad, unlike the CustomUI Editor, is capable of doing find-and-replace-style searches. This is a major benefit of the XML Notepad, and you will have ample opportunities to use it.
- XML Notepad includes a "Nudge" feature, which will move a block of code up or down as a unit. This feature does not exist in either Notepad or the CustomUI Editor.
- The stepped layout displayed in XML Notepad makes it easy to identify what elements are nested where, a feature that is not evident in Notepad or the CustomUI Editor.
- Because XML Notepad is linked to an XML schema, it can do live validity checking on-the-fly and report the errors that it finds, another feature that is not available in Notepad.

The Drawbacks of XML Notepad

Aside from the obvious problems of getting your file into and out of the editor, there are some other things that the CustomUI Editor offers that XML Notepad does not:

- The error-checking features of XML Notepad and the CustomUI Editor look for different things. Although selecting from the drop-down lists will build well-formed XML, XML Notepad does not actually validate your code. Therefore, these two programs should be used in tandem to give your code the best chance of being validated to perfection.
- The CustomUI Editor can generate callback signatures for you. You'll learn in later chapters that you can look these up, but it is much easier to have them generated for you automatically. XML Notepad has no facility to do this.
- The CustomUI Editor was written to make building your custom user interface easy. In addition to automatic setup of certain code portions, it also provides an easy interface for attaching pictures to your files. XML Notepad lacks this capability.
- If you start your modification by creating your `customUI.xml` file in XML Notepad instead of the CustomUI Editor, you'll need to manually link your `.rels` file, as shown earlier in this chapter. Therefore, we recommend that you use the CustomUI Editor to set up your initial linkage. However, the construction of the CustomUI code could still be done in XML Notepad and then copied to the CustomUI Editor for inclusion, as we did in the example.

A Final Word on Excel and Word Customizations

This section has covered how to open Excel and Word files for customization, and it demonstrated a couple of tools that can be used to make the job easier. It's important to realize that the CustomUI Editor and XML Notepad tools work in tandem with each other, and that they each have their own benefits and drawbacks.

Despite the difficulty in porting code back and forth between the two programs, they offer complementary benefits, and neither program should be relied on to provide a solo solution for creating and editing XML files.

Microsoft Access Customizations

Unlike Word and Excel files, which are based on the new OpenXML file standard, Microsoft Access is still a binary file. While the basic XML used for customization is virtually the same between all the applications, the binary file structure dictates that Access Ribbon customizations are loaded through a completely different method from that used with Open XML files, such as Excel or Word.

At first glance, customizing Access's UI via a table may seem quite complex, but Access is actually rather flexible when it comes to customization, as you'll see as you progress through this section.

Storing the CustomUI Information in Tables

The most logical starting point when dealing with Ribbon modifications in Access is to hold the XML code in a table. It also happens to be the easiest route to a customized UI in Access. The following customization example demonstrates how to accomplish this.

Creating an Access UI Modification Using a Table

This example builds the custom tab shown in Figure 2-22 in a new database project.

Figure 2-22: My Very Own Tab tab in Access

To get this customization up and running, you'll want to do the following:

1. Open Access and create a new database.
2. Right-click Table1 on the left, and choose Design View.
3. When prompted, give the table the name `USysRibbons`.
4. Make sure that the table has the following three fields:
   - ID (an autonumber field to serve as the index for the UI records)
   - RibbonName (it should be a text type field)
   - RibbonXml (it should be a memo type field)
5. Close the table, saving it when prompted.

NOTE **If your table disappears in the All Tables view, simply right-click All Tables and choose Navigation Options. Check the box that says "Show system objects" and click OK.**

TIP **Naming the table with the "USys" prefix — for example, USysRibbons — ensures that the table will be hidden in the Navigation Pane unless the Show System Objects option is checked under the Navigation Options dialog.**

Next, open the `USysRibbons` table and add a new record to it. For the RibbonName field, type in a meaningful name (perhaps something such as `MainRibbonUI`). In the RibbonXml field, paste the following XML code:

```
<customUI xmlns="http://schemas.microsoft.com/office/2006/01/customui">
   <ribbon startFromScratch="false">
      <tabs>
         <tab id="rxtabCustom"
            label="My Very Own Tab"
            insertBeforeMso="TabHomeAccess">
            <group idMso="GroupRichText">
            </group>
            <group idMso="GroupRecords">
            </group>
         </tab>
      </tabs>
   </ribbon>
</customUI>
```

TIP **The preceding code is available from the chapter download files, but if you are typing this by hand, you may want to do so in the CustomUI Editor discussed earlier in this chapter. While the CustomUI Editor cannot directly place the XML code in your Access database, it is a viable tool for checking your XML code for consistency. Keep in mind that this is sensitive to case, space, and punctuation.**

Your table may resemble Figure 2-23 after you paste the XML code into the RibbonXml field:

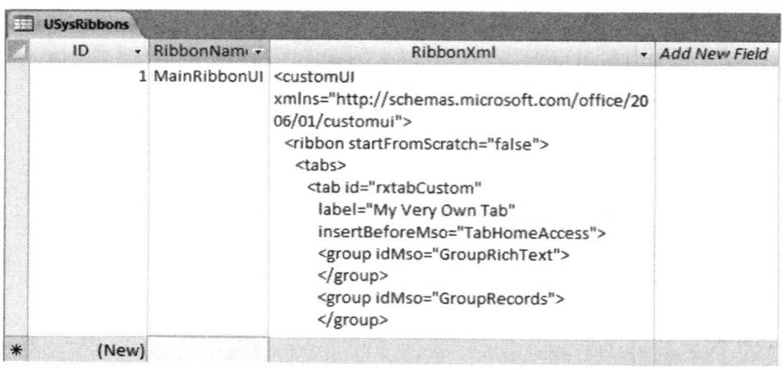

Figure 2-23: Pasting XML code into the USysRibbons table

Next, save the table, and then close and reopen the database file. When it reopens, go to Access Options (in the Office Menu) and select the Current Database option. There, under Ribbon and Toolbar Options, you will find an option (Ribbon Name) to select your custom Ribbon UI from the drop-down list, as shown in Figure 2-24.

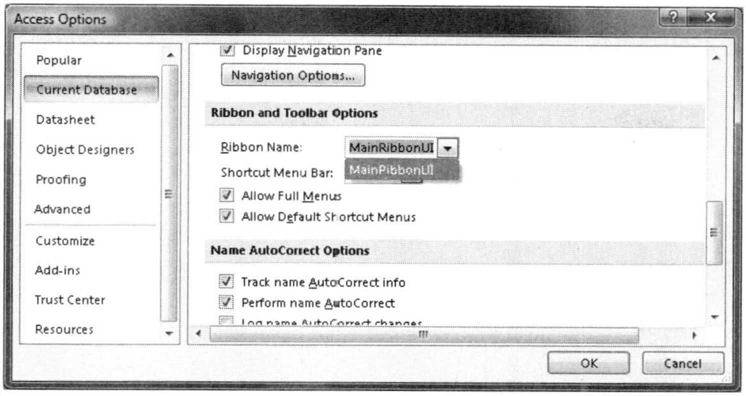

Figure 2-24: Linking the RibbonUI to your database

Unfortunately, you'll now be required to close the file one more time to allow the changes to take effect. Upon reopening the database, however, your UI should be loaded.

Without question, this method is very time consuming. You have to go through many steps in order to have your UI recognized by the system before you can finally get the Ribbon to show. Even worse, it seems to force you to reopen the database more times than you have to do restarts after applying a service pack! You'd think that there would be a more efficient way, but apparently not yet.

If you are testing many different UIs and need to swap between them, a better approach would be to use VBA to carry out this task for you. Obviously, you still need to spend some time writing your VBA code, but once it is done, you can reuse it as many times as you want.

We will come back to such issues later in the book when you are introduced to some advanced concepts of Ribbon customization.

CROSS-REFERENCE **See Chapter 16 for other deployment methods for your custom UI.**

Access USysRibbons Caveat

Despite the shuffle of opening and reopening the database to do the initial link up of the new UI, you'll probably agree that this is a relatively minor hassle. Once you are through that initial pain, you're off to the races and can customize to your heart's content, right? Well, before you can sit back and relax, you should know that Access also suffers from a limitation in terms of using the `USysRibbons` table.

For seasoned Access developers, it is a well-known fact that the maximum number of characters allowed in a memo field is 65,535. And while that seems like a lot, and it may be sufficient for most projects, you may have realized that a very complex UI could easily run into hundreds of thousands of characters. Therefore, it is quite conceivable that it could surpass the field's character limit.

What would happen if you tried to paste XML code that exceeded this limitation into the RibbonXml field? Well, it simply is not possible. Due to the character limitation, you would not be allowed to paste the UI into this field.

Great, so now what can you do to get around this limitation? Luckily, when you are using DAO instead of the UI, the Memo field has a 1GB limit, which is also restricted to text and numbers (not binary data). So, although the 65K limit should be enough to contain most customizations, there's actually a significant capacity that should be more than enough for even the most complex UI. But in the event that you need even more, we'll mention some other techniques.

Other Techniques for Access UI Customizations

By now you're likely wondering what the heck to do if your customization becomes much bigger than you expected, and it blows past the 65,535 character limit. Fortunately, there are actually several ways to store your custom UI code, and only one has that limit. So far, some of the known methods you can use to store your UI XML are as follows:

- Store the XML in a table (as you've already seen).
- Read the XML from external files.
- Store the XML in another Access database.
- Link to Excel worksheets that contain XML.

In addition, if you run into the character limitation problem and are absolutely determined to store your XML code in the `USysRibbons` table (instead of having it in an external file), you can also turn to VBA for help. This does involve another layer of programming, but it is an available alternative.

Because there are many more things that you need to know before becoming fluent in customizing the new UI, we're going to hold off on discussing these additional methods. Rest assured, however, that there are indeed ways to get around the character limit. Chapter 16 illustrates some of these methods, providing examples of your UI customizations from external files and other Access databases.

Conclusion

In this chapter, you have seen how to get your XML/RibbonX code for ribbon modification into the appropriate files.

For Excel and Word files, you've seen the hard way to accomplish this task, as well as the easier ways to build and edit your code with a variety of free tools available on the internet. Unfortunately, while each of these tools is useful in its own way, each lacks the cohesion that would be nice in a single product. Some are better for setup and others are better for editing, but none come without drawbacks. It seems that playing in this field will involve some application switching until someone builds an all-in-one tool to work with Ribbon modification.

For Access files, you've learned that there are several ways to implement the customizations, and you've walked through a simple example of using a table to do so. We've also alerted you to the limitations of storing customizations in a table. Finally, we've promised that later in this book, we will share some secrets about overcoming such limitations.

CHAPTER

3

Understanding XML

This chapter explores the fundamentals of building a custom user interface in Office 2007. Chapter 2 discussed how to access the customization layer, so you are now ready to learn how to create the core XML framework needed to access and manipulate the built-in Ribbon.

This chapter begins by exploring what XML is and how it factors into customizing the new UI. It then follows with an explanation of each of the core elements needed to create or modify the Ribbon. Each section builds on the ones before, and they each employ only XML code.

If you've never programmed anything before, don't worry. No programming knowledge is required to get started — at least, nothing more complicated than how to open the file for customization, which was covered in Chapter 2.

As you are preparing to work through the examples, we encourage you to download the companion files. The source code and files for this chapter can be found on the book's web site at `www.wiley.com/go/ribbonx`.

What Is XML and Why Do You Need It?

XML is an acronym for Extensible Markup Language, originally published by the W3C World Wide Web Consortium. It is not truly a programming language, as it lacks any mechanism to perform actions, but rather is a set of rules intended to simplify the sharing of data across platforms.

As you saw in detail in Chapter 2, Office 2007 files are deployed in Microsoft's OpenXML format, which is simply a zipped container holding several XML files. So why XML?

The great selling point of XML is data structure. By leveraging XML technology, the Office 2007 programs are able to split like data into "chunks" and store them in the XML portions of the file. For example, you can envision a Word document with an XML table of "strings" (or words) in it.

Assume that you have an entire story written that uses the word "magical" 100 times. Rather than store the seven-character string 100 times in the document, the XML structure may refer to string 102, saving four characters each time. This is a very simplified example, of course, but you can see that this kind of operation could quickly result in saving space. That is just one of the benefits of the XML structure.

In addition, by having your data structured, it can be quickly indexed. This is important, as it enables other programs to search the index for specific strings (words) or other terms.

A great example to demonstrate how indexing can add valuable functionality is to think of a banking process. Each time an e-mail is sent, the indexed XML underlying any attachments can quickly be checked for strings matching key fields or patterns (such as bank account numbers, social security/insurance numbers, and the like.) If these strings are found, confidentiality can be enforced by programmatically removing or encrypting the data.

Both of the aforementioned benefits are great, but for the developer there is yet another factor that can prove its weight in gold. You can link XML schemas within certain programs to validate XML and thereby ensure that it will work as intended. The CustomUI Editor and XML Notepad, both discussed in Chapter 2, make use of XML schemas. Without these schemas, the CustomUI Editor would not be able to validate code, and XML Notepad would not be able to provide IntelliSense, which provides or prompts with the available object or functions when writing code.

Again, this is all wonderful, and it's nice to know what XML is all about, but why should we care?

We care about XML because it is the heart of the Ribbon. In order to customize the Office 2007 user interface, you must write XML code; and while it is true that Visual Basic for Applications (VBA) can also play a huge part in customization, it is not always necessary. XML, on the other hand, almost always is. We say "almost always" because we will show you the proverbial exception that proves the rule by providing a customization that does not require XML, such as pop-up menus and some VBA customizations that appear on the Add-Ins tab. These are discussed in Chapters 15 and 16, respectively.

The rest of this chapter focuses strictly on how to build your XML framework from the ground up. Beginning with creating a placeholder for your first button, this chapter will guide you through the XML required to build and modify the Ribbon. These concepts must be mastered before you can move on to fluently work with more complex customizations.

Essential Background

Before you can start running with XML, you need to learn essential background information — namely, how XML is structured and how to write it. If you have used HTML in the past, certain things will be familiar to you. Otherwise, don't to worry if you are starting from scratch; these concepts are straightforward and easy to learn.

Tags

An XML document, such as the `customUI.xml` file you learned about in Chapter 2, works by placing verbal cues among the content, giving the document an immediately obvious structure. (This is true even if what is being structured is not that obvious.) The collection of all of these cues is referred to as *markup* (the *M* in XML).

The verbal cues are known as *tags*, and they take a consistent format to be considered valid. Consider the following snippet of code:

```
<group id="rxgrpTest">
   <button idMso="Bold"/>
   <button idMso="Italic"/>
   <splitButton id="rxsbtnTest">
        <button idMso="Underline"/>
   </splitButton>
</group>
```

Looking at the structure of the preceding code, note the use of the `<`, `>`, and `/` signs. These characters have very special uses in XML: they denote where tags start and end. For example, notice that everything between the opening `<group>` tag and the closing `</group>` tag is included within the group as it appears on the Ribbon.

The splitButton that is listed within the group uses a structure that is identical to the group. It starts with the `<splitButton>` tag and holds all the items following until the splitButton is closed by the `</splitButton>` tag. In the preceding example, only the Underline button would appear on the splitButton.

Now look at the code for the buttons themselves. Notice that the / character sits at the end of the tag and that it doesn't require a separate tag to close the element.

This demonstrates two methods that can be used for opening and closing XML tags. You need to understand and use both methods to build the structure for your customUI. Both methods are listed in Table 3-1.

Table 3-1: Forms for Opening and Closing Tags

TYPE	FORM
Open and Close separate	`<element attribute(s)="value"></element>`
Open and Close in one	`<element attribute(s)="value"/>`

At this point, you should understand that each tag in XML contains at least one element and usually at least one attribute. If you examine the preceding code snippet, you'll see that the first line uses a `group` element, which has an `id` attribute: `<group id="rxgrpTest">`. Whereas the elements and attributes are the portions within the angle brackets, the tag refers to the entire clause, from the < to the >.

How, then, would you know which method to choose? Which do you use for a group and when? What about a button? These are all great questions that this chapter will clarify, leading to your understanding of the fundamental concepts being covered. The answers lie in the relationship between parent and child objects in the XML code.

If you have much experience with programming, this concept will not be new to you. If you are new, however, you need to become familiar with it, so bear with us as we explain the coding "facts of life."

When working with code, every item that we deal with is referred to as an *object*. For example, objects include a group on the Ribbon, a button, a checkBox, or even a menu. Like humans, many (but not all) objects have children, and when a control has children, we refer to it as a *parent control*. One thing that should be made clear here is that, in the code world, a parent object usually (but not always) has child objects of a different type. A tab will have one or more group objects as children, and a group may have a combination of button, checkBox, and dynamicMenu child objects. The `dynamicMenu` object, however, is especially talented, and can have `dynamicMenu` children in addition to other children object types. Some parent objects even have an entire horde of children, referred to as a *collection*.

As you would expect, each child can also be a parent to its own children. This is where the structure of XML can actually come in quite handy, as the relationships between parent and child can be easily seen. Every child control must be "nested" within its parent's opening and closing tags. It should be noted that unlike humans, however, every child object may only have one parent.

In the following snippet (from the code shown earlier), you can see that the `splitButton` object contains one child button and that the button does not have any children of its own. This is why the button ends with the / character, whereas the splitButton has separated opening and closing tags. Likewise, the group parent contains the splitButton child (with its own children), as well as two other button controls:

```
<splitButton id="rxsbtnTest">
     <button idMso="Underline"/>
</splitButton>
```

You should understand a few other things in order to create well-formed (valid) XML:

- All tags, be they elements or attributes, are case sensitive (a `SPLITBUTTON` element is not the same as a `splitButton` element).
- Attribute values must be enclosed in single or double quotation marks (it doesn't matter which).
- The nesting of child elements within a parent is precise. *Every* start tag must be matched with *its own* end tag, whether it is closed within the same tag (via "`/>`") or by a separate tag later.

These rules help highlight a quick visual flag, so to speak. If the / is by the closing > (as shown in the button line of the preceding code), you know that the tag is a complete, standalone tag. However, if the / directly follows the opening < (</), it signals that the tag is closing an element that was opened earlier. This is clearly illustrated on the last line of the preceding code sample as it provides the closing tag of the splitButton element. This is an important style to remember as you learn to read through and interpret XML or HTML code.

Elements

When working with the Ribbon's XML, each element can be seen as referring to the particular portion of the Ribbon's controls (or structure) that you wish to work with. As you build your custom UI, you will find that you reference elements on a very regular basis.

The difference between a tag and an element can be unclear to a novice, but is actually easily defined: whereas a `group` is an element, `<group>` is a tag. Therefore, the tag is essentially the label that you use to identify any block of code surrounded by the < and > characters.

Each tag must include one, and only one, element. In addition, the element will always be in the first part of an XML tag. It tells the compiler which specific item you wish to start working with or stop working with.

Attributes

Attributes are a very important aspect of XML as well. Unlike tags, which tell the compiler what object to work with, attributes tell the compiler about the object's properties. Some examples include the object's name, the caption that shows on the screen, and whether or not the object is visible.

Unlike elements, you may set more than one attribute for an object within a given tag. The following code snippet shows an example of a tag with multiple attributes:

```
<button id="rxbtnProtectAll"
   size="normal"
   label="Protect All Sheets"
   imageMso="ReviewProtectWorkbook"
   onAction="rxbtnProtectAll_click"/>
```

The preceding code gives a button a unique id and specifies a size, label, and image for the button. In addition, it provides an `onAction` callback signature that will launch a VBA procedure when the button is clicked.

CROSS-REFERENCE **VBA callbacks are explained in great detail in Chapter 5.**

The next two sections discuss two very important attributes that are used virtually everywhere: `id` and `label`.

The id Attribute

Before we create additional objects, we need to discuss how to identify them in code. The `id` attribute is used to identify a specific object within your custom XML code, giving it a name that you can use to refer to it later. As this is the only way to refer to your objects, some form of an `id` attribute is required for each object that resides within any of the following containers:

- `contextualTabs`
- `officeMenu`
- `qat`
- `tabs`

There are several different types of `id` attributes and each one has a different use. Table 3-2 describes the different types of `id` attributes and their main purposes.

Table 3-2: Table of id Attributes

ATTRIBUTE	WHEN TO USE
id	This is used to uniquely identify your control. If you're loading items dynamically, these will be assigned for you.
idMso	This is used to uniquely identify a built-in control, tab, command, etc. Use this to interact with built-in objects.
idQ	This is used to refer to objects across a shared namespace. Shared namespaces are covered in detail in Chapter 16.

The following examples demonstrate the use of the `id` and the `idMso` attributes to refer to controls. You will learn how to construct the XML later, but for now we are focused on grasping concepts related to the `id`.

In order to identify an object, you simply add the `id` attribute within the opening tag. For example, to refer to a tab by `id`, you'd provide the following XML:

```
<tab id="rxtab">
   <!-- Other tab attributes would go here! -->
</tab>
```

NOTE **The preceding snippet provides an example of how to include a comment by preceding it with the opening `<!--` and closing it with the ending `-->`. XML comments are discussed later in this chapter.**

Likewise, if we were trying to refer to the built in `Font` group, we'd point to it by using the following XML:

```
<group idMso="Font">
   <!-- Other group attributes would go here! -->
</group>
```

NOTE **It is critically important that all `id` and `idQ` attributes be unique. Using an `id` that exists, or that is reserved by Microsoft, will result in an error and prevent your UI from loading.**

You can see where naming conventions can be your friend. This also raises a concern about the potential for conflicts when you start sharing customizations. In order to avoid conflicts with built-in Microsoft controls, it is advisable to prefix all of your custom controls using a standardized naming convention. A list of suggested prefixes, which we use throughout this book, can be found in Appendix E. Because each developer assigns the `id` of custom objects, you should employ common sense and good practices to minimize confusion or frustration.

The label Attribute

Another important attribute is the `label`. The label is what the user can read onscreen. This does not need to be unique, but it should be logical, concise, and consistent.

Whereas the `id` attribute is used to keep track of objects by the system, the `label` attribute is used to provide clear guidance to the user. As demonstrated earlier, adding a label merely requires adding a line of code to the XML. You simply follow the opening tag with as many attributes as you wish and then add the closing tag, as illustrated in the following snippet:

```
<tab id="rxtab"
   label="My Custom Tab">
</tab>
```

Tips for Laying Out XML Code

If you have seen any XML for the new UI, you may have despaired at the coding mess that can come along with it. Who wouldn't feel bewildered the first time they saw a block of text like the following?

```
<tab id="rxtab" label="My Custom Tab" insertBeforeMso = "TabHome" >
<group id="rxgrp" label='My First Group">
<button id="rxbtn1" imageMso="Italic" label="Large size button"
size="large" onAction="rxbtn1_Click"/>
<button id="rxbtn2" imageMso="Bold" label="Normal size button"
size="normal" onAction="rxbtn2_Click"/>
<button id="rxbtn3" imageMso="WrapText" label="Normal size button"
size="normal" onAction="rxbtn3_Click"/>
<button id="rxbtn4" imageMso="ConditionalFormatting" label="Normal size
button" size="normal" onAction="rxbtn4_Click"/>
</group>
</tab>
```

In fact, the preceding code is relatively short, and by now it should be reasonably easy to understand. After all, it has only a few clearly marked groups and buttons. This code creates a new tab, "My Custom Tab," and inserts it before the default Home tab. The new tab has the group My First Group, which contains four buttons. You might have noticed that the first label is large, but the remaining three labels are normal. This XML also states that the buttons will invoke an action when clicked, but it does not actually include the code to implement the action. We'll get to that in Chapters 4 and 5, when we discuss the basics of VBA that are associated with Ribbon customizations, and how to implement callbacks.

As you read through the XML, you might feel as though it isn't quite as clear as you first thought, and you might also realize that it is not enough to deploy a custom group on the Ribbon. This is where the trouble starts. It's obvious that we need to add all sorts of attributes to tabs, groups, commands, and so on. Moreover, as you might expect, the code can grow rather rapidly and become nearly impossible to read.

Obviously, trying to find a specific control in hundreds of lines of code similar to the preceding example can be aggravating. To that end, we suggest that you break up your code into logical blocks using hard returns and tabs. Fortunately, the XML code ignores these characters!

TIP Unlike VBA, you can include hard returns and tabs in the XML without affecting the code. Therefore, we highly recommend that you divide the code into easy-to-read-and-interpret blocks. Several good models are provided throughout this book and in the chapter downloads.

Have a look at the following adjusted example. Clearly, it is much easier to read:

```
<group
   id="rxgrp"
   label="My First Group">

   <button
        id="rxbtn1"
        imageMso="Italic"
        label="Large size button"
        size="large"
        onAction="rxbtn1_Click"/>

   <button
        id="rxbtn2"
        imageMso="Bold"
        label="Normal size button"
        size="normal"
        onAction="rxbtn2_Click"/>

   <button
        id="rxbtn3"
        imageMso="WrapText"
        label="Normal size button"
```

```
        size="normal"
        onAction="rxbtn3_Click"/>

    <button
        id="rxbtn4"
        imageMso="ConditionalFormatting"
        label="Normal size button"
        size="normal"
        onAction="rxbtn4_Click"/>
</group>
```

On the one hand, in the preceding reformatted example, the code is definitely longer. On the other hand, it is clear that the buttons belong to one specific group, as the command button is stepped inside its tag bracket. In addition, because each button's attributes have also been indented, you can easily refer to them and edit them as necessary. Space really isn't an issue, so it makes sense to use the whitespace to make it easy to read, interpret, and edit. Trust us, you'll thank yourself when you are trying to work with something you wrote six months ago!

Creating Comments in XML Code

It is inevitable that at some point you will want to place a comment in the XML code. Comments are excellent tools to give yourself or someone else a clue about what the code is doing. Comments can be invaluable in complex or unique situations. To include a comment, you start by opening it with a "less than" sign (<). Then you type the exclamation mark (!) followed by two hyphens (--). Closing a comment requires two hyphens followed by a "greater than" sign (>).

```
<!--This is a comment -->
```

If you think your comment may run to several lines, you might want to break it down between the opening and closing tags, as shown in the following example:

```
<!--
This is a comment that has become extremely long. Since you decided that
you do not want to have short, one line comments to describe what you
are doing, you let it run over several lines.
-->
```

NOTE **Because this is a comment, the block is opened with** `<!--` **and closed with** `-->`**. You will also notice that there is no need to include special characters to create a carriage return or to precede each line. Everything between the** `<!--` **and** `-->` **is treated as one continuous comment.**

In a situation like this you do not have to worry about running into several lines of comments. You simply keep typing until you've said everything you need to, as the comment is not closed until you reach the `-->` tag. The comment will automatically adjust to the text wrapping provided by the editor.

Another important point worth noting is that you cannot put a comment in the middle of an open block of XML code. To demonstrate this, we will look at three brief variations of inserting a comment for a button.

The first example shows how to make a comment that precedes a button:

```
<!-- This is my first button -->
<button id="rxbtn"
   label="This is my button"
   imageMso="HappyFace"
   size="large"
   onAction="rxbtn_Click"/>
```

The preceding XML code is perfectly valid, and probably reflects the most common placement: with the comment preceding the button. It would be equally acceptable to insert the comment after the button was closed by the "`/>`" characters.

The following variant is also acceptable, although it requires extra typing:

```
<button id="rxbtn"
   label="This is my button"
   imageMso="HappyFace"
   size="large"
   onAction="rxbtn_Click">
   <!-- This is my first button -->
</button>
```

If you examine the preceding code, you will see that it is actually formed as `<button [attributes]><!--comment--></button>`. Because the initial button tag was closed by the `>` character, you can now insert child objects, including comments. Remember that this button tag still needs to be closed, though, hence the `</button>` at the end.

Conversely, the following XML variation is not acceptable and will generate an error because the note is inside an open set of tags:

```
<button id="rxbtn"
   <!-- This is my first button -->
   label="This is my button"
   imageMso="HappyFace"
   size="large"
   onAction="rxbtn_Click"/>
```

The difference with this last example is that the comment was inserted in an unclosed block of code. If you look carefully, you will see that it reads as follows: `<button<!--comment-->[attributes]/>`. Notice how the button tag is still open? Each comment must exist between the tag that closes an element (`>`) and a tag that opens the next element (`<`).

As a general rule, comments are placed throughout other portions of the XML, such as within the code that creates a custom tab or group. The examples provided throughout the book demonstrate where and how to place comments.

The Core XML Framework

From this point forward, we will explore the core XML framework needed to manipulate the Ribbon. Every customization begins with the `customUI` and `Ribbon` elements that follow. This applies whether you decide to build your own UI from scratch, make minor adjustments to the order of built-in controls, or build some combination of both. In addition to the elements already listed, we will also explore the `tabs`, the `tab`, and the `group` elements, as you will use these elements in almost all of your customizations.

The customUI Element

To create a well-formed XML document, it is essential that it contains one and only one "outermost element," within which all the others are nested. This outermost element is called the *root element*, and in the case of Ribbon customizations, is the `customUI` element.

In plain English, this means that all the other tags we end up using will be nested within the `customUI` tag.

To begin this exercise, open the CustomUI Editor. You will now be staring at a blank code pane. Don't worry about opening a specific file, as you just need the editor open in order to follow along with the example.

Enter the following code in the window:

```
<customUI xmlns="http://schemas.microsoft.com/office/2006/01/customui">
   <!-- All other instructions go here -->
</customUI>
```

As you proceed through this book, you will notice that we repeatedly emphasize that at this point you should validate your code. Therefore, click the validate button as shown in Figure 3-1.

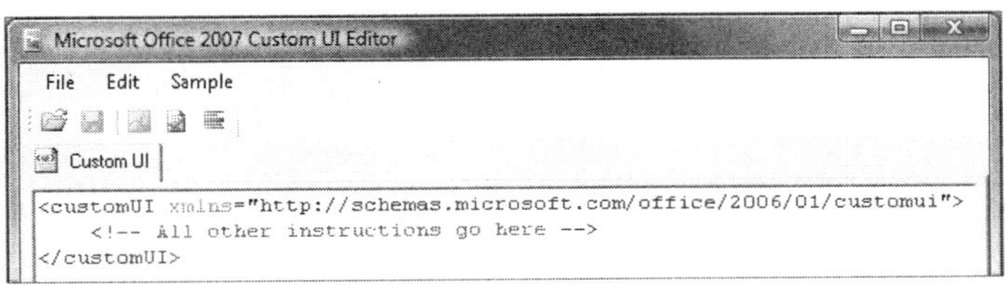

Figure 3-1: Validating XML code

Getting into the validation habit will eliminate much grief when trying to test your files, so it is imperative that you do this each time you think your customization is complete, or even when you have added a significant section that is complete.

At this point, even if you were to save your code, it wouldn't do anything. By using the CustomUI Editor on a live file, however, you would have created the link to the `.rels` file, as described in Chapter 2. The code that you have written to date has also opened the `customUI` tags, and you're now ready to start referencing content in your custom UI.

Required Attributes of the customUI Element

Before we move on to content, it is worth exploring what attributes are required for the `customUI` element. Every `customUI` tag must specify the `xmlns` attribute shown in Table 3-3.

Table 3-3: Required Attribute of the `customUI` Element

STATIC ATTRIBUTE	ALLOWED VALUES
xmlns	http://schemas.microsoft.com/office/2006/01/customui

CAUTION **The `xmlns` attribute must be specified exactly as shown in Table 3-3 or your custom UI will not work. Remember that this is case sensitive!**

Optional Static and Dynamic Attributes with Callback Signatures

In addition to including the required attribute specified above, you may also add any or all of the attributes shown in Table 3-4 to the `customUI` tag. Although you may not be ready to use these attributes yet, we provide the table now so that it serves as a convenient reference when you do need it. We have taken this approach throughout the book.

Table 3-4: Optional Attributes for the `customUI` Element

STATIC ATTRIBUTE	DYNAMIC ATTRIBUTE	ALLOWED VALUES	DEFAULT VALUE	VBA CALLBACK SIGNATURE FOR DYNAMIC ATTRIBUTE
xmlns:Q	(none)	1 to 1024 characters	(none)	(none)
(none)	onLoad	1 to 1024 characters	(none)	Sub onLoad (Ribbon as IRibbonUI)
(none)	loadImage	1 to 1024 characters	(none)	Sub loadImage (imageID as String, ByRef returnedVal)

These attributes are covered in later chapters, but just as a reference, adding the `onLoad` attribute would make the code look as follows:

```
<customUI
   xmlns="http://schemas.microsoft.com/office/2006/01/customui"
```

```
    onLoad="rxiRibbonUI_onLoad">
    <!-- All other instructions go here -->
</customUI>
```

Notice that the `onLoad` attribute is just nested within the same <> brackets that hold the `customUI` element. This would also be true of any of the other optional attributes as well. And, again, you list one attribute per line without any need to include code for continuation or line breaks.

Allowed Children Objects of the customUI Element

The `customUI` tag is a container that may, and undoubtedly will, hold other objects. As explained earlier in the chapter, it is the parent object, so it may hold child objects. Actually, the `customUI` container may only hold either or both of the following elements/objects:

- `commands`
- `ribbon`

At this point, we're ready to explore the `ribbon` element.

The ribbon Element

Now that you know how to open the `customUI` object for editing, you are ready to move on to the next step. In order to start any modification to the Ribbon itself, you would nest the `ribbon` element within the `customUI` tag, as shown here:

```
<customUI xmlns="http://schemas.microsoft.com/office/2006/01/customui">
   <ribbon>
        <!-- All other instructions go here -->
   </ribbon>
</customUI>
```

At this point, you should insert the `<ribbon>` and `</ribbon>` tags around the XML comment and revalidate the code.

Pay careful attention to how we are "encapsulating" tags according to hierarchy, generating the parent-child relationships that you learned about earlier. Each tag will be nested within the other, building a logical pyramid of modifications that is easy to read.

Required Attributes of the ribbon Element

Unlike the `customUI` element, and indeed most of the other elements that you will see, the `ribbon` element does not have any required attributes and can be used entirely on its own.

Optional Static Attributes

While the `ribbon` element may not have any required attributes, it does have one very special attribute, shown in Table 3-5.

Table 3-5: Optional Attribute of the ribbon Element

STATIC ATTRIBUTE	DYNAMIC ATTRIBUTE	ALLOWED VALUES	DEFAULT VALUE	VBA CALLBACK SIGNATURE FOR DYNAMIC ATTRIBUTE
startFromScratch	(none)	true, false, 1, 0	false	(none)

The `startFromScratch` attribute is the attribute that enables you to hide the entire built-in Ribbon that Microsoft worked so hard to create.

Notice that because it has a default value of `false`, we omitted it in the code snippet earlier. We could have achieved the same results with the following XML:

```
<customUI xmlns="http://schemas.microsoft.com/office/2006/01/customui">
   <ribbon startFromScratch="false">
            <!-- All other instructions go here -->
   </ribbon>
</customUI>
```

CROSS-REFERENCE **This attribute is essential learning if you want to create your own UI entirely from the ground up, so it is covered in much more detail in Chapter 13.**

Allowed Children Objects of the ribbon Element

The `ribbon` object may only hold any (or all) of the following elements:

- `contextualTabs`
- `officeMenu`
- `qat`
- `tabs`

Graphical View of ribbon Attributes

Using the code provided above, which included the `startFromScratch` attribute set to `false`, would have no effect on the display of the Ribbon, as no tabs, groups, or other modifications have been made.

Conversely, consider Figure 3-2, which shows how the user interface would have displayed had the `startFromScratch` attribute been set to `true`!

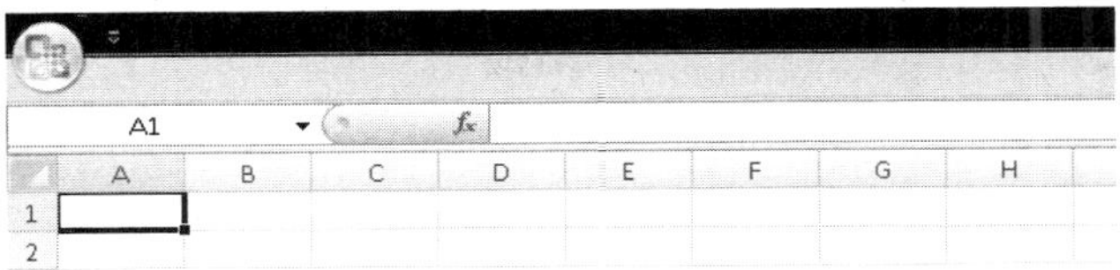

Figure 3-2: The Ribbon, with the `startFromScratch` attribute set to `true`

As you can see, the default Ribbon would be hidden, so only the Office Button and the drop-down for the QAT are displayed. Just because features aren't visible, though, doesn't mean that they aren't available. In Chapter 13, we'll build a Ribbon from scratch and discuss some of the features that remain, such as the shortcut keys.

The tabs Element

Now that we have the `customUI` container and the `ribbon` container, the next major tag in the hierarchy is the `tabs` element. This is yet another container, which must nest within the Ribbon block. Modify your code to reflect the code that follows, and remember to validate your XML:

```
<customUI xmlns="http://schemas.microsoft.com/office/2006/01/customui">
   <ribbon>
        <tabs>
            <!-- All other instructions go here -->
        </tabs>
   </ribbon>
</customUI>
```

The purpose of the `tabs` tag is to collect the elements for each and every individual tab that you choose to reference, create, or modify.

NOTE **Be aware that the preceding code, despite being well formed, will actually fail validation in the CustomUI Editor. That is because the XML code is expecting a `tab` child element. At this point, even if you open your file in the application, nothing would seem to happen.**

Required Attributes of the tabs Element

The `tabs` element is one of the easiest elements to use, as it does not have a single attribute of any kind, either required or optional!

Allowed Children Objects of the tabs Element

The `tabs` element is a container element that is used to hold specifically referenced (or created) tab controls.

The tab Element

At long last, we are finally at the place where we can do something that will show up! The `tab` element resides in the `tabs` container, and is used to create or refer to an individual tab on the ribbon.

It is extremely important to understand the difference between the `tabs` object and the `tab` object. While `tabs` (plural) refers to the entire collection of tabs, `tab` (singular) indicates a specific tab among many possible tabs (the collection of tabs). If you are familiar with VBA, you will recognize the use of collections.

If you have customized any of the Office applications in Office 2003 or earlier, you are already familiar with this sort of hierarchy in the form of the application's `Commandbars` object, which represents the collection of toolbars (command bars). By contrast, the `Commandbar` object refers to a specific object command bar object within the entire group.

Required Attributes of the tab Element

The `tab` object is the first element in the hierarchy that requires an `id` attribute. One selection, and only one selection, must be made from the available options shown in Table 3-6, which also includes suggestions regarding when to use each type of `id` attribute.

Table 3-6: id Attributes of the tab Element

ATTRIBUTE	WHEN TO USE
id	When creating your own tab
idMso	When using an existing Microsoft tab
idQ	When creating a tab shared between namespaces

The reason why an `id` attribute is required is quite simple: If the tab didn't have an `id` attribute, how would you know which tab you were referencing?

NOTE **While you can employ multiple `tab` (or other) elements using a mixture of `id` and `idQ` attributes in a single customization file, it is unlikely that you would do so. For most purposes, you will simply create new `tab` elements using the `id` attribute and refer to existing `tab` elements using the `idMso` attribute. The `idQ` attribute is discussed in detail in Chapter 16.**

Optional Static and Dynamic Attributes with Callback Signatures

The `tab` element also provides developers with several optional static attributes. In order to set the position of a tab in relation to any other existing tab, you may want to use one of the insert attributes shown in Table 3-7.

Table 3-7: Optional insert Attributes for the tab Control

INSERT ATTRIBUTE	ALLOWED VALUES	DEFAULT VALUE	WHEN TO USE
insertAfterMso	Valid Mso Tab	Insert after last tab	Insert after Microsoft tab
insertBeforeMso	Valid Mso Tab	Insert after last tab	Insert before Microsoft tab
insertAfterQ	Valid Tab idQ	Insert after last tab	Insert after shared namespace tab
insertBeforeQ	Valid Tab idQ	Insert after last tab	Insert before shared namespace tab

NOTE **If you do not specify an insert attribute, then the tab is added immediately after the last tab, whether it's a custom tab or a built-in tab.**

The `tab` control will also optionally accept any or all of the attributes shown in Table 3-8.

Table 3-8: Optional Attributes and Callbacks of the tab Control

STATIC ATTRIBUTE	DYNAMIC ATTRIBUTE	ALLOWED VALUES	DEFAULT VALUE	VBA CALLBACK SIGNATURE FOR DYNAMIC ATTRIBUTE
keytip	getKeytip	1 to 3 characters	(none)	Sub GetKeytip (control As IRibbonControl, ByRef returnedVal)
label	getLabel	1 to 1024 characters	(none)	Sub GetLabel(control As IRibbonControl, ByRef returnedVal)
tag	(none)	1 to 1024 characters	(none)	n/a
Visible	getVisible	true, false, 1, 0	true	Sub GetVisible(control As IRibbonControl, ByRef returnedVal)

CROSS-REFERENCE Dynamic callbacks are used to dynamically modify the ribbon while the file is in use. They use Visual Basic for Applications (VBA) code to function. We explain how to use dynamic callbacks in Chapter 5.

Allowed Children Objects of the tab Element

The `tab` object may only hold group elements such as the built-in Clipboard group or custom groups of your own making.

Graphical View of tab Attributes

Figure 3-3 shows a custom tab on the Ribbon. The tab was inserted before the Home tab, and it has the custom keytip of S.

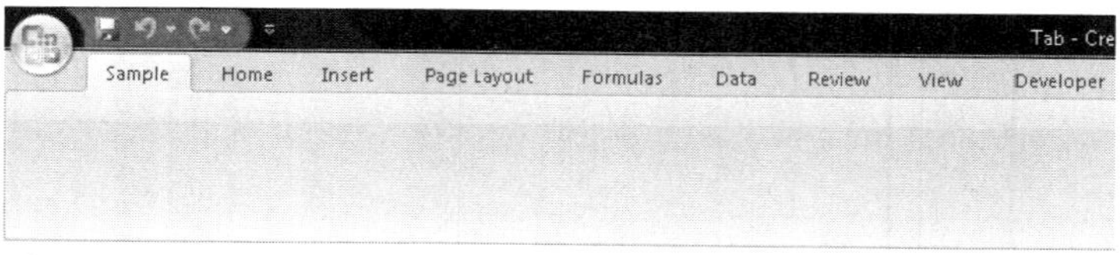

Figure 3-3: A new tab on the ribbon

Built-in Tabs

When working with tabs on the Ribbon, there are two distinct kinds that you may play with: built-in and custom. The built-in tabs are tabs are provided by Microsoft, whereas the custom tabs are, of course, your own creation. We get into custom tabs later; for now we focus on built-in tabs.

Referring to Built-in Tabs

Every built-in tab has its own unique `idMso` attribute, and you refer to the tab by calling that attribute. Indeed, the hardest part of referring to a tab is figuring out its `idMso`!

Table 3-9 shows some of the more common tab names for Excel, Access, and Word. As with other code, the use of CamelCase is critical, as your code will fail if these appear completely in lowercase.

CROSS-REFERENCE Appendix B contains tables of all the built-in tab names for all three applications.

Table 3-9: Built-in Tab Names for the Most Common Tabs

TAB NAME	idMso FOR EXCEL	idMso FOR WORD	idMso FOR ACCESS
Home	TabHome	TabHome	TabHomeAccess
Insert	TabInsert	TabInsert	(none)
PageLayout	TabPageLayoutExcel	TabPageLayoutWord	(none)
Formula	TabFormulas	(none)	(none)
Data	TabData	(none)	(none)
Review	TabReview	TabReviewWord	(none)
Create	(none)	(none)	TabCreate
External Data	(none)	(none)	TabExternalData
Database Tools	(none)	(none)	TabDatabaseTools

Modifying a Built-in Tab

Being able to reference built-in tabs gives us a little power to modify and leverage the built-in user interface. Our next example demonstrates this using Excel.

Open Excel and create a new workbook. Because the example does not require any dynamic callbacks, you can save the file in Excel's default, macro-free (`xlsx`) workbook format (as opposed to `xlsm` for files that contain macros). When you are done, close Excel and open the file in the CustomUI Editor. Apply the RibbonBase template from the Sample menu.

CROSS-REFERENCE The RibbonBase template was created in Chapter 2 and is used throughout this book.

NOTE Notice how the RibbonBase template includes the `customUI`, `ribbon` and `tabs` elements. This template was created because these items rarely change, unlike the tab controls and their child objects. Therefore, applying the template gives you a consistent baseline and beginning point for all of the examples.

Between the `<tabs>` and `</tabs>` tags, insert the following XML code:

```
<tab idMso="TabHome"
   visible="false">
</tab>
```

Remember to validate and save the code. Close the file in the CustomUI Editor and then open it in Excel. The Home tab is gone! Don't worry, though. Closing the file will make the Home tab reappear.

TIP **The preceding XML code works equally well if you try using it in a Word document instead of an Excel file. To use it in Access, however, you need to change** `TabHome` **to** `TabHomeAccess`**. A quick review of the** `idMso` **names in Table 3-9 will show you why.**

CROSS-REFERENCE **To deploy the preceding code in Access, review the steps outlined in Chapter 2.**

Custom Tabs

While hiding built-in tabs can make for a great practical joke on an unsuspecting co-worker, there is only so much use that you can get out of this capability. Fortunately, we have the toolset that enables us to create our own tabs.

Creating Custom Tabs

To create a custom tab, we don't reference the `idMso`, but instead for a new tab by specifying a unique `id` attribute. You'll recall that `idMso` is reserved for tabs provided by Microsoft.

Building on the previous exercise, close your example file in Excel, reopen it in the customUI Editor, and replace the code from `<tab` through `</tab>` with the following XML:

```
<tab id="rxtabDemo"
   label="Demo">
</tab>
```

As always, validate and save the file. Close the file in the CustomUI Editor and then reopen it in Excel. You will now have an empty tab on your ribbon, as shown in Figure 3-4.

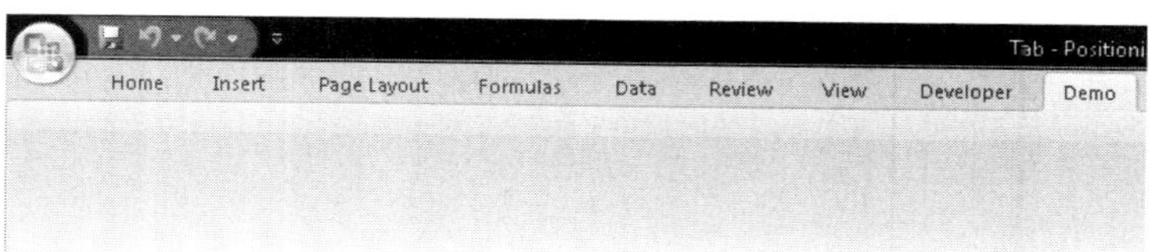

Figure 3-4: A new custom tab on the Ribbon

Positioning Custom Tabs

Now that you've created your own tab, it seems a shame to relegate it to the end of the line, so to speak. After all, if you're creating your own tools, it is because they are important! To reflect the tab's importance, let's take a look at how to slot it into the Ribbon just after the Home tab.

The secret to this action is to use of one of the optional insert attributes listed in Table 3-7. Specifying a valid `idMso` name for a tab in one of these attributes will enable you to position your custom tab exactly where you want to see it.

Since you already know that the Home tab is called "TabHome," you can easily insert your tab immediately after the Home tab using the `insertAfterMso` attribute.

Once again, close your Excel file and reopen it in the CustomUI Editor. Adjust the code used to create the custom tab so that it includes the `insertAfterMso` attribute as follows (this is only a portion of the code; do not delete the other parts):

```
<tab id="rxtabDemo"
   label="Demo"
   insertAfterMso="TabHome">
```

Validate your code to catch any pesky typing errors, save the file, and close it in the CustomUI Editor. Now open the file again in Excel and note how the tab has moved, as shown in Figure 3-5.

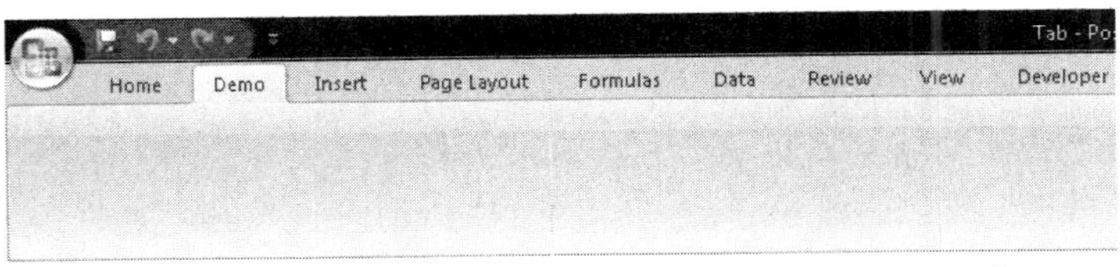

Figure 3-5: A custom tab between the Home and Insert tabs

NOTE **Although you inserted your tab *after* the Home tab, you could have inserted it *before* the Insert tab by specifying** `insertBeforeMso="TabInsert"`**. Whichever route you chose, you'd still end up with the same result, at least for now. Naturally, how you approach this depends on where your object is going, and what other tabs may be present or might be added.**

As you can see, the task of placing tabs is fairly straightforward. However, it can involve a bit of foresight and planning when working with multiple custom tabs.

NOTE When multiple controls declare that they should be inserted, they are inserted in the order in which the XML code is written. For example, assuming that you have three controls in your file that specify `insertAfterMso="TabHome"`, the first control will be added after the Home tab. When the next line is read, it will place the second control immediately after the Home tab, bumping your first control to the right. This will continue with all subsequent controls that specify this position. This also holds true for multiple opened files. The most recent file will bump the earlier file's customizations to the right, as its controls are inserted immediately after the specified control.

The group Element

So far, we've managed to create a new tab in the Ribbon, but it's still empty. Obviously, it won't be very useful in that state, so the next thing we'll cover is how to add items to a tab. This is where we add the `group` element.

The job of the `group` element is to create placeholders for the actual buttons, check-boxes, menus, and other rich commands that the Ribbon allows us to deploy. While this section lays the groundwork for the individual commands, you can also place a large variety of built-in groups on your tabs.

Required Attributes of the group Element

Like the `tab` element, every group requires one unique `id` attribute, as shown in Table 3-10.

Table 3-10: id Attributes of the group Element

ATTRIBUTE	WHEN TO USE
id	When creating your own group
idMso	When using an existing Microsoft group
idQ	When creating a group shared between namespaces

Optional Static and Dynamic Attributes with Callback Signatures

The `group` element, like many others, also has several optional static attributes. In order to set the position of a group in relation to any other existing group, you need to specify one of the insert attributes shown in Table 3-11.

Table 3-11: Optional insert Attributes for the group Control

INSERT ATTRIBUTE	ALLOWED VALUES	DEFAULT VALUE	WHEN TO USE
insertAfterMso	Valid Mso Group	Insert after last group	Insert after Microsoft group
insertBeforeMso	Valid Mso Group	Insert after last group	Insert before Microsoft group
insertAfterQ	Valid Group idQ	Insert after last group	Insert after shared namespace group
insertBeforeQ	Valid Group idQ	Insert after last group	Insert before shared namespace group

NOTE **If you do not specify an insert attribute, then the group is added immediately after the last group that currently exists on the tab. In the case of a built-in tab, a new group would be added at the end. In the case of a custom tab, groups without an insert attribute are added from left to right in the order that they appear in the XML code.**

The `group` control will also optionally accept any or all of the attributes shown in Table 3-12.

Table 3-12: Optional Attributes and Callbacks of the `group` Control

STATIC ATTRIBUTE	DYNAMIC ATTRIBUTE	ALLOWED VALUES	DEFAULT VALUE	VBA CALLBACK SIGNATURE FOR DYNAMIC ATTRIBUTE
image	getImage	1 to 1024 characters	(none)	Sub GetImage (control As IRibbonControl, ByRef returnedVal)
imageMso	getImage	1 to 1024 characters	(none)	Same as above
keytip	getKeytip	1 to 3 characters	(none)	Sub GetKeytip (control As IRibbonControl, ByRef returnedVal)
label	getLabel	1 to 1024 characters	(none)	Sub GetLabel (control As IRibbonControl, ByRef returnedVal)

Continued

Table 3-12: *(continued)*

STATIC ATTRIBUTE	DYNAMIC ATTRIBUTE	ALLOWED VALUES	DEFAULT VALUE	VBA CALLBACK SIGNATURE FOR DYNAMIC ATTRIBUTE
screentip	getScreentip	1 to 1024 characters	(none)	Sub GetScreentip (control As IRibbonControl, ByRef returnedVal)
supertip	getSupertip	1 to 1024 characters	(none)	Sub GetSupertip (control As IRibbonControl, ByRef returnedVal)
tag	(none)	1 to 1024 characters	(none)	(none)
visible	getVisible	true, false, 1, 0	true	Sub GetVisible (control As IRibbonControl, ByRef returnedVal)

NOTE **While all of the attributes listed in Table 3-12 are valid attributes, the *only* attributes that seem to be useful are the `label` and `visible` attributes and their associated callback signatures. Why the rest are valid attributes is somewhat of a mystery as the controls that nest within the groups provide all the needed functionality in this regard.**

Allowed Children Objects of the group Element

The `group` element can hold any combination of the following objects:

- `box`
- `button`
- `buttonGroup`
- `checkBox`
- `comboBox`
- `control`
- `dialogBoxLauncher`
- `dropDown`
- `editBox`
- `gallery`
- `labelControl`

- `menu`
- `separator`
- `splitButton`
- `toggleButton`

Graphical View of group Attributes

Figure 3-6 shows a custom group on a custom Ribbon tab. It isn't quite what one might expect, and we'll explain that momentarily.

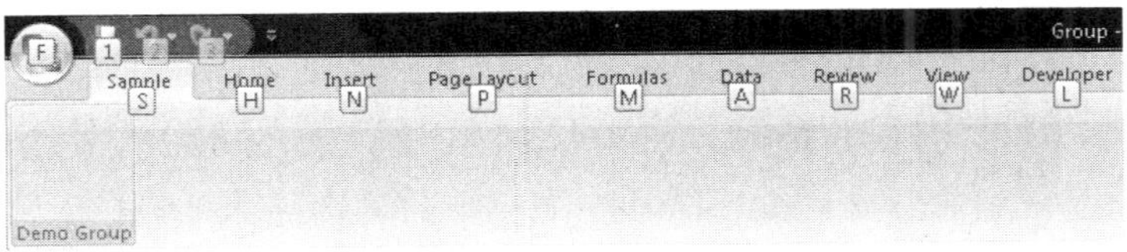

Figure 3-6: A custom group on a custom tab

What is especially interesting about this image is that it was created with the following XML code:

```
<group id="rxgrpDemo"
   label="Demo Group"
   imageMso="HappyFace"
   keytip="D"
   screentip="This is my screentip"
   supertip="This is my supertip">
</group>
```

Notice that of the properties set in the XML, only the `label` actually manifested itself on the Ribbon. In fact, the `visible` setting does as well, although it is implied because the default is `true` and so is not even included in the code. The `keytip` represented by (S) is for the tab, rather than the group; and as our earlier note pointed out, group `screentip` and `supertip` commands do not appear, and neither does an `imageMso`. Again, this begs the question of why one would bother to list the attributes if they are going to be ignored. Although we don't have the answer to that question, this little exercise does illustrate a point and may help you avoid some needless coding.

TIP **The majority of the optional attributes, such as `imageMso`, will not have a visible effect on a group control.**

Because it is unlikely that you will ever specify the `visible` property manually, it appears that you can focus your attention on the `label` and `insert` attributes for a group, safely ignoring the rest of the optional attributes.

Built-in Groups

Using built-in groups and controls can come in handy when you want to start a UI from scratch but still be able to offer users some of the built-in features. In addition, it also gives you the capability to create custom tabs that contain the groups of controls which are frequently used together. After all, you may choose to arrange controls somewhat different from the way that Microsoft organized them by default.

Using Microsoft's built-in groups is often much easier than referencing all the individual controls; and since the groups are available, why not make use of the convenience?

Referring to Built-in Groups

Similar to working with tabs, you can identify custom groups by referring to their `id` attribute, and built-in groups by referring to their `idMso` attribute.

Table 3-13 lists some of the built-in groups in Excel, Access, and Word.

Table 3-13: Common Groups Across Excel, Access, and Word

DISPLAY NAME	idMso NAME
Clipboard	GroupClipboard
Font	GroupFont
Shapes	GroupShapes

CROSS-REFERENCE **For a full list of all the built-in group names, refer to Appendix B.**

Armed with what you have learned so far, you could hide the Clipboard group on the Home tab. Why not give it a try using Word? Create a new Word document and save it in the macro-free `docx` format. (As before, no macros will be necessary, as we are not setting anything dynamically.) Close the file in Word and open it in the CustomUI Editor. Apply the RibbonBase template and insert the following XML code between the `<tabs>` and `</tabs>` tags:

```
<tab idMso="TabHome">
   <group idMso="GroupClipboard"
        visible="false">
   </group>
</tab>
```

Validate and save the code, and then close the file in the CustomUI Editor. Reopen the document in Word. As shown in Figure 3-7, the Clipboard group has disappeared.

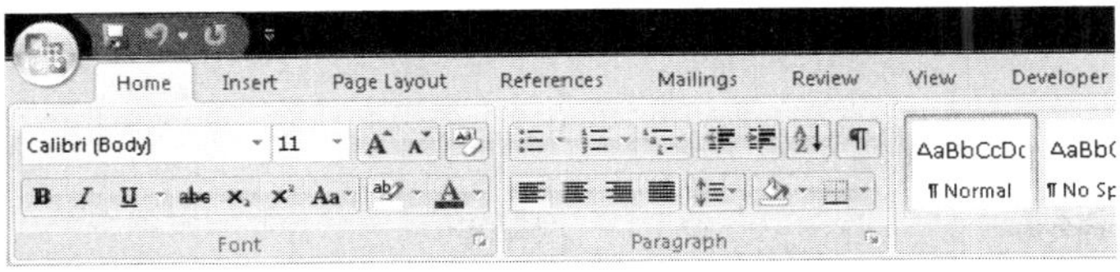

Figure 3-7: The Home tab with a hidden Clipboard group

NOTE **While hiding the clipboard may appear to eliminate the cut, copy, and paste commands, this is not the case. These commands are merely hidden, and remain available through contextual (right-click) menus and keyboard shortcuts.**

CROSS-REFERENCE **Methods of truly overriding and disabling controls are covered in detail in Chapter 13.**

Using a Built-in Group on a Custom Tab

Like hiding tab controls, hiding groups will really only get us so far. Fortunately, you are also able to use these built-in groups on your own tabs!

The ability to create copies of the built-in groups is a key feature in Office 2007. While Microsoft invested a huge amount of time and money into studying user habits, the default order of controls isn't always going to be the best fit for your purpose. With the capability to reuse Microsoft's groups, you can easily place your most frequently used commands on a single tab so that they aren't just convenient (supposedly, the Ribbon is convenient), but also visible and at your disposal with literally just one click!

The controls for this type of custom tab are obviously based on usage patterns. For example, assume that you spend much of your time reviewing Excel workbooks for consistency. In the default Ribbon implementation, you may constantly be jumping back and forth among the Ribbon tabs to leverage the controls you need. Table 3-14 shows just some of the groups that may be required, and highlights how many different tabs you would have to work with.

Table 3-14: Location of Common Auditing Tools in Excel

GROUP NAME	DEFAULT TAB	NAME
Clipboard	Home	GroupClipboard
Font	Home	GroupFont
Formula Auditing	Formulas	GroupFormulaAuditing
Comments	Review	GroupComments
Editing	Home	GroupEditingExcel

Since it is possible to reuse these groups, why not save yourself the time involved in tab switching by populating a custom tab with the commands you repeatedly use? In many work environments, creating a custom, consolidated tab could save countless keystrokes and significantly boost productivity — to say nothing of reducing the levels of frustration and tedium.

In the next exercise, we create a custom tab with the groups listed in Table 3-14. To begin, create a new workbook in Excel and save it in the Macro-free (`xlsx`) format. Close the file in Excel and open it in the CustomUI Editor. Apply the RibbonBase template and insert the XML below between the `<tabs>` and `</tabs>` tags:

```
<tab id="rxtabMyTools"
   label="My Tools"
   insertBeforeMso="TabHome">
   <group idMso="GroupClipboard"/>
   <group idMso="GroupFont"/>
   <group idMso="GroupFormulaAuditing"/>
   <group idMso="GroupComments"/>
   <group idMso="GroupEditingExcel"/>
</tab>
```

CROSS-REFERENCE **If you want to add other controls, remember that you can find the entire set of group `idMso` identifiers in Appendix B.**

There is something worth paying extra attention to in the preceding code. Until now, all of the examples have used separate open and close tags for the `group` element. In this code, however, the `group` is dealt with on one line by closing it immediately with a `/>` ending. When you validate the code, you'll see that it works just fine, but you may be wondering why we've done this.

It's very simple, actually. The previous examples were building custom groups with the expectation that controls would be nested within the group. In this case, we do not wish to make any modifications to the groups; we merely wish to place them on our tab. Therefore, there is no need for additional code, and the tag can be opened and closed on the same line.

Once you are satisfied that your XML is "well formed" (validated), save and close the file in the CustomUI Editor. Open it in Excel and have a good look at the new tab that contains all of your favorite controls, as shown in Figure 3-8.

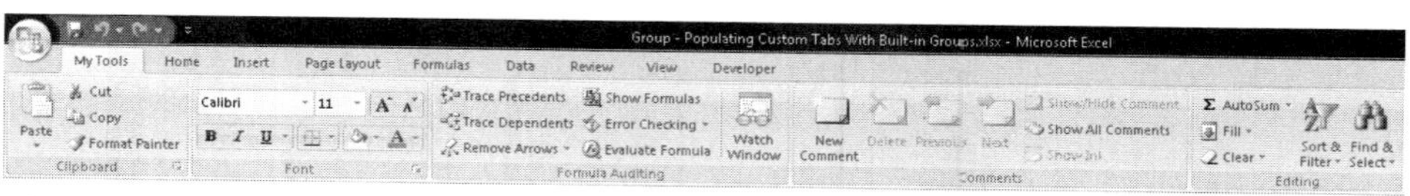

Figure 3-8: A custom tab populated with built-in groups

When taking this tab for a test drive, you'll notice that the controls within the groups function exactly as they do in their native locations. You should also take note of the fact that the groups still reside in their default locations; a copy has merely been placed on the custom tab.

Custom Groups

The painful reality of Ribbon customization is that despite the hard work that Microsoft has done, they just can't anticipate exactly how we want our controls displayed. We may want only specific Microsoft controls arranged in our groups, we may want tabs of our own creation, and we may even want a mixture of the two.

Creating Custom Groups

Like `tab` elements, custom groups are created by specifying a unique `id` attribute, rather than referencing the `idMso` of a built-in group.

Close your example file in Excel, if it's still open, and reopen the file in the CustomUI Editor. Immediately after the last `group` tag, add the following lines of XML code just before the `</tab>` tag:

```
<group id="rxgrpMyGroup"
   label="My Group">
</group>
```

Did you notice that this group does not open and close the group within the same line of code? Although this is a topic beyond the scope of this chapter, the reason is because you would only create a new group in order to fill it with other controls, such as the `button`, `checkBox`, or `dynamicMenu`. Separating the opening and closing tags establishes the framework for adding additional controls.

Now validate the XML, save the file, and close it in the CustomUI Editor. Open it in Excel again. Notice that the My Group tab shows up as the empty group that it is, as expected, to the right of the other groups, as displayed in Figure 3-9.

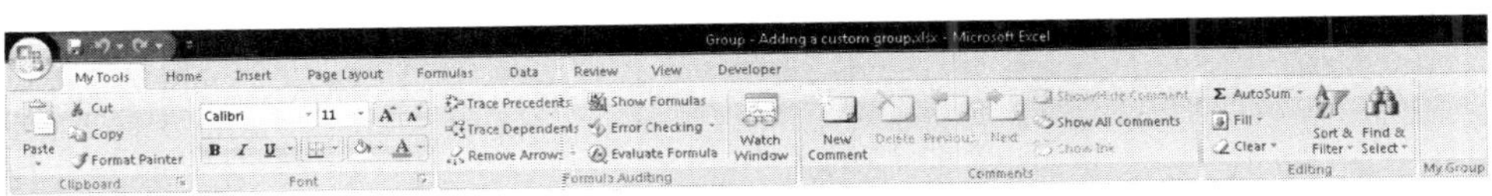

Figure 3-9: A custom group on a custom tab

CROSS-REFERENCE **The various types of controls that can be contained within a group container are discussed in detail in Chapters 6 through 11.**

Positioning Custom Groups

While the custom group did show up on our tab, perhaps it is not where we would like to see it. Suppose that you would rather have the custom group appear between the Clipboard and Font groups. It turns out that there are actually two ways to accomplish this.

The first way to accomplish this would be to reference the `idMso` of the group that you want to appear either before or after. We demonstrated that earlier, so you'll recognize the last insert line used here. This may cause the XML to look like the following:

```
<tab id="rxtabMyTools"
   label="My Tools"
   insertBeforeMso="TabHome">
   <group idMso="GroupClipboard"/>
   <group idMso="GroupFont"/>
   <group idMso="GroupFormulaAuditing"/>
   <group idMso="GroupComments"/>
   <group idMso="GroupEditingExcel"/>
   <group id="rxgrpMyGroup"
        label="My Group"
        insertBeforeMso="GroupFont">
   </group>
</tab>
```

TIP **You could also swap the** `insertBeforeMso="GroupFont"` **attribute with** `insertAfterMso="GroupClipboard"` **to achieve exactly the same results.**

While the preceding XML works, it also makes the code a little bit hard to follow as the groups are no longer created in the order in which they are displayed. This brings us to the second (and preferred) method for positioning a group. You can create the groups on the custom tab in the order you wish them to appear. Using that approach, the code would be as follows:

```
<tab id="rxtabMyTools"
   label="My Tools"
   insertBeforeMso="TabHome">
   <group idMso="GroupClipboard"/>
   <group id="rxgrpMyGroup"
        label="My Group">
   </group>
   <group idMso="GroupFont"/>
   <group idMso="GroupFormulaAuditing"/>
   <group idMso="GroupComments"/>
   <group idMso="GroupEditingExcel"/>
</tab>
```

Try updating the code in the CustomUI Editor yourself. Whichever version you decide to use, it will display as shown in Figure 3-10 when you reopen the file in Excel.

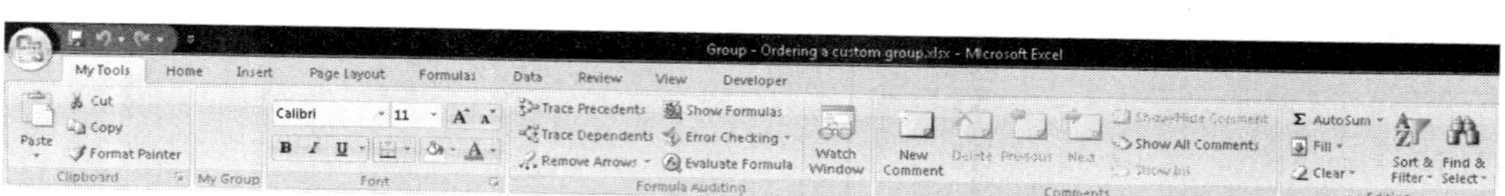

Figure 3-10: The custom group is now displayed between the Clipboard and Font groups

Custom Groups on Built-in Tabs

While the preceding example placed a custom group on a custom tab, it is just as easy to insert your own group in one of Microsoft's built-in tabs. We'll demonstrate that here in Word.

Create a new document in Word and save it in the macro-free docx format. Close Word, open the file in the CustomUI Editor, and apply the RibbonBase template. Between the <tabs> and </tabs> tags, enter the following XML code:

```
<tab idMso="TabHome">
   <group id="rxgrpMyGroup"
        label="My Group"
        insertBeforeMso="GroupFont">
   </group>
</tab>
```

Once you've validated and saved the code, close the file in the CustomUI Editor. Upon reopening the file in Word, you will now see a custom group on the Home tab, as shown in Figure 3-11.

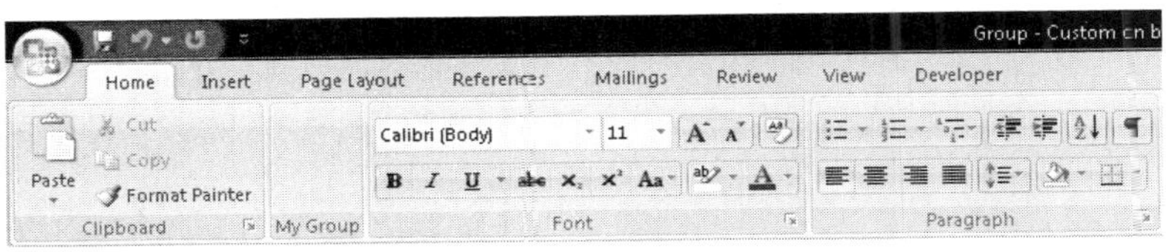

Figure 3-11: A custom group on Word's Home tab

As you can see, we have added the custom group My Group to the built-in Home tab. In addition, we've positioned the group to be second, or at least to remain just to the left of the Font group. That's all there is to it. You are now ready to create your own groups to hold the controls you wish to add.

NOTE **If you try to create this example in Access using the steps outlined in Chapter 2, you would expect to be able to use the same code. Access's font group on the Home tab is actually called GroupTextFormatting, not GroupFont as you'd expect. You can easily modify the code to work with Access simply by replacing "GroupFont" with "GroupTextFormatting".**

Conclusion

This chapter began with a discussion of what XML is and why it is important to the Office 2007 user interface. You learned about tags, which are comprised of elements and attributes, and how they add structure to an XML document. The essential id and `label` attributes were explored, as well as tips on how to lay out your XML code to make it more readable. Because we can't always rely on things being completely intuitive to the user (or our own memory for that matter), you also learned the syntax required to leave comments in your XML code.

With the essential background out of the way, we turned our attention to the actual elements that are at the core of all Ribbon modifications. From the root `customUI` element to the `ribbon` element to the `tabs` element, we looked at how to nest the tags within one another to build the required customization hierarchy.

Upon reaching this critical level of understanding, you should now be able to write some code that actually accomplishes visible results in the Office 2007 user interface. We started by creating and positioning new tabs. Of course, empty tabs aren't of much use, so you learned how to place Microsoft's built-in groups on your tabs. With that knowledge, you can quickly build a user interface that groups together the tools you use, and with minimal work on your part.

Following the example of using the built-in groups, we also explored how to create custom groups. While the placement of controls in these groups is covered in Chapters 6 through 11, you have now learned how to create the fundamental building blocks to modify your UI.

Where you proceed from here depends on whether you want to merely modify your Ribbon to organize the controls as you like, or you actually want to build custom controls into your files.

If you are only interested in repositioning Microsoft's built-in controls to make your Ribbon more efficient, you can learn about the individual controls in Chapters 6 through 11. Armed with the information from this chapter, you will be able to create your own tabs and groups, and fill them with built-in controls.

If you are interested in creating your own controls, however, you need to learn about Visual Basic for Applications (VBA), which is covered in the next chapter.

CHAPTER

4

Introducing Visual Basic for Applications (VBA)

In Chapter 3, you looked at some simple examples showing how to customize the Ribbon using XML. However, in order to create true custom solutions, you will need to add functionality. This is when Visual Basic for Applications (VBA) comes into play.

This chapter has seven sections, each covering different aspects of VBA, such as recording macros, writing subprocedures and functions, debugging code, and error handling.

Each section builds your knowledge and awareness of VBA. At this stage, the code is as simple as possible. The goal here isn't to teach you all there is to know about VBA, but rather to provide a strong enough foundation for you to interpret, modify, and write code or code snippets to customize the Ribbon.

Bear in mind, however, that this chapter is about learning the basics of VBA in order to add functionality to Ribbon customization; and because the visual effects are accomplished using XML code, which was introduced in Chapter 3, the examples in this chapter don't even work with the Ribbon.

As you are preparing to work through the examples, we encourage you to download the companion files. The source code and files for this chapter can be found on the book's web site at `www.wiley.com/go/ribbonx`.

Getting Started with Visual Basic for Applications (VBA)

In Chapter 3 you were introduced to XML code, which is used to add or remove tabs, groups, and controls from the Ribbon. However, just adding those is not enough. To add functionality to your customization, you need to work with VBA code. After all, what good is a new button on the Ribbon if it doesn't do anything when clicked? Now it's time to learn some of the fundamental principles and rules for programming with VBA.

NOTE **When you work with built-in controls they will work as advertised — that is, all you need to do is to reference them and the customization will inherit all the behaviors and features of the built-in control, unless you state otherwise. Chapter 13 deals with overriding built-in controls and commands.**

If you are fluent with VBA, you may choose to skip this chapter, but you may benefit from breezing through the material to see some of the new ways that things work, such as how to get to the macro recorder. In addition, for those of you who have relatively little experience with VBA and/or macros, we highly recommend that you not only read through this chapter, but that you also spend some time practicing the exercises, as they lay the foundation for the rest of the book. Of course, you can always refer back to this chapter as you are working through the examples in later chapters.

How VBA will apply to your work depends on the application you are working with. In Excel, you find a set of objects that are associated with Excel; similarly, there is a separate set of objects for Access and for Word. Therefore, although you may be comfortable with using VBA and macros in one application, you might need a refresher in the other applications.

In this chapter, we will look at some important aspects of the object model (or OM) for these three applications in order to provide key insights into how you can interact with the program to add the functionality you want.

Generally speaking, the set of instructions you give in a VBA procedure is called a *macro* in Excel and Word. However, Access also has objects called macros, which come with some predetermined instructions you can readily use in your project, instead of writing the process in a VBA function or subroutine. You should not confuse Excel and Word macros with Access macros. They are not the same entities. Moreover, you should *not* mistake macro (a procedure in Excel or Word) with the `macro` object in Excel.

Another significant difference between the applications is that Excel and Word have a macro recorder, but Access does not. As you'll soon discover, the macro recorder is a very useful tool. For one thing, it enables you to quickly expose certain properties and methods that otherwise would take a lengthy time to ascertain by inspecting the object's model. However, Access 2007 does have a very nice Macro Designer that includes fields for users to provide the macro name, condition, action, arguments, comments, and more. In addition, starting with 2007, the Access wizards generate macros instead of VBA code.

Although VBA is not the only programming language you can use to program the Ribbon — you could also use languages such as C# (C-Sharp), C++, VB.NET, and VB (using COM) — we discuss only VBA in this book because not only is VBA powerful, but it is also available to anyone who owns a copy of Microsoft Office. Therefore, everything in this book is much more accessible to anyone venturing into programming the UI for the first time and whose programming experience is limited.

What Is VBA?

We've been referring to VBA, so it's time that we explain what we're taking about. VBA is a coding language that enables people to do things that would otherwise be impossible using the built-in tools. It can also be used to improve upon and automate certain tasks.

Broadly speaking, for Excel and Word, VBA can be divided in two categories of code: recordable code and nonrecordable code. These two categories don't apply to Access, as it does not offer the macro recorder feature. In addition, although Access wizards generate macros, none of the wizards relate to Ribbon customizations. Therefore, the discussions and examples using Access rely mostly on VBA, but there are also a few examples that show how to use Access macro objects.

In the first case, to create recordable code, simply turn on the macro recorder (detailed steps explaining how to do this are provided later). Any user can record and play back a macro; it requires no special training or skills. You don't even have to be able to interpret the code to be able to use it.

In the second case, which uses nonrecordable code, although you may not need a lot of specialized training, you will need some knowledge of VBA; you'll also need some familiarity with the object models of the particular application that you will be working with.

The Developer Tab on the Ribbon contains the developer's tools that you'll use to work with VBA and to inspect the XML schema. This tab is not displayed by default, so you may want to add it to your Ribbon now. We include instructions for displaying the Developer tab in Chapter 1, in the section "Showing the Developer Tab."

The following sections introduce some tools that are useful for writing and working with code. If you are not familiar with VBA, you should study the tools, as they play a critical role in adding functionality to the Ribbon and creating a custom UI.

Macro-Enabled Documents

Before delving into VBA code, you need to be aware that Excel and Word have two new file formats. One of the file formats for each application does not allow you to save embedded macros with it.

If you have saved your Excel workbook or Word document as plain documents instead of macro-enabled ones, any code in the files will be permanently removed when you confirm that the file should be saved. Fortunately, you are warned and given an option to change your mind, as shown in Figure 4-1.

WARNING **If code is commented – flagged so that it will not run – in a workbook, sheet, or document module, be aware that both Excel and Word will delete the code when the file is closed. In addition, it doesn't matter whether the file is macro-enabled or not. In order to avoid this unpleasant surprise, you must ensure that a standard module or class module is present in your project (with or without code).**

Figure 4-1: Choosing the correct file format

Because most Ribbon customizations require code, the document must allow macros to run. Therefore, it is good to establish the practice of saving your workbooks and Word documents as macro-enabled. This is not a blanket requirement for Microsoft Access, as it handles many things differently, as you are already learning. We'll go into more detail about the relevant security settings in Chapter 17.

Using the Visual Basic Editor (VBE)

After you've ensured that your workbook or document is macro-enabled, it is time to get started with the Visual Basic Editor (or VBE). The VBE is where you will be writing VBA code.

To access the VBE window, do one of the following:

- Click the Developer tab ➪ Visual Basic (for Excel/Word only).
- Press Alt+F11 (for Excel/Access/Word).

If you are using Access you have two additional avenues:

- Click Create ➪ Other ➪ Macro ➪ Module.
- If you are in Design View, under the Design tab select Tools ➪ View code.

Table 4-1 describes some of the elements of the VBE window. We refer to several of these throughout the book as we walk through the examples.

Table 4-1: Important Elements of the VBE Window

ELEMENT	WHEN TO USE
Code window	The code window is where you type your VBA code (or where the recorded code goes). Each major object has its own code window. Standard modules and class modules also have their own code window.
Code window close button	Use this button to close the code window of an opened object.
Code window maximize/ restore button	Use this button to maximize/restore the code window of an object.

Table 4-1 *(continued)*

ELEMENT	WHEN TO USE
Code window minimize button	Use this button to minimize the code window for the opened object.
Immediate window	Use the immediate window to debug code. You send results from your code to this window or you can type instructions directly in the window.
Menu bar	This is the VBE menu and it remains the same as previous versions not only in terms of content but also in terms of looks.
Project explorer	This is a container for your project's objects.
Properties window	A window that shows the available properties for the object that has the current focus
Title bar	If you're having a hard time figuring out to which object the code window refers, look at the title bar. This is where the name will be.
Toolbars	Toolbars contain useful commands to help you to get your coding job done more easily.
VBE close button	Use this button to close the VBE working environment.
VBE maximize/restore button	Use this button to maximize/restore the VBE working environment.
VBE minimize button	Use this button to minimize the VBE working environment.

To make it easy to find an element when you're ready to use it, Figure 4-2 provides callouts to each VBE element listed in Table 4-1.

Recording Macros for Excel and Word

The best way to get to know the object model in Excel or Word is to record a macro. When you record a macro, Excel or Word will keep track of almost anything that you do in the working environment and record these actions as VBA code.

We say "almost anything" because not all actions you perform are macro-recordable. Therefore, if you need to do something that cannot be recorded by a macro, you will have to generate the code on your own, or at least with the guidance of this book. For example, you cannot record the steps to create a function. However that's one of the things that we'll be covering later.

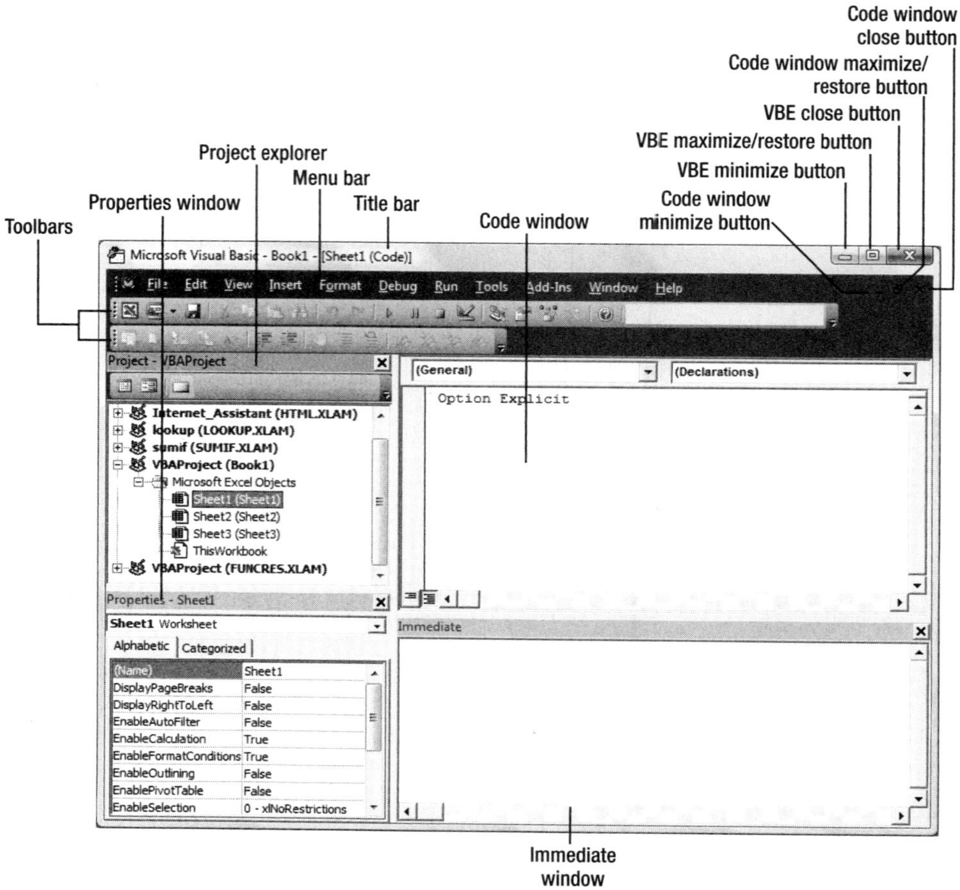

Figure 4-2: Visual Basic Editor window explained

NOTE **Although recording a macro is a great way to discover a lot about the object model, you'll also find that the macro recorder actually records a lot of stuff that you don't need or want in your code. Therefore, cleaning up recorded code is a must.**

To get started with recording a macro (in Excel or Word), just follow three easy steps:

1. From the Developer tab, select Code group ➪ Record Macro.
2. The Record Macro dialog box will open (they are slightly different for Excel and Word, but similar enough that this example works for both).
3. With the dialog box open, define the following options (because they are options, you can skip them if you like. Both Excel and Word provide values for non-optional items). Figure 4-3 shows the Record Macro dialog box for Word and Excel, respectively.

TIP **You can also find a handy macro recording button on the application's status bar at the left bottom corner. You can show/hide this button by right-clicking on the status bar and choosing Macro Recording from the pop-up list.**

- **Macro Name (Excel/Word):** Use this text box to enter a meaningful name for the actions you are about to record. If you do not specify a name for your macro, Excel/Word will create a sequential name starting at Macro1, incrementing each macro by 1.

NOTE **Macro names need to follow good naming conventions. The name cannot include spaces or other special characters. We discuss naming conventions later in this chapter.**

- **Button (Word only):** Use this option to assign the recorded macro to a button.
- **Shortcut keys (Excel) and Keyboard (Word):** Use these options to specify a keyboard shortcut for your macro. If you click Keyboard in Word, then another window is opened so that you can insert the key combination you want. This even includes using uppercase or lowercase letters, but you shouldn't use numbers, spaces, or special characters.
- **Store macro in:** This text box specifies where the macro being recorded should be stored. By default, Excel stores the macro in the workbook that called the recorder, whereas Word will store the macro in the `Normal.dotm` file. It is not a very good idea to store customization and code in startup files. For the purposes of all the examples discussed in the book, we always save both, customization and VBA code, in the example files.
- **Description:** Use this option to specify a description for your recording.

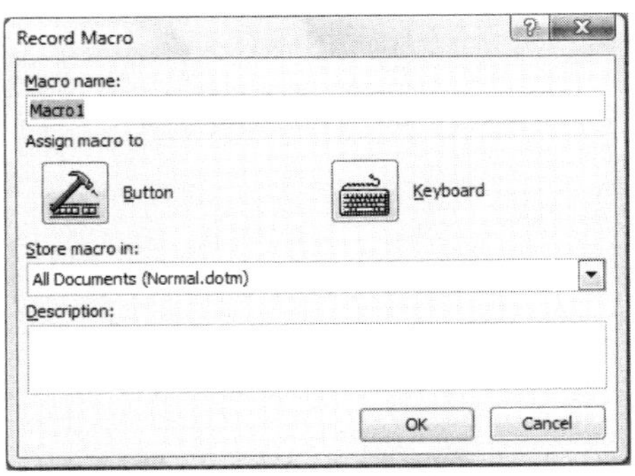

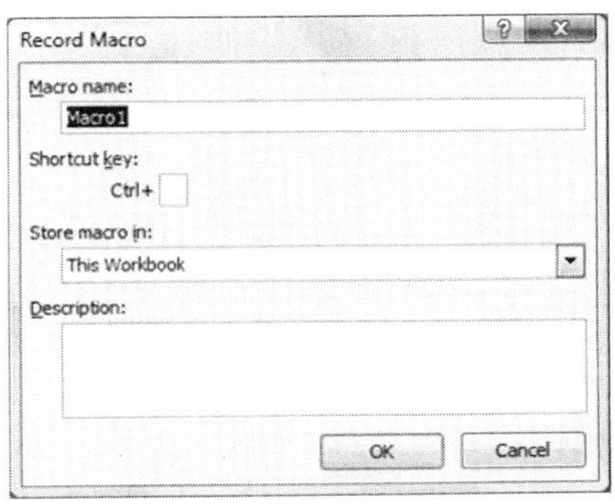

Figure 4-3: Record Macro dialog boxes for Word and Excel, respectively

After filling in the text boxes, click the OK button to start your recording session.

When you have finished recording, simply click the Stop Recording button under the Developer tab ⇨ code group (or on the status bar if you decided to use our tip).

NOTE The macro recorder does not record how long you take to perform your actions, only what you do. Hence, don't worry if it is taking you what seems like forever to get things done while recording. However, be aware that it will record almost everything, including errors, so it's a good thing that you can clean these up later.

After you've stopped the recorder, open the VBE and the module code window, and then open the `Modules` folder and select the new module. When you open the module, you will see the code that was created to automate your actions. You can add comments and modify the code as necessary. Otherwise, if it does exactly what you want, simply leave it as it is.

One critical difference between Excel and Word that you need to keep in mind when recording a macro is that Excel allows you to use the mouse while recording your actions. Word, conversely, records only keyboard entries. This means that although you can use the mouse to select text in Excel and then perform some kind of action with the text and the process will be recorded, in Word you cannot use the mouse in the document window. Any action performed with the mouse is not recordable in Word.

NOTE Although you cannot use the mouse to perform actions on the document, you can use the mouse to select commands on the Ribbon and/or select elements in the UI.

A Recording Example

This section walks through a simple example of recording a macro. Suppose you have certain calculations in Excel for which you always insert a specific comment. Instead of typing the comment each time, you can record the actions associated with inserting the comment and then simply play back the recording.

Here are the steps for recording such a macro:

1. Go to Developer ➪ Code ➪ Record Macro. The Record Macro dialog box will open.
2. Type the macro name (we used InsertComment).
3. Define a shortcut for it. We use Ctrl+Shift+C (simply hold down the Ctrl and Shift keys when typing the letter C in the box and Excel will show the full shortcut).
4. Click OK to start recording.

Now you need to insert the comment. Follow these steps:

1. Select the cell in which the comment should go.
2. Go to Review ➪ Comments ➪ New comment.
3. Type in your comment (we typed "This is the comment!").
4. When you're done, go to Developer ➪ Code ➪ Stop recording.

TIP **You might find it quicker to right-click and select Insert Comment from the pop-up menu list.**

That's it! You've saved your macro and you're done! In the code window for the standard module created, you should see something similar to what is shown in Figure 4-4.

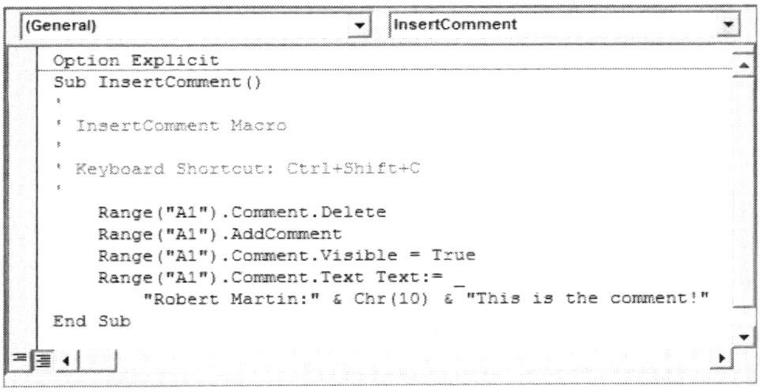

Figure 4-4: Code window for a standard module containing the recorded actions performed

Editing the Recorded Macro

The first thing to notice about this procedure is that it will always insert the comment on cell A1, or whichever cell you created the comment in during the recording process. This may not be exactly what you want, as it's more likely that you want to insert the comment on whichever cell you select.

Also note that if a comment already exists in cell A1, then you will get the error message shown in Figure 4-5, which will grind your code to a halt.

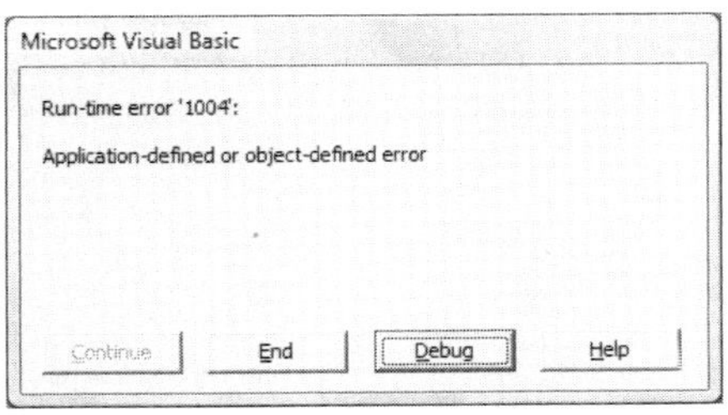

Figure 4-5: Error when trying to overwrite an existing comment

Pity. You were just getting started and you end up in a situation like this. Don't panic, however, as this can be resolved in several ways. For now we describe one possible solution; later we explain how to resolve some error-handling issues.

To make this macro more feasible for reuse, we can edit the code to accomplish the following:

- Remove the old comment before adding a new one.
- Ensure that the comment is always visible.

The amended VBA code is shown here, followed by a detailed explanation:

```
Sub InsertComment()
' InsertComment Macro
' Keyboard Shortcut: Ctrl+Shift+C
    Range("A1").Comment.Delete
    Range("A1").AddComment
    Range("A1").Comment.Visible = True
    Range("A1").Comment.Text Text:= _
        "Robert Martin:" & Chr(10) & "This is the comment!"
End Sub
```

Because we already have a comment in cell A1, we can use the `Delete` method of the `Comment` object to clear it up before inserting a new comment. Note, however, that if there is no comment in the cell, you get an error — just as you previously got an error message when trying to insert a comment in a cell that already had one.

But that's really just the beginning of the modifications, because you also want to insert the comment in the active cell, rather than always in A1. To put the comment in the active cell, replace `Range("A1")` in the code with `ActiveCell`:

- Except for the second line, all the other lines refer to the `Comment` object. The `Comment` object does not have an `Add` method (such as the `AddComment` method, which is available in the `Range` object, as shown in the recording example), which is what allowed us to add a comment to the cell.
- You could add the comment directly on the second line by specifying its text in the method's argument: `Range("A1").AddComment("Robert Martin:" & Chr(10) & "This is the comment!")`

For now, this is all we will do in terms of recording, but we'll come back to this example later, when we develop error handling and again when we are working with block constructs of code.

Editing Macro Options After Recording

Up until this point, we've assumed that you would record and change all of your macro options when you started. However, what if you wanted to change something later? This is not a major issue; in fact, it is relatively easy, as you'll see by going through the following steps in Excel:

1. With your workbook open, click Developer ➪ Code ➪ Macros to open the Macro list dialog box.
2. Select the macro you want to change and then click Options to open the Options dialog.
3. Change the details and click OK to continue.

As you might expect, the process is slightly different for Word. In the previous example, you could change the assigned shortcut keys directly in the Options dialog box. However, if you are working with Word, you need to go to a different location. To get you familiar with the process, we'll use that location in the following example.

With your Word document open, follow these steps:

1. Click Office Button ➪ Word Options ➪ Customize.
2. Under Keyboard shortcuts, click the Customize button.
3. Under Category, scroll to Macros and select it.
4. Under Macros, select the macro for which you want to reassign the shortcut keys.
5. Specify the key sequence.
6. Choose where you want to save the macro and click OK to finish.

Figure 4-6 shows the Customize Keyboard window, where you change the shortcut key for a Word macro.

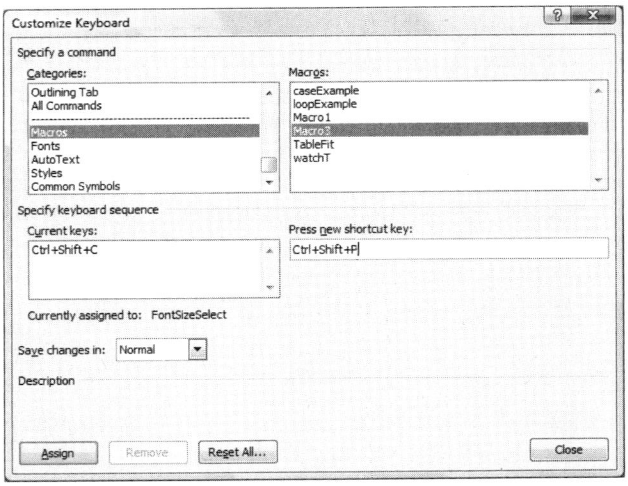

Figure 4-6: Editing macro options in Word

Subprocedures versus Functions

Unlike the previous section, the subprocedures and functions described here apply to all three applications: Excel, Word, and Access. The differences are only relevant when dealing with specific object models that are unique to one application. However, the object models can be referenced and used across all three applications. (Referencing is covered later in this chapter.)

We point out any instances of application-specific code in the examples — otherwise, the code should run without a problem in any of the three applications. We also provide more information about the individual objects as they are used in the examples.

Object Model

The object model (OM) enables you to access and control objects in the application. The Office OM has the `Application` object as the highest ranking object in the hierarchy of OMs. As such, it is commonly referred to as the *root object*.

The OM is basically a set of objects and collections of objects that expose properties and methods that can be used to perform a variety of actions. Although some of these properties and methods are not directly accessible from an object, they can be reached by following the hierarchical path in the model. This is why it is important to understand both the concept and syntax for working with the OM.

For example, suppose that you want to add a table to a Word document. Although it might be tempting to jump from the `Application` object straight into the `Add` method of the `Tables` collection, that would be skipping some steps. Instead, you must include the complete path from the root object to what you want to work with, as demonstrated in the following line of code:

```
Application.Documents("Document1").Tables.Add
```

The number of objects varies depending on the application and object; and each object has its own properties and methods. In the preceding example, we start at the root object and move to the `Documents` collection, singling out `"Document1"` in the collection. We then use the `Add` method to add a `table` object to the `Tables` collection. Notice that collections are in the plural, whereas an object is in the singular.

Similar to the way in which we move from the highest-ranking object to the lowest-raking object along the path, we can also move from the lowest-ranking object to the highest-ranking object by using the `Parent` property of the low-ranked object. This is particularly helpful when you want to learn something about the parent object, such as the directory of a file, or the name of a parent object. Consider the following line:

```
MsgBox ThisWorkbook.Parent
```

In the preceding example, the message box will show `Microsoft Excel` as the parent (or higher-ranked object) of the `ThisWorkbook` object in the OM hierarchy.

If you wish to study the hierarchy of the object models for the applications discussed in this book, you can open the VBA Help and inspect the Object Model Map. In order to access this resource, open the Help window and then click the Home button ➪ Application Object Model Reference ➪ Application Object Model Map ➪ Object Model Map.

Subprocedures

Now that you know a little more about the object model, we can move on to subprocedures. We're going to use them, so it's helpful for you understand a little bit about what they are. A subprocedure is basically a set of instructions designed to perform a certain task or set of tasks when it is executed.

For example, you could create a procedure that opens a report in Access, or create a procedure that turns formulas into text in Excel.

Take a moment to review the following procedures and then we'll explain the parts and what they do. The following snippet demonstrates an Excel example:

```
Sub WorkingWithCell()
   ThisWorkbook.Windows(1).ActiveCell.ClearContents
   ThisWorkbook.Windows(1).ActiveCell.Value = Now()
   ThisWorkbook.Windows(1).ActiveCell.NumberFormat = _
      "dd-mm-yyyy hh:mm:ss"
End Sub
```

Here is the Access example:

```
Private Sub cmdExit_Click()
    CloseCurrentDatabase
End Sub
```

Finally, the following illustrates a Word example:

```
Sub TableFit()
    ThisDocument.Tables(1).AllowAutoFit = True
End Sub
```

In the first example, we are working with a cell.

NOTE **Because the term** `ActiveCell` **is used, this is not specifying a particular cell, but instead will work with whatever cell is currently the active cell in an Excel (the application) window.**

In the second example, we're dealing with a database in Access. In the final example, we're dealing with a table in Word.

In looking at the three examples, you can discern a few important objects:

- **ThisWorkbook:** This is native to Excel and refers to the workbook that contains the code. There are other ways to refer to a workbook, but if you need to work with workbook-level elements, use this object to do so (`ThisWorkbook` is also a property of the `Application` object, which returns a `workbook` object).
- **ThisDocument:** Similar to Excel, Word uses `ThisDocument` as the means to access relevant properties and methods for the document that contains the code.
- **CurrentProject:** This object is native to Access and is used to retrieve important information about the database project that contains the code, such as the connection string, the path, and so on.

For example, you could use `ThisWorkbook` in the following way to identify the author of a workbook:

```
Sub ThisWB()
    MsgBox ThisWorkbook.BuiltinDocumentProperties("Author")
End Sub
```

Conversely, you could retrieve the entire connection details from your DB project with this code:

```
Sub connectionDetails()
    MsgBox CurrentProject.Connection
End Sub
```

If you haven't seen the complete connection details before, you'll be surprised by how much information is returned. Figure 4-7 shows an example of what you will see.

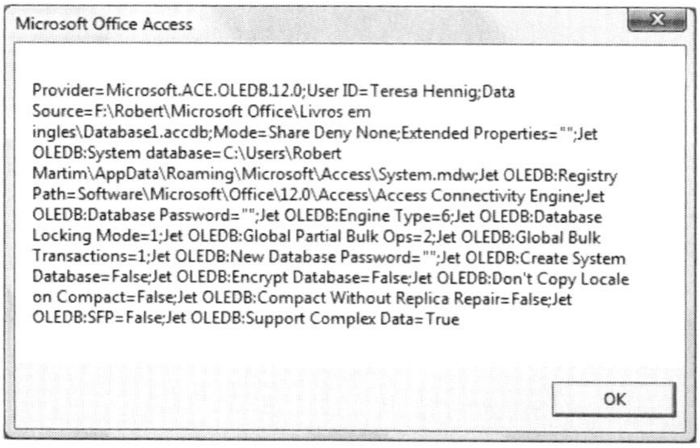

Figure 4-7: Message box showing connection details for an Access database

Functions

Functions are normally used to return values, unlike subprocedures, which typically perform a task. For example, if you want to get the results of a calculation, then you would use a function. As an example, the following function calculates the *n*th root of a number:

```
Function nthRoot(number As Double, nth As Integer) As Double
    nthRoot = number ^ (1 / nth)
End Function
```

This function can be used as written in all three applications. These terms and the syntax perform equally well in Excel, Access, and Word.

Functions can be used directly or indirectly. This means that you can use the function to calculate values in forms or in a worksheet; or you can call the function from another procedure within your VBA project. The call could come from another function whose final value depends on an intermediate calculation or it could come from a subprocedure.

Using an Access form, you could implement the `nthRoot` function as shown in Figure 4-8.

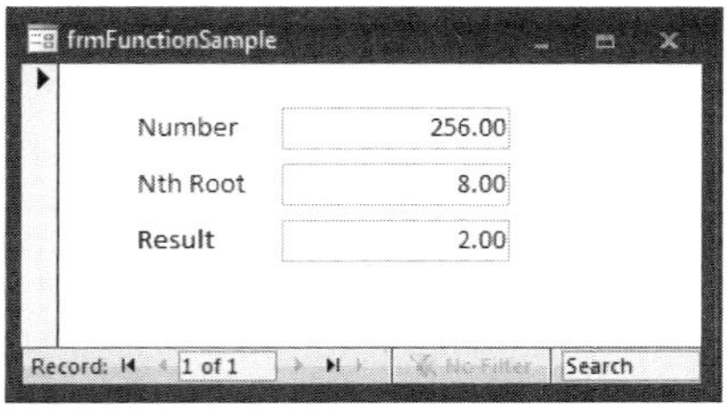

Figure 4-8: Implementing the user-defined function (UDF) in Access

The text box for the result contains the following formula `=nthRoot([txtNumber],[txtnthRoot])`, where `txtNumber` is the text box containing the number and `txtnthRoot` is the text box containing the Nth Root.

This formula calls the function that returns the *n*th root of the chosen number.

Of course, this is a simple example, and a function can be as complex as needed or imagined. Now that you've seen some basic aspects of subprocedures and functions, in the following section we turn our attention to some advanced aspects of VBA programming.

VBA Coding Techniques

We've already discussed some basic aspects of VBA, such as macro recording, macro-enabled documents and workbooks, and we've briefly covered subprocedures and functions. However, this only scratches the surface of VBA.

In this section you are introduced to some coding techniques that are extremely useful when developing in VBA. You will find yourself in situations where you are unable to finish a task unless you use loops to repeat a process a certain number of times or until a specified result occurs. In other scenarios, you might need to structure your code so that it becomes more readable — in other words, using code blocks such as `With-End With`. In others, you will need to make decisions within the code, which is typically done using `If-Then` and `Select Case` statements (aka constructs).

In addition to providing the desired functionality, code blocks also make it easier for you and other developers to interpret your code and make modifications when appropriate to accommodate changes in processes or business rules. All these scenarios are discussed here so that you can start implementing more advanced coding techniques in your projects.

Looping Statements

Our first stop is to see some examples of looping constructs. Loops enable your code to run through a sequence and perform some sort of action — either a set number of times (as below) or until a condition changes (True/False).

Loops come in a variety of flavors. We will look at each of them separately. If you're not familiar with loops, you should study the examples, as loops are extremely important in some of the coding that we will develop later.

For-Next Loops

This kind of loop can work as a counter or as a loop of elements within a predetermined set. We'll provide a working example momentarily, but first let's review the syntax and the definition of the elements. The syntax for the counter is as follows:

```
For counter = start To end [Step step]
    [statements]
[Exit For]
    [statements]
Next [counter]
```

In the `Next [counter]` part, you can omit the `[counter]`. However, if you have many nested loops, you may want to explicitly specify which counter you refer to by the `Next` keyword, as we'll explain shortly.

Table 4-2 lists each part of the loop statement, along with an explanation of what it does and whether it is required or optional.

Table 4-2: Elements of the For-Next Loop

PART	DESCRIPTION
counter	Required after the `For` keyword. Not required after the `Next` keyword. You must specify a numeric variable to be used as the loop counter. You cannot specify a Boolean or an array as a counter element.
start	Required. This is the initial value of `counter`.
end	Required. This is the initial final value of `counter`.
step	Optional. This specifies by what amount the counter is changed each time through the loop. If not specified, `step` defaults to one. A step can be negative if you wish to reverse the start-end position to "step up" the loop.
statements	Optional. Specifies one or more statements between `For` and `Next` keywords, which are executed the specified number of times.

This kind of loop will run through the specified items within the specified range, as shown in the following example:

```
Sub loopExample()
    Dim i       As Integer
```

```
    Dim iCount  As Integer

    For i = 1 To 100
        iCount = iCount + 1
    Next i
    MsgBox iCount
End Sub
```

In the preceding example, the loop runs from 1 to 100 and adds 1 to the counter variable each time the loop occurs until it is over. This example will work with any of the applications discussed in this book. Keep in mind that the terms "group" and "collection" are often used interchangeably when discussing these types of processes.

TIP **You may want to step through the code by pressing F8, as it runs very fast. By stepping through the code using the F8 key, you can watch the loop doing its magic.**

In the same manner as the `For-Next` loop, you do not need to explicitly specify the element after the `Next` keyword. However, as before, if you have many nested loops, you may want to explicitly specify it.

The syntax for the elements loop is as follows:

```
For Each element In group
   [statements]
[Exit For]
   [statements]
Next [element]
```

Table 4-3 describes each element of the `For Each-Next loop` statement.

Table 4-3: Elements of the For Each-Next Loop

PART	DESCRIPTION
element	Required. Variable used to iterate through the elements of the collection or array. For collections, `element` can only be a `Variant` variable, a generic object variable, or any specific object variable (e.g., `Worksheet`, `Document`, `Database`). For arrays, `element` can only be a `Variant` variable.
group	Required. Name of an object collection or array (except an array of user-defined types). As noted, a `group` can also be referred to as a `collection`.
statements	Optional. One or more statements that are executed on each item in group.

As shown in Table 4-2, you can also step the loop — that is, you can specify a value for the loop increment other than 1. You can obtain the exact effect as the preceding loop as follows:

```
Sub loopExample()
    Dim i       As Double
    Dim iCount  As Integer

    For i = 0 To 1 Step 0.01
        iCount = iCount + 1
    Next i
    MsgBox iCount
End Sub
```

What we did above is akin to dividing a one-dollar bill into 100 cents (or 0.01). Thus, between 0 and 1 we have one hundred units, which is the same as counting from 1 to 100 in the first loop.

Notice, however, that we changed the data type from `Integer` to `Double` for the `i` variable. This is necessary because the step is not an integer. If you left `i` as an integer, you would get an infinite loop because you would never manage to move from 0 to the next step, as 0.01 would be considered 0.

The next example, `Sub listFileNames`, is applicable to Excel (it can also be adapted for Access and Word). The code reads through each file in the folder where the workbook is located and lists the files in the active worksheet.

For this example, we reference the Windows Script Hosting Model in order to be able to use objects such as `FileSystemObject`, `Folder`, and `File`. This is a critical reference, as the following code will fail without this reference:

```
Sub listFileNames()
    Dim fsoObj        As New FileSystemObject
    Dim fsoFolder     As Folder
    Dim fsoFile       As File
    Dim lngRow        As Long
    Dim strPath       As String

    strPath = ThisWorkbook.Path
    Set fsoFolder = fsoObj.GetFolder(strPath)

    lngRow = 1

    For Each fsoFile In fsoFolder.Files
        ActiveSheet.Cells(lngRow, 1) = fsoFile.Name
        lngRow = lngRow + 1
    Next fsoFile

    Set fsoFile = Nothing
    Set fsoObj = Nothing
End Sub
```

NOTE **The workbook must be saved in order for the procedure to work as the file will not have a path until then.**

CROSS-REFERENCE **See "Referencing," later in this chapter, for details on referencing libraries.**

Do-While/Do-Until Loops

These loops are useful when you want to loop through certain instructions until a condition is met and it equates to `true`.

The syntax for these two types of loops is as follows:

```
Do [{While | Until} condition]
    [statements]
    [Exit Do]
    [statements]
Loop
```

In the preceding case, you specify the condition prior to entering the loop. You could also evaluate the condition after you enter the loop:

```
Do
    [statements]
    [Exit Do]
    [statements]
Loop [{While | Until} condition]
```

Note that either version of the code will execute at least once.

As pointed out, these two types of loops are useful when you want the loop to occur until a certain criterion is met, as shown here:

```
Sub DoUntilLoop()
    Dim lngRow As Long
    lngRow = 1
    Do Until IsEmpty(ActiveSheet.Cells(lngRow, 1))
        lngRow = lngRow + 1
    Loop
    MsgBox ActiveSheet.Cells(lngRow, 1).Address
End Sub
```

The preceding loop will occur until it reaches an empty cell in the active worksheet. Once that point is reached, the address of the first empty cell is shown in a message box.

The next example applies to Access (it can also apply to Excel and Word if those applications are accessing a recordset and looping through it):

```
Sub DoWhileLoop ()
    Do While (Not (rst.EOF))
```

```
        rst.MoveNext
    Loop
End Sub
```

The preceding loop will occur while it is not the end of file (`EOF`). At each stage, you move to the next record in the recordset. When the end is reached, the loop finishes.

A variation of the `Do While` loop could be the following:

```
While (Not (rst.EOF))
    rst.MoveNext
Wend
```

This loop does exactly the same thing as the previous example, but some people don't like the syntax of the `Wend` keyword because the consolidated format does not list the elements separately and the condensed style isn't as easy to interpret.

With . . . End With Statement

This statement is extremely useful when you need to execute a series of statements in a single object or a user-defined type.

The general syntax for this statement is as follows:

```
With object
    [statements]
End With
```

Table 4-4 describes each element of the `With-End With` statement.

Table 4-4: Elements of the With Statement

PART	DESCRIPTION
object	Required. The name of an object or user-defined type.
statements	Optional. One or more statements to be executed on the object.

The great advantage of using the `With` statement is that you can execute a series of statements with the same object (or property) without the need to repeat the object's name over and over.

You will remember our example for subprocedures where we were working with the `ActiveCell` property in Excel:

```
ActiveCell.ClearContents
ActiveCell.Value = Now()
ActiveCell.NumberFormat = "dd-mm-yyyy hh:mm:ss"
```

You can see that the `ActiveCell` property is repeated at every single line, but you could avoid that repetition by using the `With` statement. For example, the preceding code rewritten to use `With - End With` would be as follows:

```
With ActiveCell
    .ClearContents
    .Value = Now()
    .NumberFormat = "dd-mm-yyyy hh:mm:ss"
End With
```

As you can see, you qualify the `ActiveCell` property and then assign the values for each property of the object or call a method to be executed (in the case of the `ClearContents` method).

This not only saves you the time of requalifying the `ActiveCell` property at each line, it also structures your code so that it has a cleaner layout, which makes it easier to read and understand. You can easily imagine how much time this approach will save if you are going to repeat the process with several objects. You merely write the code once, copy and paste it numerous times, and then replace the name of the object — and modify other relevant commands and values.

If . . . Then . . . Else . . . End If Statement

The `If-Then-Else-End If` statement is a decision statement that executes a block of instructions according to whether the specified condition is met or not. Which statement (either the `Then` statement or the `Else` statement) should be executed depends on whether the condition is met or not.

The short syntax for this statement is as follows:

```
If condition Then [statements] [Else elsestatements]
```

Although this syntax is perfectly acceptable from the point of view of evaluating the condition and executing the statement, a better choice is to break the statement into blocks, as shown in the following example:

```
If condition Then
    [statements]
[ElseIf condition-n Then
    [elseifstatements]
[Else
    [elsestatements]]
End If
```

Table 4-5 describes each element of the `If...Then...Else` statement. As you can see, only a few of the elements are required. The optional elements make this a very versatile and powerful tool that can be expanded to handle multiple conditions.

Table 4-5: Elements of the If...Then...Else Statement

PART	DESCRIPTION
condition	Required. Refers to the condition that needs to be evaluated during the decision process.
statements	Optional in block form. Required in a single-line form that has no `Else` clause. One or more statements separated by colons; executed if the condition is `True`.
condition-n	Optional. Same as `condition`.
elseifstatements	Optional. One or more statements are executed if the associated `condition-n` is `True`.
elsestatements	Optional. One or more statements are executed if no previous condition or `condition-n` expression is `True`.

The following example shows a function that compares a part-string against a full string:

```
Function isLike(varValue As Variant, strLike As Variant) As Boolean
    If varValue Like strLike Then
        isLike = True
    Else
        isLike = False
    End If
End Function
```

The preceding function can be used in any of the applications discussed in this book. How you call the function depends on its use. In Excel, you could call it from a formula in a cell. In Access, you could use it in a formula or call it using a subroutine:

```
Sub compare()
    MsgBox isLike("robson", "rob*")
End Sub
```

This subroutine compares the part-string `"rob*"` (starting with `"rob"` and ending in anything) against the `"robson"` string. In the preceding case, the function returns `True`. It would also return `True` if the main string were `"robert"`, `"robertson"`, or any other string containing `"rob"` in the first three letters and ending in anything.

The last example uses a direct message box, but the comparison could also evaluate a condition:

```
Sub compare()
    If isLike("robertson", "mar*") Then
        MsgBox "The comparison is true.", vbInformation
    Else
        MsgBox "The comparison is false.", vbInformation
    End If
End Sub
```

Select Case Statement

The `Select Case` statement is also used in decision making. When a case is evaluated as `true`, its statement is executed. In addition, at the end, you also have a general case (`Case Else`), which can be evaluated in the event that all other case expressions evaluate to `false`.

This provides a lot of flexibility and can make it easier to read complex operations than it is by using a series of `If...Then...Else` statements.

Additionally, with the `Select Case` statement, the conditional portion is taken care of within the evaluation of each case, instead of using several nested `If...Then` statements.

The general syntax for the `Select Case` statement is provided here:

```
Select Case testexpression
  [Case expressionlist-n
    [statements-n]]
  [Case Else
    [elsestatements]]
End Select
```

Table 4-6 describes each element of the `Select Case` statement.

Table 4-6: Elements of the Select Case Statement

PART	DESCRIPTION
testexpression	Required. Any numeric expression or string expression.
expressionlist-n	Required if a `Case` appears. Delimited list of one or more of the following forms: `expression`, `expression To expression`, `Is comparison operator expression`. The `To` keyword specifies a range of values. If you use the `To` keyword, the smaller value must appear before `To`. Use the `Is` keyword with comparison operators (except `Is` and `Like`) to specify a range of values. When not supplied, the `Is` keyword is automatically inserted.
statements-n	Optional. One or more statements executed if the test expression matches any part of `expressionlist-n`.
elsestatements	Optional. One or more statements are executed if the test expression doesn't match any of the `Case` clause(s).

Keep a few things in mind when using the `Select Case` statement:

- The case being evaluated must match exactly the expression text specified, and it is case sensitive. Thus, if an expression specifies "text" but the case is "Text", then it will evaluate to `false`.
- If the expression can be matched to more than one case, then only the expression text belonging to the first case after the expression is evaluated.
- Use `Case Else` to evaluate an expression when there is no match in the cases specified.

The following example helps illustrate what the second bullet above means:

```
Sub caseExample()
    Dim Number    As Integer
    Number = 1
    Select Case Number
        Case 1
            MsgBox 1
        Case 1
            MsgBox 2
        Case 1
            MsgBox 3
    End Select
End Sub
```

Because all cases are 1 and the number is 1, only the first case is evaluated, and only MsgBox 1 will be displayed. You typically won't find code that matches this example, however, because there would be little benefit to having the second and third message boxes. Nonetheless, it effectively illustrates an important aspect of case statements — namely, that because the comparisons are made in sequential order, you only get the results specified by the first match.

The next example demonstrates how the `Case Else` occurs when there is no match:

```
    Number = 2
    Select Case Number
        Case 1
            MsgBox 1
        Case 1
            MsgBox 2
        Case Else
            MsgBox "There is no case for the specified number."
    End Select
```

Here, the case number is 1; and since the number passed is 2, the `Case Else` is evaluated.

Writing Your Own Code

You've now reviewed the basics of VBA and learned some important programming aspects. This section introduces some concepts that will be useful for writing your own code, such as naming conventions and data types.

Also included in this section is a discussion of referencing libraries, which are extremely important when you need to bring external components into your own application.

Naming Conventions

This book is about a new technology, and as you'd expect, people are writing XML code and declaring names in various ways. While this may be convenient to them, it can be a problem if the code needs to be interpreted or used by others.

The idea behind naming conventions is to provide an easy way for others to understand your code, and you as well for that matter. Trust us, it is not uncommon to be baffled by code in a project that you wrote years or even months before.

For the purposes of standardization, we use RVBA (Reddick VBA, see note below) as the naming convention for the VBA code presented here. For the XML, we devised our own naming convention based on RVBA and the naming conventions used in VBA itself. We discuss them in this chapter in a moment. You can also refer to the appendix for some tables of the more common names.

Do you have to use a naming convention? The answer is "no," but we strongly recommend that you do. The benefits are worth the slight effort to learn the standards. Implementing naming conventions offers several benefits:

- It makes code easier for you and others to read and interpret.
- It reduces the chances of using a reserved word or special character.
- It avoids name conflicts between the objects that you create and those in code from other sources, such as third-party add-ins.
- It makes it easier for you to interpret code from others — whether you're adapting it to your own project, helping someone else find a solution, or just learning what the code is intended to do.

Admittedly, if you're writing the code only for yourself, then you can typically get away with using whatever names you are comfortable with – providing that you don't use reserved words or special characters. Even then, however, you'll probably notice that you've adopted your own convention. Moreover, as soon as you start incorporating code from other sources, you will see that following naming conventions can avoid conflicts and save a tremendous amount of time troubleshooting and debugging.

When you are working with many people on a project or you need to share your code with others, following a standard naming convention is the way to go. Think of it as a language (like English itself); while it is OK to have slang in any language, not everyone understands such parlance (vernacular). Conversely, almost everyone can quickly and consistently interpret the meaning of standard English.

NOTE **The Reddick convention can be found at** `www.xoc.net/standards/rvbanc.asp`**.**

That said, now it's time to focus on the naming convention that we've adopted for the XML code that you write. It consists of the following parts:

- **Prefix:** We have adopted the `rx` prefix to differentiate code written in VBA from Ribbon customization from that written directly on your project for your project.

- **Tag:** We have adopted the RVBA tagging system to tag Ribbon controls. The tag is very important because it tells the reader of your code what the control or object really is. For example, a `label` control in VBA would have the `lbl` tag. When we translate this into our Ribbon naming convention, it would become `rxlbl`. By doing so, we know by the VBA code that this label comes from the Ribbon and not from a label control within the VBA project.
- **BaseName:** This is the description of the control. For example, you could have a Ribbon button and define its prefix and tag as `rxbtn`; however, what does this button do? If it were a demo button you could name it `rxbtnDemo`, making it more meaningful.
- **Event suffix:** You already have a button, but what happens when a user clicks it? Well, an event will be triggered. In order to make life easier, we use the common VBA event suffixes to describe such actions. Therefore, if you have an `onAction` attribute attached to the Demo button, the procedure should be named `rxbtnDemo_click`.
- **Shared event:** In the previous example, we have a click for the Demo button. However, what if you wanted to share this event with other buttons? Or with other controls that have the `onAction` attribute? You would not be able to add the tag as we did before, so you'd use a generic tag to indicate that the `onAction` attribute is shared among many different controls. For example: `rxshared_click`. Now you know that this click is shared by many other controls that have an `onAction` attribute. However, the `click` event can perform different actions depending on the control that called it. You will learn how to make that happen in Chapter 5.
- **Repurpose suffix:** We already mentioned that we use event suffixes to match the events of VBA. However, when you use a built-in command, you may want to repurpose its action using the `onAction` attribute. Since `onAction` returns a `click` suffix, it would not be clear to a reader of the code that it was a built-in command being repurposed. In such cases, we use the `rx` prefix followed by the `idMso` attribute of the control as the base name, followed by an underscore and the word "Repurpose" to make it clear that the built-in command is being repurposed. For example, `rxFileSave_Repurpose` means that the `FileSave` command has been repurposed to perform some other action.

The naming convention we adopted for the Ribbon certainly doesn't have the force that an International Treaty on Naming Conventions might have, but it is very appropriate for the scope of this book, and it is an excellent way to jump-start a naming convention for the Ribbon XML code.

Data Types

As you start to develop code, you will want to be aware of data types. Knowing what a data type can contain and how it can function will prevent you from looking for a solution to a problem that could have been easily avoided in the first place.

If you recall from the loop section, when we created the stepped loop, we had to change the data type from `Integer` to `Double`. If you have not run through the example yet, this is a good time to do so. Keep the data type as `Integer` and try to run the stepped loop. What happens? You're probably stuck in a never-ending loop. Why? Because you have the wrong data type and the loop is unable to match the step. That's a perfect example of our point that understanding data types can help you avoid problems.

NOTE If you are stuck in a loop and can't get out of it, press `CTRL+BREAK` to break the code and end it.

Table 4-7 lists the data types VBA supports. The table includes storage sizes and value ranges.

Table 4-7: Some Fundamental Data Types

DATA TYPE	STORAGE SIZE	VALUE RANGE
Byte	1 byte	0 to 255
Boolean	2 bytes	True or False
Integer	2 bytes	-32,768 to 32,767
Long (long integer)	4 bytes	-2,147,483,648 to 2,147,483,647
Single (single-precision floating-point)	4 bytes	-3.402823E38 to -1.401298E-45 for negative values; 1.401298E-45 to 3.402823E38 for positive values
Double (double-precision floating-point)	8 bytes	-1.79769313486231E308 to -4.94065645841247E-324 for negative values; 4.94065645841247E-324 to 1.79769313486232E308 for positive values
Currency (scaled integer)	8 bytes	-922,337,203,685,477.5808 to 922,337,203,685,477.5807
Decimal	14 bytes	+/ 79,228,162,514,264,337,593,543,950,335 with no decimal point; +/-7.9228162514264337593543950335 with 28 places to the right of the decimal; smallest non-zero number is +/-0.0000000000000000000000000001
Date	8 bytes	January 1, 100 to December 31, 9999
Object	4 bytes	Any Object reference
String (variable-length)	10 bytes + string length	0 to approximately 2 billion
String (fixed-length)	Length of string	1 to approximately 65,400

Continued

Table 4-7 *(continued)*

DATA TYPE	STORAGE SIZE	VALUE RANGE
Variant (with numbers)	16 bytes	Any numeric value up to the range of a Double
Variant (with characters)	22 bytes + string length	Same range as for variable-length String
User-defined (using Type)	Number required by elements	The range of each element is the same as the range of its data type.

Working with Events

You had a taste of events when we provided a sample of code for the old customization. Now it's time to learn more about events. As with loops, events also come in a variety of flavors. You can use built-in events or you can write custom events to handle specific tasks. In this section, you will learn how to harness the power of events and how you can use events to interact with other programs and files.

Excel, Access, and Word can monitor many different types of events. Events are normally associated with objects that you commonly use. This section covers the following events:

- **Workbook events:** As the name suggests, these events are associated with Excel workbooks. There are many workbook events, such as `Open`, `BeforeClose`, `SheetActivate`, and so on. Workbook-level events must be stored in the workbook in which events are being monitored. Application-level events are discussed later in this section.
- **Worksheet events:** Again, this is native to Excel and is associated with events happening in a worksheet. For example, you could have a `SelectionChange`, `Change`, `BeforeRightClick`, and so on.
- **Form events:** These are events occurring in Microsoft Access forms, and include events such as `Load`, `Open`, `MouseWheel`, and so on. (Although there are events associated with other types of forms, for our purposes we're limiting this to forms in Access).
- **Report events:** These are events occurring in Microsoft Access reports. Among these events you will find `Open`, `Close`, and so on.
- **Document events:** Document events are associated with Word documents. Here you will find events such as `New`, `Open`, and `Close`.
- **Application-level events:** Application-level events monitor events that you find in a document or workbook, for example, but which are not locked in the document or workbook container. There may be cases you need to monitor when a new workbook or document is created, when a file is sent to print, and so on. Here, you will need to add custom classes to handle such application-wide events.

Any event handler can be directly typed into the code window of the object you're dealing with. However, this method is extremely prone to typing errors and entering the procedure incorrectly. If you intend to work with an event, the best way is to simply let VBE write the procedure stub. Momentarily, we'll show you how to make that happen.

Workbook Events

Figure 4-9 shows how to initiate the process.

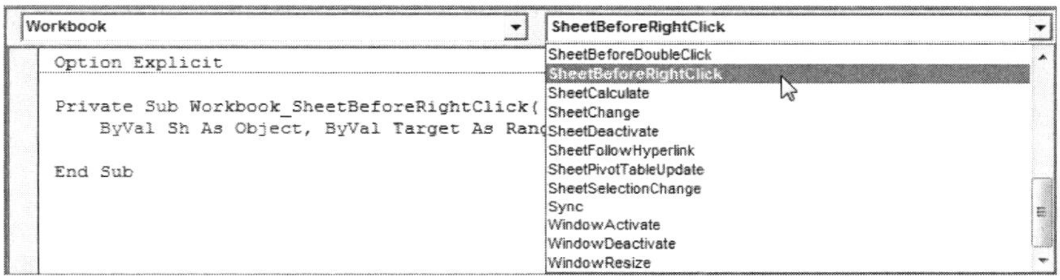

Figure 4-9: Choosing workbook events in the workbook's code window

The image is for Excel, but the process is the same whether you're using Excel, Access, or Word. In this particular example, you are working with the code window for a workbook. The event is the `Workbook_SheetBeforeRightClick`.

The first two steps to get VBE to add the procedure are as follows:

1. Select the object you want to work with from the object list (the left drop-down menu in the code window).
2. Select the event from the object's event list (the right drop-down menu in the code window).

This produces the procedure you use to handle the event. Our example generated the following procedure:

```
Private Sub Workbook_SheetBeforeRightClick(ByVal Sh As Object, _
    ByVal Target As Range, Cancel As Boolean)
'   Your event handler code goes here
End Sub
```

Note that this event controls the right-click event of all sheets in the workbook. Later in this chapter, when you learn about worksheet events, you will also learn how to control the right-click event on a particular worksheet.

In looking at the following code snippet, you will notice that the `Open` event does not have any arguments. It is important to recognize that although most events have arguments, some do not. The `Open` event is an example of an event that does not have any arguments:

```
Private Sub Workbook_Open()
'   Your event handler code goes here
End Sub
```

Now let's take a look at the arguments for our first example, the `SheetBeforeRightClick` event. As written, the `sub` has the following arguments:

- `Sh`: Refers to the sheet where the right-click occurred. The sheet is passed as an object because it can be either a chart sheet or a worksheet.
- `Target`: Refers to the target of the right-click and represents a range. The range can be a single cell or multiple cells.
- `Cancel`: Determines whether the return on the right-click should be canceled or not. You would normally get a pop-up menu when right-clicking. By setting `Cancel` equal to `true`, the pop-up menu is canceled.

To provide code to block the use of the right-click in the range A1:C25, you could use the following:

```
Private Sub Workbook_SheetBeforeRightClick(ByVal Sh As Object, _
    ByVal Target As Range, Cancel As Boolean)
    If Union(Target.Range("A1"), Range("A1:C25")).Address = _
        Range("A1:C25").Address Then Cancel = True
End Sub
```

NOTE The preceding code assumes you're dealing with a worksheet. If the object is a chartsheet, then the code will not behave as expected because a chartsheet does not have a selectable range as defined in the code.

The preceding procedure will cancel the right-click on any cell within the specified range. You could, of course, choose any other range:

```
    If Union(Target.Range("A1"), Range("C10:E20")).Address = _
        Range("C10:E20").Address Then Cancel = True
```

Keep in mind that the preceding code affects every single sheet in your workbook. If you need to cancel the right-click on a specific sheet, you can use the preceding code in the worksheet module, instead of in the workbook module. We discuss worksheet modules next.

Table 4-8 lists some of the workbook-level events. In order to view the list of available events, follow the process depicted in Figure 4-9.

Table 4-8: Some Useful Workbook-Level Events

EVENT	WHEN IT OCCURS
BeforeClose	The workbook is about to be closed
BeforeSave	The workbook is about to be saved
NewSheet	A sheet is added to the workbook
Open	The workbook is opened

Table 4-8 *(continued)*

EVENT	WHEN IT OCCURS
SheetActivate	A sheet in the workbook is activated
SheetBeforeRightClick	The right-click of the mouse button is actioned
SheetChange	A change occurs on any sheet in the workbook

Worksheet Events

The previous events are for the workbook, but they were also able to control what happened to sheets. When you want to work with events happening in one specific worksheet, you could not use the previous example, as it affects all sheets simultaneously.

When it is necessary to work events on just one worksheet, a better alternative is to use the events for the worksheet itself. Take the example for the right-click. You could apply the same logic to just Sheet1, as shown in the following example, instead of to every worksheet in the workbook, as we did in the previous example:

```
Private Sub Worksheet_BeforeRightClick(ByVal Target As Range, _
    Cancel As Boolean)
    If Union(Target.Range("A1"), Range("A1:C25")).Address = _
        Range("A1:C25").Address Then Cancel = True
End Sub
```

You might immediately notice a few differences between the two examples:

- As a worksheet-level event, the argument for the sheet no longer appears in the procedure.
- The procedure is prefixed by `Worksheet` instead of `Workbook`.

Now let's look at a scenario in which a worksheet event can be remarkably helpful. Suppose that you have validated column A to accept only unique values. Everything will work just fine, as long as the user inputs data into each cell and does not copy and paste within the range. That is a critical restriction, because if the user does copy and paste within the range, your validation will be wiped out. It's times like these that event procedures really demonstrate their value.

You can use the `Change` event to check what is happening in the column, and if the user pastes something, the procedure can reverse the pasting so that no duplicates occur in the column. The following code will accomplish your goal:

```
Private Sub Worksheet_Change(ByVal Target As Range)
    Dim rngSelected     As Range
    Dim rngValue        As Range
    Dim lngCount        As Long

'   Disable further events while we check what is happening
    Application.EnableEvents = False
```

```
'   The range being monitored
    If Union(Target.Range("A1"), Range("A1:A1048576")).Address = _
        Range("A1:A1048576").Address Then

        On Error Resume Next

'       Sets the selected range
        Set rngSelected = Selection

'       count the occurrence of the pasted value in the upper most
        For Each rngValue In rngSelected
            lngCount = WorksheetFunction.CountIf(Range("A1:A1048576"), _
                rngValue)

'       If the occurrence is greater than one
        If lngCount > 1 Then

'           Show the error message
            MsgBox "Column A only accepts unique values. " _
                & "The value/s you typed has/have already been" _
                &"entered. Try again.", vbCritical, _
                "Value duplicated in column A..."

'           Undo the pasting action
            Application.Undo

            Application.CutCopyMode = xlCut
            Exit For
        End If
        Next rngValue

    End If

'   Enable events so that monitoring can continue
    Application.EnableEvents = True
End Sub
```

Note that because the code also causes a change in the worksheet, you need to temporarily disable events. If you do not, the process may end up in an infinite loop. (That is accomplished in the line `Application.EnableEvents = False`.) In addition, of course, it is critical to enable events before exiting the `Sub`. In the preceding example, the first and last step in the routine take care of this.

NOTE **It is standard practice to include the enabling of features in error handling routines. You'll learn more about that later in this chapter when we discuss error handling.**

Table 4-9 lists some common worksheet-level events and when they occur.

Table 4-9: Some Useful Worksheet-Level Events

EVENT	WHEN IT OCCURS
Activate	The worksheet is activated
BeforeDoubleClick	The left button of your mouse is pressed/clicked quickly twice
BeforeRightClick	The right button of your mouse is pressed/clicked
Change	Something in your worksheet changes
SelectionChange	A selection in your worksheet changes

Form and Report Events in Access

Now that we've covered some of the basics with Excel, let's look at some events in Access. Here we'll focus on the events for forms and reports, as these comprise the primary user interface.

Envision a scenario in which a user opens a report, but there is nothing to see — that is, there is no data to be placed in the report. This suggests several undesirable possibilities. If there is no error trapping, then the user will get an error message. And even if you didn't get an error message, what good is a report without data? A blank report can give the impression that there was an error in processing, rather than that there was no data to report.

You can avoid many of these issues and potentially confusing outcomes by using the `NoData` event to determine whether the report should be canceled. In addition to canceling the report `print` event, the following code provides a nice explanation to the user:

```
Private Sub Report_NoData(Cancel As Integer)
    MsgBox "No data available at present. The report will be" _
    &"canceled..."
    Cancel = -1  'True would also work here as -1 equates to true.
End Sub
```

By setting the `Cancel` value to `-1`, you effectively set its value to `True` (meaning the report should be canceled). You could also use `True` as the value instead of the integer.

Another useful event is the `Open` event. You can use this event to ensure that important elements are loaded before the report is shown. Quite often, users will provide information on a form that is then used to filter the data (the recordsource) for the report — for example, choosing an account and dates to filter the report. The report could open the form, be called from the form, or check to see whether the form is open, as shown in the following code snippet:

```
Private Sub Report_Open(Cancel As Integer)
    DoCmd.OpenForm "frmInputData", , , , , acDialog, "Transactions"
```

```
    If Not IsLoaded("frmInputData") Then
       Cancel = True
    End If
End Sub
```

This example checks whether a particular form (`frmInputData`) is loaded before the report can be shown. If it is not loaded, then the report is canceled.

A report also contains other elements that have events. For example, the Detail part of a report has events such as `Format`, which can be used to do such things as add lines or color to alternating rows as a report is about to print. By now, you should be able to interpret the following code, so give it a whirl and then read the explanation that follows:

```
' Module private count variable
Private mRowCount As Long
Private Sub Detail_Format(Cancel As Integer, FormatCount As Integer)
'   Counts the number of rows in the details at each pass
    mRowCount = mRowCount + 1

'   Determines the remainder of a division by 2.
'   If zero, then BackColor 16777215 is applied (white background)
    If mRowCount Mod 2 = 0 Then
      Me.Detail.BackColor = 16777215

'   Else, BackColor 15263976 (grey) is applied
    Else
      Me.Detail.BackColor = 15263976
    End If
End Sub
```

In this example, the formatting event fires for each line in the Details section of the report. When the line number is an even number, no color is applied, but if it is odd, a grey background is applied.

NOTE **Although it required special code to add this type of formatting in prior versions of Access, 2007 provides some impressive formatting options that do not require code. In the report, go to Layout View and you can easily change the appearance of the report by selecting Report Layout Tools ⇨ Format ⇨ AutoFormat.**

Like reports, forms also share some of the same events, plus they allow you to add other objects that will have events of their own, such as combobox, textbox, and so on. If you have a data entry form, you can use the `Open` event to open the form to a new record, rather than display existing data. The following code snippet is just one of the ways to do that:

```
Private Sub Form_Open(Cancel As Integer)
    DoCmd.RunCommand acCmdRecordsGoToNew
End Sub
```

Just as a report has a Details section, so does a form. You will recall that when you right-click on a form, you get the contextual pop-up menu. We showed you how to cancel such pop-ups in Excel, and the same technique will work in Access. In fact, you may prefer to swap out the pop-up menu and use your own, as shown in Figure 4-10.

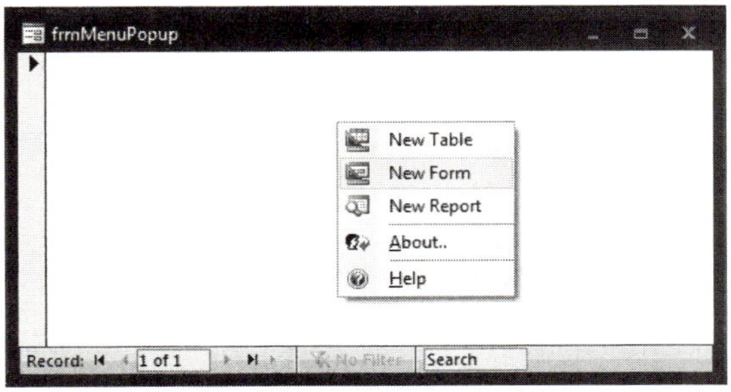

Figure 4-10: Pop-up menu triggered by a right-click event

The following code enables you to display your custom pop-up menu, whether it is replacing the standard pop-up or adding a pop-up where Access does not provide one:

```
Private Sub Detail_MouseDown(Button As Integer, _
    Shift As Integer, X As Single, Y As Single)
    If Button = acRightButton Then
        DoCmd.CancelEvent
        CommandBars(gcCMDBARNAME).ShowPopup
    End If
End Sub
```

You first need to determine whether the click came from the right-hand button. If it did, then you cancel the event and show your own pop-up menu. In looking at the previous code sample, you can determine that the pop-up is globally defined as `gcCMDBARNAME`.

CROSS-REFERENCE **See the section "Replacing Built-in Pop-up Menus in Their Entirety" in Chapter 15 for complete examples showing how to swap built-in pop-up menus with your own.**

Table 4-10 lists some common report/form events and when they occur. The order of events can be very important, considering that the outcome of one event may prevent subsequent events from firing.

Table 4-10: Some Useful Report and Form-Level Events*

EVENT	WHEN IT OCCURS
Click	A mouse is clicked over the report/form
Close	A report/form is closed and removed from the screen
Current	The focus moves to a record (in a form or report), making it the current record, or the form is refreshed or requeried
Load	Occurs when a form/report is opened and its records are displayed
NoData	Access formats a report for printing that has no data, but before the report is printed
OnFormat	Access is determining which data belongs in a report section, but before Access formats the section for previewing or printing
Open	A form is opened, but before the first record is displayed. For a report, it occurs before a report is previewed or printed.

*Includes events for the Detail part of a report/form

Document-Level Events in Word

Document-level events, as the name suggests, are events happening within a particular document in Word. For example, an event can be printing or it can be creating a new document.

In Word, as in Excel and Access, you will find some common events, such as `Open` and `Close`, which you can use to perform some sort of action:

```
Private Sub Document_Open()
'   Your event handler code goes here
End Sub
```

Although Excel provides other events straight from the code window for the object you want (such as the `Document` equivalent `ThisWorkbook`), Word does not do that. Instead, you need to create a class module to handle events for a particular document. You can also apply this method to global templates or to add-ins that control application-level events in Word.

The key to making this work is to use the `WithEvents` keyword to declare a public Word object that can be used across the project, as shown in Figure 4-11.

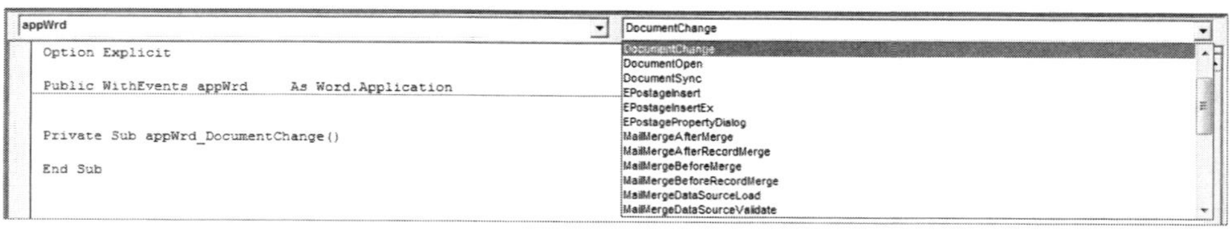

Figure 4-11: Choosing an event in a class window in Word

The first thing you need to do is add a class module to your project. In order to add a class module, with the VBE opened, click Insert ➪ Class Module (or press the Alt ➪ I ➪ C sequence). For this example, name it `clsEvents`. Now that you have named the module, open its code window (if it is not opened yet) and enter the following lines of code:

```
Public WithEvents appWrd     As Word.Application
Private Sub appWrd_DocumentChange()
End Sub
```

The first line of code says that the events for Word should be monitored. The procedure under it says that a document change should be monitored.

As it is, nothing will happen. However, you can use the `Open` event at the document level to set the application-level events for Word:

```
Dim mappWrd     As New clsEvents
Private Sub Document_Open()
    Set mappWrd.appWrd = Application
End Sub
```

Once you have done that, you're ready to use the event that you just declared in the class module, `clsEvents`. Remember, though, that you must write all your events first; otherwise, the class will be terminated because it has no events to monitor.

Having said that, we'll add an event that might be useful, as it will enable you to keep track of the printing of a certain document. We do that with the following code:

```
Private Sub appWrd_DocumentBeforePrint(ByVal Doc As Document, _
    Cancel As Boolean)
    If Doc = ThisDocument Then
        'Log code goes here
    Else:
        'Code for when printing another document
    End If
End Sub
```

Notice that the `WithEvents appWrd` will monitor the entire Word application, so when you intend to monitor just the document that contains the code, you should construct the code to only execute if it is the correct document. In our example, we used the `ThisDocument` object to stipulate the document containing the code.

Application-Level Events

Application-level events can be used to control what happens in different parts of the application. Because we just addressed this for Word, we'll move on to Excel and Access. Before diving into this, however, it is important to note the differences in how each program opens. Access does not open multiple projects on the same Access window; instead, it opens multiple instances of Access. Excel, however, can open various workbooks in the same window. This difference is a critical factor when determining the scope of application-level events.

We'll start by looking at events for Excel and then move on to Access.

As you have already seen in Word, if you plan to deploy application-level event, you need to use a class module. Thus, all examples here use a class module. To practice these examples, you should use the standard name `clsEvents`, as it is the name we will be referencing throughout our processes.

The first example demonstrates how to monitor the printing of a particular workbook and only allow the specified workbook to print.

Start by opening Excel and adding a new class module. Insert the following code:

```
Public WithEvents appXL     As Excel.Application
Private Sub appXL_WorkbookBeforePrint(ByVal Wb As Workbook, _
    Cancel As Boolean)
    If Not Wb.Name = "AllowedWorkbook.xslm" Then
        MsgBox "Printing is not allowed, except for the " _
            & "AllowedWorkbook.xslm workbook", vbCritical
        Cancel = True
    End If
End Sub
```

Once you have created the preceding code, you can use the local `Open` event to set this application-level event:

```
Dim mappXL      As New clsEvents
Private Sub Workbook_Open()
    Set mappXL.appXL = Application
End Sub
```

Once this has been set, only the allowed workbook will print. All other printing attempts will be canceled, and the message shown in Figure 4-12 will be displayed.

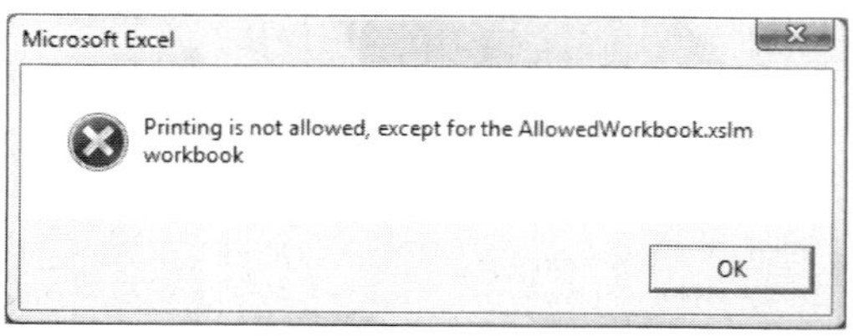

Figure 4-12: Message box triggered by printing event

Now let's look at an example using Access. The need for data validation is fairly universal, so we'll use an example that provides one way to validate data before it is accepted into a table.

In this scenario, assume a text box is used to enter data into a field that should only contain positive values. Therefore, if the text box appears on multiple forms, you might be tempted to write validation code for each occurrence of the text box. However, you can save a lot of time by writing a simple procedure within a class module and then using it throughout the project.

Start by creating the class module shown below. Although this has some new material, you should recognize the terms that we've previously used; and because we are using standard naming conventions, you can probably discern the rest. Read through and interpret the code, and then review the explanation that follows:

```
Public WithEvents clsTextBox    As TextBox
Private Sub clsTextBox_AfterUpdate()
    With Me
        If .clsTextBox.Value < 0 Then
           MsgBox "Negative values are not allowed in this field...", _
             vbCritical
           .clsTextBox.Value = 0
        End If
    End With
End Sub
```

NOTE **The code example does not test for text typed into the** `textbox` **control.**

Now that the class module has been created, you need to call it from any form that will use this text box. Note that the text box must have the same name on every form. The steps will be the same for each form with the text box, so open an applicable form in Design View and enter the following code:

```
Dim mtxtbox As New clsTextBoxEvents
Private Sub Form_Load()
    Set mtxtbox.clsTextBox = Me.txtValue
End Sub

Private Sub txtValue_AfterUpdate()
' This procedure has no use.
' It only serves to ensure the class is executed.
End Sub
```

The `TextBox` instance is set when the form is loaded. The `AfterUpdate` event, which would normally contain the code that is now in the class module, is now used only to subclass (trigger) the event. In other words, if you do not have the `AfterUpdate` event signature (or whatever event signature you plan to use) present in the code module of your form, the public event declared in the class is not triggered.

You should now be able to reuse the class anywhere in your project without having to write the same code repeatedly. This is a very useful technique that can be applied to many scenarios.

The Object Browser

As no doubt you've come to realize, each object model has hundreds of member properties and methods. This can seem overwhelming and make you wonder how you're supposed to remember them all. Thankfully, you don't need to know them off the top of your head. However, you certainly need to know where to go in order to get some help and to find out what objects, properties, and methods are available.

The best place to find such help is in the Object Browser, where you will be able to inspect each object and its corresponding members.

To work with the Object Browser, follows these steps:

1. Open the VB editor (Alt+F11).
2. Press F2 (or go to View ➪ Object Browser).

Figure 4-13 shows the Object Browser open to all libraries.

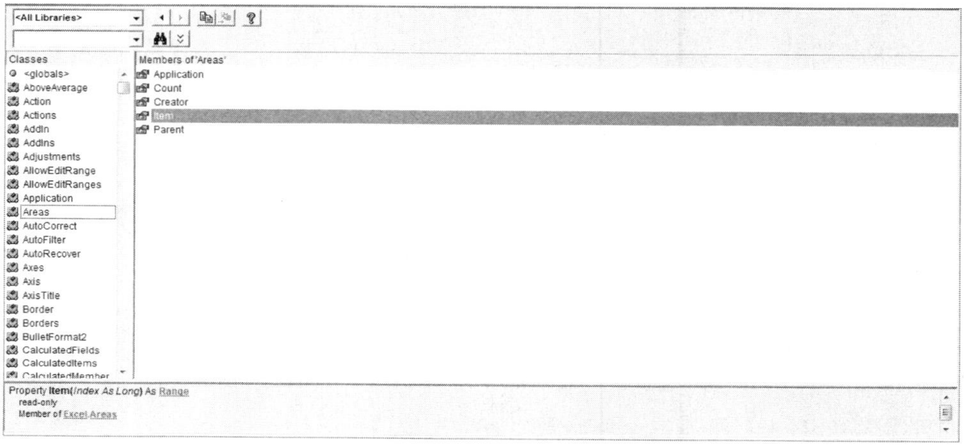

Figure 4-13: Inspecting libraries using the Object Browser

From the Project/Library drop-down list, you can filter which library to show. Figure 4-13 shows all libraries available in the project, but if you had referenced a library, then you could filter to see only the classes belonging to that library. You could then review the members of each class by selecting the class you want to inspect. (See the following section for information about how to reference libraries.) When you finally select a member of a class, the Object Browser will provide information about that member.

In this particular case, as you can see from the details pane at the bottom of the window, `Item` is a property, and it is a member of Excel and of the `Areas` class.

Referencing Libraries

In many cases, you will find yourself in a situation where you must reference other libraries. For example, you might want to use PDF objects to read PDF files from your application or to write PDF files. In such cases, you would not need to reinvent the wheel in order to create links to other programs. All you need to do is reference the appropriate library. Obviously, you would still need to know how to use the library, but once the library is referenced you can inspect its object model.

This probably sounds a little more complicated and intimidating than it really is. Actually, it is very simple to reference a library — as long as it is installed on your computer or at least accessible to the computer. Just follow these steps:

1. Open the VB editor (Alt+F11).
2. Go to Tools ➪ References.
3. When the reference dialog box opens, scroll through the list to find the desired reference, check the box in front of it, and then click OK to finish.

You can now use the Object Browser to inspect the library that you just referenced (see Figure 4-14). From the Project/Library drop-down, choose the library that you just installed.

Figure 4-14: Referenced library viewed in the Object Browser

In this case, we have referenced the Outlook library. That's all it takes to make Outlook's objects available to your Excel, Access, or Word project. You can now do such things as save a report, attach it to an e-mail, and have it waiting for the user to complete the address block. In addition, you can further automate the process to automatically fill in the address line and send the e-mail — a routine that can be quite helpful in obtaining error reports without imposing on the user.

Keep in mind that just because you reference a library in one application, that does not mean that it is referenced in the others. If you want to work with PDF files in all three applications, you need to set the reference in all three. Moreover, reference settings do not travel with the files from one computer to another. Although there are certain scenarios in which references can be set at the project level and essentially installed on the user's machine, that is beyond the scope of what we cover here. Nevertheless, knowing that it is possible might avoid some confusion and frustration if you see different libraries referenced.

We've only provided a glimpse at how powerful and versatile VBA can be, and although you're probably intrigued and want to explore more right now, we have to stay focused on covering all the fundamentals so that you will be prepared for customizing the Ribbon. So now we'll move on to figuring out why code doesn't always work the way we want it to.

Early and Late Bindings Explained

When working with external objects — that is, objects that do not belong to the object model you are working with — you must create an instance of that external object. You do that with either *early* or *late binding*.

When you install references to other libraries you work with early binding. This means you bind the objects you dimension in your code to match those of the library you referenced, as shown in the following example:

```
Dim olEmail      As Outlook.MailItem
```

Using the referenced Outlook library shown in Figure 4-14, you can dimension an Outlook e-mail object from either Excel, Access, or Word.

Early binding not only speeds up the programming process, as you now have all the library's objects exposed to you, along with all of their properties and methods, but it also improves code performance. The drawback is that users of your project will need the library registered in their installation of Office as well.

Late binding, conversely, does not rely on referencing. You simply declare generic objects and use their properties and methods, and these will be resolved at runtime (when that part of the code is running). Following is an example:

```
Dim appOL        As Object
Dim Email        As Object
Set appOL = CreateObject("Outlook.Application")
Set Email = appOL.CreateItem(olMailItem)
```

The preceding example does a late binding of the `appOL` object (representing the Outlook application) and then does the same with the `Email` object (representing an Outlook mail item). Because these are generic objects, they can be used to represent any object you like.

The `CreateObject` function will always create a new instance of the object you want — that is, if you have an instance of the object already opened, then another one is created (this is not the case with applications that only run one instance of the object at any given time, such as Outlook). If you do not want to use up resources by creating new instances of an application object, you can use the `GetObject` function instead:

```
Set appWrd = GetObject(, "Word.Application")
```

The preceding example will fetch the Word `application` object if it is already open so that you do not need to create another instance of the application. Of course, if the instance of the application doesn't exist, then the code will return an error. You can get the best of both situations and avoid the error with the following code:

```
On Error Resume Next
Set appWrd = GetObject(, " Word.Application")
If appWrd Is Nothing Then _
    Set appWrd = CreateObject("Word.Application")
```

You use `On Error Resume Next` in order to ignore the possible error of not having an instance already running. If the error occurs, then the object is not set and it remains as `"nothing"`. You check whether it is nothing and if it is, you create a new instance of the object.

For more on error handling, see "Error Handling" later in this chapter. At this point, we will turn our attention to debugging code.

Debugging Your Code

More often than not, users spend a lot of time trying to figure out why a certain piece of code does not behave as expected. When you write code, it is interpreted according to rules of logic, not according to what is perceived as truth. This is where a lot of developers get bogged down.

There is no a priori correlation between the logic of your code and what you consider to be true, which has no bearing on the result; rather, the result is completely based on the premises set out in your code. Therefore, if the premises of the code are true, the result of running the code will also be true. However, this is not at all the same as saying that the code is true (that the code will perform as written) and the desired result of running the code is true (will create the desired/expected result). Sound confusing? Actually, it doesn't have to be; but the more complex the code, the more confusing it can become. And that's when debugging comes into play.

The following syllogism will help illustrate what is meant by following logically to a conclusion, rather than trying to figure out what the truth is:

All Excel users are weirdos.

My pet snake is an Excel user.

Conclusion: My pet snake is a weirdo.

Obviously, we know that not all Excel users are weirdos, let alone that my pet snake is an Excel user. However, if you were to put this into your code, the logic dictates that you must accept the conclusion (the result) that can be drawn from the first two premises; therefore, the code would provide the logical conclusion and state that my pet snake is also a weirdo. This is exactly what code will always do, no matter what you think or know about Excel users, or whether you believe that my pet snake is a fingerless but competent Excel user.

In other words, what you think about the truth of the premises has no bearing on the conclusion itself because the conclusion flows directly from the premises. Once you're committed to the premises, you must accept the conclusion.

The preceding example could be written as an `If...Then` statement. In doing so, you will quickly realize why it is critical to state the premises correctly in order to achieve the desired results.

This section explains how to debug your code. Debugging code is about checking the logic of your code to ensure that it performs as expected. Sometimes, even after a lot of debugging, you will still find bugs, even after months of running smoothly. That's just part of the dynamics of programming and the never-ending changes in programs and the ways users do things. You will definitely benefit from learning how to debug and troubleshoot code.

Debug.Print and Debug.Assert

The `Debug` object is used to send output to the Immediate Window (see Figure 4-15 and the "Immediate Window" section later in this chapter). It has two methods:

- **Print**: This method is used to print some sort of output to the Immediate Window.
- **Assert**: This method is used to assert a condition that evaluates to `False` at runtime when the expected result should evaluate to `True`.

The first method is very useful when you need to see the value a variable has taken or how this value behaves during the course of executing the code:

```
Sub debugPrint()
    Dim x       As Long
    Randomize
    x = Int((100 - 0 + 1) * Rnd + 0)
    Debug.Print "The value for x is: " & x
End Sub
```

This is a simple example that will generate a random number between 0 and 100 and display the result in the Immediate Window. This little bit of code could easily be used for selecting random winners, to draw numbers for a bingo, and a myriad of other purposes.

The `Assert` method can come in handy when you have a logical situation to evaluate, such as the syllogism involving the pet snake. Although we can all agree that the scenario is absurd, the point is that the conclusion is logical given the premises.

You might be wondering at this point what would happen when you write code that should return a true value or is based on true assumptions, but actually returns a false value. You can assert the code so that when it is evaluated to false, it stops at the assertion line, as shown in the following example:

```
Sub debugAssert()
    Dim lngRow              As Long
    Dim blnAssertNotEmpty   As Boolean
```

```
    lngRow = 1

    Do Until IsEmpty(Cells(lngRow, 1))
        blnAssertNotEmpty = Not (IsEmpty(Cells(lngRow + 1, 1)))
        lngRow = lngRow + 1
        Debug.Assert blnAssertNotEmpty
    Loop
End Sub
```

In this example, you loop through the specified cells in a worksheet checking whether the next one is empty or not. When an empty cell is encountered, the `Boolean` value becomes `False` and the code stops at the assertion line.

Stop Statement

The `Stop` statement is used to suspend execution of code at a particular point. Suppose you need to stop the code when the workbook, document, report, or form is opened. You could add a `MsgBox` and enter the code after the message is shown. However, that may create unwanted interruptions, as you would have to deal with the message box and the code every time the line is executed. A better alternative may be to use the `Stop` statement — and avoid the message box.

Using a `Stop` statement will suspend execution, enabling you to analyze your code. The following code includes a `Stop` statement that halts processes before you set the `Ribbon` object. If you stopped the execution at this point, then the UI will still load, but the `Ribbon` object would not be available to work with:

```
Sub rxIRibbonUI_onLoad(ribbon As IRibbonUI)
    Stop
    Set grxIRibbonUI = ribbon
End Sub
```

Notice that using `Stop` has a similar effect to adding a breakpoint to your code. However, you would not be able to add a breakpoint to closed files. Thus, when the file is closed, the breakpoint would lose its effect. The `Stop` statement, however, ensures that the code is suspended at the precise location you've set. Therefore, every time the file is opened, the process stops at that point, enabling you to check the condition and correctness of variables and other processes in your code.

If you already have the file open, another alternative is to use breakpoints. These also stop the code, and they enable you to step through the code to see the effects, one line at a time. To add a breakpoint, go to the line where you want to add a break/stop and then press F9 (or go to Debug ➪ Toggle Breakpoint). The code will now stop when it reaches that point. As you can see from the toggle option, it is just as easy to remove the breakpoint.

Immediate Window

The Immediate Window, shown in Figure 4-15, is an inconspicuous part of the VBE but it is an invaluable tool for debugging code. Many developers use the Immediate Window to display a value, but it can do so much more, including the following:

- Test code you've written or debug problems in your code.
- Query or change the value of a variable.
- Query or change the value of a variable while execution is halted.
- Assign the variable a new value.
- Query or change a property value.
- Run subprocedures or functions.
- View debugging output.

Figure 4-15: The Immediate Window

If you recall, this is the window where we sent our x variable earlier in this section.

Additional ways to open the Immediate Window include going to View ➪ Immediate Window or pressing Ctrl+G.

You have already learned how to send variable values to the Immediate Window so that you can have a look at them. However, you may encounter scenarios where you actually do not want to flood the Immediate Window with all sorts of variable values, lists, and the like.

Study the following piece of code, and you'll understand what we mean:

```
Sub immediateWindow()
    Dim i           As Integer
    Dim blnAssert   As Boolean

    For i = 1 To 10
        If i Mod 2 = 0 Then
            blnAssert = False
        Else:
            blnAssert = True
        End If
        Debug.Assert blnAssert
    Next i
End Sub
```

Here, the `Assert` method is being used to stop the code, although a more realistic scenario might have halted the code for some other reason, such as when a modal dialog box is shown. What matters here is only that the code halted, so now you need to find out what the value of `i` is at that specific point.

Figure 4-16 shows how to use the Immediate Window to query the value assigned to a variable at the point where the code stopped.

Figure 4-16: Querying a variable value in the Immediate Window

At this point, all you need to do is type **?i** (or the name of any other variable) and press Enter. The Immediate window will give you the value of the variable at the point where the `Assert` method stopped the code.

You're now probably thinking, "So what?"

Well, the Immediate Window's usefulness does not stop there. You can also evaluate expressions, such as comparing the variable to a set value or to another variable. The following expression compares the current value of `i` to the value of the variable `j`:

```
?i=j
```

This will return `true` if the expression is equal (if `i` indeed equals `j`); otherwise, it returns `false`. You could also type the following query into the Immediate Window to retrieve the entire connection string of an Access database. The results are shown in Figure 4-17.

```
?CurrentProject.Connection
```

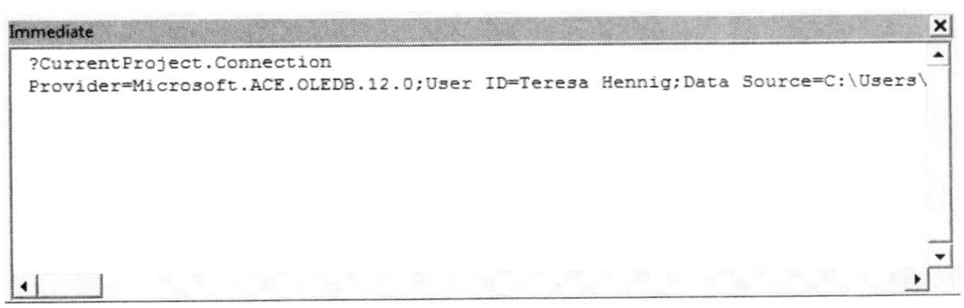

Figure 4-17: Querying a property in the Immediate Window

Note that you use a question mark before typing anything. This question mark means you are querying something. In the previous examples, we have queried the value of a variable, the result of a comparison, and the connection string of an Access database.

It does not have to stop there. Suppose you wanted to query the result of a custom function. In Word, you can query the result of your custom function as follows:

```
?ThisDocument.myCustomFunction
```

You can do something similar with Excel:

```
?RibbonXFunctions.hasSuperTip ("rxbtnDemo")
```

With Access, you could use the following:

```
?IsLoaded("myForm")
```

What if it were a subprocedure instead of a function? Not a problem — all you have to do is remove the question mark to call the procedure and display the results in the Immediate Window.

Note that in the case of Word and Excel you explicitly identify where the function is located (`ThisDocument` and `RibboXFunctions` standard module). It makes life simpler if you do this, because then you can clearly refer to the location of the subprocedure.

Locals Window

The Locals Window is used to show variable values as well as other objects that belong to the procedure being executed. If it isn't currently showing, you can open the Locals Window (shown in Figure 4-18), by going to View ➪ Locals Window.

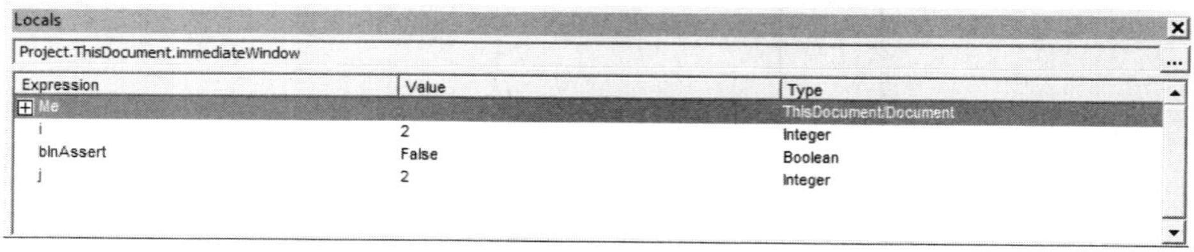

Figure 4-18: Locals Window

From Figure 4-18, you can identify the expression, its type, and the current value, as described here:

- The `Me` object, which refers to `ThisDocument`
- The `i` variable, which takes a value equal to `2` and is an `Integer` data type
- The `blnAssert` variable, which takes a `false` value and is a `Boolean` data type
- The `j` variable, which takes a value equal to `2` and is an `Integer` data type

As you can see, the Locals Window will show you the values of variables as well as objects that come under the procedure, so it is a very handy way to view how variables behave as each line of code is executed.

If you have several variables, values, or objects to monitor, using the Locals window is probably one of the best ways to do so.

Watches Window

The Watches Window is another great tool for debugging code. It enables you to specify instructions for watching the value of an object, such as a variable, an expression, a function call, and so on.

Similar to some of the prior examples, a watch will pause code execution when the criterion is met (such as when the expression is true) or the variable that is being watched changes.

If the Watches Window, shown in Figure 4-19, is not yet displayed, you can open it from View ➪ Watch Window.

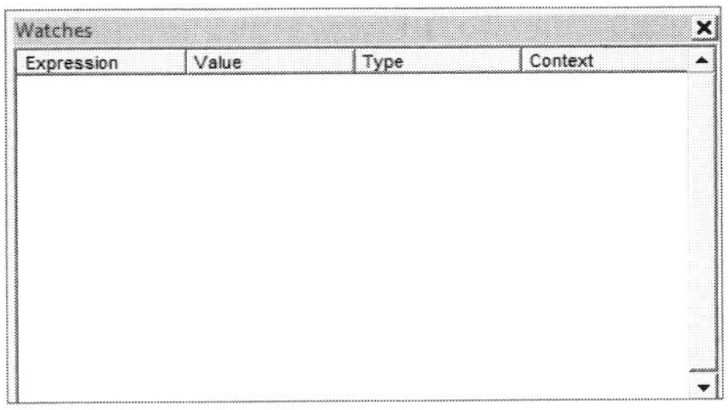

Figure 4-19: The Watches Window

Now that you have the Watches Window open, you need to specify a watch. You do that with the `Add Watch` dialog box, shown in Figure 4-20. To open the Add Watch dialog box, do one of the following:

- Right-click on the Watches Window and choose Add Watch from the pop-up menu.
- Go to Debug ➪ Add Watch.

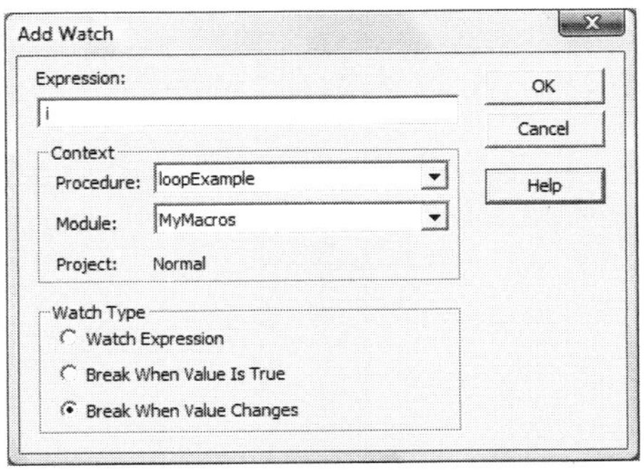

Figure 4-20: The Add Watch dialog box

Once you've set up a watch, every time an expression meets the criterion or a variable changes, the watch will be listed in the Watches Window, as shown in Figure 4-21.

TIP **You might find it easier to right-click on the variable and then select Add Watch from the pop-up menu.**

Table 4-11 shows the expressions available in the Add Watch dialog box and explains how each of the expressions is used.

Table 4-11: Add Watch Dialog Elements

ELEMENT	DESCRIPTION
Expression	Refers to the expression to be watched. It can be a variable, a property, a function call, or any valid expression that you may have in mind.
Procedure	Refers to the procedure where the term is located. By default, it shows the details for the selected term in the Watches Window. You can choose all procedures or just a specific one.
Module	Refers to the module where the term is located. By default, it shows the details for the selected term in the Watches Window. You can choose all modules or just a specific one.
Project	Shows the name of the current project. You cannot evaluate expressions that are outside the current project context.
Watch expression	Shows the watch expression and its value in the Watches Window. When its value changes, the result is updated in the Watches Window.
Break When Value Is True	Code execution will break when the expression evaluates to `true` or is non-zero (does not apply to strings).
Break When Value Changes	Code execution will break when the value of the expression changes within the defined context.

Now that you have all the explanations, the following example creates a simple watch to monitor a string (ensure that the Watches window is visible):

```
Sub watchT()
    Dim strT        As String
    strT = "This is a T-string"
    strT = "This is no longer a T-string"
End Sub
```

TIP **As well as typing your expression in the Add Watch dialog box, you can also drag and drop it onto the Watches Window. If you drop in an expression that is a value, VBE will take care of the rest for you. Otherwise, you will get an error message indicating the problem.**

In setting up the watch, choose `Break When Value Changes` so that the code execution enters break mode when the string changes from the first to the second. The code and Watches Window are shown in Figure 4-21.

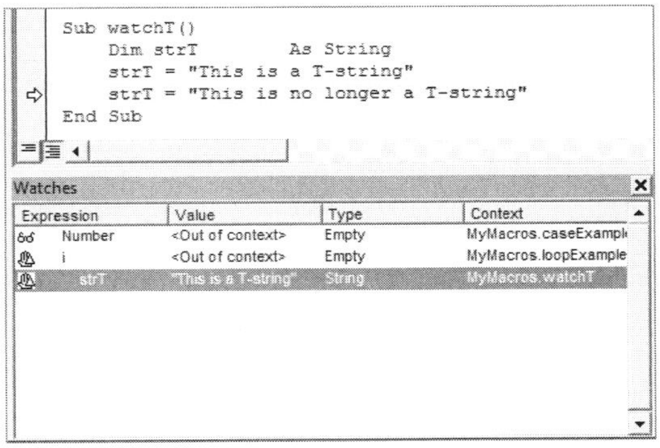

Figure 4-21: Watching strT for a change in value

NOTE **When selecting a context, you should narrow the scope so that you do not include procedures or modules that are irrelevant to the specific action or watch. This will improve performance, as there will be less to watch during the execution process.**

Error Handling

As you write more and more code, you will realize that it is virtually impossible to predict everything that could happen. You could come across overflows, infinite loops, locked tables, and so on. All of these will generate some sort of error, many of which are almost impossible to predict. In order to ensure that your code does not crash the program, you need to add error handling.

There are some very simple ways to tackle unresolved or unpredictable problems that the end user may encounter. In this section, we cover some of the basics of error handling. In addition to enabling you to deliver more stable projects, it will also help you write more robust code.

On Error Resume Next

Maybe the simplest and most frequently used error handler for VBA is `On Error Resume Next`. In lay terms, what the instruction does is simply ignore whatever error happens and continue execution on the next line. The problem with that, of course, is that the error has not been handled. It has been ignored, which can have implications in your code because other parts of the code may be dependent on the line where the error occurred.

Consider the following code and then we'll discuss it. The example applies to Excel, but it can be adapted to Word and Access. Because we're working with the `FileSystem` object, you need to set the reference to the Windows Script Host Model before continuing.

```
Sub onErrorResumeNext()
    Dim fsoObj       As FileSystemObject
    Dim fsoFolder    As Folder
    Dim fsoFile      As File
    Dim lngRow       As Long

    lngRow = 1
    On Error Resume Next
    Set fsoFolder = fsoObj.GetFolder("C:\YourFolder")

    For Each fsoFile In fsoFolder
        ActiveSheet.Cells(lngRow, 1) = fsoFile.Name
    Next fsoFile
End Sub
```

The flaw in this code is that the `fsoObj` has not been set. By instructing VBA to ignore the error and resume processing from the next line, all subsequent errors will also be ignored. The `Folder` object needs a `FileSystem` object, so it will fail; and because the `File` object depends on the `Folder` object, it will also fail. This causes a chain reaction in the entire code, which means it won't provide the expected result — i.e., a list of files in `YourFolder`.

As you can see, although `On Error Resume Next` is useful, it can also cause bigger problems than the error itself. This could have been a critical error that needed proper handling, but if the error is ignored you may be oblivious to its existence.

Thus, you should use this method of error handling sparingly and only when you know it will not impair anything critical in your project. A better option for handling exceptions in code is to direct them to an error-handling process, the subject of the next section.

On Error GoTo

This form of error handling can appear in the form of `On Error GoTo 0` or `On Error GoTo <label>`, where `<label>` stands for a label of your choice. You will typically find that most people use labels such as `ErrHandler` or `Err_Handler` (`<label>` merely represents the name a procedure or function. In this case, that might be `ErrHandler`, `Err_Handler`, or something meaningful to the purpose of the instruction). The point is to clearly communicate that if the error occurs, the process must move to the code that handles the error rather than continuing with the next line of code.

The first option (`On Error GoTo 0`) is VBA's default error handling. It will simply return the usual VBA error message (refer to Figure 4-5 to refresh your memory regarding what it looks like). Essentially, with that message, the user has two options: choose End to close the program and hope that all data is preserved and the file works when reopened, or choose Debug and be faced with the code window with the failed line of code highlighted.

Since neither of these options is very appealing, you can appreciate why effective error handling is so important.

NOTE `On Error GoTo 0` **does not mean that error handling begins at line 0 of your code. Rather, it is akin to having no error handling enabled in your code (error handling is disabled). Even if you have other error handlers in the procedure, once this line is triggered it is essentially the end of the road, and the default message appears. Or, worse yet, the program just shuts down after indicating that it encountered a problem.**

Generally speaking, error handling is written in the following format. We'll review the parts and then go through a working example.

```
Sub onErrorGoTo()
    On Error GoTo Err_Handler
    'insert body of procedure/function here
     Exit Sub

Err_Handler:
    'insert error handling code here
    Resume Next
End Sub
```

Notice that before the `Err_Handler` label we place an `Exit Sub` instruction. This is necessary because without this line, the error handling code will be executed as part of the procedure. You'll also notice that we place a `Resume Next` after the error handling procedure. This implies that the code should be resume with whatever would otherwise have happened after the line where the error occurred. You could use `Resume <label>` to send the code to another label within the code that handles something else, such as cleaning up objects.

NOTE **When handling errors in a function, use** `Exit Function`**. When handling errors in a property, use** `Exit Property`**.**

In order to practice this, go back to the example of the previous section and add error handling code as follows:

```
Sub onErrorResumeNext()
    Dim fsoObj      As FileSystemObject
    Dim fsoFolder   As Folder
    Dim fsoFile     As File
    Dim lngRow      As Long

    lngRow = 1
    On Error GoTo Err_Handler
    Set fsoFolder = fsoObj.GetFolder("C:\MyFolder")

    For Each fsoFile In fsoFolder
        ActiveSheet.Cells(lngRow, 1) = fsoFile.Name
    Next fsoFile

    Set fsoObj = Nothing
    Set fsoFolder = Nothing
    Exit Sub

Err_Handler:
MsgBox "The following error occurred: " & vbCr & _
    Err.Description, vbCritical, "Err number: " & Err.Number
    Resume Next
End Sub
```

As the errors now occur, you will be able to analyze each one and then take appropriate measures to correct it. Because the errors may occur with the end user of your project, you may also want to devise a means to log the errors. In addition, as mentioned earlier, it can also be helpful to silently e-mail the error notices or log files to a designated recipient. Having a log enables you to track errors and improve error trapping, and it strengthens your ability to fix bugs. Moreover, it can be an invaluable tool for troubleshooting and delivering more stable and robust solutions.

Working with Arrays

Because you may also use arrays in your customizations, we'll provide a brief introduction. An array is basically a group of indexed data that VBA treats as single variable. If that sounds confusing, then take a look at the following declaration, and you'll start to get the picture:

```
Dim InflationRate(2000 To 2007) As Double
```

The indexes in this case are the years between 2000 and 2007, and the data we would be interested in is the inflation rate. You can assign and retrieve values from an array as follows:

```
Sub ExampleArray()
    Dim InflationRate(2000 To 2007) As Double
```

```
    InflationRate(2000) = 0.043

    Debug.Print InflationRate(2000)
    Debug.Print InflationRate(2005)

End Sub
```

In this exercise, we assign the imaginary inflation rate of 4.3% for the year 2000. We then print the values for the years 2000 and 2005 to the Immediate Window. Because no inflation rate is assigned to the year 2005, the value returned is zero (be careful here; otherwise, you might think that the inflation rate for 2005 was actually zero).

Notice that although there are several inflation rates, there is only one variable `InflationRate`.

Although we used a `Double` data type, arrays can use other data types — for example, when referring to objects. The next example demonstrates how to use an array that contains worksheet objects:

```
Sub ExampleArray2()
    Dim MyWorksheet(1 To 2) As Worksheet

    Set MyWorksheet(1) = ThisWorkbook.Sheets(1)
    Set MyWorksheet(2) = ThisWorkbook.Sheets(3)

    Debug.Print MyWorksheet(1).Name
    Debug.Print MyWorksheet(2).Name

End Sub
```

The second index of our array (`MyWorksheet(2)`) does not match the index of the sheet to which it refers (`ThisWorkbook.Sheets(3)`). This illustrates that items can go into the array in whatever order you choose, but it is critical to know where they are so that you can call the correct object.

Determining the Boundaries of an Array

Suppose you have an array but you don't know its lower or upper limits. In that case, you can use the `LBound` and `UBound` functions to determine the lower bound and upper bound of the array.

Using the inflation rate array we created earlier, you can check the upper bound as follows:

```
MsgBox UBound(InflationRate)
```

In this particular example, you would get 2007 as the upper bound. This is substantiated by the settings in code (2000 to 2007), but in most cases the limits will not be so obvious, so you can use the two handy functions to quickly retrieve the answers.

Resizing Arrays

Looking again at the inflation rate example, you'll see that we declared an array which has a fixed size — that is, you can only use the indexes specified to fill the array with data. An alternative is to create a dynamic array that can be resized later. You use the `ReDim` keyword to resize an array, as shown in the following example:

```
Sub ExampleArray(ByVal StartingYear As Long, _
    ByVal EndingYear As Long)

    Dim InflationRate() As Double

    ReDim InflationRate(StartingYear To EndingYear)

    Debug.Print LBound(InflationRate)
    Debug.Print UBound(InflationRate)

End Sub
```

The problem with this approach is that if the array contains any data already, then that data will be cleared. If you want to keep the previous information contained in the array, you can use the `Preserve` keyword alongside the `ReDim` keyword, like so:

```
ReDim Preserve InflationRate(StartingYear To EndingYear)
```

Here, you set the lower and upper bounds of the array without losing existing data. Now you can add items to the array by changing its upper limit. What you cannot do is change its lower bound. Rather than having to build a new array, you can pass the original array to a `variant` data type, redimension the array (clearing all its contents), and finally pass back the information from the `variant` data type. We'll do that with our final example:

```
Dim InflationRate() As Double
Dim varArray        As Variant

Sub RunExampleArray()
    Call ExampleArray(1990, 2000)
    Call ExampleArray2(1980, 2007)
End Sub

Sub ExampleArray(ByVal StartingYear As Long, _
    ByVal EndingYear As Long)

    ReDim InflationRate(StartingYear To EndingYear)

    InflationRate(1990) = 2.4
    InflationRate(2000) = 1.9

    varArray = InflationRate()
```

```
End Sub

Sub ExampleArray2(ByVal StartingYear As Long, _
    ByVal EndingYear As Long)

    ReDim InflationRate(StartingYear To EndingYear)

    InflationRate(1990) = varArray(1990)
    InflationRate(2000) = varArray(2000)


    Debug.Print LBound(InflationRate)
    Debug.Print UBound(InflationRate)

    Debug.Print InflationRate(1990)
    Debug.Print InflationRate(2000)

End Sub
```

Notice that both variables used in this example are declared in the general declaration area of the module, so your data is back in the new array, and you are set to work with data from 1980 through 2007, instead of the original array from 1990 to 2000.

Conclusion

This has been a very long chapter, and although we have introduced many aspects of VBA, we have barely scratched its surface. We will return to VBA in Chapter 12, when you are introduced to some more advanced concepts regarding VBA programming. However, from this point forward, our work with VBA will be fully integrated with the Ribbon customization process.

It is hard to determine what requires a solid understanding and what does not, as many things can be useful in a certain context and not in another. Our goal with this chapter was to cover the fundamentals of VBA, while emphasizing the things that we will use throughout the book. With that in mind, we encourage you to pay particular attention to working with decision statements such as `If...Then...Else` and `Select Case`. You will also need to be comfortable with the various ways you can loop through objects and handle events. Finally, of course, you will find that debugging and error handling are critical skills. As we just demonstrated, error handling is particularly important because you do not want your customization bombing for the end user. We cannot overemphasize that programs will change and users will do unexpected things, so you have to test beyond your own routines; and if you have any doubts, go back, revise, and practice.

Now that you've learned the basics for XML and VBA, you are ready for Chapter 5, where you will learn the nuts and bolts of callbacks.

CHAPTER

5

Callbacks: The Key to Adding Functionality to Your Custom UI

If you've worked through the earlier chapters, you already know some of the basics relating to Ribbon customization, such as XML structure, and you've had an introduction to VBA. This chapter introduces you to *callbacks* — the code that makes your customization work.

Without callbacks, your UI may look beautiful, but that's all it will be: just a pretty Ribbon — that is, of course, unless you are drawing from built-in controls, as they don't require custom callbacks. However, for custom controls, looks just aren't enough. What really matters is that your UI adds value for the user. In this chapter you learn the basics about how callbacks provide the functionality required for custom controls to work.

In the following pages you learn a combination of XML and VBA, as you will need to specify a callback in your XML code and then write VBA code to match and handle that callback. As you are preparing to work through the examples, we encourage you to download the companion files. The source code and files for this chapter can be found on the book's web site at `www.wiley.com/go/ribbonx`.

Callbacks: What They Are and Why You Need Them

Callbacks are subprocedures and functions used by your custom UI to make your customization work. A callback simply represents the movement of the instruction given. For example, when you set the `onAction` attribute for a button and load the UI, once the button is clicked it generates a callback on the action specified in the attribute.

If nothing is found, then the callback fails because it has an exception in the code: In other words, the callback specified in the attribute does not exist in VBA, so it fails. Figure 5-1 shows how the callback flows from the UI project to the VBA code project, in much the same way that an event calls a procedure or function.

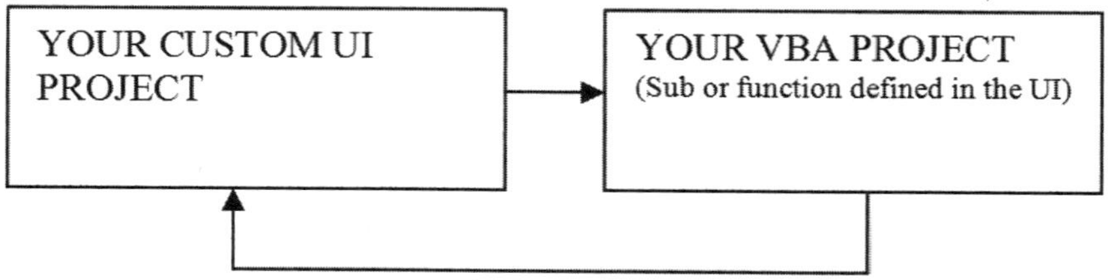

Figure 5-1: Callback flow

Your UI will call on your VBA project as soon as it loads, searching for the specified functions or procedures. If they are found, then the value is passed back to UI. If the specified functions or procedures are not found, then an error results.

There are two primary ways to create callbacks:

- Type the procedure or function directly into a standard module in the VB editor.
- Generate the procedures using a tool such as the Office 2007 CustomUI Editor.

The key advantage of using tools such as the Office 2007 CustomUI Editor is that they sweep the XML code and return a callback signature, also known as a *subprocedure stub*, for each attribute in the XML code that has a callback needing handling. Attributes that take a callback as a value include `onAction`, `getVisible`, and `getImage`.

In addition to saving time, using the custom editor also helps you avoid mistakes that can easily be made when manually writing callback signatures. Each of the preceding attributes generates a different callback signature that must be handled using code in order for the UI to function properly. This book relies on VBA, but you can use other code languages, such as C#.

Another thing to keep in mind is that some callbacks are called upon, and need to run, when the project loads. This means you will get an error message if the callback handler (the VBA code that responds to the callback) is not present in the project. However, there is no need to panic if that happens, as you will learn how to mitigate this type of error. More important, you will learn how to avoid them altogether.

Setting Up the File for Dynamic Callbacks

In this section you learn some of the basic techniques that are fundamental to all customizations. One of the critical elements is that the file must be macro-enabled in order for custom controls to work. In fact, a file must be macro-enabled, otherwise you will not be able to add or run VBA code.

The macro-enabled constraint applies to Excel and Word only. Access has another constraint, addressed later in this chapter in the section "Handling Callbacks in Access."

Capturing the IRibbonUI Object

An important part of the customization is related to the `IRibbonUI` object. This object refers to the Ribbon user interface and can be used to control how things respond.

One of its key uses in VBA is to invalidate the entire `Ribbon` object (so that certain features of the Ribbon can be changed) or to invalidate specific controls in the Ribbon (so that certain features of the control can be changed).

CROSS-REFERENCE **See "Invalidating UI Components" later in this chapter for more information about invalidating the Ribbon and its components.**

Adjusting the XML to Include onLoad

In order to use the `IRibbonUI` object, you need to set it in VBA. We'll explain more about that later, but for now we're going to stay focused on how you get to that stage. First, you need to specify a value for the `onLoad` attribute of the UI. That is done by specifying a callback for the `onLoad` attribute, as shown here:

```
<customUI
   xmlns="http://schemas.microsoft.com/office/2006/01/customui"
   onLoad="rxIRibbonUI_onLoad">
```

Because the value of the `onLoad` attribute is a callback, it needs to be handled in the VBA code. This, in turn, enables you to use the `IRibbonUI` object in your project.

Setting Up VBA Code to Handle the onLoad Event

You likely noticed that we previously referred to `onLoad` as an attribute, but are now calling it an *event*. This is because you can define values for a number of attributes, such as `onAction`, `getLabel`, and `onLoad`, in the XML file. Once a value has been assigned to an attribute, if it can be triggered in any way it will cause an event to occur, and thus we make the distinction between attribute and event.

Because the `IRibbonUI` object is used throughout the application, it needs to be declared in the Global Declarations area of a standard module, as shown in the following code. Recall from Chapter 4 that the `g` prefix indicates a global variable. We have adopted and built upon the Reddick naming conventions, but you can implement whatever standard you choose. The critical part here is that global variables must be declared at the beginning of the module, before any other type of variable or any code.

```
'The global ribbon object
Dim grxIRibbonUI        As IRibbonUI
```

We use the standardized form `grxIRibbonUI` to refer to the `IRibbonUI` object. The next step is to add a callback to set the object:

```
Sub rxIRibbonUI_onLoad(ribbon As IRibbonUI)
    Set grxIRibbonUI = ribbon
End Sub
```

CROSS-REFERENCE There are other ways to set custom properties of the Ribbon object. Chapter 12 has additional examples and instructions.

After you have globally set the object, it will be available throughout the project. Note, however, that the Ribbon object is very "sensitive" to change. This means that if you step into the code at any time to make changes, the object instance will be lost and any operation requiring the `Ribbon` object will fail. Therefore, it isn't just as simple as test, tweak, test — you need to save, close, and reopen the project any time you make a change.

Generating Your First Callback

The previous topic explained how to set the `IRibbonUI` object, and since you know that you need to get a callback signature, you're probably wondering how you're supposed to know which signature to use. That's the next step in the process, so we'll explain that now.

A `toggleButton`, for example, would have the following signature:

```
Sub rxtgl_Click(control as IRibbonControl, pressed as Boolean)
```

A generic button would have this signature:

```
Sub rxbtn_Click(control as IRibbonControl)
```

You have already seen that the `onLoad` attribute generates a callback with a different signature. We realize that this may seem like a lot of minor nuances, so the goal of this chapter is to make it perfectly clear how all these details affect the Ribbon. This is a complex subject with endless variations, but the more you work through it, the better you'll understand it.

Writing Your Callback from Scratch

To learn how to write a callback from scratch, begin by taking a look at the previous example using a callback signature for a `toggleButton`:

```
Sub rxtgl_Click(control as IRibbonControl, pressed as Boolean)
```

This seems pretty straightforward , but it is not the entire story. As with most code, there is a lot more to it than what meets the eye. For example, if you happen to know the callback signature, you do not necessarily need to declare the arguments using the standard form given above.

The following example helps to demonstrate this point. Suppose you have a `toggleButton` that uses the following XML:

```
<toggleButton
   id="rxtgl"
   label="Toggle"
   size="large"
   onAction="rxtgl_Click"
   imageMso="FormatPainter"/>
```

You could then write the `rxtgl_click` callback as follows:

```
Sub rxtgl_Click(rxctl As IRibbonControl, toggled As Boolean)
    If toggled Then
        MsgBox "I am toggled...And my ID is " & rxctl.ID, vbInformation
    End If
End Sub
```

Because the click on the `toggleButton` triggers the callback, the arguments are passed as usual; hence, the change in the signature will not cause the procedure to fail as long as you have the correct arguments of the correct type. Yes, "correct arguments of the correct type" sounds a bit like double-talk. This is a time when examples work best. In the example, the arguments are used to identify the specific controls: `rxctl As IRibbonControl` and `toggled As Boolean`. Notice that the initial `As` keyword identifies the control. Next, `As` is used with the argument type to specify that the value of the control must be a certain data type. In this case the `toggleButton` will require a `Boolean` value.

CROSS-REFERENCE **If you need a refresher on data types, refer to the section "Data Types" in Chapter 4.**

With this under your belt, you could also change the `onLoad` callback signature to suit your needs, as shown next. This callback sets the `Ribbon` object in the same way the standard signature does:

```
Sub rxIRibbonUI_onLoad(MyRibbon As IRibbonUI)
    Set grxIRibbonUI = MyRibbon
End Sub
```

The problem you may have now is that your code differs from the standard format, so it may not be easily understood by other developers; indeed, it may seem foreign to you in a few weeks or months. Therefore, even though it is good to have options, you may find that it is better to stick with the standard format. Table 5-1 lists some callback signatures that will be handy if you choose to write your callbacks from scratch.

Table 5-1: Callback Signatures for Different Object Attributes

ATTRIBUTE	CALLBACK SIGNATURE
onLoad	(ribbon as IRibbonUI)
getLabel, getPressed, getEnabled, getImage, getScreentip, getVisible, etc	(control as IRibbonControl, ByRef returnedVal)
onAction (for toggleButtons)	(control as IRibbonControl, pressed as Boolean)
onAction (for buttons)	(control as IRibbonControl)

Unless you are a glutton for punishment, we do not advise you to type each signature on your own — just consider the number of callbacks that you need to handle! Of course, you could reduce the amount of work by using shared callbacks, so that several controls are handled by just one callback. That is a subject beyond the scope of this discussion, but you can look forward to learning about shared callbacks later in this chapter, in the section "Using Global Callback Handlers."

An alternative to writing the callbacks is to use a tool such as the CustomUI Editor. This will read the XML code, identify where a callback is necessary, and generate the subprocedure stub, which brings us to the next topic.

Using the Office CustomUI Editor to Generate Callbacks

An easy and hassle-free way to generate callbacks is to use the CustomUI Editor. This little wonder-tool will sweep together all of the attributes that return a callback and then generate the callbacks that are needed.

The greatest advantage of using this type of editor is that you do not need to keep track of all the callbacks in the XML. This is almost invaluable if the XML code becomes quite long.

With the CustomUI Editor, you can use the following steps to automatically generate the necessary callbacks:

1. Use the CustomUI Editor to open the Excel or Word file that contains the XML code. (For an Access file, copy and paste the XML code into a blank CustomUI Editor code window.)
2. Click the Generate Callbacks button.
3. A new Callbacks tab will appear. Highlight all the callbacks that were generated and then copy and paste them into the VBA project.

NOTE **Make sure you validate the code before continuing — just click the Validate button on the CustomUI Editor toolbar. Because this does not guarantee a full validation, refer to the section "Showing CustomUI Errors at Load Time" in Chapter 1 for more detailed instructions.**

Figure 5-2 shows the result of automatically generating callbacks using the CustomUI Editor.

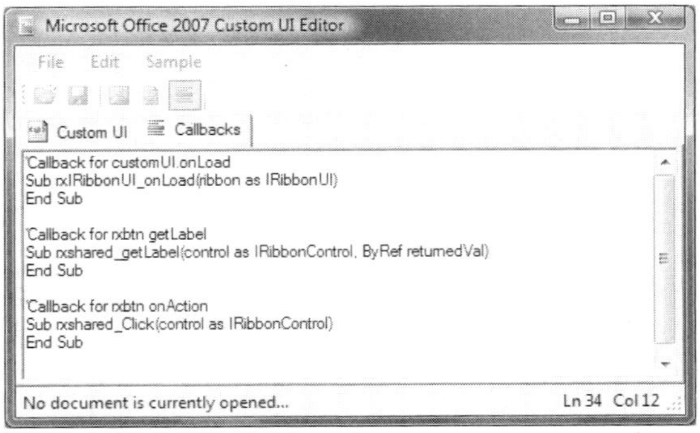

Figure 5-2: The CustomUI Editor generates callbacks on-the-fly.

The preceding example has three callbacks. The first two (`onLoad` and `getLabel`) occur when the UI loads. The last callback, `onAction`, occurs when the button is clicked by the user. The last callback is a shared callback, used by multiple controls that share a common `onAction` attribute and have a common signature.

Understanding the Order of Events When a File Is Open

As you add callbacks to your project, certain procedures will be called when the document is open. Which specific procedures are called varies depending on whether or not your customization has the focus when the project opens. Keep in mind that some procedures are called only when the tab containing the customization has the focus, whereas others are called when the mouse hovers over the control.

Understanding the order in which these procedures are called can be tricky because calling order is influenced by numerous variables. However, the event that tops the list is the `onLoad` event. To help you anticipate the typical order of events, Table 5-2 lists the events for the Ribbon tabs and their corresponding order.

Table 5-2: Event Order When Tab Has Focus After Project Is Opened

EVENT	TAB GETS FOCUS	TAB HAS FOCUS	ALT KEY IS PRESSED	MOUSE OVER
onLoad	Top most event. It will occur when the UI is loaded.			
getVisible	First	First	N/A	N/A
getLabel	Second	Third	N/A	N/A
getImage	Third	Fourth	N/A	N/A

Continued

Table 5-2 *(continued)*

EVENT	TAB GETS FOCUS	TAB HAS FOCUS	ALT KEY IS PRESSED	MOUSE OVER
getEnabled	Fourth	Second	N/A	N/A
getKeytip	N/A	N/A	First	N/A
getScreentip	N/A	N/A	N/A	First
getSupertip	N/A	N/A	N/A	Second

The preceding table lists only a few examples of common attributes that you might use. You should also keep in mind that order will be affected by the introduction of other attributes, such as `getDescription`, `getTitle`, and so on. Nonetheless, the table can serve as a general guide when you plan the best way to tackle the UI in terms of performance.

Can I Have Two Callbacks with the Same Name But Different Signatures?

VBA will not allow two callbacks in the same project to have the same name but different signatures. If you try to do this, it will fail, as it would with any other code language.

However, the same callback name can have different signatures if the callbacks are in different projects. Therefore, if you have more than one Word and/or Excel document and add-ins opened simultaneously, you might find yourself in an unusual situation that causes a callback return to have an unexpected result. That's because if there is more than one action (signature) associated with a callback name, then the callback for the active document will run. Because Access uses a different process to manage multiple database instances, we cover that in a separate section of this chapter.

The following example will help illustrate how this works in Excel; it is essentially the same in Word. Suppose you have an open Excel workbook with two add-ins installed, and all three items have a custom UI with a control that calls `rxbtnnsQaShared`.

When you click the button on the UI, you expect to add a new workbook. However, the message box shown in Figure 5-3 appears instead.

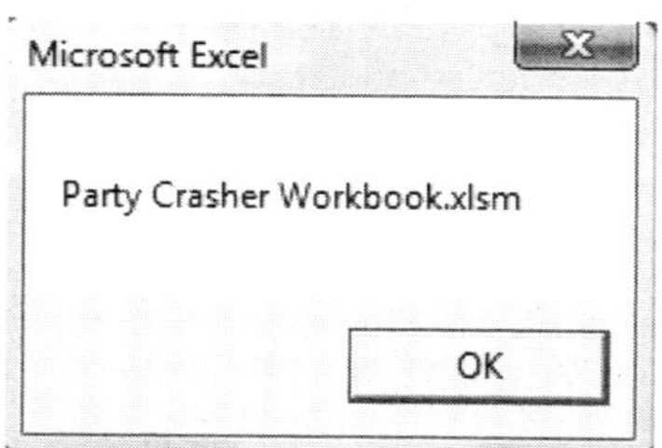

Figure 5-3: Message box shown instead of adding a new workbook

Upon investigating this, you discover that you have used the same callback for all three buttons. Even so, you might assume that if you click the button in the UI, then you should get the response for that specific button, so you add a breakpoint to the VBA to see exactly what is happening with the `click` event, and then you click the button again. This shows that because your Party Crasher Workbook is active when the button is pressed, Excel runs the code associated with that control. In other words, although we are allowed to use identical names with different signatures as long as they are in different projects, it is not necessarily a good idea (see Figure 5-4).

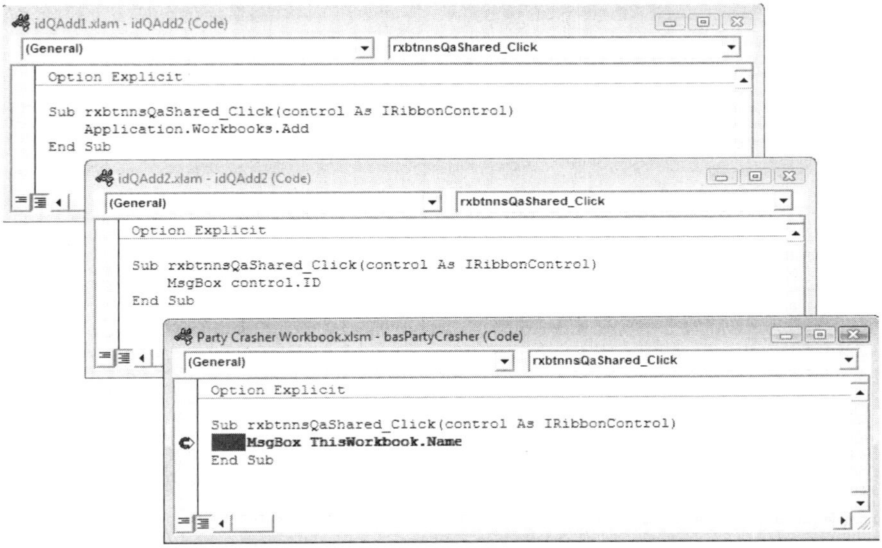

Figure 5-4: Callbacks with same names in different locations can cause unexpected behavior.

We've captured the three callbacks in Figure 5-4. As you can see in the title bars, two of the callbacks are in add-ins and the third is in the Party Crasher workbook. All three are in the same Excel file. You can also run into a similar scenario if you are sharing controls from different documents, as it is likely that they will also have a shared callback, or the same callback name may be repeated in multiple documents. Keep in mind that you will only have a problem if the callback has a different function than the one you are expecting. In general, however, shared callbacks in the same document won't have an operational impact.

Calling Procedures Located in Different Workbooks

In the previous example you saw how having the same procedure name in different files can cause some unexpected behavior depending on which file is active or has the focus.

You can also run into a similar problem if your XML code runs VBA that is located in a different workbook. Suppose you have two workbooks: Book1.xlsm and Book2.xlsm. You want to add a button to the first workbook to run a procedure located in the second workbook. You could do that using the following XML code to build the UI:

```
<customUI xmlns="http://schemas.microsoft.com/office/2006/01/customui">
   <ribbon>
      <tabs>
         <tab id="rxtabDemo"
            label="My Custom Tab"
            insertBeforeMso="TabHome">
            <group id="rxgrpDemo"
               label="My Demo Group">
               <button id="rxbtnDemo"
                  label="My Demo Button"
                  size="large"
                  onAction="Book2.xlsm!rxbtnDemo_Click"
                  imageMso="FileStartWorkflow"/>
            </group>
         </tab>
      </tabs>
   </ribbon>
</customUI>
```

NOTE **Using the `BookName.xlsm!rxctl_click` structure will cause the CustomUI Editor to struggle with generating the callback. In fact, the callback (shown in the following code) must be modified in order to work. To correct the problem, you merely need to remove the `xlsm!`**

```
Sub xlsm!rxbtnDemo_Click(control as IRibbonControl)
End Sub
```

The preceding code is an incorrectly generated subprocedure stub. As indicated in the note, you merely need to remove the `xlsm!` and it will work just fine, as demonstrated in the following code sample.

We now have the XML in `book1.xlsm` with the `onAction` attribute pointing to `Book2.xlsm`, so when you click the button created by `Book1`, it will look to `Book2.xlsm` for the `onAction` VBA code — so let's do that. Place the following code in a standard module in `Book2`:

```
Sub rxbtnDemo_Click(control As IRibbonControl)
    MsgBox "You called a procedure located at: " _
       & ThisWorkbook.Name
End Sub
```

Remember that both workbooks must be open for this to run. If you wanted the `onAction` attribute to point to a loaded add-in, rather than a workbook, then you would simply prefix the `onAction` code name with `[add-in name].xlam`, rather than `[workbook name].xlsm`. e.g., `onAction="myAddIn.xlam!rxbtnDemo_Click"` and then place the callback VBA code in a standard module in the add-in:

```
Book3.xlam!rxbtnDemo_Click
```

Keep in mind that this event will run the code contained in the active workbook if both the `xlsm` and `xlam` have the same name for a procedure specified under the `onAction` attribute of the UI. You likely also noticed that although we had to remove the `xlxm!` from our previous callback, `xlam!` is required to work with the add-in.

Organizing Your Callbacks

As you progress in your Ribbon customization coding skills, you will notice that there are different ways to organize the callbacks. You can have an individual callback handler or you can have a global callback handler that takes care of multiple controls at once.

The way you want your VBA code (as well as your XML code) to look will determine which method or combination of methods you use.

We start our look at callback organization by working with individual callback handlers.

Individual Callback Handlers

When you write XML code, you can specify various attributes that return a callback such as `onAction`, `getLabel`, `getVisible`, `getEnabled`, and so on. Each of these callbacks has to be handled. The following example illustrates the process by generating three buttons in a group. Although this example is for Word, it also works in Excel. Access is handled differently, so we will work through an Access example later in this chapter.

```
<customUI xmlns="http://schemas.microsoft.com/office/2006/01/customui">
   <ribbon>
      <tabs>
         <tab id="rxtabDemo"
            label="My Custom Tab"
            insertBeforeMso="TabHome">

            <group id="rxgrpDemo"
               label="My Demo Group">
```

```
                <button id="rxbtnPaste"
                   label="My Paste Button"
                   size="normal"
                   onAction="rxbtnPaste_click"
                   imageMso="Paste"
                   tag="Custom Paste Button"/>

                <button id="rxbtnCopy"
                   label="My Copy Button"
                   size="normal"
                   onAction="rxbtnCopy_click"
                   imageMso="Copy"
                   tag="Custom Copy Button"/>

                <button id="rxbtnCut"
                   label="My Cut Button"
                   size="normal"
                   onAction="rxbtnCut_Click"
                   imageMso="Cut"
                   tag="Custom Cut Button"/>
             </group>
          </tab>
       </tabs>
    </ribbon>
```

As you can see, each button is assigned its own `onAction` attribute, which means that each attribute must be handled if you intend to add functionality to the button:

```
Sub rxbtnPaste_Click(control As IRibbonControl)
    MsgBox "You clicked on " & control.Tag, vbInformation
End Sub

Sub rxbtnCopy_Click(control As IRibbonControl)
    MsgBox "You clicked on " & control.Tag, vbInformation
End Sub

Sub rxbtnCut_Click(control As IRibbonControl)
    MsgBox "You clicked on " & control.Tag, vbInformation
End Sub
```

As you might anticipate, dealing with each attribute individually can become very cumbersome and hard to maintain. Keep in mind that you need to handle each `onAction` attribute as well as any other attribute that generates a callback.

An alternative to this is to handle multiple attributes at once. As you will appreciate, this is where following a naming convention becomes a blessing. If you're using our suggested method, you will readily see how easy it is to handle all the callbacks in one tidy process.

Using Global Callback Handlers

As their name implies, global callback handlers can be used to handle several controls at once, and it gets even better if you standardize the way you name global handlers, because then you can immediately differentiate a global callback handler from an individual callback handler just by glancing through your VBA. This is yet another benefit of planning ahead when creating callbacks.

The reason why you can use global callbacks is because some instructions may overlap; and even when the instructions do not overlap, you can still benefit from the fact that certain controls share the same attribute for a specific action — such as the `onAction` attribute. In addition, if the actions are the same, then the procedures can be grouped together in a single callback handler.

You can take advantage of this to reduce the number of callbacks to be handled, and instead of handling individual callbacks, you can handle the control itself through a common callback.

Take, for example, the following objects: tab, group, and button. Each one of these controls shares a common attribute — namely, `getLabel`. Therefore, building on our previous statements, this tells you that you do not need to write a `getLabel` callback for each control in your XML code when you need to dynamically apply a value to each control. Instead, you can bring them together in a single process by sharing the task in a VBA procedure. Moreover, because it's a callback, you do not need to loop through the controls specified in the XML. It will automatically go through the controls until they all have their required values.

We can use the example from the previous section so that you can compare both methods and decide what is best for a given situation.

All you need to do is change the `onAction` attribute for each of the buttons in the previous XML code to the following:

```
onAction="rxshared_click"
```

This will generate a single callback that can be used to handle any control that has an `onAction` attribute and shares this signature.

The next step is to handle this callback for each button in VBA. That is accomplished with one small code snippet, as follows:

```
Sub rxshared_click(control As IRibbonControl)
    MsgBox "You clicked on " & control.Tag, vbInformation
End Sub
```

Obviously, the preceding code is not really "handling" anything just yet, but it illustrates that there is no need to repeat the message box line inside each individual callback. It also gives you a taste of how handling various procedures through a single callback handler can save you a lot of time and hassle.

As you would probably want to add individual code to each button, you can use a `Select Case` statement to structurally separate each button and assign it a specific piece of code:

```
Sub rxshared_click(control As IRibbonControl)
    Select Case control.ID
```

```
            Case "rxbtnPaste"
'           Your code goes here for the rxbtnPaste button
            Case "rxbtnCopy"
'           Your code goes here for the rxbtnCopy button
            Case "rxbtnCut"
'           Your code goes here for the rxbtnCut button
        End Select
    End Sub
```

As you can see, there is no need to handle a callback for each custom control in the UI. Instead, you can use a global (shared) callback and then handle each control within the VBA procedure. We used a `Select Case` statement because it is concise and easy to interpret. You could also use an `If ... Then ... ElseIf... End If` statement.

Handling Callbacks in Access

When it comes to customization, Access is unique in many ways. As you have already seen with something as basic as attaching the XML code to your project's UI, Access uses a table, rather than a zipped group of XML files as in Excel and Word.

CROSS-REFERENCE **See Chapter 16 for other methods of deploying a custom UI in Access.**

In Access, you can use VBA or macros to handle your callbacks. When working with Word and Excel, the word "macro" typically refers to a VBA procedure, but in Access a macro is an object that you create. In addition, because macros have predefined instructions that typically only need an argument, there is little need to know much about programming in VBA.

The next two sections describe how to use VBA and macros in Access to add functionality to your UI.

Using VBA to Handle Callbacks

The obvious way to handle callbacks in Access is to use the same method that we used for Excel and Word. In Access, the biggest difference is that you need to reference the Office 12 Object Library. If you don't reference this library, you will get the error message shown in Figure 5-5.

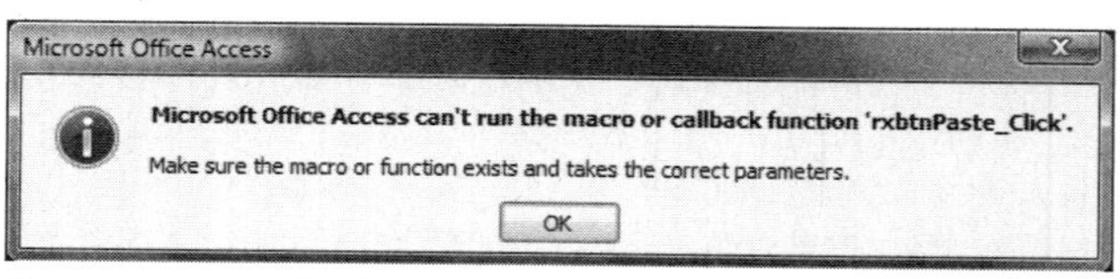

Figure 5-5: Error due to uninstalled Office 12 Object Library

CROSS-REFERENCE See Chapter 4 for instructions on how to reference libraries in your project.

The problem with the message is that it can be misleading. As you can see in Figure 5-5, the message doesn't indicate the true root of what we know to be the problem. Although it may be true that a callback subprocedure or function is missing, it can also indicate that Access is unable to identify an existing object because the library itself is missing from the project. Either scenario will generate the same message.

Therefore, considering that forewarned is forearmed, let's get started with a simple example. The following XML code creates a single button for your custom tab/group in Access:

```
<customUI xmlns="http://schemas.microsoft.com/office/2006/01/customui">
   <ribbon>
      <tabs>
         <tab id="rxtabDemo"
            label="My Custom Tab"
            insertBeforeMso="TabHomeAccess">

            <group id="rxgrpDemo"
               label="My Demo Group">

               <button id="rxbtnReport"
                  label="My Report Button"
                  size="large"
                  onAction="rxbtnReport_Click"
                  imageMso="CreateReport"
                  tag="Create Report"/>

            </group>
         </tab>
      </tabs>
   </ribbon>
</customUI>
```

Now add a standard module to your project, to which the following code should be added for testing purposes:

```
Sub rxbtnReport_Click(control As IRibbonControl)
    On Error GoTo Err_Handler
    DoCmd.OpenReport "MyReport", acViewPreview
    Exit Sub
Err_Handler:
    MsgBox Err.Description, vbCritical, "Err number: " & Err.Number
End Sub
```

In this example, after the button is clicked it will open the report named `MyReport` in `View Preview` mode. However, if it encounters an error, instead of the report, it will display a message box with the error description and number.

Using Macros to Handle Callbacks

With Access 12, the `macro` object is an alternative to using standard VBA code to handle your callbacks. If you plan to use macros to handle your callbacks in Access, you need to know that they are slightly different from VBA, and they need to be handled in XML and in Access.

Suppose you want to handle an `onAction` attribute using a macro. You would need to specify the `onAction` attribute as follows:

```
onAction="rxMacroName.ObjectName"
```

Notice that, similar to the Excel example that runs a procedure in a different workbook, this procedure also consists of two parts:

- `rxMacroName` refers to the name of the macro object to be created in Access.
- `ObjectName` refers to the object `id` that was created in the XML code; which, in turn, refers to a macro name. Do not mistake the macro object, which has a name, with the macro name itself, which is merely the identifier for the macro object.

If that last bulleted point sounds confusing, Figure 5-6 should help it make more sense. It shows the macro object named `rxsharedMacro`, which contains three named macros: `rxbtnPaste`, `rxbtnCopy`, and `rxbtnCut`. Of course, we're about to explain how to name and refer to macros.

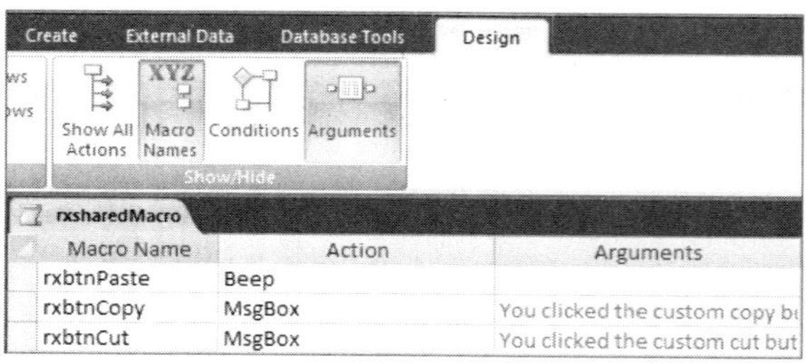

Figure 5-6: Access's macro window

Note that the tab of the macro window contains the macro object name, whereas the field `Macro Name` refers to the Ribbon object id (the object in your XML code). The reason for choosing the syntax `rxMacroName.ObjectName` is that the first part refers to the macro object itself; the second part refers to a macro name within the macro object; and that, in turn, points to an object in your XML code. By naming the macros in this manner, you should be able to identify the object in your XML code and match it to the macro object by looking up its name in the Macro Name field (column), as shown in Figure 5-6.

NOTE **If the Macro Name column is not visible, just click the Macro Names toggleButton to display it. That is the button with the XYZ shown in Figure 5-6.**

To see a demonstration of how to use a macro for the callbacks, create a new tab and group and add the following buttons to it:

```
<button id="rxbtnPaste"
   label="My Paste Button"
   size="normal"
   onAction="rxsharedMacro.rxbtnPaste"
   imageMso="Paste"
   tag="Custom Paste Button"/>
<button id="rxbtnCopy"
   label="My Copy Button"
   size="normal"
   onAction="rxsharedMacro.rxbtnCopy"
   imageMso="Copy"
   tag="Custom Copy Button"/>
<button id="rxbtnCut"
   label="My Cut Button"
   size="normal"
   onAction="rxsharedMacro.rxbtnCut"
   imageMso="Cut"
   tag="Custom Cut Button"/>
```

Now add a new macro object in Access and name it `rxsharedMacro`. After doing so, open the macro in Design View and add three new macro instructions, each one named using the text after the dot in the `onAction` attribute in your XML code. You're now set to go. Your macro should look similar to the one shown in Figure 5-6. For demonstration purposes, we added three simple macro instructions: a beep and two messages. Although you wouldn't find these in a functional application, their simplicity makes them effective learning tools.

As shown in Figure 5-7, the message box generated by the third macro displays the comment in the macro's argument. This demonstrates that the parameters set in the action's argument grid (as shown in Figure 5-6) will display in the message box.

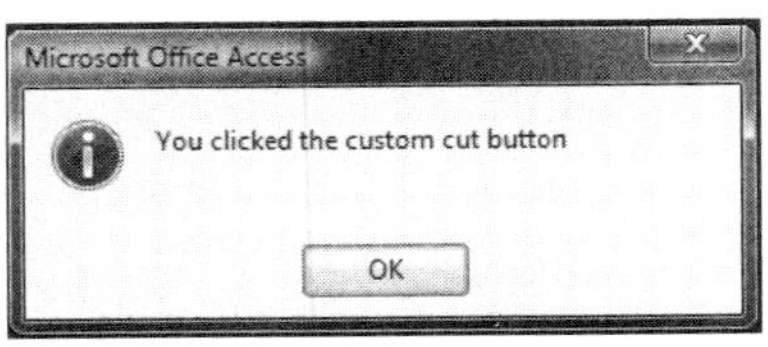

Figure 5-7: Message box generated by the macro `rxbtnCut`

Although the messages relate to the buttons, in a real application the macro name would have more relevance to the action involved. For example, in a case like the one shown in this example, in a real application the macro name would likely be something like `rxbtnMsgCut` instead of `rxbtnCut`. We wanted to use a simple example to make it easier to grasp the principles. Once you understand the process, you can expand the actions by either writing a more complex macro instruction or by pointing the macro to a VBA function that runs more complex instructions.

Invalidating UI Components

One important aspect of the Ribbon relates to invalidating the Ribbon or specific controls. As you will see, some actions can only be carried out if you invalidate the entire Ribbon, but other actions can be accomplished by just invalidating a specific control.

This section explains how to invalidate the Ribbon, how to invalidate specific controls, and how to harness the invalidation power to your benefit.

What Invalidating Does and Why You Need It

Before moving on to invalidation of the Ribbon and its controls, you need to understand what it actually means to you and your project.

The `IRibbonUI` object contains two methods: `Invalidate` and `InvalidateControl`. These are described in Table 5-3.

Table 5-3: IRibbonUI Object Methods

METHOD	WHAT IT DOES
Invalidate()	Marks the entire Ribbon (consequently marking every control in it) for updating
InvalidateControl(strControlID)	Marks a specific control for updating. The control to be updated is passed as a string in the argument of the method. (strControlID)

A key to understanding the `Invalidate` method is to remember that it invalidates every control in the UI — meaning that it will force a call on all callbacks defined in the UI. In addition, it will cause a refresh on all controls whether they have a callback or not. That means that when the Ribbon is invalidated, a call is made on the Ribbon, and every procedure specified in the UI will run.

This is likely to place a performance stress on your code, and it can slow things down considerably. Think of the `Invalidate` method as a way to refresh the controls in your UI, but do not confuse *refreshing the controls in the UI* with *reloading the UI*. In other words, refresh simply refreshes the controls already loaded in the UI when you opened the project, whereas reloading implies unloading and reloading the entire project along with the UI.

Unless you truly need to affect the entire Ribbon, a better option is to invalidate individual controls at specific moments during execution. That way, you only invalidate controls when necessary.

In order to invalidate either the entire Ribbon or specific controls in the Ribbon, you need to set a global variable representing the `IRibbonUI` object. This is done by specifying a callback on the `onLoad` attribute, as previously shown. For your convenience, the XML syntax is repeated here:

```
<customUI xmlns="http://schemas.microsoft.com/office/2006/01/customui"
   onLoad="rxIRibbonUI_onLoad">
</customUI>
```

Next, you need to write a piece of VBA code to handle the callback specified in the `onLoad` attribute:

```
Public grxIRibbonUI             As IRibbonUI
Sub rxIRibbonUI_onLoad(ribbon As IRibbonUI)
    Set grxIRibbonUI = ribbon
End Sub
```

Notice that the variable representing the `IRibbonUI` object is declared in the Global Declarations area of a standard module. That is because the object needs to be accessible to other parts of the project.

Now that you've seen how to create a global variable to represent the entire Ribbon object, we'll look at an example showing how to invalidate the entire Ribbon, and then we'll discuss how to invalidate a specific control.

Invalidating the Entire Ribbon

Now that you know how the invalidation process works, and you're acquainted with the two methods available in the `IRibbonUI` object, you are ready to build a simple example. This first example demonstrates how invalidating the entire Ribbon will affect the controls in it.

NOTE The example discussed here is for Excel, but the chapter download also includes a file for Access and a file for Word that will replicate the example for those programs.

First, create a new Excel file and save it as a macro-enabled workbook. Next, using the CustomUI Editor, attach the following XML code to the file:

```
<customUI xmlns="http://schemas.microsoft.com/office/2006/01/customui"
   onLoad="rxIRibbonUI_onLoad">
   <ribbon>
      <tabs>
         <tab id="rxtabDemo"
            label="My Custom Tab"
```

```
                insertBeforeMso="TabHome">

                <group id="rxgrpDemo"
                    label="My Demo Group">

                    <button id="rxbtn"
                        getLabel="rxshared_getLabel"
                        size="normal"
                        onAction="rxshared_Click"
                        imageMso="FillRight"/>

                    <button id="rxbtn2"
                        getLabel="rxshared_getLabel"
                        size="normal"
                        onAction="rxshared_Click"
                        imageMso="FillRight"/>

                </group>
            </tab>
        </tabs>
    </ribbon>
</customUI>
```

After pasting in the code, save the file. With the CustomUI Editor still open, use the following steps to add the callbacks:

1. Click the Generate Callback button to generate the callbacks.
2. Copy the callbacks to the clipboard and close the workbook.
3. Open the workbook in Excel and add a standard module (don't worry about the error message that appears).
4. With the standard module open, enter the following code (this is a great time to copy and paste from the online file):

```
Public grxIRibbonUI As IRibbonUI
Public glngCount1 As Long
Public glngCount2 As Long

Sub rxIRibbonUI_onLoad(ribbon As IRibbonUI)
    Set grxIRibbonUI = ribbon
End Sub

Sub rxshared_Click(control As IRibbonControl)
    grxIRibbonUI.Invalidate
End Sub

Sub rxshared_getLabel(control As IRibbonControl, ByRef returnedVal)
    Select Case control.ID
        Case "rxbtn"
            returnedVal = _
```

```
                "Ribbon invalidated: " & glngCount1 & " times."
            glngCount1 = glngCount1 + 1
        Case "rxbtn2"
            returnedVal = _
                "Ribbon invalidated: " & glngCount2 & ' times."
            glngCount2 = glngCount2 + 1
    End Select
End Sub
```

5. Finally, in order for the code to take effect, you need to save the workbook, close it, and then open it again. You'll appreciate that the count displayed on the button has been added merely to illustrate our point. As you work through the next example, you'll gain a better understanding of the rest of the code.

Now click one of the new buttons that appears in the custom tab. The result will look like Figure 5-8. Note that as you click either button, both labels are updated. This is because both controls are invalidated when either button is clicked because the code invalidates the entire Ribbon. You'll also see that the shared `getLabel` procedure is called once for the first button and again for the second button.

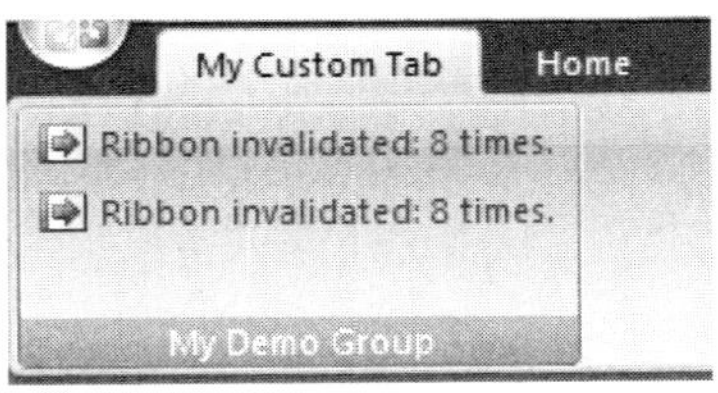

Figure 5-8: Invalidating the `IRibbonUI` object causes all controls in it to be invalidated.

The next example repeats this exercise but only invalidates the button clicked.

CAUTION **There is a slight MS bug in here. If you click too fast on one control they can become out of sync. This does not seem to apply to Word, but both Excel and Access have demonstrated this slightly erratic behavior.**

Invalidating Individual Controls

A more realistic scenario would not require the entire `IRibbonUI` object to be invalidated. Instead, it would more likely need to invalidate a specific control. We demonstrate that now using exactly the same XML code as the previous example; however, instead of invalidating the entire `IRibbonUI` object, we invalidate only the button that triggered the `click` event. We will thereby be able to create a count indicating how many times the specific control was invalidated.

As before, you need to declare the variables. You'll notice that the `onLoad` event does not change. However, you need to modify the shared `click` and the shared `getLabel` events to read as follows:

```
Public grxIRibbonUI             As IRibbonUI
Public glngCount1               As Long
Public glngCount2               As Long
Sub rxIRibbonUI_onLoad(ribbon As IRibbonUI)
  Set grxIRibbonUI = ribbon
End Sub

Sub rxshared_Click(control As IRibbonControl)
    Select Case control.ID
        Case "rxbtn"
            glngCount1 = glngCount1 + 1
        Case "rxbtn2"
            glngCount2 = glngCount2 + 1
    End Select
    grxIRibbonUI.InvalidateControl (control.ID)
End Sub

Sub rxshared_getLabel(control As IRibbonControl, ByRef returnedVal)
    Select Case control.ID
        Case "rxbtn"
            returnedVal = "I was invalidated " & glngCount1 & " times."
        Case "rxbtn2"
            returnedVal = "I was invalidated " & glngCount2 & " times."
    End Select
End Sub
```

You can now click on an individual control and the count will increment only on the control that was invalidated by the click, as illustrated in Figure 5-9.

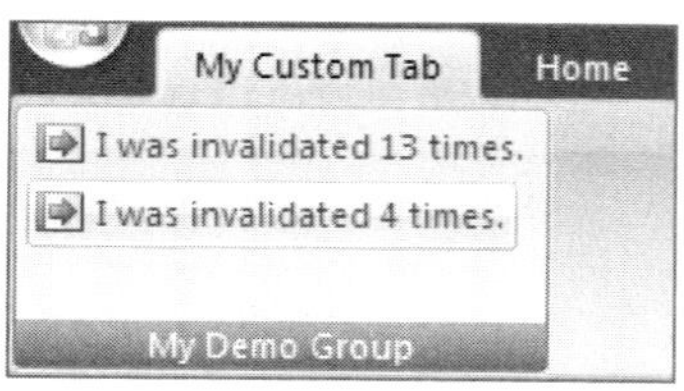

Figure 5-9: Have more control over the UI by invalidating control objects only.

Unlike invalidating the entire Ribbon, when you click the buttons on the UI, the button you click is the one that is invalidated; and therefore its click count is increased by one. Although you won't notice a performance change with this few controls, you can easily understand the concept.

Conclusion

This chapter discussed a key aspect of customizing the Ribbon: adding functionality through callbacks. You learned how to capture and use the Ribbon object, and how to organize your procedures through either individual or shared callbacks.

Although writing callbacks from scratch can be a very complex process, you saw how to do it in case you choose that option. However, given the advantages of using the Custom UI Editor to generate the callbacks, we will rely on that for the remainder of the book.

Another complexity that we covered involved scenarios in which a callback name is associated with different functions. This was demonstrated in a single Excel file and then extended to demonstrate how it can affect multiple projects or files.

Because Access has some unique ways of handling customizations, this chapter also included sections devoted to Access. These showed you how to use macro objects in Access to handle callbacks, and how to amend the XML code accordingly.

Finally, we described how to invalidate the entire Ribbon, and discussed some of the relevant implications. Based on our examples, we hope you agree that in most situations a better approach is to invalidate individual controls as needed.

Now it is time to turn our attention to some basic Ribbon controls. Some of these have already cropped up in examples in this chapter, but they are explained in more detail in Chapter 6.

CHAPTER

6

RibbonX Basic Controls

It's time to start exploring the controls that reflect the RibbonX experience. This chapter begins that process by examining four of the most basic, yet most frequently used, Ribbon controls: `button`, `checkBox`, `editBox`, and `toggleButton`.

This chapter is divided into four main sections, each of which discusses an individual control in great detail. Because the XML and VBA code required to make these controls function is supposed to be agnostic across the several Office applications, in theory they can all be covered once. However, we all know the benefit of seeing how something works in our primary application, so each section also includes examples that are specific to Excel, Word, and Access. When working through the examples, we encourage you to download the companion files. The source code and files for this chapter can be found on the book's website at `www.wiley.com/go/ribbonx`.

The button Element

Without question, the button is the most well known of all the tools in the developer's toolbox. From early versions of the applications, users have had access to buttons on toolbars, menus, and even in other forms such as ActiveX controls. Some have pictures and others have text, and they can vary in size and shape, but they all have one thing in common: When you click a button, something happens.

The Ribbon gives you control over a very rich button experience. You can use built-in images or supply your own; you can specify that you'd like a large button, or use its smaller form. With very little extra code you can even supply a label to go with it. In addition, you have access to a wide variety of callback procedures that can be leveraged to make the button experience quite dynamic. The button offers several attributes — or elements — that are used to customize the look and response. Some attributes are required, others are optional, and a few allow you to pick one from a short list of candidates.

The following tables will be a good reference when you are creating buttons; but for now, the acronyms, lists, and terms may seem a little overwhelming to those of you who are relatively new to XML, VBA, and programming. Keep in mind that each section and chapter in this book contains examples with detailed steps to walk you through the processes. In addition, you can always refer to Chapter 3 for a refresher on working with XML, or Chapter 4 to review VBA fundamentals. Namespaces, which you'll see mentioned in the tables throughout this chapter, are explained in Chapter 16, in the section "Creating a Shared Namespace."

Required Attributes of the button Element

The `button` requires any one of the `id` attributes shown in Table 6-1.

Table 6-1: Required Attributes of the button Element

ATTRIBUTE	WHEN TO USE
id	When creating your own button
idMso	When using an existing Microsoft button
idQ	When creating a button shared between namespaces

Each `button` also requires the `onAction` callback from Table 6-2.

Table 6-2: Required Callback of the button Element

DYNAMIC ATTRIBUTE	ALLOWED VALUES	VBA CALLBACK SIGNATURE
onAction	1 to 4096 characters	Sub OnAction (control As IRibbonControl)
onAction	Repurposing	Sub OnAction (control As IRibbonControl, byRef CancelDefaultcancelDefault)

CROSS-REFERENCE **The second version of the `onAction` callback is used when "repurposing" a built-in control. You'll learn more about repurposing in Chapter 13.**

Optional Static and Dynamic Attributes with Callback Signatures

With a `button`, you have the option to use any one `insert` attribute from Table 6-3.

Table 6-3: Optional insert Attributes of the button Element

INSERT ATTRIBUTE	ALLOWED VALUES	DEFAULT VALUE	WHEN TO USE
insertAfterMso	Valid Mso Group	Insert at end of group	Insert after Microsoft control
insertBeforeMso	Valid Mso Group	Insert at end of group	Insert before Microsoft control
insertAfterQ	Valid Group idQ	Insert at end of group	Insert after shared namespace control
insertBeforeQ	Valid Group idQ	Insert at end of group	Insert before shared namespace control

You may also provide any or all of the attributes from Table 6-4.

Table 6-4: Optional Attributes and Callbacks of the button Element

STATIC ATTRIBUTE	DYNAMIC ATTRIBUTE	ALLOWED VALUES	DEFAULT VALUE	VBA CALLBACK SIGNATURE FOR DYNAMIC ATTRIBUTE
description	getDescription	1 to 4096 characters	(none)	Sub GetDescription (control As IRibbonControl, ByRef returnedVal)
enabled	getEnabled	true, false, 1, 0	true	Sub GetEnabled (control As IRibbonControl, ByRef returnedVal)
image	getImage	1 to 1024 characters	(none)	Sub GetImage (control As IRibbonControl, ByRef returnedVal)

Continued

Table 6-4 *(continued)*

STATIC ATTRIBUTE	DYNAMIC ATTRIBUTE	ALLOWED VALUES	DEFAULT VALUE	VBA CALLBACK SIGNATURE FOR DYNAMIC ATTRIBUTE
imageMso	getImage	1 to 1024 characters	(none)	(Same as above)
keytip	getKeytip	1 to 3 characters	(none)	Sub GetKeytip (control As IRibbonControl, ByRef returnedVal)
label	getLabel	1 to 1024 characters	(none)	Sub GetLabel (control As IRibbonControl, ByRef returnedVal)
screentip	getScreentip	1 to 1024 characters	(none)	Sub GetScreentip (control As IRibbonControl, ByRef returnedVal)
showImage	getShowImage	true, false, 1, 0	true	Sub GetShowImage (control As IRibbonControl, ByRef returnedVal)
showLabel	getShowLabel	true, false, 1, 0	true	Sub GetShowLabel (control As IRibbonControl, ByRef returnedVal)
size	getSize	normal, large	normal	Sub GetSize (control As IRibbonControl, ByRef returnedVal)
supertip	getSupertip	1 to 1024 characters	(none)	Sub GetSupertip (control As IRibbonControl, ByRef returnedVal)
tag	(none)	1 to 1024 characters	(none)	(none)
visible	getVisible	true, false, 1, 0	true	Sub GetVisible (control As IRibbonControl, ByRef returnedVal)

Allowed Children Objects of the button Element

The `button` control does not support child objects of any kind. We mention that to save you some of the time and frustration of looking for something that isn't there. If you are accustomed to VBA programming, you might anticipate the ability to leverage children objects.

Parent Objects of the button Element

The `button` control can be placed within any of the following controls:

- `box`
- `buttonGroup`
- `dialogBoxLauncher`
- `documentControls`
- `dynamicMenu`
- `gallery`
- `group`
- `menu`
- `splitButton`
- `officeMenu`

Graphical View of button Attributes

Figure 6-1 shows a sample customization that displays all of the visible graphical attributes that you can set on the `button` control.

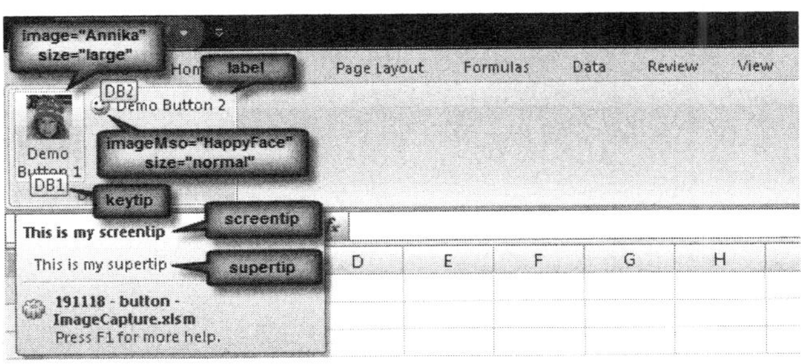

Figure 6-1: Graphical view of button attributes

Using Built-in button Controls

Adding built-in controls to a group is actually fairly simple. Let's say that you are working in Excel and would like that nice, pretty little "$" from the Accounting Number Format control sitting in your own custom group. Intuitively, you'd expect it to be as easy as doing the following:

1. Create a new `.xlsx` file and save it as `Excel Built In Button Example.xlsx`.
2. Close the file in Excel the open it in the CustomUI Editor.
3. Apply the RibbonBase template to the file.
4. Insert the following XML between the `<tabs>` and `</tabs>` tags:

```
<tab id="rxtabCustom1"
   label="Demo"
   insertBeforeMso="TabHome">
   <group id="DemoGroup"
      label="Demo Group">
      <button idMso="AccountingFormat"/>
   </group>
</tab>
```

Lo and behold, it doesn't create what you were expecting. Figure 6-2 shows the group that will be created by the preceding code.

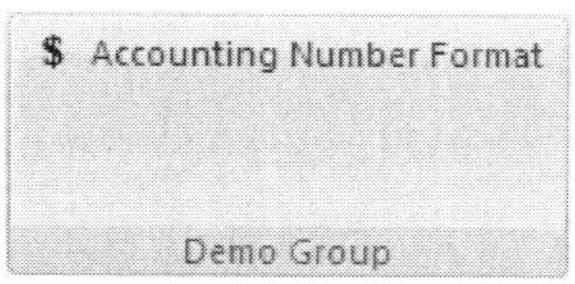

Figure 6-2: Built-in control's default appearance

You didn't ask for that text . . . or did you?

Be aware that when you are working with built-in controls, you get the entire package: image, label, pre-programmed callbacks, and all. Therefore, if you want just the image and the functionality, you need to set the `showLabel` attribute to `false` in addition to requesting the desired `idMso`. To do that, you simply modify the code to read as follows:

```
<tab id="rxtabCustom1"
   label="Demo"
   insertBeforeMso="TabHome">
   <group id="DemoGroup"
      label="Demo Group">
      <button idMso="AccountingFormat"
         showLabel="false"/>
   </group>
</tab>
```

Now you will create a nice little button that shows only the image, and not the label, as shown in Figure 6-3. Of course, it still has all the other properties of the built-in control. In other words, clicking the control will change the number style, just as you'd expect.

Figure 6-3: Built-in controls with showLabel="false"

A button Idiosyncrasy: The showLabel Attribute

Now suppose you've decided that the little icon that you received when working with the prior example just won't do, and you've gone back to make it larger. Based on the original example, you might think that you could just change the portion of the code that deals with the button to reflect the larger size:

```
<button idMso="AccountingFormat"
   showLabel="false"
   size="large"/>
```

The result of using the preceding code is shown in Figure 6-4. What's going on here? The label is showing up even though the code explicitly dictates that it should not!

Figure 6-4: Built-in control's default large appearance

As it turns out, this is a strange idiosyncrasy of the button model. While the approach will work as expected for a button that is of `size="normal"`, it won't work for a button that is specified as `size="large"`. As you can see, when the button is size large, the default values override custom settings for attributes other than the size of the symbol and label text.

Despite this, it is still possible to get the button to display in a large format without the label. The secret is to specify the label text as a blank space. This kind of coding is generally frowned upon in practice, as it is not very elegant, but you must supply at least one character for a label, so it is currently the only way to accomplish our goal.

The XML would therefore look like the following:

```
<group id="DemoGroup" label="Demo Group">
   <button idMso="AccountingFormat"
      label=" "
      size="large"/>
</group>
```

As shown in Figure 6-5, this achieves the desired label-free button with a large image.

Figure 6-5: Built-in control with the desired large icon

Creating Custom button Controls

While it's great that you can add built-in buttons to your groups, that is only the tip of the iceberg of what you want and truly need to be able to do. You're hungry for a place to store a custom macro that you built, and you don't want it attached to a simple forms button or to an ActiveX control. You want to learn how to add your own button to the Ribbon, and have it fire your macro when it is clicked.

It's time to create some buttons that do something you might want to accomplish in the real world.

An Excel Example

For this example, assume that you are an accountant, and you've built a continuity schedule for your prepaid expenses. It might look similar to the file shown in Figure 6-6, in which you'd expect the user to enter data in the shaded cells.

	A	B	C	D	E	F
1		Do It All Home Improvement (un) Ltd.				
2		Prepaid Expenses				
3		January 31, 2007				
4						
5	Vendor Name	Opening Balance	Additions	Usage	Ending Balance	Expense To
6	Mr Shingles Roofing	4,376.53		534.67	3,841.86	Roofing
7	Tremblay Gutters	8,018.98	35.00		8,053.98	Roofing
8	Light Em Up Electric	2,945.52	56.00	23.00	2,978.52	Electric
9	Dirtscapers Inc.	3,915.40			3,915.40	Landscaping
10	Green Thumb Plants	631.84			631.84	Landscaping
11		19,888.27	91.00	557.67	19,421.60	

Figure 6-6: Example of a continuity schedule

TIP **This file is included in the Chapter 6 example files under the name** Button-Monthly Roll Forward.xlsm.

Now that you have your continuity schedule built and saved as a macro-enabled file, it's time to write the macro that will run on a monthly basis to prepare the sheet for the next month. Specifically, the macro needs to do the following:

- Copy the ending balance to the opening balance column.
- Clear the Additions and Usage area (for this month's entries).
- Advance the date to the next month's end.
- Advise the user to save the file.

To do that, you need to write some VBA like the following, and save it in a standard module:

```
Public Sub RollForward()
    With ActiveSheet
        .Range("E6:E10").Copy
        .Range("B6:B10").PasteSpecial Paste:=xlValues
        .Range("C6:D10").ClearContents
        .Range("A3") = .Range("A3").Value + 40 _
            - DatePart("d", .Range("A3").Value + 40)
    End With
    MsgBox "Rolled forward successfully!" & vbCrLf & _
        "Please save the file under a new name.", _
        vbOKOnly + vbInformation, "Success!"
End Sub
```

If you'd like, you can test this macro by pressing Alt+F8 and choosing RollForward from the box. By putting data in the C6:D10 range, you'll notice that the macro does each of the tasks on the list.

Well, this is all great and wonderful, but you want to attach it to a button, rather than press the keyboard shortcut each time. To that end, save and close the Excel file and open it again with the CustomUI Editor. From there, apply the RibbonBase template to the file and insert the following code between the `<tabs>` and `</tabs>` tags:

```
<tab id="DemoTab"
   label="Demo"
   insertBeforeMso="TabHome">
   <group id="DemoGroup"
      label="Demo Group">
      <button id="rxbtnRollForward"
         label="Roll Forward"
         imageMso="CreateReportFromWizard"
         size="large"
         onAction="rxbtnRollForward_Click"/>
   </group>
</tab>
```

CROSS-REFERENCE **If you don't remember how to set up the RibbonBase template, review "Storing Customization Templates in the CustomUI Editor" from Chapter 2.**

After you've validated the code to make sure your XML is well formed, click the Generate Callbacks button and copy the code for your `onAction` callback. Once you've taken care of that little detail, save the file, close the CustomUI Editor, and reopen the file in Excel. Do not click the button yet, however, as it won't do anything except throw the error message shown in Figure 6-7.

NOTE **Remember to enable macros when running this type of file. Although using built-in controls does not require that the file be code-enabled, any file that requires VBA code needs to have macros enabled.**

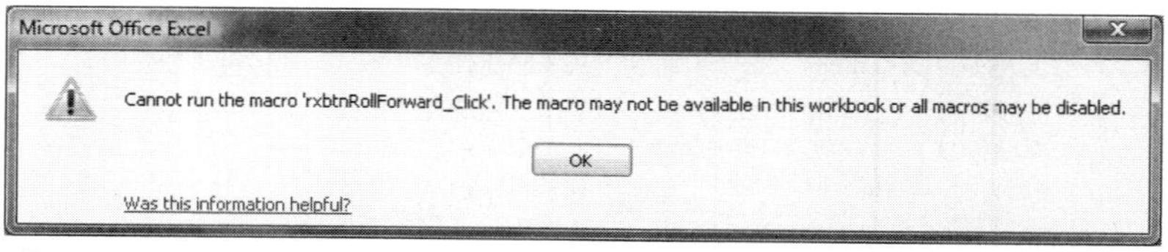

Figure 6-7: Error indicating a missing callback

Obviously, in this case, you would expect this error because the callback hasn't been programmed, so it is time to take care of that little issue. Go back into the Visual Basic Editor, enter the module in which you saved your `RollForward` subroutine, and paste the callback code that you copied from the CustomUI Editor. You'll then add a tiny bit of code to your callback so that it calls the existing procedure that you already wrote and tested. Your callback will then look like this:

```
'Callback for rxbtnRollForward onAction
Sub rxbtnRollForward_Click(control As IRibbonControl)
    Select Case control.ID
      Case Is = "rxbtnRollForward"
         Call RollForward
      Case Else
         'do nothing
    End Select
End Sub
```

That's all there is to it. Just exit the Visual Basic Editor, save your file, and start clicking your button to watch your code be called.

WARNING **If you did click the button prematurely and receive the error shown in Figure 6-7, you will need to save, close, and reopen the file in order for the code to take effect. This is because any UI errors break the hooks to the Ribbon and the file must be re-accessed in order for the hooks to be restored.**

A Word Example

In this example you add the capability to update all fields in the document at once. This is a nice automation to add because the only way to do this natively is to print the document.

You'll start by opening your favorite Word document and saving it as a `.docm` file. Open the Visual Basic Editor and add the following code in a new standard module:

```
Public Sub UpdateDocumentFields()
    Dim rngStory As Word.Range

    For Each rngStory In ActiveDocument.StoryRanges
          rngStory.Fields.Update
          Do
               If rngStory.NextStoryRange Is Nothing Then Exit Do
               Set rngStory = rngStory.NextStoryRange
               rngStory.Fields.Update
          Loop
    Next rngStory
End Sub
```

If you'd like to test this, just create a document with some calculated fields. (Alternately, you could just load the example file called `button-Update Word Fields.docm`.) You could use a formula in a table, cross-references to another section of the document, or whatever calculated field that you like.

For the purposes of building this example, the document shown in Figure 6-8 was constructed using the following field codes:

```
Reference { STYLEREF 1 \s }-{ SEQ Figure \* ARABIC \s 1}
```

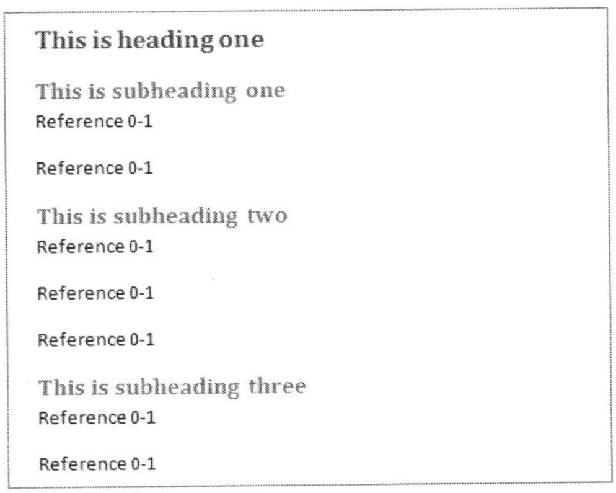
This is heading one

This is subheading one

Reference 0-1

Reference 0-1

This is subheading two

Reference 0-1

Reference 0-1

Reference 0-1

This is subheading three

Reference 0-1

Reference 0-1

Figure 6-8: Example of non-updated Word fields

After you have your choice of fields set up correctly (or you are in the example file), just copy and paste the line a few times. You'll notice that the numbers do not update for you.

Run the preceding macro and you'll notice that all the fields are updated to new index numbers. To return the document's appearance to its original state, just copy the first reference line and paste it over all of the existing ones again.

Now that you have something to work with, save the file, close it, and open it again in the CustomUI Editor. Apply the RibbonBase template to the file, and insert the following XML between the `<tabs>` and `<tabs>` elements:

```
<tab id="DemoTab"
    label="Demo"
    insertBeforeMso="TabHome">
    <group id="DemoGroup"
      label="Demo Group">
      <button id="rxbtnUpdateFields"
         label="Update Fields"
         imageMso="MailMergeRecipientsEditList"
         size="large"
         onAction="rxbtnUpdateFields_click"/>
    </group>
</tab>
```

Don't forget to validate the code before you save it, just to catch any of those pesky little typing errors in XML-specific code. After you've done that, click the Generate Callbacks button and copy the code provided. Close the CustomUI Editor, reopen the document in Word, and head straight into the VBE. Paste the callback code in the same module in which you stored the `UpdateDocumentFields` routine, and modify calling that routine as shown here:

```
'Callback for rxbtnUpdateFields onAction
Sub rxbtnUpdateFields_click(control As IRibbonControl)
   Call UpdateDocumentFields
End Sub
```

Close the VBE, save your file, and now turn your attention to the button that appears on the Demo group (right before the Home tab), as shown in Figure 6-9.

Go ahead, give it a click. Your fields should all update automatically for you.

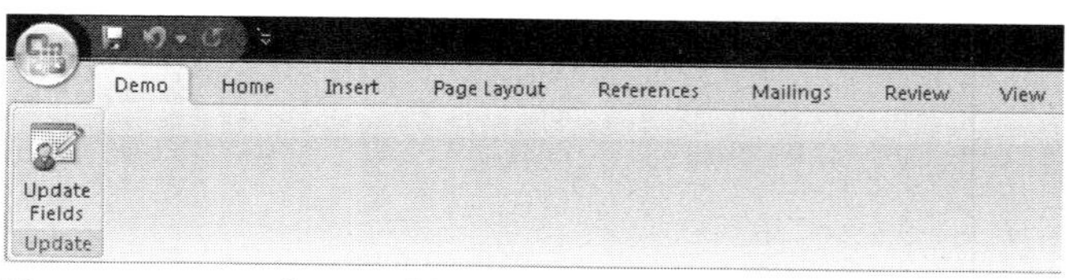

Figure 6-9: Update Fields button

An Access Example

This section describes how a button is used in Access. Assume that you're building an application and you want to provide your users with the capability to launch a form from a Ribbon group. It's your lucky day, as that's exactly what this example will do!

To start, create a database and set up the RibbonUI so that it is completely linked to the project.

CROSS-REFERENCE **If you need to work from a guide, follow the instructions in Chapter 2 to set up a new RibbonUI in a database. You'll replace the XML later, but for now it's important to get the UI linked to work with.**

Once you have that done, you need to create a little structure to work with. From the Create tab, create a new table. You'll notice that the Datasheet tab on the Ribbon is immediately activated. Click the View drop-down, choose Design View, and save the table as tblAuthors when prompted. Set up your table as shown in Figure 6-10.

tblAuthors

Field Name	Data Type
ID	AutoNumber
Author Name	Text
Country	Text
Special	Number

Figure 6-10: tblAuthors table design

Close the table, saving it when prompted, and reopen it. Populate the table with the information shown in Figure 6-11.

tblAuthors

ID	Author Name	Country	Special	Add New Field
1	Robert Martim	Brazil	20	
2	Ken Puls	Canada	22	
3	Teresa Hennig	USA	25	
(New)				

Figure 6-11: tblAuthors data

Close the table again and ensure that it is selected in the navigation window. Again, on the Create tab, click Form. Delete the ID field and its corresponding entry field, select the name, and change it to read "Author Information." Your form should now look like the one displayed in Figure 6-12.

Figure 6-12: frmAuthors display

Close the form, saving it as frmAuthors, and breathe a sigh of relief. The database structure has been completed, and you're ready to link it all to the Ribbon.

At this point, you need to create the XML code to display your Ribbon commands. Depending on how much you need to do, and how familiar you are with the tools, you may elect to do this using either the CustomUI Editor or XML Notepad. For the purposes of this example, however, you'll stick with the CustomUI Editor for the moment.

Open the CustomUI Editor and immediately apply the RibbonBase template discussed in Chapter 2. Replace the line that reads <!– Enter your first tab here –> with the following XML code:

```
<tab id="rxTabMyTools"
   label="My Tools"
   insertBeforeMso="TabHomeAccess">
   <group id="rxgrpForms"
      label="Forms">
      <button id="rxbtnFrmAuthors"
         imageMso="FileCreateDocumentWorkspace"
         size="large"
         label="Enter Authors"
         onAction="rxbtnFrmAuthors_click"/>
   </group>
</tab>
```

You'll recall that one of the reasons for writing code in the CustomUI Editor is to confirm that the code is valid, so make sure that you validate the code, and then copy everything in the window (not just what you just entered).

Don't close the CustomUI editor just yet, but head back to Access and open the USysRibbons table. Paste the code in the RibbonXML field for the MainRibbonUI and save it. Now, close your database, reopen it, and take a moment to admire your new tab, shown in Figure 6-13.

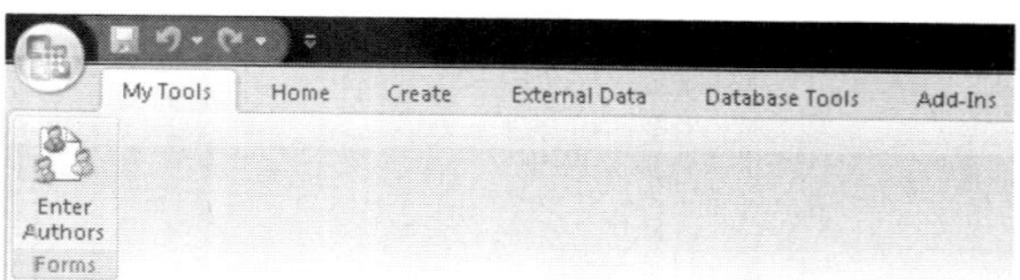

Figure 6-13: The Enter Authors button on the My Tools tab

Unfortunately, as pretty as this looks, it doesn't do anything yet, as it has not been linked to any code. Ultimately, however, you'd like to have the user click the button and launch your form. To accomplish this, you need to write a little VBA code.

The first step, of course, is to create a new VBA module to hold the VBA code. Therefore, on the Create tab, click the Macro drop-down (the last command on the right), and choose Module. This will open a new window with the VBE (Visual Basic Editor), and you'll be staring at a fresh, almost blank page.

Head back into the CustomUI Editor and click the Generate Callbacks button. Copy the resulting code and close the CustomUI Editor. When you return to Access, go to the VBE and paste the code at the end of the module that was just created. Now, modify the code to read as follows:

```
'Callback for rxbtnFrmAuthors onAction
Public Sub rxbtnFrmAuthors_click(control As IRibbonControl)
    DoCmd.OpenForm "frmAuthors", acNormal
End Sub
```

The preceding code leverages the `OpenForm` method of the `DoCmd` object. Notice that you've fed it the name of the Authors form, and you've specified that you would like the form opened in Normal View.

TIP **Don't forget to set a reference to the MS Office 12.0 Objects Library, as described in Chapter 5.**

Finally, save your module as `modRibbonX` and close it. Try clicking the button. Your form should jump open in front of you!

WARNING **If you already clicked the button and received an error, you will need to close and reopen your database to reactive the Ribbon interface again. As noted with the Excel example, this is because any UI errors break the hooks to the Ribbon; to restore the hooks you need to re-access the file.**

The checkBox Element

The `checkBox` control enables users to toggle between two states. Although these states are true and false by default, this element could indicate on/off, up/down, left/right, 1/0, or any other combination of opposite states that the developer could imagine.

There are numerous scenarios in which you might wish to use a `checkBox` to control or indicate something. A couple of practical examples might help prompt some ideas of your own. For example, you might benefit from using a `checkBox` for the following:

- To indicate whether a specific criterion has been met in a field in your database. In this case, when the criteria is met, the check would automatically appear in the box.

- To allow the user to determine whether an object should be displayed or not, such as to show or hide gridlines or even a subform.

As you explore the examples in this section, you'll begin to see how the concept of invalidation is applied in a real-world setting as well.

Required Attributes of the checkBox Element

The `checkBox` control requires any one of the `id` attributes shown in Table 6-5.

Table 6-5: Required Attributes of the checkBox Element

ATTRIBUTE	WHEN TO USE
id	Create your own checkBox
idMso	Use an existing Microsoft checkBox
idQ	Create a checkBox shared between namespaces

The `checkBox` control also requires the `onAction` callback, shown in Table 6-6.

Table 6-6: Required Callback for the checkBox Element

DYNAMIC ATTRIBUTE	ALLOWED VALUES	VBA CALLBACK SIGNATURE
onAction	1 to 4096 characters	Sub OnAction (control As IRibbonControl, pressed as Boolean)

Optional Static and Dynamic Attributes with Callback Signatures

In addition, the `checkBox` control can optionally make use of any one `insert` attribute, shown in Table 6-7.

Table 6-7: Optional insert Attributes of the checkBox Element

INSERT ATTRIBUTE	ALLOWED VALUES	DEFAULT VALUE	WHEN TO USE
insertAfterMso	Valid Mso Group	Insert at end of group	Insert after Microsoft control

Table 6-7 *(continued)*

INSERT ATTRIBUTE	ALLOWED VALUES	DEFAULT VALUE	WHEN TO USE
insertBeforeMso	Valid Mso Group	Insert at end of group	Insert before Microsoft control
insertAfterQ	Valid Group idQ	Insert at end of group	Insert after shared namespace control
insertBeforeQ	Valid Group idQ	Insert at end of group	Insert before shared namespace control

The `checkBox` element may also employ any or all of the attributes shown in Table 6-8.

Table 6-8: Optional Attributes and Callbacks of the checkBox Element

STATIC ATTRIBUTE	DYNAMIC ATTRIBUTE	ALLOWED VALUES	DEFAULT VALUE	VBA CALLBACK SIGNATURE FOR DYNAMIC ATTRIBUTE
description	getDescription	1 to 4096 characters	(none)	Sub GetDescription (control As IRibbonControl, ByRef returnedVal)
enabled	getEnabled	true, false, 1, 0	true	Sub GetEnabled (control As IRibbonControl, ByRef returnedVal)
keytip	getKeytip	1 to 3 characters	(none)	Sub GetKeytip (control As IRibbonControl, ByRef returnedVal)
label	getLabel	1 to 1024 characters	(none)	Sub GetLabel (control As IRibbonControl, ByRef returnedVal)
(none)	getPressed	true, false, 1, 0	false	Sub GetPressed (control As IRibbonControl, ByRef returnedVal)
screentip	getScreentip	1 to 1024 characters	(none)	Sub GetScreentip (control As IRibbonControl, ByRef returnedVal)

Continued

Table 6-8 *(continued)*

STATIC ATTRIBUTE	DYNAMIC ATTRIBUTE	ALLOWED VALUES	DEFAULT VALUE	VBA CALLBACK SIGNATURE FOR DYNAMIC ATTRIBUTE
supertip	getSupertip	1 to 1024 characters	(none)	Sub GetSupertip (control As IRibbonControl, ByRef returnedVal)
tag	(none)	1 to 1024 characters	(none)	(none)
visible	getVisible	true, false, 1, 0	true	Sub GetVisible (control As IRibbonControl, ByRef returnedVal)

Allowed Children Objects of the checkBox Element

The `checkBox` control does not support child objects of any kind.

Parent Objects of the button Element

The `checkBox` control can be placed within any of the following controls:

- `box`
- `dynamicMenu`
- `group`
- `menu`
- `officeMenu` (Note that when the checkbox is unchecked, only the description, but not the checkbox, appears on the menu.)

Graphical View of checkBox Attributes

Figure 6-14 shows a sample customization that displays all of the visible graphical attributes that you can set on the `checkBox` control.

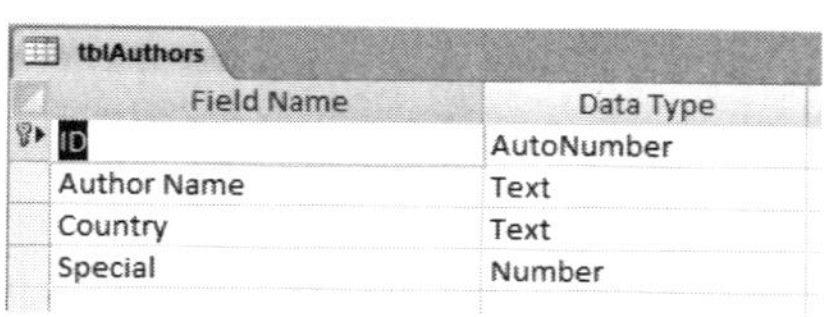

Figure 6-14: Graphical view of checkBox attributes

Using Built-in checkBox Controls

To demonstrate the use of a built-in control, you'll add a custom tab in Word, and put the View Gridlines `checkBox` on it. To do this, create a new Word document and save it as a `.docx` file.

NOTE **Because you are only using built-in controls, and do not need to program any callback macros, the file does not have to be saved in a macro-enabled format. This is an exception to the norm, because most Word and Excel files with custom Ribbons will include macros and therefore require a file extension ending with "m".**

Close the document in Word and open it in the CustomUI Editor. Apply the RibbonBase template to the file, and then insert the following XML between the `<tabs>` and `</tabs>` tags:

```
<tab id="rxtabDemo"
   label="Demo"
   insertBeforeMso="TabHome">
   <group id="rxgrpDemo"
      label="Demo Group">
      <checkBox idMso="ViewGridlinesWord"/>
   </group>
</tab>
```

Validate the code to ensure that you've typed it correctly, and then save and close the file in the CustomUI Editor. Reopen the document in Word and click the Demo tab to the left of the Home tab, as shown in Figure 6-15.

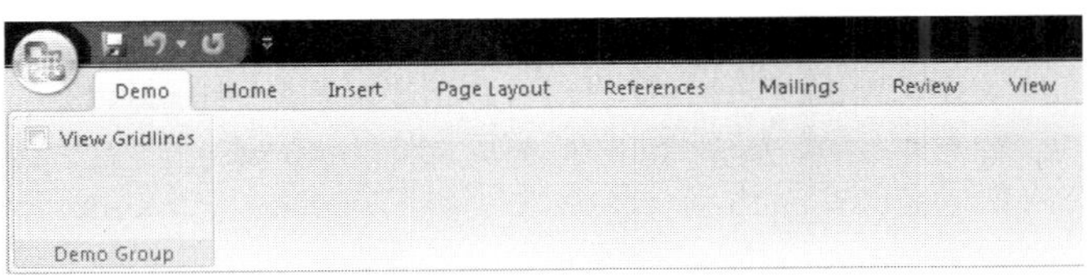

Figure 6-15: Built-in checkBox default appearance

You'll notice that the `checkBox` is there and that it works, although the name is probably not what you're after. Why not go back, edit the XML, and give it a new name. Update the XML to add a label to the code that declares the `checkBox`. Instead of one line, you will have two lines, as shown here:

```
<checkBox idMso="ViewGridlinesWord"
   label="Toggle Gridlines"/>
```

Upon reopening your document, your group should now look like what is shown in Figure 6-16.

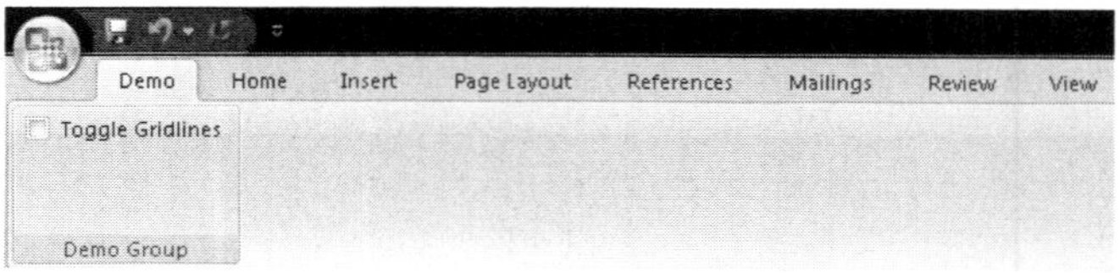

Figure 6-16: Built-in checkBox relabeled

NOTE **The preceding example will work in Excel with only one minor change: Instead of using** `idMso="ViewGridlinesWord"` **in your XML, substitute** `idMso="GridlinesExcel"` **and save it in an Excel file.**

Creating Custom Controls

Now it's time to explore some of the diversity of the Ribbon checkBox and create your own customizations. Again, you'll have the opportunity to work through an example in Excel, Word, and Access. So let's get started!

An Excel Example

One of the things that can be handy when working in Excel is the capability to quickly toggle between A1 and R1C1 formulas in your workbook. There are several scenarios in which it may be more advantageous to place your formulas via R1C1 notation, so this example demonstrates how to make it easy to quickly flip your formulas to display in the alternate notation.

NOTE **For users who may not be familiar with the difference between A1 and R1C1 notation, A1 notation enables users to specify formulas and references by pointing to the cell's coordinates in the spreadsheet grid. R1C1 notation, however, tends to be more like referring to an off-setting cell a certain number of rows and columns in any direction. Excel allows either notation type.**

This example adds a control to the Formulas tab to save you the hassle of having to dig through the Office menu to find the checkbox for that setting. The completed UI modification is shown in Figure 6-17, with the new `checkBox` control on the far right, in the Other Settings group.

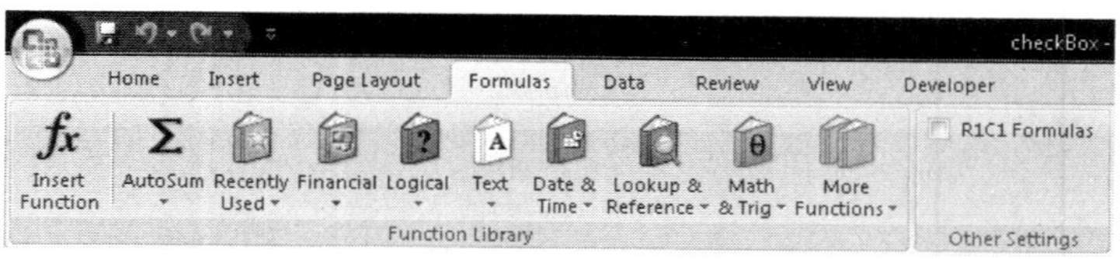

Figure 6-17: R1C1 formula checkbox

To begin, create a new workbook and insert all the required XML. There's going to be a bit of VBA code involved to set this up, so make sure you save the workbook as an .xlsm workbook, and then close the file. Open the file with the CustomUI Editor, apply the RibbonBase template, and insert the following XML code between the <tabs> and </tabs> tags:

```
<tab idMso="TabFormulas">
   <group id="rxgrpOtherSettings"
      label="Other Settings"
      insertBeforeMso="GroupNamedCells">
      <checkBox id="rxchkR1C1"
         label="R1C1 Formulas"
         getPressed="rxchkR1C1_getPressed"
         onAction="rxchkR1C1_click"/>
   </group>
</tab>
```

In addition, you need to modify the first line of the XML code to capture the Ribbon object for later use:

```
<customUI
   xmlns="http://schemas.microsoft.com/office/2006/01/customui"
   onLoad="rxIRibbonUI_onLoad">
```

NOTE **Remember that although it may seem wrong at first glance, the last two lines are </tab> and </tabs>. This is because each tag must be individually closed. The code that you are inserting has a </tab> that partners with the opening line, and the entire tab is encompassed by the <tabs> and </tabs>.**

Again, don't forget to validate it before you save the file, and be sure to copy the callback signatures before you close it. Reopen the file in Excel, open the VBE, and paste the code in a new standard module.

You'll notice that there are now three callback signatures in the file: rxIRibbonUI_onLoad, rxchkR1C1_getPressed, and rxchkR1C1_click. These have the following purposes:

- rxIRibbonUI_onLoad will store the RibbonUI object for you, enabling you to invalidate controls later to force their updates.
- rxchkR1C1_getPressed is fired when the Formulas tab is first activated (or upon invalidation) and sets the checkBox appropriately.
- rxchkR1C1_click is triggered whenever the checkbox is checked or unchecked. The purpose of this macro is to actually toggle the setting from on to off.

Before you can use this, you need to lay a little more groundwork. The rxIRibbonUI_onLoad needs a custom workbook property to operate, so that should be set up first. Browse to the ThisWorkbook module for the project, and enter the following code:

```
'Private variables to hold state of Ribbon and Ribbon controls
Private pRibbonUI As IRibbonUI
```

```
Public Property Let RibbonUI(iRib As IRibbonUI)
'Set RibbonUI to property for later use
    Set pRibbonUI = iRib
End Property

Public Property Get RibbonUI() As IRibbonUI
'Retrieve RibbonUI from property for use
    Set RibbonUI = pRibbonUI
End Property
```

Once that has been accomplished, you'll want to complete the `rxIRibbonUI_onLoad` routine. Browse back to the standard module and modify this routine to look as follows:

```
Private Sub rxIRibbonUI_onLoad(ribbon As IRibbonUI)
'Set the RibbonUI to a workbook property for later use
    ThisWorkbook.RibbonUI = ribbon
End Sub
```

Your `RibbonUI` object should now be captured when the workbook is loaded, and will be available for invalidation.

NOTE The preceding code uses public properties but it could have used public variables instead. We chose to work with the properties in this case because we will be invalidating the code in several procedures, and using properties will be more elegant.

The next step in the process is to generate the macro to toggle this setting. The easiest way to work out this bit of code is to record a macro, so start the macro recorder and create a new macro that will be stored in the workbook you just created.

CROSS-REFERENCE If you need a refresher on how to use the macro recorder, review "Recording Macros for Excel and Word" in Chapter 4.

Now, go to the Office Menu, choose Excel Options ⇨ Formulas, and check (or uncheck) the R1C1 Reference Style checkbox. Once you have done this, stop the macro recorder and jump into the VBE to examine the code. It will most likely look like this:

```
Application.ReferenceStyle = xlR1C1
```

This is a situation in which the macro recorder can really help you, as it tells you exactly what objects you need to reference. You still need to make some modifications to the code, but at least you know where to start and you have the correct syntax.

Fill in the `getPressed` callback first. It's actually not too difficult. Basically, you want to determine whether the application is in R1C1 mode, and if so return `true`. This can be accomplished by modifying the routine to read as follows:

```
'Callback for rxchkR1C1 getPressed
Sub rxchkR1C1_getPressed(control As IRibbonControl, ByRef returnedVal)
```

```
    If Application.ReferenceStyle = xlR1C1 Then returnedVal = True
End Sub
```

Next, you want to deal with the callback that handles the actual clicking of the checkbox. With your checkbox, the `pressed` parameter tells you whether the checkbox is checked (`pressed=true`) or not (`pressed=false`). This means that you can test the `pressed` argument and react accordingly:

```
'Callback for rxchkR1C1 onAction
Sub rxchkR1C1_click(control As IRibbonControl, pressed As Boolean)
    Select Case pressed
      Case True
         Application.ReferenceStyle = xlR1C1
      Case False
         Application.ReferenceStyle = xlA1
    End Select
End Sub
```

If you were to click the Formulas tab now, the `getPressed` routine would fire, setting the checkbox to indicate what display mode you're currently in. Likewise, checking the box would set it to the opposite state.

Unfortunately, there is an issue remaining with this setup: What if someone goes through the Excel Options to change the value of that `checkBox`? In that case, the `checkBox` will not be updated.

While you can't make this perfectly transparent, you can force it to update whenever you activate a new worksheet. (This will also force an update when your workbook is reactivated as well.) To do this, you make use of the capability to invalidate a specific control — in this case, the `rxchkR1C1 checkBox`.

Head back into the `ThisWorkbook` code module, and choose Workbook from the drop-down list on the left, as shown in Figure 6-18.

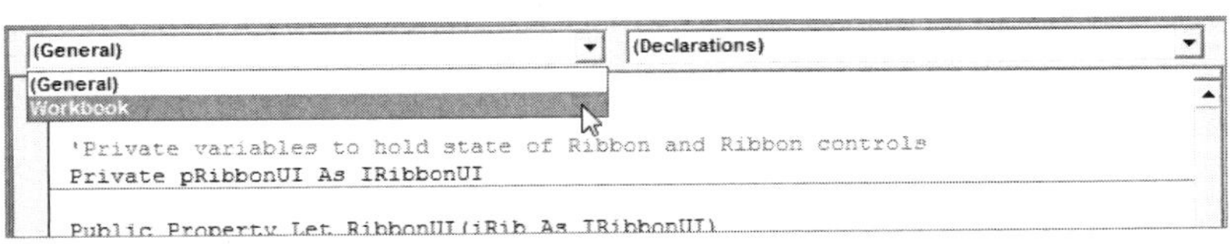

Figure 6-18: Selecting the Workbook code container

You will be greeted by a new procedure in your code called `Workbook_Open`. Before you delete it, choose Sheet_Activate from the right hand drop-down list. Modify the resulting procedure to read as follows:

```
Private Sub Workbook_SheetActivate(ByVal Sh As Object)
'Invalidate the tab each time a worksheet is activated
    ThisWorkbook.RibbonUI.InvalidateControl ("rxchkR1C1")
End Sub
```

TIP **You could have typed your code in instead of selecting the appropriate procedure from the drop-down lists, but going this route offers you the benefits of browsing the available events, and ensures that they are syntactically correct when you set them up.**

That's it. Save and reopen your workbook, and then place the following formula in cell B1: =A1

When you click the `checkBox`, it will change to =RC[-1]. Notice that changing the R1C1 setting through the Excel Options screen does not immediately update your `checkBox`, but selecting a different sheet and coming back to the first sheet does.

A Word Example

Word also has some useful tools that might seem buried, such as those in the Word Advanced Options window. For instance, it would be handy to have the capability to quickly show or hide the Style Inspector window so that you can see what styles are active in your document. This next example focuses on using a `checkBox` to control this setting on a custom Ribbon tab.

Because this setting is effective in Draft or Outline views only, it probably makes most sense to put this information on the View tab. To do this, you again begin by creating a new Word file and inserting the following code in a new standard module:

```
Private Sub ShowStyleInspector()
'Show the Style inspector window
    ActiveWindow.StyleAreaWidth = InchesToPoints(1)
    If ActiveWindow.View.SplitSpecial = wdPaneNone Then
        ActiveWindow.ActivePane.View.Type = wdNormalView
    Else
        ActiveWindow.View.Type = wdNormalView
    End If
End Sub

Private Sub HideStyleInspector()
'Hide the Style inspector window
    ActiveWindow.StyleAreaWidth = 0
End Sub
```

Because both of these routines have been marked `Private`, they are not included with the macros listed in the Macro window. To try them out, you need to enter the VBE (Alt+F11), click somewhere within the appropriate macro, and press F5 to run it. If you do decide to try the ShowStyleInspector macro, you'll notice upon leaving the VBE that you are switched to Draft view, and the Style Inspector, displaying the "Normal" style, is shown on the left side of the screen, as illustrated in Figure 6-19.

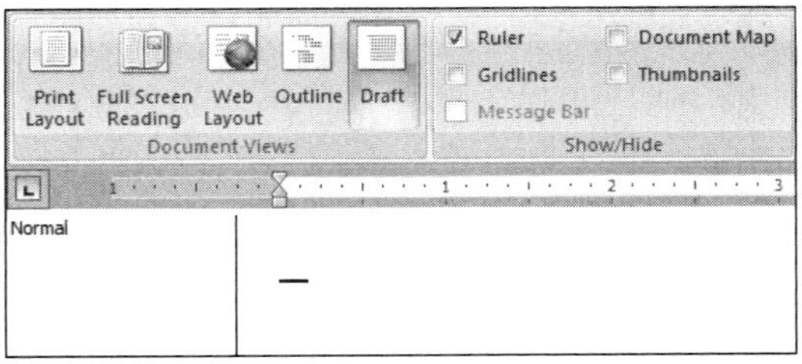

Figure 6-19: The Style Inspector

Likewise, run the `HideStyleInspector` routine to hide the Style Inspector.

The next step is to save the file as a macro-enabled document (`.docm`), exit Word, and open the file in the CustomUI Editor. Apply the RibbonBase template to the file, and insert the following XML between the `<tabs>` and `</tabs>` elements:

```
<tab idMso="TabView">
   <group id="rxgrpStyleInsp"
      label="Custom Options"
      insertBeforeMso="GroupZoom">
      <checkBox id="rxchkStyleInsp"
         label="Style Inspector"
         getPressed="rxchkStyleInsp_getPressed"
         onAction="rxchkStyleInsp_click"/>
   </group>
</tab>
```

Again, validate the code before you save it, and click the Generate Callbacks button to copy the callback code. Close the CustomUI Editor and reopen the document in Word. Do *not* click the View tab, but rather head straight into the VBE again. (If you don't, you will get an error and will need to reload the file once your callbacks have been successfully implemented.)

Paste the generated callbacks code in the module that holds the two routines you saved earlier and modify them to read as follows:

```
Sub rxchkStyleInsp_getPressed(control As IRibbonControl, ByRef
returnedVal)
'Callback for rxchkStyleInsp getPressed
    Select Case ActiveWindow.View.Type
        Case Is = wdNormalView, wdOutlineView
            If ActiveWindow.StyleAreaWidth > 0 Then
                returnedVal = True
            Else
                returnedVal = False
            End If
        Case Else
            returnedVal = False
    End Select
End Sub
```

```
Sub rxchkStyleInsp_click(control As IRibbonControl, pressed As Boolean)
'Callback for rxchkStyleInsp onAction
    Static lState As Long

    Select Case pressed
      Case True
         lState = ActiveWindow.View.Type
         Call ShowStyleInspector
      Case False
         Call HideStyleInspector
         ActiveWindow.View.Type = lState
    End Select
End Sub
```

So what's happening here?

The `getPressed` routine will fire the first time you click the View tab, and will check the width of the StyleArea. If it's greater than 0, the checkbox will be flagged as true, and display a checkmark. If not, it won't be displayed.

The `rxchkStyleInsp_click` routine is fired when you actually click the `checkBox`. It checks the state of the button; if it is true (checked), it calls the ShowStyleInspector macro. Otherwise, it calls the routine to hide the Style Inspector.

TIP **Notice the `Static variable lState` that was included in this routine. This records the view state before calling the macro to show the Style Inspector. Because it is a static variable, it holds its values in scope between macro executions, and you can then use it to return the view to its original state upon calling the macro to turn off the Style Inspector!**

Now close the VBE, save your file, and click the View tab. You will see a new group with your `checkBox`, as shown in Figure 6-20.

Figure 6-20: The Style Inspector checkbox

Give it a click and the Style Inspector will become visible. Uncheck it and it goes away. In addition, thanks to the `Static` variable, this even remembers the view setting that was active when you clicked the `checkBox`!

An Access Example

One of the things that can be a little daunting to a new user, and that causes frustration for users who frequently set up customizations, is that the USysRibbons table is a system object, and therefore it is hidden by default. It can be quite the unpleasant surprise for novice users to have their new table disappear as soon as they save it. With that in mind, this next example creates a checkbox on the Ribbon to show/hide the Systems Objects.

To make life easier, why not just add this to the project that you started working on button controls earlier? Find that file and let's get started.

TIP **You can always download the completed button example file from the website if you want to catch up, or even start fresh at this point.**

Open the previous example and open the USysRibbons table. Copy all of the code in the RibbonXML field, and then open a fresh instance of the CustomUI Editor and paste the code there. Now you will insert a new group, `rxgrpTools`. Put the cursor between the `</group>` and `</tab>` lines, and insert the following XML code:

```
<group id="rxgrpTools"
   label="Tools">
   <checkBox id="rxchkShowSysObjects"
      label="Show System Objects"
      getPressed="rxchkShowSysObjects_getPressed"
      onAction="rxchkShowSysObjects_click"/>
</group>
```

Again, validate your code and then copy the entire code listing. Leave the CustomUI Editor open, and switch back to Access. Replace the value of the RibbonXML field with what you just copied. Save and close the table.

Switch back to the CustomUI Editor and press the Generate Callbacks button. You'll notice that three callback signatures are listed. Because the example file already holds the callback signature for the `rxbtnFrmAuthors` button, you only need to worry about copying the `rxchkShowSysObjects` callbacks. After you have done so, you may close the CustomUI Editor.

Flip back to Access, open the `modRibbonX` module, and paste your new callbacks at the end of the module. You'll then need to modify them to actually do something when called, so revise them to read as follows:

```
`Callback for rxchkShowSysObjects getPressed
Sub rxchkShowSysObjects_getPressed(control As IRibbonControl, _
    ByRef returnedVal)
    returnedVal = Application.GetOption("Show System objects")
End Sub

`Callback for rxchkShowSysObjects onAction
Sub rxchkShowSysObjects_click(control As IRibbonControl, _
    pressed As Boolean)
    Application.SetOption "Show System objects", pressed
End Sub
```

The preceding code uses the `getPressed` callback to check whether the Show System Objects setting is `true` when your tab is first activated. If it is `true`, then the checkBox will appear as checked; if it is `false`, then the `checkBox` will be empty. The second routine actually toggles the setting. Because the object model requires a true/false value to be specified in order to set this option, the `checkBox` state can simply be queried and fed right to it!

The final step in making this work is to save the code module and reload the database to make the Ribbon code effective. Upon doing so, you'll notice that the new group has been added to the tab, as shown in Figure 6-21.

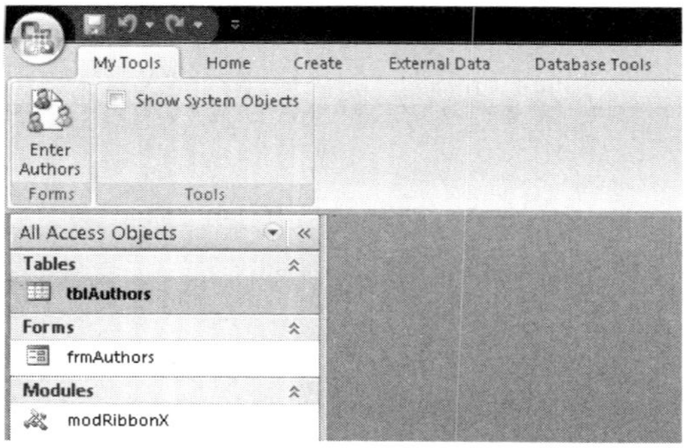

Figure 6-21: The Show System Objects checkBox set to false

Now give the `checkBox` a click. In addition to seeing all of the tables that Access creates by default, you'll be happy to see that your USysRibbons table is prominently displayed as well.

NOTE **This setting is a global setting and will affect all databases opened in your Access application. This `checkBox` is intended to make your life as a developer a little easier, but it is not something that you'd deploy to all of your users. If you use this technique, make sure that your deployment checklist includes a step to hide system tables.**

The editBox Element

The `editBox` control allows users to enter text. This is quite handy if you are looking for some kind of input from the user. You might use an `editBox` to rename a worksheet in Excel, or to assign a caption to each image in Word, for example. The basic concept is that the user is asked for the input, which is then used when the `editBox` loses focus, the event that occurs just before the next control in the sequence is activated. Although some developers may prefer to provide a second button for users to click that will run code to store the text from the edit box, we've found that using loss of focus works quite well for this purpose.

Required Attributes of the editBox Element

The `editBox` requires any one of the `id` attributes shown in Table 6-9.

Table 6-9: Required Attributes of the editBox Element

ATTRIBUTE	WHEN TO USE
id	When creating your own editBox
idMso	When using an existing Microsoft editBox
idQ	When creating an editBox shared between namespaces

The `editBox` also requires the `onChange` callback shown in Table 6-10.

Table 6-10: Required Callback for the editBox Element

DYNAMIC ATTRIBUTE	ALLOWED VALUES	VBA CALLBACK SIGNATURE
onChange	1 to 4096 characters	Sub OnChange (control As IRibbonControl, text As String)

Optional Static and Dynamic Attributes with Callback Signatures

In addition to the required attributes, your `editBox` can optionally make use of any one `insert` attribute, described in Table 6-11.

Table 6-11: Optional insert Attributes of the editBox Element

INSERT ATTRIBUTE	ALLOWED VALUES	DEFAULT VALUE	WHEN TO USE
insertAfterMso	Valid Mso Group	Insert at end of group	Insert after Microsoft control
insertBeforeMso	Valid Mso Group	Insert at end of group	Insert before Microsoft control
insertAfterQ	Valid Group idQ	Insert at end of group	Insert after shared namespace control

Continued

Table 6-11 *(continued)*

INSERT ATTRIBUTE	ALLOWED VALUES	DEFAULT VALUE	WHEN TO USE
insertBeforeQ	Valid Group idQ	Insert at end of group	Insert before shared namespace control

The `editBox` can also employ any or all of the attributes described in Table 6-12.

Table 6-12: Optional Attributes and Callbacks of the editBox Element

STATIC ATTRIBUTE	DYNAMIC ATTRIBUTE	ALLOWED VALUES	DEFAULT VALUE	VBA CALLBACK SIGNATURE FOR DYNAMIC ATTRIBUTE
enabled	getEnabled	true, false, 1, 0	true	Sub GetEnabled (control As IRibbonControl, ByRef returnedVal)
image	getImage	1 to 1024 characters	(none)	Sub GetImage (control As IRibbonControl, ByRef returnedVal)
imageMso	getImage	1 to 1024 characters	(none)	Same as above
keytip	getKeytip	1 to 3 characters	(none)	Sub GetKeytip (control As IRibbonControl, ByRef returnedVal)
label	getLabel	1 to 1024 characters	(none)	Sub GetLabel (control As IRibbonControl, ByRef returnedVal)
maxLength	(none)	1 to 1024 characters	1024	(none)
screentip	getScreentip	1 to 1024 characters	(none)	Sub GetScreentip (control As IRibbonControl, ByRef returnedVal)
showImage	getShowImage	true, false, 1, 0	true	Sub GetShowImage (control As IRibbonControl, ByRef returnedVal)

Table 6-12 *(continued)*

STATIC ATTRIBUTE	DYNAMIC ATTRIBUTE	ALLOWED VALUES	DEFAULT VALUE	VBA CALLBACK SIGNATURE FOR DYNAMIC ATTRIBUTE
showLabel	getShowLabel	true, false, 1, 0	true	Sub GetShowLabel (control As IRibbonControl, ByRef returnedVal)
sizeString	(none)	1 to 1024 characters	12*	(none)
supertip	getSupertip	1 to 1024 characters	(none)	Sub GetSupertip (control As IRibbonControl, ByRef returnedVal)
tag	(none)	1 to 1024 characters	(none)	(none)
(none)	getText	1 to 4096 characters	(none)	Sub GetText (control As IRibbonControl, ByRef returnedVal)
visible	getVisible	true, false, 1, 0	true	Sub GetVisible (control As IRibbonControl, ByRef returnedVal)

NOTE ***The default value for the `sizeString` attribute (if the attribute is not declared) is approximately 12, but this will vary based on the characters used and the system font.**

Allowed Children Objects of the editBox Element

The `editBox` control does not support child objects of any kind.

Parent Objects of the editBox Element

The `editBox` control can only be placed within the following two controls:

- `box`
- `group`

Graphical View of editBox Attributes

Figures 6-22 and 6-23 display all of the visible graphical attributes that you can set on an `editBox` control.

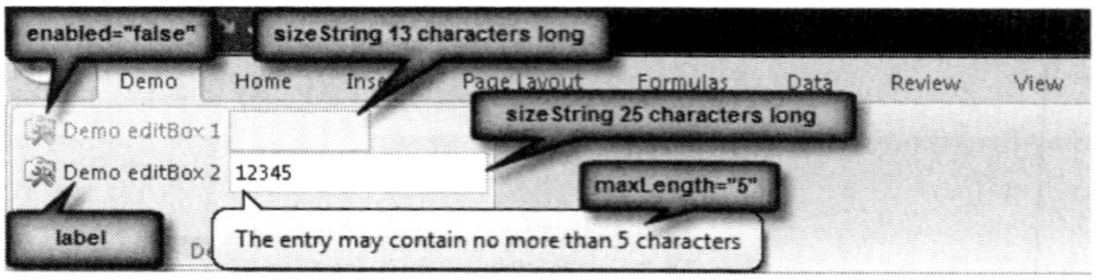

Figure 6-22: Graphical view of editBox attributes (part 1)

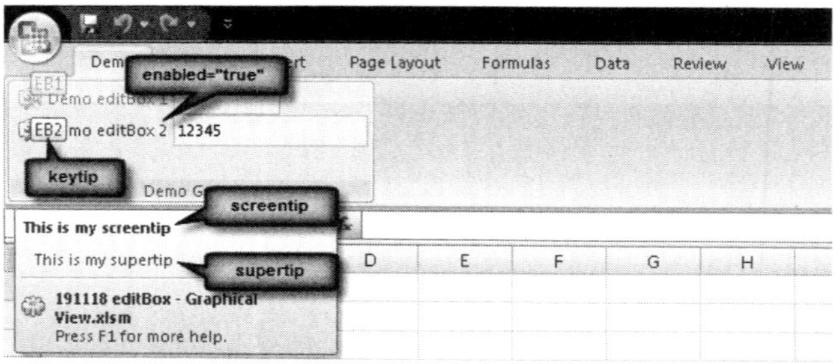

Figure 6-23: Graphical view of editBox attributes (part 2)

Using Built-in editBox Controls

Interestingly enough, there does not appear to be a way to customize any built-in `editBox` controls in Excel, Access, or Word. However, as you can see in the previous two figures, we have extensive opportunities for creating and customizing our own `editBox` controls.

Creating Custom Controls

As mentioned, the `editBox` can provide an efficient way to obtain input from a user. The following examples walk you through a couple of popular uses, such as to change a file or worksheet name. By now you are familiar with many of the individual steps so they aren't repeated in the examples. However, you can always get a refresher by following the detailed processes described earlier in this chapter.

An Excel Example

For this example, assume that you are building an application within Excel that takes control of the entire user interface. This is actually fairly common in practice. It involves hiding every built-in facet of the provided UI, and replacing the standard UI with a custom setup that limits the user to only those actions that you explicitly allow. There are some specific Ribbon tricks for doing this, which are covered in later chapters, but for now you'll focus on giving the user a way to rename a worksheet.

You'll start, once again, by going into Excel and creating a new Excel file. Save it in a macro-enabled (`.xlsm`) format, as you'll need to rely on macros to work your magic.

With the Excel file open, the next step is to build your macro so that you can link it up to the `editBox` later. For now, create VBA code similar to the following, and store it in a standard module:

```
Private Function shtRename(sCallSheet As String) As Boolean
    On Error Resume Next
    ActiveSheet.Name = sCallSheet
    If Err.Number = 0 Then shtRename = True
End Function

Public Sub RenameSheet()
   Dim sNewSheetName As String

    sNewSheetName = InputBox("Please enter a new name for the sheet.")
    If shtRename(sNewSheetName) = False Then
      MsgBox "There was a problem and I could not" & vbCrLf & _
            "rename your sheet. Please try again.", _
            vbOKOnly + vbCritical, "Error!"
    End If
End Sub
```

It's important to understand the purpose of not only these two routines but also the individual parts. Of course, these examples can also be enhanced, such as to provide more elegant error messages. The focus here, however, is on working with the `editBox`.

- `shtRename` is a function that renames the sheet. `On Error` is used to allow the routine to continue even if an error is encountered in the process. A function was used here, as it can test whether an error was encountered and return a true/false statement indicating whether the renaming was successful.
- `RenameSheet` then calls the function and tests whether it was successful. If it wasn't, it informs the user.

To test this, run the RenameSheet macro and give it a name when prompted. Notice that your worksheet will be renamed. If you supply an invalid parameter, however, such as an existing sheet name, you will get an error message.

Now that you have some functional code, save and close the file, and then open it in the CustomUI Editor.

Again, because the idea is to be running these customizations without relying on built-in tabs or groups, you need to supply your own. Apply the RibbonBase template, and insert the following XML code between the `<tabs>` and `</tabs>` tags:

```
<tab id = "rxtabCustom"
   label="My Tools"
   insertBeforeMso="TabHome">
   <group id="rxgrpCustom"
```

```
        label="Worksheet">
        <editBox id="rxtxtRename"
           label="Rename sheet to:"
           imageMso="SignatureLineInsert"
           keytip="R"
           sizeString="123456789012345"
           onChange="rxtxtRename_Click"/>
    </group>
</tab>
```

TIP **Now you will notice that even though there is no user interface to work with, the code still specifies the custom tab's position before the Home tab. This is OK, as the built-in tabs are merely hidden, not completely destroyed, when you create a new user interface from scratch.**

TIP **When working with the** `sizeString` **attribute, it can be helpful to type out the number of characters with incrementing numbers so that you can quickly determine the number of characters allowed. As shown in the example, "123456789012345" is 15 characters, and "123456789012345678901" would be 21 characters.**

Now validate your XML, copy the callback signature, and save and close the file. Upon reopening the file in Excel, you should now see the `editBox` on your custom tab, as shown in Figure 6-24.

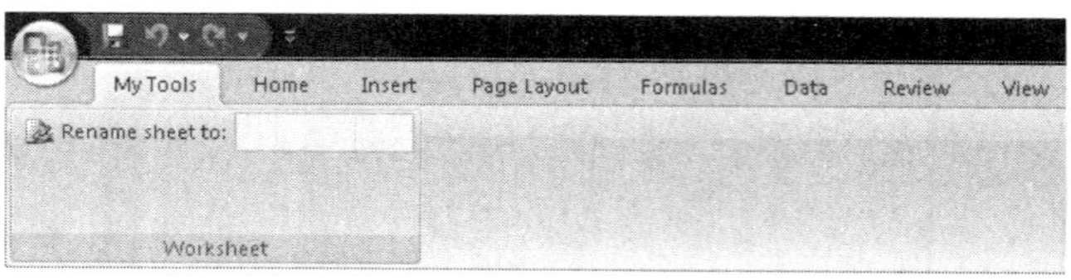

Figure 6-24: editBox example in Excel

You have not yet implemented the callbacks, so the `editBox` obviously won't work. Therefore, jump straight into the VBE, locate the standard module, and paste in the callback signature.

In reviewing the VBA that was written earlier, you can see that you could not call this procedure directly from the callback. While that worked well in other examples, in this case we needed to determine whether the name already existed and check for other errors that would require the user to provide the sheet name twice.

In order to accomplish our objective, we used the callback to run a series of functions. This may seem a little complex right now, but it is an important technique for you to become familiar with. To demonstrate this, put the following line in your callback and give it a test. Just don't forget to remove it once you're convinced:

```
Call RenameSheet
```

Fortunately, the `onChange` callback actually passes the text value that the user typed into the `editBox`. Now you have a couple of options. You could opt to pass the user's response as a parameter to the already written routine, or you could just integrate the required portions right in the callback. The latter sounds like a much better and more direct approach, so that will be your next step.

You want to copy the contents of the `RenameSheet` procedure into the callback, but make sure that you do not copy the following two lines:

```
Dim sNewSheetName As String
sNewSheetName = InputBox("Please enter a new name for the sheet.")
```

Those two lines were used to ask the user for a new worksheet name, before you had the `editBox` at your disposal. The user can now input the new sheet name right in the `editBox` before the procedure is run, so you don't need those lines at all. The only problem that causes is that the callback now refers to the `sNewSheetName` variable, which has not been declared. You need to update the name to refer to the string that is passed to the callback: `text`.

The adjusted callback will look as follows:

```
'Callback for rxtxtRename onChange
Sub rxtxtRename_Click(control As IRibbonControl, text As String)
    If shtRename(text) = False Then
      MsgBox "There was a problem and I could not" & vbCrLf & _
             "rename your sheet. Please try again.", _
             vbOKOnly + vbCritical, "Error!"
    End If
End Sub
```

Once you have your callback set up like the preceding example, jump out of the VBE, save the file, and click the My Tools tab. Type in a new name, and watch as the worksheet tab is updated.

A Word Example

In the previous Word example, you built a `checkBox` control to show and hide the Style Inspector. One thing that was lacking, however, was a way to easily set the width. The `editBox` is the perfect control for that purpose, so in this example you'll learn how two controls can be set on a Ribbon group to interact with and complement each other. You'll keep the `checkBox` control in place, but also add an `editBox` to the Ribbon group. The purpose of the `editBox` will be to give users a place to enter whatever width they'd like to see.

To get started, open the Word `editBox` example file that you worked on earlier in this chapter and save it under a new name. (Why reinvent the wheel if you already have half the code, right?) Remember to keep it in a `.docm` format, as you will still need to use the macros.

Now open the new file in the CustomUI Editor and add the following XML code right before the </group> tag:

```
<editBox id="rxtxtStyleWidth"
   label="Width"
   sizeString="1234567890"
   onChange="rxtxtStyleWidth_change"/>
```

Again, validate the XML, save the file, and copy the `rxtxtStyleWidth` callback signature. Close the document in the CustomUI Editor and open it in Word. If you activate the View tab, you'll see your UI modifications, which should look the same as what is shown in Figure 6-25. The Custom Options group now has the Width `editBox` below the Style Inspector `checkBox`.

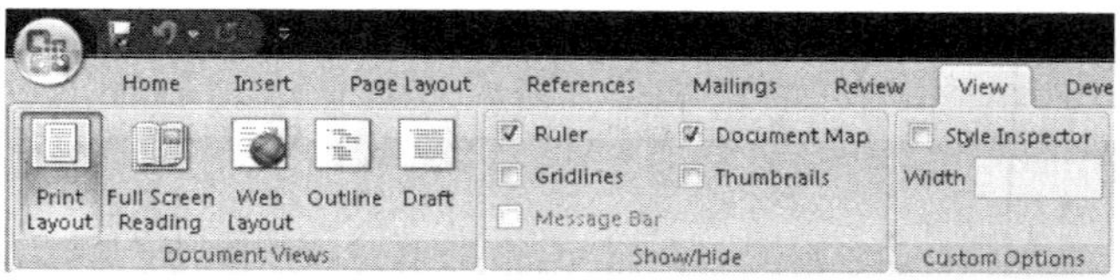

Figure 6-25: The Style Inspector Width editBox

Now that you've satisfied your curiosity about the new look, it's time to program your callbacks to fire. Head back into the VBE and paste your callback signature into the standard module that holds the rest of your Ribbon code.

The next step, if you haven't already thought this through, is to determine how the `editBox` control will interact with the existing `checkBox` control. You know that users are going to enter the width into the `editBox`, so what happens when they do this? In addition, what if they enter a value when the `checkBox` isn't true? To deal with these eventualities, you need to save that value for later access. Obviously, this isn't an exhaustive list of potential actions that a user could take, but it illustrates the need to think through a wide gamut of possibilities. It would be so much easier to write code if only we could control the user, but we do what we can to predict and provide accordingly.

For now, you'll learn a fundamental step, which is to store a value from the `editBox`. To do this, set up a new global variable at the top of your module (just under the Option Explicit line, which is at the top of all modules if you are following our recommended best practices):

```
Dim dblStyleAreaWidth as Double
```

TIP **Setting this up as a `Double`, unlike a `Long` or an `Integer` data type, enables you to hold decimal values. This is important, as not all users will want to use round numeric increments as their Inspector widths.**

Next, look at your new callback signature and modify it to read as shown here:

```
'Callback for rxtxtStyleWidth onChange
Sub rxtxtStyleWidth_change(control As IRibbonControl, text As String)
```

```
    On Error Resume Next
    dblStyleAreaWidth = CDbl(text)
    If Err.Number <> 0 Then
      MsgBox "Sorry, you must enter a numerical value in this field!"
      text = ""
    Else
      ActiveWindow.StyleAreaWidth = InchesToPoints(dblStyleAreaWidth)
    End If
End Sub
```

This might look a little confusing, but it breaks down as follows: The text from the `editBox` is passed to the routine and converted to a `Double` by way of the `CDbl` method. The reason why error handling was activated in the previous line, however, is to check whether this failed. If it did, then the user is informed that they did not enter a number, and the `editBox` is cleared. If the value was numerical, no error would be triggered, so the width is set to the value.

Keep in mind that if the `checkBox` is not set to true, then nothing will appear to happen. In fact, every time the number is changed in the `editBox`, the value is passed to the `dblStyleAreaWidth` variable and stored there for you.

The value is stored, but there is still one small thing you need to do before your function will work as intended. You might be wondering how the value is pulled *from* that variable when you need it.

The answer, currently, is that it isn't. You need to modify the `ShowStyleInspector` routine, programmed in the previous example, to make that happen. Therefore, take a look at that routine and change the first line to read as follows:

```
ActiveWindow.StyleAreaWidth = InchesToPoints(dblStyleAreaWidth)
```

That's all you need to do here. Now you can close the VBE, save the file, and start to play with the controls. Enter a new number in the `editBox`, and check and uncheck the `checkBox`. The Style Inspector window will react to your requests.

NOTE This setup does not deal with a couple of things. First, the Style Inspector width can only go so far. Currently, if you change it to a number above the maximum threshold, calculated as half of the points value of the `ActiveWindow.UseableWidth`, it just won't do anything. Second, if a user were so inclined, they could still go into the Word Options screen to set this width property and it would not be reflected in your Ribbon controls. However, the chances of this approach are quite slim.

An Access Example

This example again builds on the previously illustrated database used in the last section, so if you need a refresher on the detailed steps, you can review the process there as well. Here, you'll add the capability to rename forms from the Ribbon by specifying the old form name and then providing a new name. This involves using two `editBox` controls, and invalidating the UI.

To get started, create a copy of the project you were working on for the `checkBox` example (or download the complete `checkBox` example from the website) and open the new file. Create a new form in the database project. We'll use this new form to test the renaming procedure.

Next, navigate to the USysRibbons table and copy the XML code from the RibbonXML field into a new instance of the CustomUI Editor.

You need to add two new `editBoxes` to this project, and the most sensible place seems to be under the Show Systems Objects `checkBox` that you created earlier. To add the `editBoxes`, insert the following XML just before the last `</group>` line:

```
<editBox id="rxtxtRenameFrom"
   label="Rename Form:"
   getText="rxtxtRenameFrom_getText"
   onChange="rxtxtRenameFrom_change"/>
<editBox id="rxtxtRenameTo"
   label="Rename To:  "
   getText="rxtxtRenameTo_getText"
   onChange="rxtxtRenameTo_change"/>
```

Now you need to add one more piece to your XML in order to be able to invalidate the UI. Recall that invalidating the UI causes the entire Ribbon to reload so that it will incorporate the new objects. To accomplish this, you must capture the `IRibbonUI` object, which requires you to modify the opening `CustomUI` tag to read as follows:

```
<customUI
   onLoad="rxIRibbonUI_onLoad"
   xmlns="http://schemas.microsoft.com/office/2006/01/customui">
```

Once you've done all this, validate the XML, and then copy all the code from the CustomUI Editor. Paste this back into the RibbonXML field in your database, replacing the code that was in the field.

Now, head back into the CustomUI Editor, generate the callbacks, and copy the following callbacks into the modRibbonX module in the Access Project:

```
rxIRibbonUI_onLoad
rxtxtRenameFrom_getText
rxtxtRenameFrom_change
rxtxtRenameTo_getText
rxtxtRenameTo_change
```

Before you start modifying these routines, you need to set up two global variables. This is done by placing the following two lines just beneath the Option lines that should appear at the top of the module, as mentioned earlier:

```
Dim RibbonUI As IRibbonUI
Dim sRenameFrom As String
```

The purpose of the first variable is to hold the `RibbonUI` object in memory so that you can invalidate it, forcing the Ribbon controls to be rebuilt. The second variable will hold the name of the form that you wish to rename. This variable is important, as it can be referenced in other routines that need to use the value.

Now that the global variables are set up, it's time to modify the callback signatures. The first is the `onLoad` signature that captures the `ribbon` object. It should look as follows:

```
'Callback for customUI.onLoad
Sub rxIRibbonUI_onLoad(ribbon As IRibbonUI)
    Set RibbonUI = ribbon
End Sub
```

Next, you want to deal with the rest of the callbacks. They should look as follows:

```
`Callback for rxtxtRenameFrom getText
Sub rxtxtRenameFrom_getText(control As IRibbonControl, _
    ByRef returnedVal)
    returnedVal = sRenameFrom
End Sub

'Callback for rxtxtRenameTo getText
Sub rxtxtRenameTo_getText(control As IRibbonControl, ByRef returnedVal)
    returnedVal = " "
End Sub

'Callback for rxtxtRenameFrom onChange
Sub rxtxtRenameFrom_change(control As IRibbonControl, text As String)
    On Error Resume Next
    sRenameFrom = CurrentProject.AllForms(text).Name
    If Err.Number <> 0 Then
      'Table does not exist, so clear the editBox
      MsgBox "That table does not exist!"
      sRenameFrom = " "
      RibbonUI.InvalidateControl ("rxtxtRenameFrom")
    End If
    On Error GoTo 0
End Sub

'Callback for rxtxtRenameTo onChange
Sub rxtxtRenameTo_change(control As IRibbonControl, text As String)
    Dim sOldName As String

    On Error Resume Next
    'Check if from name is valid
    sOldName = CurrentProject.AllForms(sRenameFrom).Name
    If Err.Number <> 0 Then
      MsgBox "Specify a valid table to rename first!"
      GoTo EarlyExit
    End If

    'Attempt to rename the table to new name
    DoCmd.Rename text, acForm, sOldName
```

```
    If Err.Number <> 0 Then
MsgBox "Sorry, that is an invalid name. " _
    & "Please enter a different name"
      GoTo EarlyExit
    End If

    'Rename was successful, so clear the editBoxes
    sRenameFrom = " "
    RibbonUI.InvalidateControl ("rxtxtRenameFrom")
    RibbonUI.InvalidateControl ("rxtxtRenameTo")

EarlyExit:
    On Error GoTo 0
End Sub
```

These routines are built on the following methods:

- The `rxtxtRenameFrom_getText` routine returns the text displayed in the `RenameFrom` text box. Every time this routine is called, whether that's at the time the tab is initially activated or when the control has specifically been invalidated, it will check the value (if any) that is held in the global variable `sRenameFrom` and place the value in the `editBox`.
- The `rxtxtRenameTo_getText` callback is very similar to the above, but it does not use a global variable to hold a value. It simply returns a blank space every time it is called. This may seem strange, but you'll never need to store a value for this `editBox`. If the renaming is successful, the `editBox rxtxtRenameTo_getText` is cleared by invalidating it. If it is not successful, then the user must reconfirm the value in this `editBox` to fire its code, so storing the value is not necessary.

NOTE If you've done any programming in VBA, you'll find the use of the blank space a little jarring. To conform to best practices, most coders would never commit such an atrocity to clear a value from a control. They would instead provide the `vbnullstring` constant, which equates to a Null value. Unfortunately, XML requires that any string data type, of which the `editBox` text length is one, be at least one character long.

The `rxtxtRenameFrom_change` routine uses a trick to test whether the form name supplied is valid. It checks by asking for the supplied form's name. If it can be provided, then the form must exist. If not, then the user must have provided an invalid form because every form has a name. In the case of a user providing an invalid name, the control is cleared by invalidating it.

The `rxtxtRenameTo_change` routine is the most complicated routine in the set. It first checks to ensure that the form the user has asked to be renamed exists. This is necessary in case the first `editBox` has been left blank. If this test passes successfully, then the routine tries to rename the form to the value provided by the user in the `rxtxtRenameTo editBox`. Because it is possible for a user to provide an invalid name (one reserved by Access, that of an existing form, or one that uses forbidden characters), the code checks whether an error was encountered during the renaming process. If so, then the user receives an error message and the editBox is cleared. If there was no error and this test passes, the renaming was successful, and therefore both editBoxes are cleared by invalidation.

Finally, you are ready to save the VBA project. You need to close and reload your database so that the RibbonUI modifications can take effect.

In your new UI, type the name of the temporary table that you created in the first `editBox`, and the new name that you'd like to call it in the second `editBox`, as shown in Figure 6-26.

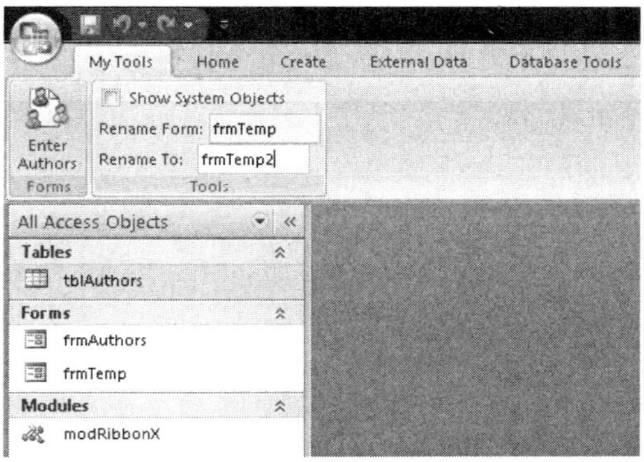

Figure 6-26: Renaming a form

Upon pressing the Enter key, you'll see that the `frmTemp` form will be renamed to the name that you provided. Try providing an invalid name in the first `editBox`, or try to give the form the same name of an existing object, such as repeating a table name. Note how the error handling informs the user about the issue.

The toggleButton Element

A `toggleButton` is used to alternate between states — such as turning some feature on and off — when it is pressed. For example, you could use this button to turn the ruler in Word on and off, or to switch from the Page Break view in Excel, or to hide/unhide a form in Access. Whatever way you use it, you are alternating between two possible states of an object, control, and so on.

Required Attributes of the toggleButton Element

The `toggleButton` requires any one of the `id` attributes listed in Table 6-13.

Table 6-13: Required Attributes of the toggleButton Element

ATTRIBUTE	WHEN TO USE
id	When creating your own toggleButton
idMso	When using an existing Microsoft toggleButton
idQ	When creating a toggleButton shared between namespaces

The `toggleButton` also requires the `onAction` callback shown in Table 6-14.

Table 6-14: Required Callback of the toggleButton Element

DYNAMIC ATTRIBUTE	ALLOWED VALUES	VBA CALLBACK SIGNATURE
onAction	1 to 4096 characters	Sub OnAction (control As IRibbonControl, selectedId As String, selectedIndex As Integer)

Optional Static and Dynamic Attributes with Callback Signatures

The `toggleButton` may have one of the `insert` attributes shown in Table 6-15.

Table 6-15: Optional insert Attributes of the toggleButton Element

INSERT ATTRIBUTE	ALLOWED VALUES	DEFAULT VALUE	WHEN TO USE
insertAfterMso	Valid Mso Group	Insert at end of group	Insert after Microsoft control
insertBeforeMso	Valid Mso Group	Insert at end of group	Insert before Microsoft control
insertAfterQ	Valid Group idQ	Insert at end of group	Insert after shared namespace control
insertBeforeQ	Valid Group idQ	Insert at end of group	Insert before shared namespace control

In addition, it may have any or all of the attributes listed in Table 6-16.

Table 6-16: Optional Attributes and Callbacks of the toggleButton Element

STATIC ATTRIBUTE	DYNAMIC ATTRIBUTE	ALLOWED VALUES	DEFAULT VALUE	VBA CALLBACK SIGNATURE FOR DYNAMIC ATTRIBUTE
description	getDescription	1 to 4096 characters	(none)	Sub GetDescription (control As IRibbonControl, ByRef returnedVal)
enabled	getEnabled	true, false, 1, 0	true	Sub GetEnabled (control As IRibbonControl, ByRef returnedVal)
image	getImage	1 to 4096 characters	(none)	Sub GetImage (control As IRibbonControl, ByRef returnedVal)
imageMso	getImage	1 to 4096 characters	(none)	Same as above
keytip	getKeytip	1 to 3 characters	(none)	Sub GetKeytip (control As IRibbonControl, ByRef returnedVal)
label	getLabel	1 to 4096 characters	(none)	Sub GetLabel (control As IRibbonControl, ByRef returnedVal)
(none)	getPressed	true, false, 1, 0	(none)	Sub GetPressed(control As IRibbonControl, ByRef returnedVal)
screentip	getScreentip	1 to 4096 characters	(none)	Sub GetScreentip (control As IRibbonControl, ByRef returnedVal)
showImage	getShowImage	true, false, 1, 0	true	Sub GetShowImage (control As IRibbonControl, ByRef returnedVal)
showLabel	getShowLabel	true, false, 1, 0	true	Sub GetShowLabel (control As IRibbonControl, ByRef returnedVal)
size	getSize	normal, large	normal	Sub GetSize (control As IRibbonControl, ByRef returnedVal)

Continued

Table 6-16 *(continued)*

STATIC ATTRIBUTE	DYNAMIC ATTRIBUTE	ALLOWED VALUES	DEFAULT VALUE	VBA CALLBACK SIGNATURE FOR DYNAMIC ATTRIBUTE
supertip	getSupertip	1 to 4096 characters	(none)	Sub GetSupertip (control As IRibbonControl, ByRef returnedVal)
tag	(none)	1 to 4096 characters	(none)	(none)
visible	getVisible	true, false, 1, 0	true	Sub GetVisible (control As IRibbonControl, ByRef returnedVal)

Allowed Children Objects of the toggleButton Element

The `toggleButton` does not support any child objects.

Parent Objects of the toggleButton Element

The `toggleButton` control can be placed within any of the following controls:

- `box`
- `buttonGroup`
- `dynamicMenu`
- `group`
- `menu`
- `officeMenu`
- `splitButton`

Graphical View of toggleButton Attributes

Figure 6-27 is a sample customization that displays all of the visible graphical attributes that you can set on the `toggleButton` control.

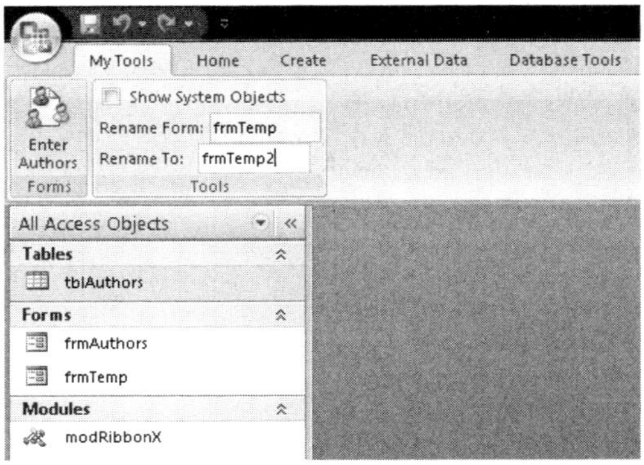

Figure 6-27: Graphical view of toggleButton attributes

Using Built-in toggleButton Controls

Quite a few built-in `toggleButton` controls are used by Microsoft in the Ribbon. They range from font styles to borders to paragraph alignment tools. This example adds four built-in `toggleButtons` to a custom tab. It includes one of the controls not prominent in the Ribbon, despite being a built-in control.

Create a new Word file to house the example. You won't need any macros for this example, so a `.docx` file type will work just fine. After saving the file, open it in the CustomUI Editor, apply the RibbonBase template, and insert the following XML code between the `<tabs>` and `</tabs>` tags:

```
<tab id="rxtabCustom"
   label="My Tools"
   insertBeforeMso="TabHome">
   <group id="rxgrpFormats"
      label="Formatting">
      <toggleButton idMso="Bold"/>
      <toggleButton idMso="Italic"/>
      <toggleButton idMso="Underline"/>
      <toggleButton idMso="UnderlineDouble"/>
   </group>
</tab>
```

Once you've validated your code, save the file and open it in Word. After clicking the My Tools tab, you should be looking at the group shown in Figure 6-28. It can be a little frustrating to have the label displayed, but it helps to illustrate the next point.

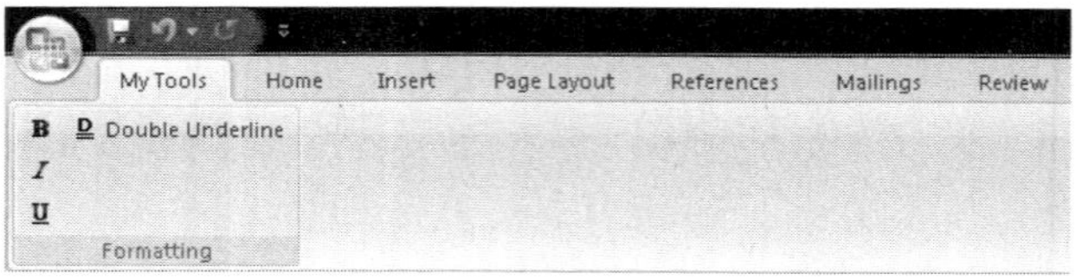

Figure 6-28: The My Tools tab in Word

Although there are consistencies between the applications, there are also some inconsistencies present. Try creating a new Excel file and using the exact same XML code to create your new UI. The result will look like what is shown in Figure 6-29.

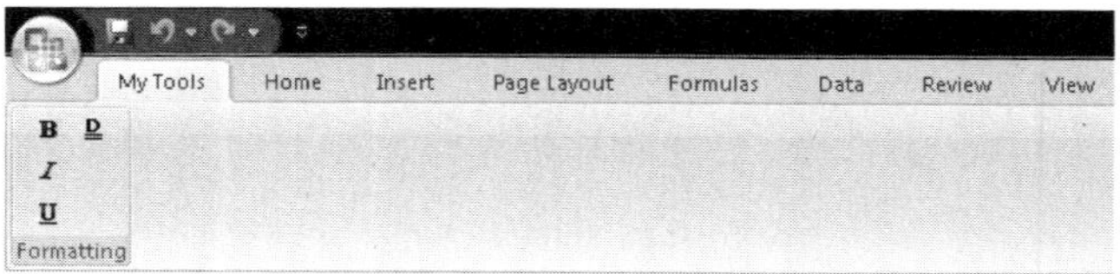

Figure 6-29: The My Tools tab in Excel

Notice how Excel hides the caption for the Double Underline, whereas Word prominently displays it. Hiding the caption was covered in the button control example at the beginning of the chapter, so you already know how to do that. The point is to illustrate some of the nuances that you should be aware of.

Before moving into the following examples, try typing some text in your document (or worksheet) cell and playing with the formatting controls. They will toggle on and off with the setting. Isn't it reassuring that it is becoming relatively easy to insert a customization that functions just as you'd expect?

Creating Custom Controls

It is now time to look at some examples of creating your own custom controls in Excel, Word, and Access. The Word example provides a new tool that enables you to use image placeholders, rather than store the entire image in a document. The Excel and Access examples continue to build upon previous examples by adding extra functionality.

An Excel Example

To show off the features of the `toggleButton`, this example revisits the Prepaid Expense schedule that was used earlier in this chapter in the custom button example. We'll add the capability to turn a custom view on or off, thereby allowing users to show or hide the Expense To column, shown in Figure 6-30.

	A	B	C	D	E	F
1		Do It All Home Improvement (un) Ltd.				
2		Prepaid Expenses				
3		January 31, 2007				
4						
5	Vendor Name	Opening Balance	Additions	Usage	Ending Balance	Expense To
6	Mr Shingles Roofing	4,376.53		534.67	3,841.86	Roofing
7	Tremblay Gutters	8,018.98	35.00		8,053.98	Roofing
8	Light Em Up Electric	2,945.52	56.00	23.00	2,978.52	Electric
9	Dirtscapers Inc.	3,915.40			3,915.40	Landscaping
10	Green Thumb Plants	631.84			631.84	Landscaping
11		19,888.27	91.00	557.67	19,421.60	

Figure 6-30: Prepaid Expense schedule showing the Expense To column

Are you ready to get started? Open the previous example, or use the file `button-Monthly Roll Forward.xlsm` from the book's website. Save the file with a new name, but don't head over to the CustomUI Editor quite yet. There's a bit of work to be done here first.

It's time to set up the custom views that you will need to make this work. Therefore, before you do anything else, go to the View tab and click Custom Views. Select Add and call the view `cvw_Show`. This view will be used to return to a full view of the worksheet, with all columns showing.

Next, you'll want to set up the second view that will hide the Expense To column. To do that, click Close to close the Custom Views window and return to the main Excel interface, and then hide column F. You'll notice now that your cursor is missing, and that the line between columns E and G seems to be selected. This is a cosmetic issue that can be resolved by selecting cell A1, and then returning to Custom Views. This time, add a new custom view called `cvw_Hide`. Close the Custom Views window again.

TIP **If you make a mistake when setting up your view, you can replace it by setting up a new view the way you like it and then saving it with the name of the view that you want to replace.**

Now it's time to record the macro to toggle the views on and off. Click the Record Macro button, which is found on both the status bar and the Developer tab. With the recorder on, use the following steps to record the process:

1. Go back to the View tab.
2. Click Custom Views.
3. Select the `cvw_Hide` view and choose Show.
4. Click Custom Views again.
5. Select the `cvw_Show` view and choose Show.
6. Go back to the Developer tab and stop the Macro recorder.

You may be wondering why you did this. The answer will become obvious when you open the VBE and look at the code that was recorded. You'll see the following:

```
ActiveWorkbook.CustomViews("cvw_Hide").Show
ActiveWorkbook.CustomViews("cvw_Show").Show
```

Notice that it generated only two lines, which are fairly self-explanatory. These will come in very handy in a moment, when you are programming the callbacks.

Your next step, though, is to set up the new `toggleButton` on the Ribbon. Save your file, close it in Excel, and open it in the CustomUI Editor. Insert the following XML just before the `</group>` tag:

```
<toggleButton id="rxtglHideExpense"
   label="Hide Expenses"
   imageMso="FieldList"
   size="large"
   onAction="rxtglHideExpense_Click"/>
```

As always, validate the code, save the file, and remember to copy the new `rxtgl-HideExpense_Click` callback signature before closing the file. Open the file in Excel, jump into the VBE, and paste the callback signature into the standard module that contains the existing code.

It's now time to modify the callback to do what you need. Once again, you'll want to set up a `Select Case` statement to evaluate which action to take when the button is clicked. Like the `checkBox`, the RibbonX code passes a parameter named `pressed` to the routine when it is fired. This makes your job very easy, as you merely need to paste the appropriate lines into the case statement, as shown here:

```
`Callback for rxtglHideExpense onAction
Sub rxtglHideExpense_Click(control As IRibbonControl, _
    pressed As Boolean)
    Select Case pressed
        Case True
            ActiveWorkbook.CustomViews("cvw_Hide").Show
        Case False
            ActiveWorkbook.CustomViews("cvw_Show").Show
    End Select
End Sub
```

Now that the callback is programmed and completely operational, head back to the Excel interface and click the Demo tab. Congratulations! You've successfully added automation. Note that when the sheet opens, the `toggleButton` is not highlighted and column F is visible. However, clicking the Hide Expenses button changes the view to that shown in Figure 6-31.

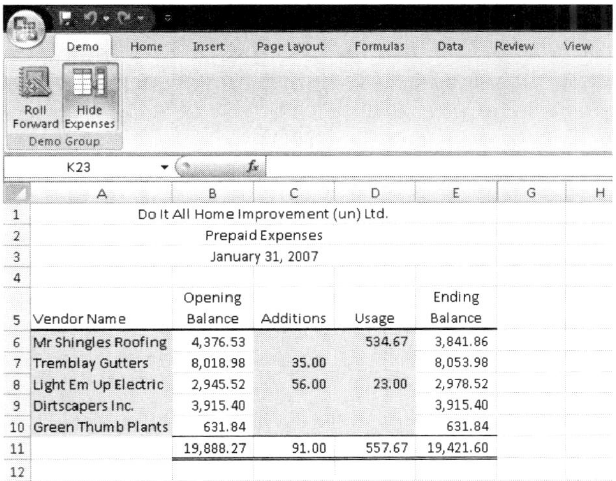

Figure 6-31: Prepaid Expense schedule under mask of a custom view

Clicking the Hide Expenses button again will display Column F, and revert the Hide Expenses `toggleButton` to its unselected state, as shown in Figure 6-32.

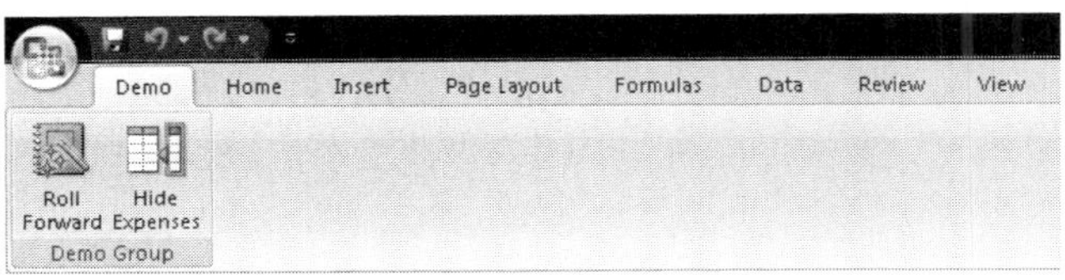

Figure 6-32: Hide Expenses toggleButton in its unselected state

You should be aware that this example is not set up to deal with the issue caused when the workbook is saved with the `cvw_Hide` view active. In that case, when the workbook was opened, the `toggleButton` would show unselected, but the view with the hidden column would be active. A couple of clicks by the user would resolve the disparity, but it's better to manage this with code. There are two ways to fix this issue:

- Set up a `Workbook_Open` procedure that sets the `cvw_Show` view to active when the workbook is opened.
- Set up the `getPressed` callback to test which view is active when the workbook is opened and return that state to the toggleButton.

A Word Example

If you work with long documents that contain numerous images, you will likely perceive a performance hit. Fortunately, there is a setting in Word that allows us to show placeholders for pictures, rather than render the entire image. Logically, this should provide a noticeable improvement in response time, and make users rather happy. The `toggleButton` is the ideal control for turning this setting on and off.

Since the previous example started a collection of custom tools, we'll add the `toggleButton` to the same group, as shown in Figure 6-33.

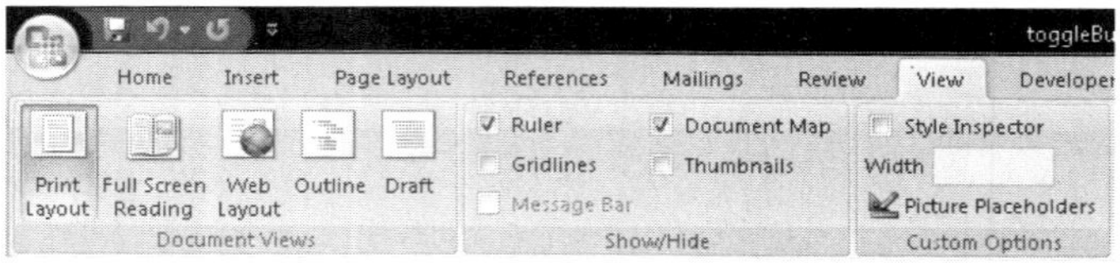

Figure 6-33: Using a toggleButton control

NOTE **If you want to create this in a new file, feel free to do so, as none of the VBA routines overlap. Be aware that you'll also need to create the XML framework.**

Start by saving a new copy of the example file from the previous illustration (or open a copy from the example files available at the website for this book). Make sure that the file is a macro-enabled (`.docm`) file, as this will require a little more work in the VBE.

Before you move to the XML arena, we recommend that you start in Word and record a macro that will do what you are trying to accomplish — that is, change the `ShowPicturePlaceholders` property. After all, if the VBA macro doesn't work, all the XML code in the world won't do any good.

In the Word file, start the Macro recorder. Once you've given the recorder a name for the macro, go to the Office button, choose Word Options, and click the Advanced button. Under the Show Document Content header, you'll find the setting for Show Picture Placeholders. Check the box, say OK, and stop the macro from recording. If you now check the VBE, you'll see that your code looks like the following:

```
ActiveWindow.View.ShowPicturePlaceHolders = True
```

This is fantastic, as it provides a short, concise, and fairly intuitive code snippet. You can easily change this value by setting it to true or false. Moreover, you can test it to determine the current value.

Confident that the code that will work, you can now set the XML markup in the CustomUI. Save the file, open it in the CustomUI Editor, and then insert the following XML just before the `</group>` tag:

```
<toggleButton id="rxtglPicHold"
   label="Picture Placeholders"
   getPressed="rxtglPicHold_getPressed"
   getImage="rxtglPicHold_getImage"
   onAction="rxtglPicHold_click"/>
```

There is just one more step in this part of the process. In this example, you want to invalidate a control, which means that you need to capture the `ribbon` object to a variable. To do this, you must include an `onLoad` statement in your XML. Therefore, at the top of the XML code, modify the opening tag to read as follows:

```
<customUI
   onLoad="rxIRibbonUI_onLoad"
   xmlns="http://schemas.microsoft.com/office/2006/01/customui">
```

As always, before you close the file in the CustomUI Editor, you need to validate the code. In addition, you also need to copy all three `rxtglPicHold` callback signatures and the `rxIRibbonUI_onLoad` signature.

Because activating your tab will generate missing callback errors, you might as well skip that for now and head straight into the VBE. Paste your callback signatures into the standard module that holds the rest of the code.

Now it's time to set the groundwork for linking your file together. First, create a variable to hold the `RibbonUI` object. At the top of your module, just under the Option Explicit line, insert the following line:

```
Private ribbonUI As IRibbonUI
```

Next, update your callback signatures. Because there are several signatures, it's best to review them one at a time. As we go through them in order and explain what each one does, keep in mind that all four functions will appear together in your code.

The first routine is triggered at load time, and captures the `ribbon` object to the `ribbonUI` variable for later use:

```
Private Sub rxIRibbonUI_onLoad(ribbon As IRibbonUI)
'Store the ribbonUI for later use
    Set ribbonUI = ribbon
End Sub
```

The `getPressed` routine, shown in the following code, is fired when the tab is first activated, and attempts to determine whether the control should show as pressed or not. In this case, it evaluates whether the `ShowPicturePlaceHolders` setting is true or false, and passes that back to the `returnedVal` parameter:

```
Public Sub rxtglPicHold_getPressed(control As IRibbonControl, _
    ByRef returnedVal)
    `Callback for rxtglPicHold getPressed
    returnedVal = _
        ActiveDocument.ActiveWindow.View.ShowPicturePlaceHolders
End Sub
```

The `getImage` routine was inserted to update the picture on the toggleButton depending on the state of the setting. If it is true, then it uses one picture (`SignatureInsertMenu`); and if it is false, then it displays the `DesignMode` image. This routine isn't strictly necessary, but it is an relatively easy way to jazz up your controls:

```
Public Sub rxtglPicHold_getImage(control As IRibbonControl, _
    ByRef returnedVal)
```

```
 'Callback for rxtglPicHold getImage
   Select Case ActiveDocument.ActiveWindow.View.ShowPicturePlaceHolders
       Case True
           returnedVal = "SignatureInsertMenu"
       Case False
           returnedVal = "DesignMode"
   End Select
End Sub
```

Last but not least is the actual `Click` routine. This is the routine that really controls what's going on. Whenever it is clicked, it sets the `ShowPicturePlaceHolders` property to the `toggleButton's pressed` state. (Remember that each click toggles the `pressed` state between `true` and `false`.) In addition, it invalidates the control, forcing the Ribbon to rerun the `getImage` and `getPressed` routines. By running those two routines, it can toggle the image with each press of the `toggleButton`.

```
Public Sub rxtglPicHold_click(control As IRibbonControl, _
    pressed As Boolean)
    `Callback for rxtglPicHold onAction
    ActiveDocument.ActiveWindow.View.ShowPicturePlaceHolders = pressed
    ribbonUI.InvalidateControl "rxtglPicHold"
End Sub
```

It's time to save and reload the document. Give it a try and take a moment to appreciate your handiwork!

An Access Example

This example builds on the prior database by adding some really neat functionality. Specifically, you'll build a group that only shows up when a specific form is opened, a truly contextual group. The new group will provide the capability to toggle between the DataSheet and Normal views.

To get started, make another copy of the database that we were working with in the previous example. Open the file and then copy the `RibbonUI` code from the USysRibbons table and paste it into the CustomUI Editor. Because you will typically want to hide this entire group, you'll need to create a brand-new group. It makes the most sense to put the new group between the two existing groups, so paste the following code between the `</group>` and `<group>` lines:

```
<group id="rxgrpFormTools"
   label="Form Tools"
   getVisible="rxgrpFormTools_getVisible">
   <toggleButton
      id="rxtglViewDataSheet"
      label="Show DataSheet View"
      onAction="rxtglViewDataSheet_click" />
</group>
```

Validate the code to ensure that it was typed correctly, and then copy the entire code listing, and paste it back into the RibbonUI field in your database. You'll then need to go back and copy the new callbacks into your modRibbonX VBA project as well. This time, you'll be copying the following:

```
rxgrpFormTools_getVisible
rxtglViewDataSheet_click
```

Again, you need to set up a global variable, so just underneath the existing ones, add the following:

```
Public bShowFormTools As Boolean
```

The purpose of the variable is to hold the state indicating whether the form is currently active, which in turn will determine whether the new group should be visible or not.

NOTE Because this will be referred to from another module later, it should be marked as *public*. Public variables can be "seen" from the other modules. In addition, the RibbonUI variable should also be marked as a public variable.

Now it's time to program your callbacks. Add code to the signatures so that they look as follows:

```
`Callback for rxgrpFormTools getVisible
Sub rxgrpFormTools_getVisible(control As IRibbonControl, _
    ByRef returnedVal)
    returnedVal = bShowFormTools
End Sub

`Callback for rxtglViewDataSheet onAction
Sub rxtglViewDataSheet_click(control As IRibbonControl, _
    pressed As Boolean)
    `Open the correct view
    Select Case pressed
        Case True
            DoCmd.OpenForm "frmAuthors", acFormDS
        Case False
            DoCmd.OpenForm "frmAuthors", acNormal
    End Select
End Sub
```

The `getVisible` callback pulls its value from the global variable the first time the group is activated, as well as whenever it is invalidated. The `rxtglViewDataSheet_click` routine, however, is a little more complex. It checks the state of the toggleButton, (`true` for clicked, `false` if not), and opens the form in Data Sheet or Normal View as appropriate. It also toggles the `Show Totals` variable to ensure that it will be hidden if in Normal View. By invalidating the control after the `Show Totals` variable is set, you know that it will always be in the correct state.

At this point, you may be wondering how this `toggleButton` ever shows up at all. The answer is that it will be triggered by launching the Enter Authors form. To do this, you need to add some event code that will be triggered by various form actions.

The easiest way to set up the required code is to open the form and set it to Design View. (You can change the view via the View button on the Home tab.) Once there, on the Design tab, click the Property Sheet button on the Tools group. Next, click the Event tab of the Property Sheet window, and then in the blank space next to the On Activate line. You'll notice that a little drop-down arrow and an ellipses (. . .) button appear. From the drop-down arrow, select [Event Procedure], and then click the . . . button to be taken to the VBE.

Notice that a new Forms module was created, and that you are now looking at an event procedure for the `Forms` object. Change this procedure to read as follows:

```
Private Sub Form_Activate()
   bShowFormTools = True
   RibbonUI.Invalidate
End Sub
```

MS Office forms have Activate and Deactivate events that fire each time the Ribbon UI is invalidated, so these are ideal events for controlling when a contextual group is visible or not. The preceding routine takes care of making sure that the group shows up when the form is activated, but you'll also need to set up the Deactivate event.

On the left side of the code pane, Form is selected; the right side shows Activate. On the right drop-down, select Deactivate, and notice how the event signature is placed in your code module. Adjust it to read as follows:

```
Private Sub Form_Deactivate()
   bShowFormTools = False
   RibbonUI.Invalidate
End Sub
```

These routines toggle the `bShowFormTools` values and invalidate the entire Ribbon in order to show or hide the group when the form is active or inactive, respectively.

TIP **In order to get a group's callbacks to fire, you may have to invalidate the entire Ribbon, instead of just the individual control.**

NOTE **Because there are rare instances when the Activate and Deactivate events aren't triggers, some developers might be tempted to use the** `onLoad` **and** `onClose` **events. However, these would leave the custom group visible when the user moves from one form to another without closing the "target" form.**

Now it's time to try it out. Save everything, and then close and reload your database. When you click the Enter Authors button, the form will still launch, and you should see the My Tools tab with the Form Tools group, as shown in Figure 6-34.

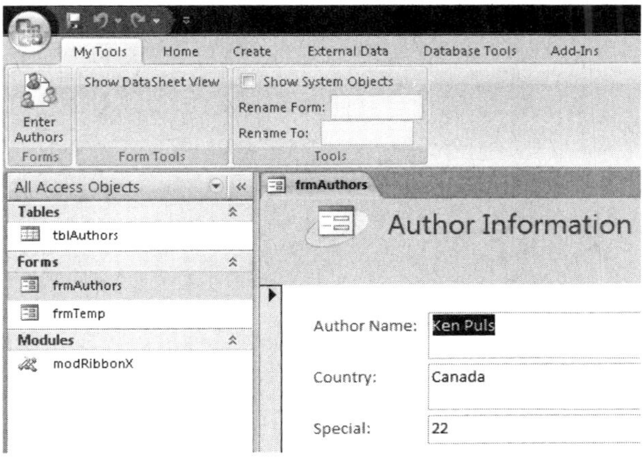

Figure 6-34: The visible Form Tools group

Now try clicking the Show DataSheet View toggleButton; both the form's display and the Ribbon group will change to appear as shown in Figure 6-35.

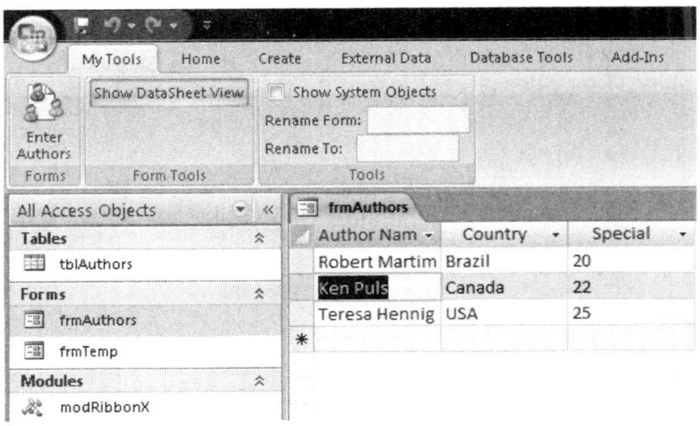

Figure 6-35: DataSheet view

Conclusion

This chapter provides several reference tables so that you can conveniently find the attributes and callback signatures associated with the various Ribbon controls. We also included images to illustrate where you can add visible attributes.

Our examples demonstrated a variety of required and optional features so that you will have the experience and confidence to expand and extrapolate the processes to work with your projects. We covered many of the most popular controls, such as the `button`, `checkBox`, `editBox`, and `toggleButton`. As the examples began to build on one another, you were exposed to just some of the richness that can be attained by using

Ribbon controls, both alone and in concert with other controls. Even with the variety of examples provided here, we've only begun to explore the limits of these and other controls. By now you are likely realizing that the appearance of your UI is limited only by your own imagination.

Now that you have a firm understanding of the most common Ribbon controls, you are ready to move into some more robust features. Chapter 7 is the next step, as it focuses on the `dropDown and comboBox` elements.

CHAPTER

7

comboBox and dropDown Controls

In the previous chapter, you learned about the button, checkBox, editBox, and toggleButton controls. This chapter explores two new controls: the comboBox and the dropDown. The comboBox and dropDown list are similar in a great many ways, including design, implementation, and appearance. They also have some important differences that are discussed in this chapter.

Before you can start exploring these two controls, you need to learn about the fundamental element that supports them: the item element. The chapter begins by exploring this critical piece.

Following the section on the item element, you'll find both the comboBox and dropDown sections, which explore these two elements in great detail. As in the previous chapter, examples are included for each application, some of which display the creation of static versions of controls, while others create fully dynamic versions. Whether you're working through the examples or just reading the chapter, you will appreciate seeing a fully functioning version. As you are preparing to work through the examples, we encourage you to download the companion files. The source code and files for this chapter can be found on the book's web site at www.wiley.com/go/ribbonx.

The item Element

The item element is used to create static items that must be used within a gallery, dropDown, or comboBox. This particular element is not intended for use on its own, but rather must be an integral part of other controls, such as those mentioned above.

Unlike other sections of this book, where we provide full working examples of the element being discussed, we review only the XML construct and discuss the structure of the `item` element. This departure from the pattern reflects the fact that the `item` element is so tightly integrated with the `comboBox`, `dropDown`, and gallery `controls` that it cannot be separated from them. Because of this, you need to know a little bit about `item` before you can move on. The way these are used may seem rather complicated for now, but rest assured that the processes will become surprisingly clear when you examine the `comboBox` and `dropDown` RibbonX elements later in this chapter.

Required Attributes of the item Element

Each `item` requires a unique `id` attribute, as described in Table 7-1.

Table 7-1: Required Attribute of the item Element

ATTRIBUTE	WHEN TO USE
id	Use this attribute to create your own item.

The `item` element has only one attribute, the `id`. As we just mentioned, the `item` control must be used in conjunction with other elements; therefore, it relies on the other elements for all other attributes.

NOTE Unlike other elements, there is no `idMso` or `idQ` attribute available for the `item` control.

Optional Static and Dynamic Attributes with Callback Signatures

Each `item` element can optionally make use of any or all of the attributes shown in Table 7-2.

Table 7-2: Optional Attributes for the item Element

STATIC ATTRIBUTE	DYNAMIC ATTRIBUTE	ALLOWED VALUES	DEFAULT VALUE	VBA CALLBACK SIGNATURE FOR DYNAMIC ATTRIBUTE
image	(none)	1 to 1024 characters	(none)	(none)
imageMso	(none)	1 to 1024 characters	(none)	(none)
label	(none)	1 to 1024 characters	(none)	(none)

Table 7-2 *(continued)*

STATIC ATTRIBUTE	DYNAMIC ATTRIBUTE	ALLOWED VALUES	DEFAULT VALUE	VBA CALLBACK SIGNATURE FOR DYNAMIC ATTRIBUTE
screentip	(none)	1 to 1024 characters	(none)	(none)
supertip	(none)	1 to 1024 characters	(none)	(none)

Did you notice the lack of callback signatures in Table 7-2?

It is important to understand that the `items` in the XML code underlying Ribbon modifications are always static. This is actually a good thing, as it means that you can provide a static list of items to the control without having to write a single line of VBA.

Don't misunderstand this to mean that you can't create items for a control on-the-fly using VBA, as that is not the case. When you create an item for a control, the callback is actually associated with the `Parent` object (i.e., the `comboBcx`, `dropDown`, or `gallery` control), not the actual item itself.

NOTE As you design your XML code, you are given a choice between using static `item` elements (specified in your XML), or dynamic elements (generated via the parent control's callback signature.) Whichever route you choose is mutually exclusive of the other. In other words, if you specify static items for a control, you cannot also specify dynamic `items` for that control as well.

Allowed Children Objects of the item Element

The `item` element does not support child objects of any kind, so it cannot have any embedded controls.

Parent Objects of the item Element

An `item` may only be used in the following controls:

- `comboBox`
- `dropDown`
- `gallery`

Graphical View of item Attributes

Figure 7-1 shows a `dropDown` control on a Ribbon group. It houses three static `item` elements that are written into the XML code. The callouts annotate where the `item`'s static attributes are displayed.

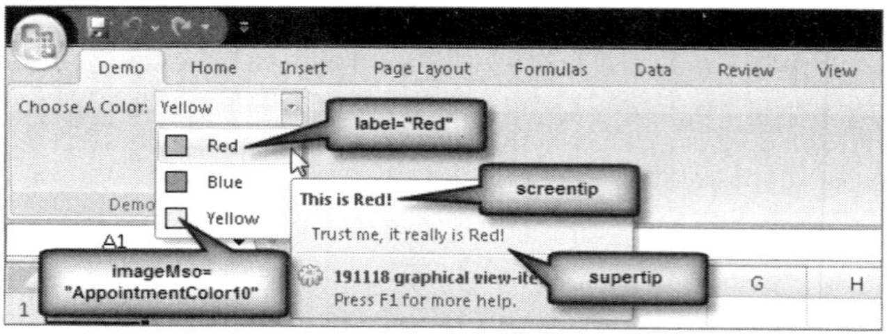

Figure 7-1: Graphical view of the item elements

Using Built-in Controls

You don't have the opportunity to leverage built-in `item` elements because Microsoft does not expose them for our use, but the chances are fairly good that you wouldn't want to use them anyway, so it's not really a big loss. If you did want to have some of these items in a control, you could just include the entire parent element in your Ribbon.

Creating Custom Controls

We explore the setup for the parent controls shortly, so this section focuses on the underlying XML code needed to create the static `item` elements demonstrated in Figure 7-1.

As mentioned earlier, Figure 7-1 makes use of a `dropDown` control to house these items. The `dropDown` control should be constructed, like all controls, with opening and closing XML tags. The following code goes between those tags:

```
<item id="rxitemddColor1"
    imageMso="AppointmentColor1"
    label="Red"
    screentip="This is Red!"
    supertip="Trust me, it really is Red!"/>
<item id="rxitemddColor2"
    imageMso="AppointmentColor2"
    label="Blue"
    screentip="This is Blue!"
    supertip="Trust me, it really is Blue!"/>
<item id="rxitemddColor3"
    imageMso="AppointmentColor10"
    label="Yellow"
    screentip="This is Yellow!"
    supertip="Trust me, it really is Yellow!"/>
```

As you review Figure 7-1, you will see each of the elements in the live representation on the Ribbon.

The comboBox Element

The `comboBox` control displays data based on a designated record source, and it is a hybrid of the `editBox` that we covered in Chapter 6 and the `dropDown` control that we review next.

One of the great features of a `comboBox` control is that, in addition to being able to pick something from the list, the user can also type something into the text box. In searching and selecting from the list, it acts like a "hot lookup," enabling users to skip to the closest match. As the user keeps typing, the choices are narrowed down. At any time, users may accept one of the displayed values or they may keep typing to create a new entry.

The `comboBox` is best used in the following situations:

- The list is very long and you wish to give users the capability to quickly jump to the appropriate place by typing a few keys. (The `fonts` control is a good example of this.)
- You wish to present users with a pre-defined list, but also want them to be able to add items to the list.

As mentioned earlier in the chapter, you can populate the `comboBox` with both static lists and dynamically created lists.

Required Attributes of the comboBox Element

The `comboBox` control requires any one of the `id` attributes shown in Table 7-3.

Table 7-3: Required id Attributes of the comboBox Element

ATTRIBUTE	WHEN TO USE
id	When creating your own comboBox
idMso	When using an existing Microsoft comboBox
idQ	When creating a comboBox shared between namespaces

Optional Static and Dynamic Attributes withCallback Signatures

In addition to the required `id` attribute, the `comboBox` control will optionally accept any one of the `insert` attributes listed in Table 7-4.

Table 7-4: Optional insert Attributes of the comboBox Element

INSERT ATTRIBUTE	ALLOWED VALUES	DEFAULT VALUE	WHEN TO USE
insertAfterMso	Valid Mso Group	Insert at end of group	Insert after Microsoft control
insertBeforeMso	Valid Mso Group	Insert at end of group	Insert before Microsoft control
insertAfterQ	Valid Group idQ	Insert at end of group	Insert after shared namespace control
insertBeforeQ	Valid Group idQ	Insert at end of group	Insert before shared namespace control

Finally, the `comboBox` may also be configured to use any or all of the optional attributes or callbacks shown in Table 7-5.

Table 7-5: Optional Attributes and Callbacks of the comboBox Element

STATIC ATTRIBUTE	DYNAMIC ATTRIBUTE	ALLOWED VALUES	DEFAULT VALUE	VBA CALLBACK SIGNATURE FOR DYNAMIC ATTRIBUTE
(none)	onChange	1 to 4096 characters	(none)	Sub OnChange (control As IRibbonControl, text As String)
enabled	getEnabled	true, false, 1, 0	true	Sub GetEnabled (control As IRibbonControl, ByRef returnedVal)
image	getImage	1 to 1024 characters	(none)	Sub GetImage (control As IRibbonControl, ByRef returnedVal)
imageMso	getImage	1 to 1024 characters	(none)	Same as above
(none)	getItemCount	1 to 1024	(none)	Sub GetItemCount (control As IRibbonControl, ByRef returnedVal)
(none)	getItemID	1 to 1024 characters	(none)	Sub GetItemID (control As IRibbonControl, index As Integer, ByRef id)
(none)	getItemImage	Unique text string	(none)	Sub GetItemImage (control As IRibbonControl, index As Integer, ByRef returnedVal)

Table 7-5 *(continued)*

STATIC ATTRIBUTE	DYNAMIC ATTRIBUTE	ALLOWED VALUES	DEFAULT VALUE	VBA CALLBACK SIGNATURE FOR DYNAMIC ATTRIBUTE
(none)	getItemLabel	1 to 1024 characters	(none)	Sub GetItemLabel (control As IRibbonControl, index As Integer, ByRef returnedVal)
(none)	getItem ↵ Screentip	1 to 1024 characters	(none)	Sub GetItemScreenTip (control As IRibbonControl, index As Integer, ByRef returnedVal)
(none)	getItemSupertip	1 to 1024 characters	(none)	Sub GetItemSuperTip (control As IRibbonControl, index As Integer, ByRef returnedVal)
keytip	getKeytip	1 to 3 characters	(none)	Sub GetKeytip (control As IRibbonControl, ByRef returnedVal)
label	getLabel	1 to 1024 characters	(none)	Sub GetLabel (control As IRibbonControl, ByRef returnedVal)
maxLength	(none)	1 to 1024	1024	(none)
screentip	getScreentip	1 to 1024 characters	(none)	Sub GetScreentip (control As IRibbonControl, ByRef returnedVal)
showImage	getShowImage	true, false, 1, 0	true	Sub GetShowImage (control As IRibbonControl, ByRef returnedVal)
showItem ↵ Attribute	(none)	true, false, 1, 0	true	(none)
showItemImage	(none)	true, false, 1, 0	true	(none)
showLabel	getShowLabel	true, false	true	Sub GetShowLabel (control As IRibbonControl, ByRef returnedVal)
sizeString	(none)	1 to 1024 characters	12*	(none)
supertip	getSupertip	1 to 1024 characters	(none)	Sub GetSupertip (control As IRibbonControl, ByRef returnedVal)

Continued

Table 7-5 *(continued)*

STATIC ATTRIBUTE	DYNAMIC ATTRIBUTE	ALLOWED VALUES	DEFAULT VALUE	VBA CALLBACK SIGNATURE FOR DYNAMIC ATTRIBUTE
tag	(none)	1 to 1024 characters	(none)	(none)
(none)	getText	1 to 4096 characters	(none)	Sub GetText (control As IRibbonControl, ByRef returnedVal)
visible	getVisible	true, false, 1, 0	true	Sub GetVisible (control As IRibbonControl, ByRef returnedVal)

NOTE **The default value for the `sizeString` attribute (if the attribute is not declared at all) is approximately `12`, but this varies depending on the characters used and the system font.**

Allowed Children Objects of the comboBox Element

The only child object that can be used with the `comboBox` element is the `item` element.

Parent Objects of the comboBox Element

The `comboBox` element may be nested within the following elements:

- `box`
- `group`

Graphical View of comboBox Attributes

Figure 7-2 gives a graphical representation of the visible attributes that can be set on the `comboBox` control.

Figure 7-2 shows all of the `comboBox` attributes except for the `screentip` and `supertip`. These two attributes only show when the `dropDown` list portion is not active; consequently, they could not be captured while showing the `dropDown` list.

Using Built-in Controls

Of all the controls in Excel and Word, probably the best known is the Fonts `comboBox`. If you are creating custom Ribbon tabs to group your most commonly used controls together, then you will certainly want to add this control. It is therefore the first one that we look at.

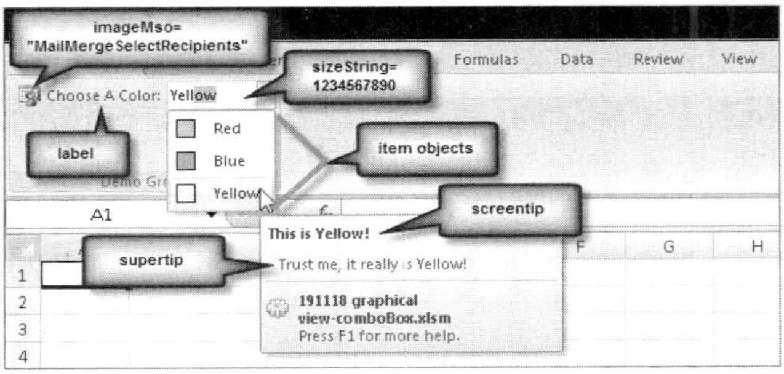

Figure 7-2: Graphical view of the comboBox elements

The XML code for the example that you are about to build is almost completely application agnostic; it will work equally well in Excel and Word, and it only requires a very minor change to work in Access. We'll go through examples for each application so that you will be comfortable and confident in all three.

NOTE The completed example files (`comboBox-Fonts.xlsx`, `comboBox-Fonts.docx`, and `comboBox-Fonts.accdb`) can be downloaded from the book's website at `www.wiley.com/go/ribbonx`.

Because we are only using built-in controls, this example does not require VBA. We'll begin with Excel, so start by creating and saving a new `xlsx` file. Open the file in the CustomUI Editor, apply the RibbonBase template you created in Chapter 2, and insert the following code between the `<tabs>` and `</tabs>` tags:

```
<tab id="rxtabDemo"
    label="Demo"
    insertBeforeMso="TabHome">
    <group id="rxgrpDemo"
        label="Demo">
    <comboBox idMso="Font"/>
    <comboBox idMso="FontSize"/>
    </group>
</tab>
```

Remember to validate your code to catch any pesky typing errors. Once you have done this, save the file, and open it in Excel. Navigate to the Demo tab and you will see the UI shown in Figure 7-3.

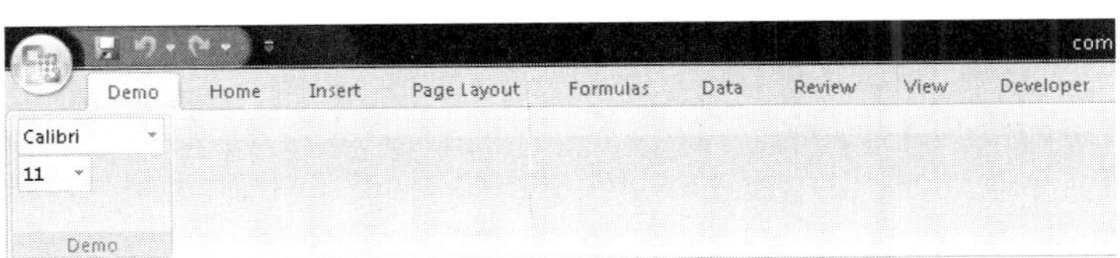

Figure 7-3: The Font and FontSize comboBox controls on a new Excel tab

With regard to differences between Excel and Word, this code is 100% application agnostic. Try it for yourself — create a new `.docx` file and open it in the CustomUI Editor. Enter the same XML code and save the file. (Remember to validate the code if you retyped it all by hand!) Upon opening Word, you'll see the Ribbon as it appears in Figure 7-4.

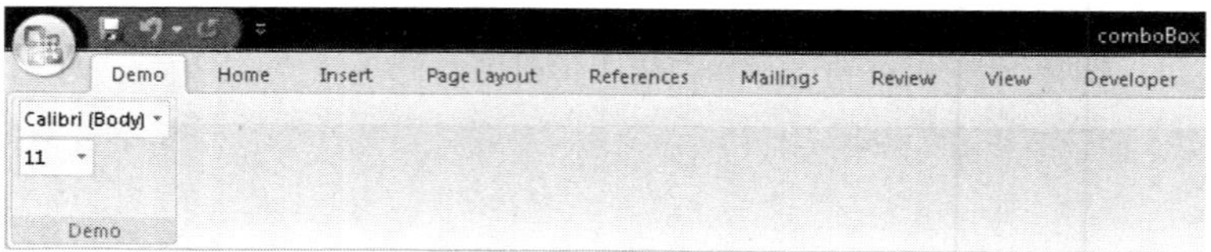

Figure 7-4: The Font and FontSize comboBox controls on a new Word tab

As we mentioned, there is a minor change required to get this code to work in Access. You merely need to revise the `insertBeforeMso` attribute, as `TabHome` is not a defined tab in Access. In other words, the `Demo` tab's `insertBeforeMso` attribute for Access should read as follows:

```
insertBeforeMso="TabHomeAccess"
```

With this code in place, when you reopen the database, the UI will appear as shown in Figure 7-5.

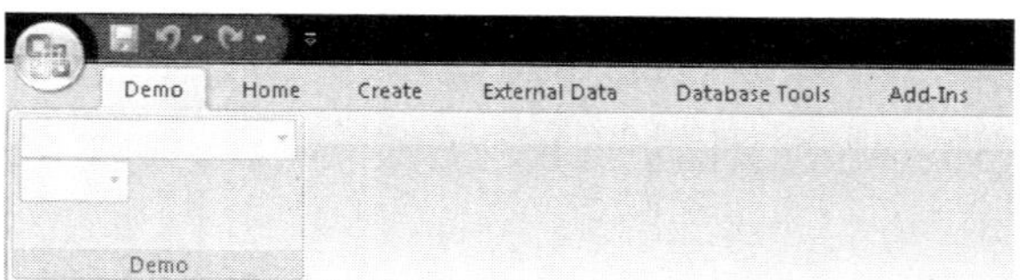

Figure 7-5: The Font and FontSize comboBox controls on a new Access tab

"But wait," you say, "that does not look exactly the same!" That's true — the name of the font is not displayed because nothing is open that has a font that can be edited. If you open a table or a form, you'll find that these controls are immediately enabled. Our example was intended to provide the added benefit of demonstrating when you might see the blank list, so you needn't be alarmed that your code might have failed.

Creating Custom Controls

Demonstrating how to use Font and FontSize `comboBox`es as was an easy example that you will reuse many times, but we can only get so far using Microsoft's built-in `comboBoxes`. It's time to look at some examples of building items that do things that Microsoft hasn't allowed for.

The Excel and Word examples in this section display how to employ static lists in the comboBox controls and incorporate the item controls that were covered in the first section of this chapter. With the Access example, we start to explore a dynamic comboBox control.

An Excel Example

For this example, we again assume that you have hidden the entire user interface. In addition, also imagine that in an attempt to make your application look less like Excel, you have hidden all the worksheet tabs. You still want users to be able to move between the three worksheets, however, so you need to provide some vehicle to accomplish this. In many ways, the comboBox can be an ideal control for this kind of navigation: It lists all the "pages" in your application, and allows users to type in a specific one that they may wish to jump to.

Naturally, you need a macro or two to make this work, so create a new macro-enabled Excel file (.xlsm). Save it, and then open it in the CustomUI Editor. Apply the RibbonBase template, and insert the following code between the <tabs> and </tabs> tags:

```
<tab id="rxtabDemo"
    label="Navigation"
    insertBeforeMso="TabHome">
    <group id="rxgrpNavigate"
        label="Navigate To">
        <comboBox id="rxcboSelectSheet"
            label="Activate:"
            onChange="rxcboSelectSheet_Click">
            <item id="rxitemcboSelectSheet1"
                label="Sheet1"/>
            <item id="rxitemcboSelectSheet2"
                label="Sheet2"/>
            <item id="rxitemcboSelectSheet3"
                label="Sheet3"/>
        </comboBox>
    </group>
</tab>
```

Notice that the comboBox makes use of the onChange callback to take action when an item is selected. In addition, this comboBox holds three items: Sheet1, Sheet2, and Sheet3. These items are static and cannot be changed from within the file; nor will the user be able to add additional items. This is a perfect fit for the goal of ensuring that users are able to navigate only to these worksheets.

Before you close the CustomUI Editor, be sure to validate your code for typing errors, and then copy the onChange callback.

CROSS-REFERENCE **For a refresher on working with callbacks and the CustomUI Editor, see Chapter 5.**

When you are back in Excel, open the VBE and paste the callback into a new standard module. Now you need to edit the callback to make it react as you wish. You can figure out how to do that by thinking through the order of events:

1. The user will select an item from the Worksheet list.
2. The callback will be triggered.
3. The selected value of the `comboBox` (in this case, the worksheet name) will be passed to the routine.
4. The worksheet will be activated.

So far so good, but there is one more piece that may cause a glitch: We stated that users can only select one of the sheets specified in the code. And what happens if they type in a different value? To deal with these eventualities, you should edit the callback signature to read as follows:

```
'Callback for rxcboSelectSheet onChange
Sub rxcboSelectSheet_Click(control As IRibbonControl, text As String)
    On Error Resume Next
    Worksheets(text).Activate
    If Err.Number <> 0 Then
        MsgBox "Sorry, that worksheet does not exist!"
    End If
End Sub
```

The second line of code attempts to activate the worksheet that has been passed to the callback. Items chosen from the list will always be a valid name, but text typed in by the user may not match an item in the list. The `On Error` statement at the beginning of the routine deals with this by telling the code to continue to the next line even if an error is present.

At this point, you can check whether the `Err` property is zero. If the `Err` property does not equal zero, then an error must have occurred; therefore, the value the user typed is not valid. In addition, because you want the user to know that their input wasn't acceptable, you include a message box. Of course, you can display whatever message that you'd like and even add other options, but message box customization is outside our focus, so let's keep moving.

Now that your callback is set up correctly, click the Navigation tab and play with the `comboBox`. Try selecting items from the list, as well as typing in a value, as shown in Figure 7-6.

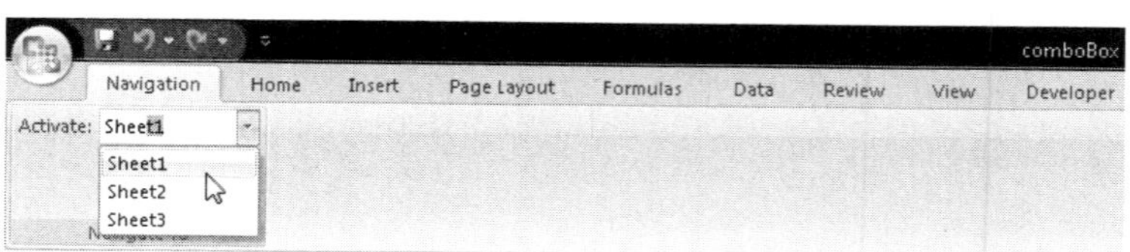

Figure 7-6: Using a comboBox to change worksheets in Excel

A Word Example

Recall that in Chapter 6 we built a customization that allowed the user to enter the width of the Styles pane in an `editBox`. Although this works nicely for giving users the capability to control the width, it isn't very intuitive, as there is no indication of what type of values to put in the box. There are some techniques that provide this information to the user, but those are more complex, and we cover them in Chapter 11. For now, you can use the `comboBox` to provide the user with a pre-set list of options from which to choose.

To make things easy for the user, we keep the `checkBox` that we used to toggle the Styles pane on and off. In addition, rather than create everything from scratch, you can use the `editBox` example file created in Chapter 6. In that, we replaced the `editBox` with the `comboBox` control.

NOTE **Instead of using the `editBox` example you created in the previous chapter, you can also download the complete `editBox` example, `editBox-Style Inspector Width.docm`, from the book's website.**

To get started, open the existing file in the CustomUI Editor and replace the editBox-specific XML with the following:

```
<comboBox id="rxcboStyleWidth"
    label="Inspector Width"
    sizeString="1234"
    onChange="rxcboStyleWidth_Click">
    <item id="rxitemcboStyleWidth1"
        label="1.00"/>
    <item id="rxitemcboStyleWidth2"
        label="2.00"/>
    <item id="rxitemcboStyleWidth3"
        label="3.00"/>
    <item id="rxitemcboStyleWidth4"
        label="4.00"/>
    <item id="rxitemcboStyleWidth5"
        label="5.00"/>
    <item id="rxitemcboStyleWidth6"
        label="6.00"/>
    <item id="rxitemcboStyleWidth7"
        label="7.00"/>
    <item id="rxitemcboStyleWidth8"
        label="8.00"/>
</comboBox>
```

As usual, validate the XML code before saving the file, and because you already have the `checkBox` callbacks programmed in the file, you only need to copy the callback signature for the `rxcboStyleWidth_click` event.

If you examine this XML, you will see that we have added eight options to the `comboBox`'s drop-down list portion: the numbers 1.00 through 8.00. Remember that while each item's `id` must be unique, it is the item's label that will be passed to the callback when the control is accessed.

TIP **In this example, a four-character `sizeString` is declared even though we only show three digits. This is because we want to allow a number with two decimal places and one leading digit. The decimal also counts as a character, so we must include it in our maximum size.**

Upon opening Word, you will again want to jump into the VBE right away to paste your callback. Recall that earlier in the chapter we mentioned that the `comboBox` control is a hybrid between the `editBox` and `dropDown` controls. This works very much to your benefit in this case because the `editBox` callback already exists in the file.

To port the code from the `editBox` to the `comboBox`, you have two options:

1. Copy the code from the `rxtxtStyleWidth_getText` routine to the `rxcboStyleWidth_Click` routine and delete the original `rxtxt` routine.
2. Replace the `rxtxtStyleWidth_getText` signature line with the `rxcboStyleWidth_Click` line.

TIP **If you elect to rewrite the signature line, it is a good idea to get into the practice of making sure that you rewrite all of the parameters as well, not just the name of the callback. This will ensure that if you are updating from one type of callback to another it will still run.**

TIP **If you paste a callback signature line into your module and then update another callback to an identical signature, be sure to delete or rename the original. Otherwise, you will receive an error that an "Ambiguous Name Has Been Detected."**

Once you have updated your procedure, save the file and select the View tab. Your updated Style Options will look like what is shown in Figure 7-7.

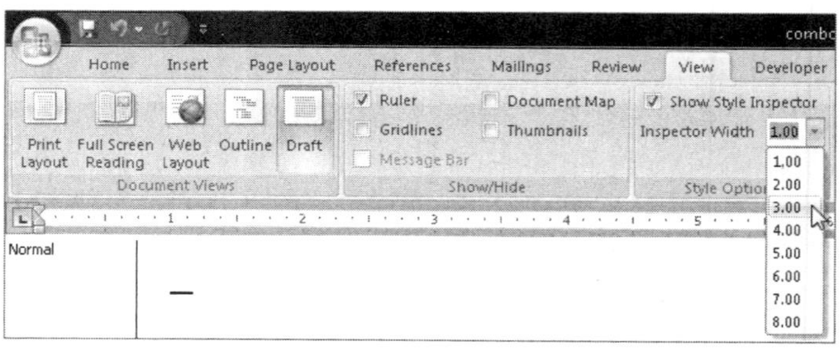

Figure 7-7: Using a comboBox to change Word's Style Inspector width

Try using the `comboBox` to change the width of the Style Inspector pane. Notice the following:

- It only shows when the checkbox is checked.
- The width changes each time you select a new value.
- Typing a custom value also changes the Style Inspector width.
- Typing text will return a custom error message.

An Access Example

In this example, we again build on the Access database used in the last chapter. This time, we add a new group containing a `comboBox` that opens a form directly to a specific field.

Unlike previous examples that used static callbacks, this customization makes use of callbacks to dynamically populate the `comboBox` with a list of all the authors in the tblAuthors table. To do this, we repopulate the `comboBox` every time the form is closed. We recognize that the data in the `comboBox` and the table may become out of sync, but it could be impractical to maintain the XML code for each and every record added to the database, as frequent updates would have a significant performance impact.

To get started, open the Access example from the previous section or download the `toggleButton-Form Tools.accdb` file from the book's website. Copy the RibbonX information from the RibbonXML field of the USysRibbons table and paste it into a fresh instance of the CustomUI Editor. Between the `</group>` and `<group id="rxgrpTools">` tags, enter the following XML for the `comboBox` control:

```
<group id="rxgrpSearch"
    label="Search Tools">
    <comboBox id="rxcboSearchAuthor"
        label="Review Author:"
        onChange="rxcboSearchAuthor_Click"
        getItemID="rxcboSearchAuthor_getItemId"
        getItemCount="rxcboSearchAuthor_getItemCount"
        getItemLabel="rxcboSearchAuthor_getItemLabel"/>
</group>
```

As you can immediately see, the `comboBox` specification looks much different than that shown in the Excel and Word examples. A host of callbacks are declared and no `item` controls are listed. Because the items will be provided dynamically by the callbacks at run-time, it isn't necessary to declare any static items.

NOTE Although it has been mentioned before, it is worth repeating a very important point: Even if you did want to declare one or more static item controls that will show up in every `comboBox` control you use, it must be done through the callback if you elect to populate any controls dynamically. Use of dynamic (or static) callbacks is an "all or nothing" approach.

CROSS-REFERENCE **Another thing to notice about the preceding XML code is that there is no `</comboBox>` tag. Instead, the `comboBox` declaration ends with a /> instead of the / character. As discussed in Chapter 3, this is possible because no child elements are declared for the `comboBox` control.**

Once you have the code validated and copied into the RibbonXML field of the USysRibbons table, generate and copy all of the `rxcboSearchAuthor` callbacks.

If you are keeping track, you will notice that we have declared four callbacks, but only three callouts are generated by the CustomUI Editor. Specifically, the `rxcboSearchAuthor_getItemId` callback signature is missing, which appears to be a bug in the CustomUI Editor program.

Fortunately, you can consult Table 7-5, earlier in this chapter, and obtain the signature for this callback. It is declared as follows:

```
Sub GetItemID(control As IRibbonControl, index As Integer, ByRef id)
```

NOTE **If for some reason you don't have this book with you when you're attempting this in a project, you can also search for these callback signatures on the Internet. An article containing all of the callback signatures can be located on the MSDN site at the following URL:** `http://msdn2.microsoft.com/en-us/library/ad7222523.aspx`

Most of the callback signatures have been generated for you, so copy and paste them into the code module that holds the rest of the code. Next, you need to manually type in the `GetItemID` callback signature.

Before we start writing the code, it's time to figure out exactly how this works. Again, you do this by thinking through the steps in a logical manner. We want to do the following:

1. Create a list of all the authors currently in the database.
2. Submit that list to the `comboBox`.
3. Open the form when the user clicks on (or manually enters) an author's name.
4. Let the user know when an author cannot be found (and close the form).
5. Start again at Step 1 when the form is closed (to ensure that the list is current if any authors were added).

As with all code, the methods by which you accomplish these things are limited only to your imagination and ability. What is detailed below can certainly be done differently, but it works well for the purposes of this example.

To begin, the code needs a place to store the list of author names, and a count of those names. To do this, you add two global variables to the top of your project, just underneath the Option lines. The first is a variant array (a dynamically sized space to hold the list of names), and the second is a `Long` data type, which can hold the count of the names in the array. They read as follows:

```
Public gaAuthorList As Variant
Public glngItemCount As Long
```

CROSS-REFERENCE **For a review of variant arrays, please see Chapter 4.**

Now that you have a variable to hold the list of names, it makes sense to work on the routine that populates the list. Because we indicated that the list will be populated when the file is loaded and every time a form is closed, it makes sense to build the process into a routine, and to call the routine whenever we need to check the table and populate the list. The routine looks as follows:

```
Sub PopulateAuthorArray()
'Populate the global array of author names
    Dim db As DAO.Database
    Dim rst As DAO.Recordset
    Dim lngLoopCount As Long

    'Open the recordset for the authors table
    Set db = CurrentDb()
    Set rst = db.OpenRecordset("tblAuthors", dbOpenTable)

    'Store list of all authors in an array
    On Error Resume Next
    lngLoopCount = 0
    With rst
        If .EOF Then .MoveFirst
        glngItemCount = .RecordCount
        ReDim gaAuthorList(glngItemCount - 1)
        Do While Not (.EOF)
            gaAuthorList(lngLoopCount) = !AuthorName.Value
            .MoveNext
            lngLoopCount = lngLoopCount + 1
        Loop
    End With

    'Release all objects
    rst.Close
    db.Close
    Set rst = Nothing
    Set db = Nothing
End Sub
```

The routine loops through all the records in the tlbAuthors table and adds them to the `gaAuthorList` array. In addition, it sets the `glngItemCount` variable to hold the total number of records that were in the table (and therefore the array.)

Next, we deal with the callbacks.

The `getItemCount` callback simply returns the number stored in the `glngItemCount` variable, telling the control how many records you have:

```
'Callback for rxcboSearchAuthor getItemCount
Sub rxcboSearchAuthor_getItemCount(control As IRibbonControl, _
    ByRef returnedVal)

    returnedVal = glngItemCount
End Sub
```

The getItemID callback is used to create a unique item ID for each of the item controls that are dynamically fed into the comboBox. The index variable is always unique (numbered from zero to the number of items you have, less one), so you can simply add the index to a string of text, as shown here:

```
'Callback for rxcboSearchAuthor getItemID
Sub rxcboSearchAuthor_getItemID(control As IRibbonControl, _
    index As Integer, ByRef ID)

    ID = "rxitemcboSearchAuthor" & index
End Sub
```

TIP **You may wonder why we didn't just set up this callback using** `ID = index` **to generate an ID for the item. We could have used that approach, but it would fail if we added another** `comboBox` **to the project and used the same logic because the IDs would no longer be unique (i.e., two controls could end up with an** `id=0`**.) It is a far better practice to ensure that your ID is tagged with your control name. Therefore, in addition to generating a unique ID, you are now generating a coding habit that will never leave you debugging this issue.**

The getItemLabel callback returns the author's name from the global array that was established earlier. When the array is created, each element has an index, or place, in the array. You can use the following callback to return the element of the array corresponding to the index number:

```
'Callback for rxcboSearchAuthor getItemLabel
Sub rxcboSearchAuthor_getItemLabel(control As IRibbonControl, _
    index As Integer, ByRef returnedVal)

    returnedVal = gaAuthorList(index)
End Sub
```

NOTE **If you are experienced with changing the base of an array and intend to apply that technique in these databases, you need to adjust these indexes to coincide with your arrays.**

The Click event is the final callback that needs programming in our example. It uses the following code:

```
'Callback for rxcboSearchAuthor onChange
Sub rxcboSearchAuthor_Click(control As IRibbonControl, text As String)
'Open the form at the requested Author

    Dim sAuthorName As String
    Dim rs As DAO.Recordset

    'Open the appropriate form
    sAuthorName = "[AuthorName] = '" & text & "'"
```

```
        DoCmd.OpenForm "frmAuthors"

        'Find the correct author
        With Forms!frmAuthors
            Set rs = .RecordsetClone
            rs.FindFirst sAuthorName
            If rs.NoMatch Then
                MsgBox "Author Not found"
                DoCmd.Close acForm, "frmAuthors", acSaveNo
            Else
                .Bookmark = rs.Bookmark
            End If
        End With

        'Release the objects
        Set rs = Nothing
    End Sub
```

This event opens the form and attempts to activate the record pertaining to the author who has either been selected from the comboBox or typed in manually. If the record can be found it is "bookmarked" and activated. If the record is not found, the user is informed (via our friendly message box) and the form is closed.

There is one final thing left to do in order for this example to work: You need to hook the PopulateAuthorArray to the appropriate routines. Without this hook, the array will never be filled and the comboBox will sit empty.

To create the hook, simply insert the following code snippet in the rxIRibbonUI_onLoad event (before or after the line that captures the RibbonUI), as well as in the frmAuthor's Form_Deactivate event (just before the line that invalidates the RibbonUI):

```
    'Populate the array of Author names
        Call PopulateAuthorArray
```

Now that you have made all of these modifications, save, close, and reopen your database. You will have a new group on the Ribbon that holds the combBox. Select an author's name from the list and you will be taken to their record, as shown in Figure 7-8.

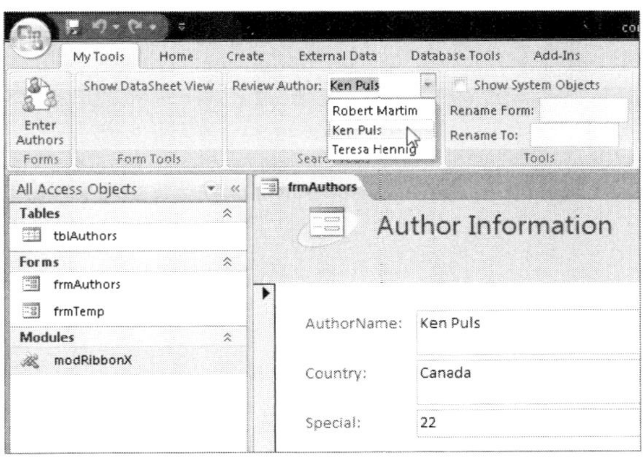

Figure 7-8: Using a comboBox to jump to a specific

record in a form

Now try adding your name to the Author's table. After all, you have done a lot of work just to get to this point! After adding your name, close the form and check the comboBox list. Voilà, your name in print!

The dropDown Element

Like the `comboBox`, the `dropDown` control presents the user with a pre-defined list of options from which to choose. In addition, it too can be populated either at design-time using XML to provide a static list, or dynamically at run-time via callbacks.

The biggest of differences between the `comboBox` and `dropDown` controls lies in the ability of the `comobBox` to accept user-entered data; the `dropDown` control has no such facility, forcing the user to select an item from the pre-defined list and only from that list.

At first glance, you may ask yourself why anyone would want to use a `dropDown` over a `comboBox`. After all, wouldn't you always want to make the controls more robust and accessible? The answer depends upon your implementation, of course, but some reasons you may want to use the `dropDown` control include the following:

- You do not want users to enter their own information.
- Your list is not long, so using the "auto complete" capability is not a concern.
- You are not interested in programming the callbacks to validate user-entered data.

Required Attributes of the dropDown Element

To create a `dropDown` control, you need to define one and only one of the `id` attributes shown in Table 7-6.

Table 7-6: Required id Attributes for the dropDown Element

ATTRIBUTE	WHEN TO USE
id	When creating your own `dropDown`
idMso	When using an existing Microsoft `dropDown`
idQ	When creating a `dropDown` shared between namespaces

Optional Static and Dynamic Attributes with Callback Signatures

The `dropDown` element optionally accepts any one `insert` attribute shown in Table 7-7.

Table 7-7: Optional insert Attributes for the dropDown Element

INSERT ATTRIBUTE	ALLOWED VALUES	DEFAULT VALUE	WHEN TO USE
insertAfterMso	Valid Mso Group	Insert at end of group	Insert after Microsoft control
insertBeforeMso	Valid Mso Group	Insert at end of group	Insert before Microsoft control
insertAfterQ	Valid Group idQ	Insert at end of group	Insert after shared namespace control
insertBeforeQ	Valid Group idQ	Insert at end of group	Insert before shared namespace control

In addition to the `insert` attribute, you may also include any or all of the optional static attributes or dynamic equivalents shown in Table 7-8.

Table 7-8: Optional Attributes and Callbacks of the dropDown Element

STATIC ATTRIBUTE	DYNAMIC ATTRIBUTE	ALLOWED VALUES	DEFAULT VALUE	VBA CALLBACK SIGNATURE FOR DYNAMIC ATTRIBUTE
enabled	getEnabled	true, false, 1, 0	true	Sub GetEnabled (control As IRibbonControl, ByRef returnedVal)
image	getImage	1 to 1024 characters	(none)	Sub GetImage (control As IRibbonControl, ByRef returnedVal)
imageMso	getImage	1 to 1024 characters	(none)	Same as above
(none)	getItemCount	1 to 1024	(none)	Sub GetItemCount (control As IRibbonControl, ByRef returnedVal)
(none)	getItemID	Unique text string	(none)	Sub GetItemID (control As IRibbonControl, index As Integer, ByRef id)
(none)	getItemImage	1 to 1024 characters	(none)	Sub GetItemImage (control As IRibbonControl, index As Integer, ByRef returnedVal)

Continued

Table 7-8 *(continued)*

STATIC ATTRIBUTE	DYNAMIC ATTRIBUTE	ALLOWED VALUES	DEFAULT VALUE	VBA CALLBACK SIGNATURE FOR DYNAMIC ATTRIBUTE
(none)	getItemLabel	1 to 1024 characters	(none)	Sub GetItemLabel (control As IRibbonControl, index As Integer, ByRef returnedVal)
(none)	getItemScreentip	1 to 1024 characters	(none)	Sub GetItemScreenTip (control As IRibbonControl, index As Integer, ByRef returnedVal)
(none)	getItemSupertip	1 to 1024 characters	(none)	Sub GetItemSuperTip (control As IRibbonControl, index As Integer, ByRef returnedVal)
keytip	getKeytip	1 to 3 characters	(none)	Sub GetKeytip (control As IRibbonControl, ByRef returnedVal)
label	getLabel	1 to 1024 characters	(none)	Sub GetLabel (control As IRibbonControl, ByRef returnedVal)
screentip	getScreentip	1 to 1024 characters	(none)	Sub GetScreentip (control As IRibbonControl, ByRef returnedVal)
(none)	getSelected ↵ ItemID	Unique text string	(none)	Sub GetSelectedItemID (control As IRibbonControl, ByRef returnedVal)
(none)	getSelected ↵ ItemIndex	1 to 1024	(none)	Sub GetSelectedItemIndex (control As IRibbonControl, ByRef returnedVal)
showImage	getShowImage	true, false, 1, 0	true	Sub GetShowImage (control As IRibbonControl, ByRef returnedVal)
showItem ↵ Image	(none)	true, false, 1, 0	true	(none)
showItem ↵ Label	(none)	true, false, 1, 0	true	(none)

Table 7-8 *(continued)*

STATIC ATTRIBUTE	DYNAMIC ATTRIBUTE	ALLOWED VALUES	DEFAULT VALUE	VBA CALLBACK SIGNATURE FOR DYNAMIC ATTRIBUTE
showLabel	getShowLabel	true, false, 1, 0	true	Sub GetShowLabel (control As IRibbonControl, ByRef returnedVal)
sizeString	(none)	1 to 1024 characters	12*	(none)
supertip	getSupertip	1 to 1024 characters	(none)	Sub GetSupertip (control As IRibbonControl, ByRef returnedVal)
tag	(none)	1 to 1024 characters	(none)	(none)
visible	getVisible	true, false, 1, 0	true	Sub GetVisible (control As IRibbonControl, ByRef returnedVal)
(none)	onAction	1 to 1024 characters	(none)	Sub OnAction (control As IRibbonControl, selectedId As String, selectedIndex As Integer)

NOTE **The default value for the** `sizeString` **attribute (if the attribute is not declared at all) is approximately** `12`**, but this will vary depending on the characters used and the system font.**

Allowed Children Objects of the dropDown Element

The only child object that can be used with the `dropdown` element is the `item` element.

Parent Objects of the dropDown Element

The `dropDown` element may be used within the following controls:

- `box`
- `group`

Graphical View of dropDown Attributes

Figure 7-9 shows a `dropDown` control on a Ribbon group, which houses two dynamic items. The captions annotate the properties that can be set on a `dropDown` control.

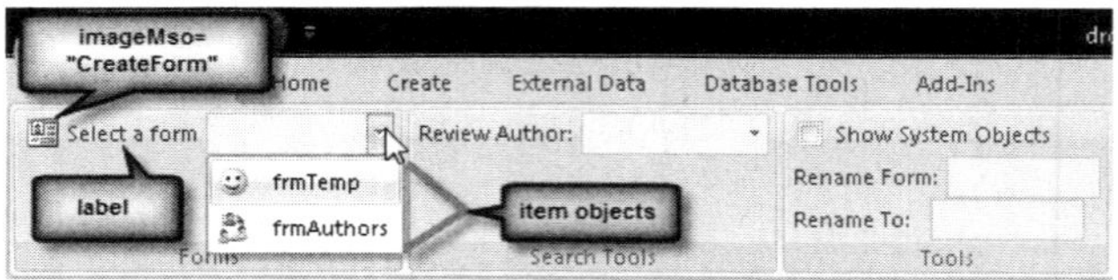

Figure 7-9: Graphical view of the dropDown element

Using Built-in Controls

Because there are no built-in `dropDown` controls that span all the applications, this example again focuses on referencing one of Excel's native `dropDown` controls: the `BorderStyle` control.

To make use of the control, create a new `xlsx` file and open it in the CustomUI Editor. Apply the RibbonBase template and place the following code between the `<tabs>` and `</tabs>` tags:

```
<tab id="rxtabDemo"
    label="Demo"
    insertBeforeMso="TabHome">
    <group id="rxgrpDemo"
        label="Demo">
        <dropDown idMso="BorderStyle"/>
    </group>
</tab>
```

Validate your XML, save the file, and reopen it in Excel. You will now see the fully functional control available on the Demo tab, as shown in Figure 7-10.

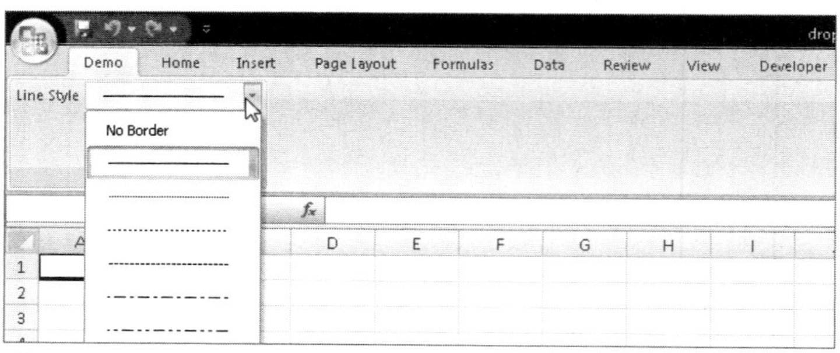

Figure 7-10: Using the BorderStyle control in a custom Excel group

Creating Custom Controls

In this section we again create custom tools, rather than reuse the commands and functionality inherent in the programs.

In addition to employing a static `dropDown` list in Excel, the previous `comboBox` example will also be revised so that it dynamically populates a `dropDown` control. The Word example will remain static, but we add another useful tool to the collection that you have been building. The Access example again creates a completely dynamic list in the `dropDown` control.

An Excel Example

This example is quite interesting because it uses two `dropDown` elements in tandem. Similar to the `comboBox` example in the previous section, the first control lists all the worksheets in the workbook. In this case, however, we employ the available callbacks to update the `dropDown` list as worksheets are added to or removed from the workbook. Pretty cool — and you can certainly see the value in the example and anticipate ample opportunities to incorporate this into your customizations.

NOTE By switching from a `comboBox` to a `dropDown`, we lose the capability to type in the worksheet we want to activate. It should be assumed that this process was a conscious choice on the part of the developer.

The second control allows us to toggle the visibility of the selected worksheet between Excel's three states: `xlSheetVisible`, `xlSheetHidden`, and `xlSheetVeryHidden`.

NOTE The `xlSheetVeryHidden` state of an Excel worksheet is not known to most users because it must be set from VBA. This is a state that enables a developer to completely hide a worksheet from the users, and it will not show in the menu that allows users to unhide sheets.

One of the best ways to highlight the differences between the two controls is to convert one to the other, so that is exactly how this example begins. If you have not completed the previous example, or are unsure how it compares to the examples in this book, download the `comboBox-Select Sheet.xlsm` file from the book's website.

Before you open the file in Excel, open it in the CustomUI Editor and replace everything from and including the `<comboBox>` to the end of and including `</comboBox>` with the following XML:

```
<dropDown id="rxddSelectSheet"
   label="Apply To:"
   visible="true"
   onAction="rxddSelectSheet_Click"
   getItemID="rxitemddSelectSheet_getItemId"
   getItemCount="rxitemddSelectSheet_getItemCount"
   getItemLabel="rxitemddSelectSheet_getItemLabel"/>
```

```
<dropDown id="rxddSheetVisible"
   label="Set To:"
   onAction="rxddSheetVisible_Click">
   <item id="rxitemddSheetVisible1"
       label="Visible"/>
   <item id="rxitemddSheetVisible2"
       label="Hidden"/>
   <item id="rxitemddSheetVisible3"
       label="VeryHidden"/>
</dropDown>
```

Notice a few things about the preceding code:

- The first `dropDown` declaration has no ending `</dropDown>` tag. This is because it contains all of its attributes within the code block and is requesting all of its child objects via callbacks; therefore, it does not require any static child objects declared in the XML, and can be closed by using `/>` at the end.
- The callback signature for the `dropDown` is different from the `comboBox`. Whereas the `comboBox` used an `onChange` callback, the `dropDown` uses an `onAction` callback when it is clicked.
- The second `dropDown` list does have a `</dropDown>` tag to close it. This is because it holds a static list of `item` objects declared directly in the XML code.

In addition, we also need to capture the `RibbonUI` object in order to update the lists dynamically. Adjust the `CustomUI` tag to include the `onLoad` element as shown below:

```
<customUI
    onLoad="rxIRibbonUI_onLoad"
    xmlns="http://schemas.microsoft.com/office/2006/01/customui">
```

As always, you should validate your code, save it, and generate and copy the callback signatures. As with the `comboBox` element, be aware that the callback for the `getItemID` callback will not be generated by the CustomUI Editor. If you were doing this on your own, you'd once again need to look this up and type it in manually (or copy it from a functional example).

Open Excel again, but don't be alarmed when you see the error message indicating that it cannot run the macro, shown in Figure 7-11.

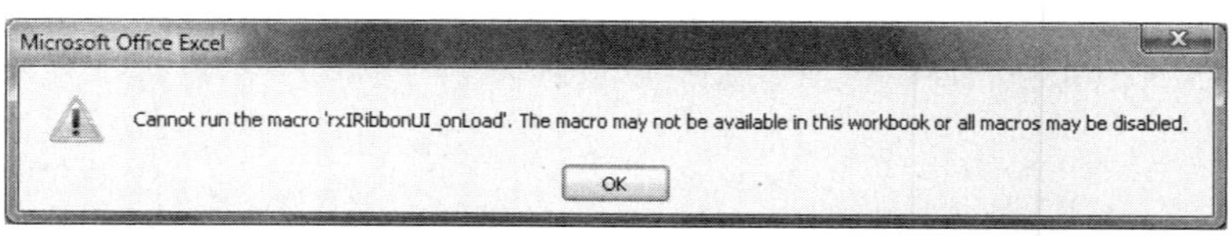

Figure 7-11: Error message indicating a missing callback

This is to be expected, as we have declared an `onLoad` callback but have not yet provided the programming. To do that, in the VBE, open the code module that holds all the RibbonX event code and paste the callback signatures at the end.

Before we go any further, let's deal with the `onLoad` callback. You want to add two variables to the top of the project. The first will hold the `RibbonUI` object, while the second will store the worksheet name that was selected. They are placed just under the Option Explicit line and should be declared as follows:

```
Public RibbonUI As IRibbonUI
Dim sSheetName As String
```

Next, we make sure that the `RibbonUI` object is captured at load time by setting the `onLoad` callback as follows:

```
'Callback for customUI.onLoad
Sub rxIRibbonUI_onLoad(ribbon As IRibbonUI)
    Set RibbonUI = ribbon
End Sub
```

Now it's time to look at the rest of the callback signatures, starting with the callback that tells the control how many items exist. Fortunately, it doesn't require much code to make this work, as the item count will always be equal to the number of worksheets in the workbook. You can use the following code:

```
'Callback for rxddSelectSheet getItemCount
Sub rxitemddSelectSheet_getItemCount(control As IRibbonControl, _
    ByRef returnedVal)

    returnedVal = Worksheets.Count
End Sub
```

Next, we set up the callback for the `getItemLabel`, which returns the text of each item to the `dropDown` list:

```
'Callback for rxddSelectSheet getItemLabel
Sub rxitemddSelectSheet_getItemLabel(control As IRibbonControl, _
    index As Integer, ByRef returnedVal)

    returnedVal = Worksheets(index + 1).Name
End Sub
```

If you haven't worked much with arrays, you might not notice a very big issue lurking in the middle of this routine. Pay careful attention to the fact that the name being returned for an item is the index + 1.

The reason for this shift is that by default VBA works in zero-based arrays (as previously mentioned, VBA starts counting at 0, not 1), but Excel's default worksheet indexes and names work in one-based arrays (Excel starts counting at 1, not 0.)

To understand the ramifications, assume that we have a workbook set up to start with the default 3 worksheets. In the `getItemCount` procedure, we asked for a count of the Worksheets 1, 2, and 3. We received a total count of 3, as we would expect. What is interesting, however, is how this actually dimensions the array. Have a look at Table 7-9 to see how the array will manifest itself.

Table 7-9: Dimensions and Values of an Array

ARRAY INDEX	ELEMENT VALUE	ACTUAL VALUE
0	Worksheets(index + 1).Name	Sheet1
1	Worksheets(index + 1).Name	Sheet2
2	Worksheets(index + 1).Name	Sheet3

NOTE **If this appears intimidating, don't worry about it. It is confusing for most users who are not accustomed to working with arrays. As a rule of thumb, if the values you are trying to pass in to or retrieve from an array appear to be out of sync by one, just adjust your index, as shown in the previous code snippet.**

Next, you will want to ensure that the callback is programmed to dynamically generate the unique ID for each of the drop-down items. The callback should read as follows:

```
'Callback for rxddSelectSheet getItemID
Sub rxitemddSelectSheet_getItemID(control As IRibbonControl, _
    index As Integer, ByRef id)

    id = "rxitemddSelectSheet" & index
End Sub
```

There is one more callback to set up: the `rxddSelectSheet_Click` callback. Because we started with the previous file, you have all the code for the `rxcboSelectSheet_Click` event that was triggered by selecting a `comboBox` item. However, you can't just rename and reuse. Take a look at Table 7-10, noting the difference between the callback signatures.

Table 7-10: Difference between dropDown and comboBox Callback Signatures

CONTROL	CALLBACK SIGNATURE
comboBox	rxcboSelectSheet_Click (control As IRibbonControl, text As String)
dropDown	rxddSelectSheet_Click (control As IRibbonControl, id As String, ↵ index As Integer)

You can see that while the `comboBox` passes the text of the control to the callback, the `dropDown` is not quite so friendly. Instead, it passes the ID and the index number. Unfortunately, we're not interested in that number at this time; we need to show the user the actual name of the sheet.

In order to work out the control's name, we can leverage one of the less obvious features of Ribbon construction. We can actually call the `getItemLabel` callback to give us this information!

If you take a good look at the `getItemLabel` callback, you'll see that it accepts three parameters. The key to making this work is the keyword that prefaces the variable in the last parameter:

```
Sub rxitemddSelectSheet_getItemLabel(control As IRibbonControl, _
    index As Integer, ByRef returnedVal)
```

In VBA, every parameter is passed to a procedure specifying that the variable is passed by either `ByVal` (which is the default, so the parameter is typically omitted, as it is implied) or `ByRef`. The difference is that when a variable is passed `ByVal`, a copy of the variable is used inside the receiving procedure. Anything that is done to it within the procedure is lost when the procedure goes out of scope (ends).

In contrast, when a variable is passed to a procedure `ByRef`, the actual variable is passed as a parameter. Anything that is done to the variable inside that procedure is passed back to the calling procedure when the called procedure ends. It's this capability that enables us to make use of the `getItemLabel` callback.

Update your callbacks so that the `rxddSelectSheet_Click` routine reads as follows, and delete the `rxcboSelectSheet_Click` event:

```
'Callback for rxddSelectSheet onAction
Sub rxddSelectSheet_Click(control As IRibbonControl, id As String, _
    Index As Integer)

    On Error Resume Next
    Call rxitemddSelectSheet_getItemLabel(control, index, sSheetName)
    If Err.Number <> 0 Then
        MsgBox "Sorry, that worksheet does not exist!"
        RibbonUI.InvalidateControl "rxddSelectSheet"
    End If
End Sub
```

Make note of how we are calling the `getItemLabel` callback, and especially how we are passing the `sSheetName` variable to the `returnedVal` parameter. Because the actual `sSheetName` variable is passed, and not a copy, the changes made in that procedure will replicate back to the global variable, and the worksheet name will be ready when we need it.

Finally, we've completed the setup for the dynamic `dropDown` control, and we can focus on setting up the sole callback for the static `dropDown`. Update the callback for this control to read as follows:

```
'Callback for rxddSheetVisible onAction
Sub rxddSheetVisible_Click(control As IRibbonControl, id As String, _
    index As Integer)

    `Check that a worksheet has been selected
    On Error Resume Next
    sSheetName = Worksheets(sSheetName).Name
    If Err.Number <> 0 Then
        MsgBox "Sorry, but you need to select a valid sheet first!"
        Exit Sub
    End If
```

```
        'Change the sheet's visibility
        Select Case id
            Case "rxitemddSheetVisible1"
                Worksheets(sSheetName).Visible = xlSheetVisible
            Case "rxitemddSheetVisible2"
                Worksheets(sSheetName).Visible = xlSheetHidden
            Case "rxitemddSheetVisible3"
                Worksheets(sSheetName).Visible = xlSheetVeryHidden
        End Select

        'Tell user if it is last visible sheet
        If Err.Number <> 0 Then
            MsgBox "Sorry, this is the only visible sheet." & vbCrLf & _
            "You can't hide them all!"
        End If
        On Error GoTo 0
    End Sub
```

This callback evaluates whether any value is contained in the `sSheetName` variable. If there is one, it then sets the visibility of the sheet as chosen by the user.

You'll recall that we experienced an error when the file was originally loaded, so we won't be able to try out our customization until we save and reload the workbook. Once you've done this, navigate to the Review tab and play with the new controls, shown in Figure 7-12.

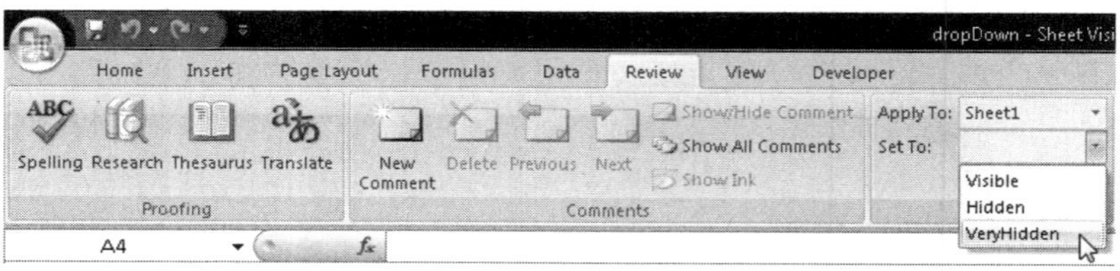

Figure 7-12: The sheet visibility dropDown menu set

A Word Example

In the tradition of adding useful tools to the Word Ribbon groups, we're going to continue adding another feature to the example that we created in the section on the comboBox.

If you frequently use Word templates, you may find that you are offered a ton of styles that you don't use, which results in a lot of unwanted clutter. Word has four distinct settings to filter the styles to make them easier to use. In this section, we'll create a customization that provides the capability to quickly select these four settings.

To start, make a copy of the Word `comboBox` example from the previous section, or download the completed `comboBox-Style Inspector Width.docm` file from the book's website. Open the new file in the CustomUI Editor and insert the following XML between the `</comboBox>` and `</group>` tags:

```
<dropDown id="rxddStylesView"
    label="Show Styles:"
    onAction="rxddStylesView_Click">
    <item id="rxitemddStylesAll"
        label="All"/>
    <item id="rxitemddStylesInCurrent"
        label="InCurrent"/>
    <item id="rxitemddStylesInUse"
        label="InUse"/>
    <item id="rxitemddStylesRecommended"
        label="Recommended"/>
    <item id="rxitemddStyles(none)"
        label="None"/>
</dropDown>
```

This will enter a static `dropDown` under the existing controls. It holds five different items: four related to the Styles view options and a final option to hide the Styles task pane.

Validate the code, as you usually do, and copy the `rxddStylesView_Click` callback. Open Word, open the VBE, and paste your callback signature in the module that holds the rest of the existing callback signatures. The next step is to record a macro that will capture as much information about the process as possible.

TIP **Never overlook the macro recorder, as it is a handy tool. Even if it can only record pieces of the process, the documentation provides a great place to start learning about the objects that you are trying to manipulate. In addition, you can save a lot of time and avoid typos by copying and pasting from the generated code.**

We're trying to capture a couple of different things here. The first is how to show and hide the Styles task pane at the side of the document. The second is how to select the desired filtered view.

Let's walk through the process. To begin, start the macro recorder and press Alt+Ctrl+Shift+S to show the Styles task pane on the side of your screen. (You could also navigate to the Home tab and click the little arrow in the bottom, right corner of the Styles group, if you prefer.)

Next, in the bottom right corner of the Styles pane, you will see an Options link. Click the link and you will see the dialog shown in Figure 7-13.

In the drop-down list, select Recommended and then click OK. Return to the Style Pane Options and select each option in turn, saying OK to each one. Finally, close the Styles task pane.

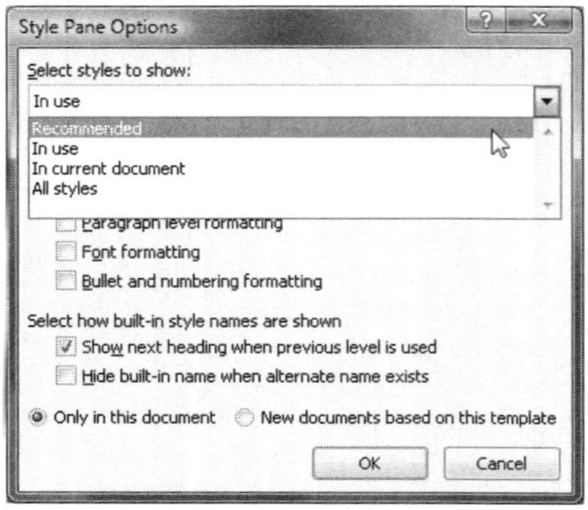

Figure 7-13: The Style Pane Options dialog

Now it's time to examine the code that was recorded. You should see something similar to the annotated version shown here:

```
Sub Macro1()
'All styles
    ActiveDocument.FormattingShowFilter = wdShowFilterFormattingInUse
'In current document Styles
    ActiveDocument.FormattingShowFilter = wdShowFilterStylesAll
'In use Styles
    ActiveDocument.FormattingShowFilter = wdShowFilterStylesInUse
'Recommended Styles
    ActiveDocument.FormattingShowFilter = wdShowFilterStylesAvailable
'Turn off the Styles task pane
    CommandBars("Styles").Visible = False
End Sub
```

NOTE **We've annotated the code because the constants that Microsoft used are less than intuitive. One might think that the** `wdShowFilterStylesAll` **would apply the All setting, not the In Current Document setting, as it does. Rather than have you waste time figuring out which is which, we've provided the clarification so that you can stay focused on the exercise.**

NOTE **There is no code recorded to launch the Styles pane, but there is code to close it. Interestingly enough, once you have opened the Styles pane in your current Word instance, you can show the Styles task pane by executing the command** `CommandBars("Styles").Visible = true`**. Until you have activated it at least once manually, however, the code will fail. This is a known bug in Microsoft Word, and it is hoped that it will be fixed in an upcoming service pack. There is a workaround for the issue, however, which is to replace** `CommandBars("Styles").Visible = true` **with** `Application .TaskPanes(wdTaskPaneFormatting).Visible = True`**.**

The good news here is that you can easily adapt this code into the callback signature, as the commands are relatively straightforward. Placing a case statement in the callback will give us the following:

```
'Callback for rxddStylesView onAction
Sub rxddStylesView_Click(control As IRibbonControl, id As String, _
    Index As Integer)

    On Error Resume Next
    Application.TaskPanes(wdTaskPaneFormatting).Visible = True

    Select Case id
        Case "rxitemddStylesAll"
            ActiveDocument.FormattingShowFilter = _
                wdShowFilterFormattingInUse
        Case "rxitemddStylesInCurrent"
            ActiveDocument.FormattingShowFilter = _
                wdShowFilterStylesAll
        Case "rxitemddStylesInUse"
            ActiveDocument.FormattingShowFilter = _
                wdShowFilterStylesInUse
        Case "rxitemddStylesRecommended"
            ActiveDocument.FormattingShowFilter = _
                wdShowFilterStylesAvailable
        Case "rxitemddStylesNone"
            CommandBars("Styles").Visible = False
    End Select
End Sub
```

NOTE The addition of the line continuations (a space followed by the underscore and a hard return) is not essential to making the code work, but it does make it easier to read.

Once you have this code fully integrated, save the file and browse to the View tab. Try using various selections on the Show Styles `dropDown`, as shown in Figure 7-14.

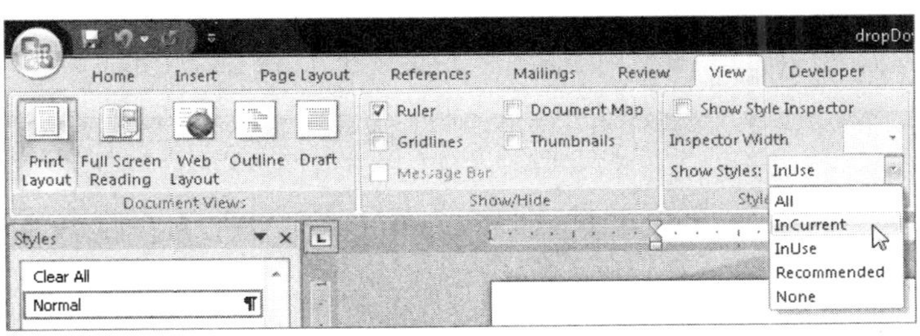

Figure 7-14: The Show Styles dropDown in use

An Access Example

The final example in this section also builds on the previous file. This time, you replace the button that was created to launch the Authors form with a dynamic `dropDown` list that will launch any of the forms. This `dropDown` will update each time a new form is added to, or removed from, the database. As an added twist, we also add a callback to retrieve an image for each item in the `dropDown` list.

Make a copy of the Access example from the previous section or download the `comboBox-Author Query.accdb` file from the book's website. Open it and copy the RibbonX information from the RibbonXML field of the USysRibbons table. Once you've done that, open the CustomUI Editor and paste the code in the blank pane. Locate the following code:

```
<button id="rxbtnFrmAuthors"
   imageMso="FileCreateDocumentWorkspace"
   size="large"
   label="Enter Authors"
   onAction="rxbtnFrmAuthors_click"/>
```

Replace it with this code:

```
<dropDown id="rxddSelectForm"
    label="Select a form"
    imageMso="CreateForm"
    onAction="rxddSelectForm_click"
    getItemCount="rxddSelectForm_getItemCount"
    getItemID="rxddSelectForm_getItemID"
    getItemImage="rxddSelectForm_getItemImage"
    getItemLabel="rxddSelectForm_getItemLabel"/>
```

Like the `comboBox` code used in the previous example, setting up a dynamic `dropDown` involves a great many callbacks.

As always, validate the XML code. Once it is error-free, copy all of the XML and replace the code that is stored in the RibbonX field of your USysRibbons table.

Next, use the CustomUI Editor to generate the callbacks, copy all of the `rxddSelectForm` signatures, and paste them to the code module that holds the rest of the callback code. Be sure to manually create the following callback that the CustomUI Editor does not generate:

```
'Callback for rxddSelectFrom getItemID
Sub rxddSelectForm_getItemID(control As IRibbonControl, _
    index As Integer, ByRef ID)
End Sub
```

Now that all of the callbacks are placed in the module, it's time to start hooking them up to do the things that we want. By examining the XML code, you can see that the `dropDown` control will be placed in the group with an icon beside it. The rest of the content, of course, will be dynamic.

In order to populate the `dropDown` list dynamically, you need to return the total number of items that the list will contain, which is done using the `getItemCount` callback. We're interested in knowing the total number of forms in the database, and that number can be retrieved with the following code:

```
'Callback for rxddSelectForm getItemCount
Sub rxddSelectForm_getItemCount(control As IRibbonControl, _
    ByRef returnedVal)

    returnedVal = CurrentProject.AllForms.Count
End Sub
```

You also know that each item in the `dropDown` list must have its own unique ID. As in the previous examples, this can easily be accomplished by setting up the callback to read as follows:

```
'Callback for rxddSelectFrom getItemID
Sub rxddSelectForm_getItemID(control As IRibbonControl, _
    index As Integer, ByRef ID)

    ID = "rxitemddSelectForm" & index
End Sub
```

Next, you need to determine how to get the label for each item. Because each form has an index number in the collection, the callback can be set up as follows:

```
'Callback for rxddSelectForm getItemLabel
Sub rxddSelectForm_getItemLabel(control As IRibbonControl, _
    index As Integer, ByRef returnedVal)

    returnedVal = CurrentProject.AllForms(index).Name
End Sub
```

One more callback needs to be set up in order to populate the items in the list box. The XML code specifies that we also want an image for each item in the list, so we need a callback to get the image. The completed callback signature will look like this:

```
'Callback for rxddSelectForm getItemImage
Sub rxddSelectForm_getItemImage(control As IRibbonControl, _
    index As Integer, ByRef returnedVal)

    Select Case CurrentProject.AllForms(index).Name
        Case Is = "frmAuthors"
            returnedVal = "FileCreateDocumentWorkspace"
        Case Else
            returnedVal = "HappyFace"
    End Select
End Sub
```

This callback looks up the name of the form by passing the index number to the `AllForms` collection. Once that name has been returned, it is evaluated by the `case` statement. If the form name matches any of the cases, it is assigned the picture specified. The `Else` portion of this code assigns Microsoft's HappyFace image to any form that is not specified in the code.

NOTE **Remember that the contents of the `dropDown` list will be populated dynamically. This is important, as a user may add a new form — so it would not likely be in the list. By using the `Else` statement to assign a default image, you don't have to worry about constantly updating the code.**

Now that all the callbacks are in place to populate the `dropDown`, we need to add the callback to handle the user's selections. We'll use the `onAction` callback, which is set up as shown here:

```
'Callback for rxddSelectForm onAction
Sub rxddSelectForm_click(control As IRibbonControl, ID As String, _
    Index As Integer)

    Dim sFormName As String
    Call rxddSelectForm_getItemLabel(control, index, sFormName)
    DoCmd.OpenForm sFormName, acNormal
    RibbonUI.InvalidateControl ("rxddSelectForm")
End Sub
```

Note that this routine again uses the trick of retrieving the item's label by leveraging the ability to set the `sFormName` variable by executing the `getItemLabel` callback. Once the selected form name has been retrieved, the form is opened.

The invalidation contained in this routine ensures that each time a form is opened, the `dropDown` is repopulated. Therefore, if a new form has been added, then it will be added to and appear in the `dropDown` list.

NOTE **Because a form needs to be opened via the `dropDown` to repopulate it, there is a one-click delay in the updating of the list each time a form is added to or deleted from the project. Ideally, the invalidation would actually be housed in a class module to monitor the creation and deletion of a form. However, this is more complicated and would distract from our demonstration of incorporating and using the `dropDown` control. We've placed the invalidation in the `onAction` callback. We encourage you to investigate creating a class module to monitor the form creation and removal events at your leisure.**

The final piece of programming work is to clean up remnant code from the button you replaced. All you need to do is locate the `rxbtnFrmAuthors_click` routine and delete it from the project.

Now that all the code is in place, close and reload the Access database, thereby saving your work and allowing the new Ribbon to be installed as the file opens.

When you return to your database, check the `dropDown` menu. Next, try adding a new form. Click on the menu to launch the Authors form and then check the `dropDown` list again. You will see that your control now also houses the new form as well, as shown in Figure 7-15.

This demonstrates that one-click delay just mentioned. The drop-down list needs to be refreshed after it is repopulated.

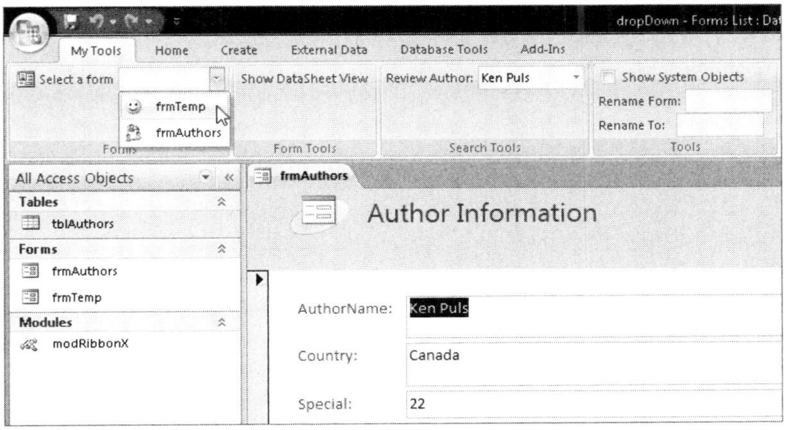

Figure 7-15: Dynamic dropDown list to select a form in Access

Conclusion

As you've seen, the `comboBox` and `dropDown` controls are extremely similar in implementation and appearance. The examples presented in this chapter covered using static items defined in the XML code, as well as leveraging VBA to provide dynamically updated controls. There is no question, however, that one of the biggest deterrents to using either of these methods to set up an effective, fully dynamic solution is the copious amount of code that would have to be manually generated.

When considering these controls, the main questions facing you are which one should you use, and when? The answer depends completely on how much latitude you wish to give your users. If, on the one hand, you need to limit users to selecting from a standard list that never changes, then you'll want to use a `dropDown` control. On the other hand, if you want to offer your users either of the following options, then you will want to use a `comboBox`:

- The ability to jump to an item in the list
- The ability to enter text that is not already defined in the list

Now that you have learned how to present users with different lists of items, it is time to learn about two controls that can add impressive richness to your applications. In Chapter 8, you will learn how to incorporate the picture and gallery controls into your customizations.

CHAPTER

8

Custom Pictures and Galleries

As you become more experienced in developing a custom UI, you will probably find that the built-in icon gallery just isn't enough. You may want to take it to the next level and add a greater personal touch by introducing your own images (icon or pictures).

In this chapter, you learn how to harness the power of custom pictures and how to use galleries, one of the coolest new features in the UI.

As you are preparing to work through the examples, we encourage you to download the companion files. The source code and files for this chapter can be found on the book's web site at `www.wiley.com/go/ribbonx`.

Custom Pictures

Many of the examples you've seen so far involve built-in pictures (or images if you prefer). Using custom pictures is a highly visible way to truly personalize your UI.

There are different ways you can add pictures to your project. You can attach them to the project itself or you can load them from external picture files. You will learn these methods as well as the unique way in which Access can work with pictures. First, however, you need to get acquainted with which formats are appropriate for the job.

Suggested Picture Formats

If you really get into planning a customized UI, you will probably also consider using your own images to add that extra touch.

Adding custom images is not rocket science, but it is important that you get to know some file formats so that you can make an educated choice as to which type you should use in particular situations. Consider, for example, Figure 8-1, which shows a customized button.

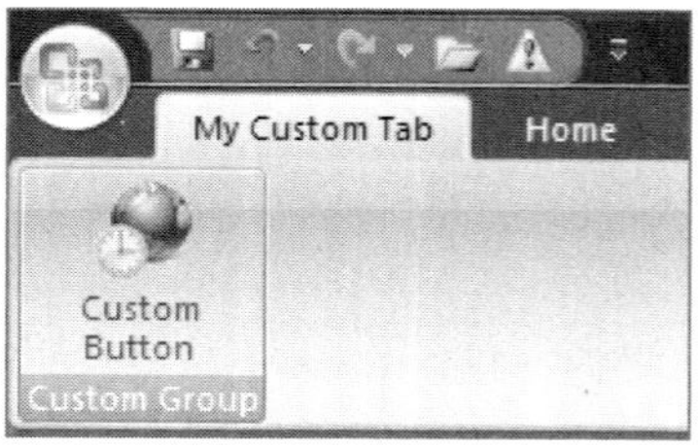

Figure 8-1: A custom image placed in a custom button to match the color scheme

The customization looks perfect because it uses an old trick that many Office power-users and programmers have long used: the image background matches the UI background. For the most part, this approach is acceptable, with one significant caveat. It can be a problem if the color scheme (or color theme, if you prefer) is changed, as illustrated in Figure 8-2.

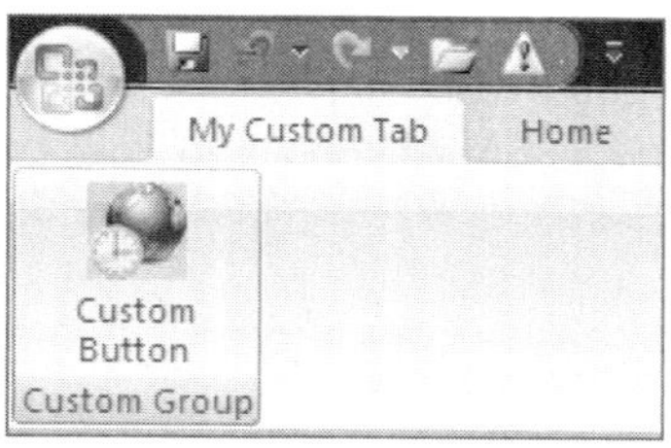

Figure 8-2: Changing color scheme disrupts the harmony of the UI

Now you can clearly see that the image no longer matches the background, and the framing makes your UI look plain ugly. By using the right file format for your pictures, you can avoid this problem.

A good format for working with custom pictures is the PNG format. PNG files allow for full transparency (something not supported by some of the other possible formats such as BMP, GIF, and JPEG), which means you should not find yourself suffering the embarrassment caused by the scenario shown in Figure 8-2 after deploying your solution. To demonstrate this, we'll save the image used for the Custom Button as a PNG file type and use the PNG file with two color schemes, shown in Figure 8-3.

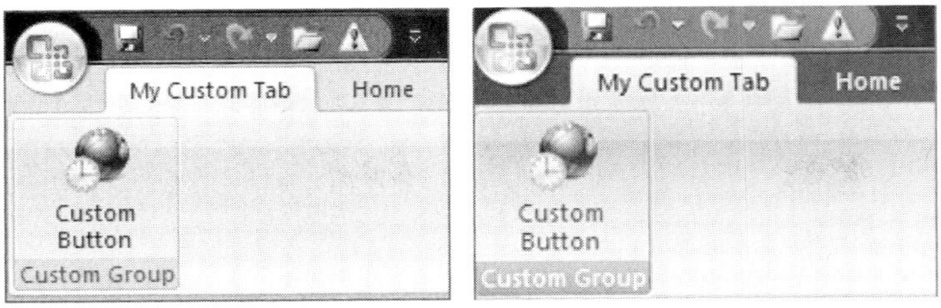

Figure 8-3: Full transparency solves the problem of differing UI color schemes.

As you can see from the composite image shown in Figure 8-3, by adding full background transparency to a PNG file you no longer need to worry about the user choosing different color schemes and destroying your cherished UI.

However, we don't live in a perfect world and, like everything else, PNG files can let you down in some circumstances. For example, if you need to load an image on-the-fly using the VBA `LoadPicture` function, you cannot use the PNG format. This limited scope of usage means that you will need to look for alternatives — either a different format or a different method to load the image.

TIP **Check the two Excel files that accompany this chapter on the book's website to contrast the differences. Change the color scheme and note the differences between a PNG file and a BMP file. You can use the same example for Access and Word.**

Table 8-1 shows some of the file formats you can use in your custom UI.

Table 8-1: Some Possible Picture Formats for the Custom UI

PICTURE EXTENSION	FORMAT
PNG	Portable Network Graphics is an excellent format to use with your custom UI if you plan to have it attached with the project. You cannot use the `LoadPicture` function with this file format.
BMP	This refers to a bitmapped picture format. It is useful for loading pictures using the `LoadPicture` function.
ICO	Refers to icon format
WMF	Refers to Windows Metafile. Also useful when loading using the `LoadPicture` function.
JPG, JPEG	JPEG (Joint Photographic Experts Group) format offers a lower quality for the image.
GIF	Graphic Interchange Format, like JPEG, offers lower image quality overall.

If your UI will be custom-picture intensive, you should choose PNG over the other file formats. PNG is the only format that provides full support for transparency, and PNG pictures are highly compressible without loss of quality. In contrast, JPG and GIF formats are generally not recommended because of their low image quality.

NOTE **If you are wondering whether PNG format is the Eighth Wonder, that question does not have a straight answer. Although the format is great, you cannot load it on-the-fly using the available tools in VBA. Instead, you need to get specialized help from the GDI+ subsystem. We explain more about this in the section "Using GDI+ to load PNG files" later in this chapter.**

Appropriate Picture Size and Scaling

Now that you know what types you can use in your custom UI, it is only appropriate that you invest some time in learning a few things about size and scaling.

These factors are important to displaying clear and crisp pictures in your UI, rather than something sloppy and distorted. As a rule of thumb, figures should be sized at 16 × 16 and 32 × 32 with 96dpi, as shown in Figure 8-4. As you can see, these are square images. Although it isn't imperative, square images minimize distortion.

Figure 8-4: 16 × 16 and 32 × 32 images are the perfect size.

The thing to keep in mind here is that you may have a picture file that has the right canvas dimensions (16 × 16 or 32 × 32) but whose picture is not in the correct dimension, meaning that the picture covers an area that is smaller than the total canvas size. This may cause distortion (or some other unexpected result) when it is added to the UI. A disparity between the image's size and its canvas size often manifests as a white band representing the background of the image. You can learn more about the image dimensions and the canvas size by opening the image in an imaging software package, where you can look at the image (as a layer) against its background.

Adding Custom Pictures to Excel or Word Projects

Because Excel and Word work differently from Access, we will present the methods separately. In this first section, we demonstrate how to get the job done in Excel and Word. We later work with Access to load images using different methods.

You can load your custom pictures in different ways. You can attach the pictures in advance within the zipped XML group or you can load them on-the-fly. In this section, you will learn both methods.

Using the Custom UI Editor

When it comes to loading images, you will find that the methods used can vary from one another. You could, for example, go through the trouble of manually packaging them all together by sorting out the UI relationship files yourself. You'd soon learn that this involves too much unnecessary work and is prone to errors. An alternative is to simply use the Custom UI Editor and let it sort all the relationship files and attachments for you. That's the approach that we're going to use here.

CROSS-REFERENCE **If you skipped the chapter on the CustomUI Editor or need a refresher, see Chapter 2.**

In order to add a custom image, you must use the `image` attribute of the control. Suppose you want to add a custom image to a button — the XML code for the button should look something like this:

```
<button id="rxbtn"
   label="Custom Button"
   image="test_img"
   size="large"/>
```

By now, you're probably fluent in interpreting such straightforward XML, so we're just going to point out some helpful factors. In the preceding example, the image name is `test_img`. Notice that it is unnecessary to specify the file extension; the relationship file takes care of that as well as pointing to the correct location of the image within the XML zipped group. In this example, if you were to inspect the relationship XML file (`customUI.xml.rels`), you'd find the following code snippet:

```
<Relationships
xmlns="http://schemas.openxmlformats.org/package/2006/relationships">
  <Relationship
Type="http://schemas.openxmlformats.org/officeDocument/2006/relationships/image"
Target="images/test_img.bmp"
  Id="test_img" />
  </Relationships>
```

This relationship file and its XML code are automatically generated by the CustomUI Editor, a very handy tool to use. The next task is to load the images.

In order to use the CustomUI Editor to load custom images, follow these steps:

1. Open your workbook/document using the CustomUI Editor.
2. Add your UI XML code. Wherever you wish to add an image, use the `image` attribute and specify the filename — for example, `image="test_img"`. You do not need to worry about file extensions.
3. Click the `Insert Icon` button on the CustomUI Editor toolbar.
4. Browse to the folder containing the images and open the image files.

Figure 8-5 shows the `test_img` file added through the CustomUI Editor. Notice that the CustomUI Editor now has an extra column to list all images attached to the project.

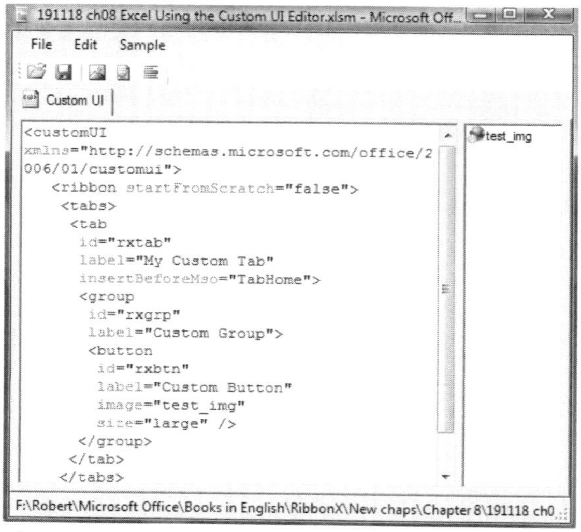

Figure 8-5: Adding custom pictures using the CustomUI Editor

This is a very easy way to load custom pictures to your UI, but it can also be very time consuming, especially if you have a lot of pictures to load. An alternative is to load the pictures on-the-fly, so we'll cover that next.

Loading Custom Pictures On-the-Fly

You now know how to load custom pictures using the CustomUI Editor, and how to identify your custom pictures in the UI. However, there may be times when you need to swap images on-the-fly, or when the volume of images is simply too large to justify a mega operation to write the XML code; in other words, you would spend more time writing XML code than anything else. In such situations, the images should not be bundled together with the XML files that make up your Excel workbook or Word document. Doing so would cause the images to sit statically on the UI because the UI will be built at design-time, not at run-time. If you need to swap images on-the-fly — for example, making a change at run-time — then you need to load the images using the `getImage` attribute of the control.

However, this brings us to yet another problem. In this case, the method for loading an image is normally through the VBA `LoadPicture` function. As pointed out previously, this function cannot handle PNG files, which are the best picture format for the Ribbon.

We'll start with something simple before getting to the details of loading custom PNG pictures. Our first example will load common BMP pictures into a `toggleButton`, as shown in the following code. We've chosen BMP files because they are very common.

After we cover how to load PNG images, which support full transparency, you can compare the results. Note that the method used to load bitmap files can also be used for icon files and Windows metafiles such as `FileName.ico`, `FileName.wmf`, and so on.

```
<toggleButton id="rxtgl"
label="Custom Button"
getImage="rxtgl_getImage"
size="large"
onAction="rxtgl_Click"/>
```

You use the `getImage` attribute to define a callback that will handle the loading of the picture. In this example, the callback is named as `rxtgl_getImage` and has the following signature:

```
rxtgl_getImage(control as IRibbonControl, ByRef returnedVal)
```

Because this example uses a `toggleButton`, you need to keep track of the toggle state — that is, is the button toggled or not? You can do this in various ways, such as by keeping its value in the registry. However, for our purposes, we will use a global Boolean variable to keep track of it. We also need an `onLoad` event to invalidate the control and ensure that the image is loaded according to the click of the `toggleButton`.

Hence, we will have the following VBA code in a standard module. Please note that this code is also provided in the download file for this chapter.

NOTE When placing code in modules, you can place them all in the same module. However, you may find it easier to separate the code into different modules for better organization and compartmentalization of the code. For example, you may wish to place callbacks in one module, custom functions in another, and so on. Remember to save the modules and name them in accordance with whatever naming conventions you have adopted.

```
Dim grxIRibbonUI As IRibbonUI
Dim gblnPressed As Boolean

Sub rxIRibbonUI_onLoad(ribbon As IRibbonUI)
    Set grxIRibbonUI = ribbon
End Sub

Sub rxtgl_getImage(control As IRibbonControl, ByRef returnedVal)
    Set returnedVal = LoadImage(ThisWorkbook.Path & "\mex.bmp")
    If gblnPressed Then Set returnedVal = _
        LoadImage(ThisWorkbook.Path & "\usa.bmp")
End Sub

Sub rxtgl_Click(control As IRibbonControl, pressed As Boolean)
    gblnPressed = pressed
    grxIRibbonUI.InvalidateControl ("rxtgl")
End Sub
```

Figure 8-6 shows the customized `toggleButton`. Note that the labels for the images are static.

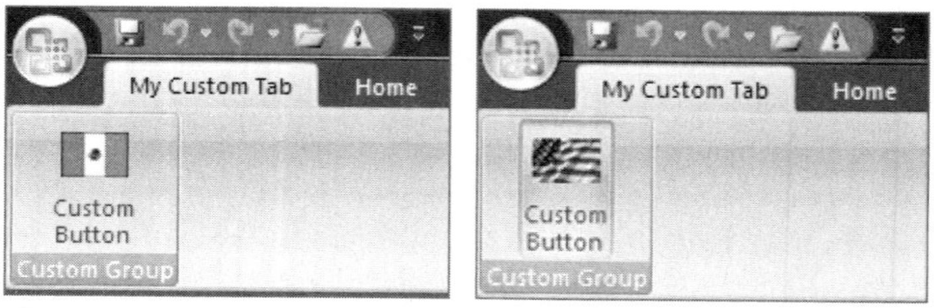

Figure 8-6: Swapping images on-the-fly

If you wish, you can use the `getLabel` attribute instead of the `Label` attribute to dynamically change the labels as you toggle and release the `toggleButton`. The following lines of code are enough to get that done:

```
Sub rxtgl_getLabel(control As IRibbonControl, ByRef returnedVal)
    returnedVal = "Mexico Rocks!"
    If gblnPressed Then returnedVal = "The US Rocks!"
End Sub
```

NOTE **Before using the preceding code, ensure that you have replaced the `Label` attribute with the `getLabel` attribute, as they cannot coexist in the XML code.**

Adding Custom Pictures to Access Projects

Access, as you have already seen, is unique when it comes to customization. You will remember that you added your XML code to a table, loaded the UI, chose the UI, and then had to close and reopen the file before you could have a glimpse of the new UI.

Just as you do not attach your XML UI file to a bundle of compressed XML files that make up an Excel workbook or Word document, you cannot bundle pictures in Access using this method. Instead, you have to rely on other means.

Despite Access's uniqueness, one of the methods presented for Excel and Word also works for Access: using the `getImage` attribute to specify a callback that will load the images into Access on-the-fly.

Loading on-the-fly is not always going to be the desired approach, though, so another option is to store the images in an attachment field (a great new feature in Access 2007) and then retrieve these files and load them to the UI. This is akin to bundling the image files in the compressed format for Excel and Word. Storing the images within the file avoids concerns about shipping images separately or suddenly missing images.

Use the following steps to store images in an attachment field:

NOTE **When adding the fields to the table, ensure that you are in Design View. If you create a field from Datasheet View by typing in the data, you cannot convert the field to an attachment field later.**

1. Add a new table and name it `USysRibbonImages`. (You may use a different name, but this name is used in the following code and examples).
2. Add the following fields to the new table:
   - ID (an auto numbering field)
   - ImageName (a text field)
   - ImageFile (an attachment field)
3. Save and close the table.
4. With the table selected (but still closed), go to Create ➪ Forms ➪ Form and create a new form based on the `USysRibbonImages` table.

Next, you need to fill in the details for each image and attach the image files to their corresponding fields in the table. You are, in fact, simply adding records to the table. After you have added a couple of records, the table (in Datasheet View) should look similar to the table shown in Figure 8-7.

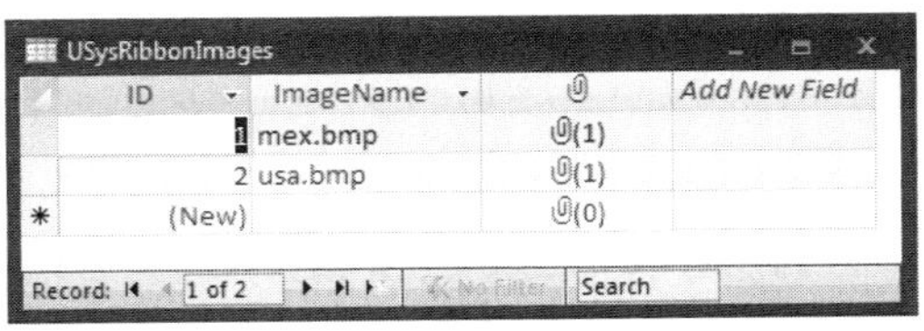

Figure 8-7: Adding image files as records in an attachment field

With the images attached to the fields and the table ready, you can now write the VBA code that will handle the swapping (loading) of the two images. We used the following code placed in a standard module (to add a standard module, click Create ➪ Other ➪ Macro ➪ Module):

```
'Declaration of global variables
Dim grxIRibbonUI          As IRibbonUI
Dim gblnPressed           As Boolean
Dim gFrmImages            As Form
Dim grstForm              As DAO.Recordset2

Sub rxIRibbonUI_onLoad(ribbon As IRibbonUI)
'    Open the form containing the records for the images
    DoCmd.OpenForm "USysRibbonImages", , , , acFormReadOnly, acHidden
```

```
'   Set the global form as being the USysRibbonImages form
    Set gFrmImages = Forms("USysRibbonImages")

'   Set the form recordset
    Set grstForm = gFrmImages.Recordset

    Set grxIRibbonUI = ribbon

End Sub

Sub rxtgl_getImage(control As IRibbonControl, ByRef returnedVal)

'   If the toggleButton is not pressed, then load the Mexican flag by...
    If Not (gblnPressed) Then
'       ... finding the Mexican flag record...
        grstForm.FindFirst "ImageName='mex.bmp'"
'       ... and setting the toggleButton image
'       equal to the image attachment
        Set returnedVal = gFrmImages.imagefile.PictureDisp
    Else
'       Otherwise, load the American flag image
        grstForm.FindFirst "ImageName='usa.bmp'"
        Set returnedVal = gFrmImages.imagefile.PictureDisp
    End If
End Sub

Sub rxtgl_Click(control As IRibbonControl, pressed As Boolean)
    gblnPressed = pressed
    grxIRibbonUI.InvalidateControl ("rxtgl")
End Sub
```

This method works fine, but you should also know that all of the images can be stored in a single record. You can do this in conjunction with using the `USysRibbons` table to save time and keep customization-specific images in a single location. Keep in mind that there may be more than one customization stored in the table, and each one of these customizations may have its own set of images.

Now it is time to demonstrate this technique. Using your current file, follow these steps:

1. Add a new field to the `USysRibbons` table and set its data type to attachment. In our example, the field is called RibbonImages.
2. Create a new form based on the `USysRibbons` table. (By default it will have the same name as the table; you can keep the name or change it if you like.)
3. Attach to this field all of the images that you want to use. You may want to match the attachments to each UI you have on the table. The attachment field will show the total number of pictures attached to it, as shown in Figure 8-8.

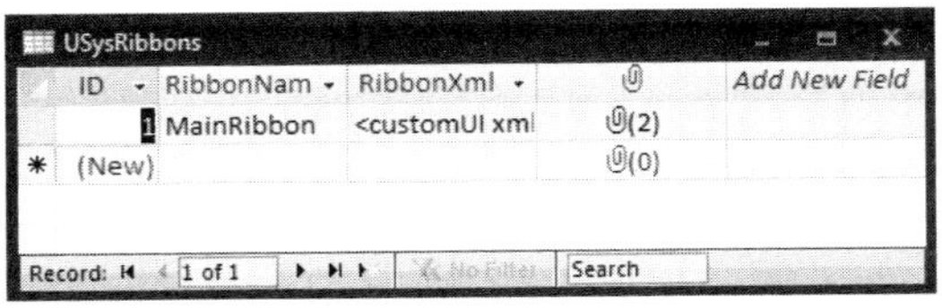

Figure 8-8: Adding image files as attachments to a single record

Next, it is time to write the VBA that will handle loading the image for the `toggleButton`. We used the following code in a standard module (you can create a new module or add this to an existing module, whichever fits best with your standard practices and naming conventions):

```
Dim grxIRibbonUI          As IRibbonUI
Dim gblnPressed           As Boolean
Dim gAttachment           As Attachment

Sub rxIRibbonUI_onLoad(ribbon As IRibbonUI)

'   Open the form and set the attachment as being the attachment
'   control on the form
    DoCmd.OpenForm "USysRibbons", , , , acFormReadOnly, acHidden
    Set gAttachment = Forms("USysRibbons").Controls("RibbonImages")

    Set grxIRibbonUI = ribbon

End Sub

Sub rxtgl_getImage(control As IRibbonControl, ByRef returnedVal)
'   Set the image according to the need. Use the file name to
'   refer to the image you want to load
    Set returnedVal = gAttachment.PictureDisp("usa.bmp")
    If Not (gblnPressed) Then Set returnedVal = _
        gAttachment.PictureDisp("mex.bmp")
End Sub
```

Everything looks great except for one significant detail: the image is a BMP that displays with a white background, which makes it look plain ugly.

As previously mentioned, you cannot load PNG images to the UI using the common methods applied here; instead, you need to use Windows APIs. That is covered in the next section, so keep working.

Using GDI+ to Load PNG Files

This section describes how to use the GDI+ (Graphics Device Interface Plus) APIs to load PNG files. However, because many of you may not be familiar with GDI+, we'll take just a moment to provide a definition before jumping into the examples.

GDI+ is one of the core subsystems of Windows. It is used as an interface for representing graphical objects when you need to send these objects to devices such as displays and/or printers. The GDI+ handles the rendering of various drawing objects, and here we use it to render PNG objects so that they can be loaded onto the UI.

Unfortunately, you cannot use `PictureDisp`, as you did in the preceding section, to refer to a PNG file, let alone use the `LoadPicture` function to load a picture from an external location. You need to use some other technique to load your pictures.

The method you will use involves the implementation of some Windows APIs, whose explanation is beyond the scope of this book. Moreover, the code for such a task is quite long, so we will not repeat it here; however, you can find it in the accompanying sample files in the download for this chapter on the book' website.

Because the focus of this example is loading images, you can use the examples from the previous sections and thereby use the same XML. Right now, it is only VBA code that we're concerned about.

The User Defined Function (UDF) based on GDI+ APIs is called `LoadImage`. Hence, if you wish to load images in Excel or Word, all you need to do is replace the `LoadPicture` function with the `LoadImage` function. The VBA code relating to the `getImage` attribute would now look like the following after making the appropriate changes:

```
Sub rxtgl_getImage(control As IRibbonControl, ByRef returnedVal)
    Set returnedVal = LoadImage(ThisWorkbook.Path & "\mex.png")
    If gblnPressed Then Set returnedVal = _
        LoadImage(ThisWorkbook.Path & "\usa.png")
End Sub
```

You can use the same method in Access, but be aware that you also have other options. For example, suppose you used a table containing an attachment field to store your PNG images (like the one you used in the first Access example). In that case, you need to modify the `rxtgl_getImage` callback. You also need to declare and instantiate a new variable.

To get started, open the VBE and, in the General Declarations area of your standard module, declare the following variable:

```
Dim gstrTempFolderFile  As String
```

For the `onLoad` event, you only need to set the `IRibbonUI` object. The form and attachment objects used previously will not be necessary this time. The `rxtgl_Click` event will remain the same. The big change occurs in the `rxtgl_getImage` callback. For that, we use the following code:

```
Sub rxtgl_getImage(control As IRibbonControl, ByRef returnedVal)
    Dim rstData          As DAO.Recordset
    Dim rstImages        As DAO.Recordset
    Dim db               As DAO.Database
```

```
    Dim objWSHShell As Object
    Dim strSQL As String

    Set db = CurrentDb
    If gstrTempFolderFile = "" Then
        Set objWSHShell = CreateObject("WScript.Shell")
        gstrTempFolderFile = _
            objWSHShell.SpecialFolders("Desktop") & "\temp.png"
    End If

    strSQL = "SELECT * FROM RibbonImages WHERE ImageName='usa.png'"
    If gblnPressed Then strSQL = _
        "SELECT * FROM RibbonImages WHERE ImageName='mex.png'"

    On Error Resume Next
    Set rstData = db.OpenRecordset(strSQL, dbOpenDynaset)
    Set rstImages = rstData.Fields("ImageFile").Value
    rstImages.Fields("FileData").SaveToFile gstrTempFolderFile

    Set returnedVal = LoadImage(gstrTempFolderFile)

    Kill gstrTempFolderFile

    db.Close
    rstData.Close
    rstImages.Close

    Set db = Nothing
    Set rstData = Nothing
    Set rstImages = Nothing
    Set objWSHShell = Nothing

End Sub
```

Now that you have the code in front of you, take a moment to review what it is doing:

1. You create a `Shell` object so that you can temporarily save the image to a location in your hard drive. Our example uses the Desktop as the temporary location.
2. You define a SQL instruction to retrieve the image and save it to the defined location (directly on the Desktop) using the `SaveToFile` method.
3. The image is loaded using the `LoadImage` function.
4. The temporary image is deleted from the Desktop.
5. You close with some good housekeeping techniques.

NOTE **If you are using Windows Vista with User Account Control switched on, you must choose an area of the hard drive for which you have permission to write. To avoid undue complications, we chose the Desktop as the destination of the temporary PNG file.**

Using the Gallery Control

The gallery control is new to Office 2007 and was conceived in conjunction with the Ribbon. The gallery was designed as a way to graphically display user options; an excellent example is the Styles gallery, which enables users to select a style by looking at a graphical representation of the style, rather than a name.

You can use galleries for such tasks as organizing photos, accessing styles, or storing color palettes. A gallery is the perfect control for a customization that requires and provides visual impact.

Figure 8-9 shows a photo gallery.

Figure 8-9: A two-column photo gallery

Note that you can also add buttons at the bottom of the gallery. With such versatility, the uses for a gallery are limited only by your imagination.

Before we get into the code for a gallery, let's briefly review how this example works. It is advisable that you download all files for this chapter before continuing. We have created various examples of image galleries for your reference.

As you can see from the image gallery examples in Access, each image represents an item in the gallery — these items are loaded from images contained in a folder. When you click on the icon to expand the gallery, it will list the images contained in the folder; clicking on a specific image will open the folder that contains the actual image files that are represented in the gallery. Note that our example only displays the PNG version of the image in the gallery, but the folders actually contain both a PNG and a BMP version of the selected photos.

When users click on an image, they will get a standard message from Access advising them that they are about to open the folder with the gallery images. Clicking Yes will then open the selected folder using Windows Explorer, so it will show all the files, not just the image files. At that point, the behavior of the files and images is controlled by the default setting on the computer. If you click on an image, it will open with the default program, such as Windows Picture and Fax Viewer (you can open the image using its associated program directly from your project through a Shell function, for example).

The markup for a gallery is as follows:

```
<gallery>
   <!-- Your XML code goes here -->
</gallery>
```

A gallery is made up of static, dynamic, and optional child attributes. It requires each of the static attributes shown in Table 8-2.

Table 8-2: Gallery Static Attributes

STATIC ATTRIBUTE	ALLOWED VALUES	VBA CALLBACK SIGNATURE FOR DYNAMIC ATTRIBUTE
columns	1 to 1024	N/A
itemHeight	1 to 4096	Sub getItemHeight (control As IRibbonControl, ByRef height)
itemWidth	1 to 4096	Sub getItemWidth (control As IRibbonControl, ByRef width)
rows	1 to 1024	N/A
sizeString	1 to 1024 characters	N/A
showItemImage	true, false, 1, 0	N/A
showItemLabel	true, false, 1, 0	N/A

A gallery may also have all of the dynamic attributes shown in Table 8-3.

Table 8-3: Gallery Dynamic Attributes

DYNAMIC ATTRIBUTE	ALLOWED VALUES	VBA CALLBACK SIGNATURE FOR DYNAMIC ATTRIBUTE
getItemCount	0 to 1000	Sub GetItemCount (control As IRibbonControl, ByRef count)
getItemID		Sub GetItemID (control As IRibbonControl, index As Integer, ByRef id)
getItemImage		Sub GetItemImage (control As IRibbonControl, index As Integer, ByRef image)

Continued

Table 8-3 *(continued)*

DYNAMIC ATTRIBUTE	ALLOWED VALUES	VBA CALLBACK SIGNATURE FOR DYNAMIC ATTRIBUTE
getItemLabel	1024	Sub GetItemLabel (control As IRibbonControl, index As Integer, ByRef label)
getItemScreentip	1024	Sub GetItemScreenTip (control As IRibbonControl, index As Integer, ByRef screentip)
getItemSupertip	1024	Sub GetItemSuperTip (control As IRibbonControl, index As Integer, ByRef supertip)
getSelectedItemID	1 to 1024 characters	Sub GetSelectedItemID (control As IRibbonControl, ByRef index)
getSelectedItemIndex	1 to 1024	Sub GetSelectedItemIndex (control As IRibbonControl, ByRef index)
onAction		Sub OnAction (control As IRibbonControl, selectedId As String, selectedIndex As Integer)

Finally, a gallery can take either or both of the objects shown in Table 8-4 as its child elements; it can also have multiple instances of each.

Table 8-4: Child Elements of a Gallery

OBJECT	WHAT IT IS FOR
button	Add a clickable button to the gallery in the same way you can add a clickable button to a group, for example.
item	Adds an item to the gallery. The item can be a graphical representation of some action that you want to perform, such as a graphical representation of a chart layout.

Now that you've seen the list of gallery attributes, let's take a look at the benefits and uses of each category.

Example of Static Attributes

Using static values for attributes means that the customization cannot be modified after the UI has been loaded. Remember that the Ribbon is built at design-time, not at run-time. After the UI is loaded, limited changes may be possible if the control is dynamic or has dynamic attributes.

Our demonstration walks through creating the gallery shown in Figure 8-9. In order to create a gallery, follow these steps:

1. Create your Excel or Word file and ensure that it is macro-enabled.
2. Save and close the file. Open it using the CustomUI Editor.
3. Paste the following XML code into it:

```
<customUI xmlns="http://schemas.microsoft.com/office/2006/01/customui">
  <ribbon startFromScratch="false">
    <tabs>
     <tab id="rxtab"
      insertBeforeMso="TabHome"
      label="My Custom Tab">

      <group id="rxgrp"
       label="My Photo Gallery">

       <!-- Starts the definition of our gallery-->
       <gallery id="rxgal"
         label="My Photo Gallery"
         image="img4"
         columns="2"
         rows="2"
         itemWidth="200"
         itemHeight="150"
         showItemLabel="false"
         size="large">

       <!-- Insert the photo gallery-->
       <!-- Import the photos you want to use first-->
       <item id="rxitem0" label="London 1" image="img0"/>
       <item id="rxitem1" label="London 2" image="img1" />
       <item id="rxitem2" label="London 3" image="img2" />
       <item id="rxitem3" label="London 4" image="img3" />
       <item id="rxitem4" label="London 5" image="img4" />
       <item id="rxitem5" label="London 6" image="img5" />

       <!-- Insert a button at the end of the gallery-->
       <button id="rxbtn"
         imageMso="RefreshStatus"
         label="Visit Wiley online..."
         onAction="rxbtn_Click"/>
       </gallery>
      </group>
     </tab>
    </tabs>
  </ribbon>
</customUI>
```

4. Load the images named `img0` through `img5` using the CustomUI Editor.

CROSS-REFERENCE **For more detailed instructions on this method of loading custom images, refer to the section "Using the Custom UI Editor" earlier in this chapter.**

Example of Built-in Controls

A good use for built-in galleries is to consolidate into one location those tools you use most often. For example, you may have galleries under the Home, Insert, and Page Layout tabs that you want to bring together under a custom tab so that you have them all in one place. That way, you don't need to navigate from one tab to another, which can be distracting and time consuming.

As you know, you refer to built-in controls by invoking the `idMso` attribute for the control that you want. The following example brings together three gallery controls onto a custom tab and group in Excel:

```
 <box id="rxbox1" boxStyle="horizontal">
   <gallery idMso="FontColorPicker" label="AAA"/>
   <labelControl id="rxlbl1" label="Font Color"/>
</box>
<box id="rxbox2" boxStyle="horizontal">
   <gallery idMso="CellFillColorPicker"/>
   <labelControl id="rxlbl2" label="Cell Color"/>
</box>
<box id="rxbox3" boxStyle="horizontal">
   <gallery idMso="ChartTypeColumnInsertGallery" size="normal"/>
</box>
```

Reviewing the code, you may have noticed two controls that we haven't yet covered: `labelControl` and `box`. Chapter 10 explains the features and attributes of these controls, as well as how to work with them. For now, we want to stay focused on working with images.

Figure 8-10 shows our new consolidation and custom group.

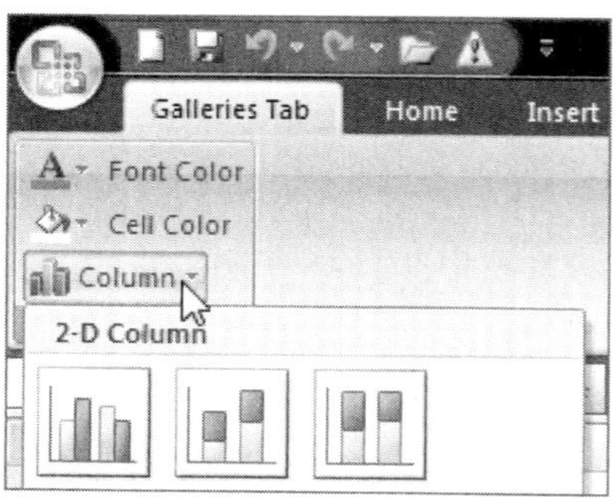

Figure 8-10: Consolidated built-in galleries

Creating an Image Gallery On-the-Fly

The previous example is fine as long as you do not have to load a lot of images. As the number of images in your gallery increases, you need to type more into the XML code. Obviously, this is not only time consuming but also complicated to maintain.

The following example helps you avoid that extra typing. Although it is for Access, it can also be used in Excel or Word. In fact, this example is drawn from the previous one, with the difference that this dynamically loads the images. You will also notice two new attributes, as well as one that you've already seen.

- `getImage`: You have already seen this attribute. You will use it to load the front picture of the gallery (not the actual gallery pictures).
- `getItemCount`: This attribute is used to return the total number of items in the gallery. You will use a constant in the VBA code to determine this value so that you can easily change the item count if you need.
- `getItemImage`: This attribute is used to load the item image — that is, each image that appears in the gallery.

Note that you do not run a loop through each item; instead, the Ribbon will call back on the `getItemImage` attribute (hence the "callback" terminology) until it runs through all the items determined for the `getItemCount` attribute. As it does so, it returns an index number for each item's image. You then use this index to grab and load each corresponding picture.

The XML code for this customization is as follows:

```
<customUI xmlns="http://schemas.microsoft.com/office/2006/01/customui">
   <ribbon startFromScratch="false">
      <tabs>
         <tab id="rxtab"
            insertBeforeMso="TabHomeAccess"
            label="My Custom Tab">

            <group id="rxgrp"
               label="My Photo Gallery">

               <!-- Starts the definition of our gallery -->
               <gallery id="rxgal"
                  label="My Photo Gallery"
                  columns="2"
                  rows="2"
                  itemWidth="200"
                  itemHeight="150"
                  getImage="rxgal_getImage"
                  getItemCount="rxgal_getItemCount"
                  getItemImage="rxgal_getItemImage"
                  onAction="rxgal_Click"
                  showItemLabel="false" size="large">

                  <!-- Inserts a button at the bottom of the gallery -->
```

```
                    <button id="rxbtn"
                        imageMso="RefreshStatus"
                        label="Visit Wiley online..."
                        onAction="rxbtn_Click"/>
                </gallery>
            </group>
        </tab>
    </tabs>
  </ribbon>
</customUI>
```

Save the XML code to your `USysRibbon` table in Access and add a standard module to which you add the following callbacks:

```
Public Const gcItemCount = 6

Sub rxgal_getItemCount(control As IRibbonControl, ByRef returnedVal)
    returnedVal = gcItemCount
End Sub

Sub rxgal_getItemImage(control As IRibbonControl, index As Integer, _
    ByRef returnedVal)

    Set returnedVal = _
        LoadPicture(CurrentProject.Path & "\img" & index & ".bmp")
End Sub

Sub rxgal_getImage(control As IRibbonControl, ByRef returnedVal)
    Set returnedVal = LoadPicture(CurrentProject.Path & "\img4.tif")
End Sub

Sub rxgal_Click(control As IRibbonControl, id As String, _
    index As Integer)

    MsgBox "You have click on image index number " & index
End Sub
```

You are now probably questioning the BMP format. No worries — if you need to load the suggested format (PNG) you can use the `LoadImage` function to do so. The Access project that accompanies this example uses the `LoadImage` function to load PNG files.

Conclusion

In this chapter, you learned the intricacies of dealing with custom images in a custom UI. You learned what file formats are appropriate and which sizes are ideal, as well as scaling and resolution of such files.

You went through the process of manually loading images, and used the `LoadPicture` function and a more specialized UDF wrapper function based on a Windows API.

You also learned some unique ways of storing and retrieving images from an attachment field of an Access table to be used in your UI and how to build custom galleries and consolidate built-in galleries.

Now you are ready to add a very personal touch to an already personalized working environment, so go have fun with your photos and other images.

The next chapter describes how to create menus and how to use the `splitButton` and `dynamicMenu` controls to organize your UI.

CHAPTER

9

Creating Menus

In implementing the Ribbon, one of Microsoft's primary goals was to provide a more intuitive user interface and to move away from the old menu-driven paradigm that had historically housed Office's commands. Therefore, it may come as a bit of a surprise to find out that menus are still very much alive and well. In fact, in selected scenarios they actually form the most dynamic of all the controls that the Ribbon has to offer.

The `comboBox` and `dropDown` controls you learned about in Chapter 7 can be viewed as menu-type controls, in that they both provide a label next to an empty box; and by clicking that box, the user is provided a list of items to pick from.

This chapter deals with three other menu-type controls: the `menu`, the `splitButton` and the `dynamicMenu`. Unlike the `comboBox` and `dropDown` controls, the `menu` and `splitButton` controls provide their menus behind a button-style interface from which the options become available. The `dynamicMenu` is similar in purpose to the `menu`, but actually creates a full menu on-the-fly.

This chapter provides a detailed discussion of these three controls and includes examples showing how to create and use each one. As you are preparing to work through the examples in this chapter, we encourage you to download the companion files. The source code and files can be found on the book's website at `www.wiley.com/go/ribbonx`.

The menu Element

On the surface, the `menu` is very similar in purpose to the `dropDown` controls we created in Chapter 7. A menu provides the user with a pre-defined list of options to pick from, and like the `dropDown` it can incorporate both images and text. Why learn about the menu control if the `dropDown` does the same thing?

One major limitation of a `dropDown` control is that it can only hold "items," whereas a `menu` control can hold a wide variety of other controls, including buttons, checkboxes, galleries, and even another menu. Although we haven't yet demonstrated these other controls in the examples, you can appreciate that the capability to nest all of these elements within a menu gives it very rich formatting possibilities, and thereby makes the `dropDown` seem quite plain in comparison.

In addition, the default display of the `dropDown` is an empty box, but the `menu` can be configured with a "face" that is independent of the actual items that appear in its list. Given that appearance and first impressions matter, being able to give the menu a face is a rather attractive feature.

The `menu` control also has an attribute that can be used to draw lines between controls in the menu. While the `menuSeparator` attribute is not explored until Chapter 10, it is nonetheless one of the reasons why the `menu` control is used; used together, these elements enable you to bring controls together in groups and then organize them into subgroups.

Required Attributes of the menu Element

To create a `menu` element, you need to define one, and only one, of the `id` attributes shown in Table 9-1.

Table 9-1: Required Attributes of the menu Element

ATTRIBUTE	WHEN TO USE
id	When creating your own menu
idMso	When using an existing Microsoft menu
idQ	When creating a menu shared between namespaces

Optional Static and Dynamic Attributes with Callback Signatures

The `menu` element will optionally accept any one `insert` attribute shown in Table 9-2.

Table 9-2: Optional insert Attributes of the menu Element

INSERT ATTRIBUTE	ALLOWED VALUES	DEFAULT VALUE	WHEN TO USE
insertAfterMso	Valid Mso Group	Insert at end of group	Insert after Microsoft control
insertBeforeMso	Valid Mso Group	Insert at end of group	Insert before Microsoft control
insertAfterQ	Valid Group idQ	Insert at end of group	Insert after shared namespace control
insertBeforeQ	Valid Group idQ	Insert at end of group	Insert before shared namespace control

In addition to the `insert` attribute, you may also include any of the optional static attributes, or their dynamic equivalents, listed in Table 9-3.

Table 9-3: Optional Attributes and Callbacks of the menu Element

STATIC ATTRIBUTE	DYNAMIC ATTRIBUTE	ALLOWED VALUES	DEFAULT VALUE	VBA CALLBACK SIGNATURE FOR DYNAMIC ATTRIBUTE
description	getDescription	1 to 1024 characters	(none)	Sub GetDescription (control As IRibbonControl, ByRef returnedVal)
enabled	getEnabled	true, false, 1, 0	true	Sub GetEnabled (control As IRibbonControl, ByRef returnedVal)
image	getImage	1 to 1024 characters	(none)	Sub GetImage (control As IRibbonControl, ByRef returnedVal)
imageMso	getImage	1 to 1024 characters	(none)	Same as above
itemSize	(none)	normal, large	normal	(none)
keytip	getKeytip	1 to 3 characters	(none)	Sub GetKeytip (control As IRibbonControl, ByRef returnedVal)

Continued

Table 9-3 *(continued)*

STATIC ATTRIBUTE	DYNAMIC ATTRIBUTE	ALLOWED VALUES	DEFAULT VALUE	VBA CALLBACK SIGNATURE FOR DYNAMIC ATTRIBUTE
label	getLabel	1 to 1024 characters	(none)	Sub GetLabel (control As IRibbonControl, ByRef returnedVal)
screentip	getScreentip	1 to 1024 characters	(none)	Sub GetScreentip (control As IRibbonControl, ByRef returnedVal)
showImage	getShowImage	true, false, 1, 0	true	Sub GetShowImage (control As IRibbonControl, ByRef returnedVal)
showLabel	getShowLabel	true, false, 1, 0	true	Sub GetShowLabel (control As IRibbonControl, ByRef returnedVal)
size	getSize	normal, large	normal	Sub GetSize (control As IRibbonControl, ByRef returnedVal)
supertip	getSupertip	1 to 1024 characters	(none)	Sub GetSupertip (control As IRibbonControl, ByRef returnedVal)
tag	(none)	1 to 1024 characters	(none)	(none)
visible	getVisible	true, false, 1, 0	true	Sub GetVisible (control As IRibbonControl, ByRef returnedVal)

Allowed Children Objects of the menu Element

The `menu` element will accept any combination of the following child objects:

- button
- checkbox
- control
- dynamicMenu
- gallery

- menu
- menuSeparator
- splitButton
- toggleButton

Parent Controls of the menu Element

The `menu` element may be used within the following controls:

- box
- buttonGroup
- dynamicMenu
- group
- menu
- officeMenu
- splitButton

Graphical View of menu Attributes

Figure 9-1 displays a custom Ribbon group in Word with a `menu` control. Because the `menu` control is shown in its expanded form, you cannot see the screentip, supertip, or keytip associated with the custom Save As menu, but they are available. The figure also illustrates the effect of the `itemSize` attribute, showing the menu items with a setting of "normal," rather than "large."

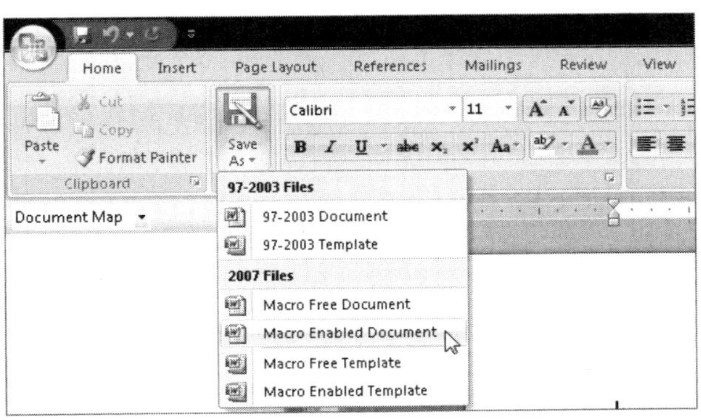

Figure 9-1: Visible attributes of the menu element

Despite the fact that this is a completely customized Save As menu, it will probably look quite intuitive. The "97-2003 Files" and "2007 Files" headers are both `menuSeparator` elements, which instantly add clarity by grouping the controls. The `menuSeparator` can also provide the dividing line, as shown in the heading lines "97-2003 Files" and "2007 Files." Chapter 10 explains how to add the various `menuSeparator` elements to a customization.

Using Built-in Controls

Microsoft exposes several `menu` controls for our use, so let's take a look at how you would go about using one of them. The Prepare menu is available in both Excel and Word. It is usually located on the Office Menu (see Figure 9-2).

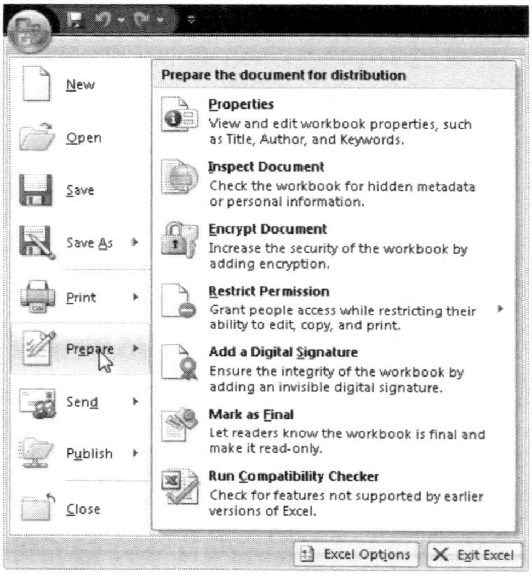

Figure 9-2: The Prepare menu in Excel

However, let's assume that due to frequent usage, it would save the users time if this were conveniently located on a custom Ribbon tab instead of being buried on the Office button. The first thing that you would want to do is create a new file to hold the code. Open either Excel or Word, create a new document, and save it in the macro-free file format (`xlsx` or `docx`, respectively). That's a benefit of working with a built-in control. No VBA code is required to make this work, so the file can be saved in a macro-free format, and the customizations will be fully functional. Once the file is saved, close the application.

CROSS-REFERENCE **Chapter 17 provides a more complete discussion of security and enabling macros.**

Launch the CustomUI Editor and open the file within it. Apply the RibbonBase template that you created in Chapter 2, and insert the following code between the `<tabs>` and `</tabs>` tags:

```
<tab id="rxtabDemo"
   label="Demo"
   insertBeforeMso="TabHome">
   <group id="rxgrpDemo"
      label="Demo">
      <menu idMso="FilePrepareMenu"
      size="large"/>
   </group>
</tab>
```

Once you have validated your code, save it and close the file in the CustomUI Editor. Reopen the file in its native application and check the Demo tab. As shown in Figure 9-3, the menu has smoothly moved into a Ribbon group.

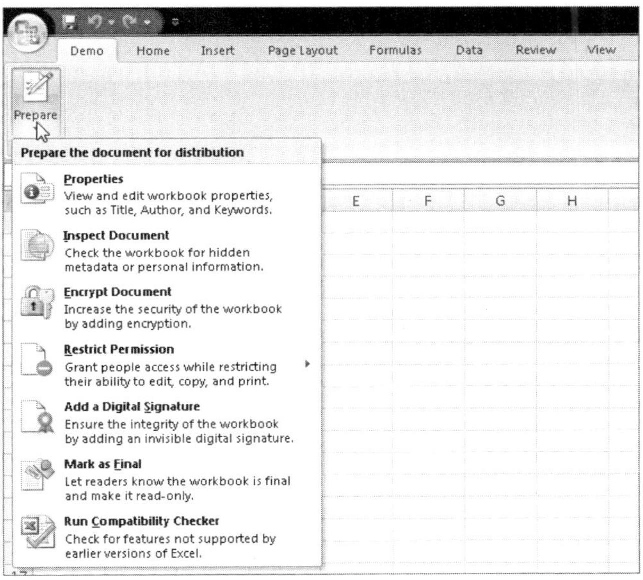

Figure 9-3: The "FilePrepareMenu" on a custom tab

Of course, this is actually just a copy of the Prepare menu, so it will still be in the default location under the Office button. That is only logical, as users are accustomed to finding commands where Microsoft places them. In other words, unless you use the `startFromScratch` setting, discussed in Chapter 13, customizations will merely create additional links to built-in commands.

Creating Custom Controls

With so many controls on the Ribbon, it is nice to know that you can use Microsoft's built-in controls pretty much wherever you'd like. It is relatively easy to provide convenient, custom groups of the controls that an individual (or department) uses the most. However, as you begin to design your own user interfaces, it will quickly become apparent that the built-in controls are just not enough. This is why we now turn our focus to some practical examples that demonstrate why you might want to create custom menu controls, and how you can do that for each of the three applications. The `menu` control is used in a variety of examples throughout the book, so you'll have more opportunities to use it in conjunction with other controls. In fact, you'll use it later in this chapter with the `splitButton` control.

An Excel Example

For this example, we create a menu that holds a few useful Internet links. It will be contained on a custom group called "Ribbon Help" and placed at the end of the Developer tab.

Naturally, Microsoft cannot provide us with this exact menu, because we want it to contain our preferred links. That means that we need to create the entire menu from scratch. That requires VBA code to react to the selected items, so open Excel, create a new workbook, and save it in the macro-enabled (`xlsm`) format. After saving the file, close Excel and open the file in the CustomUI Editor.

Apply the RibbonBase template (created in Chapter 2) to the file, and enter the following code between the `<tabs>` and `</tabs>` tags:

```
<tab idMso="TabDeveloper">
   <group id="rxgrpRibbonHelp"
      label="Ribbon Help">
      <menu id="mnuResources"
         imageMso="HyperlinkInsert"
         size="large"
         label="Useful Links">
         <menuSeparator id="rxmSepRibbon"
            title="RibbonX Resources"/>
         <button id="rxbtnMSDN"
            label="MSDN Ribbon Developer Centre"
            onAction="rxsharedLinks_click"
            tag="http://msdn2.microsoft.com/↵
en-us/cffice/aa905530.aspx"/>
         <button id="rxbtnKenPuls"
            label="The Ken Puls blog (Excel MVP)"
            onAction="rxsharedLinks_click"
            tag="http://www.excelguru.ca/blog/2006/12/01/↵
ribbon-example-table-of-contents"/>
         <button id="rxbtnRondeBruin"
            label="Ron deBruin's Site (Excel MVP)"
            onAction="rxsharedLinks_click"
            tag="http://www.rondebruin.nl/ribbon.htm"/>
         <button id="rxbtnAccessFreak"
            label="Access Freak (Access MVP)"
            onAction="rxsharedLinks_click"
            tag="http://www.access-freak.com"/>
         <button id="rxbtnPatrickSchmid
```

```
 label="Patrick Schmid's RibbonX Forum"
            onAction="rxsharedLinks_click"
            tag="http://pschmid.net/office2007/forums"/>
         <menuSeparator id="rxmSepAuthors"
            title="Authors Sites"/>
         <button id="rxbtnAuthorRobertMartin"
            label="Robert Martin"
            onAction="rxsharedLinks_click"
            tag="http://www.msofficegurus.com/"/>
         <button id="rxbtnAuthorKenPuls"
            label="Ken Puls"
            onAction="rxsharedLinks_click"
            tag="http://www.excelguru.ca/"/>
         <button id="rxbtnAuthorTeresaHennig"
            label="Teresa Hennig"
            onAction="rxsharedLinks_click"
            tag="http://www.DataDyanmicsNW.com/"/>
      </menu>
   </group>
</tab>
```

This code creates a menu that lists seven websites in all. (Four of those sites have Ribbon-specific information, while the last three are the authors' own sites.) The `menuSeparator` effectively distinguishes the two groupings. We explain how to use the `menuSeparator` in Chapter 10.

Notice that we have used the same callback for every `menu` control. While this is not necessary, it helps to make the VBA code very concise. Also note that we store the actual URLs in the `tag` attribute. The reason for that will become very clear when you read the VBA code.

CROSS-REFERENCE The standard processes for working with callbacks were discussed in detail in Chapter 5. If you feel a little less confident with any of the other steps, a quick review of Chapters 3 and 4 will provide a refresher on XML and VBA.

As usual, validate the code to ensure that no typing errors were made and then save the file. Before closing the file in the CustomUI Editor, don't forget to generate and copy the callback signature.

Reopen the file in Excel, launch the VBE, and add a new standard module to the project. Paste your callback signature within the new module and adjust it to read as follows:

```
'Callback for rxsharedLinks onAction
Sub rxsharedLinks_click(control As IRibbonControl)
    ActiveWorkbook.FollowHyperlink _
            Address:=control.Tag, _
            NewWindow:=True
End Sub
```

This code launches a hyperlink in a new Web window. It is very simple, but why do we only need the one line? Will it work for all the different menu items? The answer to this question is yes, of course, and it all revolves around how we constructed the `tag` property.

When a callback is fired, the `control` object is passed to the procedure. This object has three properties: `context`, `id`, and `tag`. A callback will normally query the ID of the control and react accordingly, but in this case it queries the tag because that is where we stored the URL. The hyperlink is then provided for whichever control is clicked. This eliminates the need to worry about which control was actually fired, and the appropriate hyperlink is launched.

Try it out. Save the code, return to the main Excel user interface, and click the Developer tab. As shown in Figure 9-4, the Useful Links menu is now at the end. Try clicking one of the items to be taken to the site listed.

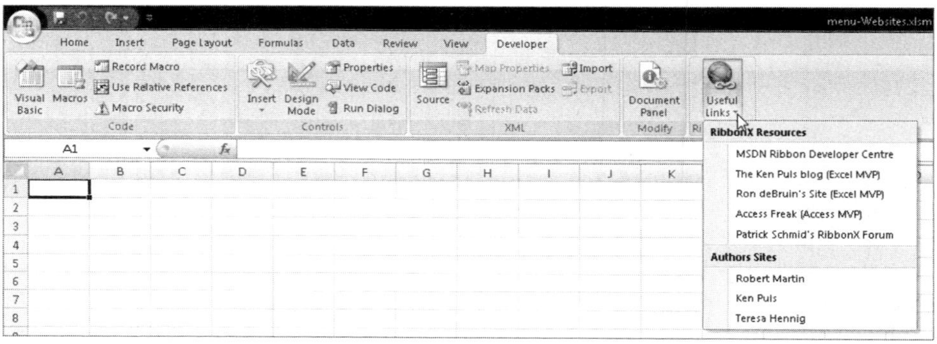

Figure 9-4: A Useful Links menu on the Developer tab

NOTE While the formatting of the individual items was left quite plain in the example, you could just as easily assign images to the buttons to spruce it up a little. Of course, URLs do change, but that will be left to you to maintain.

A Word Example

To demonstrate use of the menu in Word, we take an existing group and create a custom menu to hold all of its controls. Our goal is to thin out the Document Views group on the View tab so that we have more room to display our own groups.

This portion only uses built-in child controls, so it won't require VBA. This means that we'll start by creating a new Word document, which can be saved in the macro-free `docx` format. After saving the file, close the document in Word and open it in the CustomUI Editor. Apply the RibbonBase template and place the following code between the `<tabs>` and `</tabs>` tags:

```
<tab idMso="TabView">
   <group idMso="GroupDocumentViews"
```

```
        visible="false"/>
     <group id="rxgrpDocViews"
        label="Document Views"
        insertBeforeMso="GroupDocumentViews">
        <menu id="rxmnuDocViewsMenu"
           itemSize="normal"
           imageMso="FilePrintPreview"
           label="Document Views"
           size="large">
           <toggleButton idMso="ViewPrintLayoutView"/>
           <toggleButton idMso="ViewFullScreenReadingView"/>
           <toggleButton idMso="ViewWebLayoutView"/>
           <toggleButton idMso="ViewOutlineView"/>
           <toggleButton idMso="ViewDraftView"/>
        </menu>
     </group>
  </tab>
```

Notice that we begin by hiding the built-in Document Views group and creating our own custom group with the same name. This is a sneaky way of imposing our own mask on what the user assumes is still the built-in Microsoft group. We've also inserted our group before the group that we hid, essentially taking its place. This may seem to contradict one of the basic premises regarding consistency, but sometimes simplicity or the need for absolute control of the environment trumps consistency. For those situations, you'll want to know about this technique.

As you can also see, we've provided the Print Preview image to be the "face" of the menu. The only purpose this image serves, along with the label, is to give the menu a pretty appearance. Within the actual menu itself, we simply nested each of the `toggleButton` controls that Microsoft uses on the Document Views group.

Validate the code before saving the file. When you are done, close the file in the CustomUI editor and open it in Word. Browse to the View tab to see the changed Ribbon, as shown in Figure 9-5.

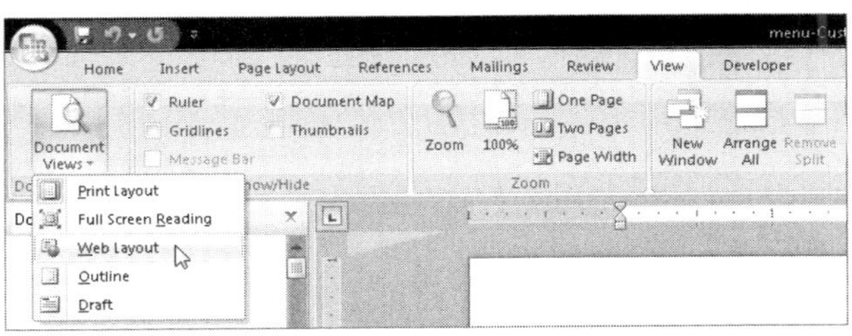

Figure 9-5: The Document Views controls moved into a menu

As you can see, the document Views group is now holding its commands in a menu, not as individual controls displayed on the Ribbon.

An Access Example

This example adds functionality to one of our previous examples by adding a menu that enables us to look up an author by country. The menu we will use offers a pre-programmed selection of the countries in the database. It does this by creating and updating a query on-the-fly.

Rather than start this whole example from scratch, we build on the `toggleButton` example from Chapter 6, where we built the Form Tools menu. If you completed this example yourself, then open it now. If not, feel free to download a copy of `toggleButton-FormTools.accdb` from the book's website.

After you have the database open on your system, enter the USysRibbons table and copy the code from the RibbonXML field of the first record. Open the CustomUI Editor and paste the code within. Browse through the XML code until you come across the following two lines:

```
</group>
<group id="rxgrpTools"
```

You probably recognize that this is the closing tag for one group and the opening tag for the Tools group. It is between these two lines that we are going to insert the required XML code to create our menu, the intention being to place the menu in a custom group immediately before the Tools group. Place the following XML code between those two lines:

```
<group id="rxgrpDataMining"
   label="Data Mining">
   <menu id="rxmnuAuthByCountry"
        label="Authors by Country"
        imageMso="OutlookGlobe"
        size="large"
        itemSize="large">
        <button id="rxbtnAuthByCountry_Brazil"
            label="Brazil"
            tag="Brazil"
            onAction="rxsharedAuthByCountry_click"/>
        <button id="rxbtnAuthByCountry_Canada"
            label="Canada"
            tag="Canada"
            onAction="rxsharedAuthByCountry_click"/>
        <button id="rxbtnAuthByCountry_USA"
            label="United States of America"
            tag="USA"
            onAction="rxsharedAuthByCountry_click"/>
   </menu>
</group>
```

As you can see, this code adds a new group, Data Mining, and populates it with a static menu of pre-defined countries. All the countries listed here will show up in our menu, but only those countries will appear. In other words, if you added "France" as a value in the tblAuthors table, it would still not show up in the menu, as it has not been specified in the XML.

Another point worth noticing here is that, like the Excel example, this uses a single shared callback to control what happens when a menu item is clicked.

NOTE **We could have placed this XML immediately before or after any group on the custom tab and still have it show up where we wanted it, simply by using one of the attributes; for example,** `insertBefore="rxgrpTools"`**.**

At this point, validate the XML code to ensure that it is well formed and then save and copy it all. Now we're ready to return to Access and replace the existing code in the USysRibbons table.

TIP **Although it's theoretically possible to just copy the new custom group portion of the XML code from the CustomUI Editor and insert it into the existing code in the Access database, it is recommended that you not take this approach. An Access field will only expand to display a limited amount of data, so it can become difficult to find exactly where you need to place your XML code. That can cause issues with XML validity, which was just checked with the CustomUI Editor. Rather than risk pasting into the wrong spot, it is faster and easier to just replace the entire XML code base.**

After the XML has been successfully replaced with the updated version, it is time to create the required VBA code to react to the menu clicks. Generate and copy the `rxsharedAuthByCountry_click` callback in the CustomUI Editor. Head back to Access, double-click the `modRibbonX` code module in the main Access window, and scroll down to the very bottom of the VBA module. Paste the callback signature there and modify it to read as follows:

```
Sub rxsharedAuthByCountry_click(control As IRibbonControl)
'Callback for rxbtnAuthByCountry_Brazil onAction

    Const cstrQueryName As String = "Query Authors"

    Dim db As DAO.Database
    Dim qry As DAO.QueryDef
    Dim strSQL As String

    strSQL = "SELECT tblAuthors.[Author Name] " & _
            "FROM tblAuthors " & _
            "WHERE tblAuthors.[Country]='" & control.Tag & "'"

    Set db = CurrentDb
    On Error Resume Next
    db.QueryDefs.Delete cstrQueryName
    Set qry = db.CreateQueryDef(cstrQueryName, strSQL)
```

```
    DoCmd.OpenQuery qry.Name, acViewNormal
    db.Close
    Set db = Nothing

End Sub
```

This routine will launch a query called "Query Authors", showing a list of authors from the country selected from the menu. Let's examine how this works.

First, a SQL query is created that requests a list of the names of each author from tblAuthors and filters the list on the country specified. By using the tag attribute of the control, you can ascertain which country this should be.

Next, the code sets a variable to hold a pointer to the database that you are working with and deletes any query that has this name — just in case one exists. (The query's name is defined at the beginning of the procedure and is held in the cstrQueryName constant.)

The routine then creates a new query, with the specified name, by using the SQL string that was defined earlier in the code. This new query is then launched, enabling the user to view the results. At that point, the reference to the database is closed and released.

We have finished writing our code, so it is now time to compile it to catch any typing errors. From the Debug menu, click Compile [*your database's filename*].

To get this to work, you will, of course, need to save your VBA code, and then close and reopen the database (in order for the Ribbon modifications to become linked to the database UI). Upon doing so, you will see the new menu on your My Tools tab, as shown in Figure 9-6.

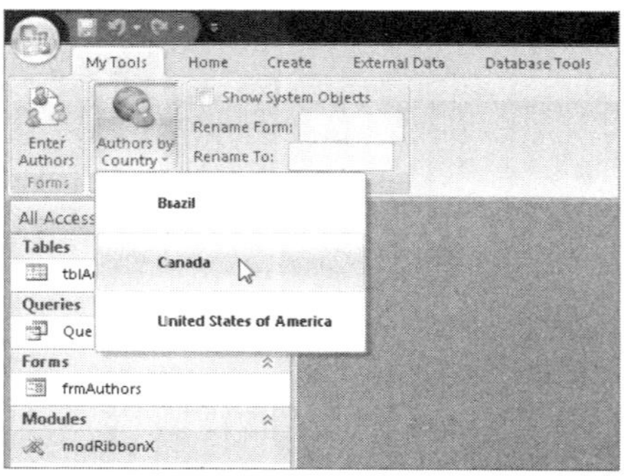

Figure 9-6: Getting a list of authors by country

Clicking the menu item launches a list of all authors who come from the specified country. After you have tried it out for yourself, close the query and open the form frmAuthors. If you have not already done so, add your own name to the list of authors. For the country, enter one of the countries that are pre-defined in the XML: Brazil, Canada, or USA. Close frmAuthors, and select your chosen country from the list. You should now see at least two entries in the query.

Finally, close the query, go back into frmAuthors, and locate your record. This time, change the country to one that is not specified in the XML code. (The country is not important, as long as it is not Brazil, Canada, or USA, so why not pick your preferred vacation destination?) Close the form again and check the menu. Nothing is different and there are still only three countries listed.

As logic dictates, while the results of the query are dynamic and include changes to data, the actual menu structure does not change. The only way to have an additional country listed is to edit the XML and then reload the database. At that point, the menu will list all of the countries in the XML, and all related records would then appear when a country is chosen from the menu.

The splitButton Element

On the outside, the `splitButton` is virtually identical to the `menu` element. As with a `menu`, when a user clicks on a `splitButton` it will either implement a command or a cascading list will display additional options. (See related comments in the "Allowed Children" section.) In fact, the only visible difference between the `menu` and `splitButton` controls is the horizontal line that gives the `splitButton` its name. Apart from that, the differences are all under the hood in the XML code.

Unlike the `menu`, which can have lines between items, the `splitButton` has no such formatting attributes. As a general rule, therefore, the `splitButton` is typically used to keep like commands together, rather than to organize a variety of commands into logical groups and subgroups.

The `splitButton` also offers the capability to provide a button or `toggleButton` as the "Face" control. While this button functions very much like using the menu's default attributes to create the control's face, the ability to use a `toggleButton` in the `splitButton` is part of what makes it unique.

In truth, aside from the dividing line in the appearance, the `menu` can do all but one thing that the `splitButton` can, and a whole lot that it can't. The one place where the `splitButton` does outshine the `menu` is in the ability to face the `splitButton` control with a `toggleButton`. In fact, this may be the main reason to choose a `splitButton` control over a `menu` control.

Required Attributes of the splitButton Element

To create a `splitButton` element, you need to define one, and only one, of the `id` attributes shown in Table 9-4.

Table 9-4: Required Attributes of the splitButton Element

ATTRIBUTE	WHEN TO USE
id	When creating your own splitButton
idMso	When using an existing Microsoft splitButton
idQ	When creating a splitButton shared between namespaces

Optional Static and Dynamic Attributes with Callback Signatures

The `splitButton` element optionally accepts any one `insert` attribute shown in Table 9-5.

Table 9-5: Optional insert Attributes of the splitButton Element

INSERT ATTRIBUTE	ALLOWED VALUES	DEFAULT VALUE	WHEN TO USE
insertAfterMso	Valid Mso Group	Insert at end of group	Insert after Microsoft control
insertBeforeMso	Valid Mso Group	Insert at end of group	Insert before Microsoft control
insertAfterQ	Valid Group idQ	Insert at end of group	Insert after shared namespace control
insertBeforeQ	Valid Group idQ	Insert at end of group	Insert before shared namespace control

In addition to the `insert` attribute, you may also include any combination of the optional static attributes, or their dynamic equivalents, shown in Table 9-6.

Table 9-6: Optional Attributes and Callbacks of the splitButton Element

STATIC ATTRIBUTE	DYNAMIC ATTRIBUTE	ALLOWED VALUES	DEFAULT VALUE	VBA CALLBACK SIGNATURE FOR DYNAMIC ATTRIBUTE
enabled	getEnabled	true, false, 1, 0	true	Sub GetEnabled (control As IRibbonControl, ByRef returnedVal)
keytip	getKeytip	1 to 3 characters	(none)	Sub GetKeytip (control As IRibbonControl, ByRef returnedVal)
showLabel	getShowLabel	true, false, 1, 0	true	Sub GetShowLabel (control As IRibbonControl, ByRef returnedVal)

Table 9-6 *(continued)*

STATIC ATTRIBUTE	DYNAMIC ATTRIBUTE	ALLOWED VALUES	DEFAULT VALUE	VBA CALLBACK SIGNATURE FOR DYNAMIC ATTRIBUTE
tag	(none)	1 to 1024 characters	(none)	(none)
visible	getVisible	true, false, 1, 0	true	Sub GetVisible (control As IRibbonControl, ByRef returnedVal)

Allowed Children Objects of the splitButton Element

According to Microsoft's original documentation, found at MSDN, the `splitButton` element must contain one button or one `toggleButton` (to be the face of the control), as well as one `menu` element, which must be defined after the button or `toggleButton` control. In reality, the button or `splitButton` is actually optional, which is why our introduction indicated that the splitButton could either directly implement a command or cascade a list of additional commands. Whether intentional or a bug, the omission of the button or `toggleButton` forces the first item in the `splitButton`'s menu to become the face of the `splitButton` control. Thankfully, the item will still appear in the list, so the intended functionality is preserved.

Parent Objects of the splitButton Element

The `splitButton` control may be used in the following controls:

- box
- buttonGroup
- dynamicMenu
- group
- menu
- officeMenu

Graphical View of splitButton Attributes

Unfortunately, it is impossible to capture any visible attributes of the `splitButton` element, as all but the `keytip` attribute are actually controlled by the button or `toggleButton` used to place a face on the control. Figure 9-7 displays the standard PivotTable `splitButton` control used in Excel.

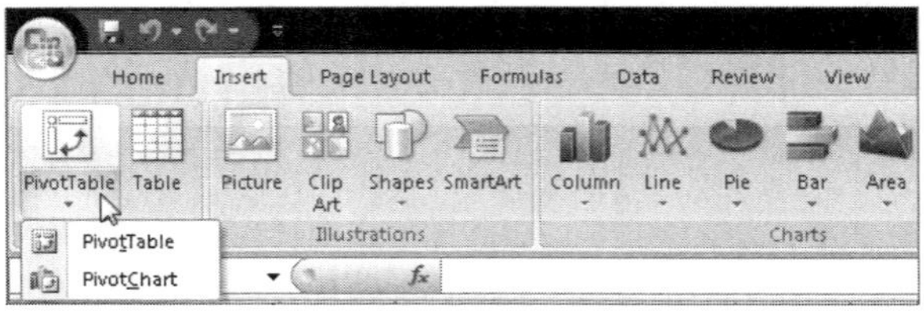

Figure 9-7: The splitButton element in use

As you can see, the horizontal separator and two-tone effect are quite distinguishing and are not offered with any other control.

Using Built-in Controls

Microsoft provides a wide variety of `splitButton` controls, one of which is the File `SaveAs` control, used in both Excel and Word. Although this `splitButton` resides on the Office Menu, we will replicate it as a custom Ribbon tab.

To begin, open either Excel or Word and create a new file. Save it as a macro-free file (either `xlsx` or `docx`) because this won't require any VBA code. Close the file and open it in the CustomUI Editor.

After applying the RibbonBase template to the file, place the following code between the `<tabs>` and `</tabs>` tags:

```
<tab id="rxtabDemo"
   label="Demo"
   insertBeforeMso="TabHome">
   <group id="rxgrpDemo"
        label="Demo">
        <splitButton idMso="FileSaveAsMenu"
            size="large"/>
   </group>
</tab>
```

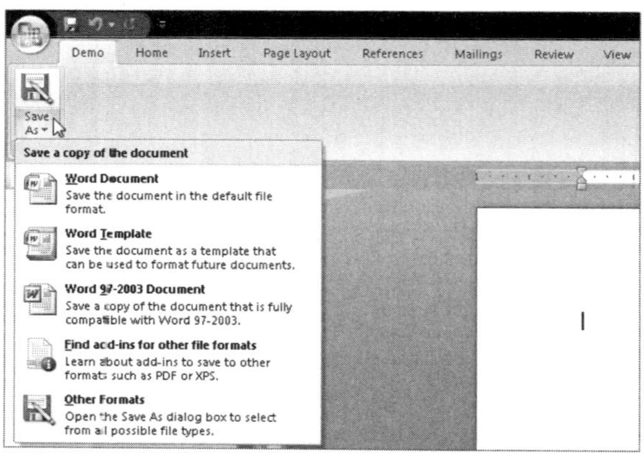

Figure 9-8: The SaveAs splitButton on a custom tab

Validate the code as you usually would, save the file, and close it in the CustomUI Editor. Now reopen the file in its original application and browse to the newly created Demo tab, shown in Figure 9-8. Go ahead and use this to save the file. The controls work just as they do on the Office Menu. Moreover, as we mentioned earlier, they are indeed still on the Office Menu.

As you can see, it is relatively easy to take entire groups of built-in controls and place them where they will be most convenient for users.

Creating Custom Controls

Of course, you can anticipate that the built-in controls will become insufficient at some point. Therefore, we will work through some examples demonstrating how to create some `splitButton` controls from scratch. A different example is used for each application.

An Excel Example

In this example, we add a `splitButton` that enables us to insert new sheets in our workbook. Rather than right-click on the Sheet tab, choose Insert, and then pick a sheet type, we enable users to insert a new sheet by using a splitButton on the Insert tab. In addition, because inserting a sheet is likely a frequent task, we put our new control at the very beginning of the Ribbon.

Of course, Microsoft hasn't given us any default controls that complete the entire process, so we need to write a little VBA code to make it happen. Open Excel, create a new workbook, and save it in the macro-enabled (`xlsm`) format. Close Excel and open the file in the CustomUI Editor.

Next, you'll want to save yourself some typing by applying the RibbonBase template. Between the `<tabs>` and `</tabs>` tags, enter the following code:

```
<tab idMso="TabInsert">
    <group id="rxgrpInsertSheet"
        label="Sheets"
        insertBeforeMso="GroupInsertTablesExcel">
        <splitButton id="rxsbtnInsertSheet"
            size="large">
            <button id="rxbtnSplitFace"
                label="Sheets"
                imageMso="CreateReportFromWizard"/>
            <menu id="mnuInsertSheet">
                <button id="rxbtnWorksheet"
                    label="Insert Worksheet"
                    imageMso="GetExternalDataFromText"
                    onAction="rxbtnInsertSheet_click"/>
                <button id="rxbtnChartsheet"
                    label="Insert Chart Sheet"
                    imageMso="PivotChartType"
                    onAction="rxbtnInsertSheet_click"/>
            </menu>
```

```
        </splitButton>
    </group>
</tab>
```

Notice that the actual `splitButton` holds a button that lacks an `onAction` callback. This is a very important aspect, as the sole purpose of this button is to be the face (image) on the `splitButton`. This initial element basically holds the image and the words that you see, and that's it.

In addition, right after the button is a menu. This particular menu holds only two buttons: Insert Worksheet and Insert Chart Sheet. As a matter of convenience, they share a callback signature.

Now that we're done perusing the code, make sure you validate it before saving. Copy the callback signature, close the CustomUI Editor, and reopen the file in Excel. Enter the VBE, insert a new standard module, and paste your callback signature. You should then modify it to read as follows:

```
'Callback for rxbtnWorkSheet onAction
Sub rxbtnInsertSheet_click(control As IRibbonControl)
   Select Case control.ID
        Case Is = "rxbtnWorksheet"
            ActiveWorkbook.Worksheets.Add
        Case Is = "rxbtnChartsheet"
            ActiveWorkbook.Charts.Add
   End Select
End Sub
```

As you can see, the callback is set up to immediately query the ID of the control that has been fired. If it is the `rxbtnWorksheet` control, then it will insert a new worksheet in the file. If it is the `rxbtnChartsheet` control, then it will insert a new chartsheet instead.

TIP **You may have also noticed that we haven't included error handling. This is worth mentioning because, in this particular case, it isn't needed. Because this is a static menu with defined controls, only two options are available. In addition, because we're handling them both with `Select Case` statements, this essentially provides the error handling as well.**

Close the VBE, save the file, and navigate to the Insert menu, which now looks like what is shown in Figure 9-9.

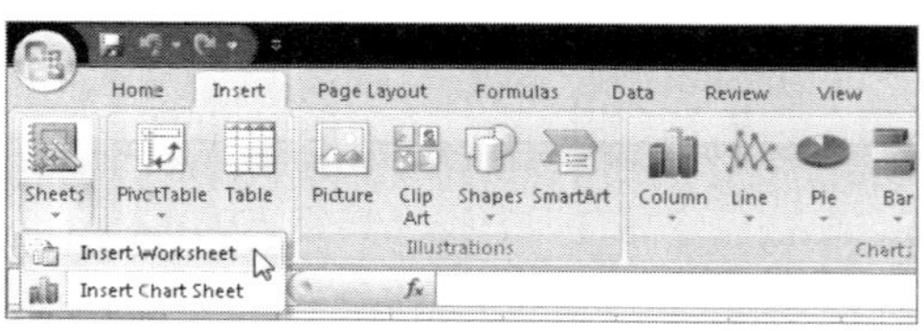

Figure 9-9: A custom splitButton in Excel

As you'd expect, the `splitButton` is there waiting for you to use. Give it a try and you'll see that it inserts new sheets exactly as if you followed the original process to do so.

A Word Example

In an effort to show the similarities and differences between the `menu` and `splitButton` elements, this example uses the same premise as the example used to showcase a custom Word menu in the first section of this chapter.

If you followed along with the previous Word example, then make a copy of the file you created and start with that. Alternately, download the `menu-CustomDocViewsMenu.docx` file from the book's website. Open the file in the CustomUI Editor and modify the entire `rxgrpDocViews` element to read as follows:

```
<menu id="rxmnuMenuVersion"
   itemSize="normal"
   imageMso="FilePrintPreview"
   label="Menu Version"
   size="large">
   <toggleButton idMso="ViewPrintLayoutView"/>
   <toggleButton idMso="ViewFullScreenReadingView"/>
   <toggleButton idMso="ViewWebLayoutView"/>
   <toggleButton idMso="ViewOutlineView"/>
   <toggleButton idMso="ViewDraftView"/>
</menu>
<splitButton id="rxsbtnSplitVersion"
   size="large" showLabel="false">
   <button id="rxbtnSplitVersionFace"
        imageMso="FilePrintPreview"
        label="Split Button Version"/>
   <menu id="rxmnuSplitVersionMenu"
        itemSize="normal">
        <toggleButton idMso="ViewPrintLayoutView"/>
        <toggleButton idMso="ViewFullScreenReadingView"/>
        <toggleButton idMso="ViewWebLayoutView"/>
        <toggleButton idMso="ViewOutlineView"/>
        <toggleButton idMso="ViewDraftView"/>
   </menu>
</splitButton>
```

While the menu control only requires minor modifications to make it look like a polished menu, it takes a few extra lines to create a basic menu using a `splitButton`. In addition, some nice features such as the `menuSeparator` (discussed in Chapter 10), just aren't available to a `splitButton`.

As usual, the next step is to validate the code, save it, and close the CustomUI Editor. Open the file in Word and navigate to the View tab. You will now see two virtually identical controls side by side in our custom group, as shown in Figure 9-10.

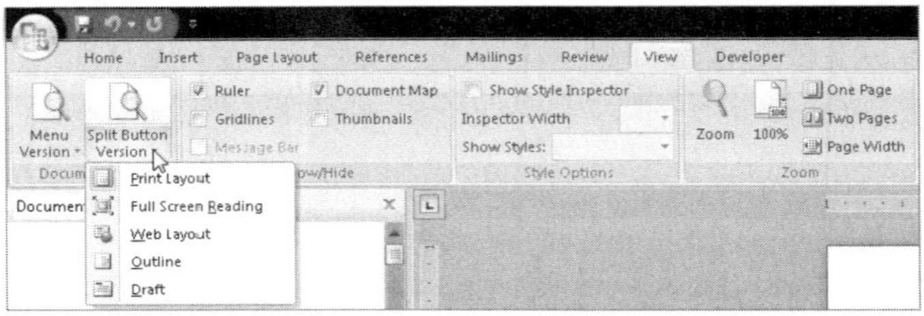

Figure 9-10: splitButton version of the Document Views menu

Do you notice the difference between the two? It comes down to only the thin horizontal line that separates the image from the text on the `splitButton` control. This line is not evident on the `menu` control.

An Access Example

To begin this example, download the partially constructed file (`splitButton-Base-File.accdb`) from the book's website. This file holds the USysRibbons table for this exercise, as well as two reports already prepared with their code modules.

In this example, we create a `splitButton` with a `toggleButton` as the main face of the button. The `toggleButton` shows as active when either or both reports are open, but inactive when the reports are closed. This is a nifty little trick that you can easily apply to other situations.

Once you have the database file downloaded and open, you need to add the code to the USysRibbons table to create the new UI. Open the USysRibbons table and replace all of the existing XML in the MainRibbon's RibbonXML field with the code listed here:

```
<customUI
   onLoad="rxIRibbonUI_onLoad"
   xmlns="http://schemas.microsoft.com/office/2006/01/customui">
   <ribbon startFromScratch="false">
        <tabs>
            <tab id="rxtab"
                insertBeforeMso="TabHomeAccess"
                label="My Custom Tab">
                <group id="rxgrpReporting"
                    label="Reporting Tools">
                    <splitButton id="rxsbtnReporting"
                        size="large">
                        <toggleButton id="rxtglFace"
                            imageMso="LookUp"
                            label="Open Report"
                            getPressed="rxtglFace_getPressed"/>
                        <menu id="rxmnuReporting"
                            label="Reporting Menu"
                            imageMso="CreateReportInDesignView"
                            itemSize="large">
                            <button id="rxbtnAListing"
```

```
                        label="Account Listing"
                        imageMso="CreateReportFromWizard"
                        onAction="rxbtnshared_Click"/>
                    <button id="rxbtnASummary"
                        label="Account Summary"
                        imageMso="CreateReport"
                        onAction="rxbtnshared_Click"/>
                </menu>
            </splitButton>
        </group>
    </tab>
  </tabs>
 </ribbon>
</customUI>
```

TIP Remember that when you are building your XML from scratch, you should do it in the CustomUI Editor. This enables you to validate it before copying it to Access, and the editor will also generate the callback signatures.

As you can see from reading the code, a new group is created on a custom tab. Our `splitButton` will be housed in that group, and will contain a list of two individual menu items that trigger a shared callback. Of course, we need to update the `toggleButton` to ensure that it indicates whether one of the reports is open, so we include the `onLoad` callback; and because it needs to check the state of the `toggleButton` within the splitButton control, the `getPressed` callback is used as well.

Once you are confident that your XML code has been typed correctly, close the USysRibbons table and we will turn our attention to writing the necessary VBA code. We need to start by inserting a new code module to hold our code, so click the `Create` tab on the Ribbon and choose Macro\Module.

As you'll recall, we need the `onLoad` statement to fire before anything else, so we'll deal with that first. Add the following code to the end of the module:

```
Public rxRibbon As IRibbonUI

'Callback for customUI.onLoad
Sub rxIRibbonUI_onLoad(ribbon As IRibbonUI)
    Set rxRibbon = ribbon
End Sub
```

That part was fairly simple, so let's move on to something a little more challenging: the `getPressed` callback. The beauty of our scenario is that we know we only have two reports, which makes it tempting to consider using a public variable. Why not set up a public variable, adding 1 to it each time a report is opened, and subtracting 1 each time a report is closed. That way, we will always know that if the number is greater than zero, then a report must be open.

To do this, you need to create a new public variable, in addition to the `getPressed` routine. Insert the following code between the public variable declaration for the `rxRibbon` object and the `onLoad` callback signature:

```
Public lReportsOpen As Long

'Callback for rxtglFace getPressed
Sub rxtglFace_getPressed(control As IRibbonControl, ByRef returnedVal)
    If lReportsOpen > 0 Then
        returnedVal = True
    Else
        returnedVal = False
    End If
End Sub
```

Next up, you need to write a routine to react when a menu item is selected. This routine needs to open the form and increment the `lReportsOpen` variable by 1. Naturally, it should also invalidate the `toggleButton` to ensure that it is displaying in its pressed state when a user does open a report. You need to be careful that you don't increment the counter when the button is clicked but it does not open a new instance of a report. (If you did, you would not have an accurate count for resetting to the untoggled state when the count reaches 0.) To accomplish all of this, use the following callback, which makes use of a function to check whether the report has already been opened. Place these routines somewhere after the public variable declarations:

```
Sub rxbtnshared_Click(control As IRibbonControl)
    Dim sReport As String

    'Record name of report to open
    Select Case control.Id
        Case "rxbtnAListing"
            sReport = "rptAccountListing"
        Case "rxbtnASummary"
            sReport = "rptAccountSummary"
    End Select

    If IsReportOpen(sReport) = False Then
        'Open new report, increment report counter and refresh
        DoCmd.OpenReport sReport, acViewReport
        lReportsOpen = lReportsOpen + 1
        rxRibbon.InvalidateControl ("rxtglFace")
    Else
        MsgBox "That report is already open!"
    End If
End Sub

Function IsReportOpen(ByVal strReportName As String) As Boolean
    IsReportOpen = False
    If SysCmd(acSysCmdGetObjectState, acReport, strReportName) <> 0 Then
```

```
        If Reports(strReportName).CurrentView <> 0 Then
            IsReportOpen = True
        End If
    End If
End Function
```

We're almost finished setting up the code, but there is one thing left to do: You need to decrement the `lReportsOpen` variable each time a report is closed. If you had several reports to deal with, you would write your own class module to monitor when any report is unloaded, but since there are only two that would be overkill here.

While you are still in the VBE, browse to the `Report_rptAccountListing` and `Report_rptAccountSummary` class modules. Double-click them to open their code windows (an alternative method is to right-click and choose View Code). At the end of each of these class modules, paste the following code:

```
Private Sub Report_Close()
    lReportsOpen = lReportsOpen - 1
    rxRibbon.InvalidateControl ("rxtglFace")
End Sub
```

Finally, it is time to compile the code, close the VBE, and then close the database itself, as you need to reload the entire database to have it compile the new XML customizations. Upon returning to the database, look at My Custom Tab. You'll now find the split button that enables you to open the reports. Notice that it is currently not glowing. Selecting a report, however, will toggle it to "pressed," as shown in Figure 9-11. Opening the other report will have no effect at this point, but closing them both will set the `toggleButton` back to its unselected state.

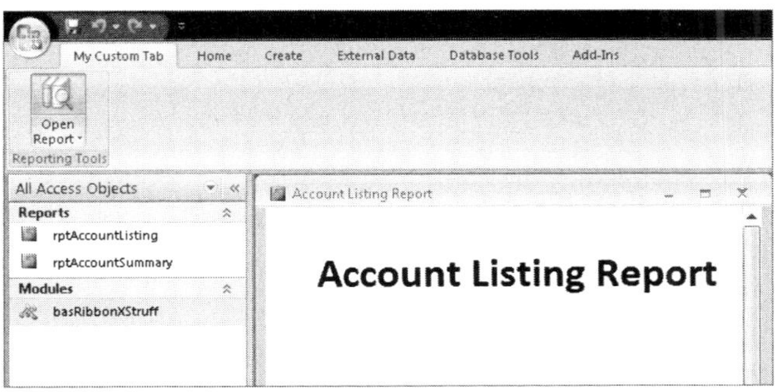

Figure 9-11: The splitButton, showing that a report is open

The Open Report `toggleButton` is toggled on when a report is opened, and, thanks to our nifty code to count the number of open reports, the Open Report button will "glow" until all reports are closed.

The dynamicMenu Element

The main purpose of the `dynamicMenu` is to build a menu "on-the-fly" from XML code that is fed back to the control through a VBA callback.

The `dynamicMenu` is, without a doubt, the crown jewel of flexibility in the Ribbon. Although it can take a fair amount of work to set up, the `dynamicMenu` offers unparalleled options that give it a major role in many Ribbon customizations. It is so robust that it is a shame to not find comparable functionality in both tabs and groups.

The `dynamicMenu` works by using a `getContent` callback to request the XML code needed to build a Ribbon menu. The XML for ID, images, callback signatures, and all other attributes can be compiled by VBA code and passed to the `dynamicMenu`. This code is then implemented just as if it were a menu that had been coded into the XML structure typically used to build the Ribbon customization, thereby allowing for a robust and remarkably dynamic user experience.

The potential of this control is vast — from creating an updated list of all workbooks and worksheets open on the system to providing an updateable menu hierarchy of all files within a network drive. With that type of capability, this control can provide some exciting new features for your applications.

One thing that is extremely important to know before diving into the `dynamicMenu` element is that you must write a significant amount of VBA code to use it. Even if all you want to do is dynamically create a menu that uses built-in controls, the XML still needs to be compiled and fed back to the `dynamicMenu` control through the use of a VBA callback.

CROSS-REFERENCE **If you are not feeling comfortable with your VBA skills, you may want to return to Chapter 4.**

Required Attributes of the dynamicMenu Element

To create a `dynamicMenu` element, you need to define one and only one of the id attributes shown in Table 9-7.

Table 9-7: Required Attributes of the dynamicMenu Element

ATTRIBUTE	WHEN TO USE
id	When creating your own dynamicMenu
idMso	When using an existing Microsoft dynamicMenu
idQ	When creating a dynamicMenu shared between namespaces

In addition to the `id` attribute, each `dynamicMenu` must have the callback shown in Table 9-8 programmed as well.

Table 9-8: Required Callback of the dynamicMenu Element

STATIC ATTRIBUTE	DYNAMIC ATTRIBUTE	ALLOWED VALUES	DEFAULT VALUE	VBA CALLBACK SIGNATURE FOR DYNAMIC ATTRIBUTE
(none)	getContent	1 to 1096 characters	(none)	Sub GetContent (control As IRibbonControl, ByRef returnedVal)

Optional Static and Dynamic Attributes with Callback Signatures

The `dynamicMenu` element will accept any one `insert` attribute shown in Table 9-9, although it is not required.

Table 9-9: Optional insert Attributes of the dynamicMenu Element

INSERT ATTRIBUTE	ALLOWED VALUES	DEFAULT VALUE	WHEN TO USE
insertAfterMso	Valid Mso Group	Insert at end of group	Insert after Microsoft control
insertBeforeMso	Valid Mso Group	Insert at end of group	Insert before Microsoft control
insertAfterQ	Valid Group idQ	Insert at end of group	Insert after shared namespace control
insertBeforeQ	Valid Group idQ	Insert at end of group	Insert before shared namespace control

In addition to the `insert` attribute, you may also include any of the optional static attributes or their dynamic equivalents shown in Table 9-10.

Table 9-10: Optional Attributes and Callbacks of the dynamicMenu Element

STATIC ATTRIBUTE	DYNAMIC ATTRIBUTE	ALLOWED VALUES	DEFAULT VALUE	VBA CALLBACK SIGNATURE FOR DYNAMIC ATTRIBUTE
description	getDescription	1 to 1024 characters	(none)	Sub GetDescription (control As IRibbonControl, ByRef returnedVal)

Continued

Table 9-10 *(continued)*

STATIC ATTRIBUTE	DYNAMIC ATTRIBUTE	ALLOWED VALUES	DEFAULT VALUE	VBA CALLBACK SIGNATURE FOR DYNAMIC ATTRIBUTE
enabled	getEnabled	true, false, 1, 0	true	Sub GetEnabled (control As IRibbonControl, ByRef returnedVal)
image	getImage	1 to 1024 characters	(none)	Sub GetImage (control As IRibbonControl, ByRef returnedVal)
imageMso	getImage	1 to 1024 characters	(none)	Same as above
keytip	getKeytip	1 to 3 characters	(none)	Sub GetKeytip (control As IRibbonControl, ByRef returnedVal)
label	getLabel	1 to 1024 characters	(none)	Sub GetLabel (control As IRibbonControl, ByRef returnedVal)
screentip	getScreentip	1 to 1024 characters	(none)	Sub GetScreentip (control As IRibbonControl, ByRef returnedVal)
showImage	getShowImage	true, false, 1, 0	true	Sub GetShowImage (control As IRibbonControl, ByRef returnedVal)
showLabel	getShowLabel	true, false, 1, 0	true	Sub GetShowLabel (control As IRibbonControl, ByRef returnedVal)
size	getSize	normal, large	normal	sub GetSize (control As IRibbonControl, ByRef returnedVal)
supertip	getSupertip	1 to 1024 characters	(none)	Sub GetSupertip (control As IRibbonControl, ByRef returnedVal)
tag	(none)	1 to 1024 characters	(none)	(none)
visible	getVisible	true, false, 1, 0	true	Sub GetVisible (control As IRibbonControl, ByRef returnedVal)

Allowed Children Objects of the dynamicMenu Element

The `dynamicMenu` control will accept any or all of the following child objects:

- button
- checkbox
- control
- dynamicMenu
- gallery
- menu
- menuSeparator
- splitButton
- toggleButton

Parent Objects of the dynamicMenu Element

The `dynamicMenu` control can be placed in any of the following objects:

- box
- buttonGroup
- dynamicMenu
- group
- menu
- officeMenu

Graphical View of dynamicMenu Attributes

The visible attributes of the `dynamicMenu` are identical to those of the `menu` element in every way; the only visible attributes that can be set for the `dynamicMenu` are the image, label, keytip, screentip, and supertip, as illustrated in Figure 9-12.

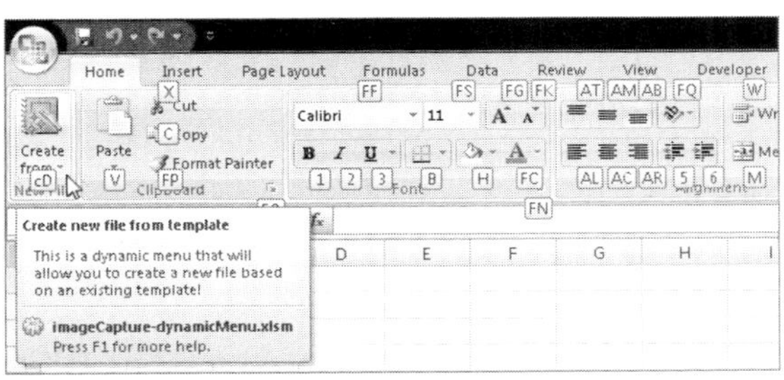

Figure 9-12: Visible attributes of a dynamicMenu

The "Create from" button shown in Figure 9-12 is a new custom dynamic menu that we create in this section.

Using Built-in Controls

Because Microsoft pre-programmed all of the controls available on the Ribbon, they had no need for a built-in `dynamicMenu` of any kind. This control has been provided solely to allow flexibility for the user.

Creating Custom Controls

Although our example won't add any new functionality to Excel or Word, it serves its purpose of showcasing the incredible power of the `dynamicMenu`. With the ability to be refreshed by the user (you), we add a dynamically created menu that creates a new file based on any of the existing templates that you may have in your personal templates folder.

We start this project by building the example in Word (available as `dynamicMenu-CreateFromTemplate.docm` from the book's website). Although we won't cover the very minor adjustments that need to be made to build the same functionality in Excel, a sample file for Excel is available from the book's website (`dynamicMenu-CreateFromTemplate.xlsm`).

As mentioned many times in this section, the key to creating a successful `dynamicMenu` is to use VBA code to provide the appropriate XML code to the `getContent` callback. That makes it sound complicated; and although it can be, we break this down into bite-size pieces so that it will be easy to understand and incorporate into your solutions.

We start at the very beginning: To store VBA code in your file, you naturally need to save your file in a macro-enabled format. You now have your first step: Create a new document in Word and save it as a macro-enabled file.

Next, you need to craft your XML code, so close the file in Word and open it in the CustomUI Editor. Again, apply the RibbonBase template to the file, and then insert the following code below between the `<tabs>` and `</tabs>` tags:

```
<tab idMso="TabHome">
     <group id="rxgrpNewFile"
          label="New File"
          insertBeforeMso="GroupClipboard">
          <dynamicMenu id="rxdmnuTemplates"
               label="Create from..."
               imageMso="CreateReportFromWizard"
               size="large"
               getContent="rxdmnuTemplates_getContent"/>
     </group>
</tab>
```

As you can see, the actual XML code used to create the `dynamicMenu` is actually quite short. You have given it a label and a large image for the face of the menu. Apart from that, it also requires a `getContent` callback that will be used to build the actual menu items on-the-fly.

Before we can call this job done, however, remember that we want to give the user the ability to refresh this menu at will. That requires invalidating the Ribbon, so you need to add the `onLoad` attribute to the `customUI` element. You'll recognize the line when you update the opening `customUI` tag to read as follows:

```
<customUI
   onLoad="rxIRibbonUI_onLoad"
   xmlns="http://schemas.microsoft.com/office/2006/01/customui">
```

Now it's time to validate the XML code and save the file. Before closing it, remember to generate and copy the callback signatures.

Let's head back into Word and open the document. If you enable macros, you will immediately receive an error because the `rxIRibbonUI_onLoad` macro cannot be found. Just ignore the error message, as you know that it was generated because you haven't yet programmed any callbacks.

You've likely noticed the new group on the Home tab that will hold your new `dynamicMenu`. Of course, clicking it now only generates an error, so there is not much reason to do so at this point. Instead, open the VBE and add a new standard module to the VBA project.

Paste the callback signatures that you copied from the CustomUI Editor into the module. As you learned in Chapter 5, the `onLoad` callback required to capture the `RibbonUI` object can be set up as follows:

```
Dim rxIRibbonUI As IRibbonUI

Sub rxIRibbonUI_onLoad(ribbon As IRibbonUI)
'Callback for onLoad to capture RibbonUI
    Set rxIRibbonUI = ribbon
End Sub
```

TIP **Remember that the first line of the preceding code must be placed before the first Sub or Function in the module, and it must come after any** `Option` **statements (such as** `Option Explicit`**).**

The next thing you need to do is create the `getContent` callback for the `dynamicMenu`. This is the tricky part of using the `dynamicMenu`, and it takes considerable thought and planning. Fortunately, we've done this for you and have come up with the following code:

```
Sub rxdmnuTemplates_GetContent(control As IRibbonControl, ByRef content)
'Callback for GetContent to return XML used to create dynamicMenu

    Dim objFSO As Object
    Dim objTemplateFolder As Object
    Dim file As Object
    Dim sXML As String
```

```
Dim lBtnCount As Long

'Open the XML string
sXML = "<menu xmlns=""" & _
    "http://schemas.microsoft.com/office/2006/01/customui"">"

'Create FSO object and set to templates folder
Set objFSO = CreateObject("Scripting.FileSystemObject")
Set objTemplateFolder = _
    objFSO.getfolder( _
    Application.Options.DefaultFilePath(wdUserTemplatesPath))

'Add template files
If objTemplateFolder.Files.Count > 0 Then
    For Each file In objTemplateFolder.Files
        'Check if file is a temporary file
        If Not Left(file.Name, 2) = "~$" Then
        'File is not a temp file, so check extension
            Select Case LCase(Right(file.Name, 4))
                Case ".dot", "dotx", "dotm"
                    'Word template.
                    If Not LCase(Left(file.Name, 6)) = "normal" Then
                        sXML = sXML & _
                            "<button id=""rxbtnDyna" & _
                            lBtnCount & """ " & _
                            "label=""" & file.Name & """ " & _
                            "imageMso=""FileSaveAsWord97_2003"" " & _
                            "tag=""" & file.Path & """ " & _
                            "onAction=""rxbtnDyna_onAction""/>" & vbCrLf
                            lBtnCount = lBtnCount + 1
                    End If
                Case Else
                    'Unknown format. Ignore.
            End Select
        End If
    Next file
End If

'Release the FSO objects
Set file = Nothing
Set objTemplateFolder = Nothing
Set objFSO = Nothing

'Check if any items buttons were created
'Create a "No Templates" button if not
If lBtnCount = 0 Then _
    sXML = sXML & "<button id=""rxbtnDyna0"" label=""No Templates _
Found""/>"
```

```
    'Add Refresh button & close the menu tags
    sXML = sXML & _
           "<button id=""rxbtnRefresh"" " & _
           "label=""Refresh List"" " & _
           "imageMso=""RecurrenceEdit"" " & _
           "onAction=""rxbtnDyna_onAction""/>" & _
           "</menu>"

    'Feed the XML back to the Ribbon
    content = sXML
End Sub
```

Wow, does that ever look complicated! Let's break it down a bit and examine what everything does. The first portion of the code begins the creation of an XML string, (held in the `sXML` variable) which will eventually be passed back to the `dynamicMenu` element. This XML string will contain an entire menu hierarchy and must begin with a specific XML namespace. Like the `customUI` element, every dynamic menu callback must include this line so that the Ribbon knows how to interpret the code and compile it.

The next step is to actually look at the individual files in the `templates` directory to determine whether any menu items should be added. To do this, you make use of a handy little object called the *file system object (FSO)*. While not specifically part of VBA, this little fellow has been around in Visual Basic for many years, and it gives us the capability to look at folders, subfolders, and files. The code we have used creates an FSO object, sets a folder object to reference our templates folder, and then looks at each file within that folder.

TIP **While full coverage of FSO is outside the scope of this book, the Internet offers a wealth of information about how to use the FSO. Type FSO VB6 into any search engine and you will find a large number of pages that expose how to use FSO for various purposes: moving files, copying files, renaming files, and so on.**

CROSS-REFERENCE **If you do run into a wall trying to create or debug your VBA code, don't forget to consult Appendix F, which lists several sources of help!**

Next, the code checks whether the file starts with `~$`, which indicates it is a temp file. If it is, the file is ignored, as we're not interested in temporary files.

Following that, you check the extension to see whether it is a document template. Notice that you actually check the last four characters. This is because the new file formats have four characters, but you also list the old "dot" format as `.dot` so that it will return all Word templates. In addition, you use the `LCase()` function to convert the filename to lowercase before checking it. Use of the `LCase()` function is a standard way to ensure that you do not run into issues with case sensitivity, and it will effectively treat "dot", "Dot" and "DOT" as equal, whereas they may not have been before.

Finally, you also eliminate the files that start with "Normal." Word bases its files on the normal templates, so they are for Word's internal use and should not be launched directly by a user. Therefore, you want to ensure that you don't include the Normal templates.

If a file passes all of these tests, then you finally create the XML to add a button for it to the menu. This XML is then added to the end of the `sXML` string that you used earlier, with each successive button's XML code being appended to the string. You also increment the `lBtnCount` variable to indicate how many buttons you have.

TIP **When trying to include the " character in a VBA string, you actually need to provide two quotes instead of one. If this seems confusing, it's time for a refresher about the proverbial collapsing quotes.**

Using a quote mark (") within a VBA string requires two quotes. This makes sense when you consider that the quote mark is typically a command. Therefore, the first quote essentially indicates that the next quote should be taken literally. For example, to derive an `sXML` value of `id="rxbtnHello"`, you would need to enclose both the complete string and the quote itself in quotes. The required code would therefore look as follows: `sXML="id=""rxbtnHello"""`.

This is a very important piece of information to become familiar with, as missing quotes are a common cause of errors when writing XML and VBA code.

After working through each file in the `templates` subfolder, you tell the FSO objects that you are finished with them, setting each of them to nothing. (This is a good programming practice, as it releases them from memory.)

The code then evaluates the number of buttons that were added to the XML string. If the `lBtnCount` variable's value is still zero, you must not have added any buttons, so a button is created to let the user know that no templates were found (a polite way of providing consistency and avoiding any questions about whether the code is working properly). As you can read in the code, this button has no `onAction` callback, so instead of firing any action, it acts as an informative label.

As mentioned at the outset of the example, you also want users to be able to refresh the button; for example, they might create a new template and want to see it in the list. Again, you will need to append the code to the XML string, along with a closing `</menu>` tag, which will finish off the XML code.

Assuming that you had one template in your templates folder and it was named `MyTemplate.dotx`, the `sXML` variable would end up holding the following XML code:

```
<menu xmlns="http://schemas.microsoft.com/office/2006/01/customui">
   <button id="rxbtnDyna0"
      label=" MyTemplate.dotx "
      imageMso="FileSaveAsWord97_2003"
      tag="C:\Users\YourName\AppData\Roaming\Microsoft\Templates↵
\MyTemplate.dotx"
      onAction="rxbtnDyna_onAction"/>
   <button id="rxbtnRefresh"
      label="Refresh List"
```

```
        imageMso="RecurrenceEdit"
        onAction="rxbtnDyna_onAction"/>
</menu>
```

Ultimately, the real purpose of the `dynamicMenu`'s `getContent` callback is to feed back well-formed XML code to the `dynamicMenu` object so that it will create the menu for you. Your goal when programming a `dynamicMenu` is to build a routine that generates clean and valid XML to feed out of the `getContent` callback.

NOTE The "YourName" portion included in the tag attribute would be your username. In addition, the tag would need to reference a slightly different path depending on whether you are running Windows XP (or another platform) instead of Windows Vista.

Pay attention to a couple of things in the preceding XML output. The first item ensures that the path to the template is stored in the `tag` attribute. This enables us to easily reference the file path when we want to launch a specific template.

The second item is to note that we created a single callback that works with all of the buttons that were created. The reason for this is actually quite simple: If you created `onAction` routine names on-the-fly, then you would have to write VBA code to write the VBA callbacks as well. While this is certainly possible, it is definitely an unnecessary complication that we can do without.

Each button will fire the `rxbtnDyna_onAction` callback, so we'll build it now. The code for this routine is surprisingly simple:

```
Sub rxbtnDyna_onAction(control As IRibbonControl)
'Callback for button onAction
    If control.ID = "rxbtnRefresh" Then
        rxIRibbonUI.InvalidateControl ("rxdmnuTemplates")
    Else
        Documents.Add (control.Tag)
    End If
End Sub
```

As you can see, the routine is set up to check whether it was called by the "Refresh" button and to invalidate the dynamicMenu if so. However, if it wasn't, it simply creates a new document based on the template stored in the control's `tag` attribute.

That was a lot to cover, but you're ready to try this out. Close the VBE and then save and close the file. Reopen it and try clicking on the menu. Wait a minute . . . this may not be what you expected: a message telling you that no templates were found, as shown in Figure 9-13.

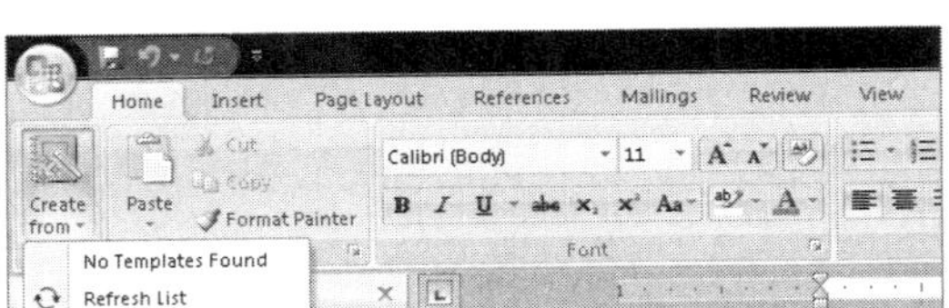

Figure 9-13: The dynamicMenu showing No Templates Found

Fortunately, this is a very easy problem to overcome. Just create a template! Create a new document and then immediately go to the Office Menu and choose Save As. Change the file format to Document Template (`dotx`), call it something interesting like "My Template," and make sure it is saved in your default `templates` directory.

TIP **The standard location for your `templates` directory on Windows Vista is**

```
C:\Users\username\AppData\Roaming\Microsoft\Templates
```

On Windows XP it is

```
C:\Documents and Settings\username\Application Data\Microsoft\Templates
```

(Note that in both cases, `username` will be the username that is currently logged into Windows.)

Save and close the file and then return to the `dynamicMenu` file. Now click the menu and choose Refresh List. Voilà! You will now see your new template as shown in Figure 9-14.

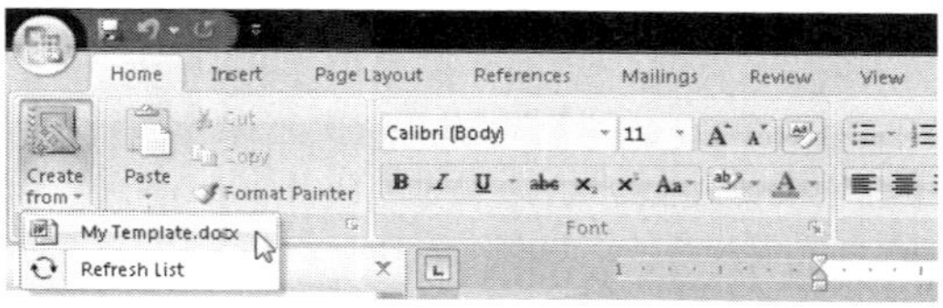

Figure 9-14: The dynamicMenu showing a template

OK, it may have been mean to make you suffer the initial disappointment of getting the No Templates Found message, but we wanted to demonstrate that portion of the code. Of course, if there are templates in your default directory, you missed that part of the fun.

Conclusion

In this chapter, you have seen three different elements that can be used to create menus on the Ribbon: `menu`, `splitButton`, and `dynamicMenu`.

While the `menu` and `splitButton` controls can both be used to deliver menu solutions with static items, it appears that virtually everything a `splitButton` can do, a menu can do better — with two exceptions: the `splitButton` has an attractive separating line when selected, and it can be faced with a `toggleButton`. Beyond that, however, the variety and richness you can create with a `menu` control is far more vast and exciting. Unless either of the `splitButton`'s specific benefits is needed, it makes sense to use the more robust `menu` element, especially when you consider that it also takes less XML code to produce.

Unlike the former two controls, which restrict the application's users to specified lists, the `dynamicMenu` offers incredible flexibility and can be used to create context-sensitive menus. With the ability to create and reload XML on-the-fly, you are given a huge amount of contextual ability. Just think about it — these are just a few of the things that can be done:

- React to user-driven choices, providing controls that are appropriate settings (see Chapter 15 for information about context-sensitive controls).
- Compile different menus based on security settings.
- List directories and files on a system.
- Build a table of contents that changes as worksheets or sections are added or removed.

Of course, this list is just the proverbial tip of the iceberg, and it is limited only by your own imagination and skill set.

Ultimately, the power of the `dynamicMenu` is so great that it is a shame that Microsoft has yet to offer a similar control at the tab or group level. With a `dynamicTab` control, we could reload entire tabs on-the-fly, creating the ultimate contextual solutions, but alas this is not currently possible. The best we can hope for is that Microsoft adds this functionality in future versions of the Ribbon.

The next step in our journey is to look at controls that can be used to format the Ribbon. In Chapter 10, we explore how to group controls and add other visual effects that not only enhance the look of the Ribbon, but also make it more intuitive and efficient.

CHAPTER

10

Formatting Elements

So far, this book has focused on setting up environments and controls to interact with the user. Each control discussed in this book thus far has a specific purpose — to allow the user to make a choice. Whether the control is a `button`, `checkBox`, or `comboBox`, each provides the user with the opportunity to do something.

The controls in this chapter, however, have different purposes than those that we've been working with. Our new focus here is strictly on formatting. (None) of the controls discussed in this chapter are provided for the user to work with in any way. While these controls will not react to clicks, they do retain a certain dynamic so that they can react to other controls, should you so choose.

We begin the chapter by looking at two grouping elements: the `box`, and its close cousin, the `buttonGroup`. Following that, we explore the `labelControl`, which is purely a textual control. Finally, we discuss the `separator` and `menuSeparator` controls. These final two controls enable us to divide menus and controls into logical groupings.

Because the concepts for working with formatting controls apply equally to Excel, Access, and Word, we do not demonstrate working with the controls in each program. However, you can rest assured that the XML elements, attributes, and callbacks are indeed equally applicable to each of the applications, and you will have little or no difficulty adding them to your projects, regardless of the program.

As you prepare to work through the examples in this chapter, we encourage you to download the companion files. The source code and files for this chapter can be found on the book's website at `www.wiley.com/go/ribbonx`.

The box Element

Based on its name, you might expect the `box` object to place a visible box around the specified controls in your group. As logical as that may seem, it is not the case, because the box itself is invisible. Therefore, although the box is an element used for visual grouping, it does not provide the dividing lines to aid the user in quickly recognizing and navigating through controls.

The main purpose of the `box` control is to group controls together as one unit. This is important, as it enables us to manage the way controls are displayed within groups. Normally, each control that we assign to a group is placed underneath the prior control until the column is filled. At that point, the next control is placed in the top row of the column to the right. By grouping our commands within a box, however, we can treat several controls as one entity and place the entire group on the Ribbon at once. This has the great benefit that we can easily organize the order of display and not have to fiddle around with dummy buttons or create other workarounds just to provide "whitespace."

Required Attributes of the box Element

Every `box` element requires a unique `id` attribute (see Table 10-1).

Table 10-1: Required Attributes of the box Element

ATTRIBUTE	WHEN TO USE
id	When creating your own box
idQ	When creating a box shared between namespaces

TIP **Keep in mind that the `id` for each control, including each box, must not conflict with (i.e., be the same as) any other control.**

NOTE **To save you some time searching for something that isn't there, Microsoft does not provide any built-in `box` elements, so the `idMso` attribute cannot be specified.**

Optional Static and Dynamic Attributes with Callback Signatures

Although specifying a position is optional, if you choose to position a box in relation to another element, you must use one of the `insert` attributes listed in Table 10-2.

Table 10-2: Optional insert Attributes for the box Element

INSERT ATTRIBUTE	ALLOWED VALUES	DEFAULT VALUE	WHEN TO USE
insertAfterMso	Valid Mso group	Insert at end of group	Insert after Microsoft control
insertBeforeMso	Valid Mso group	Insert at end p of group	Insert before Microsoft control
insertAfterQ	Valid group idQ	Insert at end p of group	Insert after shared namespace control
insertBeforeQ	Valid group idQ	Insert at end of group	Insert before shared namespace control

NOTE **If you are not concerned with positioning the box adjacent to a specific control, then you do not need to provide an `insert` attribute. As with other controls, the default action is to append the control to the UI in the order that it is listed in the XML code.**

The `box` element will also accept either or both of the optional attributes and callbacks shown in Table 10-3.

Table 10-3: Optional Attributes and Callbacks of the box Element

STATIC ATTRIBUTE	DYNAMIC ATTRIBUTE	ALLOWED VALUES	DEFAULT VALUE	VBA CALLBACK SIGNATURE FOR DYNAMIC ATTRIBUTE
boxStyle	(none)	horizontal, vertical	horizontal	(none)
visible	getVisible	true, false, 1, 0	true	Sub GetVisible (control As IRibbonControl, ByRef returnedVal)

Allowed Children Objects of the box Element

The `box` control can hold a great variety of RibbonX controls, each of which is shown in the following list. While one might assume that there is a limit to the number of controls that can be in one `box` control, we have not found any documentation to indicate such a limit. Moreover, we have successfully inserted dozens of controls — so many, in fact, that the box extended past the edge of the screen, leaving a "more. . ." arrow. Since the focus should be on making things logical and easy for the user, it is hard to imagine a scenario where you would hit the limit, if indeed there actually is one.

- box
- button
- buttonGroup
- checkBox
- comboBox
- control
- dropDown
- dynamicMenu
- editBox
- gallery
- labelControl
- menu
- splitButton
- toggleButton

Notice that the `box` control will also hold other `box` controls. This concept, known as *nesting,* can be very useful when you are trying to get controls to display in exactly the right order. We demonstrate several layouts for nesting `box` controls later in this chapter.

Parent Objects of the box Element

The `box` control may only be nested within one of the following two controls:

- box
- group

Graphical View of box Attributes

Figure 10-1 displays a Ribbon group with nested `box` controls used to create whitespace on the Ribbon.

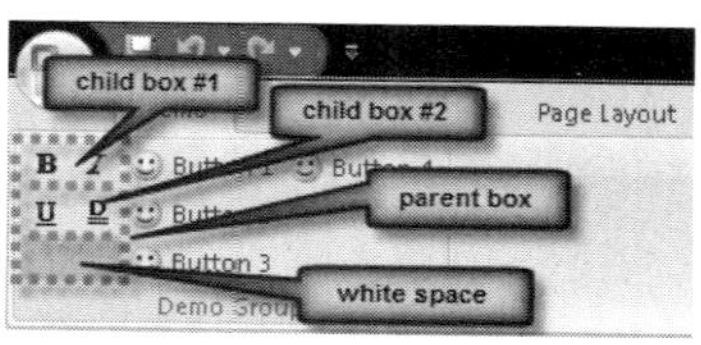

Figure 10-1: Nested box controls

Figure 10-1 uses three box controls to create the desired grouping and spacing. The first is a vertical box element holding two horizontal box elements. The first horizontal box contains the Bold and Italic toggleButton controls, while the second horizontal box holds the Underline and Double Underline toggleButton controls. There are no box elements defined around the happy face buttons, and the buttons fill the space, top down and then moving to the next columns on the right. Since you're familiar with the Ribbon, you'll immediately recognize that the dotted lines have been added to provide clarity to the image; they are not part of the Ribbon itself.

The important thing to notice here is that the space under the box elements is left blank. This is because the vertical box control has space for three horizontal box controls, so an empty space is created by only using two of the three rows. Had the vertical box been left out of the XML code, the Button1 control would have filled that blank space.

Using Built-in box Elements

The only purpose of the box element is to group other controls, so it makes sense that Microsoft does not expose any built-in box controls for use as commands. Therefore, there it has no need for an idMso.

Creating Custom box Elements

Now that we've explained the basics, it is time to actually construct some custom box elements to organize our Ribbon controls. The examples that follow will give you a thorough understanding of the box control and how to use it in any configuration, whether it be horizontal, vertical, nested, or any combination thereof. While the examples that follow are all drafted in Excel, the concepts can be applied to Access or Word just as easily.

Horizontal Alignment

Our first example demonstrates the effect of using a horizontal box control. Start by creating a new Excel file. This example won't require using any VBA code, so feel free to save it as a macro-free (xlsx) workbook.

Close the file, open it in the CustomUI Editor, and apply the RibbonBase template, (created in Chapter 2) to the file. Between the <tabs> and </tabs> tags, enter the following XML:

```
<tab id="rxtab_Demo"
   label="Demo"
   insertBeforeMso="TabHome">
   <group id="rxgrp_Demo"
      label="Demo Group">
      <box id="rxboxFormat1"
         boxStyle="horizontal"
         visible="true">
         <toggleButton idMso="Bold"/>
```

```
<toggleButton idMso="Italic"/>
         <toggleButton idMso="Underline"/>
         <toggleButton idMso="UnderlineDouble"/>
      </bcx>
      <button id="rxbtnHappy1"
         imageMso="HappyFace"
         label="Button 1"/>
      <button id="rxbtnHappy2"
         imageMso="HappyFace"
         label="Button 2"/>
      <button id="rxbtnHappy3"
         imageMso="HappyFace"
         label="Button 3"/>
      <button id="rxbtnHappy4"
         imageMso="HappyFace"
         label="Button 4"/>
   </group>
</tab>
```

As always, validate the file before you save it. Then, because no callbacks are required here, you can just close the file in the CustomUI Editor and reopen it in Excel.

Figure 10-2 shows the results of the preceding code sample. It creates a horizontal box, (highlighted by the added dotted lines) to group the four formatting elements together, allowing them to be moved as one unit. In addition to allowing the buttons to span more than one column, the horizontal group also creates "whitespace" to the right of Button 1 and Button 2. You'll notice that Button 3 and Button 4 do not have this "padding," so to speak.

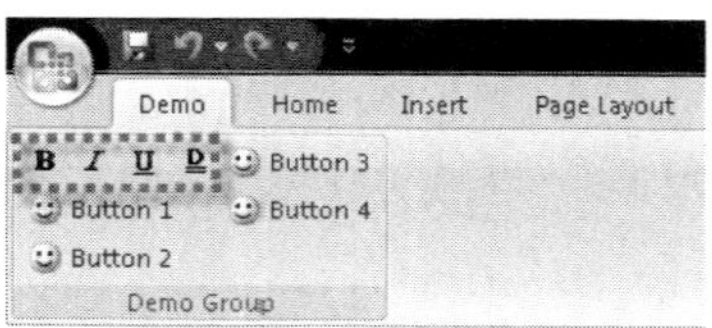

Figure 10-2: The box element, using a horizontal alignment

Vertical Alignment

Using the example presented in the "Horizontal Alignment" section, let's look at what happens when we select a vertical alignment. Close the Excel file and reopen it in the CustomUI Editor. Scan the XML for the following line and replace `horizontal` with `vertical`:

```
boxStyle="horizontal"
```

Now save the file, close the CustomUI Editor, and reopen the workbook in Excel. Your group will now look like the one shown in Figure 10-3 (minus the dotted lines added for illustrative purposes, of course).

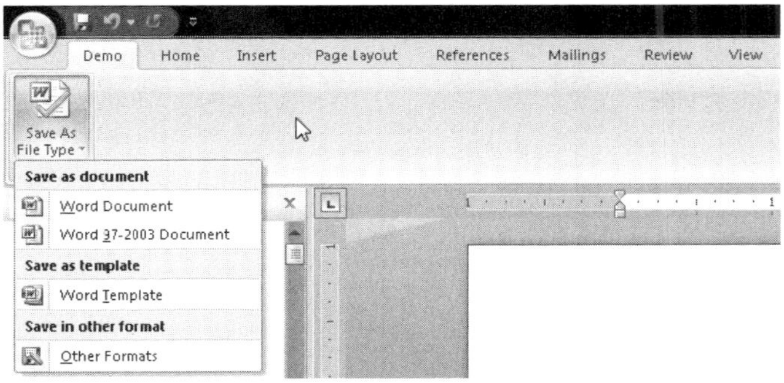

Figure 10-3: The box element, using a vertical alignment

As you can see, the controls are now aligned top to bottom, left to right, almost as though it did not use a `box` control. What is different, however, is the whitespace under the Double Underline `toggleButton`. That, of course, would not be there if the four format controls were not in a `box` control. By using the box, that space is reserved for controls in the box, and other controls cannot infringe on the space.

Nesting box Controls

Now that you have seen how the `box` control is displayed using both the horizontal and vertical attributes of the `boxStyle` element, it is time to see what happens when you nest boxes within each other. In addition to the nesting aspect, this next example also shows the effects of using the `getVisible` callback to control the visibility of the box.

This example houses two `box` controls, each containing two of the formatting controls used in the previous examples. In addition, each of these boxes is housed within a parent box, allowing us to reserve vertical space on the Ribbon so that no other buttons can end up below our controls. We'll also use three checkboxes to select which boxes are visible.

Since the previous two examples were built in Excel, we will construct this one in Word. If you prefer, you can just as easily go through the steps in either Excel or Access. Regardless of the program, you will need to use a macro-enabled file format because we will be using callbacks to make the Ribbon group dynamic.

The first step is to create a new Word file and save it as a macro-enabled (`docm`) document. Close Word, open the file in the CustomUI Editor, and apply the RibbonBase template. Between the `<tabs>` and `</tabs>` elements, enter the following XML code:

```
<tab id="rxtabDemo"
   insertBeforeMso="TabHome"
   label="Demo">
   <group id="rxgrpDemo"
```

```
                label="Demo Group">
                <box id="rxbox1"
                    boxStyle="vertical"
                    getVisible="rxboxShared_getVisible">
                    <box id="rxbox11"
                        boxStyle="horizontal"
                        getVisible="rxboxShared_getVisible">
                        <toggleButton idMso="Bold"/>
                        <toggleButton idMso="Italic"/>
                    </box>
                    <box id="rxbox12"
                        boxStyle="horizontal"
                        getVisible="rxboxShared_getVisible">
                        <toggleButton idMso="Underline"/>
                        <toggleButton idMso="UnderlineDouble"/>
                    </box>
                </box>
                <checkBox id="rxchkVisibleBox1"
                    label="Box 1 Visible?"
                    getPressed="rxchkShared_pressed"
                    onAction="rxchkShared_click"/>
                <checkBox id="rxchkVisibleBox11"
                    label="Box 1-1 Visible?"
                    getPressed="rxchkShared_pressed"
                    onAction="rxchkShared_click"/>
                <checkBox id="rxchkVisibleBox12"
                    label="Box 1-2 Visible?"
                    getPressed="rxchkShared_pressed"
                    onAction="rxchkShared_click"/>
                <button id="rxbtnReset"
                    imageMso="HappyFace"
                    label="Reset All"
                    onAction="rxbtnReset_click"/>
           </group>
       </tab>
```

Notice that in this case we actually have a total of three `box` controls, two of which are nested in the first. All three of these controls will use a shared callback to make the programming a bit easier.

CROSS-REFERENCE **For a review of shared callbacks, see Chapter 5.**

Of course, you need to be able to invalidate the Ribbon to force your `box` controls to hide or show, and to do this you need to capture the `RibbonUI` object. Naturally, this means that you need to modify the `CustomUI` tag to include an `onLoad` statement, so modify your opening line to read as follows:

```
<customUI
    onLoad="rxIRibbonUI_onLoad"
    xmlns="http://schemas.microsoft.com/office/2006/01/customui">
```

Validate the code and copy the callback signatures before you close the file in the CustomUI Editor and reopen it in Word. Ignoring the error about the missing `onLoad` macro, press Alt+F11 to open the VBE, create a new standard module, and paste the callback code.

Each of the callbacks is explained in detail as we go through the examples, but for now we focus on completing the code. At the top of your module (below any lines beginning with `Option` — such as `Option Explicit` — but above any callbacks), add the following code:

```
Dim rxIRibbonUI As IRibbonUI
Dim bBox1_Visible As Boolean
Dim bBox11_Visible As Boolean
Dim bBox12_Visible As Boolean
```

You'll recognize the first line as the variable that will store the `RibbonUI` object and enable you to invalidate the Ribbon later. The other three variables will hold the visible state of the various groups. Since you are controlling these through `checkBox` controls, you can also use these variables to store the state of the `checkBox` that is related to each box.

In addition to capturing the `RibbonUI` at load time, you need to ensure that each `box` control is visible. To do this, the `onLoad` callback should read as follows:

```
'Callback for customUI.onLoad to make each box control visible
Sub rxIRibbonUI_onLoad(ribbon As IRibbonUI)
    Set rxIRibbonUI = ribbon
    bBox1_Visible = True
    bBox11_Visible = True
    bBox12_Visible = True
End Sub
```

You've probably noticed the rather boilerplate comments that precede each callback. Those are graciously provided by the CustomUI Editor. To stay focused on the project, we have left the comments pretty much as generated and merely added the elements when creating shared callbacks. In following code snippets, we added "shared" and the two additional elements `rxbox11` and `rxbox12`. Feel free to modify the comments to suit your style and needs.

The next step is to set up the shared `getVisible` callback for the `box` controls. This should read as follows:

```
'Shared Callback for rxbox1, rxbox11 and rxbox12 getVisible
Sub rxboxShared_getVisible(control As IRibbonControl, ByRef returnedVal)
    Select Case control.ID
        Case "rxbox1"
            returnedVal = bBox1_Visible
        Case "rxbox11"
            returnedVal = bBox11_Visible
        Case "rxbox12"
            returnedVal = bBox12_Visible
    End Select
End Sub
```

As you can see, a `case` statement evaluates which control fired the callback, and retrieves the appropriate value from the variable to return to the `RibbonUI`.

The `getPressed` callback to handle the `checkBox` controls is also based on the same variables, so it looks very similar. The main difference is the name of the controls. The `getPressed` code should read as follows:

```
'Shared Callback for rxchkVisibleBox1, -Box11 and -Box12 getPressed
Sub rxchkShared_getPressed(control As IRibbonControl, ByRef returnedVal)
    Select Case control.ID
        Case "rxchkVisibleBox1"
            returnedVal = bBox1_Visible
        Case "rxchkVisibleBox11"
            returnedVal = bBox11_Visible
        Case "rxchkVisibleBox12"
            returnedVal = bBox12_Visible
    End Select
End Sub
```

Next you want to create the routine that fires when a `checkBox` is clicked. It changes the value of the visible variable to the current "pressed" state (`true` or `false`), and then triggers an invalidation of the Ribbon. This invalidation not only triggers the `getVisible` callbacks for each of the `box` controls, it also ensures that all of the `checkBox` controls are up to date:

```
'Shared Callback for rxchkVisibleBox1, -Box11, -Box 12 onAction
Sub rxchkShared_click(control As IRibbonControl, pressed As Boolean)
    Select Case control.ID
        Case "rxchkVisibleBox1"
            bBox1_Visible = pressed
        Case "rxchkVisibleBox11"
            bBox11_Visible = pressed
        Case "rxchkVisibleBox12"
            bBox12_Visible = pressed
    End Select
    rxIRibbonUI.Invalidate
End Sub
```

Finally, you have the `onAction` callback for the button that you added. While this callback is not really required for your UI to run, it is a handy shortcut to set each and every control back to the default state of visible:

```
'Shared Callback to make buttons visible for rxbtnReset onAction
Sub rxbtnReset_click(control As IRibbonControl)
    bBox1_Visible = True
    bBox11_Visible = True
    bBox12_Visible = True
    rxIRibbonUI.Invalidate
End Sub
```

Now it's time to take this UI for a test drive! Save your code, close the file, and reopen it. You should see the new tab that holds the group you just created, as shown in Figure 10-4.

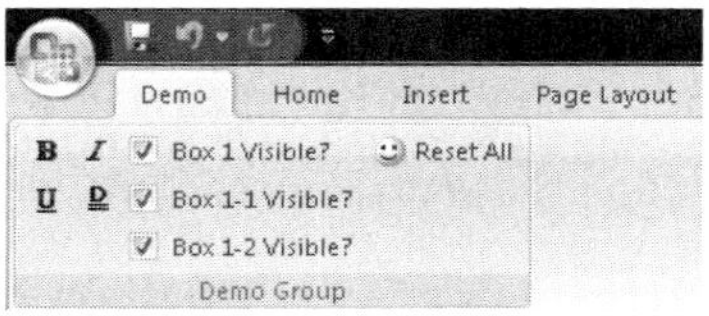

Figure 10-4: Nested box controls on the Ribbon

Now try clearing the check from the `checkBox` marked Box 1-1 Visible? You'll see the Bold and Italic icons vanish! Uncheck Box 1-2 Visible? and all of the formatting buttons will disappear! Click the Reset All button to set everything back to visible, or you can recheck the individual `checkBox` controls.

This time, uncheck the `checkBox` labeled Box 1 Visible? This will toggle the parent box. Notice how it appears as though nothing happened? However, there is a different reaction if you now toggle the visibility of one of the nested `box` controls. Go ahead and try a few different combinations. In addition to demonstrating how to nest boxes, this exercise provides some good tools for experimenting with the synergistic effects of controls.

NOTE While you are permitted to use the `getVisible` callback to set a parent box to `visible="false"`, this will not hide the parent box and all child controls as you might expect. Instead, both the parent and child `box` controls will be frozen in their current state — visible or not. The controls themselves will all be visible (if they were before the parent was toggled) and work, but any attempts to change the state of the nested controls by callbacks will be ignored. The effects of this will be reversed when the `getVisible` callback for the parent box is again set to `true`.

NOTE The only way to hide a parent `box` control is to hide all of the child items. Upon doing so, the parent box will collapse and therefore appear invisible, even though the box's `visible` property is set to `true`.

The buttonGroup element

The `buttonGroup` element is similar to the `box` element but it has some unique features as well. The biggest difference in appearance between the `buttonGroup` and the `box` controls is that although the `box` does not place a visible perimeter around the group, the `buttonGroup` element actually displays a border. The `buttonGroup` cannot be aligned vertically, however, and unlike the `box`, it will not accept either the `box` or `buttonGroup` elements as children.

The main differences between the `box` element and the `buttonGroup` element are summarized in Table 10-4.

Table 10-4: Differences Between the box and buttonGroup Elements

ABILITY	BOX	BUTTONGROUP
Align controls horizontally	✔	✔
Align controls vertically	✔	
Will accept a nested box control	✔	
Will accept a nested buttonGroup control	✔	
Places a visible outline around the controls		✔

Based on this information, you may conclude that the `box` is a far more robust control. While this may be true, keep in mind that the `buttonGroup` is the only control that allows you to place a visible border around a collection of controls.

In truth, it is a shame that the Ribbon designers did not add a "`showBorder`" attribute to the `box` control. Had they done so, the `buttonGroup` attribute probably would not be needed at all.

Required Attributes of the buttonGroup element

Each `buttonGroup` object requires one of the two unique `id` attributes listed in Table 10-5.

Table 10-5: Required Attributes of the buttonGroup Element

ATTRIBUTE	WHEN TO USE
id	When creating your own `buttonGroup`
idQ	When creating a `buttonGroup` shared between namespaces

NOTE **Like the `box` element, Microsoft does not provide any built-in `buttonGroup` controls, so the `idMso` attribute cannot be specified, as no controls can be referenced.**

Optional Static and Dynamic Attributes with Callback Signatures

In order to position your `buttonGroup` in relation to an existing control, you must use one of the `insert` attributes listed in Table 10-6.

Table 10-6: Optional insert Attributes for the buttonGroup Element

INSERT ATTRIBUTE	ALLOWED VALUES	DEFAULT VALUE	WHEN TO USE
insertAfterMso	Valid Mso Group	Insert at end of group	Insert after Microsoft control
insertBeforeMso	Valid Mso Group	Insert at end of group	Insert before Microsoft control
insertAfterQ	Valid Group idQ	Insert at end of group	Insert after shared namespace control
insertBeforeQ	Valid Group idQ	Insert at end of group	Insert before shared namespace control

The `buttonGroup` element also accepts the optional visible attribute or callback shown in Table 10-7.

Table 10-7: Optional Attribute or Callback of the buttonGroup Element

STATIC ATTRIBUTE	DYNAMIC ATTRIBUTE	ALLOWED VALUES	DEFAULT VALUE	VBA CALLBACK SIGNATURE FOR DYNAMIC ATTRIBUTE
visible	getVisible	true, false, 1, 0	true	Sub GetVisible (control As IRibbonControl, ByRef returnedVal)

NOTE **While the `buttonGroup` has a `getVisible` callback available, there was a bug with the callback at the time this was written. This bug stymies the callback if the value is set to `false`; however, the callback works properly when the value is set to `true`. It is hoped that this will be fixed in an upcoming service release.**

Allowed Children Objects of the buttonGroup Element

The `buttonGroup` element may contain any or all of the following controls:

- button
- control
- dynamicMenu
- gallery
- menu
- splitButton
- toggleButton

Parent Objects of the buttonGroup Element

A `buttonGroup` may only be nested within one of the following two elements:

- box
- group

Graphical View of a buttonGroup

Figure 10-5 gives a clear picture of how a `buttonGroup` is displayed in a group.

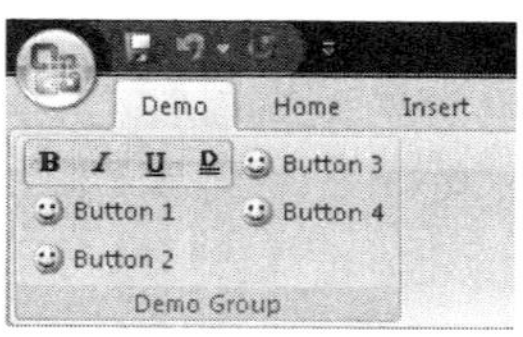

Figure 10-5: A buttonGroup displayed in a group

While it may be difficult to see in print, not only does the `buttonGroup` display a border around the four supplied formatting buttons, each button is also separated by a faint line.

Using Built-in buttonGroup Elements

Like the `box` element, the only purpose of the `buttonGroup` is to help format the Ribbon. For this reason, it makes sense that Microsoft doesn't expose any `buttonGroup` controls, as we would undoubtedly want to use nested controls other than those provided.

Creating Custom buttonGroup Elements

In the next example, we build a modified version of the Ribbon shown in Figure 10-5. Rather than leave empty space under the `buttonGroup`, we will bump all of the buttons over to the second column of controls.

To start this process, create a new Word document. We won't be adding any dynamic controls to this file, so you can save it in the macro-free (`docx`) format. Close Word and open the file in the CustomUI Editor, apply the RibbonBase template, and enter the following code between the `<tabs>` and `</tabs>` elements:

```
<tab id="rxtab_Demo"
   label="Demo"
   insertBeforeMso="TabHome">
   <group id="rxgrp_Demo"
      label="Demo Group">
      <box id="rxboxCustom"
         boxStyle="vertical">
         <buttonGroup id="rxbgrpMsoControls">
            <toggleButton idMso="Bold"/>
            <toggleButton idMso="Italic"/>
            <toggleButton idMso="Underline"/>
            <toggleButton idMso="UnderlineDouble"
               showLabel="false"/>
         </buttonGroup>
      </box>
      <button id="rxbtnHappy1"
         imageMso="HappyFace"
         label="Button 1"/>
      <button id="rxbtnHappy2"
         imageMso="HappyFace"
         label="Button 2"/>
      <button id="rxbtnHappy3"
         imageMso="HappyFace"
         label="Button 3"/>
   </group>
</tab>
```

In reviewing this code, note that the `buttonGroup` control is encapsulated within a vertical `box` control. As you learned earlier in this chapter, using the `box` control enables you to reserve the whitespace under your controls by forcing all the `button` controls into the next column.

The next step, of course, is to validate the code. There are no dynamic features to this example, so no callback signatures are required. Save the file, close the CustomUI Editor, and reopen the document in Word. You will now see the `buttonGroup` displayed on the custom tab, as shown in Figure 10-6.

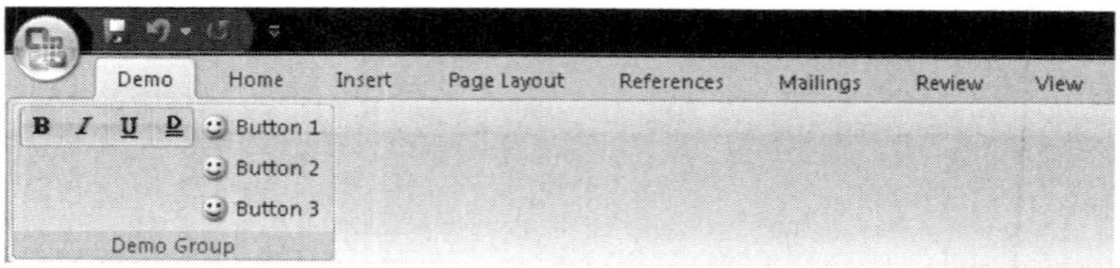

Figure 10-6: A buttonGroup with whitespace below

Notice that the font controls, which are in a horizontal button group, are displayed on one line at the top of the vertical `box` control. The vertical control reserves the entire area for its contents, so three happy-face buttons appear in a column to the right.

The labelControl Element

The `labelControl` gives developers a way to show a text label on the Ribbon. This control has no actions and is typically used for headings or descriptions of other controls. It is mostly used to give context to buttons that are arranged in a column.

Required Attributes

Each `labelControl` requires one of the three `id` attributes shown in Table 10-8.

Table 10-8: Required Attributes of the labelControl Element

ATTRIBUTE	WHEN TO USE
id	When creating your own `labelControl`
idMso	When using an existing Microsoft `labelControl`
idQ	When creating a `labelControl` shared between namespaces

Optional Static and Dynamic Attributes with Callback Signatures

As with other controls, the `insert` attribute is again optional. It is only needed when you want to position a `labelControl` in relation to another control. Table 10-9 lists the `insert` attributes.

Table 10-9: Optional insert Attributes for the labelControl Element

INSERT ATTRIBUTE	ALLOWED VALUES	DEFAULT VALUE	WHEN TO USE
insertAfterMso	Valid Mso Group	Insert at end of group	Insert after Microsoft control
insertBeforeMso	Valid Mso Group	Insert at end of group	Insert before Microsoft control
insertAfterQ	Valid Group idQ	Insert at end of group	Insert after shared namespace control
insertBeforeQ	Valid Group idQ	Insert at end of group	Insert before shared namespace control

The `labelControl` will also accept any combination of the attributes or callback equivalents shown in Table 10-10.

Table 10-10: Optional Attributes and Callbacks of the labelControl Element

STATIC ATTRIBUTE	DYNAMIC ATTRIBUTE	ALLOWED VALUES	DEFAULT VALUE	VBA CALLBACK SIGNATURE FOR DYNAMIC ATTRIBUTE
enabled	getEnabled	true, false, 1, 0	true	Sub GetEnabled (control As IRibbonControl, ByRef returnedVal)
label	getLabel	1 to 1024 characters	(none)	Sub GetLabel (control As IRibbonControl, ByRef returnedVal)
screentip	getScreentip	1 to 1024 characters	(none)	Sub GetScreentip (control As IRibbonControl, ByRef returnedVal)
showLabel	getShowLabel	true, false, 1, 0	true	Sub GetShowLabel (control As IRibbonControl, ByRef returnedVal)
supertip	getSupertip	1 to 1024 characters	(none)	Sub GetSupertip (control As IRibbonControl, ByRef returnedVal)

Continued

Table 10-10 *(continued)*

STATIC ATTRIBUTE	DYNAMIC ATTRIBUTE	ALLOWED VALUES	DEFAULT VALUE	VBA CALLBACK SIGNATURE FOR DYNAMIC ATTRIBUTE
tag	(none)	1 to 1024 characters	(none)	(none)
visible	getVisible	true, false	true	Sub GetVisible (control As IRibbonControl, ByRef returnedVal)

Allowed Children Objects of the labelControl Element

The `labelControl` does not support child controls of any kind.

Parent Objects of the labelControl Element

The `labelControl` element may only be used within the following controls:

- box
- group

Graphical View of a labelControl

The `labelControl` is a very simple text label that can appear either on a group or in a box. While it can contain `screentip` and `supertip` attributes (which you learn about in Chapter 11), Figure 10-7 shows it in its most basic format. The `labelControl` is the portion marked "Audit Formulas" at the top of the custom-built Audit group.

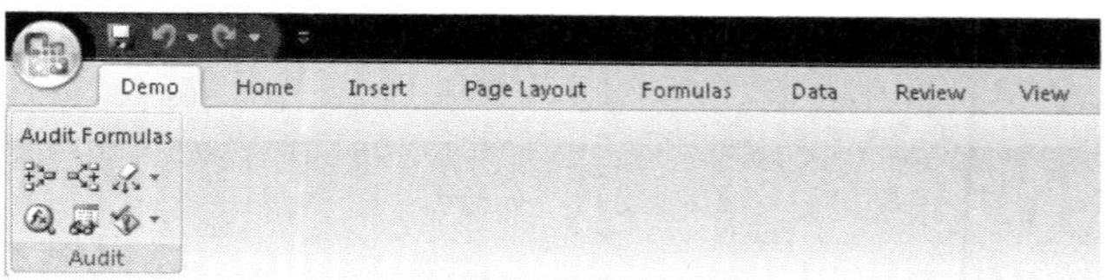

Figure 10-7: The labelControl on a group

As you can see, the `labelControl` takes the space of one entire row of controls. You will want to keep this in mind when planning the layout of control groups.

Using Built-in labelControl Elements

Believe it or not, Microsoft actually does expose six of its own `labelControl` elements in Excel; and it exposes two `labelControl` elements in Word. However, when it comes to Access, none of the `labelControl` elements are exposed. In any case, it is difficult to imagine why you would ever want to use these elements, as it is much quicker to build a custom label of your own design than to look up one of theirs.

Consider for a moment how long this process would take. You would first have to look up the `idMso` for an existing `labelControl`, and then you would still have to put the name in the CustomUI Editor and build a `lableControl` element that references the `idMso` name. Again, why bother? Since you have to write XML anyway, it is faster and more straightforward to create a custom `labelControl` and give it the exact name that you want.

Creating Custom labelControl Elements

A rather cool use of the `labelControl` is to use it as a flag — a visual indication that something has been done. After all, it's right there on the Ribbon, so all you have to do is draw attention to it and make it change. Maybe you have a procedure that only runs once per session. Rather than have users click the button and have a message box advise them if the procedure has been run or not, you could provide a visual cue first so they don't need to click the button.

Our next example works through that scenario. Rather than hide the buttons, which might be disconcerting for the users, we instead change the label above the button. Just for fun, we also change the image on the button as well. We again work through the process in Excel, although it could just as easily be implemented in Access or Word.

Start by creating a new Excel file. You need to invalidate the Ribbon to change the `labelControl`, so save the file in the macro-enabled format (`xlsm`). Close the file and open it in the CustomUI Editor. Apply the RibbonBase template and insert the following XML between the `<tabs>` and `</tabs>` elements:

```
<tab id="rxtabDemo"
   insertBeforeMso="TabHome"
   label="Demo">
   <group id="rxgrpDemo"
      label="Demo Group">
      <labelControl id="rxlblFeedback"
         getLabel="rxlblFeedback_getLabel"/>
      <button id="rxbtnProcess"
         getImage="rxbtnProcess_getImage"
         onAction="rxbtnProcess_click"/>
   </group>
</tab>
```

In addition, you also need to edit the CustomUI element to request an `onLoad` event. You're quite familiar with the prerequisite code, so modify the first line of the XML to read as follows:

```
<customUI
   onLoad="rxIRibbonUI_onLoad"
   xmlns="http://schemas.microsoft.com/office/2006/01/customui">
```

Now it's time to validate the code, copy the callbacks, save and close the file, and reopen it in Excel. Again, ignore the error messages about the missing `onLoad` callback and just open the VBE to paste your callbacks in a new module.

Before we deal with the callbacks themselves, it is important to think through the entire process. We want the label to read Process Accounts before the button is clicked, and Accounts Complete afterward. We need a variable to store the value that indicates whether the button has been clicked or not, so insert the following code snippet at the top of the module, but below any lines prefaced with the `Option` keyword:

```
Dim bButtonClicked as Boolean
```

Of course, you need to include a global variable to store the `RibbonUI`, and this should be placed with the variable to store the button's clicked state. We can now proceed to create the individual callbacks. Notice that there are four callbacks in all. The first callback, `onLoad`, is shown here and should look very familiar:

```
Dim rxIRibbonUI As IRibbonUI

'Callback for customUI.onLoad
Sub rxIRibbonUI_onLoad(ribbon As IRibbonUI)
    Set rxIRibbonUI = ribbon
End Sub
```

Next, create the `getLabel` callback for the `labelControl`. The easiest way to evaluate whether the button has been clicked or not is to check the `bButtonClicked` variable. You can do that using a `select case` statement, as follows:

```
'Callback for rxlblFeedback getLabel
Sub rxlblFeedback_getLabel(control As IRibbonControl, ByRef returnedVal)
    Select Case bButtonClicked
        Case False
            returnedVal = "Process Accounts"
        Case True
            returnedVal = "Accounts Complete"
    End Select
End Sub
```

You can use a similar construct to return the image for the button. Which image or label is displayed is determined by the evaluation of the `Select` statement. You can see that this can be a powerful and flexible tool.

```
'Callback for rxbtnProcess getImage
Sub rxbtnProcess_getImage(control As IRibbonControl, ByRef returnedVal)
    Select Case bButtonClicked
        Case False
            returnedVal = "CreateReportFromWizard"
        Case True
            returnedVal = "DeclineInvitation"
    End Select
End Sub
```

Finally, you need to deal with your button. Again, you check the value of `bButtonClicked`. If it is `False`, you change the value of `bButtonClicked` to `true`, run your routine, and then invalidate the Ribbon. The invalidation will, of course, trigger the rebuild, and your controls will update to show the user it has been done. If the value of `bButtonClicked` is already `true`, you tell the user that they have already completed the routine. The following code will accomplish this:

```
'Callback for rxbtnProcess onAction
Sub rxbtnProcess_click(control As IRibbonControl)
    Select Case bButtonClicked
        Case False
            bButtonClicked = True

            'Code to process accounts goes here

            rxIRibbonUI.Invalidate
        Case True
            MsgBox "You have already run this routine!"
    End Select
End Sub
```

Now that the necessary code has been entered, save, close, and reopen the workbook. You will see the tab displayed in Figure 10-8.

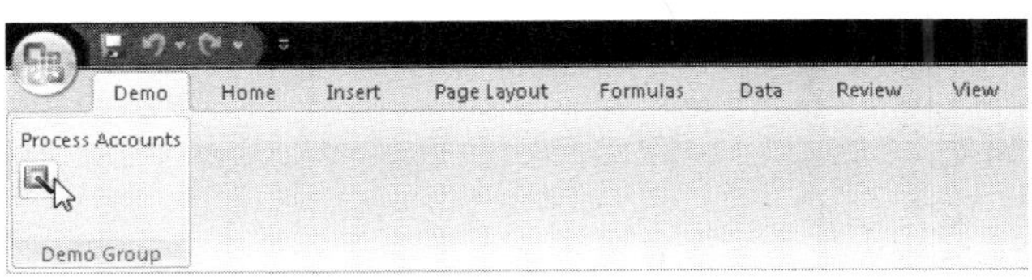

Figure 10-8: The Process Accounts label on the group

Click the button, and the group will update to the view shown in Figure 10-9.

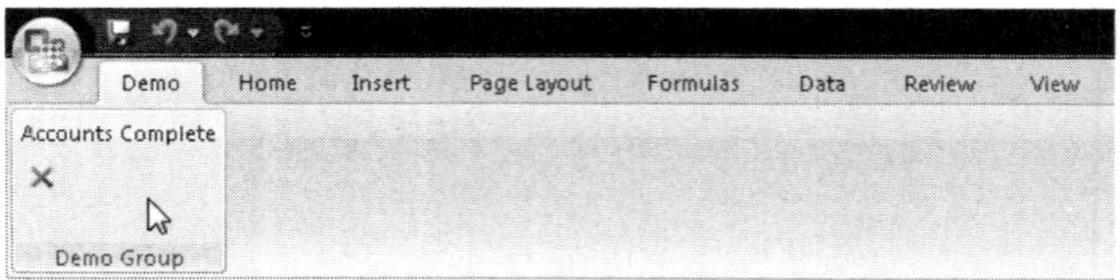

Figure 10-9: The Process Accounts labelControl updated via a callback

As shown in the code, we have used both the label and the graphic to call the user's attention to the status — or change in status. It is hoped that this example has sparked some ideas about how you can use a `labelControl` to alert users about the status of an object or an event.

The separator Element

The `separator` control is quite different from the three controls covered so far in this chapter. While it is the job of the `box` and `buttonGroup` to collect controls into a unit, it is the job of the `separator` to draw clear and logical boundaries and to essentially create subgroups within a tab's groups.

The `separator` control manifests itself as a vertical line break between items in a group. It spans from the top of the group to the bottom of the group, and cannot be set to any other orientation or size. It can, however, provide whitespace on the Ribbon, similar to the space that you can create using a vertical `box` control.

Required Attributes of the separator Element

Every `separator` requires a unique `id` attribute from the two listed in Table 10-11.

Table 10-11: Required Attributes of the separator Element

ATTRIBUTE	WHEN TO USE
id	When creating your own `separator`
idQ	When creating a `separator` shared between namespaces

NOTE **There is no `idMso` for this control, as there would be no benefit to referencing a built-in separator.**

Optional Static and Dynamic Attributes with Callback Signatures

The placement of a `separator` control in relation to an existing control requires use of one of the `insert` attributes listed in Table 10-12. As is usual, ignoring this attribute enables the XML code to be executed in the order in which it is written.

Table 10-12: Optional insert Attributes for the separator Element

INSERT ATTRIBUTE	ALLOWED VALUES	DEFAULT VALUE	WHEN TO USE
insertAfterMso	Valid Mso Group	Insert at end of group	Insert after Microsoft control
insertBeforeMso	Valid Mso Group	Insert at end of group	Insert before Microsoft control
insertAfterQ	Valid Group idQ	Insert at end of group	Insert after shared namespace control
insertBeforeQ	Valid Group idQ	Insert at end of group	Insert before shared namespace control

The `separator` element will accept the static visible attribute or the callback equivalent shown in Table 10-13.

Table 10-13: Optional Attributes and Callbacks of the separator Element

STATIC ATTRIBUTE	DYNAMIC ATTRIBUTE	ALLOWED VALUES	DEFAULT VALUE	VBA CALLBACK SIGNATURE FOR DYNAMIC ATTRIBUTE
visible	getVisible	true, false, 1, 0	true	Sub GetVisible (control As IRibbonControl, ByRef returnedVal)

NOTE Up to and including the release of Office 2007 Service Pack 1 (released as we write this chapter), the `separator` control suffered from a fairly serious bug. While the XML schema allows you to specify `false` as the value for the separator element's `visible` attribute, (using either static XML or using a callback), the value has no effect. Regardless of the settings or combinations of settings, the `separator` control always remained visible during our testing.

Allowed Children Objects of the separator Element

The `separator` element does not support child objects of any kind.

Parent Objects of the separator Element

The `separator` control may only be used in the following three elements:

- documentControl
- group
- sharedControl

Graphical View of a Separator

As shown in Figure 10-10, adding a `separator` control places a dividing line between existing controls in a group.

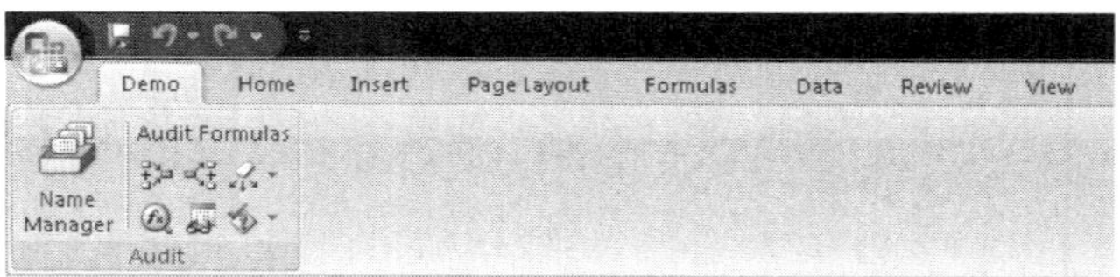

Figure 10-10: A separator control brings order to a Ribbon group

In this example, the `separator` makes it instantly clear that the label Name Manager refers to the control above it, and that the `labelControl` bearing the title Audit Formulas refers to the six controls under it.

Using Built-in separator Elements

The `separator` element is essentially a visible line. Since it would take us much more typing to refer to a built-in version than to just create our own, there is absolutely no reason for us to use one of Microsoft's built in `separator` controls, even if we could access them.

Creating Custom separator Elements

Because the `separator` control has one primary function and very few options, this example shows how you can use the `separator` to create whitespace on the Ribbon.

In the section on `box` controls, we demonstrated how you can nest a horizontal box within a vertical box and create whitespace (because the vertical box prevents buttons from encroaching into its area). However, this requires multiple controls and can take a bit of planning. That's what makes the `separator` so convenient: it works independently. One of the key benefits of the `separator` is that it forces a break between controls, so the whitespace is preserved without the effort of adding nested `box` controls.

We demonstrate this here using the Excel workbook used earlier in this chapter in the "Horizontal Alignment" portion of the box examples. (You can also download box-horizontal.xlsx from the book's website.) Open the file in the CustomUI Editor and place the following code right after the </box> line:

```
<separator id="rxsep1"/>
```

Upon saving and opening the file in Excel, the Ribbon group should look like the one displayed in Figure 10-11.

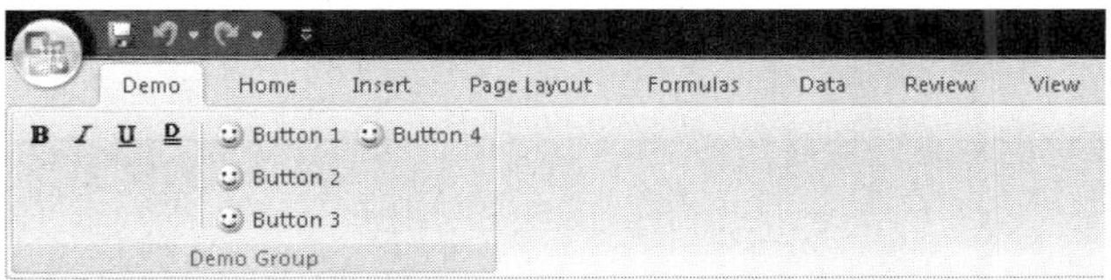

Figure 10-11: The custom separator

Wow — that is so much easier than nesting horizontal box controls in a vertical box. Don't get us wrong; there are other reasons for nesting controls. We're just not recommending it as the first choice for creating whitespace.

The menuSeparator Element

The menuSeparator is somewhat of a hybrid between the separator and labelControl elements. While this might seem like a strange combination, you will see that, in the right circumstances, it can be quite useful.

Like the separator control, the menuSeparator can be used to draw a line, except this control creates a horizontal line instead of vertical line. Before you get excited, be aware that this control is reserved for specific types of menu controls (listed in the section on parent objects). It cannot be used to format standard groups.

On the upside, however, you can provide text with the menuSeparator control, and this nifty option enables you to add some pizzazz and distinction by adding headers between menu items. That will be demonstrated in just a moment.

Required Attributes of the menuSeparator Element

Each menuSeparator requires a unique id attribute from the two shown in Table 10-14.

Table 10-14: Required Attributes of the menuSeparator Element

ATTRIBUTE	WHEN TO USE
id	When creating your own menuSeparator
idQ	When creating a menuSeparator shared between namespaces

NOTE **As with the `separator` control, there is no `idMso` for this control, as there would be no benefit to referencing a built-in `menuSeparator`.**

Optional Static and Dynamic Attributes with Callback Signatures

Placing a `menuSeparator` relative to any existing menu item requires one of the `insert` attributes listed in Table 10-15. The alternative is to default to the order in which the control is listed in the XML code. If you construct a menu following our example, the desired positioning is achieved even without this attribute.

Table 10-15: Optional insert Attributes for the menuSeparator Element

INSERT ATTRIBUTE	ALLOWED VALUES	DEFAULT VALUE	WHEN TO USE
insertAfterMso	Valid Mso Group	Insert at end of group	Insert after Microsoft control
insertBeforeMso	Valid Mso Group	Insert at end of group	Insert before Microsoft control
insertAfterQ	Valid Group idQ	Insert at end of group	Insert after shared namespace control
insertBeforeQ	Valid Group idQ	Insert at end of group	Insert before shared namespace control

The `menuSeparator` control accepts the title element or callback equivalent shown in Table 10-16.

Table 10-16: Optional Attribute and Callback of the menuSeparator Element

STATIC ATTRIBUTE	DYNAMIC ATTRIBUTE	ALLOWED VALUES	DEFAULT VALUE	VBA CALLBACK SIGNATURE FOR DYNAMIC ATTRIBUTE
title	getTitle	1 to 1024 characters	line	Sub GetTitle (control As IRibbonControl, ByRef returnedVal)

NOTE **There is no visible attribute or callback for the** `menuSeparator`**. If you decide to use this control, it will show on your menu in one way or another – either as a textual header, using whatever text you specify for the title attribute, or simply as a line if no title is provided.**

Allowed Children Objects of the menuSeparator Element

The `menuSeparator` does not support child objects of any kind.

Parent Objects of the menuSeparator Element

A `menuSeparator` may only be used within the following three controls:

- menu
- officeMenu
- dynamicMenu

Graphical View of the menuSeparator Element

Building from the menu example shown in Chapter 9, this example adds a few `menuSeparator` elements to make it more readable, as shown in Figure 10-12. Note that there are actually four `menuSeparator` elements in this image. Three of them were provided a title element, and are displayed as the headings within the menu: Save in 2007 format, Save in 97-2003 format, and Save in other format. The last one was declared in the XML with the `title` attribute omitted, and manifests as the shaded line between the Macro Enabled and Binary menu items in the first section.

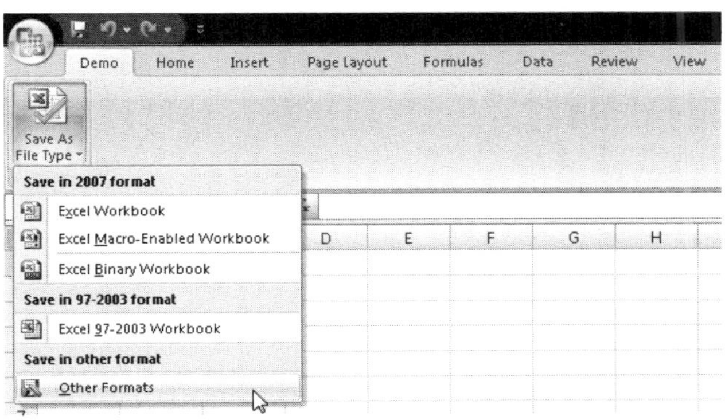

Figure 10-12: menuSeparator attributes used to divide a menu

The `title` attribute provides the bonus of adding shading to the line. Combined with the lack of an image, it makes the headings stand out and clearly differentiates them from the clickable controls.

Using Built-in menuSeparator Elements

Like the `separator` and `labelControl` elements, Microsoft does not expose any `menuSeparator` controls for our use. As before, this is neither surprising nor of particular concern, as it takes less effort to create our own `menuSeparator` than it does to find and reference one of theirs.

Creating Custom menuSeparator Elements

To demonstrate how to build custom `menuSeparator` controls, we will construct the UI modification displayed in Figure 10-12.

To begin, create a new Excel document and save it in the macro-free (`xlsx`) file format. Close the file and open it in the CustomUI Editor. Apply the RibbonBase template and insert the following XML between the `<tabs>` and `</tabs>` elements:

```
<tab id="tabDemo"
   label="Demo"
   insertBeforeMso="TabHome">
   <group id="grpSaveFiles"
        label="Save File">
        <menu id="mnuNewFile"
        label="Save As File Type"
        size="large"
        imageMso="FileCompatibilityChecker">
        <menuSeparator id="rxmSep01"
                title="Save in 2007 format"/>
        <button idMso="FileSaveAsExcelXlsx"/>
        <button idMso="FileSaveAsExcelXlsxMacro"/>
        <menuSeparator id="rxmSep02"/>
        <button idMso="FileSaveAsExcelXlsb"/>
        <menuSeparator id="rxmSep03"
                title="Save in 97-2003 format"/>
        <button idMso="FileSaveAsExcel97_2003"/>
        <menuSeparator id="rxmSep04"
                title="Save in other format"/>
        <button idMso="FileSaveAsOtherFormats"/>
        </menu>
   </group>
</tab>
```

In this XML code, notice that unlike the other `rxmSep` controls, `rxmSep02` does not specify a `title` attribute. This is how we will create a thin line to separate the menu items, rather than use a title bar with a line.

Now you are ready to validate the code, save the file, and close it in the CustomUI Editor. Upon reopening the file in Excel, you will see a newly formatted menu (refer to Figure 10-12).

Of course, the menuSeparator element is provided purely to support your formatting goals. Generally, it won't be necessary to show lines between your items. For example, there wouldn't be much benefit to adding lines to the menu shown in Figure 10-13.

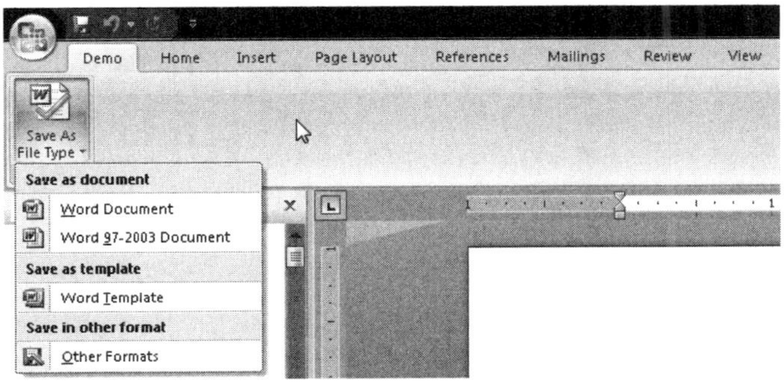

Figure 10-13: Separating a custom Word menu with textual separators

Alternately, maybe you prefer to have thin lines and to avoid the distraction created by titles, as Figure 10-14 illustrates. The uniform appearance of a menu with just faint lines and no titles gives the menu a totally different feel.

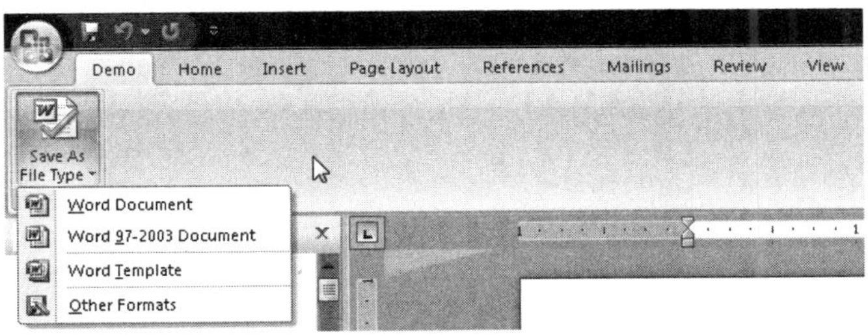

Figure 10-14: Separating a custom Word menu with linear separators

The great thing about the menuSeparator element is that you can quickly flip it between different views to see which you prefer. Let's do exactly that. Create a new Word document and save it as a macro-free (docx) file. Close the file and open it in the CustomUI Editor. Apply the RibbonBase template and insert the following XML between the <tabs> and </tabs> elements:

```
<tab id="tabDemo"
   label="Demo"
```

```
      insertBeforeMso="TabHome">
      <group id="grpSaveFiles"
           label="Save File">
           <menu id="mnuSaveFile"
               label="Save As File Type"
               size="large"
               imageMso="FileCompatibilityCheckerWord">
               <menuSeparator id="rxmSep01"
                   title="Save as document"/>
               <button idMso="FileSaveAsWordDocx"/>
               <button idMso="FileSaveAsWord97_2003"/>
               <menuSeparator id="rxmSep02"
                   title="Save as template"/>
               <button idMso="FileSaveAsWordDotx"/>
               <menuSeparator id="rxmSep03"
                   title="Save in other format"/>
               <button idMso="FileSaveAsOtherFormats"/>
           </menu>
       </group>
   </tab>
```

Validate the code, save the file, and close it in the CustomUI Editor. When you open the file in Word, you should see a menu like the one shown in Figure 10-13.

Now that you're satisfied that the menu exists, close the file and reopen it in the CustomUI Editor. Find every `menuSeparator` element and remove the `title` attribute from it so that they all read similarly to the following:

```
<menuSeparator id="rxmSep01"/>
```

Again, validate the code, save the file, close it in the CustomUI Editor, and reopen it in Word. Notice that the menu now looks like the image shown in Figure 10-14.

It is also worth pointing out that the first `menuSeparator` actually becomes invisible during this process. While the code still calls the element, it is ignored because it is above the first menu item. In fact, it could have just as easily been omitted, but sometimes you may wish to keep it there. If you are building a very complex menu, you may want to create a numbering convention, using your `menuSeparator` controls as logical breaks between selected numbers. As you can see, using invisible `menuSeparators` could be a very useful tool for that purpose.

Conclusion

This chapter focused exclusively on the elements that can be used to format the Ribbon, making it more intuitive and visually appealing. You first learned how to use the `box` element. While the `box` itself is invisible, the effects that it creates can appear quite dramatic. The `box` not only enables us to group controls together, it can also be used to reserve whitespace on the Ribbon, thereby providing a more attractive and understandable UI.

We also demonstrated that the `buttonGroup` is a close cousin to the `box` element. Similar in purpose, this element is actually very obvious, putting a border around the group of controls nested within it. While this can add great visual effect to your Ribbon, the `buttonGroup` is limited in the types of controls that it can contain.

Next, we took a detailed look at the `labelControl`. This element, used to provide text on the Ribbon, can really add flair and distinction, to say nothing of the vital information that it can convey to users. By placing a `labelControl` over one or more groups of controls, you can immediately indicate their purpose to users, without forcing them to rely on a screentip.

While the `box` and `buttonGroup` controls are intended to bring different controls together in logical groups, it is the job of the `separator` element to draw clear boundaries between the controls. The `separator` can only be a vertical line running from the top of the Ribbon group to the bottom.

That brings us to the final control in this section. We ended the chapter by looking at the `menuSeparator` control. Similar in purpose to the `separator`, the `menuSeparator` is a horizontal line used to separate the items on menu-style controls. Although it can only be used with the `menu` controls, it is still more robust than its group-level counterpart, the `separator`. The `menuSeparator` can have a text title so that it will display both a horizontal line and a title.

Ultimately, Microsoft has provided us with a fairly good collection of elements with which we can format and layout our Ribbon customizations. While improvements can always be made, these controls will accomplish most of the formatting that you want.

The next chapter focuses on the controls and attributes that help users. You'll learn how you can create a Ribbon that makes it easier for users to get their work done. Chapter 11 is the final chapter in this part, covering the fundamental concepts that are the prerequisites for creating truly customized Ribbons. After the next chapter, we move into more advanced concepts and work a lot more with VBA.

CHAPTER

11

Using Controls and Attributes to Help Your Users

One of the things developers often overlook when building programs is ease of use. Indeed, this is one aspect of development that the Ribbon was designed to fix. Even so, it is still the developer's responsibility to ensure that needed controls are logically placed, have meaningful labels, and are easily understood by the user. Despite our best efforts, sometimes even we developers are unable to make things completely intuitive — and that is where providing help to your users comes in.

In this chapter you'll learn techniques for providing custom help and tips to users, when and where they need it most. We'll examine one control and three attributes, and show you how to give a face-lift to existing controls. When used together, these can effectively become the first level of help for users.

We start by looking at the `dialogBoxLauncher` control, which is used to display custom userforms or built-in dialogs. While the main purpose of this control is to enable the user to choose from a wide array of options, it can also be used to provide informational forms. This chapter describes both uses for this control.

Following the `dialogBoxLauncher`, three specific attributes are explored: `keytip`, `screentip`, and `supertip`. Each of these attributes can be used in its own special way to make the Ribbon more accessible, easier to navigate, and more logical to follow.

Finally, we demonstrate how to replace some of the attributes of built-in controls. By modifying some of the built-in controls to be consistent with your custom controls, you can provide a more uniform user interface. This enables users to become more comfortable and fluent with the controls specific to the application. At the same time, it enables you to avoid creating everything from scratch.

By the end of the chapter, you will have the tools and knowledge to create easy-to-use custom UIs, and you'll be able to incorporate strategically placed help files and tips. As you are preparing to work through the examples, we encourage you to download the companion files. The source code and files for this chapter can be found on the book's website at `www.wiley.com/go/ribbonx`.

The dialogBoxLauncher Element

The `dialogBoxLauncher` is a little, almost invisible, gadget that you can use on your group. This tiny square with an arrow in it, shown in the lower-right corner of each group in Figure 11-1, launches a dialog box (either custom or built-in).

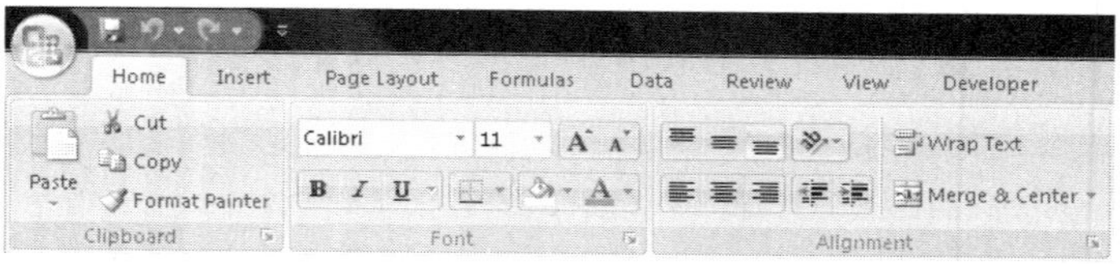

Figure 11-1: Three groups with dialogBoxLauncher elements in place

In most cases, the `dialogBoxLauncher` is used to provide users with many more options than you could, or would want to, fit on the Ribbon. It does this by launching one of Microsoft's built-in dialogs. Fortunately, we are not limited to simply using the built-in dialogs provided by Microsoft. Indeed, as demonstrated later in the chapter, you can create your own userforms, which can be used to provide users with additional options or help documentation.

This section looks at three ways to use the `dialogBoxLauncher`: using a built-in version to launch the default dialog that Microsoft has assigned; creating a custom `dialogBoxLauncher` to launch a built-in dialog; and creating a custom `dialogBoxLauncher` to launch your own custom userform. First, though, we explore the XML structure of the `dialogBoxLauncher`.

Required and Optional Attributes

The `dialogBoxLauncher` is somewhat unusual compared to the rest of the fleet of RibbonX elements. Whereas normally we provide a table of all the required and optional attributes for the element, the `dialogBoxLauncher` does not have any — not even an `id`!

While it may seem very strange at first, the sole job of this element is to launch another element; therefore, it does not need any attributes. Instead, the `dialogBoxLauncher` relies on the child object to provide its own attributes.

Allowed Children Objects

The `dialogBoxLauncher` is a container, nothing more. Therefore, it not only accepts a child object, it requires a child object in order to function. The `dialogBoxLauncher` must have one button, and only one button, as a child object. In fact, it is actually the job of the button to launch the application's dialog, so the `dialogBoxLauncher` doesn't even do that!

NOTE `dialogBoxLauncher` **is unique in that it has no attributes. In addition, it must have one, but only one, child button. Although it might be easiest to use a built-in button, this has the extra challenge of ensuring that the correct built-in** `dialogBoxLauncher` **button is selected.**

Parent Objects

The only place where a `dialogBoxLauncher` may be used is on a group.

Examples of Using the dialogBoxLauncher Element

As mentioned earlier, there are three different ways to implement a `dialog-BoxLauncher` in the UI:

- Use one of the defaults that Microsoft has made available,
- Create a custom launcher to use one of Microsoft's other dialogs.
- Create a custom launcher to launch your own custom userform.

Each of these approaches is now explored in detail.

Built-in dialogBoxLaunchers

The easiest way to add a `dialogBoxLauncher` to your group is to use one of Microsoft's built-in `dialogBoxLauncher` buttons as the child object. Because Microsoft provides several built-in `dialogBoxLauncher` buttons, it makes sense to use them where you can, rather than program the callbacks to launch the dialogs yourself.

The example that follows will be created in Microsoft Word, but it can also be completed in Access or Excel. As it only uses built-in controls, it does not require VBA, so it can be saved in a macro-free file format.

Begin by creating a new Word file and opening it in the CustomUI Editor. After applying the RibbonBase XML template designed in Chapter 2, insert the following XML code between the `<tabs>` and `</tabs>` tags:

```
<tab id="rxtabDemo"
   label="Demo"
   insertBeforeMso="TabHome">
   <group id="rxgrpTest"
      label="Test">
      <box id="rxboxFormat">
         <comboBox idMso="Font"/>
         <comboBox idMso="FontSize"/>
      </box>
```

```
        <dialogBoxLauncher>
            <button idMso="FontDialog"/>
        </dialogBoxLauncher>
    </group>
</tab>
```

NOTE **Remember that if you are following along in Access, you need to replace** `"TabHome"` **with** `"TabHomeAccess"` **in the** `insertBeforeMso` **attribute.**

Notice that the `dialogBoxLauncher` is merely a shell that holds one button. The trick to using the `dialogBoxLauncher` is to ensure that the correct built-in `dialog-boxLauncher` button is used.

Once you have validated and saved your XML, reopen the file in Word. On the Demo tab, you'll see that the `dialogBoxLauncher` is now showing in the bottom right-hand corner of the Test group. Clicking the arrow will launch the dialog, as shown in Figure 11-2.

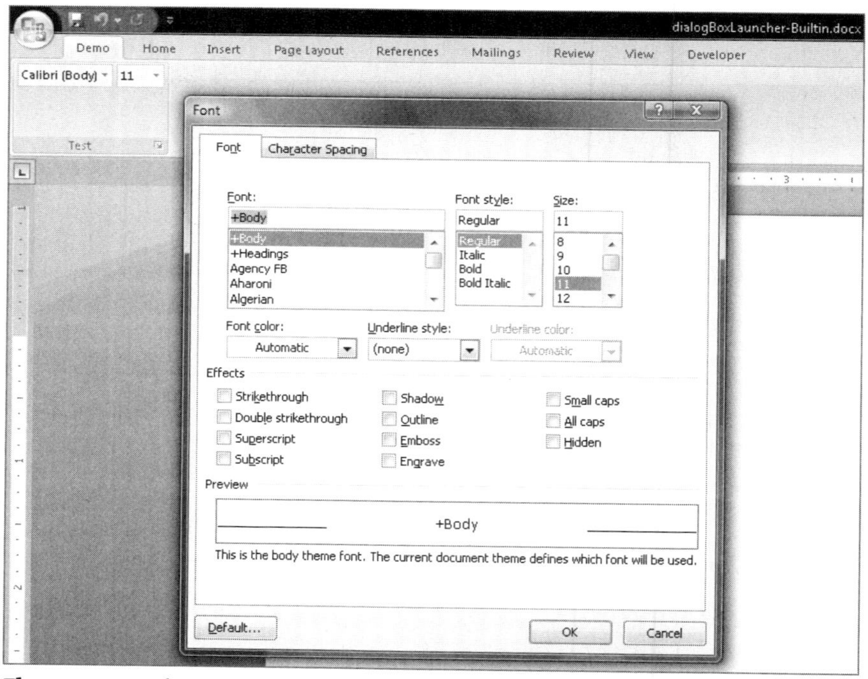

Figure 11-2: The Font dialog launched from a built-in dialogBoxLauncher

A Custom dialogBoxLauncher with Built-in Dialogs

While Microsoft has pre-programmed many `dialogBoxLauncher` buttons, they certainly did not provide one for each of their many application dialogs. Sometimes it is just easier to look up the dialog you are after, and then program the callbacks to launch the dialog yourself. The following example, again focused on the Font group, walks you through the process.

Rather than start from scratch, we'll reuse the file created for the previous example.

NOTE **You can download a completed version of the previous example from the book's website.**

One immediate change that we need to make to our prior file is to save it in a macro-enabled format. Because the changes we're about to make require callbacks, the file has to allow VBA to run. Therefore, open the file in Word, save it as a macro-enabled (`docm`) file, and then close it again. Now open the file in the CustomUI Editor so that you can make the necessary changes to the `dialogBoxLauncher` button.

The only section of the XML that you need to replace is the following line within the `dialogBoxLauncher` tags:

```
<button idMso="FontDialog"/>
```

Change the preceding line to read as follows:

```
<button id="rxbtnDialog"
   onAction="rxbtnDialog_click"
   screentip="Launch Dialog"/>
```

Note here that no image is associated with the button. This may not seem like a big deal, but we point it out so that you don't try to add one. In fact, even if you did supply a button image, it would be overwritten by the `dialogBoxLauncher` image anyway.

As usual, validate the code and generate and copy your callback before you save the file. Reopen Word, launch the VBE, and insert a new standard module to hold the callback signature.

Now comes the tricky part. You want your callback signature to read as follows:

```
'Callback for rxbtnDialog onAction
Sub rxbtnDialog_click(control As IRibbonControl)
    Application.Dialogs(wdDialogFormatAddrFonts).Show
End Sub
```

The hard part in this callback is finding the appropriate constant for the dialog (the `wdDialogFormatAddrFonts` portion). Figuring this part out tends to be a bit of an educated guess at the best of times, so it can quickly become very frustrating to anyone new to the game.

There are two common ways for reviewing lists of constants: using the Object Browser and using IntelliSense. To use the Object Browser, access the Visual Basic Editor and open the Object Browser. Start by searching the Word library for the term "wdDialog." Once you have successfully narrowed the object model to the `wdDialog` constants, as shown in Figure 11-3, it is merely a matter of scanning the right-hand column for a constant that looks promising and then trying it out. If you've seen the dialog in action somewhere in the application, it *will* be in this list, but the challenge is figuring out what it is called.

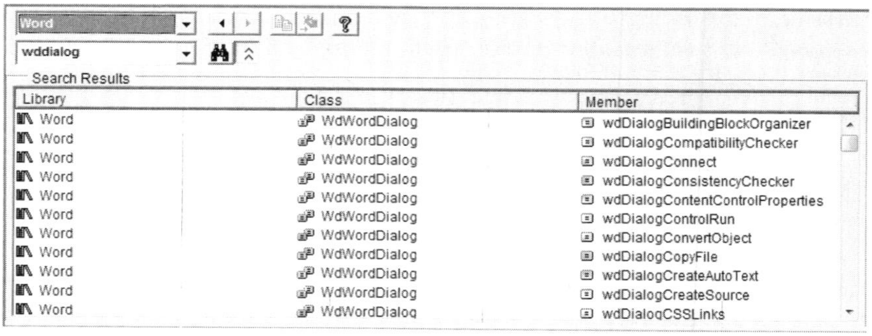

Figure 11-3: The Object Browser searching for dialog constants

CROSS-REFERENCE **For a review of the Object Browser, revisit Chapter 4.**

The other approach is to use IntelliSense. You're probably familiar with that by now, and can anticipate that as you type **"Application.dialogs("** the IntelliSense will kick in when "(" is typed and provide a list of applicable constants. Here, again, you'll be scrolling through the list; but at least as you keep typing, the list continues to zero in on matching the existing text.

Our example again uses `wdDialogFormatAddrFonts`. Now that we have our dialog launcher callback in place, we are ready to exit the VBE and close the file and try it out. Return to the Demo tab in Word and click the dialog launcher icon. The dialog will pop up, front and center, just as it did in the previous example.

Once you're satisfied that the dialog is working the way you want, try going back into the VBE and substituting a different dialog constant. Click the launcher and it will quickly become apparent how versatile this callback tool can be. Even better, note how many dialogs are now available to you!

Custom dialogBoxLauncher with Custom Userforms

No matter how many built-in dialogs Microsoft provides, it is inevitable that you will eventually want to create your own. In this section you will learn to do just that. While it is possible to create complete userform interfaces to set different options, that's a topic beyond the scope of this book. Instead, we will confine our example to a simple implementation of a userform that provides help.

We start with the file we just finished in the previous example. The XML is ready to use, but we need to make some changes to the VBA.

NOTE **A completed version of the previous example (**`dialogBoxLauncher-BuiltinDialog.docm`**) can be downloaded from the book's website.**

If you are not already in the Word document, open it and go to the VBE (Alt+F11). Make sure that both the Project Explorer and Properties windows are showing, because you'll need to use both.

TIP **To show the Project Explorer window, just press Ctrl+R, and F4 for the Properties window. In both cases, the windows will be opened or activated if already open.**

Insert a new userform in your project and add a `label` and a `CommandButton` to it. Add some text to the `label` control, and change the caption on the `CommandButton` to "Close." For now, leave the name of the userform and all the controls at their defaults.

Next, right-click the `CommandButton` and choose View Code. You will be taken to the code module behind the userform, where you will be able to see that the `CommandButton1_click` event has been created for you. Modify the procedure to read as shown here:

```
Private Sub CommandButton1_Click()
    Unload Me
End Sub
```

This line will unload the userform when the `CommandButton` is clicked.

TIP **Confused about the difference between hide and unload when it comes to userforms? Whereas "hide" merely makes the userform invisible, "unload" actually closes the form and unloads it from memory completely.**

Now you need to modify the callback so that it launches your own userform instead of the Microsoft userform used in our previous example. Browse to the standard module where you stored the callback signature and edit the code to read as follows:

```
'Callback for rxbtnDialog onAction
Sub rxbtnDialog_click(control As IRibbonControl)
    UserForm1.Show
End Sub
```

Close the VBE, save the changes, and return to the Word document. By clicking on the `dialogBoxLauncher`, you'll now see your very own userform pop up. Figure 11-4 shows an example of such a userform, and should leave you with no doubts about its versatility.

NOTE **Naturally, your forms will vary depending upon the controls and text that you used. In addition, while many of the colors and formatting can be set when designing the userform, some settings (such as title bar color, font, and size,) are controlled at the system level.**

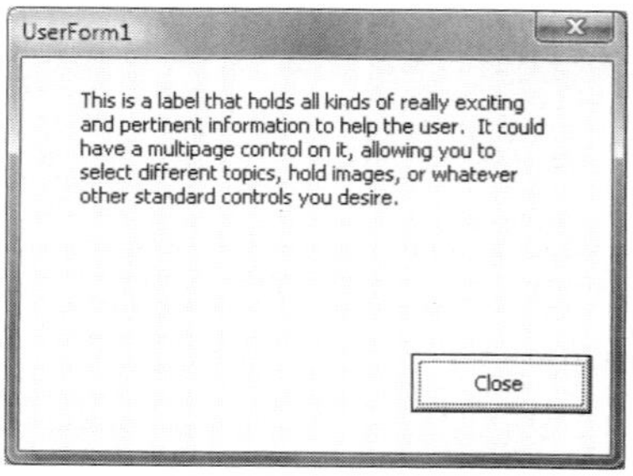

Figure 11-4: A custom userform launched from a dialogBoxLauncher

The keytip Attribute

Contrary to what the name implies, the keytip does not have anything to do with displaying tips or help. Rather, the keytip is the feature that enables users to navigate the Ribbon via the keyboard, in lieu of the mouse. While keytips are not required in a simple UI, they are appreciated by users who do not like to use the mouse, and they also help make the UI more accessible. Thankfully, setting up a keytip for a command is very easy, and only a tiny bit of planning is required to successfully implement some time-saving options.

Pressing the Alt key puts the keyboard into *keytip navigation mode*. This enables users to navigate the tab, group, and control hierarchy without ever having to grab the mouse. Simply press the characters(s) of a command and it will be activated. You definitely want to keep in mind that keytips are context sensitive, so some invoke different actions depending on the program, the application, and even which window or Ribbon tab is active.

While the `keytip` attribute accepts up to three characters, remember that they are used in an attempt to grant a more efficient access path through your UI than using the mouse. It therefore makes sense to try to keep them as short as possible.

Likewise, just because the keytip will accept either textual, numeric, or mixed data, it is not supposed to be cryptic. Rather than make these challenging, every attempt should be made to keep the key selection as logical as possible. The more the keytip departs from the name of the control that it activates, the harder it will be for users to remember, and therefore the less useful it will be.

TIP **Remember that you can display the available keytips just by pressing the Alt key. At that point, typing the key has the same effect as clicking on the control.**

Figure 11-5 displays Excel's Ribbon tabs and Quick Access Toolbar in keytip navigation mode.

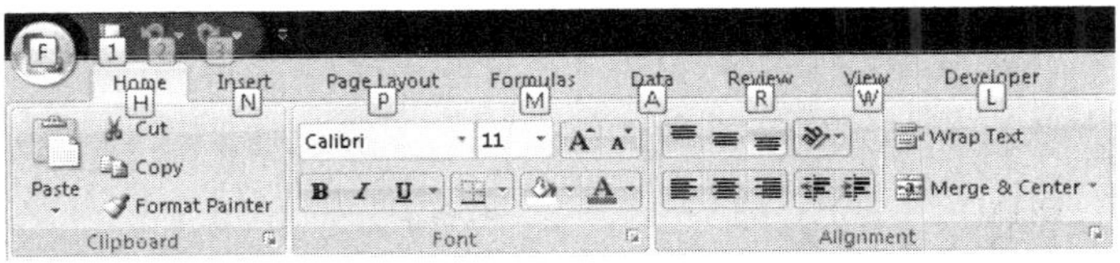

Figure 11-5: The keytip attributes of Excel's tabs and QAT

If you were to press the letter H, which represents the shortcut for the Home tab, you would be presented with the shortcuts for the each of that tab's commands, as shown in Figure 11-6.

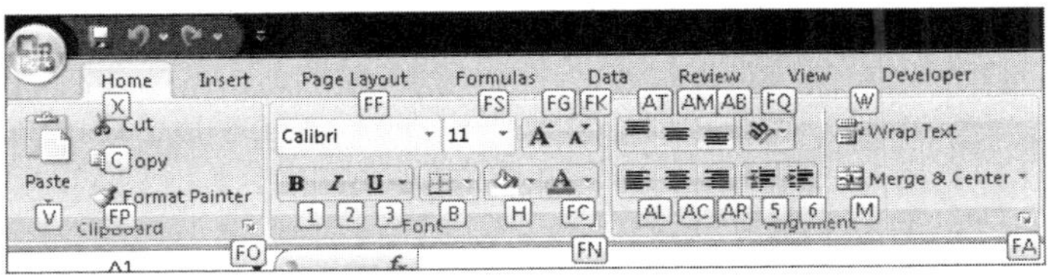

Figure 11-6: keytip attributes for the controls of Excel's Home tab

Fortunately, it's easy to display keytips, because it would be quite a challenge to remember all the common commands, let alone figure out the underlying logic to their designation.

Creating a Keytip

So how do you go about creating your own keytip attributes? As mentioned earlier, it is actually quite easy — you simply add an appropriate `keytip="abc"` tag to the parent element in the XML structure.

To illustrate, create a new file in your favorite application (this can be saved in a macro-free format), and insert the following XML code:

```
<customUI xmlns="http://schemas.microsoft.com/office/2006/01/customui">
   <ribbon startFromScratch="false">
      <tabs>
         <tab id="rxtabDemo"
            label="Demo"
            keytip="cD"
            insertBeforeMso="TabHome">
            <group id="rxgrpDemo"
               label="Demo Group">
               <button id="rxbtnDemo"
               label="Testing"
               keytip="B"
               imageMso="HappyFace"/>
            </group>
         </tab>
```

```
        </tabs>
    </ribbon>
</customUI>
```

As you can see, you are simply creating a new group that contains a happy-face button.

TIP **If you build the example in Access, the** `insertBeforeMso` **attribute needs to be updated from** `TabHome` **to** `TabHomeAccess`**.**

Once the file has been reopened (and after pressing the Alt key), the new UI will look like the one shown in Figure 11-7.

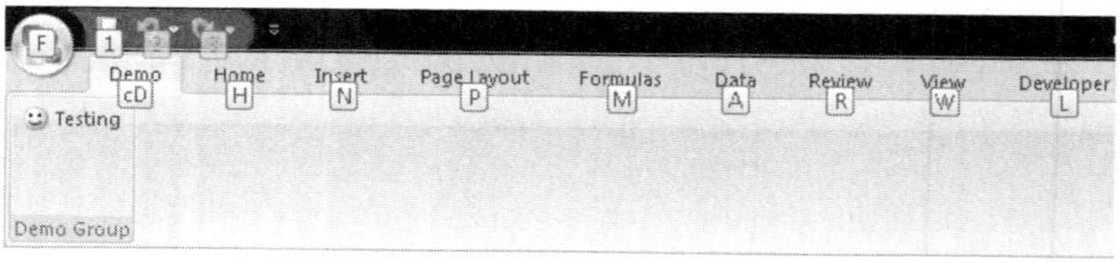

Figure 11-7: A custom keytip in place on the Ribbon

Notice that while the keytip is displayed in whatever format or case that is typed in the code, a keytip is not case sensitive. In the preceding example, pressing the "c" and then "d" keys will take you into the Demo Group, which displays the Testing button with its keytip of "B".

NOTE **You can also populate your keytip attributes dynamically using the** `getKeytip` **callback signatures in lieu of a static keytip.**

Keytip Idiosyncrasies

One thing that may seem odd about Figure 11-7 is the decision to use a keytip that is two characters long. Moreover, it uses a mixture of uppercase and lowercase characters! You may be thinking that it makes more sense to use an uppercase D to be consistent with the rest of the tabs, rather than make the keytip stick out like a sore thumb.

The painful reality is that had you decided to use a "D" for your keytip, pressing the Alt key would have revealed the keytips shown in Figure 11-8. Frustrating as it may be, there is no warning about the impending switch. In addition, the XML code will not be updated for you either, so it will continue to state that the keytip should display a "D".

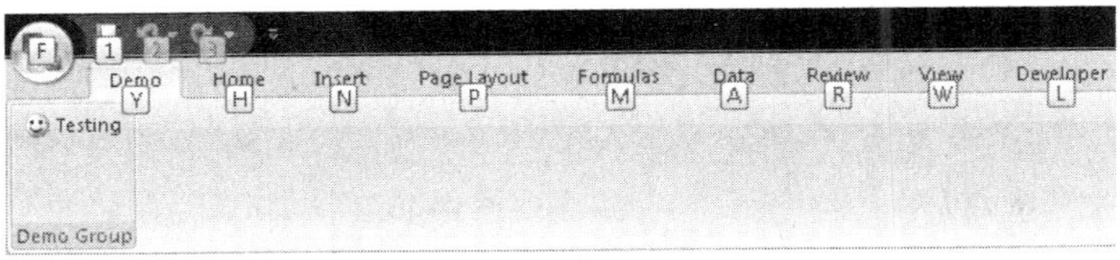

Figure 11-8: The Demo tab with a programmed keytip="D"

What is going on here? Is "D" already used as a keytip? Even if it is, this should not prevent assigning a letter a second time. You can see that "H" is in use by the Home tab. Strangely, if you had assigned "H" to your keytip, the results would look like what is shown in Figure 11-9. Note both an H1 and an H2.

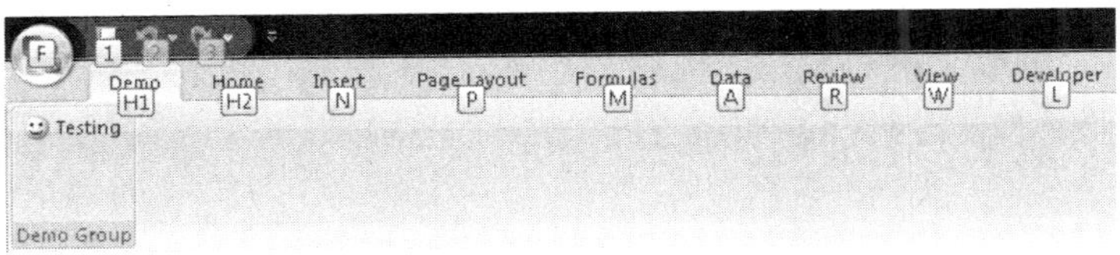

Figure 11-9: The Demo tab with a programmed keytip="H"

Because using "H" modifies both your keytip and the default keytip, you know that there isn't an issue with assigning a keytip that is already in use. However, it certainly alerts you to the issue that the original keytip became H2. This is *not* good, as it is contrary to convention and would shock users who might be rapidly typing a succession of keytips and suddenly find themselves in unfamiliar territory. It also begs the question of whether this is related to positioning and whether the numbers will always ascend from left to right so that additional Hs will become H1 and these two would be bumped up yet another number.

As it turns out, the Alt+D keystroke combination is reserved by Microsoft to place the user in Office 2003 keystroke mode. Microsoft actually recommends beginning all keytips with a "Z" character. Ironically, starting a keytip with an uppercase "Z" will yield an effective keytip of "Y" on the ribbon, but using a lowercase "z" as the first character works just fine.

Before you do anything, however, think about this for a moment. How many developers currently use Z as a flag for objects that are pending deletion? We're all for naming conventions, but "Z" certainly isn't the answer, and "z" is questionable at best. Besides, the keytips should benefit the user, and how many users are going to think, "I'm about to use a custom keytip, so it must begin with "z"?

Unfortunately, despite all your best planning in this regard, you may still have to play around a bit to select a logical keytip, and even then it might not be exactly the one you prefer. Thankfully, it only takes a moment to create, test, view, and even revise a keytip, so you can immediately change the character if it doesn't seem appropriate. One thing in your favor is that with the Ribbon being essentially all icons with very few words, when keytip mode is used, the keytip letters virtually leap out at the user.

screentip and supertip Attributes

The `screentip` and `supertip` attributes enable you to provide helpful text for your controls when a user moves the mouse over them. One of Microsoft's very rich screentip and supertip combinations is shown in Figure 11-10.

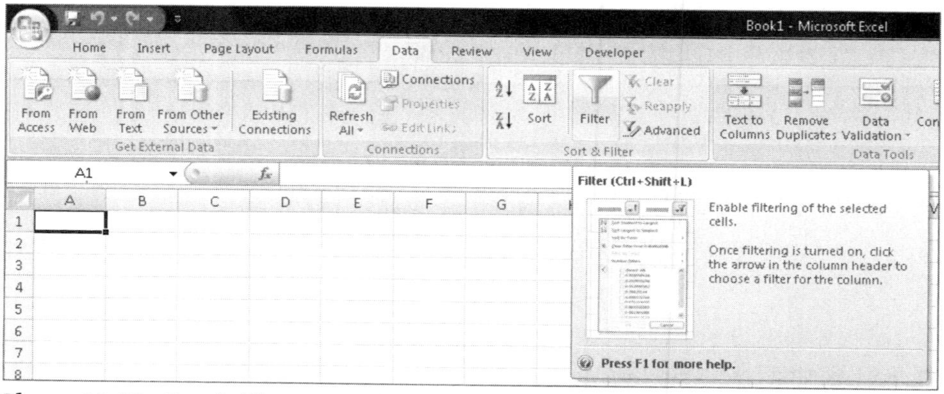

Figure 11-10: Excel's Filter screentip and supertip attributes

NOTE **The screentip portion is the bolded line at the top of the box that gives the keystroke shortcuts, while the supertip is the rest of the information within the drop-down pane.**

Now that we've teased you with a peek at this incredible attribute, we also need to put a cap on your excitement. Microsoft does not let us add our own images to supertips. This is a shame, but it certainly doesn't render these attributes useless. It simply deprives them of some additional luster. It also gives us something to hope for in version 2.0 of the Ribbon.

Focusing once again on the purpose of these attributes, they are intended to share information with the user — specifically, to indicate the purpose of the control. This is the first or second line of help for users, and it should be kept clean and concise. Use the screentip to tell users what the control is, and use the supertip to provide a slightly longer explanation of what the control does.

Creating screentip and supertip Attributes

Like the keytip, it is very easy to add screentip and supertip attributes to a control. For use of static screentip and supertip attributes, you simply code them into the XML. When you want to assign these dynamically, they have the prerequisite callback signatures.

For this example, we will again work with static versions of the attributes. Locate the previous example file that you created, or download the completed version (`CustomKeytip.xlsx`) from the book's website. Replace the XML used to create the button with the following:

```
<button id="rxbtnDemo"
   label="Testing"
   screentip="This is very accurate information!"
   supertip="It tells you nothing... which is exactly what this button↲
does!"
   imageMso="HappyFace"/>
```

After you save the file and reopen it in the application, rolling the mouse over the button will display the tips that were programmed, as shown in Figure 11-11.

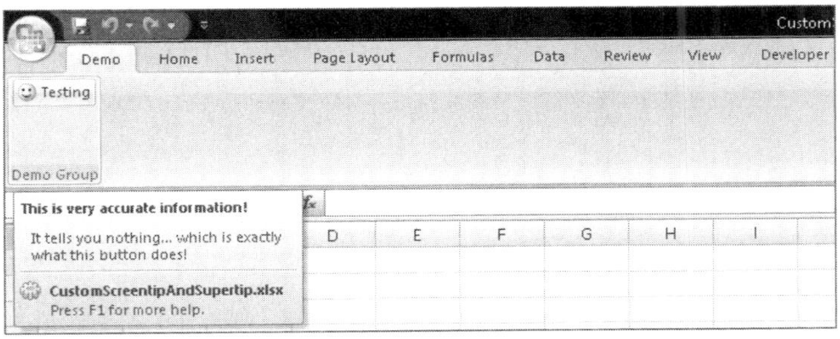

Figure 11-11: Custom screentip and supertip attributes for a button

TIP **When working with text that spans multiple lines in your XML, the tab character can be used to align the XML code without affecting what the user sees. However, entering an extra hard return or space will insert a space in the text displayed for the attribute.**

TIP **If you want to force a line break in your outputted text, you need to add the** `
` **characters to your XML. These five characters force a hard return in the output. Try it for yourself, changing the screentip line in the preceding example to read** `screentip="This is very accurate &#13 information!"`

While it is unfortunate that we can't add images to our supertips, it is even more frustrating that we can't customize or remove the filename, gear icon, or help label that shows at the bottom of the supertip window. Although users may become accustomed to and even ignore these, it definitely counters any attempt to make things completely seamless with the existing application; and to add insult to injury, so to speak, pressing F1 for help, as advised by the supertip, offers no assistance whatsoever.

Overwriting Built-in Control Attributes

Suppose you are creating your application's entire Ribbon interface from scratch. Chances are very good that you will want to use some of Microsoft's built-in controls, but most likely some of them won't be labeled quite right for your purposes. Rather than confuse the user, it would be better to rename them, but it doesn't seem worth having to create the control from scratch. Thankfully, you can change some attributes, and that is precisely what we cover in this final section.

For this example, we use a Microsoft Access database and change the Home tab to contain a label stating Start Here. In addition, it only seems logical that the keytip to go with it should be "S," not "H," as shown in Figure 11-12.

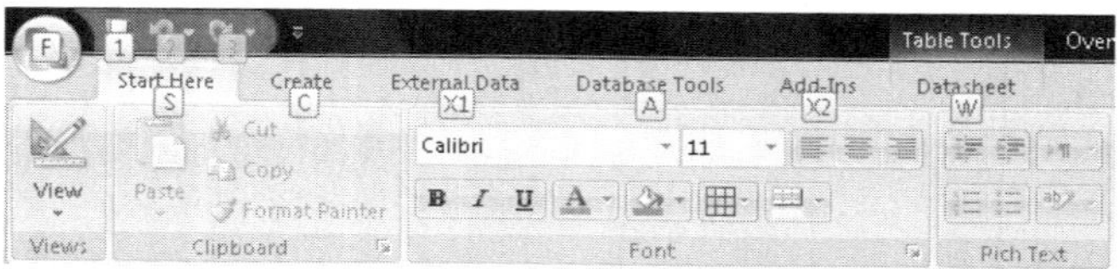

Figure 11-12: Overwriting a tab's label and keytip attributes

To accomplish the customization shown in Figure 11-12, you merely need to refer to the `idMso` of the control that needs to changed, as shown in the following XML:

```
<customUI xmlns="http://schemas.microsoft.com/office/2006/01/customui">
   <ribbon startFromScratch="false">
       <tabs>
           <tab idMso="TabHomeAccess"
               label="Start Here"
               keytip="S">
           </tab>
       </tabs>
   </ribbon>
</customUI>
```

To try this out, create a new database and copy the preceding code into the field on the USysRibbons table responsible for holding your XML. Of course, you could also use this same code in Excel or Word if you changed TabHomeAccess to TabHome.

CROSS-REFERENCE **For a refresher on how to do this in Access, review the "Microsoft Access Customizations" section in Chapter 2.**

This technique can also be used to change a great many other attributes of built-in controls; probably the most common use is to rename buttons or hide their labels.

One frustrating exception to this technique, however, is that we are not permitted to modify any of the properties of built-in groups. It isn't clear why Microsoft chose to exclude groups, as it would have been made things so much easier. For example, it would be nice (and a lot less work) to simply set a group's `visible` property to `false`, rather than have to create a custom tab to contain the existing groups that you do want to use.

Conclusion

In this chapter, you learned how to use several tools to create a more helpful and intuitive user interface. You learned not only how the `dialogBoxLauncher` control can be used to display built-in dialogs full of options, but also how to create a custom version to display help that is specific to the controls on your group.

We also covered the `keytip`, `screentip`, and `supertip` attributes, and showed how each one can be customized and incorporated into an application. By employing these easy-to-create attributes, you can put information and guidance literally at a user's fingertips. In doing so, you not only help them navigate more efficiently, but also expose them to more features so they can use the programs more effectively.

Finally, you learned how to replace some of the attributes of built-in Microsoft controls, which enables you to rename certain aspects in the UI without having to re-create everything from scratch.

This is the final chapter for covering the basics. By now, you understand the fundamentals for creating customizations. At this point, you're ready to move into more advanced VBA techniques that can really make your work shine.

Part

II

Advanced Concepts in Ribbon Customization

In This Part

CHAPTER

12

Advanced VBA Techniques

Now that you've learned about the basic building blocks for Ribbon customizations, it's time to delve into some more advanced VBA techniques. We're calling these advanced because they require specialized knowledge of VBA, not necessarily because they are difficult to implement.

In this chapter you learn how to implement custom properties, methods, and events through classes. You also learn how to add custom properties to built-in objects such as `ThisWorkbook`, `Sheet`, `ThisDocument`, `Form`, and so on. These techniques help you to streamline your code and make it more manageable when implementing the UI across your entire project.

As you are preparing to work through the examples, we encourage you to download the companion files. The source code and files for this chapter can be found on the book's website at `www.wiley.com/go/ribbonx`.

Working with Collections

A `Collection` object is a set containing various elements. Because it is a set, it can be referred to as a single unit. A `Collection` object is very handy when it comes to collecting information about related elements — although they do not necessarily need to be related or even have the same data type.

When working with classes, for example, a `Collection` object can work as a container for elements that you need to add to your custom object.

CROSS-REFERENCE For a refresher on classes, you might want to review "Document-Level Events" in Chapter 4.

A `Collection` object can be created as follows:

```
Dim myCollection As New Collection
```

A custom collection is made up of four methods, as shown in Table 12-1.

Table 12-1: Methods Present in a Custom Collection

METHOD	DESCRIPTION
Add	Adds an item to the collection. You can define the item, its key, and its position.
Count	Counts how many items are in the collection
Item	Returns a specific item within the entire collection. You can use the index or the key to return the corresponding item.
Remove	Removes an item from the collection. Use the index or key to refer to which item is to be removed.

When working with built-in `Collection` objects, you will recognize them because they are written in the plural form. Notice in the following example that we `dim` (dimension) each database as a `DAO.database`, and later in the code we use the databases in the line `For Each db In wrkSpace.Databases`.

```
Sub dbCollection()

    Dim wrkSpace    As DAO.Workspace
    Dim db1         As DAO.database
    Dim db2         As DAO.database
    Dim db          As DAO.database
    Dim strBD       As String
    Dim tbl         As DAO.TableDef
    Dim fld         As DAO.Field

    On Error Resume Next
    Set wrkSpace = CreateWorkspace("Sample_WrkSpace", _
      "admin", "", dbUseJet)

'   Set the first database in the workspace
    strBD = CurrentProject.Path & "\Northwind.mdb"
    Set db1 = wrkSpace.OpenDatabase(strBD)

'   Set the second database in the workspace
    strBD = CurrentProject.Path & "\Northwind - Copy.mdb"
    Set db2 = wrkSpace.OpenDatabase(strBD)
```

```
    Debug.Print " Workspace Name: " & wrkSpace.Name
    For Each db In wrkSpace.Databases
        With db
            Debug.Print db.Name
            For Each tbl In db.TableDefs
                Debug.Print tbl.Name
                For Each fld In tbl.Fields
                    Debug.Print "    " & fld.Name
                Next fld
        Next tbl
        End With
    Next db

   db1.Close
   db2.Close
   wrkSpace.Close

End Sub
```

The preceding example opens two databases under the `Sample_WrkSpace` workspace. These databases, in turn, make up the databases collection of the workspace. We can then run through each database in the workspace to work with each one individually.

You use the same logic to work with the `workbooks` and `documents` collections in Excel and Word:

```
Sub wbCollection()
    Dim wb           As Workbook

    For Each wb In Application.Workbooks
        Debug.Print wb.Name
    Next wb

End Sub


Sub docCollection()
    Dim wrdDoc           As Document

    For Each wrdDoc In Application.Documents
        Debug.Print wrdDoc.Name
    Next wrdDoc

End Sub
```

In the same way, you use the `Add` method in custom collections to add elements to the collection; you can also use this method to add elements to built-in collections, as shown in the following code snippet:

```
Set wrdDoc = Application.Documents.Add
```

Note that with Access we use the `OpenDatabase` method. Excel and Word also provide an `Open` method that adds a workbook/document to the `Workbooks/Documents` collection. The difference is that the first method adds a new workbook/document (that is, either blank or based on a template), and the second method opens an existing workbook/document.

Referring to an item within the collection follows the same pattern (the number in parentheses refers to the database item):

```
wrkSpace.Databases(1).TableDefs.Count
```

The preceding example accesses the database collection and then, looking at the database with the index count of 1, counts the number of table objects — returning that value. A similar approach can be used to obtain the number of sheets in an Excel workbook. You can also use this approach to obtain other information about the files within a collection. For example, the following line of code would return the name of the second Word document in the `Documents` collection:

```
Application.Documents.Item(1).Name
```

As you can see from the previous two examples, once you get the hang of working with collections, many of the techniques used in one application can be immediately transferred to another application within the Office suite.

TIP **It is important to remember that the index count starts with 0, which is why the (1) returns the value associated with the second item in a collection.**

In some cases, you will come across items in a built-in collection that have pre-defined values for the indexes — for example, the `Borders` collection:

```
With ActiveCell.Borders.Item(xlEdgeRight)
    .LineStyle = xlDouble
    .ColorIndex = 5
End With
```

For the `Borders` collection, we have a pre-defined value for each item that belongs to the collection. The preceding example uses the index number of the pre-defined value of the color to specify that the item (`xlEdgeRight`) is blue. If you are accustomed to setting format properties of text and lines, you're probably familiar with some of the numbers associated with the color pallet.

TIP `xl[something]`, `wd[Something]`, **and so on, are global constants that mask the underlying index number. If you type** `?xlEdgeRight` **in the Immediate window, you will get the index number. In this example, you would get 10 as the value for** `xlEdgeRight`**.**

Determining Whether an Item Belongs to a Collection

One of the things that immediately comes to mind when dealing with collections relates to how you retrieve an item from the collection. By using the `Item` method, you can refer to a specific element by passing the index number as the argument; you can also refer to an item's key, to the pre-defined index of an item, or to the name of the object in the collection. The trouble starts when you have several elements and you do not know whether the element that you are looking for is actually in the collection.

You could, of course, loop through all the elements until you locate what you are looking for, or you could simply pass the index value and pray that it is there. The problem with this approach is that if it's not there, it will return an error. The good news about the error is that it indicates that an element is not present; hence, you can use this error to determine the absence or presence of an element in a collection. The following example should help clarify what we mean:

```
Function ItemExists(ByVal strItemKey As String, _
    ByVal objColName As Object) As Boolean
    Dim objGeneric      As Object

    On Error Resume Next
    ItemExists = False
    Set objGeneric = objColName(strItemKey)
    If Err = 0 Then ItemExists = True
End Function
```

This generic function can be used to determine whether an item exists within a collection. For example, you could determine whether a specific Word document (`Document3`, for example) is currently open by using the following code snippet:

```
?ItemExists("Document3",Application.Windows)
```

Simply type the request in the Immediate window of whatever application you are currently working in. Because it is a generic function, it will also work in Excel and Access just by tweaking the syntax, as illustrated by the following examples:

```
?ItemExists("WBName",gWBCollection)
```

The preceding code applies to a custom collection that collects workbook objects. You test for a specific workbook presence by passing the item's `Key` value (filename). This example searched for the Excel file named `"WBName"`. In Access, you could check for the presence of a specific table using the following line of code:

```
?ItemExists("MSysQueries",Application.DBEngine.Workspaces(0)↵
.Databases(0).TableDefs)
```

Note that this example checked for the presence of a system table, `MSysQueries`. This method enables you to accurately determine whether a system or hidden table exists without the need to expose it. In this example, we use the default Workspace (which has the index value of zero) and the default Database (which also has the index value of zero) to specify the current project.

Class Modules

We touched on classes in Chapter 4, where you learned a few things that can be done with them, such as writing application-level events, as well as control-specific events. We now introduce you to some other concepts that will be relevant as you start creating more complex code.

Class modules are normally underutilized because a lot of people tend to pack everything into standard modules. Although there is nothing wrong with using standard modules, certain things cannot be achieved relying solely on standard modules.

A class module (class) basically enables you to create new objects that have their own methods and properties in the same way that application objects, such as `Workbook`, `Document`, and `Database`, have their own set of properties and methods. In this way, class modules serve as the perfect type to encapsulate complex code and expose only the methods and properties associated with the object you create. Once the methods and properties are exposed, you simply call on them and the class does the rest.

Implementation becomes very simple, as developers do not need to understand anything that goes on inside the class module. All they need to do is call it. Consider how many times you used the `Add` method to add a new workbook or Word document. You rely on it to perform as intended, but you don't know how the code for the methods works behind the scenes. That's how you should be able to rely on your class modules.

Properties, Methods, and Events

As you write code for your classes, you will be interested in some specialized segments of it. When you create an object, this object can have properties, methods, and events. For example, suppose the object is a tree. This object will have properties (such as `Height`, `Width`, etc.), methods (such as `Grow`, etc.), and events that will occur (such as `Die`).

- **Properties:** These refer to certain characteristics such as `Name`, `Creator`, `Height`, and `Width`. The properties can be read-only, write-only or they can be write/read. When naming properties, you should use nouns to refer to them — for example, `MyComputer.Name` where `MyComputer` is the object and `Name` is its property.
- **Methods:** Methods refer to actions that can happen during the life of the object. For example, your tree object could grow throughout its life until it dies. When naming methods, choose a verb or a verb phrase to refer to them — for example, `MyComputer.GetIP`.
- **Events:** Events refer to what happens to your object. When your tree dies (in class parlance, when the object "terminates"), an event occurs. Metaphorically speaking, if you are environmentally conscious and your tree dies, you can hook the event, put it in your diary, and attend the memorial services.

As you have seen, you can have methods that use the same verb as an event. For example, we have an `Open` event as well as an `Open` method. How do you know which is which? The method is an instruction; you instruct the application to `Open` a document, a workbook, or a database. The event is what actually has happened in the process.

The following illustration should help to distinguish between methods and events. Consider `MyComputer.GetIP` (a method for retrieving the IP of my computer) and `MyComputer_OnGetIP` (an event that is triggered when the IP addressed is retrieved). Typically, you would not add the `On` prefix to an event, but thinking about it in this way makes it a little easier to understand and differentiate between the nomenclature for methods and events.

Working with Properties

Properties are an important aspect of an object. Take an Excel workbook, for example. You can retrieve its path by using the `Path` property or you can change the name of a worksheet by changing the `Name` property of the `Worksheet` object. By the same logic, you can read the connection string of your Access project by accessing the `Connection` property of the `CurrentProject` object. You might find it particularly helpful to use this to confirm the location of the data files when moving or replacing applications, and even when you are providing a new Ribbon customization.

Setting the properties is the first step in creating a class module.

Property Let

The first thing you need to do is declare a global variable to hold the property value. Assume your object will take a `Name` property — in the general declaration of your class module, you will have the following:

```
Dim gstrName          as String
```

The next step is to write the code for the property:

```
Property Let name(ByVal strName As String)
    gstrName = strName
End Property
```

You can now change this property in the same manner you change the `name` property of other objects:

```
Sub clsProperty()
    Dim MyComputer       As New clsProperty
    MyComputer.Name = "My Computer Name"
    Set MyComputer = Nothing
End Sub
```

This procedure is placed in a standard module, and you declare your object variable as being a new instance of your class. (In this case, `clsProperty` is the name of the class module.)

Note that the only property you have is defined by the keyword `Let`, so at this point this is a write-only class. You can change its value by writing a new value to it, but you cannot read its property value.

Property Get

You know now how to write to a property. This is great, but you certainly need to know how to retrieve its value as well. This is done by writing another property using the `Get` keyword:

```
Property Get Name() As String
   Name = gstrName
End Property
```

You can test this in a standard module as follows:

```
Sub clsProperty()
     Dim MyComputer       As New clsProperty
     MyComputer.Name = "My Computer Name"
     MsgBox MyComputer.Name
     Set MyComputer = Nothing
End Sub
```

The preceding code simply uses both the `write` and `read` properties to change the property value — that is, the `Name` property. Remember that `Let` allows you to write to the property (think of this as it "lets" you specify a value for the property), whereas `Get` allows you to retrieve its value. In the first example, we used the `Let` keyword to give the computer the name of *"My Computer Name."* Then, in the second example, we used the `Get` keyword to retrieve the name of the computer, and it returned *"My Computer Name."* At the end of each routine, we used the `Set` keyword to set the value of the variable to `Nothing`. This is important because it removes the value from temporary memory and helps to prevent memory leaks.

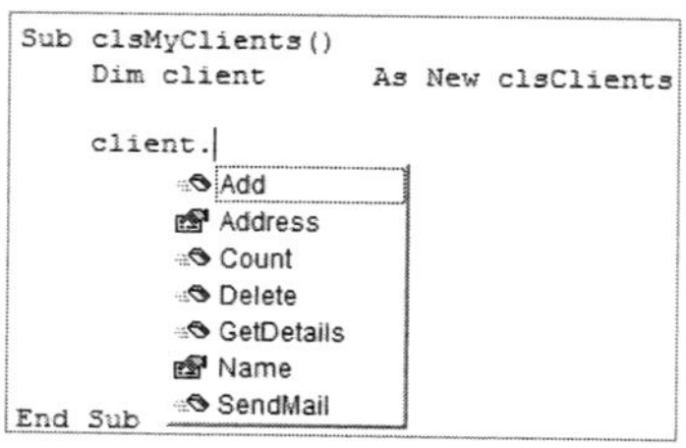

Figure 12-1: Exposing properties and methods

Working with Methods

Methods refer to such actions as `Add`, `Update`, `MoveNext`, `Clear`, `Delete`, and so on. Working with methods in classes can save you a lot of hassle in terms of implementing complex code. Suppose you have code for sending e-mails that bypass the security warning of Outlook. In this case, your class can expose a `SendMail` method that requires only the recipient as the argument of the method. The person who implements the code only needs to instantiate the class object and call upon the method. There is no need to understand what goes on behind the scenes.

Figure 12-1 shows a scenario in which a `client` object is declared as a new instance of the `clsClients` class. You can now add a new client, count the number of clients, define the name, or send an e-mail to a client, and so on.

Methods are simply subprocedures or functions written in a class module. If you need a value to be returned, then you need to use a function. Otherwise, you would use a subprocedure to perform a certain action.

Now let's create some of the methods displayed in the previous image. Here, you will use a `Collection` object to store information about the client. The first thing you need to do is declare a global variable representing this collection of clients:

```
Dim gcolClients     As New Collection
```

Now you are ready to write the methods. In this example, you create `Add`, `Count`, `Delete`, and `GetDetails` methods. The VBA code for these methods is as follows:

```
Sub Add(ByVal strName As String)
    Dim lngIDClient     As Long
    On Error Resume Next
    lngIDClient = gcolClients.Count + 1
    gcolClients.Add strName, CStr(lngIDClient)
End Sub

Function Count() As Long
    Count = gcolClients.Count
End Function

Sub Delete(ByVal strIDClient As String)
    On Error Resume Next
    If gcolClients.Count = 0 Then Exit Sub
    gcolClients.Remove (strIDClient)
    repopulate
End Sub

Function GetDetails(ByVal strIDClient As String) As Variant
    On Error Resume Next
    If gcolClients.Count = 0 Then
        GetDetails = vbNullString
        Exit Function
    End If
    GetDetails = gcolClients.Item(strIDClient)
End Function
```

It is always good to test as you go. Therefore, in a standard module, you can run a simple test to check how things respond:

NOTE **To test, ensure that you insert the name property; otherwise, you'll get an error.**

```
Sub clsMyClients()
    Dim client      As New clsClients

    With client
        .Add ("Ken Puls")
        .Add ("Robert Martin")
        .Add ("Teresa Hennig")
        .Name = .GetDetails(2)
        MsgBox .Name
        .Delete (2)
        .Name = .GetDetails(2)
        MsgBox .Name
        MsgBox .Count
    End With
    Set client = Nothing
End Sub
```

In the preceding case, we add three clients. We then get the details for the second client, whose index is two (2) and display the details through a message box. Next, we delete this client and again request the client with index two (2) to check what happened to the order and count. We show the client name and then count how many customers are left in the collection. Sound complicated? Actually, it is not. Run the code using F8 to step through each line and you will see how simple it is; and by seeing the results after each line, you'll have a much better understanding of what the code actually does.

NOTE Indexes normally start at zero, which might leave you wondering why the index in the preceding example matches the number and position of the items in the collection. The key is in the `Add` method that we created. We specified that the next index (client ID) is the count of items in the collection plus one, so if the collection starts with zero items, then the first item will have an index equal to one and the index will match the count. As demonstrated in our example, this technique can be very helpful.

Working with Events

An event simply refers to something that happens when you perform an action such as opening a document, opening a form, and so on. Events can be specific to an object or they can have wider implications, as application-level events do. For example, the class you developed in the previous section has two basic events attached to it. One is triggered when the class is initialized and the other when the class is terminated:

```
Private Sub Class_Initialize()
'   Your code goes here
End Sub
```

```
Private Sub Class_Terminate()
'   Your code goes here
End Sub
```

You can use these two events to control your own class, but you can also add events to the class to control the application or other objects.

CROSS-REFERENCE **See Chapter 4 for an overview of application-level events.**

Web Services and CustomUI

You're probably familiar with Web services, and maybe have even used some. They are services provided via Internet portals, such as Amazon, stock brokerages, and geographic locator services. In most cases, Web services enable you to link to a datasource and incorporate the data in your applications. Microsoft Office provides a toolkit that can be used to harness the power of Web services to your advantage. For example, you can use Web services in your UI to provide useful working tools to your clients or users.

We're about to show you how to utilize this power and leverage it in a neat UI implementation.

NOTE **You must download and install the toolkit from** `www.microsoft.com/downloads/details.aspx?FamilyId=4922060F-002A-4F5B-AF74-978F2CD6C798&displaylang=en` **before you can continue. Close all running applications before installing the toolkit, and check the system requirements outlined in the URL.**

Once the toolkit is installed, a new command will be available on the Tools menu of the VB Editor, as shown in Figure 12-2.

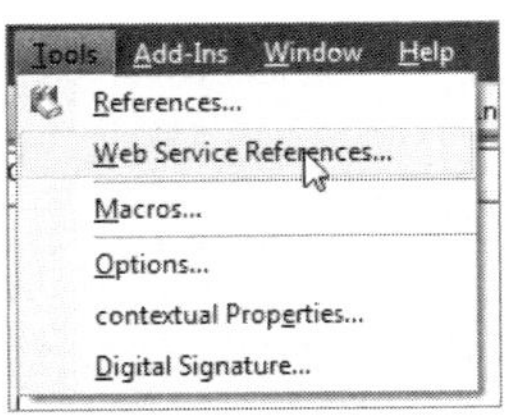

Figure 12-2: Web services tools for Office

All you have to do now is click this command to open the Web Service Reference form. Using the form, you can either search for a Web service using keywords or you can type in a URL. Our example uses the following Web service for currency conversion: `www.webservicex.net/CurrencyConvertor.asmx?WSDL`. Type this URL into the

URL box and click Search. Once the search is finished, the results will be displayed in the Search Results section of the form, as shown in Figure 12-3.

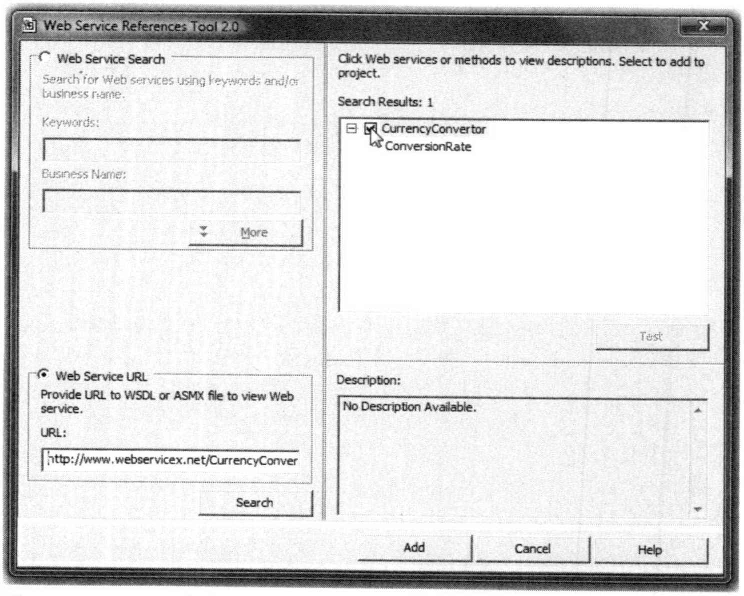

Figure 12-3: Web Service References form

Click Add to continue and a new class module will be inserted for you. Note that all the class code is added, including initialization and termination events. In addition, as pointed out earlier, you do not need to know anything about how the Web service code is written. All you have to do is to implement the class. We will not repeat the class code here, but it is available in the `Web Service.accdb` download file for this chapter.

Once the class has been created, add a standard module and insert the following code:

```
Public gclsCurConverter As clsWebservices

Function getRates(ByVal countryOrigin As String, _
    ByVal countryDestination As String) As Double

    If countryOrigin = "" Or countryDestination = "" _
        Then Exit Function

    If gclsCurConverter Is Nothing Then _
        Set gclsCurConverter = New clsWebservices

    countryOrigin = ExtractCurCode(countryOrigin)
    countryDestination = ExtractCurCode(countryDestination)

    On Error Resume Next
```

```
    getRates = gclsCurConverter.wsm_ConversionRate(countryOrigin, _
        countryDestination)
End Function

Function ExtractCurCode(ByVal strCurrency As String) As String
    ExtractCurCode = Replace(Right(strCurrency, 4), ")", "")
End Function
```

Here, we have two functions. The first function does most of the work and returns the exchange rate by passing the arguments to the Web service function declared in the class module. The second function simply extracts the currency code from the currency string. For example, the string passed could be "Canadian Dollar (CAD)" but we are only interested in the currency code, i.e., the CAD part, because this is what is used by the Web service.

The next step is to create the UI. Two `comboBox` controls will hold the country names and currency codes for the first and second currency, as shown in Figure 12-4. We will also add a `labelControl` in order to show the conversion result.

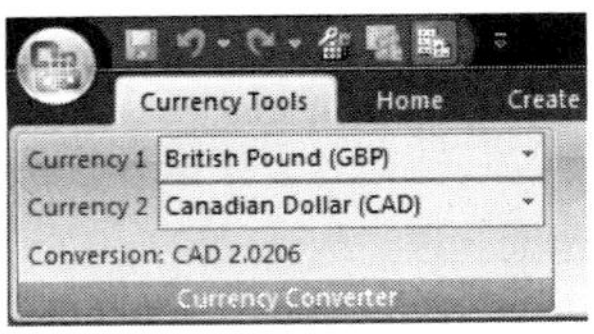

Figure 12-4: Currency conversion UI based on Web services

Up to this point, the same code works for Excel, Word, and Access. The remainder of the example applies only to Access, but the code can easily be adapted for Word and Excel.

NOTE **You must reference the Microsoft SOAP Type Library in your project in order to be able to access the Web services.**

The code that goes into the class module is written for you by the toolkit. You already have the implementation function. Now you need to write the XML code and VBA code to add functionality to it. The XML code for this example is as follows:

```
<comboBox id="rxcboCurrencyOrigin"
   label="Currency 1"
   sizeString="mmmmmmmmmmmm"
   screentip="Click here to select the currency of origin..."
   getItemCount="rxshared_getItemCount"
   getItemLabel="rxshared_getItemLabel"
   onChange="rxshared_onChange"/>
```

```
<comboBox id="rxcboCurrencyDestination"
   label="Currency 2"
   sizeString="mmmmmmmmmmmm"
   screentip="Click here to select the currency of destination..."
   getItemCount="rxshared_getItemCount"
   getItemLabel="rxshared_getItemLabel"
   onChange="rxshared_onChange"/>

<labelControl id="rxlblResult"
   getLabel="rxlblResult_getLabel"/>
```

The preceding code adds the two `comboBoxes` and the `label` control to your CustomUI. Once you have generated the callbacks, you can copy and paste them into a standard module in Access.

We used the following function to implement the class:

```
Public gclsCurConverter        As clsWebservices

Function getRates(ByVal countryOrigin As String, _
    ByVal countryDestination As String) As Double

    If countryOrigin = "" Or countryDestination = "" _
        Then Exit Function

    If gclsCurConverter Is Nothing Then _
        Set gclsCurConverter = New clsWebservices

    On Error Resume Next
    getRates = gclsCurConverter.wsm_getRate(countryOrigin, _
        countryDestination)
End Function
```

`clsWebservices` is the name we've given to the class. When this class is automatically generated, it will have a different name. You can either use the suggested name or change it to whatever name you like. We strongly recommend changing the name and following standard naming conventions.

Inside the function, we check whether the names of the countries have already been passed or not. If not, the class does not get involved in anything, as this would create an unnecessary performance hit. We also leave the class initialized during the life of the session, so that it is not initialized and terminated each time the Web service is called upon.

NOTE **Because you're dealing with an Internet connection and service, there may be a slight delay when returning the value from the Web service. Of course, you must also have an active Internet connection.**

Finally, it is time to write the code for your UI. Start by declaring the following variable in the general declarations area of your standard module:

```
Public grxIRibbonUI              As IRibbonUI
```

```
Public gaCountries            As Variant
Public glngItemCount          As Long
Public glngCount              As Long
Public gstrCountry1           As String
Public gstrCountry2           As String
```

Next, enter the following procedures. It's a lot to type, so you might want to save time and avoid errors by copying the text from the chapter download. Although by now you could probably interpret these on your own, we'll provide a brief explanation of what each procedure is intended to do.

```
Sub rxIRibbonUI_onLoad(ribbon As IRibbonUI)
    Dim rst          As DAO.Recordset
    Dim db           As DAO.Database
    Dim strSQL       As String

    On Error GoTo ErrHandler
      strSQL = "SELECT * FROM tblCountries ORDER BY " _
        & "tblCountries.CountryName;"

    Set db = CurrentDb()
    Set rst = db.OpenRecordset(strSQL, dbOpenSnapshot)

    glngItemCount = rst.RecordCount

    ReDim gaCountries(glngItemCount - 1)

    glngCount = 0
    With rst
        If .EOF Then .MoveFirst
        Do While Not (.EOF)
          gaCountries(glngCount) = !CountryName.Value & " (" _
                & !CountryCurCode.Value & ")"
            .MoveNext
            glngCount = glngCount + 1
        Loop
    End With

    Set grxIRibbonUI = ribbon
    rst.Close
    db.Close
    Set rst = Nothing
    Set db = Nothing
    glngCount = 0
    Exit Sub

ErrHandler:
    MsgBox Err.Description, vbCritical, Err.Number
End Sub
```

```
Sub rxshared_getItemCount(control As IRibbonControl, ByRef returnedVal)
    returnedVal = glngItemCount
End Sub

Sub rxshared_getItemLabel(control As IRibbonControl, index As Integer, _
    ByRef returnedVal)

    On Error GoTo ErrHandler
    returnedVal = gaCountries(index)
    Exit Sub

ErrHandler:
    MsgBox Err.Description, vbCritical, Err.Number
End Sub

Sub rxlblResult_getLabel(control As IRibbonControl, ByRef returnedVal)
    returnedVal = "Conversion: $" & Round(getRates(gstrCountry1, _
        gstrCountry2), 4)
End Sub

Sub rxshared_onChange(control As IRibbonControl, text As String)
    Select Case control.id
        Case "rxcboCurrencyOrigin"
            gstrCountry1 = text
        Case "rxcboCurrencyDestination"
            gstrCountry2 = text
    End Select
    grxIRibbonUI.InvalidateControl ("rxlblResult")
End Sub
```

Now that you've added the procedures to your module, let's review what they do.:

- **rxIRibbonUI_onLoad:** This procedure loads, as usual, your `IRibbonUI` object. You also use this same event to read through a list of countries in `tblCountries` and load them into a global array. It also gets the number of countries to be added to the `comboBoxes`.
- **rxshared_getItemCount:** Because we have two `comboBoxes` and they both use the same list of countries, you pass the same total count as the attribute value for both controls. If it happened to be a different count, you could handle each control (case) separately by referring to the control id case. We've covered that in previous examples, so you could just grab some code from one of those and tweak it to fit your needs.
- **rxshared_getItemLabel:** Each item requires a label and each label is retrieved from the global array (populated when the UI was loaded) using the label index.
- **rxlblResult_getLabel:** This `labelControl` receives the result of the currency conversion after calling on the function that uses the Web service class.
- **rxshared_onChange:** This passes the country name to the global string variable so that it can be used to retrieve the quotes for conversion.

Web services are a great way to add tremendous functionality to your projects. They enable you to leverage the work of others without having to write a lot of your own code, and they enable you to consume information that is normally very expensive to generate. Be aware, though, that most Web services have subscription fees. We've only touched the tip of an iceberg here, and it is hoped that you are enticed to explore more.

Using VBA Custom Properties

In addition to creating custom properties using classes, you can also create custom properties for many objects (such as Workbooks, Sheets, Documents, and Forms). In addition, after the custom properties are defined for an object, the properties are exposed as a member of the object, as shown in the following example:

```
ThisWorkbook.MyRibbon
```

As you can see from the preceding line, this makes it very easy to refer to the UI objects directly from a parent object (in this case, the `ThisWorkbook` object), which can save a lot of hassle when you are referring back to the `Ribbon` object. Considering that users frequently have multiple programs open at the same time, and each program could easily have an object named `MyRibbon`, it is critical that the code can clearly specify the exact object to which it is referring.

Setting Up the Custom Properties

Setting up a custom property for a built-in object is the same as creating a custom property using a standard class module, as you've already learned. The only difference is that the property must reside within its container object so that the property can be exposed as a member of that specific object.

You can use custom properties to simulate contextual tabs to easily access visibility properties, to determine label values, and more. In the example that follows, we develop custom properties to control visibility. Basically, the example creates the following:

- A custom property to show/hide a tab associated with a worksheet
- Two checkboxes that control the visibility of two built-in groups (Font and Table)

The key attribute in this example is the `getVisible` attribute. We will turn it into a custom property so that we can change its value through the property, rather than directly in the subprocedure. Notice that the groups we will hide/show through these custom properties are located under different tabs. The Font group is under the same tab as the customization, but the Table group is under the Insert tab. We included this configuration to demonstrate the behavior when you can see it happen, as well as when the change occurs in a group that is not currently visible. In the second scenario, you won't have proof that everything worked as expected until you activate the tab on which the group is located.

We demonstrate this technique using Excel. Start with the following XML (just seeing how many lines you'd be writing will give you a new appreciation for being able to download the code from the book's website):

```
<customUI xmlns="http://schemas.microsoft.com/office/2006/01/customui"
   onLoad="rxIRibbonUI_onLoad">
   <ribbon startFromScratch="false">
      <tabs>
         <tab id="rxtabSheet"
            label="Sheet Tab"
            insertBeforeMso="TabHome"
            getVisible="rxtabSheet_getVisible">

            <group id="rxgrp1"
               label="My Custom Group">
            </group>
         </tab>

         <tab idMso="TabHome"
            label="Modified Home">
            <group id="rxgrp2"
               insertBeforeMso="GroupClipboard"
               label="My CheckBox">

               <!— Add a checkBox —>
               <checkbox id="rxchkHideFontGroup"
                  getLabel="rxchkHideFontGroup_getLabel"
                  onAction="rxchkHideFontGroup_Click"
                  screentip="Hide the Font Group"
                  supertip="Click here to hide/unhide the Font Group"/>

               <!— Add a checkBox —>
               <checkbox id="rxchkHideTableGroup"
                  getLabel="rxchkHideTableGroup_getLabel"
                  onAction="rxchkHideTableGroup_Click"
                  screentip="Hide the Tables Group"
                  supertip="Click here to hide the Tables Groups"/>
            </group>
         </tab>

         <tab idMso="TabHome">
            <group idMso="GroupFont"
               getVisible="GroupFont_getVisible"/>
         </tab>

         <tab idMso="TabInsert">
            <group idMso="GroupInsertTablesExcel"
               getVisible="GroupInsertTablesExcel_getVisible"/>
         </tab>
      </tabs>
   </ribbon>
</customUI>
```

The code creates the Modified Home tab, adds the My CheckBox before the Clipboard group, and adds a custom tab (Sheet Tab) with a blank group (for example purposes only). The complete UI should look like what is shown in Figure 12-5.

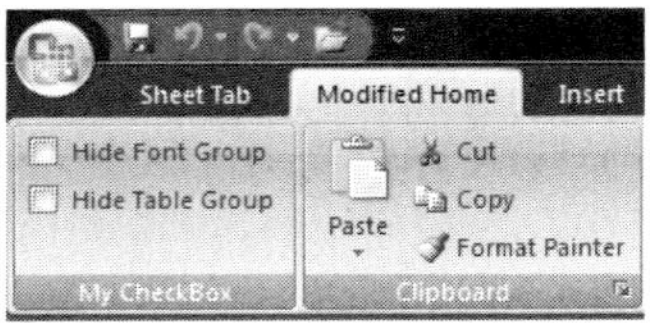

Figure 12-5: Defining custom properties for built-in objects

The next step is to define the properties. Open the code window for the `ThisWorkbook` object to define the following properties:

```
Private pRibbonUI              As IRibbonUI
Private pblnGrpTblVisible      As Boolean
Private pblnGrpFontVisible     As Boolean

'Sets the Ribbon object such that it can be accessed
'as a member of ThisWorkbook
Public Property Let rxIRibbonUI(iRib As IRibbonUI)
    Set pRibbonUI = iRib
End Property

Public Property Get rxIRibbonUI() As IRibbonUI
    Set rxIRibbonUI = pRibbonUI
End Property

'Sets the visibility attributes to a property such that i can
'be accessed as a member of ThisWorkbook
Public Property Let rxIRibbonUIGroupTableVisible( _
    ByVal blnVisible As Boolean)
    pblnGrpTblVisible = blnVisible
End Property

Public Property Get rxIRibbonUIGroupTableVisible() As Boolean
   rxIRibbonUIGroupTableVisible = pblnGrpTblVisible
End Property

Public Property Let rxIRibbonUIGroupFontVisible( _
    ByVal blnVisible As Boolean)
    pblnGrpFontVisible = blnVisible
End Property

Public Property Get rxIRibbonUIGroupFontVisible() As Boolean
   rxIRibbonUIGroupFontVisible = pblnGrpFontVisible
End Property
```

Note that although the variables used to determine the visibility are private to the `ThisWorkbook` module, the values set for the properties are exposed outside the scope of the module. Because the parent object, `ThisWorkbook`, is accessible anywhere in the project, so are the variables that are modified and accessed within the workbook's scope.

Before moving on to the callbacks, we need to create the custom properties for the worksheet. We will then use these custom properties to determine whether a tab associated with a sheet should be visible or not. It doesn't really matter which sheet you use for this exercise, but it might be easiest to emulate our example, which uses sheet1.

You can use the following code to set the custom properties for the worksheet:

```
Private pglnTabVisible      As Boolean

Property Let rxIRibbonUISheetTabVisible(ByVal blnVisible As Boolean)
    pglnTabVisible = blnVisible
End Property

Property Get rxIRibbonUISheetTabVisible() As Boolean
   rxIRibbonUISheetTabVisible = pglnTabVisible
End Property

Private Sub Worksheet_Activate()
    Sheet1.rxIRibbonUISheetTabVisible = True
    ThisWorkbook.rxIRibbonUI.Invalidate
End Sub

Private Sub Worksheet_Deactivate()
    Sheet1.rxIRibbonUISheetTabVisible = False
    ThisWorkbook.rxIRibbonUI.Invalidate
End Sub
```

Notice that you can now take advantage of the custom property that we created for `ThisWorkbook` to invalidate the Ribbon. We no longer refer to the property as belonging to a generic object; instead, we refer to it as a property that is a member of the `This-Workbook` object. Hence, you know at a glance that the UI is part of `ThisWorkbook`. There is no more guesswork.

Finally, provide the callbacks that will handle the calls from the UI:

```
Sub rxIRibbonUI_onLoad(ribbon As IRibbonUI)
    ThisWorkbook.rxIRibbonUI = ribbon
End Sub

Sub rxtabSheet_getVisible(control As IRibbonControl, ByRef returnedVal)
    returnedVal = Sheet1.rxIRibbonUISheetTabVisible
End Sub

Sub rxchkHideFontGroup_Click(control As IRibbonControl, _
    pressed As Boolean)
```

```
    ThisWorkbook.rxIRibbonUIGroupFontVisible = pressed
    ThisWorkbook.rxIRibbonUI.Invalidate
End Sub

Sub rxchkHideTableGroup_Click(control As IRibbonControl, _
    pressed As Boolean)
    ThisWorkbook.rxIRibbonUIGroupTableVisible = pressed
    ThisWorkbook.rxIRibbonUI.Invalidate
End Sub

Sub GroupFont_getVisible(control As IRibbonControl, ByRef returnedVal)
    returnedVal = True
    If control.ID = "GroupFont" Then
        returnedVal = Not (ThisWorkbook.rxIRibbonUIGroupFontVisible)
    Else:
        ThisWorkbook.rxIRibbonUI.Invalidate
    End If
End Sub

Sub GroupInsertTablesExcel_getVisible(control As IRibbonControl, _
    ByRef returnedVal)
    returnedVal = True
    If control.ID = "GroupInsertTablesExcel" Then
        returnedVal = Not (ThisWorkbook.rxIRibbonUIGroupTableVisible)
    Else:
        ThisWorkbook.rxIRibbonUI.Invalidate
    End If
End Sub

Sub rxchkHideFontGroup_getLabel(control As IRibbonControl, _
    ByRef returnedVal)
    Select Case
        Case True
            returnedVal = "Show Table Group"
        Case False
            returnedVal = "Hide Table Group"
    End Select
End Sub
```

You can now define various attributes associates with the UI objects through custom properties. By incorporating a few lines of code, you no longer depend on generic object variables that can become pretty much meaningless in a larger context. Instead, you use properties that are immediately associated with their container objects (in this case, a workbook and a worksheet). With these new skills, it is time to go one step further and get information from the Registry.

Saving and Retrieving Values from the Registry

The Windows Registry is a database used to store settings related to various aspects of your computer, such as user preferences, application settings, hardware settings, and so on.

When you program in VBA, the language provides ways to directly interact with the Registry. This is a powerful feature because it not only allows you to retrieve information about other programs and hardware, but also enables you to select important information about your application and store it in the Registry.

As our objective is to store and retrieve information about the UI, we will use a portion of the Registry that is set aside specifically for VBA (and VB) settings. Unlike most interactions with the Registry, our tasks do not require working with Windows APIs.

VBA provides two functions to work with the Registry: `GetSetting` and `SaveSetting`. These two functions can only access the following Registry handle key:

```
HKEY_CURRENT_USER\Software\VB and VBA Program Settings
```

Figure 12-6 shows the Registry Editor window opened to the key specific to VBA and VB projects.

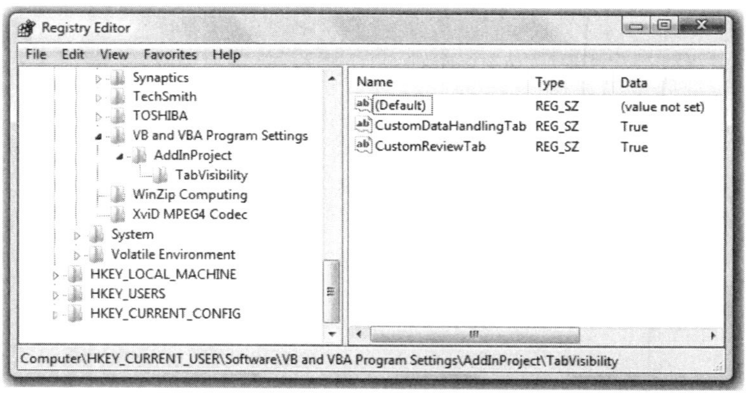

Figure 12-6: Registry Editor window

NOTE **To open the Registry Editor window, click the Windows Vista logo and in the Start Search box, type regedit and press Enter. As long as you're only working with this key, you're relatively safe and whatever you do only affects your own project (or any other project that uses this key). This book is not about the Registry, but you must not attempt to modify any other key without making a backup of it unless you're sure you actually know what you're doing. Otherwise, your actions can spell disaster.**

The folder named `AddInProject` is the application name, the subfolder `TabVisibility` refers to the section name of our customization. Inside the section folder you have the key that stores the setting for a particular part of your application. The types of values vary, and a full explanation of each one is beyond the scope of this book. The examples given here concentrate only on what we have at hand.

Figure 12-7 illustrates a scenario in which the Registry may come to the rescue. As you toggle the button, it stays toggled until you either click it again or you close the project. Once you close the project, the state is thrown out. However, you may want the button to retain the state that it had just before the project was closed.

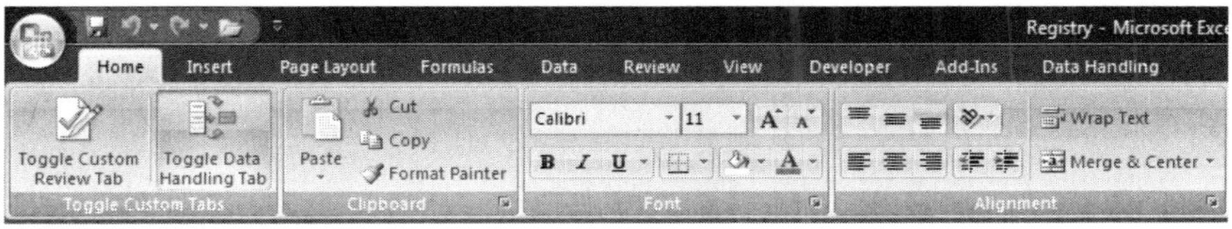

Figure 12-7: Using the Registry to keep track of toggleButton state

The complete XML code to generate the preceding UI (`toggleButtons` and custom tabs) is given here, followed by a brief explanation of the process:

```
<customUI xmlns="http://schemas.microsoft.com/office/2006/01/customui"
   onLoad="rxIRibbonUI_onLoad">
   <ribbon startFromScratch="false">
      <tabs>

<!--
*************************************************************
THE FIX STARTS HERE.
THIS ALLOWS THE TOGGLEBUTTONS TO HANDLE UI STATES.
FOR EASE OF ACCESS, THE BUTTONS ARE PLACED IN A CUSTOM GROUP
WITHIN THE HOMETAB.
*************************************************************
-->

         <tab idMso="TabHome">
            <group id="rxgrp1"
               insertBeforeMso="GroupClipboard"
               label="Toggle Custom Tabs">

               <toggleButton id="rxtglCustomReview"
                  label="Toggle Custom Review Tab"
                  imageMso="ReviewAcceptChangeMenu"
                  size="large"
                  getPressed="rxtglCustomReview_getPressed"
                  onAction="rxtglShared_Click"/>

               <separator id="rxsep1"/>

               <toggleButton id="rxtglDataHandling"
                  label="Toggle Data Handling Tab"
```

```
                imageMso="Consolidate"
                size="large"
                getPressed="rxtglDataHandling_getPressed"
                onAction="rxtglShared_Click"/>
          </group>
       </tab>

<!--
*****************************************************************
END OF FIX FOR HANDLING UI STATES.
*****************************************************************
THE CUSTOM REVIEW TAB UI STARTS HERE
*****************************************************************
-->

       <tab id="rxtabCustomReview"
          getVisible="rxtabCustomReview_getVisible"
          label="Custom Review"
          keytip="K">
          <group idMso="GroupClipboard"/>
          <group idMso="GroupFont"/>

          <group id="rxgrpProofingComments"
             label="Proofing and Comments">
             <box id="rxbox1" boxStyle="vertical">
                <button idMso="Spelling"/>
                <button idMso="Thesaurus"/>
                <button idMso="TranslationPane"/>
             </box>

             <separator id="rxsep2"/>

             <box id="rxbox2" boxStyle="vertical">
                <button idMso="ReviewNewComment"/>
                <button idMso="ReviewDeleteComment"
                   label="Delete Comment"/>
                <toggleButton idMso="ReviewShowAllComments"/>
             </box>
          </group>

          <group id="rxgrpChanges"
             label="Worksheet related changes">
             <box id="rxbox" boxStyle="vertical">
                <button idMso="ReviewHighlightChanges"/>
                <button idMso="ReviewProtectAndShareWorkbook"/>
                <button idMso="ReviewAllowUsersToEditRanges"/>
                <button idMso="SheetProtect"/>
             </box>
          </group>
       </tab>

<!--
```

```
*************************************************************
END OF CUSTOM UI REVIEW TAB
*************************************************************
-->

         <tab id="rxtabDataHandling"
            getVisible="rxtabDataHandling_getVisible"
            label="Data Handling"
            keytip="Z">
         </tab>
      </tabs>
   </ribbon>
</customUI>
```

The code contains some key callbacks that must be handled in VBA. The `getPressed` attribute is set because it returns the callback that retrieves the pressed state for the `toggleButton` from the Registry. The state is either `true` or `false`.

Next, you handle the `Click` event (which is defined as a shared callback via the `onAction` attribute). The click will save the current state of the button to the Registry every time it is clicked.

Finally, the `getVisible` attribute determines whether the tab is visible or not depending on the state of the `toggleButton`.

NOTE **The example that follows was made with Excel in mind; however, it can be replicated in Word and Access.**

For this example, encapsulate the following two VBA functions into your own function. This will give you the opportunity to hard-code certain parameters into the function itself and to practice passing arguments to UDFs (user-defined functions). The UDF doesn't do anything different from the VBA function itself, but it gives you greater control over certain aspects, as we're about to demonstrate:

```
Function getRegistry(ByVal strKey As String) As Boolean
    On Error Resume Next
    getRegistry = GetSetting("AddInProject", "TabVisibility", strKey)
    If Err <> 0 Then getRegistry = False
End Function

Function saveRegistry(ByVal strKey As String, _
    ByVal blnSetting As Boolean)
    SaveSetting "AddInProject", "TabVisibility", strKey, blnSetting
End Functionn
```

Because the `getRegistry` function will return an error if the key does not exist, you need to add error handling to the trap for that error. If an error occurs, you know that there is no key and that the `getRegistry` function should return `False`.

With the two functions ready to be used, you handle the callbacks as follows:

```
Public gblnShowCustomReviewTab          As Boolean
Public gblnShowCustomDataHandlingTab    As Boolean
```

```
Public grxIRibbonUI                          As IRibbonUI

Sub rxIRibbonUI_onLoad(ribbon As IRibbonUI)
    Set grxIRibbonUI = ribbon
End Sub

Sub rxtglCustomReview_getPressed(control As IRibbonControl, _
    ByRef returnedVal)
    returnedVal = getRegistry("CustomReviewTab")
    gblnShowCustomReviewTab = getRegistry("CustomReviewTab")
    grxIRibbonUI.InvalidateControl ("rxtabCustomReview")
End Sub

Sub rxtglDataHandling_getPressed(control As IRibbonControl, _
    ByRef returnedVal)
    returnedVal = getRegistry("CustomDataHandlingTab")
    gblnShowCustomDataHandlingTab = getRegistry("CustomDataHandlingTab")
    grxIRibbonUI.InvalidateControl ("rxtabDataHandling")
End Sub

Sub rxtglShared_Click(control As IRibbonControl, pressed As Boolean)
    Select Case control.ID
        Case "rxtglCustomReview"
            gblnShowCustomReviewTab = pressed
            saveRegistry "CustomReviewTab", pressed
            gblnCalledOnOpen = False

        Case "rxtglDataHandling"
            gblnShowCustomDataHandlingTab = pressed
            gblnCalledOnOpen = False
            saveRegistry "CustomDataHandlingTab", pressed
    End Select
    grxIRibbonUI.Invalidate
End Sub

Sub rxtabCustomReview_getVisible(control As IRibbonControl, _
    ByRef returnedVal)
    returnedVal = gblnShowCustomReviewTab
End Sub

Sub rxtabDataHandling_getVisible(control As IRibbonControl, _
    ByRef returnedVal)
    returnedVal = gblnShowCustomDataHandlingTab
End Sub
```

With that done, you can now close your project and be confident that the next time it opens, the settings for the handled control will be updated according to the values recorded in your Registry keys.

Conclusion

In this chapter, you learned several advanced concepts of VBA, coupled with UI customization. Some of the highlights included working with collections, class modules, and custom properties. With collections, you were able to use Access workspaces to enumerate databases in the collection, and we demonstrated how to determine whether an item is present in a collection. In working with class modules, you created your own properties and methods; and then you learned how to handle events.

You also saw how easy it is to connect to Web services and incorporate some of those resources directly into your Ribbon customizations. After demonstrating how to work with custom properties for built-in objects, we closed the chapter by working with the Windows Registry, and explained how to store UI values so that they can be retrieved after a session has been closed, thereby allowing the UI to return to that state the next time it is opened.

These examples only scratch the surface of what you can accomplish with these tools. Some of the tools will crop up later in the book as you advance in your understanding and begin creating a truly custom UI. The next step is to learn how to override the built-in Ribbon and controls.

CHAPTER

13

Overriding Built-in Controls in the Ribbon

In this chapter, we get into the issues and details associated with overriding built-in controls in the Ribbon. We'll also show you how easy it is to get rid of the built-in Ribbon, so if you truly want to remove all of the tabs and major controls in the Ribbon, you can do that with just one command. Thankfully, that will still leave you with some basic controls for handling the project.

Covered here are topics to help you plan and implement your customizations in the event that you deem such a drastic overhaul is the right approach for a project. We start by explaining how to build a UI from scratch.

Deciding to start a project from scratch is not an easy decision. In fact, it might seem counterintuitive, as we typically want to add new features, rather than remove existing tools. However, there may be times when this is necessary, such as when you build a front end in Excel, Access, or Word and only want selected commands to be available to the user. Whether they are custom commands, built-in commands, or a combination of the two, you need to start by removing the existing Ribbon. That means you need to use the `startFromScratch` attribute to remove the Ribbon so that you can then add back only the commands that you want to make available to users.

If you have built custom menus and toolbars in previous versions of Office, you will remember how challenging it can be to completely remove the standard menu and toolbars. Even worse was trying to recover them if someone inadvertently replaced the default menus with their customized ones.

As you are preparing to work through the examples, we encourage you to download the companion files. The source code and files for this chapter can be found on the book's website at `www.wiley.com/go/ribbonx`.

Starting the UI from Scratch

Starting your UI from scratch means just that: starting from zilch! At least that's the way it will appear. However some controls will still be available — but those are just the basics so that you can still perform certain key operations in the project, such as those listed in Table 13-1. However, starting (nearly) from scratch will do away with everything the UI has to offer in terms of accessibility. Hence, this is a feature that should be used with caution.

Setting the startFromScratch Attribute

As mentioned in the introduction to this Chapter, when you start a UI from scratch you eliminate a lot functionality that users may need. On the one hand, this can be counterproductive, as changes to the UI normally mean adding new features, not removing familiar ones. On the other hand, your project might be very specific and therefore best served by incorporating custom-tailored menus and commands. In such cases, you would normally want to do away with a lot of unwanted features in the UI, such as tabs and groups.

Starting a project from scratch is very simple — at least removing features is simple. The rebuilding is something that takes careful planning and meticulous implementation. One of the biggest risks is the potential to overlook adding back a command that is needed by end users.

Having said that, starting a project from scratch requires only the addition of the `startFromScratch` attribute and setting its value to `true`. The XML code would then read as follows. It is as simple as that: Add one short line and the Ribbon disappears:

```
<customUI xmlns="http://schemas.microsoft.com/office/2006/01/customui">
   <ribbon startFromScratch="true">
   </ribbon>
</customUI>
```

After setting the attribute to `true` and saving the UI, when the project is loaded the working environment for the project will appear as shown in Figure 13-1 (for an Excel project).

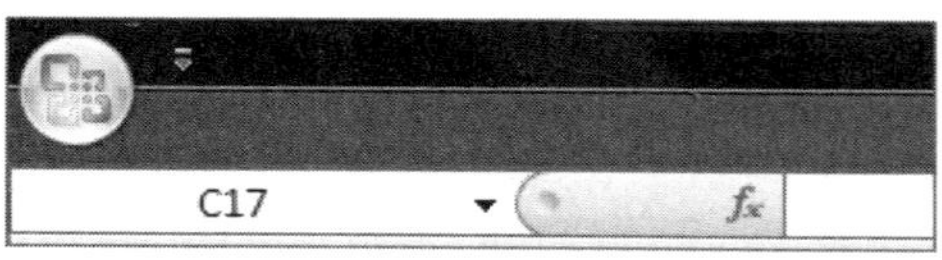

Figure 13-1: An Excel project started from scratch

However, this still leaves a few commands for you to work with. Table 13-1 lists the controls that will be available when you start a project from scratch, along with the applications in which they are available.

Table 13-1: Controls Available When Starting from Scratch

CONTROL	APPLICATION
New	Excel, Access and Word
Open	Excel, Access and Word
Save	Excel and Word
Save As	Access only
Application Options	Excel, Access and Word
Application Exit	Excel, Access and Word
Close Database	Access only

Besides these controls, you will also have default access to two additional options in the Quick Access Toolbar (QAT), as shown in Table 13-2.

Table 13-2: Additional QAT Options Available When Starting from scratch

OPTION	APPLICATION
Show Below/Above the Ribbon	Excel, Access and Word
Minimize the Ribbon	Excel, Access and Word

Although starting from scratch removes all controls with the exception of those listed in the preceding tables, it does not disable any built-in commands (starting from scratch is not the same as disabling commands associated with controls). Hence, users who know a shortcut to a command, such as copy, will be able to copy a selection by using Ctrl+c. By the same token, you could close a workbook or document by using the Ctrl+w shortcut, even though the control that executes the command is no longer displayed on the Ribbon.

Besides, if you needed to access, say, the Format Cells dialog box in Excel, you could use the Accelerator keys from Office 2003. To do so, you would use the following sequence: Alt → O → E. The keytip route, however, would not work here unless the keytip leads to the Office Button (which is equivalent to the File menu in previous versions of Office).

TIP **When accessing Accelerator keys or keytips, you can also press F10. This works the same as pressing the Alt key.**

CROSS-REFERENCE **For a list of common shortcuts, keytips, and accelerator key combinations, see Appendix D.**

Disabling such features is covered in the section "Disabling and Repurposing Commands" later in this chapter, but first we focus on adding some tabs and controls to the startlingly empty Ribbon. Adding tabs and controls is an exercise you have already covered in earlier chapters, so we combine this with activation of tabs at startup so that you do not get a fragmented picture of what we plan to show you.

Activating a Tab at Startup

You might think that all you need to do is add a tab and specify that it is to be placed in front of the Home tab; and that because it will be the first tab on the Ribbon, it will become the default tab and be automatically selected upon opening your project. Sounds logical, but it isn't that straightforward. A custom tab is selected by default, so just adding a custom tab before the Home tab does not mean that it would be selected because it is the first tab on the Ribbon — at least not in Excel. Of course, Access responds differently than the other programs. Actually, Access and Word are both more intuitive in their behavior because when a custom tab is placed at the beginning of the Ribbon, it is indeed selected by default.

Because you have to use code to specify the default tab in Excel, the example uses Excel.

NOTE **The aforementioned behavior in Access and Word is only applicable for a tab placed before the Home tab. If you plan to use the tab somewhere else, you need to select it through code. Examples for Access and Word are included in the download files for this chapter.**

In this example, selecting the tab at startup requires two steps. The first step is to define a keytip in the XML code. The second step is to define a procedure that uses the `SendKeys` method to send the keytip to the application so that it can be executed and, consequently, so that the tab be selected at startup.

As explained in the previous paragraph, the first thing to do is specify a keytip for your custom tab. You will use this keytip later in VBA (the second step) as a means to select the tab. To add a keytip to a tab (or control), you simply specify the `keytip` attribute in the XML code, as shown in the following example:

```
<tab id="rxtab"
   label="Active Tab"
   insertBeforeMso="TabHome"
   keytip="UN">
```

CROSS-REFERENCE **For more information about keytips, see Chapter 11.**

After specifying the keytip for the tab, you need to include the callback that will handle the selection of your custom tab. You might think that `Open` is the first event for the workbook, but the `OnLoad` event actually occurs first. Specify the selection instruction together with the `onLoad` event. In order to select the tab when the UI is loaded, use the `SendKeys` method, as shown in the following procedure:

```
Sub rxIRibbonUI_onLoad(ribbon As IRibbonUI)
    Application.SendKeys "%UN{RETURN}"
End Sub
```

The percent sign indicates the `Alt` key, which is necessary to trigger keytips. The `UN` is our chosen keytip. We also add the `RETURN` key so that the keytips within the tab lose focus when the tab is selected. We do that because we want the tab to have the focus, but we don't want the keytips displayed.

Table 13-3 shows combination keys you can use with the `SendKeys` method. It is important to remember and recognize the symbols representing each key when you're writing this type of code.

Table 13-3: Combination Keys for Use with the SendKeys Method

COMBINATION KEY	SYMBOL
ALT	% (percentage)
CTRL	^ (circumflex)
SHIFT	+ (plus)

You can use the keys from Table 13-3 with any other key to make up a combination. Table 13-4 shows some other keys you might find useful when using the `SendKeys` method and when a key combination is required. Although they may seem intuitive, we've included the list because it is safer to be precise than to guess and miss something. These are not case-sensitive, but we recommend using all uppercase because that way they stand out in your code.

Table 13-4: Some Special Keys and Their Respective Code

KEY	KEY CODE
BACKSPACE	{BACKSPACE} or {BS}
BREAK	{BREAK}
CAPS LOCK	{CAPSLOCK}
DELETE or DEL	{DELETE} or {DEL}
DOWN ARROW	{DOWN}
END	{END}
ENTER	~ (tilde)
ENTER (numeric keypad)	{ENTER}

Continued

Table 13-4 *(continued)*

KEY	KEY CODE
ESC	{ESCAPE} or {ESC}
F1 through F15	{F1} through {F15}
HOME	{HOME}
RETURN	{RETURN}
TAB	{TAB}

The `SendKeys` method is extremely useful for a number of tasks. This section just covered the basics before taking a look at disabling and repurposing commands.

Disabling and Repurposing Commands

Unlike previous versions, Office 2007 allows us to globally disable and repurpose commands. In the past, disabling a command entailed disabling every single instance of the control that executed the command in the UI. That was a mammoth task.

With the new UI you can globally disable and repurpose commands without much effort. It is true that there are some loopholes, but overall it is of tremendous benefit, reducing tedium and frustration; and it is much faster and easier to implement and maintain.

Disabling Commands, Application Options, and Exit

This section describes how to disable commands in Office 2007. The process is very simple and requires very little effort. The most important part is knowing the exact names of the controls whose commands you plan to disable and what type of control those commands come under. Once you have that sorted out, the rest should go very smoothly.

We've divided this into two separate sections to make it easier to learn the basic principles associated with the process. The first section looks at commands in general and the second section looks into two rather specialized commands that are exposed by the controls `Application Options` and `Exit`.

Disabling Commands

As already pointed out, disabling commands has more to do with knowing what to disable than knowing how to disable it. The main thing about disabling is that commands are disabled globally from the `commands` collection, rather than from within the Ribbon object and the object's parent container. Trying to disable a command from within the parent container will produce an error message.

When you think about it, the good news is that disabling a command does not involve, in any way, work with the Ribbon container. You can do it all with simple code. For example, suppose that you wanted to disable the `Bold` command. You can do so as follows:

```
<commands>
   <command idMso="Bold"
      enabled="false"/>
</commands>
```

That's all there is to it. The key is to ensure that you have the correct `idMso` for the command you want to disable. Now let's look at disabling the `Application Options` and the `Exit` button.

Disabling the Commands Associated with the Application Options and Exit Controls

As you have seen, when you start a project from scratch, some commands are still available by default; and although you may appreciate them as a developer, it's just as likely that you'll want to have better control over what the user can do. `Exit` is a prime example of a control that can cause some grief, as it will persist even after using `startFromScratch` to eliminate the Ribbon. For obvious reasons, you might want to ensure that the `Exit` command is disabled, as it allows users to abruptly quit a program and thus bypass all the nice shutdown and clean-up routines that you may rely on.

Although the QAT is there to provide one-click access to the most frequently used tools, it also contains the More Commands option, which gives users access to a host of other application features. Although the More Commands option is disabled when starting the UI from scratch, it still persists via the `Application Options` button under the Office Menu. Not only that, if you take a quick look at the commands available through `Application Options`, you will quickly appreciate the risk associated with making them so readily available to users. Ergo, the reason why you might decide to disable the commands associated with the `Exit` and `Application Options` controls.

Although these two controls expose commands that belong to the `officeMenu` Ribbon element, neither control can be disabled from within the `officeMenu` container. Instead, you must use the `command` element, as shown here:

```
<commands>
   <command idMso="FileExit"
      enabled="false"/>
   <command idMso="ApplicationOptionsDialog"
      enabled="false"/>
</commands>
```

NOTE **You can use this method to disable commands associated with any control in Access, Excel, and Word.**

When you have quite a few controls to disable, a better option is to have a shared callback so that you don't need to specify each case for the `enabled` attribute. In that scenario, the code would look similar to the following:

```
<commands>
   <command idMso="FileExit"
      getEnabled="rxshared_getEnabled"/>
   <command idMso="ApplicationOptionsDialog"
      getEnabled="rxshared_getEnabled"/>
   <command idMso="Bold"
      getEnabled="rxshared_getEnabled"/>
</commands>
```

Having identified the command and the attribute, the next step is to handle the callback and disable the controls themselves. This is done by setting the value of `getEnabled` to `False`, as shown in the following code snippet:

```
Sub rxshared_getEnabled(control As IRibbonControl, ByRef returnedVal)
    returnedVal = False
End Sub
```

Besides being able to disable a command associated with a control, you can also repurpose the command associated with it. This means that you can change the original function of a control to have it do something else. For example, a control that would normally save changes could be repurposed to open documents instead. Yes, we realize that this invites some imaginations to run wild with fun ideas that should never be implemented. Nonetheless, at the risk of unleashing some pranks, we'll move on to explain how to repurpose commands.

Repurposing a Command Associated with a Generic Control

Repurposing a command is accomplished in the same fashion as disabling a command, as you cannot repurpose from inside the Ribbon container; you must work in the `commands` collection.

Again, the key to a successful repurposing depends more on knowing the controls for the commands you want to repurpose than on the work involved to write the XML code itself. Another key factor to remember is that although a command may not be visible, it will still function as designed if it is called by a shortcut.

This can pose some issues for your code. More important, it can cause a lot of stress. A simple example will illustrate our point. Take a `toggleButton`; when the button is clicked, it changes from toggled to not toggled, or vice-versa. This is all fine, as long as it is an actual click. However, because the shortcut also works here, the combination of keys that triggers the shortcut occurs before the toggling event. You can see where this is going, because the shortcut will trigger the callback. That's OK so far, but the trouble starts when the button is toggled, because that will also trigger the callback. The upshot of all this is that the procedure is run twice, which is typically not a good thing and has the potential to wreak havoc in your project.

Another thing you should be aware of is that the callback signature will vary. A callback will have the following argument added to its normal signature:

```
ByRef cancelDefault
```

This means that a control such as a `toggleButton` that would normally have the signature

```
Sub rxtgl_ repurpose(control as IRibbonControl, pressed as Boolean)
```

would now need to be amended in order to avoid an error advising of a missing argument:

```
Sub rxtgl_repurpose(control As IRibbonControl, pressed As Boolean, _
  ByRef cancelDefault)
```

This added argument is used to cancel the default event. We'll provide complete examples momentarily.

NOTE When using the CustomUI Editor to generate the callbacks, note that it does not handle this properly. Because you're dealing with a generic command, it will generate a generic callback signature. Therefore, you need to modify the signature to avoid getting an error. The preceding information and the following example will be helpful guides when you are modifying callbacks.

NOTE In working through this section, recall that a generic control is much like a generic object when declared in VBA — at least in the sense that the control only takes form or delivers any functionality after it is bound to a specific object, such as a `label`, `button`, `checkBox`, and so on.

Continuing with the previous example, you could repurpose the `Application Options` button as follows:

```
<command idMso="ApplicationOptionsDialog"
   onAction="rxApplicationOptionsDialog_repurpose"/>
```

The callback could then be handled as follows (using the standard callback signature for a repurposed button):

```
Sub rxApplicationOptionsDialog_repurpose(control As IRibbonControl, _
    ByRef cancelDefault)
    MsgBox "Sorry, Word options are currently disabled.", vbCritical
End Sub
```

As with previous examples, you can use a shared procedure if the controls share the same callback signature.

CAUTION **As pointed out earlier, we realize that the capability to repurpose a command might invite some imaginations to run wild. Keep in mind that it is usually a very bad idea to repurpose a command that you know end users expect will behave in a specific way. If the command does not behave as expected it will certainly cause confusion, and it could even lead to serious problems. The approach taken in the last example of this section is probably a better option, as it explicitly informs users that the command they are attempting to use has been disabled. Bottom line: Don't disable or repurpose commands without informing the end user.**

Affecting the Keyboard Shortcuts and Keytips

There may be times when you need to overwrite built-in shortcuts as well as keytips. As you will recall, the keytip is the new feature that draws on the old accelerator keys from previous versions of Office. In order to activate keytips, you simply press and release the Alt key or the F10 function key.

It is very simple to override a keytip. You merely reference the control and then assign a new keytip to it. The following XML code shows how this is done. By assigning `$` as the keytip for the Insert tab, the keytip is effectively changed from `I` to `$`:

```
<tab idMso="TabInsert" keytip="$">
```

In addition, despite using `$`, which is a special character, the customization is displayed and functions as expected, as shown in Figure 13-2

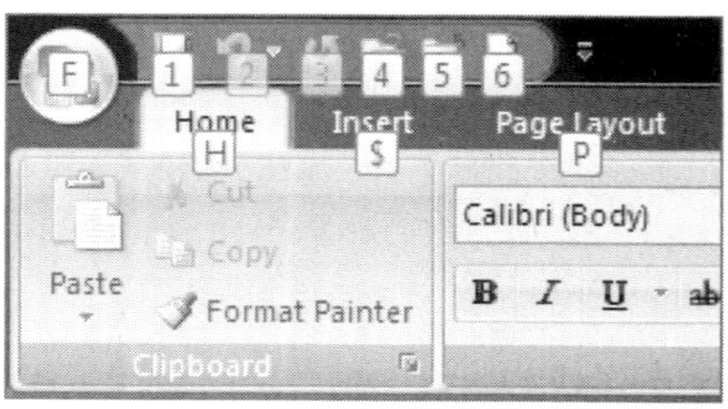

Figure 13-2: Swapping built-in keytips for preferred ones

TIP **A keytip is accessed through a "key *then* key" approach. A shortcut is accessed through a "key *plus* key" approach. In the first case you press and release one key and then press another key. In the second case, you hold down all the keys at the same time.**

The next step would be to override built-in shortcuts such as Ctrl+c, Ctrl+p, etc. We already touched on this subject when we covered how to record macros. You can assign shortcuts to macros that match built-in shortcuts, and in doing so you will effectively override the built-in shortcut key. Again, we recommend caution and prudence because changing shortcuts that are used across multiple programs and versions can be counterintuitive and counterproductive — and even counter to employment.

However, there are times when it is appropriate to establish your own set of shortcuts, so we'll cover some other methods to override built-in shortcuts such as using the `OnKey` method in Excel or an `AutoKeys` macro in Access.

CROSS-REFERENCE **For working examples using the `OnKey` method and an `AutoKeys` macro, see the "Repurposing QAT Controls" section in Chapter 14.**

The `OnKey` method in Excel is used to run the procedure that you specify. It works in a similar fashion as the `SendKeys` method works with the same values, so you can use the same key table as a reference, Table 13-4. However, the `OnKey` method is structured somewhat differently and uses the arguments shown in Table 13-5.

Table 13-5: OnKey Method Arguments

NAME	REQUIRED/OPTIONAL	DATA TYPE	DESCRIPTION
Key	Required	String	A string indicating the key or key combination to be pressed
Procedure	Optional	Variant	A string indicating the name of the procedure to be run. If the value is "" (empty text), nothing happens when the key or key combination is pressed. This form of `OnKey` changes the normal result of keystrokes. If the argument is omitted, then the key or key combination goes back to its normal behavior (any key or key combination assignments made with previous `OnKey` methods are cleared).

Thus, the general `OnKey` method can be structured as follows:

```
Application.OnKey Key, ProcedureName
```

As shown in Table 13-5, the `Key` argument refers to the key or key combination you plan to trap (override), whereas the `ProcedureName` argument refers to the procedure that must be executed when the key or key combination is pressed. Suppose you wanted to trap the print shortcut (Ctrl+p). You can do so as follows:

```
Sub print_override()
    Application.OnKey "^p", "myPrintMsg"
End Sub
```

To return things to normal, all you have to do is omit the procedure name in the argument of the `OnKey` method, as shown in the following code, and like magic, the commands will resume their default actions and no additional steps are required:

```
Sub print_override()
    Application.OnKey "^p"
End Sub
```

You will see additional examples in Chapter 14 when we discuss the QAT. You'll appreciate that the examples are more relevant to real-world situations. The goal of this chapter was to cover the basics, so although the examples may not seem to have much practical value, they made it easy to understand the concepts at work. Chapter 14 also includes a demonstration of how to incorporate a shortcut override in Access.

Conclusion

In this chapter, you've learned the basics of starting your customization from scratch, including some of the issues to be aware of. We've also looked at activating tabs on startup, and we worked with disabling and repurposing controls.

We finished by working with keytips and shortcuts, including how to override them. This is the perfect lead-in to Chapter 14, which covers some of these techniques in more detail and provides opportunities to practice them more fully as you progress into more specialized customization.

CHAPTER

14

Customizing the Office Menu and the QAT

In Office 2007, the Quick Access Toolbar (QAT) is the nearest thing that you have to the toolbars. As you have already learned, you can add buttons and entire groups to the QAT, so the tools you need are readily available to you. The Office Menu, on the other hand, is basically a menu containing various options, much the same that you would find under the old File menu in previous versions of Office. The Office Menu is accessed by clicking the Office Button.

In this chapter, you will learn more about the Office Menu and the QAT and how to customize them. These are a bit different from the customizations we've covered so far. As you are preparing to work through the examples, we encourage you to download the companion files. The source code and files for this chapter can be found on the book's website at `www.wiley.com/go/ribbonx`.

Adding Items to the Office Menu

The Office Menu is represented by the little application button at the upper-left corner of the application window. This button, also known as the Office Button, contains some common actions, or commands, that affect the document as a whole, such as Print, Save, and Publish.

As you learn how to customize the Office Menu, please keep in mind that controls are grouped under the Office Menu to reflect the concept that these commands affect the document as whole, rather than a specific part of the document, such as a paragraph or the font format.

That said, we temporarily ignore this guideline so that our examples can give you greater exposure to the Office Menu.

The Office Menu uses the following XML markup:

```
  <officeMenu>
 <! --
    Everything else goes here
 -- >
</officeMenu>
```

By now, that should be a familiar layout to you. Table 14-1 shows the child elements of the Office Menu. We will use these elements to add customizations.

Table 14-1: Child Elements of the Office Menu

OBJECT	WHAT IT IS FOR
control	Refers to a generic control object that can represent other objects such as buttons, splitButtons, groups, etc.
button	Refers to a button control used for normal clicks to perform some sort of action
checkbox	Refers to a checkbox control
gallery	Refers to a gallery control. See Chapter 8 for information on this type of control.
toggleButton	Refers to a toggle button and switches between True/False values
menuSeparator	Refers to a menu separator item
splitButton	Refers to a splitButton that can be used to hold other controls such as button controls
menu	Refers to a menu control that can be used to hold other controls such as button controls
dynamicMenu	Refers to a dynamic menu that can receive dynamic XML content at run-time

Figure 14-1 shows an example of an Office Menu customization in Access. In this example, we added the `My Tools` button with two groups, `My Toolset1` and `My Toolset2`. We're about to walk through the process of creating and adding this customization.

Figure 14-1: Adding controls to the Office Menu

In this example, we create a `splitButton` containing a menu with several buttons organized according to their specific task. The XML code for this customization is as follows:

```
<customUI xmlns="http://schemas.microsoft.com/office/2006/01/customui">
   <ribbon startFromScratch="false">
      <officeMenu>
         <splitButton id="rxsbtn"
            insertBeforeMso="FilePrintMenu">
            <button id="rxbtnSplitMain"
               label="My Tools"
               imageMso="CreateModule"/>

            <menu id="rxmnu"
               itemSize="large">

               <menuSeparator id="rxsep1"
                  title="My Toolset 1"/>
               <button id="rxbtnEmailDoc"
                  imageMso="FileSendAsAttachment"
                  label="E-mail selected table as attachment"
                  description="E-mail the selected table as an attachment↵
to an e-mail recipient..."
          onAction="rxshared_click"/>
          <buttonid="rxbtnEmailSupport"
            imageMso="MessageToAttendeesMenu"
```

```
            label="E-mail technical support"
            description="E-mail technical support about issues on this↵
application..."
            onAction="rxshared_click"/>

          <buttonid="rxbtnEmailBug"
            imageMso="ResearchPane"
            label="E-mail a bug"
            description="E-mail technical support about bugs found on↵
this application..."
            onAction="rxshared_click"/>

         <menuSeparator
           id="rxsep2"
           title="My Toolset 2"/>
          <buttonid="rxbtnPrintPDF"
            imageMso="PrintDialogAccess"
            label="Print to PDF"
            description="Print active report to PDF file format"
            onAction="rxshared_click"/>
        </menu>
      </splitButton>
    </officeMenu>
  </ribbon>
</customUI>
```

The preceding code uses a `splitButton` that encapsulates a menu. You may have noticed that a `splitButton` has a demarcation between the icon and arrow, whereas a menu does not. Figure 14-2 shows this difference. The built-in Print button is a `splitButton`; the built-in Send button is a menu button. For the most part, this is pretty much a style preference.

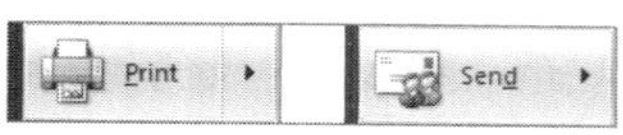

Figure 14-2: Comparing a splitButton with a menu control

The image on the left represents a `splitButton`, whereas the image on the right represents a menu. Essentially, the menu control provides the same customization without the intermediary step of a `splitButton`, which means you can do away with the `splitButton`-button combination and move straight into using menu buttons for additional functional items. For example, to redo the last `splitButton` example to use a menu control, you would use the following code:

```
<customUI xmlns="http://schemas.microsoft.com/office/2006/01/customui">
   <ribbon startFromScratch="false">
      <officeMenu>
         <menu id="rxmnu"
            insertBeforeMso="FilePrintMenu"
```

```
        imageMso="CreateModule"
        itemSize="large">

          <menuSeparator id="rxsep1"
             title="My Toolset 1"/>
          <button id="rxbtnEmailDoc"
             imageMso="FileSendAsAttachment"
             label="E-mail selected table as attachment"
             description="E-mail the selected table as an attachment↵
to an e-mail recipient..."
             onAction="rxshared_click"/>

          <button id="rxbtnEmailSupport"
             imageMso="MessageToAttendeesMenu"
             label="E-mail technical support"
             description="E-mail technical support about issues on↵
this application..."
             onAction="rxshared_click"/>

          <button id="rxbtnEmailBug"
             imageMso="ResearchPane"
             label="E-mail a bug"
             description="E-mail technical support about bugs found↵
on this application..."
             onAction="rxshared_click"/>

          <menuSeparator id="rxsep2"
             title="My Toolset 2"/>
          <button id="rxbtnPrintPDF"
             imageMso="PrintDialogAccess"
             label="Print to PDF"
             description="Print active report to PDF file format"
             onAction="rxshared_click"/>
        </menu>
      </officeMenu>
   </ribbon>
</customUI>
```

If there was any doubt in your mind about how little the difference would be, just compare your new menu control to your `splitButton`. They are virtually the same except for coloring and line, and, of course, the extra features offered by the menu control.

These two examples assume you want to add your own custom items to the Office Menu. However, you may also want to add custom or built-in items to the built-in elements within the Office Menu. In that case, you will appreciate knowing where to find the elements associated with the program that you are using. Table 14-2 provides a quick reference to Office Menu elements. Now you can quickly locate the standard elements to add items to them, using `splitButtons` or `Menus`; of course, you can also create and add your own items.

Table 14-2: Office Menu Elements

ELEMENT	TYPE	IDMSO	APPLIES TO
New	button	FileMenu	Excel/Access/Word
Open	button	FileOpen	Excel/Word
Open	button	FileOpenDatabase	Access
Save	button	FileSave	Excel/Word/Access
Save As	splitButton	FileSaveAsMenu	Excel/Word
Save As	splitButton	FileSaveAsMenuAccess	Access
Print	splitButton	FilePrintMenu	Excel/Word/Access
Prepare	menu	FilePrepareMenu	Excel/Word
Manage	menu	FileManageMenu	Access
Send	menu	FileSendMenu	Excel/Word
E-mail	button	FileSendAsAttachment	Access
Publish	menu	MenuPublish	Excel/Word/Access
Close	button	FileClose	Excel/Word
Close Database	button	FileCloseDatabase	Access

Adding Items to the QAT

The Quick Access Toolbar is the part of the new UI for which your customization efforts might seem reminiscent of the methods you used with the old Office toolbars. This section introduces you to QAT customization through XML, rather than the labor-intensive manual processes discussed in Chapter 1. Of course, we needed to cover the basics so that you know where to find — and how to work with — controls. With that behind you, you are ready to automate and streamline when possible.

CROSS-REFERENCE **If you need a refresher on manual customization, refer to Chapter 1, where the difference between a document control and a shared control is also explained.**

Customization Overview

The QAT is unique in many ways, but you will find that it is very flexible when it comes to customization, even though you may not yet think of it that way. It can contain, for example, both shared and document-specific controls. It can also include entire control groups (both built-in and custom) so that more controls are conveniently stored in a single location.

Keep in mind that when customizing the QAT, you must start it from scratch. This means that you must set the `startFromScratch` attribute to `true`; otherwise, you cannot proceed:

```
<ribbon startFromScratch="true">
```

CROSS-REFERENCE **See Chapter 13 for more information about the `startFromScratch` attribute.**

Another thing to bear in mind is that as you start from scratch, a lot of controls are removed from the Office Menu, and all tabs are removed from the Ribbon. That is probably a little more drastic than what you wanted or anticipated, but rather than letting that become a stumbling block, just take some time to plan for the future uses of the UI and determine which controls it will need, eliminating those that it won't.

NOTE **Although `startFromScratch` will remove controls from the UI, command shortcut keys will still work. Consider, for example, the Office Menu: In Excel, the menu is reduced to three basic controls: `New`, `Open`, and `Save`. However, you can still close the document using the Ctrl+w shortcut, or you can send the document to print using Ctrl+p.**

sharedControls versus documentControls

When working with the QAT, you will notice that there are two types of icons. One type has a border around it and the other one does not. This distinction indicates which control is shared and which one is specific to the document. Figure 14-3 shows two controls within the border — these are specific to the currently loaded document.

Figure 14-3: sharedControls and documentControls

This is important because you can quickly determine which controls are document controls and which are shared controls. You can use this knowledge to tailor a UI that is specific to the document that contains it or to share a custom UI with other documents, such as through an add-in. Of course, this means that the distinction is mostly for the benefit of the developer, rather than the user, but it can also alert users that new controls are conveniently placed at their fingertips, eliminating the time it takes to look for them elsewhere.

The XML markup for QAT document controls is provided by the following:

```
<qat>
   <documentControls>
      <control/>
```

```
    </documentControls>
</qat>
```

The markup for QAT shared controls is as follows:

```
    <qat>
   <sharedControls>
      <control/>
   </sharedControls>
</qat>
```

As you progress through this chapter, these outlines will be filled out in the examples.

NOTE **Groups that are added to the QAT have a different icon than shared or document-specific controls. QAT groups are discussed later in this chapter.**

Adding Custom and Built-in Commands to the QAT

Adding custom and built-in commands to the QAT is very simple. You already know the difference between a shared control and a document control. (A *control* is a generic object that can represent a button, a splitButton, a group, etc.)

A Quick Access Toolbar shared or document control has the child elements shown in Table 14-3.

Table 14-3: Child Elements of the Quick Access Toolbar

OBJECT	WHAT IT IS FOR
control	Refers to a generic control object that can represent other objects such as a button, splitButton, group, etc.
button	Refers to a button control
separator	Refers to a separator control

Let's start with a simple example that adds a built-in control and a custom button. The result is shown in Figure 14-4.

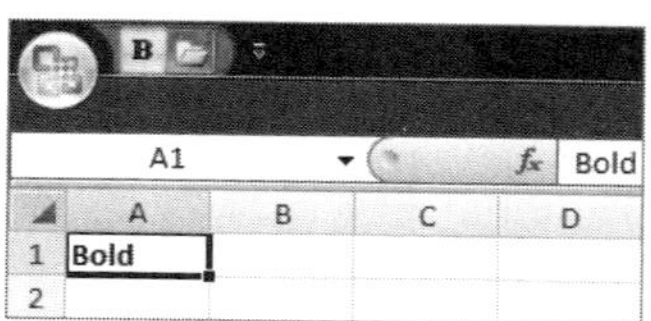

Figure 14-4: Custom button and built-in control added to the QAT

The following XML code adds both a built-in control and a custom button to the QAT:

```
<qat>
   <documentControls>
      <control idMso="Bold"
         screentip="Make it Bold"
         supertip="Click here to make the selected text bold."/>
      <button id="rxbtnOpen"
         imageMso="FileOpen"
         screentip="This is Happy"
         supertip="Click here for a happy message"
         onAction="rxbtnOpen_click"/>
   </documentControls>
</qat>
```

You use the `control` object to refer to a built-in button (in this case, the command button for Bold), and then use a button to create your own customized button. (By that we mean you can use the `control` object to refer to other controls such as a `button` or `splitButton`.) Think of it as the VBA generic `Object` class, which can morph into other objects as needed.)

In the next example, we create a `splitButton` control and then add it to the QAT. Because the QAT has no `splitButton` child element, we have to create the `splitButton` outside the QAT and then refer it back to the QAT. You do so by adding the `splitButton` control in the normal way — that is, you start by adding it to a group

```
<group id="rxgrp"
   label="My Custom Group">
   <splitButton id="rxsbtn"
      size="large">
      <button id="rxbtn2"
         imageMso="HappyFace"
         label="My Happy Split"/>
      <menu id="rxmnu">
         <button id="rxbtn3"
            label="My Happy Menu"
            imageMso="HappyFace"
            onAction="rxbtn3_click"/>
      </menu>
   </splitButton>
</group>
```

In the preceding example, we have the `splitButton` and with a menu on it. The menu, in turn, contains a button. Since QAT uses existing controls, you can now refer to the existing splitButton in the QAT, as shown in the following XML code:

```
<qat>
   <documentControls>
   <control id="rxsbtn"
      imageMso="HappyFace"
      screentip="This is Happy"
      supertip="Click here for a happy message"/>
```

```
    </documentControls>
  </qat>
```

The customization should look like what is shown in Figure 14-5.

Figure 14-5: Custom splitButton added to the QAT

You can access the full working examples of this section in this chapter's download on the book's website. If it still seems a bit confusing, just run through the file a couple of times. Then you'll be ready to move on to adding entire groups to the QAT.

Adding Custom and Built-in Groups to the QAT

Customizing the QAT is not just a matter of adding a button or two. As you have already seen, you can add entire groups to the QAT, which enables you to have frequently used commands just two clicks away. Of course, we had to jump through a few hoops to get what we wanted, but so far it's been worth it.

You are now ready to move a step further and use XML code to build your own groups. These can be added to the QAT along with built-in groups and individual controls.

If you look at the XML schema for the QAT you will not find anything about groups, which, at first glance, may seem odd. However, the QAT draws controls from the tabs. What this means is that you must first create the groups; then, from the QAT, you can refer to the id specified for the group (in the same way we did with the `splitButton` in the previous example).

The good news is that you can add groups to a tab and keep them invisible on the tab but visible on the QAT. Figure 14-6 illustrates this scenario.

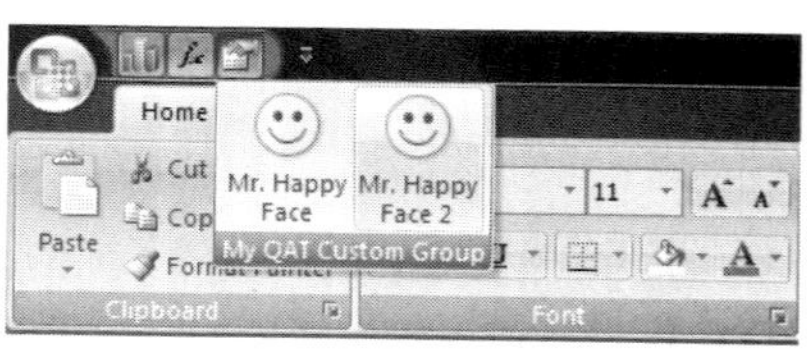

Figure 14-6: Built-in groups and customs groups on the QAT

`My QAT Custom Group` belongs to the custom `Home` tab (this is "custom" because we started from scratch and placed a "Home" tab in the UI). However, we keep its visibility set to `false`. In doing so, we can add other groups and controls to the tab and keep only those critical groups on the QAT. In fact, you could have all the built-in tabs on the

Ribbon and add hidden groups to any of the built-in tabs, only showing your groups on the QAT.

Have a look at the XML code for the preceding example and then we'll explain how it functions:

```
<customUI xmlns="http://schemas.microsoft.com/office/2006/01/customui">
   <ribbon startFromScratch="true">
      <tabs>
         <tab id="rxtabHome"
            label="Home">
            <group id="rxgrp"
               label="My QAT Custom Group"
               getVisible="rxshared_getVisible">
               <button id="rxbtnHappy"
                  label="Mr. Happy Face"
                  imageMso="HappyFace"
                  size="large"
                  onAction="rxshared_click"/>
               <button id="rxbtnHappy2"
                  label="Mr. Happy Face 2"
                  imageMso="HappyFace"
                  size="large"
                  onAction="rxshared_click"/>
            </group>
         </tab>
      </tabs>

      <qat>
         <documentControls>
            <control idMso="GroupInsertChartsExcel"/>
            <control idMso="GroupFont"/>
            <control id="rxgrp"
               imageMso="GroupFunctionLibrary"/>
         </documentControls>
      </qat>
   </ribbon>
</customUI>
```

Here's how it works:

- We start the customization from scratch — a requirement when working with the QAT.
- We set up a custom tab and group in the normal way and add two buttons to it as an example.
- We set the `getVisible` attribute to `False` so it does not show up on the tab.
- With the group set up within a tab, we open the QAT tag. We add two built-in groups to the QAT (Clipboard and Font) and use the generic `control` object to refer back to the custom group we want on the QAT. We also assign a built-in image to the group (if you don't, a generic image is shown instead).

That's all there is to it.

NOTE **If you ran through this example and could not see a group loaded to the QAT, read the section "QAT Caveats" later in this chapter.**

Repurposing QAT Controls

Repurposing a control in the QAT is very similar to general repurposing of a control in any group. Figure 14-7 shows two commands repurposed in Word.

When you repurpose a control in the QAT, you in fact repurpose a command associated with it. (A command would typically be an element that is available throughout the project, such as the `Paste` command.) You then add the same command to the QAT as a control (either shared or document specific).

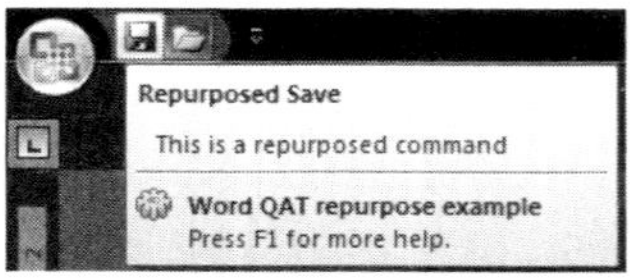

Figure 14-7: Repurposing QAT commands

One great advantage of repurposing is that it has a global effect on the control, unlike previous versions of Office in which you had to disable each instance of the control.

In this Word example, we devised the following XML to repurpose the two controls `File Open` and `File Save`:

```
<customUI xmlns="http://schemas.microsoft.com/office/2006/01/customui">
   <commands>
      <command idMso="FileSave"
         onAction="rxFileSave_repurpose"/>
      <command idMso="FileOpen"
         onAction="rxFileOpen_repurpose"/>
   </commands>

   <ribbon startFromScratch="true">
      <qat>
         <documentControls>
            <control idMso="FileSave"
               screentip="Repurposed Save"
               supertip="This is a repurposed command"/>
            <control idMso="FileOpen"
               screentip="Repurposed File Open"
               supertip="This is a repurposed command"/>
         </documentControls>
      </qat>
   </ribbon>
</customUI>
```

In the preceding XML code, we begin by declaring the commands we want to repurpose and assigning a macro to each control. Next, we open the Ribbon tag and define the commands we want to appear on the QAT.

As pointed out, this has a global effect. Thus, if you click on any of the commands or use shortcuts that point to the command (in this specific case, Ctrl+0 and Ctrl+s), then the command will point to the callback you assigned for the `onAction` attribute.

NOTE The preceding paragraph applies to Word. If you repurpose commands in Excel or Access, then the shortcut remains fully operative, even though the command itself is disabled globally.

In Excel and Access, you would use a different approach. Excel has a handy method named `OnKey` that is triggered when a specific key or combination of keys is pressed. This is an application-wide method, so once you disable a command in a workbook, all other workbooks opened during the same session will have the same commands disabled. Access, conversely, treats each project independently. Hence, what you do in one project does not affect other projects.

We begin by looking at how to handle this problem in Access. We won't give you the UI XML code, as you can adapt it from the Word example already given. The main difference is not in the XML code, but in how you will handle it in VBA or through macro objects in Access. Here we concentrate on blocking the shortcuts keys. You accomplish this in Access by adding a macro object named `AutoKeys`. When you have added the macro, open it in Design View and ensure that the Macro Name column is toggled to display. Figure 14-8 shows the `macro` object set up.

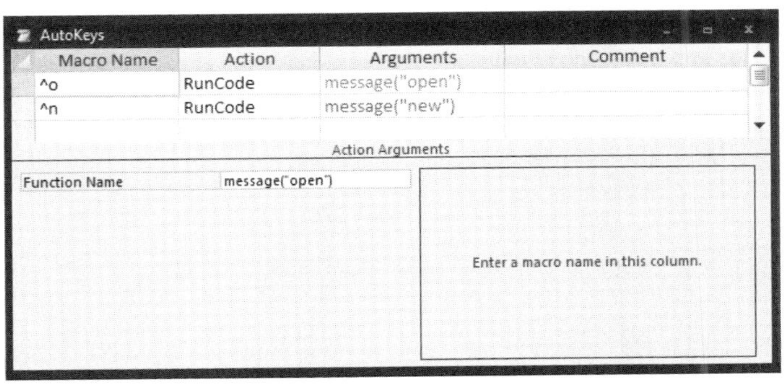

Figure 14-8: Repurposing QAT commands

The `Macro Name` represents the shortcut we want and the `Action` determines what should be done once the keys are pressed. Finally, the arguments point to a custom function placed in a standard module, which takes a string argument that represents the name of the actions we want to perform (`"open"` and `"new"`).

Once that has been set up, all you need to do is handle the function referenced in the `macro` object. The following function is an example of what you could do:

```
Function message(ByVal strCaller As String)
    Select Case UCase(strCaller)
```

```
        Case "OPEN"
            MsgBox "The 'Open Database' " _
                & "button "has been " _
                & "repurposed.", vbExclamation
        Case "NEW"
            MsgBox "The 'File New Database' " _
                & "button has been " _
                & "repurposed.", vbExclamation
    End Select
End Function
```

Table 14-4 shows the shortcut combination keys that you can use in Access macros. We "repurposed" the commands to provide a message box that advises the user that the command does not function as anticipated.

Table 14-4: Shortcut Combination Keys for Access

KEY	REPRESENT BY THE SYMBOL
Control	^
Function	{F1}
Shift	+

If you define the macro name as `^+o`, this states that the shortcut is represented by the combination Ctrl+Shift+O.

Excel, on the other hand, works differently, so you may need to evaluate different scenarios to decide when the shortcut should be cancelled. If the shortcut is to be cancelled only for the workbook that contains the UI, you need to undo the shortcut cancellation when you move to another workbook, when a workbook is opened, and so on. Because this is an application-wide event, you would need to use a class module to monitor for and respond to moves between workbooks.

CROSS-REFERENCE **See Chapter 4 if you need a refresher on class modules and events.**

Add a new class module to the Excel project. You can name the class whatever you like, but the name used in our example is `clsAppExcelEvents`. The class module will contain the following procedures:

```
Public WithEvents appXL     As Excel.Application

Private Sub ShortcutsEnabled(ByVal blnEnabled As Boolean)
    Select Case blnEnabled
        Case Is = True
            Application.OnKey "^o"
            Application.OnKey "^s"
```

```
        Case Is = False
            Application.OnKey "^o", _
              "commandDisabled"
            Application.OnKey "^s", _
              "commandDisabled"
    End Select
End Sub

Private Sub setEnabled(ByVal Wb As Workbook)
    Select Case Wb.Name
        Case Is = ThisWorkbook.Name
            ShortcutsEnabled False
        Case Else
            ShortcutsEnabled True
    End Select
End Sub
```

Notice that we declare the Excel application in the General Declarations area of the class module. There are two procedures to carry out the task: One procedure checks which workbook is the active one and the other specifies the `OnKey` method. For the two key combinations we're after, we point to another procedure, named `commandDisabled`, which must be placed in a standard module.

In the class module, you can specify which events to monitor. For example, you could monitor the activation or deactivation of a workbook to decide whether the shortcut should be cancelled or not:

```
Private Sub appXL_WorkbookActivate(ByVal Wb As Workbook)
    setEnabled Wb
End Sub

Private Sub appXL_WorkbookDeactivate(ByVal Wb As Workbook)
    setEnabled Wb
End Sub
```

Finally, you need to set the class when the project opens. This is done using the `Open` event of the workbook that contains the project:

```
Dim XL      As New clsAppExcelEvents

Private Sub Workbook_Open()
    Set XL.appXL = Application
End Sub
```

This section provided a variety of sample files for Excel, Access, and Word. The files are available for download from the book's website.

The next section discusses how to build customization with the help of tables to hold information about the UI.

Table-Driven Approach for QAT Customization (Excel and Word)

A lot has been said about how much flexibility was lost when it comes to building a custom UI in Office 2007. One of the biggest complaints stems from the fact that we can no longer take a table-driven approach to customizing the UI.

Although it is true that you cannot build the entire UI on-the-fly from tables, you can still accomplish lot with tables. In fact, using tables can simplify some of the work you do in XML prior to moving it to the UI.

Figure 14-9 shows one such example of customization that uses tables to load details to the QAT.

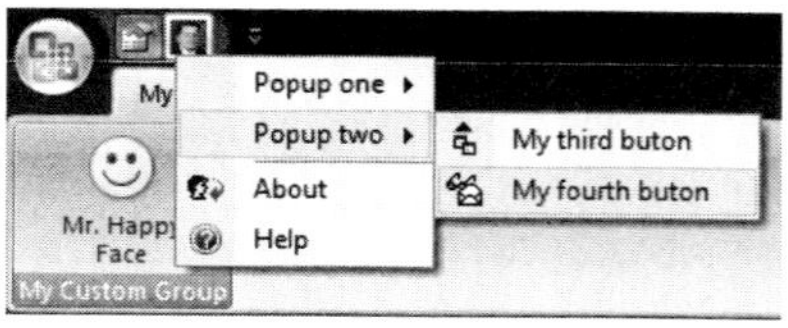

Figure 14-9: Table-drive QAT customization

This type of customization has been around for quite a while and has always applied to toolbar customization. The first step to successfully implement this solution is to build your XML code containing your UI and a QAT button to take the menu. We created a document control button as follows:

```
<documentControls>
   <control id="rxgrp"
      imageMso="AdvancedFileProperties"/>
   <button id="rxbtnShowPopup"
      image="rob"
      onAction="rxbtnShowPopup_Click"/>
</documentControls>
```

This XML code will generate the two QAT buttons you see in Figure 14-9. The key here is the callback assigned to the `onAction` attribute. This is the click that will show the menu after the custom button is clicked.

The next step is to create the table that will contain your menu details. Figure 14-10 shows a suggestion.

	A	B	C	D	E
1	TYPE	CAPTION	DIVIDER	FACEID	ONACTION
2	POPUP	Popup one		126	
3	BUTTON	My first buton		1024	
4	BUTTON	My second buton	TRUE	630	
5	POPUP	Popup two		412	
6	BUTTON	My third buton		525	
7	BUTTON	My fourth buton		324	
8	BUTTON_STANDALONE	About	TRUE	326	showAbout
9	BUTTON_STANDALONE	Help		984	showHelp
10					
11	POPUP BUTTON				
12	BUTTON_STANDALONE				

Figure 14-10: Table containing the suggested customization items

This table is just a suggestion because you may consider adding more options to it. With the table set up with all the details you want, you're ready for the VBA that will read through the table and built the menu:

```
Public Const POPNAME As String = "MY POPUP"

Sub loadPopup()
    Dim mnuWs As Worksheet
    Dim cmdbar As CommandBar
    Dim cmdbarPopup As CommandBarPopup
    Dim cmdbarBtn As CommandBarButton
    Dim nRowCount As Long

    Call unloadPopup
    Set mnuWs = ThisWorkbook.Sheets("MenuItems")
    Set cmdbar = Application.CommandBars.Add(POPNAME, msoBarPopup)

    nRowCount = 2
    With mnuWs
        Do Until IsEmpty(.Cells(nRowCount, 1))

            Select Case UCase(.Cells(nRowCount, 1))
                Case "POPUP"
                    Set cmdbarPopup = _
                        cmdbar.Controls.Add(msoControlPopup)
                    cmdbarPopup.Caption = .Cells(nRowCount, 2)
                    If .Cells(nRowCount, 3) <> "" Then
                        cmdbarPopup.BeginGroup = True
                    End If

                Case "BUTTON"
                    Set cmdbarBtn = _
                        cmdbarPopup.Controls.Add(msoControlButton)
                    cmdbarBtn.Caption = .Cells(nRowCount, 2)
                    If .Cells(nRowCount, 3) <> "" Then
                        cmdbarBtn.BeginGroup = True
                    End If
                    cmdbarBtn.FaceId = .Cells(nRowCount, 4)
                    cmdbarBtn.OnAction = .Cells(nRowCount, 5)

                Case "BUTTON_STANDALONE"
                    Set cmdbarBtn = _
                        cmdbar.Controls.Add(msoControlButton)
                    cmdbarBtn.Caption = .Cells(nRowCount, 2)
                    If .Cells(nRowCount, 3) <> "" Then
                        cmdbarBtn.BeginGroup = True
                    End If
                    cmdbarBtn.FaceId = .Cells(nRowCount, 4)
                    cmdbarBtn.OnAction = .Cells(nRowCount, 5)
            End Select
```

```
            nRowCount = nRowCount + 1
        Loop
    End With
End Sub
```

Finally, you need the VBA for the callbacks. You use the `onLoad` event to call the `loadPopup` procedure so that the pop-up is built and ready to use when you click its button on the QAT. We also have the click event that will show the pop-up menu when the click occurs:

```
Sub rxIRibbonUI_onLoad(ribbon As IRibbonUI)
    On Error Resume Next
    Set grxIRibbonUI = ribbon

    Application.Workbooks.Add
    If ActiveWorkbook.Name <> ThisWorkbook.Name Then
        With ActiveWorkbook
            .Saved = True
            .Close
        End With
    End If

'   You can load the popup menu from this event or
'   from the Open event of ThisWorkbook
    Call loadPopup
End Sub

Sub rxbtnShowPopup_Click(control As IRibbonControl)
    On Error Resume Next
    Application.CommandBars(POPNAME).ShowPopup
End Sub
```

NOTE **You can find a similar example for Word in the sample files available from the book's website.**

Table-Driven Approach for QAT Customization (Access)

You've learned how to load a custom pop-up menu in Excel, and it is hoped that you have worked through the last example and even downloaded and tested the example for Word. Now we'll look at an example for Access, which works a bit differently for this technique. The goal is to build something similar to what's shown in Figure 14-11.

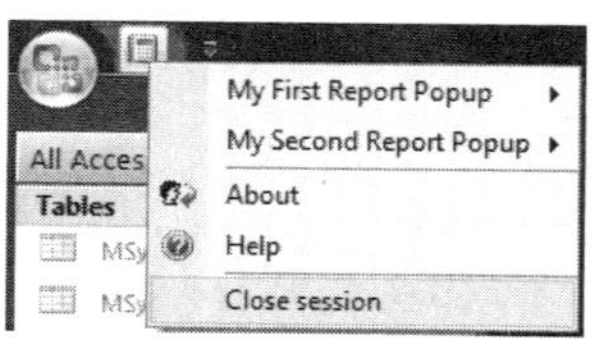

Figure 14-11: Table-driven QAT customization in Access

The idea behind this example is pretty much the same as the Excel and Word examples. We use a table to store information about the menu, which is in turn loaded when the database is open. Figure 14-12 shows a suggested table layout (and name: `tblMenuDetails`).

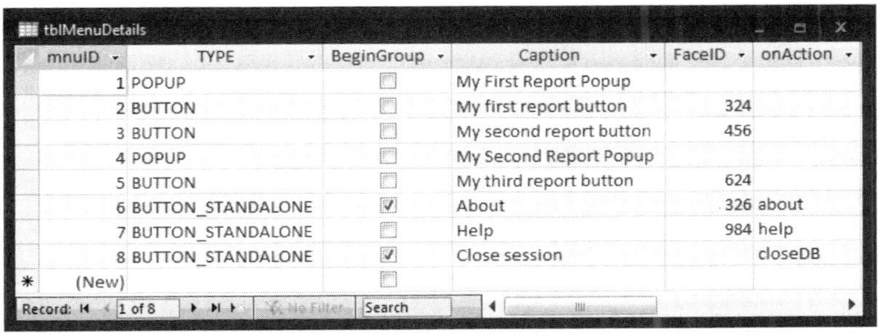

tblMenuDetails

mnuID	TYPE	BeginGroup	Caption	FaceID	onAction
1	POPUP	☐	My First Report Popup		
2	BUTTON	☐	My first report button	324	
3	BUTTON	☐	My second report button	456	
4	POPUP	☐	My Second Report Popup		
5	BUTTON	☐	My third report button	624	
6	BUTTON_STANDALONE	☑	About	326	about
7	BUTTON_STANDALONE	☐	Help	984	help
8	BUTTON_STANDALONE	☑	Close session		closeDB
(New)		☐			

Record: 1 of 8 Search

Figure 14-12: Table containing the suggested customization items

Again, you can expand the contents of the table to suit your needs. Our goal is to keep the example short and simple so that we can focus on the technique, rather than the product.

One of the key points here is to specify when to run the code that builds the pop-up menu. Obviously, it must be run when the project opens. You can choose from various methods, such as using an auto-executable macro, or a less conventional method, such as through a form. We believe that using the `onLoad` event (placed in a standard module) of the Ribbon is the perfect time to run the code:

```
Function rxIRibbonUI_onLoad(ribbon As IRibbonUI)
    Set grxIRibbonUI = ribbon
    Call mnu
End Function
```

In this example, we use a built-in control and repurpose it so that when it is clicked, the pop-up menu is shown. We do not repeat the XML code here because it is a single control and by now you have quite a bit of experience with creating a single control for the QAT.

The step that we are concerned with is ensuring that the pop-up menu is shown when the repurposed control is clicked. This is accomplished with a simple line of code in the callback of the repurposed control:

```
Sub rxCreateReport_repurpose(control As IRibbonControl, _
    ByRef cancelDefault)
    Application.CommandBars(POPNAME).ShowPopup
End Sub
```

NOTE `POPNAME` **is a string constant representing the name you want to give to your menu. This was shown on the previous example for Excel and Word. We use exactly the same structure for the benefit of the example, making it easier to follow.**

You now have the two callbacks for the Ribbon: `rxIRibbonUI_onLoad` and `rxCreateReport_repurpose`. Now we need the procedure that will build the menu. We will use the procedure `Sub mnu()` (outlined in the following example) in the `onLoad` event. In order to compartmentalize the procedures, you may want to add a new standard module with this code, which builds the menu into the new module. A more detailed explanation is provided at the end of the code:

```
Public Const POPNAME   As String = "MY POPUP"

Sub mnu()
    Dim cmdbar As CommandBar
    Dim cmdbarPopup As CommandBarPopup
    Dim cmdbarBtn As CommandBarButton
    Dim db As Dao.Database
    Dim rst As Dao.Recordset
    Dim strTYPE As String

    Set db = CurrentDb ()
    Set rst = db.OpenRecordset("tblMenuDetails", dbOpenTable)

    On Error Resume Next
    CommandBars(POPNAME).Delete

    If (rst.EOF) Then
        MsgBox "Sorry, there are no items to add to your custom popup!", _
            vbInformation
    Else
        Set cmdbar = Application.CommandBars.Add(POPNAME, msoBarPopup)
        Do While (Not (rst.EOF))
            strTYPE = UCase(rst![Type])

            Select Case strTYPE
                Case "POPUP"
                    Set cmdbarPopup = _
                        cmdbar.Controls.Add(Type:=msoControlPopup)
                    With cmdbarPopup
                        .Caption = rst![Caption]
                        .Width = rst![Width]
                        .BeginGroup = rst![BeginGroup]
                    End With

                Case "BUTTON"
                    Set cmdbarBtn = _
                        cmdbarPopup.Controls.Add(Type:=msoControlButton)
                    With cmdbarBtn
                        .BeginGroup = rst![BeginGroup]
                        .Caption = rst![Caption]
                        .FaceId = rst![FaceId]
                        .OnAction = rst![OnAction]
                    End With

                Case "BUTTON_STANDALONE"
```

```
                Set cmdbarBtn = _
                    cmdbar.Controls.Add(Type:=msoControlButton)
                With cmdbarBtn
                    .BeginGroup = rst![BeginGroup]
                    .Caption = rst![Caption]
                    .FaceId = rst![FaceId]
                    .OnAction = rst![OnAction]
                End With
            End Select

            rst.MoveNext
        Loop
    End If

    rst.Close
    db.Close
    Set rst = Nothing
    Set db = Nothing
End Sub
```

We use DAO to get an instance of the database and a recordset because DAO is native to Access and does not require adding or changing the priority of references, as you need to do when using ADO. After instantiating the database and opening the recordset, the code removes the pop-up menu. This is just a precaution in case it was left behind from previous customization, as you do not want duplicates.

You then check for records that define the buttons in the group. If no records are available, then there is nothing to be placed in the pop-up menu. Conversely, if there *are* items in the recordset, the code loops through the records and builds the pop-up menu. You close with a few clean-up tasks, such as closing the database and setting the record set and database equal to nothing.

QAT Caveats

Although the QAT is a great way to customize your working environment, it does seem to suffer from a few drawbacks that might be considered bugs in the current build of Microsoft Office. And, being the considerate people that we are, we thought we'd mention a few of those issues here and help fellow developers avoid unnecessary frustration.

Inability to Load Controls

When working with custom controls such as buttons and groups, you will find that Excel, Access, and Word sometimes fail to load the controls upon opening the project. This is particularly common when using `sharedControls`. Be assured that this is not a fault in your customizations; instead, it can be attributed to a bug that sporadically manifests itself. (As with other known bugs, we want to advise you of the situation and provide some options that you can consider using pending a fix.)

One workaround is to refresh the window by either minimizing it and then maximizing it back or by loading and then promptly unloading a blank file on top of the window containing the problematic custom UI.

That brings us to another problem: loading custom images to QAT.

Inability to Load Custom Images to Controls

Loading custom images can also be tricky in the same way that loading custom controls and groups can be. All the applications discussed in this book encounter problems when loading custom images to the QAT if the QAT contains both shared and document-specific controls. Shared controls seem particularly tricky because they tend to behave erratically, and therefore do not provide a reliable and coherent interface. For the time being at least, we recommend not using custom images in the shared controls area.

As for document controls, you can work around the problem by using the following procedure to refresh the window that contains the UI:

```
Sub rxIRibbonUI_onLoad(ribbon As IRibbonUI)
    Set grxIRibbonUI = ribbon
    On Error Resume Next
    Application.Workbooks.Add
    If ActiveWorkbook.Name <> ThisWorkbook.Name Then
        With ActiveWorkbook
            .Saved = True
            .Close
        End With
    End If
End Sub
```

The preceding procedure is for Excel, but it can be replicated to function equally well in Word. All you have to do is replace the `ActiveWorkbook`, `Workbooks`, and `ThisWorkbook` objects with `ActiveDocument`, `Documents` and `ThisDocument` objects, respectively.

Regretfully, we did not discover an acceptable workaround for Access. The only alternative seems to be to repurpose built-in controls.

NOTE The preceding example can be used to work around the inability to load custom controls, especially when working with custom groups that normally do not load on opening the project.

Duplication of Controls on XML-Based and XML-Free Customizations

Duplication of controls in the QAT normally happens when you switch between workbooks or documents. Suppose you have a workbook or document that contains a QAT customization. When you press Alt+Tab to move to another document and then return to the customized workbook or document, the controls on the QAT are duplicated, triplicated, quadruplicated . . . well, you get the point.

Figure 14-13 shows this duplication scenario, taken from an example already shown in this chapter.

Figure 14-13: Duplication of controls on the QAT

This duplication can propagate to other workbooks and documents that do not even contain any XML customization. They seem to be most susceptible when they contain document controls, but it can affect workbooks and documents that contain any form of Ribbon customizations. Therefore, if you (or others using your files) are moving between documents, you may think that you are working too hard and seeing double, as shown in Figure 14-14.

Figure 14-14: Duplication of controls on the QAT on a XML-free customization

Although we don't have a vaccine, the antidote will reverse the effect. To get rid of the extra controls, you simply need to close and reopen the document. In the worst-case scenario, you may need to exit the application and reopen it.

Conclusion

This chapter covered customization of the Office Menu and the Quick Access Toolbar, and provided a lot of new material. You learned the difference between a shared control and a document control, and even how to distinguish document controls based on the border that surrounds them. You also learned the key ideas behind adding items to the QAT, including both custom and built-in controls and groups.

In addition, this chapter kept you busy with topics such as a table-driven approach to customizing the QAT, adding custom pictures, and repurposing built-in commands. It also explained how to handle shortcuts in Excel and Access that are not disabled through repurposing. You also learned about a few inconvenient issues with QAT customization, such as duplication of controls and some of the peculiar challenges you face when loading custom controls and images.

At this point in the book, you have been introduced to all the tools you need to professionally customize both the Office Menu and the QAT. With that under your belt, you're ready to move on to contextual controls, which you to make your customizations appear when, and only when, they are relevant.

CHAPTER

15

Working with Contextual Controls

Contextual tabs offer a tremendous boost to the functionality of the new UI. These are specialized tabs that appear when the user is performing a specific task on certain objects. For example, when working with a chart in Excel, a contextual tab provides additional options specific to chart handling. The same goes for tables in Word, and forms and reports in Access.

In this chapter, you learn how to create and implement these specialized tabs, as well as how to modify built-in ones. You also learn how to customize or replace the built-in pop-up menus and how to create your own contextual pop-up menus. Finally, we discuss creating a multilingual UI.

As you are preparing to work through the examples in this chapter, we encourage you to download the companion files. The source code and files can be found on the book's website at `www.wiley.com/go/ribbonx`.

Making Your Items Contextual

Making an item contextual implies that it must react to the context of what is being done, such as manipulating a table or a picture. According to the pure definition of context-sensitive controls, you would need to use a contextual tab collection to carry out the task in the new Office UI. However, this is not always possible or practical, so we will show you some alternatives and workarounds.

This section introduces you to the concept of contextual controls, such as tabs, groups, and general controls.

Tabs

When it comes to context-sensitive commands, what immediately comes to mind are the contextual tabs. An integral part of the Ribbon's functionality, these specialized tabs will appear and disappear from the Ribbon depending on which object is selected or has the focus, such as a chart, pivot table, tabs, or picture. For example, when you are working on a picture in Microsoft Word, you have the special Picture Tools tab, with the commands that are relevant to working with pictures, as shown in Figure 15-1.

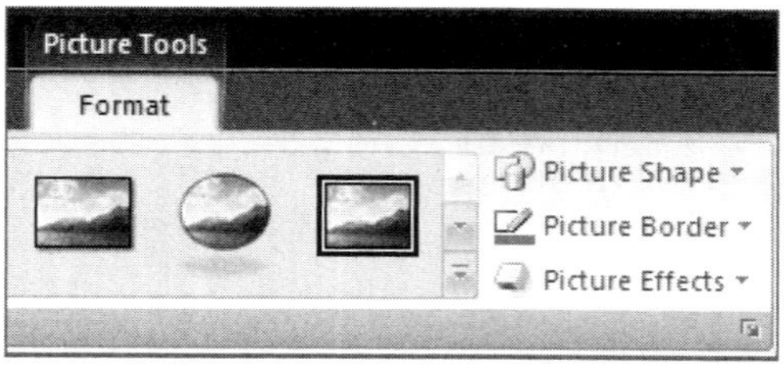

Figure 15-1: Picture Tools contextual tabSet with the Format tab

Figure 15-1 shows a `tabSet` named Picture Tools that contains one tab, which is named Format. In order to implement such a solution, you need to use the contextual tabs collection and the `tabSet` element. The following XML markup works as the container for contextual `tabSets` and the corresponding tabs:

```
<customUI xmlns="http://schemas.microsoft.com/office/2006/01/customui">
   <ribbon>
      <contextualTabs>
         <tabSet>

            <!-- Your contextual tab code goes here -->

         </tabSet>
      </contextualTabs>
   </ribbon>
</customUI>
```

The `contextualTabs` collection is the parent object for each `tabSet` in the same way that the tab's `collection` object is the parent object for a tab.

You can use the preceding code to create your own context-sensitive functionality and to access built-in `tabSets` to modify them. Unfortunately, the extensibility of such `tabSets` does not apply to Excel or Word; only Access's forms and reports offer such extensibility. When working with custom contextual `tabSets` in Access, you need to refer to the extensibility `tabSet` in the following manner:

```
<tabSet idMso="TabSetFormReportExtensibility">
```

It is within this `tabSet` that you will build the contextual UI.

For Excel and Word, you need to work around this deficit by either taking full control over a built-in contextual tab or by using events combined with the `getVisible` attribute to make tabs behave as though they are contextual. This is essentially the process that is used in our upcoming example for working with groups in Excel worksheets.

CROSS-REFERENCE **See Chapter 12 for a full working example of how to use `getVisible` to imitate contextuality.**

Groups

Groups are not contextual objects per se — that is, they are dependent on the `tabSet` and tab to which they belong — so by default they will only appear and disappear in conjunction with the parent `tabSet`. In order to give a group the appearance of being context sensitive, we recommend using the `getVisible` attribute.

To demonstrate this, consider a scenario in which you want to have the group Font and the group Insert Chart visible only when the user is working with Sheet1 in an Excel workbook.

Begin by inspecting the XML code used in this example:

```
<customUI xmlns="http://schemas.microsoft.com/office/2006/01/customui"
   onLoad="rxIRibbonUI_onLoad">
   <ribbon startFromScratch="false">
      <tabs>
         <tab idMso="TabHome">
            <group idMso="GroupFont"
               getVisible="rxShared_getVisible"/>
         </tab>
         <tab idMso="TabInsert">
            <group idMso="GroupInsertChartsExcel"
               getVisible="rxShared_getVisible"/>
         </tab>
      </tabs>
   </ribbon>
</customUI>
```

CROSS-REFERENCE **This example is based on the material covered in Chapter 12. If that seems like the distant past at this point, a quick review might be all it takes to get up to speed.**

The XML code is very simple. You start with an `onLoad` callback that sets the `Ribbon` object. Then you assign a shared callback to the `getVisible` attribute for the two groups, `GroupFont` and `GroupInsertChartsExcel`.

Using the shared callback defined in the XML, you can now determine the attribute's returned value by using a custom property for the particular worksheet you want to monitor. That is accomplished with the following code:

```
Sub rxShared_getVisible(control As IRibbonControl, ByRef returnedVal)
    Select Case control.id
        Case "GroupFont"
            returnedVal = Sheet1.rxGroupFontVisible
        Case "GroupInsertChartsExcel"
            returnedVal = Sheet1.rxGroupInsertChartsExcel
    End Select
End Sub
```

The attribute value is set according to the custom property value. First, set the `Ribbon` object when the document is opened so that you have set the Ribbon as a property of the `ThisWorkbook` object. The following code must be inserted in the `ThisWorkbook` code window:

```
Private pRibbonUI               As IRibbonUI

Public Property Let rxIRibbonUI(iRib As IRibbonUI)
    Set pRibbonUI = iRib
End Property

Public Property Get rxIRibbonUI() As IRibbonUI
    Set rxIRibbonUI = pRibbonUI
End Property
```

Second, specify the custom property for the sheet you want to monitor, which is done using the following code. This custom property is read/write so that a value can be reassigned to the property at any time during execution:

```
Private pblnGroupFontVisible        As Boolean
Private pblnGroupChartVisible       As Boolean

Property Let rxGroupFontVisible(ByVal blnVisible As Boolean)
    pblnGroupFontVisible = blnVisible
End Property

Property Get rxGroupFontVisible() As Boolean
   rxGroupFontVisible = pblnGroupFontVisible
End Property

Property Let rxGroupInsertChartsExcel(ByVal blnVisible As Boolean)
    pblnGroupChartVisible = blnVisible
End Property

Property Get rxGroupInsertChartsExcel() As Boolean
   rxGroupInsertChartsExcel = pblnGroupChartVisible
End Property
```

Finally, you can change the custom property according to your needs. Here, we want to show the groups when a specific worksheet is active, so we use the `Worksheet_Activate` and `Worksheet_Deactivate` events to change the properties values, as shown here:

```
Private Sub Worksheet_Activate()
    Sheet1.rxGroupFontVisible = True
    Sheet1.rxGroupInsertChartsExcel = True
    ThisWorkbook.rxIRibbonUI.Invalidate
End Sub

Private Sub Worksheet_Deactivate()
    Sheet1.rxGroupFontVisible = False
    Sheet1.rxGroupInsertChartsExcel = False
    ThisWorkbook.rxIRibbonUI.Invalidate
End Sub
```

As the sheet activates/deactivates, the groups are shown or hidden accordingly.

Working Through Nonvisibility Methods

Using visibility to create context-sensitive tabs and groups may be somewhat unorthodox, but it is an effective way to achieve your goals. However, this approach is not available in all circumstances — especially if you are working with built-in controls in built-in groups.

In cases where it is not feasible to make a control visible or invisible, we suggest yet another workaround: Plan B is to enable and disable the controls.

Enabling and Disabling Controls

As you have already seen, you can use the `enabled` attribute to determine whether a control is enabled or not. We've also provided some techniques for circumventing some of the issues that may be associated with disabling controls.

NOTE **Although disabling controls has its advantages, it also carries the risk of removing some functionality that is critical to end users.**

We now look at providing context-sensitive controls through the use of the `getEnabled` property. This method is actually quite simple and follows the same logic as the visibility examples. The difference, of course, is the method used. As you will remember, to disable a command, you must refer to the command itself and the button or a generic control. For example, the XML code for disabling the two commands `Copy` and `Cut` would look something like the following:

```
<customUI xmlns="http://schemas.microsoft.com/office/2006/01/customui"
   onLoad="rxIRibbonUI_onLoad">
```

```
    <commands>
       <command idMso="Copy" getEnabled="rxshared_getEnabled"/>
       <command idMso="Cut" getEnabled="rxshared_getEnabled"/>
    </commands>
</customUI>
```

The next step is simply to add a shared callback to handle procedures to be executed:

```
Sub rxshared_getEnabled(control As IRibbonControl, ByRef returnedVal)
    Select Case control.id
        Case "Copy"
            returnedVal = Sheet1.rxCopyEnabled
        Case "Cut"
            returnedVal = Sheet1.rxCutEnabled
    End Select
End Sub
```

Again, you use custom properties to specify the returned value for the callbacks, which results in a much neater way to work through the standard module holding the callbacks for the Ribbon.

Working with Contextual Tabs and tabSets

You already know something about the contextual tab container, and that it is the parent for a `tabSet`. When customizing Access, you must use the extensibility `tabSet`. We start this section by looking at how things work in Access, as this will provide the most comprehensive exposure to contextuality. After that, we analyze examples in Excel and Word.

Creating a Custom Contextual Tab in Access

As you have learned in previous chapters, Access is unique when it comes to customization. One of the unique aspects refers to contextual tabs for forms and reports. In this section, we will use that feature to create the custom, context-sensitive tab that is shown in Figure 15-2.

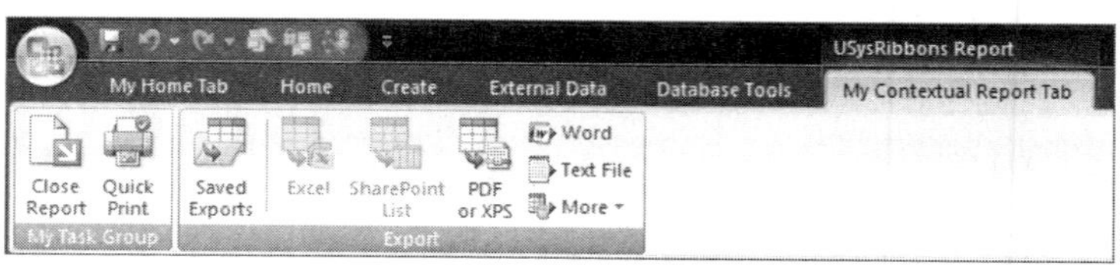

Figure 15-2: Custom contextual tab for an Access report

Figure 15-2 shows our usual custom tab (My Home Tab), which contains a button to open the report. Once the report is open, the contextual tab My Contextual Report Tab is shown. Because this is based solely on the opening and closing of the report, it does not require a callback to handle the contextual tab's visibility.

The first task, as usual, is to prepare the XML code. The following example provides the complete code that will generate the UI shown in Figure 15-2. After reading through the code, you can compare notes with our explanation of what is happening:

```
<customUI xmlns="http://schemas.microsoft.com/office/2006/01/customui">
   <ribbon>
      <contextualTabs>
         <tabSet idMso="TabSetFormReportExtensibility">
            <tab id="rxtab"
               label="My Contextual Report Tab">

               <group id="rxgrp"
                  label="My Task Group">
                  <button id="rxbtnCloseRpt"
                     label="Close Report"
                     imageMso="FileCheckOut"
                     supertip="Click here to close the active report..."
                     size="large"
                     onAction="Macros.closeReport"/>
                  <button idMso="FilePrintQuick"
                     supertip="Click here to print the active report..."
                     size="large"/>
               </group>

               <group idMso="GroupExport"/>
            </tab>
         </tabSet>
      </contextualTabs>
   </ribbon>
</customUI>
```

Here, we use the `TabSetFormReportExtensibility tabSet` to be able to present the user with the contextual tab shown previously. We created the tab "My Contextual Report Tab" to hold the custom group "My Task Group." That group has two custom buttons for closing and printing reports. Obviously, you would need to add additional code to carry out any actions, but the purpose of this exercise is to create a contextual tab.

With this XML code ready to copy, add a new record to your `USysRibbons` table in Access, enter a name for this Ribbon, and paste the XML code into its corresponding field.

Unlike the main Ribbon that loads when the Access project opens (which you select from the Access options window), for a report or a form the UI is loaded using the `Ribbon Name` property found in the property window for these two objects.

The `Ribbon Name` property can be obtained by one of the following methods:

- Open the report/form in Design View (or Layout View, if you prefer) and make sure you are viewing the properties for the report/form itself and not an object on the report (by default, Access shows the property of whatever object currently has the focus). If the property window is not open, press F4 or Alt+Enter to activate it.
- Select the Other tab and scroll down to the `Ribbon Name` property.
- From the drop-down list, choose the contextual tab you originally saved in the USysRibbons table (the record that was just added).

TIP You can also click in the little square at the top, left corner of the object to select it. For example, to get the focus on the report, click the uppermost square on the top, left corner and you will have selected the report. You can check this by looking at the selection type in the properties window.

You need to close and open your Access project before the new Ribbon functionality is fully loaded and ready to use.

Renaming a tabSet

You've probably noticed that Figure 15-2 shows the `tabSet` caption as USysRibbons Report. This is probably not what you want. Instead, you may want to give it a more meaningful name. Figure 15-3 shows a renamed `tabSet`.

Figure 15-3: Changing the tabSet caption

Changing the `tabSet` caption is another simple process, especially if it is done in conjunction with specifying the Ribbon name. Just follow these steps:

1. Open the report/form in Design View (or Layout view, if you prefer) and make sure you are viewing the properties for the report/form.
2. Select the `Format` tab.
3. Change the `Caption` property to whatever you want as the caption of your contextual tab.
4. Return to `View` mode.

Unlike many of the other changes that you've made, you do not need to restart the project for this to take effect. The caption is updated immediately.

The same logic and processes can be used to create a contextual UI for forms.

Modifying Built-in Contextual Tabs

The previous example demonstrated how to implement a contextual solution for a report in Access. We will now use Excel to demonstrate how to change a built-in contextual tab.

Seasoned Excel developers have come to realize that it is no longer possible to customize certain pop-up menus, such as the one for Excel charts. In the past, you could add customization to these pop-ups and everything would work smoothly. With the advent of the Ribbon, we can no longer use some of these favored features.

Although we lost our custom pop-ups, we gained another feature that might be even more powerful and flexible: the contextual tab. Figure 15-4 shows how you can harness the power of built-in contextual tabs.

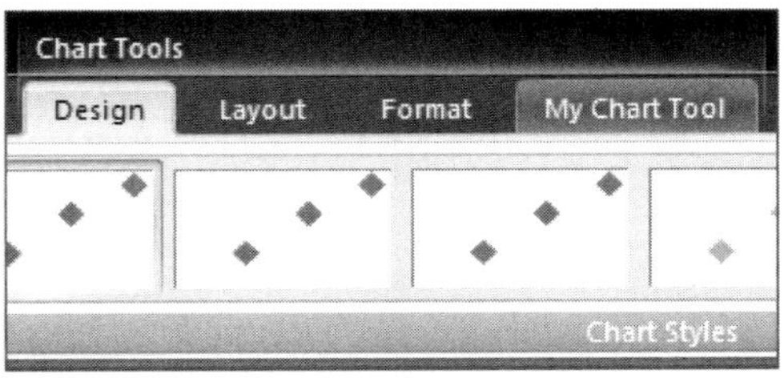

Figure 15-4: Adding a custom tab to a built-in contextual tabSet

Figure 15-4 shows the addition of a custom tab to the contextual `tabSet` for the built-in Chart Tools. This may not always be the perfect solution, but we believe that it is the next best alternative for most situations. As we previously noted, the tab is immediately visible, you can add all your customization to it; and the tab can expand to accommodate its contents rather than cramming all of the controls into a preset pop-up menu size.

The key to getting this right is knowing the `idMso` for the `tabSet` that you plan to customize. In this particular case, we want to change the `TabSetChartTools tabSet`.

CROSS-REFERENCE **For a fairly extensive list of `tabSets`, refer to Appendix B.**

Therefore, the XML code for adding your custom tab to a built-in `tabSet` would be as follows:

```
<customUI xmlns="http://schemas.microsoft.com/office/2006/01/customui">
   <ribbon>
```

```
        <contextualTabs>
           <tabSet idMso="TabSetChartTools">
              <tab id="rxtab"
                 label="My Chart Tools">
              </tab>
           </tabSet>
        </contextualTabs>
     </ribbon>
  </customUI>
```

Of course, this assumes that you actually want to add to built-in controls and `tabSets`, rather than replace them altogether. However, there may be times when you have a dashboard with loads of charts, in which case you might prefer to remove all the built-in tabs in the contextual chart tab and add only some very specific editing tools to the `tabSet`.

We'll work through both scenarios, but before we do, let's take a look at the tabs under the Chart Tools `tabSet`. These three tabs are described in Table 15-1.

Table 15-1: Default Tabs under the Chart Tools tabSet

TAB NAME	DESCRIPTION
TabChartToolsDesign	Gives the user tools for designing the selected chart, such as built-in style options, data selection, chart type, etc.
TabChartToolsLayout	Gives the user tools for laying out the selected chart, such as labels, trend lines, etc.
TabChartToolsFormat	Gives the user tools for formatting the selected chart, such as shape styling, text fills, text effects, arrangement, etc.

Tabs do not come with an `enabled` attribute like buttons do; therefore, you will use its `visible` attribute to manage their appearance. Keep in mind that by making the tabs invisible, all of their objects will also disappear from the UI. However, you'll also remember that making them invisible does not disable the controls contained in them.

Building on the previous example, you can simply add the following XML to the contextual chart `tabSet`:

```
<tab idMso="TabChartToolsDesign"
   visible="false"/>
<tab idMso="TabChartToolsLayout"
   visible="false"/>
<tab idMso="TabChartToolsFormat"
   visible="false"/>
```

If you inserted it correctly, you should now have the customization shown in Figure 15-5 when, and only when, a chart is selected.

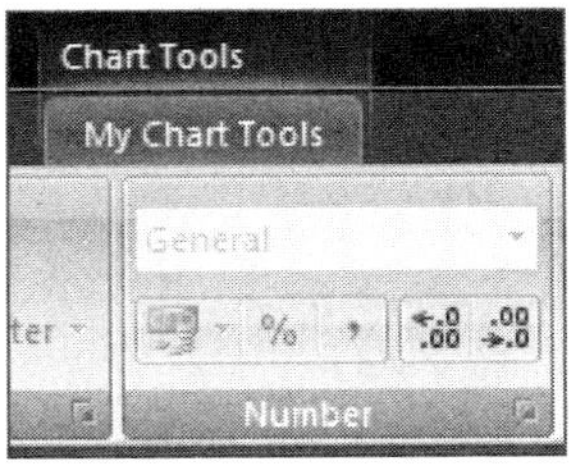

Figure 15-5: Changing visibility of built-in tabs in a contextual tabSet

That's all it takes to add a custom tab to a built-in contextual `tabSet`.

Working with Contextual Pop-up Menus

Contextual pop-up menus are our familiar friends from previous versions of Microsoft Office. They are visible when you right-click on an object or anything on your working environment that has a pop-up attached to it. Similar to contextual tabs, pop-up menus display the options that are relevant to the active object.

Pop-ups are based on VBA and do not require XML code, as they are still based on the command bar's objects. Therefore, these will seem like old friends to anyone who has worked with them in Office 97 through 2003. Most pop-ups can be customized, but we're sorry to report that the ones based on the new OfficeArt cannot be customized. However, you can still do quite a lot in terms of customization, and many of the old pop-ups are still accessible for customization. Figure 15-6 shows an example of a built-in pop-up in Excel.

NOTE **If you use a lot of graphics, keep in mind that pop-ups based on the new OfficeArt cannot be customized. However, things are constantly improving, so there is hope for the next release.**

The pop-up shown in Figure 15-6 is called "Cell" and has an index equal to 36. The next section gets into the mechanics of working with these contextual controls. We begin with some useful examples in Excel and then move on to Word and Access.

NOTE **The "floatie" (Mini toolbar) is not currently customizable, but it can be switched on and off from the Application Options under the Popular group.**

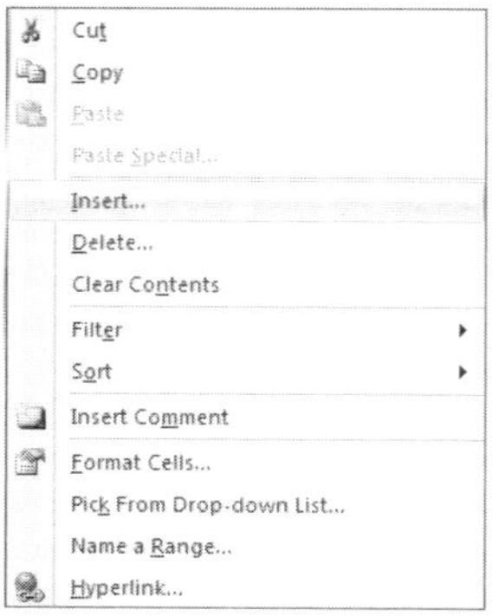

Figure 15-6: Excel's contextual pop-up menu "Cell"

Replacing Built-in Pop-up Menus in Their Entirety

When you right-click on a cell in an Excel worksheet, you get the Cell pop-up (refer to Figure 15-6). However, you may have a range for which a custom pop-up would be preferable. Figure 15-7 clearly illustrates this type of situation.

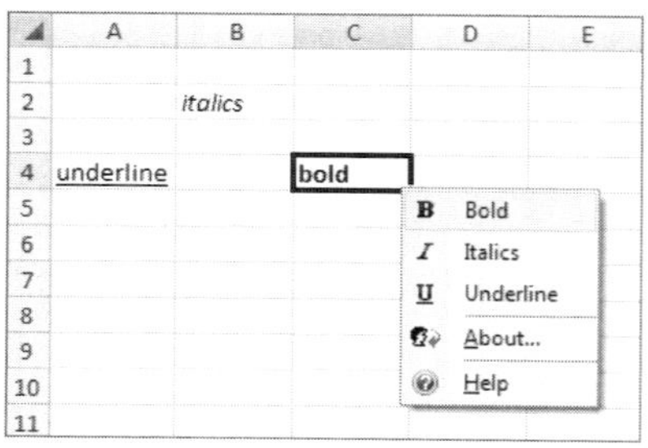

Figure 15-7: Custom pop-up replacing the built-in Cell pop-up

This is one of the few customizations that you can achieve in Office 2007 without using XML. This example is accomplished solely through use of VBA code.

Before we delve into the code, let's review what needs to happen for the pop-up customization:

- It must be shown in place of the "Cell" pop-up.
- It must be shown only in a predetermined area. The example uses the range A1:O32.

With these two points in mind, you are ready to build the pop-up. The first step is to add the following code to the worksheet code window in which the pop-up replaces the built-in Cell pop-up:

```
Private Sub Worksheet_BeforeRightClick(ByVal Target As Excel.Range, _
    Cancel As Boolean)
    If Union(Target.Range("A1"), Range("A1:O32")).Address = _
        Range("A1:O32").Address Then
        CommandBars(MYPOPUP).ShowPopup
        Cancel = True
    End If
End Sub
```

This code performs the following operations: First, the code checks for the union of the target address with the range defined (A1:O32). If the right-click occurs within this range, then the pop-up named MYPOPUP is called (please note that MYPOPUP is a global constant; you will look at the associated code momentarily). Finally, the code cancels the built-in pop-up menu by setting the `Cancel` return value to `true`.

For the second step of this example, you need to add two procedures to the workbook code window. One procedure refers to the `open` event of the workbook and the other refers to the `close` event of the workbook. In the first case, it creates the pop-up menu, and in the second it deletes the pop-up menu. The deletion is necessary so that the pop-up is not left in the customization. The two procedures are provided here:

```
Private Sub Workbook_Open()
    Call mnuPopup
End Sub

Private Sub Workbook_BeforeClose(Cancel As Boolean)
    Call delPopup
End Sub
```

The third and final step is to add a standard module to the project. This module will contain the code that generates the pop-up, as well as the code that deletes it. This means you need to insert both the `mnuPopup` and `delPopup` procedures, as presented here. Notice that the module starts by declaring a public constant, MYPOPUP. As mentioned earlier, this must be a public constant so that the value is available to both of the subprocedures:

```
Public Const MYPOPUP As String = "MY POPUP"

Sub mnuPopup()
    Dim cmdBar  As CommandBar
    Dim mnu     As CommandBarButton

    delPopup

    Set cmdBar = CommandBars.Add _
      (Name:=MYPOPUP, Position:=msoBarPopup, Temporary:=True)
```

```
        Set mnu = cmdBar.Controls.Add(Type:=msoControlButton)
        With mnu
            .Caption = "Bold"
            .OnAction = "bold"
            .FaceId = 113
        End With

        Set mnu = cmdBar.Controls.Add(Type:=msoControlButton)
        With mnu
            .Caption = "Italics"
            .OnAction = "italics"
            .FaceId = 114
        End With

        Set mnu = cmdBar.Controls.Add(Type:=msoControlButton)
        With mnu
            .Caption = "Underline"
            .OnAction = "underline"
            .FaceId = 115
        End With

        Set mnu = cmdBar.Controls.Add(Type:=msoControlButton)
        With mnu
            .Caption = "&About..."
            .OnAction = "about"
            .FaceId = 326
            .BeginGroup = True
        End With

        Set mnu = cmdBar.Controls.Add(Type:=msoControlButton)
        With mnu
            .Caption = "&Help"
            .OnAction = "help"
            .FaceId = 984
            .BeginGroup = True
        End With

    End Sub

    Sub delPopup()
        On Error Resume Next
        CommandBars(MYPOPUP).Delete
    End Sub
```

The first procedure is executed when the workbook is opened; the second procedure is executed when the workbook is closed (although the first procedure calls on the second upon opening the file).

The only task left is to add the functionality to the button in the pop-up. The sample file in the chapter download contains some simple functionality code, as follows:

```
Sub bold()
    Selection.Font.bold = Not Selection.Font.bold
End Sub

Sub italics()
    Selection.Font.Italic = Not Selection.Font.Italic
End Sub

Sub underline()
    If Selection.Font.underline = xlUnderlineStyleSingle Then
       Selection.Font.underline = xlUnderlineStyleNone
    Else
        Selection.Font.underline = xlUnderlineStyleSingle
    End If
End Sub
```

These are simple procedures to illustrate the point, but you should note that the functionality is added in the same manner as it is in XML code — that is, you use the `onAction` property (called `attribute` in XML) to refer to a subprocedure or function in your VBA project containing the code that needs to execute.

The examples that follow are for Word and Access. The VBA code to build the pop-up menus is pretty much the same, so we do not repeat them. However, we provide and discuss the event code for each example.

Starting with the example for Word, you first need to add a class module. We named it `clsRightClick`, but you're free to name it anything you like as long as you make the correct reference to it later in your code. To this class module, add the following code:

```
Public WithEvents appWord       As Word.Application

Private Sub appWord_WindowBeforeRightClick _
    (ByVal Sel As Selection, Cancel As Boolean)

    Dim selectionExists     As Long
    selectionExists = Len(Sel)

    Select Case selectionExists
        Case Is > 1
            Cancel = True
            Call showMyPopup
    End Select
End Sub
```

The main objectives of the preceding code are to capture the right-click and to show the pop-up menu. The pop-up menu is only shown if the selection length is greater than one. Figure 15-8 shows how this example works.

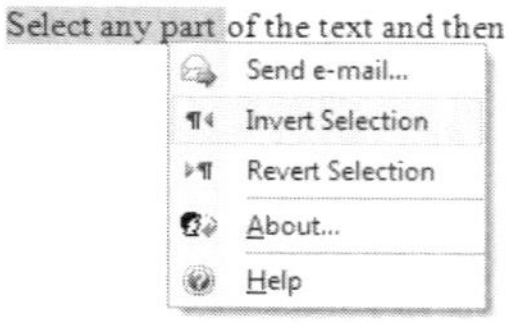

Figure 15-8: Right-click selection on a Word document

We use an application-wide event, so if you right-click on another document with a selection length greater than one, it will also show the pop-up menu in that document. You can add code to limit the scope to the current document by checking whether the click happens in the document containing the code.

Our next example is for Access and involves a right-click on a form detail. You can, of course, extrapolate the process to add the right-click to another object. Access works a bit differently than Excel and Word, as it allows you to determine which mouse button was actually clicked. This is handy if you want to provide different responses depending on whether the user right-clicked or left-clicked.

The first step is to add a form to your Access project. Then, open the code window for the new form and add the following event procedure:

```
Private Sub Detail_MouseDown(Button As Integer, _
    Shift As Integer, X As Single, Y As Single)
    If Button = acRightButton Then
        DoCmd.CancelEvent
        CommandBars(MYPOPUP).ShowPopup
    End If
End Sub
```

Figure 15-9 shows the pop-up menu when a right-click is applied on the detail area of your form.

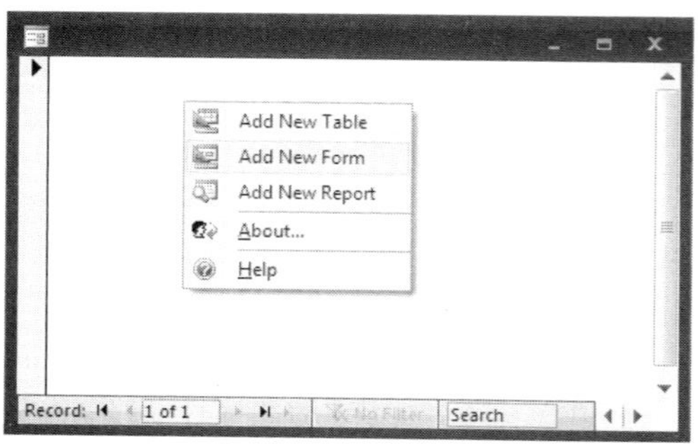

Figure 15-9: Custom pop-up menu in Access

Note that this will work fine as long as your form is in the same language as the example. Because the forms have been translated by Microsoft, the event needs to be added in whatever language you're programming your project in.

Adding Individual Items to Pop-up Menus

Another useful way to customize built-in pop-ups is to add new functionality. For example, you could add a button to the `Ply` pop-up menu in Excel so that, with just two clicks, you have a handy tool that puts the worksheets in alphabetical order. Figure15-10 shows the ply pop-up menu with a custom button added to it.

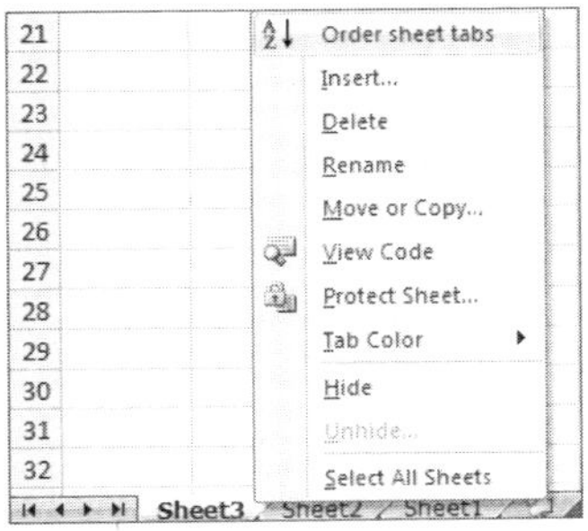

Figure 15-10: Adding custom controls to built-in pop-up menus

Try it out. Add a button to the pop-up that enables users to quickly alphabetize the worksheets. The first step is to add the button. This can be done placing the following procedure in a standard module:

```
Sub addButton()
    Dim cmdbar   As CommandBar
    Dim btn      As CommandBarButton

    Application.CommandBars("Ply").Reset

    Set cmdbar = Application.CommandBars("Ply")

    Set btn = cmdbar.Controls.Add(Type:=msoControlButton, Before:=1)

    With btn
        .Style = msoButtonIconAndCaption
        .Caption = "Order sheet tabs"
        .FaceId = 210
        .OnAction = "orderTabs"
    End With

End Sub
```

If you want to automate this, you could run the preceding procedure when the workbook opens just by adding a call to it. In addition, while you are at it, you could also add a close event to the workbook so that it triggers the following procedure:

```
Sub resetPopup()
    Application.CommandBars("Ply").Reset
End Sub
```

NOTE **If you use the `Reset` procedure shown in the preceding code, you can substitute the line equivalent to it in the `addButton` procedure. Simply make a call to the `resetPopup` procedure in the `addButton` procedure.**

This procedure will reset the `Ply` pop-up menu to its original state so that it does not leave any customization hanging around after the workbook is closed.

OK, back to the original focus, which is to add customization to the right-click function. The next step for that is to write a procedure to put the sheets in order when the button is clicked. We used the following procedure:

```
Sub orderTabs()
    Dim i       As Long
    Dim j       As Long
    Dim n       As Long

    n = ActiveWorkbook.Sheets.Count

    If n = 1 Then
        MsgBox "There is only one worksheet in this work-book!", _
            vbInformation
        Exit Sub
    End If

    For i = 1 To n - 1
        For j = i + 1 To n
            If Sheets(j).Name < Sheets(i).Name Then
                Sheets(j).Move Before:=Sheets(i)
            End If
        Next
    Next
End Sub
```

That's all there is to it! The key to this sort of customization is to know the command bars that you plan to customize. Figure 15-11 shows a compilation of lists that we've created in Access. These lists can come in handy, especially as they are updated every time they are generated.

This database is one of the sample files for this book. As a nice bonus, in addition to demonstrating how to use the right and left mouse clicks, we've provided a database that creates lists of the command bars and controls in your projects. Surely you have to agree that *that* is truly a nice bonus, thank you very much. The lists are created at runtime and you can run it to list the command bars and child controls. The code creates three tables and adds a relationship to them so that you can easily identify the hierarchy between the tables. Although the database lists the controls in Access, the code can be adapted to accomplish the same task in Excel and Word.

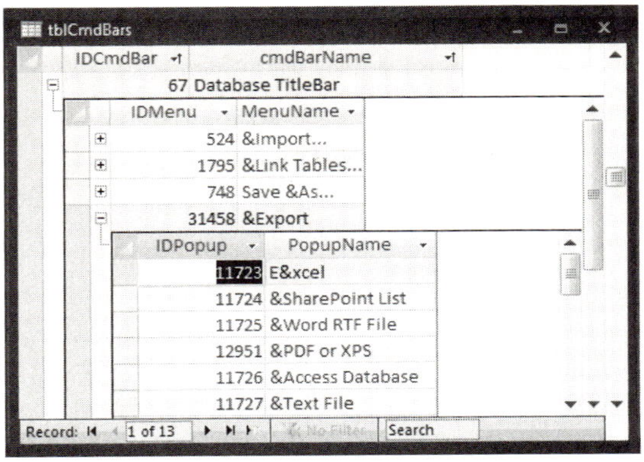

Figure 15-11: List of built-in command bars and child controls

Multilingual UI

The possibilities regarding what you can accomplish with contextual elements can take different turns depending on your needs and imagination. We now look at the multilingual UI to see how the contextual elements can support multilingual projects. Many approaches could be considered, but the current objective is to enable users to choose the language that they prefer.

Our example will offer two languages. Figure 15-12 shows the example that we will build in Excel. You could also modify the steps to work with either Word or Access. For Word, you would want to use an external file, to simplify maintenance; but when working with Access, you can easily use either table or an external source file. The process is fairly straightforward and doesn't even require XML in order to work with the resource file — the file that contains the control names and their translations. You'll notice that because we have to provide the translations, the resource file contains only the languages we are offering.

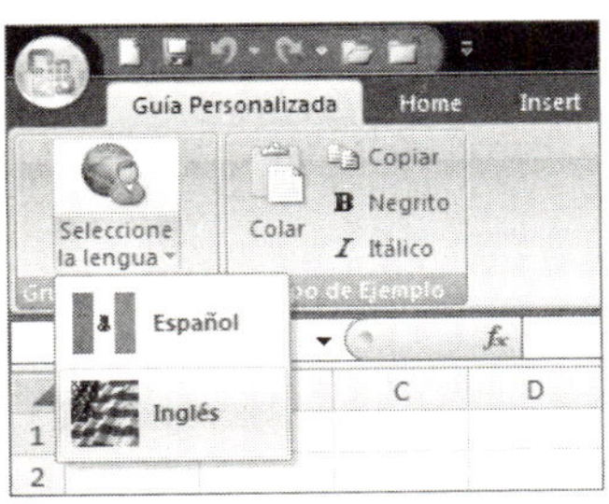

Figure 15-12: Multilingual UI in Excel

The process is quite simple. Basically, building the solution can be broken down into four essential tasks:

- The label for each control must be changed at run-time; thus, we use the `getLabel` attribute in each one of them.
- Because this is an attribute shared among all the controls, we use a shared callback to handle the change. This avoids a lot of coding.
- We use a worksheet (aka a resource file) to keep the controls' names and translations. The worksheet can be hidden so that it is not readily accessible to users.
- We use the `VLookup` function to search for the controls in the list and return the label value.

As you can see from the list, the resource for, or the worksheet with, the control names and translations is a key element in the implementation of this solution. An example of the spreadsheet is shown in Figure 15-13.

	A	B	C
1	Control	English	Spanish
2	rxtab	My Custom Tab	Guía Personalizada
3	rxgrpLanguages	Language Group	Grupo de Idiomas
4	rxbtnUN	Choose Language	Seleccione la lengua
5	rxbtnSpanish	Spanish	Español
6	rxbtnEnglish	English	Inglés
7	rxgrpDemo	Demo Group	Grupo de Ejemplo
8	rxbtnDemo1	Paste	Colar
9	rxbtnDemo2	Copy	Copiar
10	rxbtnDemo3	Bold	Negrito
11	rxbtnDemo4	Italics	Itálico

Figure 15-13: Worksheet table containing controls' translations

Although you can define a dynamic range for the area containing the translation, this might require a rather lengthy explanation of how dynamic ranges work. Another option would be to convert the range into a table. However, because we're focused on Ribbon enhancements rather than Excel formulas, our example uses the straightforward approach of a fixed range. For this example, we also concentrate on VBA and do not expand into options that require XML.

Given those caveats, we are now ready to begin. We first define a few variables that will be used throughout the example. Declare the following global variables in the general declarations area of your standard module:

```
Public grxIRibbonUI          As IRibbonUI
Public giColControls         As Integer
Public gWS                   As Worksheet
```

The first variable is the `Ribbon` object; the second variable refers to the column in which the language version is located; and the last variable refers to the worksheet object that contains the translations.

Next, use the `onLoad` event to set these variables for later use:

```
Sub rxIRibbonUI_onLoad(ribbon As IRibbonUI)
    Set grxIRibbonUI = ribbon
    giColControls = 2
    Set gWS = ThisWorkbook.Sheets("Languages")
    Application.SendKeys "%UN{RETURN}"
End Sub
```

This code does the following:

- Sets the ribbon object
- Determines the initial column in which the translation is located
- Sets the worksheet that contains the translation
- Sends the shortcut `Alt+UN` to the application so that the custom tab is selected upon opening the workbook

CROSS-REFERENCE **For a refresher on `SendKeys` and how to specify which tab has the focus when the file opens, see Chapter 13.**

The initial labels will be loaded when the document is opened, so you need to handle the shared `getLabel` callback. That is done as follows:

```
Sub rxshared_getLabel(control As IRibbonControl, ByRef returnedVal)
    On Error Resume Next
    returnedVal = Application.WorksheetFunction.VLookup( _
        control.id, gWS.Range("A1:C200"), giColControls, 0)
End Sub
```

Using the `VLOOKUP` function, you take the control `id` to determine the value being looked up in the table. You then use a fixed range (A1:C200) indicating where the details are, including the column containing the values that will be returned (i.e., displayed on the controls).

This code will be called back when the user chooses a different language from the `splitButton/menu` in the UI. When the user clicks on the chosen language command, you need to invalidate the Ribbon so that the values can be reloaded onto the UI. This is done with the following code:

```
Sub rxbtnshared_Click(control As IRibbonControl)
    Select Case control.id
        Case "rxbtnSpanish"
            giColControls = 3
        Case "rxbtnEnglish"
            giColControls = 2
    End Select
    grxIRibbonUI.Invalidate
End Sub
```

You use a `Select` statement to choose between the two languages available. If the language chosen is Spanish, then the column where the look up must occur is set to `3`. If English is selected, then the column is set to `2` (the default value).

Conclusion

In this chapter, you learned how to create context-sensitive customizations. We used an Access example to explore some new ways of adding contextual controls. In addition to creating custom groups, you learned how to customize built-in contextual tabs and harness their power and flexibility.

We also demonstrated a couple of less conventional methods for adding context-sensitive controls by using the `getVisible` and `getEnabled` attributes to hide/show and enable/disable Ribbon objects. This chapter also covered pop-up menus, a legacy from previous versions of Office, and described how to replace built-in pop-up menus with your own, as well as how to modify built-in ones.

We closed the chapter by providing a very handy tool that lists old command bars and pop-up menus, which you can use to access the information necessary to modify legacy UIs in Office 2007. You also created a multilingual UI. Who would have thought that context sensitivity covered such a wide range of controls and features?

We packed a lot into a few pages, but it is all important for preparing you for the next chapter, because now you are ready to move on to "Sharing and Deploying Ribbon Customizations."

CHAPTER 16

Sharing and Deploying Ribbon Customizations

Throughout this book, we've focused on customizing the Ribbon to best suit your needs, emphasizing functionality and convenience. It is now time to learn how to deploy customizations.

It is important to realize that every customization we built in this book was contained in a workbook, database, or document, and each customization was evident in that file only. As soon as you switched to another file, even within the same application, you would see a fresh and clean UI, with none of your customizations present. While this is a great feature to ensure that the UI is reset and not cluttered with irrelevant information, sometimes you will want to develop and use customizations across all files for a specific program.

That's why we'll now discuss how to share customizations. This chapter covers several methods, complete with both the pros and the cons of each approach. As each application deals with deployment in a slightly different manner, we cover each one separately to demonstrate the available techniques.

We begin by reviewing three ways to deploy custom solutions in Excel, and provide an in-depth discussion of the code and the modifications necessary to share customizations. The second section of this chapter covers similar material as it relates to Word.

The third portion of this chapter looks at our final RibbonX attribute: `idQ`. This attribute is specifically geared toward sharing elements across files, and it enables users to load and unload Ribbon customizations from a central source.

After that, you will learn some techniques for deploying Word and Excel solutions in an environment where prior versions of Office may also still be active. This is an invaluable section, as many people use different machines on a regular basis, and they need their files to work with Office 2000 and newer.

Finally, we cap off the chapter by discussing techniques to deploy Ribbon customizations in Microsoft Access. By the time you finish this chapter, you will have both the knowledge and the confidence required to successfully deploy solutions in a real-world environment. As always, we encourage you to download the companion files. They are an invaluable resource for working through the examples in this chapter. The files can be found on the book's website at `www.wiley.com/go/ribbonx`.

Excel Deployment Techniques

This section is geared primarily for Excel users and provides very specific information about how to deploy Ribbon customizations built for Microsoft Excel. Here, we discuss the three methods that are available for deploying customizations: workbooks, templates, and add-ins. In addition to describing what to do, we also provide some recommendations about what works best for each of these scenarios.

NOTE **Word users should also read this section, as the "Distributing Workbooks" and "Using Templates" sections contain many parallels with the way that Word operates. The "Word Deployment Techniques" section of this chapter highlights the differences between the two applications, rather than cover everything from scratch.**

Distributing Workbooks

So far, the Excel solutions that we've created would be termed "workbook-level deployments." Each was created and saved as a workbook in either a macro-free (`xlsx`) or macro-enabled (`xlsm`) file format.

This is the most common format for a novice programmer to create, and there is certainly nothing wrong with it. All the required XML and VBA code is saved within the file and travels with the workbook wherever it goes.

A workbook-level deployment has some great advantages over other deployment methods. It creates a nice, portable little package that is very easy to deploy. Simply send it to a user and it will run without issues, providing the following:

- The end user's security setting permits any code to run
- Any VBA code is correctly crafted for changes in environments (such as variable file paths, etc.)

CROSS-REFERENCE **Security is discussed in detail in Chapter 17.**

There are also some disadvantages that attend the workbook-level deployment methods. The largest of these issues revolves around the maintainability of the file.

Packaging a solution using the workbook-level approach actually violates one of the best-practice guidelines generally accepted in the development industry: separating business logic from data. Consider the scenario in which you have released a customization in the same file as your critical business data. How do you go about updating the file? Do you take it offline for as long as you need to write the update? What happens if you accidentally destroy the data while updating the code?

Another maintainability issue relates to replicated workbooks. This could lead to hundreds of copies of the same customization. Consider what it would take to track down all of the copies and roll out an update. Worse yet, what happens if you've updated the code, and the file is overwritten by an old version? Granted, this may be a worst-case scenario, because it also means that you have much bigger problems than just code maintainability, as the data would also be lost. You may think, "That could never happen to me," but we have seen this type of compounding of errors.

It is hard to beat the portability of a workbook deployment for creating simple VBA functionality enhancements, such as copying data to historical tables or clearing input cells, but this may not be the file type that is best suited to deploying Ribbon customizations.

Using Templates

The next method for deploying Excel solutions is to store the file as a template. This provides a quick way to create a new file built on the specified underlying structure.

As mentioned in the previous section, many fledgling developers create solutions, save them in a workbook format, and then distribute the files to other users. Many times, the intention is to use these files as a template. The end user may be given instructions to save the workbook under a new filename before starting, to always overwrite the old data, or to simply clear old data from the file before working with it. As the developer picks up more VBA skills, he or she may even create a button for users to clear the data cells. Sadly, these steps are an unnecessary waste of time.

The purpose of the template is to provide a fresh clean workbook when the file is called. It simply requires the developer to set up the workbook correctly and then save it as a template. Once installed in the end user's `templates` folder, it is as simple as choosing Office Menu ➪ New ➪ My Templates and double-clicking on the appropriate file. A new workbook will be created in the selected template's image. The new file is immediately given a new name so that the template cannot be overwritten.

Creating a template is much easier than you might think. We'll go through the process now. But, rather than create a brand-new file with a Ribbon customization, download one of our completed examples. For the purposes of this example, we've used the `editBox-RenameWorksheets.xlsm` file from the Chapter 6 downloads.

After you have the file open, go to the Office Menu and choose Save As. From the Save As Type drop-down list, choose Excel Macro-Enabled Template.xltm. Give the file a name and save it in the default directory, as specified in Table 16-1.

Table 16-1: Default Locations for the Local Templates Folders

PLATFORM	PATH
Windows Vista	C:\Users\username\AppData\Roaming\Microsoft\Templates
Windows XP	C:\Documents And Settings\username\Application Data\Microsoft\Templates

That's it! It really is that simple. The file is still open in the template format (it may end with `.xltm` in the application title bar), so close it now. Then go to the Office Menu and choose New ➪ My Templates to browse the Excel templates on your system. Select and open the file that you just saved.

The file opens and looks just like it did when saved, but notice the name of the file in the application's title bar. As shown in the circled area of Figure 16-1, it ends in 1 and shows no extension. Why is this?

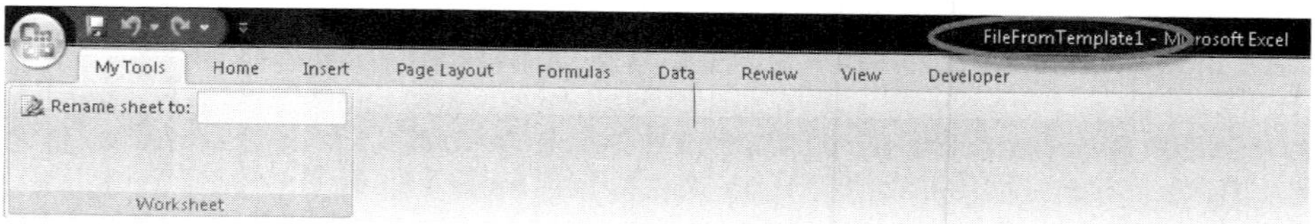

Figure 16-1: A new file created from a template

Actually, this is a fundamental selling point for the template file type. The file lacks an extension because you have not yet saved it. As soon as you hit the Save button, you will be prompted for a new filename and type. The file will *not* be saved over the template file.

NOTE **The file number will increment each time a new file is created from the same template. (You can prove this by deleting the newly created file and repeating the process.) The program increments the filename to ensure that it doesn't create a new file with the name of an existing (open) file.**

The template provides the ability to create files from a consistent and approved base. Because templates can be stored within the user's own `templates` directory, or a network directory, you can easily deploy and update your workbook templates, ensuring that all new files are built from that source.

NOTE **You *must* configure template directories through Microsoft Word, as Excel has no way of changing any of the default template locations. Changing these settings is covered in the discussion of Word, later in this chapter.**

If your template makes use of VBA, then rest assured that the VBA will still work just fine. However, be aware that the default file format for saving a file is macro-free (`xlsx`). Therefore, unless users consciously select `xlsm`, they will delete the VBA and remove all macro functionality. Currently, the only way to work around this issue is to program a custom `Workbook_BeforeSave` event to save the file in the `xlsm` file format. Although that programming is outside the scope of this book, you can quickly find additional information online.

WARNING **XML travels with the document based on a template, even if the file is saved in a macro-free file format! This means that even though any required VBA code is stripped from the document, the Ribbon customizations still travel with the file.**

At this point, you may be asking how you would update a template if you can't make changes to it. The secret lies in how the file is opened.

If you are going to use templates, it is paramount that you train users to select Office ➪ New (file) to create new files. If they instead open the file by choosing Office ➪ Open, they will have full access to the template. Any changes that they save will then become part of the template. Fortunately, templates are generally not stored in directories that users access frequently, such as the default folder for user documents. Instead, the default location is buried quite deeply in the Windows folder hierarchy. This provides an inherent level of protection, as most users have no idea where to browse to find the template files. For the same reason, workgroup template directories should not be stored within directories that users typically access.

Templates can be an ideal deployment option for creating standardized workbooks that always need to start fresh — for example, purchase orders or checklists. If you need to add data, save the file and return later to add or change data. However, workbook-level distributions may be better suited to this task.

Keep in mind that templates can also provide the foundation for a workbook deployment that has a limited shelf life. For example, a monthly reconciliation of transactions may be created from a template on the first of the month and saved. Throughout the month, data is added and passed around in the workbook until it is complete at the end of the month. At that point, a new month is started from the template, ensuring that all the necessary formulas are again whole and complete. Clearly, this can be a convenient way to distribute new features, as interim changes to the Ribbon customizations in the template would be available to users when they use the new template.

Creating and Deploying Add-ins

The next deployment vehicle is the Excel add-in. This solution is a little more complex to create and deploy, but it adds considerable flexibility for developers. Add-ins separate the data from the code required to provide the tools. Another significant benefit for Ribbon customizations is that unlike workbooks and templates, whose customizations are hidden when switching to another file, the add-in makes the customizations visible and accessible to all files.

NOTE **Although we prefer to do our development in the add-in format, this is a personal preference. Some think that those who are new to creating add-in files may find it easier to edit and modify files in the** `xlsx` **and** `xlsm` **formats, rather than develop in the Add-in format. Regardless of the format used while creating the customization, all functionality should be tested before the add-in conversion is deployed.**

To demonstrate the construction of an add-in in Excel, we will convert the dynamicMenu example that was created in Chapter 9. This file, if you recall, added the capability to create a new file from a template with a few less clicks than the method outlined above. To follow along, download the `dynamicMenu-CreateFromTemplate.xlsm` example from the Chapter 9 example file.

Preparing a Workbook for Conversion to an Add-in

When preparing to convert a file to an add-in, it is important to ensure that all the VBA code will transfer across seamlessly. If your file contains only XML customizations, you may skip this section, but if it uses any VBA code, you will want to pay careful attention. The specific things that need to be checked are as follows:

- Instances where `ThisWorkbook` is referenced in the code
- Instances where the subroutines and functions are not prefaced by the words `Public` or `Private`

Because the majority of add-ins start as `xlsm` files, many of them reference the `ThisWorkbook` object in the code. This is fine for a regular file, as the code and data are both contained within the same workbook, but once the file is converted to an add-in, the data that you will be working with will rarely be stored in the actual add-in.

NOTE **It is considered a best practice to separate all data from the actual add-in, which should serve only as a code container. This is true even for data related to custom settings for the add-in, such as languages or number of items shown in a listbox. Separating this type of data from the code allows you to deploy updates to the add-in without worrying about overwriting user settings.**

CROSS-REFERENCE **One method for storing user settings data outside a file is to store it in the Registry. We'll use this technique later in this chapter (it was also demonstrated in Chapter 12).**

Open the `dynamicMenu-CreateFromTemplate.xlsm` file in Excel, launch the VBE, and open the standard code module. Using the Find or Find Next commands from the Edit menu, search through the code to locate all instances of `ThisWorkbook`.

If you find an instance of `ThisWorkbook`, you need to determine whether it should be replaced with `ActiveWorkbook` instead. Keep in mind that the target of the code is most likely the workbook with the data (`ActiveWorkbook`) and not `ThisWorkbook`, which would refer to the add-in itself.

Take care, however, not to use a blanket "Find and Replace" of the term. There are frequently legitimate reasons to reference `ThisWorkbook`, including referring to workbook properties, as well as referring to any data tables that may be stored in worksheets of the add-in, such as a list of postal codes used to populate a UserForm ListBox.

Fortunately, our current example file contains no instances of `ThisWorkbook` in the code, so we don't need to worry about this.

The second item that you need to be aware of is the distinction between `Public`, `Private`, and unspecified routines and functions. By default, all routines and functions that are not prefaced with the `Public` or `Private` keyword are treated as `Public`. This is an important distinction because `Public` means that they are viewable when pressing the Alt+F8 keystroke sequence in the Excel UI.

It is a good practice to mark routines as `Private` whenever possible. Certain routines must be public, so that the user can run them, but if routines or functions are called only from other procedures or functions, they should be marked as `Private`.

As you review the code in the example, you will find that none of the routines have been prefaced with `Private` or `Public`. Modify each routine to start with the `Private` keyword, as shown here:

```
Private Sub rxIRibbonUI_onLoad(ribbon As IRibbonUI)
```

CAUTION **Private routines and functions cannot be called from other modules. Assume that you have decided to hold all of your Ribbon callbacks in one code module and all other "global" routines in another so that they can be called from callbacks, userforms, or class modules; you will not be able to set your "global" routines as private, as they would not be found when needed.**

As with all code, you may not get things right the first time, but don't worry about it. Code in add-ins can still be edited, so if you do make a mistake you haven't backed yourself into a corner.

Now that we have updated the code, let's turn the project into an add-in.

Converting a Workbook to an Add-in Format

The process of converting a workbook to an add-in is quite simple. From the Office Menu, choose SaveAs ⇨ Other Formats. When prompted for the filename and type, choose the Excel Add-in (*.`xlam`) format. At this point, that location changes to the `Add-ins` folder. Make sure that the file is named `CreateFromTemplate.xlam` and click the Save button.

NOTE **If multiple users will simultaneously use your add-in, you'll need to do two things. First, save the add-in in a network folder instead of in a personal Add-ins folder. Second, locate the file (through Windows), right click the add-in file, and set it to be "Read-only." This will force each user to load a copy of the file, while still letting you overwrite it if you have a new version that you'd like to deploy. If you do not change this property, then the first user to open your add-in puts an exclusive lock on the file and no one else can use, delete, or replace the file until the lock is released. For more details on this topic, please visit** `www.excelguru.ca/node/45`.

Notice that once the file is saved, the original filename still graces the title bar of the Excel application. This is to be expected, as the add-in is created as a copy of the original file. Close the original file and we'll get to work on the installation portion.

Installing an Add-in

Because you created the add-in on your system, it is stored in the local `Add-ins` directory. If you send this to a user and want it to be as easy as possible to install, you should direct the user to save the file to their local `Add-ins` folder. This folder can be found in the locations shown in Table 16-2.

Table 16-2: Local Add-ins Folder Locations

PLATFORM	PATH
Windows Vista	C:\Users\username\AppData\Roaming\Microsoft\AddIns
Windows XP	C:\Documents And Settings\username\Application Data\Microsoft\Addins

TIP **It is not necessary to place the file in the default `Add-ins` directory. Indeed, if the `Add-in` file will be shared by multiple users, this is the last thing that you should do. However, it does make the installation a few clicks easier in Excel.**

Now, ensure that your add-in is installed. Open Excel, go to the Office Menu, and choose Excel Options ⇨ Add-Ins ⇨ Go. This will bring you to the dialog shown in Figure 16-2.

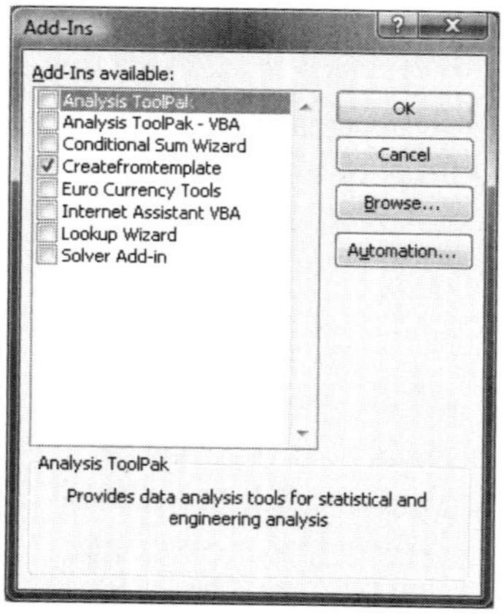

Figure 16-2: Installing a new add-in

If you stored the add-in in your local `Add-ins` folder, it will be in the list. Simply check the box next to it. If you stored the add-in in another location, however, you'll need to click the Browse button to locate the file. To complete the loading of the add-in, simply check the box next to the file and say OK.

Upon returning to the Excel UI, you'll see that the Ribbon customization you created in the Chapter 9 example is loaded, as shown in Figure 16-3.

You will also find that the add-in functions exactly as you'd expect. Click the menu for a list of all the templates stored in your `Templates` directory. If it doesn't list any templates, you can create some by following the steps outlined earlier in this chapter.

Why did we go through all of this? Open any other Excel file on your system and you'll notice that the New File menu is still there. As you can see, creating an add-in enables you to share your customizations no matter which file is open.

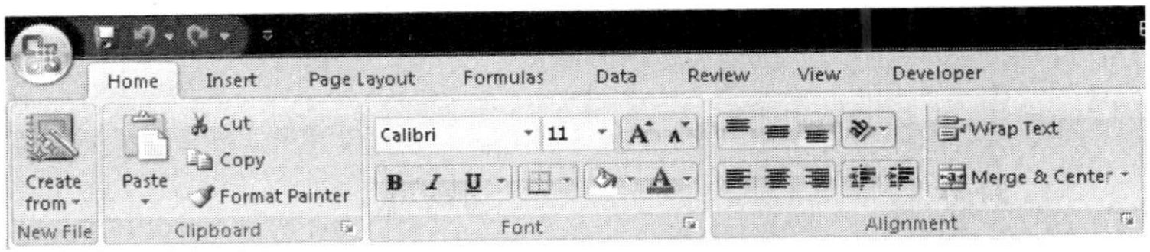

Figure 16-3: The "CreateFromTemplate" add-in in action

Unloading and Removing Add-ins

Add-ins require memory when they load, so it is a common practice for users to turn Excel add-ins on and off as needed. It is easy to turn an add-in off, but it requires a few additional steps to completely remove an add-in. One of the reasons to remove an add-in is so that you can change it from a local deployment to a network deployment.

To unload an add-in but still leave it available for loading in the future, go to the Office Menu and choose Excel Options ➪ Add-Ins ➪ Go. This will again bring you to the dialog shown in Figure 16-2. This time, simply uncheck the box next to the add-in(s) that you wish to unload. These add-ins will not be removed from your system but they will be unloaded, freeing up the portions of Excel's memory that were reserved by the add-in(s). The add-in(s) will remain in the list so that they can be easily loaded when needed.

To completely remove an add-in from your system, begin by unloading it as just described. Then close Excel and locate the actual add-in file so that you can move it or delete it from your system. Next, reopen Excel and return to the Add-ins interface, where you'll notice that the add-in is still listed. As there is no button to remove an add-in from this list, check the box next to the add-in. If you successfully moved or deleted the correct file, you will be prompted with a message to delete it from the list, as shown in Figure 16-4.

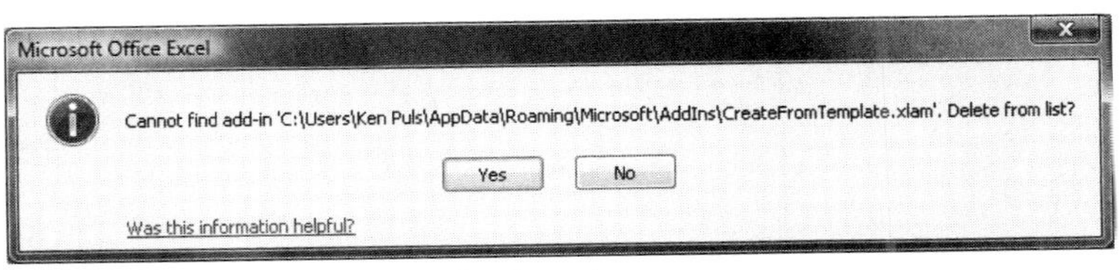

Figure 16-4: Add-in cannot be found

Select Yes and then make sure you close Excel. This is important, as closing Excel sets the change in the Registry, where the list of add-ins is maintained.

Toggling the IsAddin Property

In the discussion about add-ins, we mentioned that all is not lost if you make a mistake with any portion of the add-in. For example, perhaps you need to add a list of data to one of the worksheets in an add-in that is used in a `vlookup` formula or some other method. You can temporarily re-expose the worksheets by setting the `IsAddin` property of the add-in to `False`.

To do this, open the VBE and ensure that the Properties window is open. (Press Ctrl+R to show it if it isn't.) Browse to the `ThisWorkbook` class module in the Add-in project, select it, and press F4. This will change the view of the Properties window to show the properties of the `ThisWorkbook` object, launching the Properties window if it is not open.

Browse down the list until you find the `IsAddin` property, as shown in Figure 16-5.

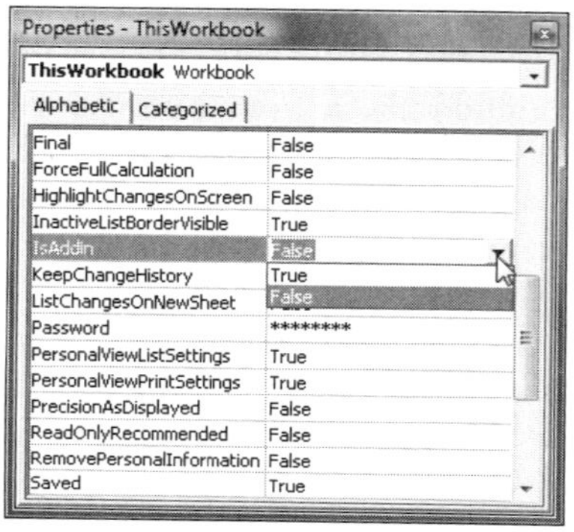

Figure 16-5: Properties of the ThisWorkbook module

Changing the `IsAddin` property to `False` tells Excel to treat the file as a regular workbook. All sheets will become visible again and the file can be modified. To turn the file back into an add-in again, access the `IsAddin` property by following the preceding steps, setting the property to `True`.

CAUTION **Once you have made your changes, you will want to ensure that you save your add-in again. You can do this by ensuring that one of the add-in's code modules is activated in the VBE's Project Explorer and pressing the Save button.**

NOTE **Toggling the `IsAddin` property may cause your RibbonX customizations to collapse — that is, they not only disappear, but they are gone until you reload Excel.**

A Note on the PERSONAL.XLSB Workbook

Users of Excel who are experienced with writing VBA macros in earlier versions of Office will undoubtedly be familiar with Excel 97–2003's `PERSONAL.XLS` workbook — a hidden workbook that was used to hold self-developed VBA procedures. As this workbook was the primary repository in which most budding developers could store their code libraries, it is completely understandable that users would try to store their personal Ribbon customizations in Excel 2007's new `PERSONAL.XLSB` file. Save yourself some time and don't bother, as it doesn't work the way you would expect.

While Ribbon customizations can be attached to the `PERSONAL.XLSB` workbook, the workbook remains hidden and so will all the Ribbon customizations. Changing the workbook to visible does display the Ribbon customizations, but that defeats the purpose of the `PERSONAL.XLSB` workbook, as the customizations are only available while that workbook is active. As with all workbooks, switching from the workbook that holds the customization discards the customizations until the workbook is activated again, so any tools you've programmed will not be available in the workbook(s) for which you created them.

In previous versions of Excel, we also had a trick to set the `IsAddin` property of the `PERSONAL.XLS` file to `True`, which would force the file to behave like an add-in. This was a great feature, as it avoided the irritating message "This workbook is in use" when a second instance of Excel was opened. Changing this setting in an effort to treat the file as an add-in causes some strange behavior in Excel 2007:

- The `IsAddin` property reverts to `false` every time you open the file.
- Changing the `IsAddin` property causes the `PERSONAL.XLSB` workbook to open as a normal, visible workbook.

Because the `PERSONAL.XLSB` workbook does not seem to work well with RibbonX customizations, it is recommended that you use a separate add-in to store customizations that will be shared globally across Excel workbooks.

Word Deployment Techniques

In this section we turn our attention to deploying our customization in Microsoft Word. Like Excel, Word offers three methods for deploying solutions: documents, templates, and global templates. Again, we will demonstrate how to make your solutions work with each of these file types.

Distributing Documents

As with Excel's workbook-level deployment, each of the Word examples in this book were deployed within the document. Whether saved in a macro-free (`docx`) or macro-enabled (`docm`) file format, these documents contain all the required XML and VBA code within the file.

While this method may seem attractive at first, it is far less functional in Word than in Excel. That's because Excel files are typically used to process data, and occasionally warehouse it. A single Excel file may be used repeatedly to add data to an ever-growing store, whereas a Word document is generally created for a single use.

While deployment on a document level may be a good way to keep specialized tools in place for a specific report, most Word customizations will be needed on a more global scale. Because of this, Word is built around templates and the use of "boilerplate" forms and documents, which can be used repeatedly.

If you have created a very specialized set of tools for a specific document, then storing it within the file may work well for you. However, if you need the tools on a larger scale, it may be time to investigate templates and global templates.

Using Templates

Templates are the lifeblood of Microsoft Word. Properly constructed, they enable users to focus on creating content, as new documents are created with the majority of the document framework already in place.

Creation and deployment of Word's templates are quite similar to the methods used in Excel. There are some minor differences, however, which we will look at now.

Configuring Template Directories

Before we begin the discussion of how to create templates, it makes sense to look at where the templates will be stored. Without this information, you cannot hope to save your files in the correct locations.

Open the Office Menu and choose Word Options ➪ Advanced. Scroll to the bottom of this window until you find the File Locations button. Upon clicking it, you will be taken to the interface shown in Figure 16-6.

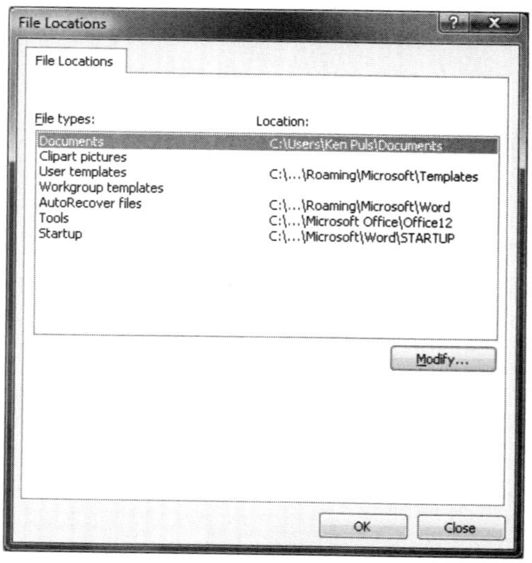

Figure 16-6: The File Locations tab

This tab provides the option to choose or modify the folder for both User Templates and Workgroup Templates. The `User Templates` folder is usually set on the user's own PC and holds templates specific to the user who is logged in. The `Workgroup Templates` directory, however, is usually placed on a network folder, and holds all of the templates that are approved for use within the corporation — of course, subject to network permissions and other controls.

CAUTION **Any template installed in the template folders listed here will open without macro warnings, even if it holds code. This is because the template folders are treated as "trusted locations." For more about trusted locations, see Chapter 17.**

Regardless of which template folder the template is in, it will open in an identical interface, as you'll see in a moment.

To find the full path for any of the locations listed in this window, highlight the item and click the Modify button. You will immediately be taken to the directory. The default locations of the local `Templates` folders are listed in Table 16-3. You'll probably notice that these are the same locations used by Excel (refer to Table 16-1).

Table 16-3: Default Locations for the Local Templates Folders

PLATFORM	PATH
Windows Vista	C:\Users\username\AppData\Roaming\Microsoft\Templates
Windows XP	C:\Documents And Settings\username\Application Data\Microsoft\Templates

Make a note of your template directories as you will use this information shortly when you create a new template.

Creating Templates

Creating a new template in Word is virtually identical to doing so in Excel, as you will see in this example. Open Word and create a new document. Type some text into the document and then go to the Office Menu and choose SaveAs ⇨ Word Template. Save the file, using a macro-free template (`dotx`) format, to either the local or workgroup template folder that you recorded earlier. As expected, the document stays active after saving, so close it.

Now try out the new template. As you did with Excel, go to Office Menu ⇨ New ⇨ My Templates. Double-click the new template to create a new document. When the file opens, you will see the words that you saved in the template file.

NOTE **As with Excel, there are two different template formats for Word: macro-free (`dotx`) and macro-enabled (`dotm`). Be aware that even when the file is saved as a macro-enabled template, new documents created from the template will default to the macro-free (`docx`) format.**

TIP **When creating VBA code for a template, use the `Document_New` event procedure, rather than the `Document_Open` procedure, if you want the macro to run when a new file is created from the template. The `Document_Open` event will not fire when a document is created from a template. However, after the file is saved and closed in a macro-enabled format, opening the file will trigger the `Document_Open` macro but not the `Document_New` procedure.**

CAUTION **Like in Excel, XML travels with the document based on a template, even if it is saved in a macro-free (`docx`) file format. Again, this means that if Ribbon customizations stored in a template rely on VBA, then they will fail if the user saves the resulting file in a macro-free document format.**

The strengths and weaknesses of deploying solutions using templates are virtually identical in Word and Excel. While you can be assured that any customizations will travel with the documents created on the template, you cannot guarantee that the VBA will go with it, as the user may save in a macro-free format. This can lead to serious frustration when the tools do not work.

In addition, as with document-level deployments, customizations are only good for files that are created using the template. If the tools need to be accessible by all documents, a better option is to use Word's global templates.

Global Templates

Word actually has two slightly different formats for add-in files: add-in templates and global templates. The difference between the two is solely the manner in which they are loaded. The add-in template is loaded by clicking the Document Template button on the Developer tab and then selecting a standard Word template; this method must be repeated each time Word is loaded. Global templates, conversely, load every time Word is launched.

Both methods result in identical functionality: the ability to share Ribbon customizations and other custom functionality across all documents and templates in the application. Unlike standard templates, XML and VBA from active global template or add-in files are not stored within regular documents that are created. This leaves the files free from clutter, while still allowing use of the tools that have been developed.

Here, we focus on Word's automatically loading global template, as it is the equivalent of the Excel add-in. Using an add-in template is explored later in this chapter, during the discussions of sharing tabs and groups in Word.

While the global template is identical in purpose to the Excel add-in, the methods of creation, deployment, and management are quite different. Global templates are not stored in regular template directories, and they are never directly referenced by the user; rather, they sit under the surface and share their functionality with the user.

To demonstrate the construction of a global template in Word, we will convert the `button-UpdateWordFields.docm` example that was created in Chapter 6. This file, available in the Chapter 6 downloads package on the book's website, adds a button to the Review tab, which allows you to update all fields — something that you normally can't do without printing the document.

Preparing a Document for Conversion to a Global Template

Three major steps are required to prepare a document for deployment as a global template:

1. Save the file as a template.
2. Review any VBA code for references to the `ThisDocument` object.
3. Verify that subroutines and functions are prefaced by the words `Public` or `Private`.

To begin the preparation process, download and open the `button-UpdateWordFields.docm` file from the book's website. You'll notice immediately that it still has all of the example text in the document. As the document will be hidden when the file is converted to a global template, you won't need this data, so delete it.

The first step to preparing the document for conversion is to save it as a template. For those files that employ XML only, you may save the file as a macro-free (`dotx`) file and skip ahead to the section entitled "Converting a Template to a Global Template." However, if the template uses any VBA, it needs to be saved in the macro-enabled template (`dotm`) format.

The next step is to check whether the file contains any references to the `ThisDocument` object in the VBA code. Where the commands are targeted at the document that holds the code, this will work just fine. Remember, though, that the purpose of the global template is to use the created functionality with *other* documents, so these references may need to be updated.

Open the VBE and browse to the code module named `Module1` in the Project Explorer.

TIP **If the Project Explorer window is not visible, you can press Ctrl+R to display it.**

For your reference, the VBA code for this module is reproduced here:

```
Public Sub UpdateDocumentFields()
     Dim rngStory As Word.Range
     For Each rngStory In ThisDocument.StoryRanges
          rngStory.Fields.Update
          Do
               If rngStory.NextStoryRange Is Nothing Then Exit Do
               Set rngStory = rngStory.NextStoryRange
               rngStory.Fields.Update
```

```
            Loop
        Next rngStory
    End Sub

    'Callback for rxbtnUpdateFields onAction
    Sub rxbtnUpdateFields_click(control As IRibbonControl)
        Call UpdateDocumentFields
    End Sub
```

Take a moment to review the code, looking for any references to `ThisDocument`. You should see one instance: the line beginning `For Each`, where the code references `ThisDocument.StoryRanges`.

The most difficult part of making these conversions is to determine whether using `ThisDocument` is appropriate or not. In this example, we are converting the file to a global template, so the template will not store data of its own and therefore will rarely contain anything in the `StoryRanges` object for `ThisDocument`. Conversely, the active Word document will likely have text in its `StoryRanges`. Because the template will provide functionality for the active document, update this line to read as follows:

```
For Each rngStory In ActiveDocument.StoryRanges
```

As that is the only reference to `ThisDocument` in the code, we can now move on to the next step: checking for `Public` and `Private` subroutines and functions.

You'll notice that in the original routine, `UpdateDocumentFields` was already declared as a public subroutine. This means that it will be available in the Macros dialog, which is accessed by pressing Alt+F8. If you want users to press your fancy button on the Ribbon, you can change this to a `Private Sub` declaration, which would hide it from the Macros dialog.

As a matter of good practice, you should also specify your callback signatures as `Private` routines, as there is no reason to have the routine declared as `Public`. After you have finished making the modifications, close the VBE and save the file.

CAUTION **Remember that private routines and functions cannot be called from other modules. Make sure that you completely test the functionality of your application after setting all your routines, just to ensure that you haven't created a problem.**

The document is now prepared for deployment as a global template.

Converting a Template to a Global Template

Compared to creating an Excel add-in, creating a global template is surprisingly easy. You do not need to save the file in a specific add-in format, and you don't need to install it through the Add-ins interface. All you need to do is copy the file into Word's `STARTUP` folder, as listed in Table 16-4.

Table 16-4: Location of Microsoft Word's Startup Directory

PLATFORM	PATH
Windows Vista	C:\Users\username\AppData\Roaming\Microsoft\Word\STARTUP
Windows XP	C:\Documents And Settings\username\Application Data\Microsoft\Word\STARTUP

After the template is saved in Word's `STARTUP` folder, you must restart Word in order for the global template to become active, so do that now. After Word has reloaded, navigate to the Review tab. Your button now appears between the Changes and Compare groups, as shown in Figure 16-7.

Figure 16-7: The Update Fields button deployed via a global template

Try it out. Open any file that you have with updateable fields. If you don't have one handy, download the `UpdateFieldsExample.docx` file from the Chapter 16 example files on the book's website.

Upon opening the document, note two things. One, the button works and updates the fields for you. Two, you can actually see this button, even though it is not part of the example file. Try closing the example and creating a new document — you'll see that the customization stays in place!

Editing Global Templates

If you recall from working through the Excel section, you can edit the VBA code in an Excel add-in while the add-in is in use. You can also toggle the `IsAddin` property, forcing the file to revert to workbook format, thereby enabling you to review the otherwise hidden worksheets. The bad news is that Word is not quite so friendly.

Although you can see the VBA project for a global template (or add-in template) listed in the VBE's Project Explorer window, clicking on it will result in the error message shown in Figure 16-8.

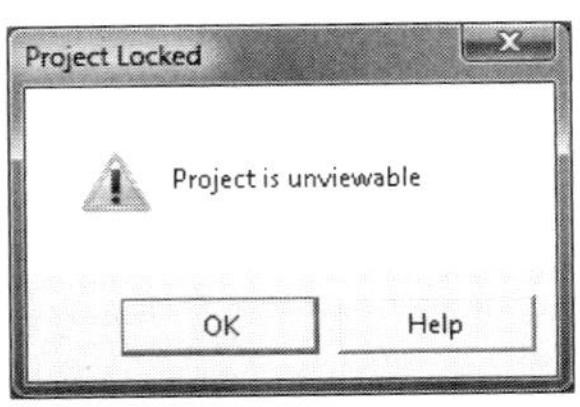

Figure 16-8: Error message generated by attempting to access a global template's code module

In order to edit the VBA code of an active global or add-in template, you must do the following:

1. Close Word.
2. Move the templates out of Word's STARTUP directory to another location.
3. Reopen Word.
4. Choose Office Menu ➪ Open and open the template.
5. Make your changes and save the file.
6. Close Word.
7. Copy the file back to the STARTUP directory.
8. Reopen Word again.

This tedious process underscores the importance of testing a template thoroughly before deploying it as a global template.

NOTE Add-in templates do not need to be moved, they just need to be opened via Office Menu ➪ Open, instead of through the Add-ins interface.

Removing Global Templates

Another drawback of Word's global template implementation is that you cannot deactivate the templates as easily as you can Excel's add-ins. Whereas Excel allows you to unload unnecessary add-ins from memory by going into the Add-Ins Manager (refer to Figure 16-1) and unchecking them, Word has no such option. Every global template is loaded into memory, whether you need it or not. The only way to stop a global template from loading (and therefore consuming your PC memory), is to remove it from Word's `STARTUP` folder!

NOTE Remember that you can find the location of Word's `STARTUP` folder in Table 16-4.

A Note on the Normal.dotm Template

If you are developing solutions for Word, it is generally not advisable to store work in the `Normal.dotm` template.

RibbonX customizations and macros can be stored in the `Normal.dotm` file. This is, in fact, the default location for storing recorded macros. The `Normal.dotm` file even works as a global template: While code and Ribbon customizations will be present in the UI, documents based on the file will not inherit its code or Ribbon customizations. Why, then, do we recommend not using `Normal.dotm` in this way?

It is not uncommon for the `Normal.dotm` file to become corrupted. One of the first troubleshooting steps to take when diagnosing issues with Word is to delete the `Normal.dotm` file. This forces Word to create a replacement file from scratch the next time Word is started, so any customizations stored in the template file will also be deleted. Our recommendation is to invest the extra effort to create a global template file and avoid this potential loss.

Sharing Ribbon Items Across Files (Word and Excel)

As you've seen earlier in this chapter, you can share your Ribbon customizations across all files in the application by deploying your solution as an Excel add-in or as a Word global template. As you begin to send Ribbon customizations to co-workers or clients, you may begin to find that you don't want to do everything in a single file. For example, you may simply want to add a button to a standard add-in when a specific document or template is opened.

One way to make writing code more efficient is to break it down into reusable subroutines or functions, thereby enabling a routine to be written once and used repeatedly. The same is true for Ribbon customizations through the use of a namespace that is shared across files. The namespace gives you the ability to create a master file that holds tab and group controls, after which documents and add-ins can add to those tabs. This is the same way that Microsoft's built-in tabs work — you can add custom groups to their built-in tabs. Using a shared namespace also enables you to load contextual controls into the UI, and it reduces consumption of computer memory by unloading files that are not required.

This section focuses on creating a *host* file that holds a shared tab and group, as well as separate *leech* file that adds its own commands to the host file's tab. To make comparisons easy between Word and Excel, we will create similar structures in each application, which will enable you to see the idiosyncrasies that come into play.

The techniques demonstrated are mainly used when creating add-ins, and work as follows:

- The Ribbon customization for a shared tab (at a minimum) is created in the host UI file.
- Groups or commands that are desired globally are added to this file.
- Additional contextual customizations or commands are contained in other files or add-in formats.
- Other (leech) files are loaded as required, attaching their commands to the host file's customizations.

To create shared tabs and groups, we must begin by exploring how to create a shared "namespace" in our XML code.

Creating a Shared Namespace

Throughout this book, we have been using namespaces, without saying so explicitly. Every UI customization requires association with a namespace, so you have been doing exactly that every time you opened a customUI tag.

Let's take a good look at the standard opening customUI tag, shown here:

```
<customUI xmlns="http://schemas.microsoft.com/office/2006/01/customui">
```

As you can see, the customUI element has been given an xmlns attribute, which happens to be a URL. The part between quotes is, in fact, the XML namespace that you wish to attach to. As stated in Chapter 3, this xmlns attribute is very specific, and now it's time to understand why.

The URL that is provided is simply a name for the XML namespace that you wish to work with. This particular URL is just a textual value that Microsoft decided to use — there is no Web page at the other end. This is important, as it means that Ribbon customizations do not require Internet access.

Microsoft could have just as easily used the name "CustomRibbon" for their defined namespace or any other wording they liked, but they elected to use the URL instead. The important point for us is that if we want to work with Microsoft's tabs, groups, and controls, we must point to this namespace, which holds all of their built-in RibbonX elements.

Microsoft has also given us the ability to create our own namespaces, enabling us to share our tabs and groups in the same way that theirs are shared. To set this up, add another xmlns attribute to the customUI tag, as shown in this example:

```
<customUI
   xmlns="http://schemas.microsoft.com/office/2006/01/customui"
   xmlns:Q="Custom Namespace">
```

You'll notice immediately that Microsoft's default namespace remains in the customUI tag. Again, this ensures that we can still access all of Microsoft's default tabs, groups, and other controls. In addition to the default namespace, we have also added the xmlns:Q attribute.

CROSS-REFERENCE **The xmlns:Q attribute is listed as one of the available attributes for the customUI element in Table 3-2 of Chapter 3.**

In the preceding code, Q is the local name you declare for your namespace. The name can be anything you like, but we recommend prefixing the local name with the characters "ns" in accordance with the list of naming conventions provided in Appendix E. As the local name is the portion that is used to refer back to the namespace, it is also recommended that it be both identifiable and short, as it could potentially be typed many times.

Assuming that we decided to use a local name of "Custom," our custom xmlns:Q would be edited to read as follows:

```
xmlns:nsCustom="Custom Namespace"
```

The portion of the line between the quotes is used to refer to customizations across files, and is purely of a textual nature. For example, if you wanted to make your customization look very official, you could put in a URL to your own website. As this is strictly a textual reference, it does not matter whether a page is there or not. You could also dedicate it to your grandparents if you preferred:

```
xmlns:nsCustom="This is for my Granny and Granddad"
```

The key point about this field is that it will be referenced at the beginning of each file that is designed to attach to your custom namespace.

NOTE **If you are developing add-ins for the Office suite using VB.NET, then the description of the namespace needs be the `ProgID` of the add-in. Associating a `ProgID` enables you to do things that you cannot do through a VBA solution, such as trigger callbacks for shared buttons. As this book focuses on building applications from within the Office suite and we cannot assign a `ProgID` to our files, the field may contain any text that you choose.**

Creating the `xmnls:Q` attribute is the fundamental piece that enables you to share your tabs and groups across multiple files in Office. We'll now explore these concepts using Excel and Word examples. The example files provide a simple demonstration of creating a "host" add-in in Excel, along with a workbook that adds to the host's tabs. The Word example accomplishes the same job, but also adds the complexities of loading Word add-ins on-the-fly, and using callbacks to dynamically set the properties of Ribbon controls.

Sharing Tabs and Groups in Excel

This example is divided into two parts: creation of the host Excel add-in file, and creation of the file that attaches to the host's custom tab.

To begin this example, open Excel and save a new workbook in the Excel add-in (`xlam`) file format. We will refer to this file as `UIHost.xlam`, storing it in the default add-ins directory, as listed in Table 16-2, earlier in this chapter. After you have created the new add-in, you may close Excel.

NOTE **If you would prefer to just download the completed versions of these files, they are included in the sample files for this chapter on the book's website. The files that you'll need are `UIHost.xlam` and `Leech.xlsm`.**

Open the `UIHost.xlam` file in the CustomUI Editor and insert the following code:

```
<customUI
   xmlns="http://schemas.microsoft.com/office/2006/01/customui"
   xmlns:nsHost="My Shared Ribbon">
   <ribbon startFromScratch="false">
```

```
        <tabs>
           <tab idQ="nsHost:rxTabUI"
              label="UI Test"
              insertBeforeMso="TabHome">
              <group idQ="nsHost:rxGrpUI"
                 label="UI Host">
                 <button id="rxHost_Btn1"
                    label="Host UI Button"
                    onAction="rxHost_Buttons"
                    imageMso="HappyFace"/>
              </group>
           </tab>
        </tabs>
     </ribbon>
  </customUI>
```

In reviewing the code, notice that we have created a custom namespace called `nsHost` for our shared Ribbon controls. Within our `customUI` container, we have also opened the `ribbon` and `tabs` containers as we usually do.

Take a good look at the `tab` element though. Notice that instead of the `id` attribute, it uses an `idQ` attribute. This ensures that the tab is created in the shared namespace, and allows other files to place groups within it.

The `idQ` attribute always takes the following form:

```
idQ="localname:id"
```

For our customization, the local name is `nsHost`. This is defined in the `xmlns` attribute of the `customUI` element.

The local name is then followed by a `":"` to show where the name ends, and then the unique identifier for the control. Keep in mind that the `id` is unique within a specific file, but the same name will often be used in multiple files. The id should follow all the rules of the `id` attribute that we have discussed throughout this book. Based on the naming conventions that we're using, this tab will be referred to as `rxTabUI`.

NOTE Don't assume that you can reference this control using `id=rxTabUI`, as that is not the case. If it is declared as an `idQ` element, then you will need to reference it using `idQ="nsHost:rxTabUI"`. This may seem obvious, but it's one of those details that can occasionally slip past us when writing code.

In the next portion of the code, the `group` element is also declared using the `idQ` attribute. Like the `tab` element, this allows the group to be shared, thereby enabling developers to add individual controls to it.

The final portion of the code creates a button, which you will notice is not declared using the `idQ` attribute but instead uses the standard `id` attribute. There are several reasons for this:

- The button is stored in an add-in, so it will always be visible.

- Any desired dynamic abilities can be set through the callbacks associated with the button element.
- There is no way to nest a control within the button, so it does not need to be shared for that purpose. (However, as we've demonstrated in earlier chapters, there are other reasons for sharing button controls.)

At this point, validate the code and save the file. After that, it's time to copy the callback signature for `rxHost_Buttons`, close the CustomUI Editor, and reopen Excel.

We have not yet installed the add-in, so we must now do so in order to access the code modules. Open the Add-ins Manager (Office Menu ➪ Excel Options ➪ Add-ins ➪ Go), and check the box next to UIHost.

TIP **If you don't see the add-in, `UIHost.xlam`, in the list, follow the steps earlier in this chapter in order to complete the installation.**

After the `UIHost.xlam` Add-in installed, open the VBE and navigate to the `UIHost.xlam` project. Add a new standard module, paste the VBA callback signature you copied from the CustomUI Editor, and edit it to read as follows:

```
Private Sub rxHost_Buttons(Control As IRibbonControl)
'Purpose   : Manage the button events

    Select Case Control.ID
        Case Is = "rxHost_Btn1"
            MsgBox "I was called from " & ThisWorkbook.Name
        Case Else
            'Placeholder for other macros
    End Select
End Sub
```

As you can see, this procedure is actually quite simple, feeding back the name of the workbook (or add-in) that called it. Once you have the code entered and compiled, save the add-in by pressing the Save button in the VBE.

NOTE **This procedure references the `ThisWorkbook` object, which means that pressing the button will always refer to the add-in, not the active file. This is by design, as we want to know which workbook the button code is being called from.**

Close the VBE and have a look at the UI Test tab, shown in Figure 16-9.

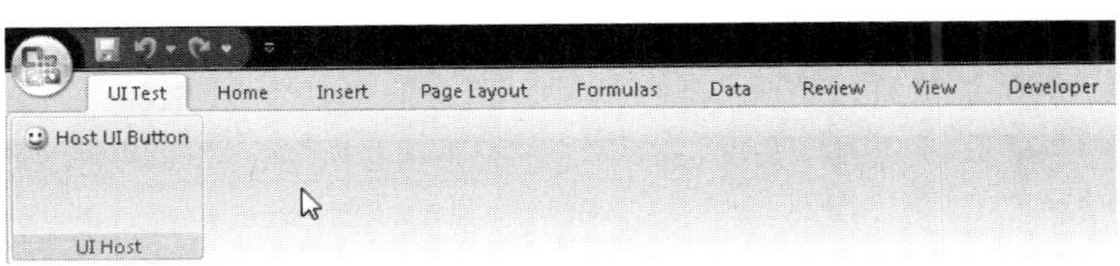

Figure 16-9: A button on a shared tab

Upon clicking the button, you will see that the routine has been called from the add-in.

The next step in this example is to create a new file that will attach its own custom group to the UIHost's shared tab. In addition, it covers both shared buttons and regular buttons, exposing some unexpected idiosyncrasies of shared controls.

To get started on this portion, create a blank workbook and save it as a macro-enabled `xlsm` file. We've called the file `Leech.xlsm` and refer to it as the Leech file, but you may call it anything you'd like. Close the Leech file in Excel, open it in the CustomUI Editor, and make sure that it contains the following XML code:

```
<customUI
   xmlns="http://schemas.microsoft.com/office/2006/01/customui"
   xmlns:nsLeech="My Shared Ribbon">
   <ribbon startFromScratch="false">
      <tabs>
      <!-- Shared tab in UI Host file -->
         <tab idQ="nsLeech:rxTabUI">

            <!-- Shared group in UI Host file -->
            <group idQ="nsLeech:rxGrpLeech"
               label="Leech"
               insertBeforeQ="nsLeech:rxGrpUI">

               <!-- Controls built using a shared namespace
                  in current file -->
               <labelControl idQ="nsLeech:rxLbl01"
                  label="Defined Namespace"/>
               <button idQ="nsLeech:rxButton01"
                  label="Button 1"
                  onAction="rxSharedCallControl_Click"
                  imageMso="HappyFace"/>
               <button idQ="nsLeech:rxButton02"
                  label="Button 2"
                  onAction="rxSharedCallControl_Click"
                  imageMso="HappyFace"/>

               <!-- Controls build without using shared namespace
                   (also in current file) -->
               <separator id="rxSeparator01"/>
               <labelControl id="rxLbl_02"
                  label="No Namespace"/>
               <button id="rxButton03"
                  label="Button 3"
                  onAction="rxSharedCallControl_Click"
                  imageMso="HappyFace"/>
               <button id="rxButton04"
                  label="Button 4"
                  onAction="rxSharedCallControl_Click"
                  imageMso="HappyFace"/>
            </group>
```

```
        </tab>
      </tabs>
    </ribbon>
</customUI>
```

You should immediately notice that we have defined our shared namespace as we did in the `UIHost.xlam` file. While we changed the name of the namespace from `nsHost` to `nsLeech`, the textual identifier remains "My Shared Ribbon."

You could have used anything for the local name, including `nsHost`, providing the name was used consistently throughout the file's XML code. The reason that we changed the namespace portion, however, is to make it clear that we are in the Leech file. This also helps to demonstrate that this portion may be different between the files. The local name is just that, local, and is used as an alias for the actual custom namespace.

Conversely, the custom namespace, `"My Shared Ribbon"`, on the other hand, *must* remain as specified in the `UIHost.xlam` file. This is the vehicle that allows us to link the files together.

As you scan down the code, note that we open the shared tab, referencing its `idQ` identifier, and then create a new group within it. In addition, we have positioned our new group immediately before the default by specifying the `insertBeforeQ` attribute.

TIP The `insertBeforeQ` attribute enables you to position shared elements in relation to each other, just as the `insertBeforeMso` attribute enables you to position elements in relation to Microsoft's built-in elements.

The next block of XML populates the new group with some custom controls that were created using an `idQ` attribute. The intention here is to have controls in a standard Excel workbook that remains available when opening a different workbook, much like the functionality provided by an add-in.

Finally, we added another block of XML to create more custom controls, but this time using the `id` attribute, rather than the `idQ` attribute. As you would expect, these controls are document specific, and are hidden when the workbook is deactivated.

One final point to note about the buttons is that they all use the same shared callback. This is simply a matter of convenience for this example; it is not a necessary restriction of shared controls.

Once you finish typing and validating the code, generate and copy the callback signature before closing the CustomUI Editor. Reopen the Leech file in Excel, open the VBE, and paste the callback signature into a new standard module. You should then modify it to read as follows:

```
Sub rxSharedCallControl_Click(control As IRibbonControl)
'Purpose   : React to the button click and inform the user where
'            it was called from
    MsgBox "You clicked " & control.ID & " from " & ThisWorkbook.Name
End Sub
```

As you saw with the `UIHost` file, this is a very simple procedure that simply lists the workbook that reacted to the button click. Now close the VBE, save the file, and have a look at your customization, shown in Figure 16-10.

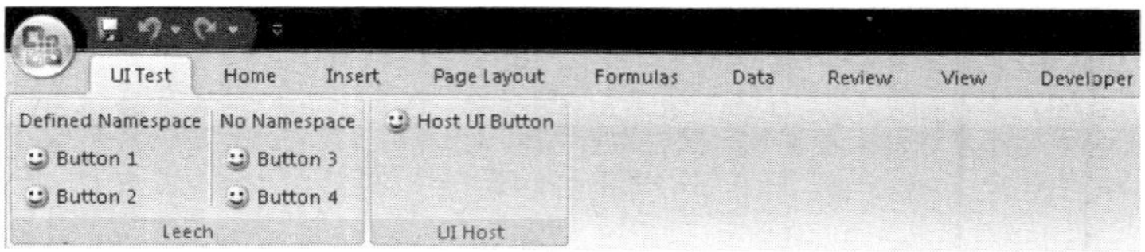

Figure 16-10: The Leech group and controls, added to a shared tab

The Leech group has been added to the UI Test tab, and all of the controls that we created, whether declared with `idQ` or `id` attributes, have been created.

Next, create a new workbook. The UI will update to appear as shown in Figure 16-11.

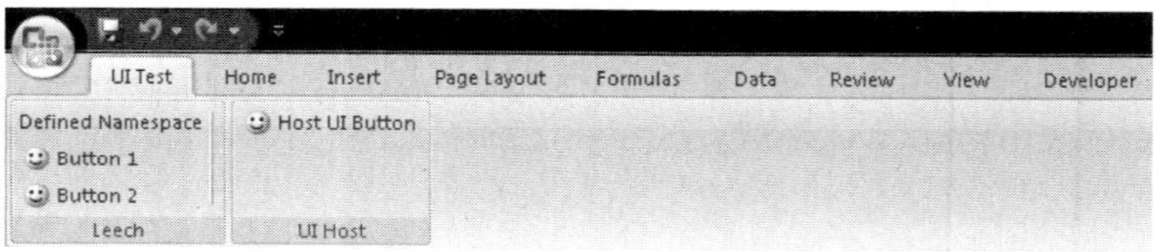

Figure 16-11: The Leech group when a different file is activated

The controls that were declared with the `id` attribute disappear, leaving only the controls that were declared with the `idQ` attribute. This is consistent with the behavior of controls that we are used to creating with the `id` attribute: They are hidden when their parent file goes out of focus. So far, so good . . . but now click Button 1.

Strangely, nothing happens. There is no message box, no error, simply nothing. You may be asking yourself whether you elected to enable macros at this point.

Toss away the workbook you just created and return to the Leech file. The UI will resume the view shown in Figure 16-10, with Buttons 3 and 4 showing. Try clicking one of them; you will receive a message similar to what is shown in Figure 16-12.

Figure 16-12: Output from Button 3's macro

Since this is working in the Leech file, macros must be enabled. Try clicking Button 1 (or Button 2) again; still nothing! So what is going on here?

A control declared using an idQ attribute, be it a button, checkBox, or whatever, will *not* trigger any callbacks. The reason behind this is related to the differences between inhabited and uninhabited namespaces, a topic that is beyond the scope of this book. Suffice it to say that there is no way in Microsoft Office to create an inhabited namespace to allow triggering callbacks for controls created with the idQ attribute.

Sadly, the lack of callback availability with idQ declared controls limits the use of the attribute to sharing tabs and groups when building solutions purely within Microsoft Office. While there is more flexibility when designing managed COM add-ins using C# or VB.NET with VSTO, it is questionable whether the added complexity actually affords us any worthwhile benefits.

NOTE **To share a** button**,** checkBox**, or similar control across multiple workbooks or documents, the controls must be deployed using an Excel add-in or using Word's global or add-in templates.**

TIP **Remember that while it is very tempting to create a shared container in your** PERSONAL.XLSB **workbook, which would allow you to attach customizations to it on-the-fly,** PERSONAL.XLSB **remains invisible to the end user.**

Sharing Tabs and Groups in Word

As with the Excel example in the last section, this example creates a UIHost file with shared tabs and groups, as well as a Leech file, which adds to it. It also includes the nonfunctional shared buttons to demonstrate the difference between how Word and Excel deal with them.

We also show you how to load a Word add-in template on-the-fly. This is similar functionality to the default behavior of Excel's Add-in manager, which provides the capability to set a file so that it can be loaded at startup when desired. Naturally, this also employs some callback signatures to record the necessary setting. Again, the example is broken down into two logical parts: the UIHost.dotm file and the Leech.dotm file.

NOTE **These files are also included in the sample downloads for this chapter.**

To begin, either open the downloaded example or create a macro-enabled template (dotm) file called UIHost.dotm. Open it in the CustomUI Editor and make sure that it contains the following XML:

```
<customUI
   xmlns="http://schemas.microsoft.com/office/2006/01/customui"
   xmlns:nsHost="My Shared Ribbon"
   onLoad="rxIRibbonUI_onLoad">
   <ribbon startFromScratch="false">
```

```
        <tabs>
          <tab idQ="nsHost:rxTabUI"
            label="UI Test"
            insertBeforeMso="TabHome">
            <group idQ="nsHost:rxGrpUI"
              label="UI Host">
              <button id="rxBtnLoadLeech"
                getLabel="rxBtnLoadLeech_getLabel"
                onAction="rxBtnLoadLeech_click"
                imageMso="HappyFace"/>
              <checkBox id="rxChkLeechStartup"
                label="Load Leech at Startup?"
                getPressed="rxChkLeechStartup_getPressed"
                onAction="rxCheckLeechStatup_click"/>
            </group>
          </tab>
        </tabs>
      </ribbon>
    </customUI>
```

Looking at this code, you can again see that we created a custom namespace and declared an `onAction` attribute. The attribute loads the callback signature to capture the `Ribbon` object required to invalidate the Ribbon, as discussed in Chapter 5. Next, we created the shared `Tab` and `Group` elements, which are declared using an `idQ` attribute, just as we did in the Excel example.

Within this group, however, things start to look a little different. We have a button to load our Leech file, as well as a `checkBox` to give users the option to load the file automatically at startup. Notice again that the clickable controls are declared with the `id` attribute, and not the `idQ` attribute. The reason for this is quite simple: We want to actually trigger a callback when we click them!

Now, validate the code and copy the callback signatures before closing the file in the CustomUI Editor. Open the file in Word, create a new standard module, and paste in all the callbacks. Before we get into creating the individual procedures, add the following three lines at the top of the module, immediately under any `Option` lines (such as `Option Explicit`):

```
Private rxIRibbonUI As IRibbonUI
Private bPressed As Boolean
Private sLabel As String
```

While the first variable, intended to capture the `Ribbon` object, is most likely quite familiar to you, the last two are specific to this application. The `bPressed` variable will hold the state of the `checkBox`, and the `sLabel` variable will hold the label that will be provided to the button. Let's look at each of the procedures in the order in which they will be called.

If an `onLoad` procedure has been declared, it will be the first procedure to fire in any Ribbon customization. This procedure is identical to the ones used throughout this book, and looks as follows:

```
Private Sub rxIRibbonUI_onLoad(ribbon As IRibbonUI)
```

```
'Callback for onLoad to capture RibbonUI
    Set rxIRibbonUI = ribbon
End Sub
```

The next two procedures that are called are the procedures to get the dynamic attributes for the Ribbon items: our `button` and `checkBox`. These procedures are also quite simple, asking only for the values to be returned from the variables that we establish for them:

```
'Callback for rxBtnLoadLeech getLabel
Private Sub rxBtnLoadLeech_getLabel(control As IRibbonControl, _
    ByRef returnedVal)
    returnedVal = sLabel
End Sub
'Callback for rxChkLeechStartup getPressed
Sub rxChkLeechStartup_getPressed(control As IRibbonControl, _
    ByRef returnedVal)
    returnedVal = bPressed
End Sub
```

You may be wondering why we set these to a variable, when the variables are empty at this stage. The callbacks will be triggered, but the button label will be blank, and the `checkBox` value will always be `false`. There is a good reason for this.

These callbacks will be used each time the `button` or `checkBox` is clicked. It is best to keep them clean, and take care of setting the default values when the "startup" routine actually runs. Remember that we've already captured the `RibbonUI` object to a variable, so we can invalidate the Ribbon to force a rebuild. In fact, this is exactly what we will do.

After all the dynamic properties have been set by callbacks, the next routines that will fire are the "startup" routines: `Document_Open` for documents, and `AutoExec` for global templates and add-ins. Because we will be converting this file to a global template, we will use the following `AutoExec` routine, placing it in the standard module with the RibbonX code. This routine contains the bulk of the settings:

```
Sub AutoExec()
'Retrieve the stored "Load at startup" behaviour
    bPressed = GetSetting("RibbonX Book", "Host/Leach Example", _
        "LoadAtStartup",

    Select Case bPressed
        Case True
            'Load the addin and store the button label
            Application.AddIns.Add Left(AddIns("UIHost").Path, _
                Len(AddIns("UIHost").Path) - 12) & "AddIns\Leech.dotm"
            sLabel = "Unload Leech"
        Case False
            'Store the button label
            sLabel = "Load Leech"
    End Select

    'Invalidate the Ribbon, updating the label and checkbox values
```

```
    rxIRibbonUI.Invalidate
End Sub
```

In reviewing the code, you will see that the very first thing it does is record the appropriate state of the `checkBox`, which has been (or will be) stored in the Registry. It then evaluates this setting and takes the appropriate action. If the setting is `True`, then it loads the `Leech.dotm` file (which we will create) from the default Add-ins directory, and sets the `sLabel` variable to read `"Unload Leech"`. If the setting is `False` (or missing), then it simply stores the text string `"Load Leech"` in the `sLabel` variable.

CROSS-REFERENCE **A full discussion of using the Registry to store data can be found in Chapter 12.**

The final step is to invalidate the Ribbon. This forces the `rxBtnLoadLeech_getLabel` and `rxChkLeechStartup_getPressed` routines to be executed a second time, returning the values to the Ribbon controls we just set.

NOTE **The line that actually loads the add-in template is set to load the file from the default** `AddIns` **directory listed in Table 16-2. This is accomplished by evaluating the full path to the** `UIHost.dotm` **document in the** `Word\STARTUP` **directory, stripping the last 12 characters and appending "AddIns." If you examine this, you will see that this converts the following file path**

`C:\Users\username\AppData\Roaming\Microsoft\Word\STARTUP`

to

`C:\Users\username\AppData\Roaming\Microsoft\AddIns`

In addition, because the Office subfolders follow the same format in Windows Vista and Windows XP, this code for determining the folder is operating-system agnostic!

Next, we need to create the routines that will actually fire when the controls are clicked. We start with the callback triggered when the `checkBox` is clicked to request that the Leech file opens at startup. That is accomplished with the following routine:

```
'Callback for rxChkLeechStartup onAction
Private Sub rxCheckLeechStatup_click(control As IRibbonControl, _
    pressed As Boolean)
    bPressed = pressed
    SaveSetting "RibbonX Book", "Host/Leach Example", _
        "LoadAtStartup", pressed
End Sub
```

This procedure sets the `bPressed` variable equal to the current state of the `checkBox`, and then it saves the state in the Registry.

Finally, we need to examine the callback for the button used to load the Leech template. The code for this is shown here:

```
'Callback for rxBtnLoadLeech onAction
Private Sub rxBtnLoadLeech_click(control As IRibbonControl)
    Select Case sLabel
        Case Is = "Load Leech"
            Application.AddIns.Add Left(AddIns("UIHost").Path, _
                Len(AddIns("UIHost").Path) - 12) & "AddIns\Leech.dotm"
            sLabel = "Unload Leech"
        Case Is = "Unload Leech"
            Application.AddIns(Left(AddIns("UIHost").Path, _
                Len(AddIns("UIHost").Path) - 12) & _
                "AddIns\Leech.dotm").Delete
            sLabel = "Load Leech"
    End Select

    'Invalidate the button, forcing the label to be updated
    rxIRibbonUI.InvalidateControl ("rxBtnLoadLeech")
End Sub
```

This callback has been structured to take the action listed on the button. The label is evaluated to determine whether the file should be loaded or unloaded, and then the appropriate steps are taken, including changing the value of the `sLabel` variable. Once this is accomplished, the button is invalidated, which triggers an update of the label.

NOTE The method to remove an add-in from Word is to "delete" it. This action actually only closes the file, which removes it from memory. It does not delete the source file itself.

It's again time to compile the code and save the file. Then, close Word and place a copy of the template in Word's STARTUP folder. Restart Word, and you will now see the `button` and `checkBox` showing on the UI Test tab, as displayed in Figure 16-13.

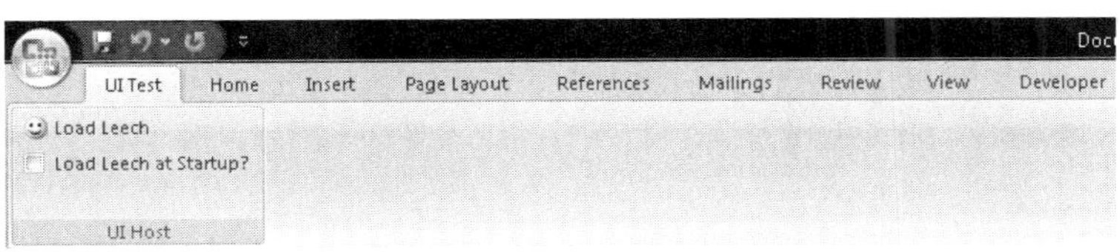

Figure 16-13: The front end loader for the Leech file

While the `checkBox` code is fully functional at this point, the `Leech` button obviously won't work because we have not created the file.

The `Leech.dotm` file is identical to the `Leech.xlsm` file created for the previous example, except that this file is saved in a macro-enabled template (`dotm`) format, rather than as a standard document. To convert the file from Excel to Word, you could do the following:

- Create a new word document and save it as a macro-enabled template (`dotm`) file.
- Copy the XML code from the Excel file and paste it in the Word file via the CustomUI Editor.
- Copy the VBA code from the Excel file and paste it in a new standard module in the Word file's VBA project.

Alternately, you could make it really easy on yourself and just download `Leech.dotm` from the example files for this chapter.

The secret to making this example work is to copy the Leech file into Office's `Add-ins` directory, which is where we saved the Excel add-ins. Once you have done this, press the Load Leech button. You will see the controls coded into the Leech file's XML, as shown in Figure 16-14.

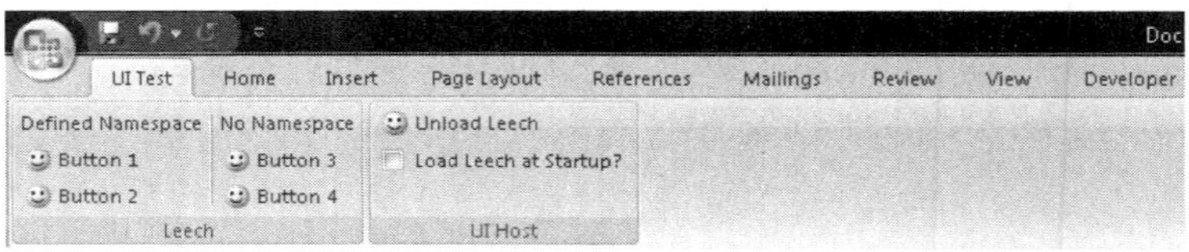

Figure 16-14: The Leech file's customizations added to the Host file

Again, clicking Button 1 or Button 2 will yield nothing, but clicking Button 3 or Button 4 will indicate that they were called from the Leech file.

NOTE **No matter what document you open, Button 3 and Button 4 still show up. This is because the Leech file was opened as an add-in template, which means that any buttons declared with an `id` attribute will show at all times.**

Now, experiment with unloading the Leech file. Upon doing so, your UI will revert to what is shown in Figure 16-13, as you would expect. Next, click the `checkBox` and restart Word. After the reboot, you should be greeted with the Leech customizations already loaded, as shown in Figure 16-15. At this point, we have confirmed that our load at startup code performs properly.

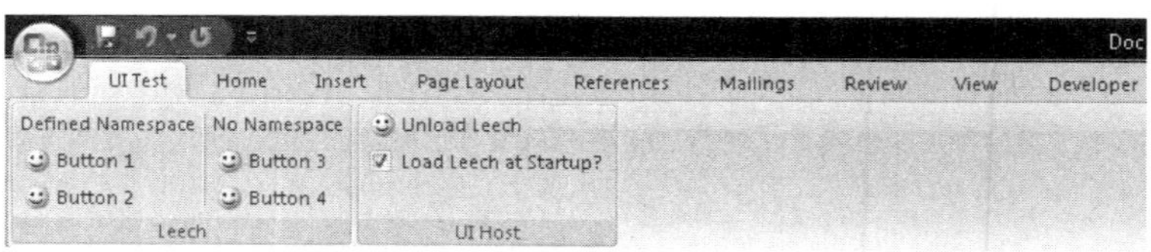

Figure 16-15: The Leech file loaded from startup

One other point worth mentioning is the difference in the way that Word and Excel treat document-level `idQ` customizations. Whereas navigating to another workbook in Excel left the `idQ` associated buttons showing and hid the buttons defined with an `id` attribute, this is not always true with Word.

If you were to save the `Leech.dotm` file as a macro-enabled document (`docm`) instead, and then open it while the host was open, you would still see the view shown in Figure 16-14, as you'd expect. (A `.docm` version of the Leech file is also included in the Chapter 6 downloads.) However, navigating to another document does *not* hide only the buttons created with the `id` attribute — it hides all of the controls, including the group in the Leech file. The results are illustrated in Figure 16-13, even though you would expect it to look like the Excel version shown in Figure 16-11.

There is no functional impact, because you cannot use the `idQ` attribute to declare buttons or other clickable controls. However, it illustrates how applications will sometimes deal with items in different ways, even in situations where you would expect them to be consistent.

Deploying Word and Excel Solutions Where Multiple Versions of Office are in Use

Unless you are working in a controlled environment where everyone has Office 2007, it would be helpful to know how to deploy an add-in file in environments that also still use legacy Office versions. Given that Office 97 is still used by many companies, this transition could take much longer than Microsoft originally anticipated.

This section does not go into the details of how to create the old CommandBar UI customizations as it is targeted at users who already know how, and who are now looking for tips on how to deploy solutions that will work seamlessly between the different Office platforms.

Do Legacy CommandBar Customizations Still Work?

One of the biggest questions facing an Office developer who considers installing Office 2007 is "Will my customizations still work, given that the Ribbon is totally different?" The answer is yes, the customizations will work, but they are sort of stuffed away in a corner.

Figure 16-16 shows what happens to an add-in, (or any other customization) that uses the legacy CommandBar code to create the menu structure. (If you're puzzling over the occasional British spelling, you can appreciate that we have a multilingual team of authors. So, in addition to English, you may see French, Portuguese, and maybe even German.)

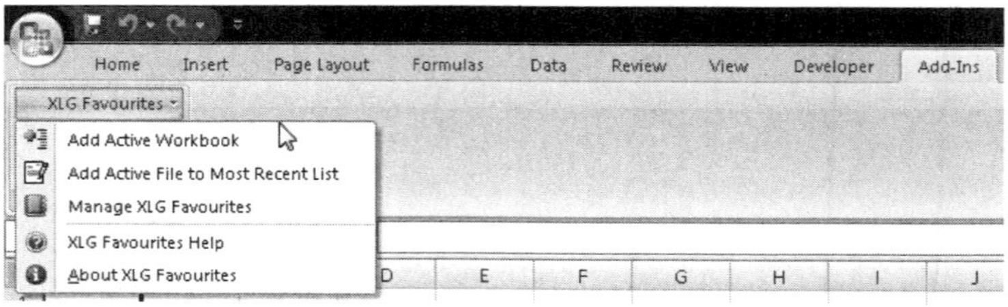

Figure 16-16: The legacy XLG Favourites add-in (from Excelguru.ca) in Excel 2007

Customizations created using the legacy CommandBar object model, whether deployed in an add-in, workbook, or template, are placed in the Add-Ins tab. This is an automatic conversion so it does not require any effort or coding on your part.

Unfortunately, with the exception of adding the entire Add-Ins tab to the QAT, there is nothing that we can do about the placement of the Add-Ins tab. Ergo, we have another incentive to migrate the files into the 2007 formats and write the XML to create a custom RibbonUI interface.

NOTE **The Add-Ins tab only appears if it is required due to automatic conversions from legacy files or because it is used in a customization.**

CAUTION **Although the CommandBar modifications appear to be converted seamlessly, this does not guarantee that the associated code will still run. VBA's** `FileSearch` **method was removed in Office 2007, for example, as was Excel's support for opening old Lotus** `wks` **files.**

There are several ways to approach deploying in mixed environments. Basically, you can *segregate*, which we cover next, or you can *integrate*. The examples in method 2, which follows, will walk you through the process of incorporating legacy customizations into Excel and Word 2007.

Method 1: Creating Separate Versions

The first method of deploying solutions in an environment with multiple versions of Office is the most obvious: create a version of the application in each file format. This is by far the most straightforward method, because it leaves the earlier customizations in their native file format and enables you to take full advantage of the new features for the 2007 files.

Creating your applications in separate file formats allows for a clear separation and focus between application versions without making compromises for other versions. This can be beneficial in that applications can be as efficient as possible in each version. Deployment can also be easier, as you simply match the version of the application to the user's needs.

The biggest drawback to this method is that it involves creating and maintaining multiple versions of the file. This is seldom desirable, as it means that every code adjustment needs to be repeated in each file format. You also run the risk of sending users the wrong file format, which may or may not work on their system.

In addition, if you are running multiple versions of Office, and you place each version of your file in a `STARTUP` directory, Office 2007 may end up loading both versions of the file. In addition to instantiating both user interfaces, this consumes more memory than just running one version.

Method 2: Calling a Previous Version from a New Add-in

The other method for working in an environment with multiple versions of Office is to create a legacy add-in or global template to contain the RibbonX interface for 2007 files. Using the `Application.Run` VBA method in the 2007 file, you can then call procedures stored in the legacy file. This way, the legacy file actually holds all of the functional code, and the 2007 file simply acts as a launcher.

To demonstrate this technique, we will modify a 2003 add-in file with a CommandBar modification to act as the back end for a 2007 add-in. This example originally created a "Forums" menu on the 2003 help menu, as shown in Figure 16-17, with two Web forums listed therein: Patrick Schmid's RibbonX Forum and VBA Express.

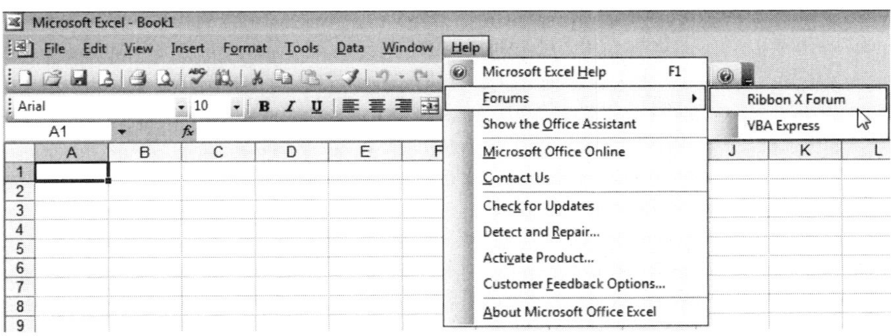

Figure 16-17: The 2003 add-in to be used as a front-end loader

While this example applies to both Excel and Word, there are differences in the way Excel add-ins and Word's global templates are loaded. The example will therefore be explored in both applications, allowing you to learn both and compare the two.

The example files are provided in the chapter downloads, and are listed along with their purpose in Table 16-5.

Table 16-5: Example Files for Front-End Loader Demonstrations

EXAMPLE FILENAME	PURPOSE
ForumLauncher_v2003_Original.xla	Starting point for following Excel example
ForumLauncher_v2003.xla	Completed Excel 2003 loader file

Continued

Table 16-5 *(continued)*

EXAMPLE FILENAME	PURPOSE
ForumLauncher_v2007.xlam	Completed Excel 2007 custom UI file
ForumLauncher_v2003_Original.dot	Starting point for following Word example
ForumLauncher_v2003.dot	Completed Word 2003 loader file
ForumLauncher_v2007.dotm	Completed Word 2007 custom UI file

Using a 2003 Excel Add-in as a Front-End Loader for a 2007 Add-in

The process of migrating a 2003 file to both handle the 2003 environment as well as act as a back end for a 2007 file is best done in three steps:

1. Create the base 2007 Ribbon customization add-in.
2. Make the required modifications to the 2003 add-in.
3. Link the 2007 file to ensure that the 2003 file is opened first.

This order of events is important so that things won't fall apart as you go along. The final point is a matter of housekeeping, to ensure that a user can never load the 2007 version of the file without the 2003 version, as the 2003 version holds all of the macro code required for the 2007 version to run.

We start by building the basic 2007 portion of the add-in, which will act as the new face of the add-in in Excel 2007. Create a new file in Excel and save it with the name `ForumLauncher_v2007.xlam` in the default `AddIns` folder. When you are done, close Excel and open the file in the CustomUI Editor.

At this point, you need to create your Ribbon customizations, which you do using the following XML code:

```
<customUI xmlns="http://schemas.microsoft.com/office/2006/01/customui">
   <ribbon startFromScratch="false">
      <tabs>
            <tab idMso="TabDeveloper">
                <group id="rxgrpForums"
                    label="Forums">
                    <button id="rxbtnRibbonX"
                        label="Patrick Schmid's RibbonX Forum"
                        onAction="rxsharedLinks_click"
                        imageMso="HyperlinkInsert"
                        tag="RibbonX"/>
                    <button id="rxbtnVBAX"
                        label="VBA Express"
                        onAction="rxsharedLinks_click"
                        imageMso="HyperlinkInsert"
                        tag="VBAX"/>
```

```
                </group>
            </tab>
        </tabs>
    </ribbon>
</customUI>
```

This code should seem relatively straightforward by now. It simply adds two buttons to a custom group at the end of the Developer tab. Notice that the buttons use a shared callback, `rxsharedLinks_click`, which will use the `tag` attribute, as you'll see shortly.

As usual, the code should be validated and saved, and the callback signatures copied before the file is closed in the CustomUI Editor.

Open Excel and install the add-in if your customizations are not showing (Office Button ➪ Excel Options ➪ Go and check the box beside ForumLauncher_v2007.xlam). Next, go into the VBE, navigate to the ForumLauncher project, insert a new module, and paste the callback signature. Modify the callback to read as follows:

```
 'Callback for rxbtnRibbonX onAction
Sub rxsharedLinks_click(control As IRibbonControl)
    Application.Run "LaunchFrom2007", control.Tag
End Sub
```

This short procedure uses the `Application.Run` method to launch a macro from another open file. It specifies the name of the macro to launch, `LaunchFrom2007`, which we will build shortly, as well as a parameter: the tag for the control.

With that modification, you have completed the first phase of the migration. Save the VBProject and uninstall the add-in.

The next major step is to make the required modifications to the 2003 add-in. Rather than retype all the code, download the sample files from the book's website. Rename the `ForumLauncher_v2003_Original.xla` to `ForumLauncher_v2003.xla`, and save it in the `AddIns` directory as well. Open Excel and install the new add-in. At this point, you now have a new menu on your Add-ins tab (see Figure 16-18).

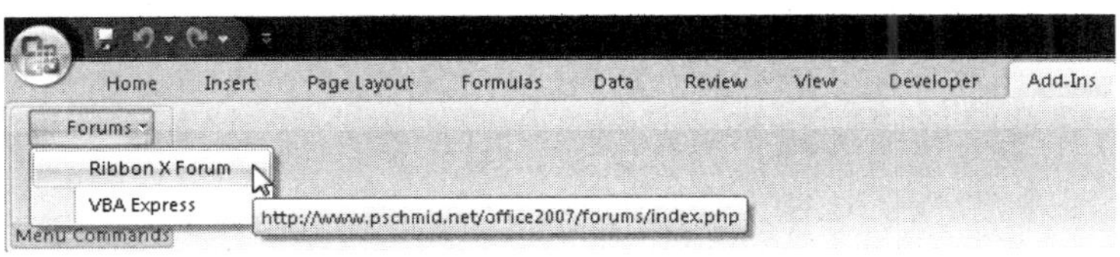

Figure 16-18: The 2003 add-in showing on the Add-ins tab

This is great, but since you've already built a Ribbon for your project, you really don't need this. Therefore, your first job is to modify the startup code to ensure that the menu is not created on the Add-Ins tab. But how do you do this? After all, you didn't write XML code for this in 2003, but Excel 2007 forces it on us.

As it turns out, you can avoid the Add-Ins manifestation simply by not creating the menu based on the CommandBar object model. Of course, you do still want the menus when you open 2003, so you need a way of ensuring that it only creates the menus if Excel 2003 or earlier is loaded. Fortunately, you can do this by testing the application version. You can also use this test to set up the event to load the 2007 file if it is required.

Use the following steps to test for versions and load the correct menus. First, open the VBE and browse to the `ForumLauncher_v2003.xla` project. Expand the `ThisWorkbook` class module and modify the `Workbook_Open` procedure to read as follows:

```
Private Sub Workbook_Open()
    Dim wbAddin As AddIn
    Dim bInstalled As Boolean
    Dim s2007FileName As String

    s2007FileName = _
    Application.WorksheetFunction.Substitute(ThisWorkbook.Name, _
        "2003", "2007") & "m"

    If Val(Application.Version) < 12 Then
        Call CreateMenu
    Else
        'Check if addin installed
        For Each wbAddin In Application.AddIns
            If wbAddin.Name = s2007FileName Then
                'Addin is installed, so open it
                Workbooks.Open ThisWorkbook.Path & _
                    Application.PathSeparator & s2007FileName
                bInstalled = True
                Exit For
            End If
        Next wbAddin

        'Install addin if required
        If Not bInstalled Then Application.AddIns.Add _
           ThisWorkbook.Path & Application.PathSeparator & s2007FileName
    End If
End Sub
```

The `Workbook_Open` event will now do the following:

- It captures the name of the 2007 add-in to a variable by substituting 2007 for 2003 in the 2003 Add-ins filename and then appending an "m" to the resulting string. (The Add-in format in Excel 2007 is an `xlam` file, not an `xla` file, as in the past.)
- The application's version is checked. If it is less than 12 (Office 2007 is version 12), it creates the menu.
- If the version is not less than 12, it checks whether the 2007 add-in is already installed.
- If the 2007 version of the add-in is installed, it loads the file and records that the 2007 version is installed.
- The `bInstalled` property is evaluated. If it is false, then the add-in is installed.

TIP **When evaluating an application version, it is a good idea to nest it within the `Val()` function. Using this function to evaluate the version strips any text characters from the value and ensures that it's actually a number. In the past, some versions were alpha-numeric, such as 9.1b, which caused numerical comparisons to fail. Using the `Val()` function deals with this issue.**

Because we have installed and opened the 2007 file when the 2003 file is launched, it also makes sense to explicitly unload the 2007 file when we are finished. To accomplish this, we need to modify the `Workbook_BeforeClose` procedure to check the version and unload the 2007 add-in when appropriate:

```
Private Sub Workbook_BeforeClose(Cancel As Boolean)
    If Val(Application.Version) < 12 Then
        Call DeleteMenu
    Else
        Workbooks(Application.WorksheetFunction.Substitute( _
            ThisWorkbook.Name, "2003", "2007") & "m").Close
    End If
End Sub
```

Again, the version of the application is tested. If the file version is less than 12, then the standard process will have loaded the 2003 menu modifications; therefore, the `DeleteMenu` routine needs to be fired. Given that this scenario only occurs when loading the 2003 version of the file, we can assume that the 2007 version was never loaded, so we don't need to explicitly close it.

As you can imagine, different code is needed if the application is version 12 or higher, as we can then assume that the 2007 version of the add-in will be loaded as well. Note that the 2007 add-in file includes code to ensure that the 2003 workbook file is already loaded. Therefore, given that both the 2003 and the 2007 add-in files will be loaded, we need to include code to close the 2007 add-in file.

The last thing that we need to do to our 2003 add-in is give it an entry point so that the 2007 version can call its procedures. Start by opening the standard module. Note that this module holds a fair volume of code, part of which is required to create and delete the menu structure as required. In addition, it also has the following two routines, which are fired when the menu buttons are clicked in Excel 2003 or earlier:

```
Private Sub Launch_VBAX()
'Launch the VBAX website
    ActiveWorkbook.FollowHyperlink (sVBAXURL)
End Sub

Private Sub Launch_RibbonX()
'Launch the RibbonX forum
    ActiveWorkbook.FollowHyperlink (sRibbonXURL)
End Sub
```

Although we could easily declare these as `Public` and evaluate the `id` of the clicked control to call the appropriate routine, this would also allow our users to run the macros by pressing Alt+F8. You may have a good reason to not allow this to happen, so to avoid the issue we are using a private routine and will create a central entry point.

One issue with running a macro from the standard interface is that the macro cannot be passed a parameter. You can use this to your benefit, as it is the perfect way to stop users from running your macros by hand, and it also happens to be the easiest way to deal with this scenario.

Now we're ready to create the central entry point. Add the following code to the end of the standard module, after all of the existing procedures:

```
Public Sub LaunchFrom2007(sSiteToLaunch)
'Act as a loader from the 2007 add-in
    Select Case UCase(sSiteToLaunch)
        Case Is = "VBAX"
            Call Launch_VBAX
        Case Is = "RIBBONX"
            Call Launch_RibbonX
    End Select
End Sub
```

If you recall, we set up a callback routine in the 2007 version, using the `Application.Run` method to call the `LaunchFrom2007` macro. The callback was constructed to pass the `tag` attribute of the control that was clicked. If you go back and review the XML code used for the 2007 UI, you'll see that the `Select Case` structure (above) is looking for these tag values. The `case` statement evaluates which control was clicked and launches the appropriate macro from the 2003 file!

TIP **Note that the `case` statement is looking for uppercase versions of the text we supplied for the tag properties. This is a technique to avoid case-sensitivity issues. You convert the string to uppercase by using the `UCase()` function in the `Select Case` statement, and then make sure that all of the variants you check against are also listed in uppercase. Even if a lowercase tag is provided, this routine will convert it to uppercase and attempt to find a match.**

Now save the 2003 `xla` add-in and uninstall it, as we have finished with the conversions that we need to make. Our final step in this process is to go back to the 2007 add-in and force the user to have the 2003 version open first.

Install the 2007 version of the add-in again. Here, in a nutshell, is the problem: We now have the 2007 file open but the 2003 file, which holds all of our required code, is not loaded. Since we are relying on a human hand to select the correct add-in, it is likely a mistake could be made here. It is probably a fair guess that if an uninformed user were in the 2007 interface and was given the option between a 2003 file and a 2007 file, they would choose the latter.

We can fix this problem by modifying the `Workbook_Open` event of the 2007 add-in, including a check to test whether the 2003 file is open. If not, we'll notify the user and shut down the 2007 version of the add-in.

Open the VBE and browse the projects until you are at the `ThisWorkbook` module for the `ForumLauncher_v2007.xla` project. Once there, insert the following code:

```
Private Const sReqdAddin = "Forum_Launcher_v2003.xla"

Private Sub Workbook_Open()
    Dim wbTest As Workbook

    On Error Resume Next
    Set wbTest = Workbooks(sReqdAddin)
    If Err.Number = 0 Then
        'Addin open
        On Error GoTo 0
        Exit Sub
    End If

    'Addin must not be open
    On Error GoTo 0
    MsgBox "You must load " & sReqdAddin & " to use " & _
        ThisWorkbook.Name
    ThisWorkbook.Close savechanges:=False
End Sub
```

Because all add-ins are shown in the `Workbooks` collection, the code begins by checking each open workbook to see whether it is the required add-in. If the name of the workbook being checked matches what is stored in the private constant, then the 2003 file must be loaded, and the routine is exited. However, if there is not a match, then the user is advised of the issue and the 2007 add-in file is closed.

Voilà, the conversion is complete. You can now save the file in the VBE and uninstall the add-in again.

Now, let's give it a test. Open the Add-ins Manager and install the 2003 version of the add-in. You should now see the fully functional group on the right side of the Developer tab, as shown in Figure 16-19.

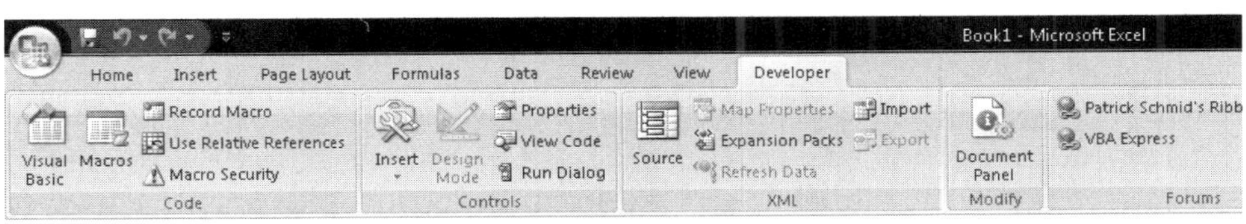

Figure 16-19: A 2007 face on a 2003 add-in

NOTE **If you haven't done so already, you may want to check out both links by clicking the buttons. They will open your Web browser and take you straight to two free forums that offer help with Ribbon and VBA programming.**

Go back into the Add-ins Manager, uninstall the 2003 version, and install the 2007 version. Upon clicking OK, you will be returned to the user interface, which displays the error message shown in Figure 16-20.

Figure 16-20: User notification to install the 2003 version in 2007

If you go into the VBE, you can confirm that neither the 2003 nor the 2007 add-in files are loaded. At this point, the only way to load the 2007 `xlam` add-in is to load 2003's `xla` file version first. Congratulations, you have indeed protected your users from inadvertently selecting the wrong add-in.

TIP **Don't change the name of the 2003 add-in or you won't be able to open the 2007 add-in. If you wish to change the names of both add-ins, open the 2003 add-in in Excel 2007 first; this will load the 2007 add-in for you. At this point, commenting out the** `Workbook_Open` **routine in the 2007 add-in will allow you to save and reopen the file without the dependency on the 2003 version.**

Using a Word 2007 Global Template as a Front-End for a 2003 Template

This example adds the same functionality to Word that we just added for Excel. It gives you the added benefit of noting the similarities and differences between the two programs. One key difference to remember is that whereas Excel allows add-ins to be installed or uninstalled and will retain this setting between sessions, Word does not have comparable functionality. That means you must create this functionality if it is important to you.

The default options in Word are to either load a global template from the `STARTUP` directory each time Word is loaded, or use an add-in template, which must be manually or programmatically opened each time the application is launched. Here, we will assume that our custom Forum menu is so useful that it should be loaded every time the application is opened.

While we could elect to go the route of loading the 2003 `dot` file as a global template at startup, installing the 2007 `dotm` file on-the-fly as an add-in template (similar to the previous Word example), that seems unnecessary in this case because anytime Word is opened, both the 2003 `.dot` file and the 2007 `.dotm` file will be launched; and when Word 2003 is opened, it simply ignores the 2007 template file formats. Given this behavior, there is no need to be concerned about memory issues, as the `dotm` file will only load in

Word 2007, and the 2003 `dot` file will be required in order for the 2007 `dotm` file to work properly. The easiest method, therefore, is to leave both the 2003 `dot` and the 2007 `dotm` files in the default Word `STARTUP` folder.

NOTE Microsoft offers a free "Compatibility Pack" which provides Office 2002(XP) and Office 2003 the ability to open files saved in the Office 2007 formats. While this enables users to use the main 2007 file formats, it does not extend to templates or add-in file formats.

Because we can keep both files in the `STARTUP` folder, and they will always, and only, be launched when needed, the modifications required to use a 2003 Word global template as a front end for a 2007 Word global template are actually a fair bit easier than the modification required for Excel add-ins. While you still need to handle the menus, you can let the application deal with loading the files. The steps to make this deployment happen in Word are as follows:

1. Make the required modifications to the 2003 add-in.
2. Create the base 2007 Ribbon customization add-in.

If you recall, with Excel we also had to ensure that the Excel 2003 file was always loaded first. Because Word templates seem to load in alphabetical order, you should not have to worry about this issue, but you still need to implement a check to ensure that the 2003 `dot` template does, in fact, exist in the `STARTUP` directory.

In addition, you may notice that we actually flipped the order of the steps from the order used to convert an Excel add-in. With Excel, we created the 2007 add-in first, so that it would be there when we made our modifications and loaded the 2003 version of the file. This isn't necessary with a Word template — both files are loaded automatically, so you don't need to add code to launch these files.

We start this example by adjusting the 2003 version of the global template contained in the chapter's download files under the name `ForumLauncher_v2003_Original.dot`. Begin the process by renaming the file to `ForumLauncher_v2003.dot`.

CAUTION Make sure that you do not save these files in Word's `STARTUP` folder yet, as there is no way to edit the code after you do, as discussed in the section "Editing Global Templates," earlier in this chapter.

The next step is to open the file in Word and locate the standard module in the `ForumLauncher_v2003.dot` Visual Basic project. Compared to the extensive editing required for Excel, you'll be surprised at just how easy this one is. Edit the `AutoExec` macro to read as follows:

```
Public Sub AutoExec()
'Create the menus if opened in Office 2003 or prior
    If Val(Application.Version) < 12 Then
        Call CreateMenu
    End If
End Sub
```

Beyond this minor edit, which suppresses menu creation if the file is opened in Excel 2007 or later, you only need to add the routine that the 2007 version will use as an entry point to the procedures contained in the 2003 template. This routine takes the exact form used in the Excel file:

```
Public Sub LaunchFrom2007(sSiteToLaunch)
'Act as a loader from the 2007 add-in
    Select Case UCase(sSiteToLaunch)
        Case Is = "VBAX"
            Call Launch_VBAX
        Case Is = "RIBBONX"
            Call Launch_RibbonX
    End Select
End Sub
```

That's it! You have now set up the 2003 global template for use with the 2007 global template. You are ready to save and close this file.

Next, we need to create the 2007 face for our 2003 global template. Start by saving a new file in the macro-enabled template (`dotm`) format.

The file then needs to have the XML code associated with it. As you might anticipate, the XML code is identical to the code for Excel, so you can grab it from the section "Using a 2003 Excel Add-in as a Front-End Loader for a 2007 Add-in" earlier in this chapter. Once you have the XML code associated with the file (follow the Excel steps in the previous example if needed), return to Word. You should now see the Forums group on the right-hand side of the Developer tab, as shown in Figure 16-21.

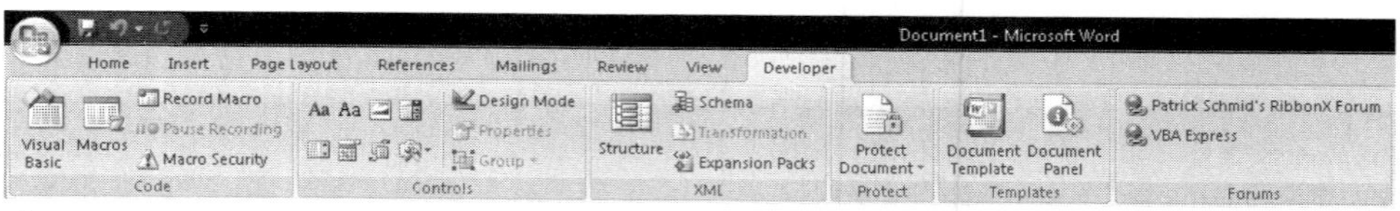

Figure 16-21: A Word 2007 skin for a 2003 global template

Next, open the VBE and ensure that the callback signature is written as shown in the following code. You'll recognize this as being identical to the Excel version:

```
'Callback for rxbtnRibbonX onAction
Private Sub rxsharedLinks_click(control As IRibbonControl)
    Application.Run "LaunchFrom2007", control.Tag
End Sub
```

At this point, things begin to get a little more complicated. As mentioned at the beginning of this section, you should test to see whether the 2003 template file exists, as it holds all the code required for the 2007 global template to function. While we expect the 2003 and 2007 versions of the template files to be shipped together, it seems prudent to warn the user if the 2003 file is missing. The following code will test for the files and generate appropriate message to warn users if something is amiss. This code should be placed at the top of the module, just below any lines beginning with the `Option` keyword (if any):

```
Private Const sReqdTemplate = "Forum_Launcher_v2003.dot"

Public Sub AutoExec()
    Dim docTest As AddIn
    On Error Resume Next
    Set docTest = AddIns(sReqdTemplate)
    If Err.Number = 0 Then
        'Template installed
        On Error GoTo 0
        Exit Sub
    End If

    'Template must not be installed
    On Error GoTo 0
    MsgBox "You must load " & sReqdTemplate & " to use " & _
        ThisDocument.Name
    Application.AddIns(ThisDocument.Name).Delete
End Sub
```

The code checks to ensure that the 2003 file is installed as an "Addin." (All global templates are part of Word's Addins collection.) If it is, then the routine exits early and all is well. However, if the 2003 template is not found, then the user is notified and the 2007 global template is disabled.

NOTE **This routine is triggered each time Word is started. If a user were to end up with only the `Forum_Launcher_v2007.dotm` file in their Word `STARTUP` directory, they would be greeted with the preceding error message each time they opened Word. The only ways to fix this are to remove the 2007 template file or to place the 2003 `dot` file in the same directory.**

Now that these changes have been made, we are ready to deploy the files as global templates. Save the current file, close Word, and copy both the `Forum_Launcher_v2003.dot` and `Forum_Launcher_v2007.dotm` files into Word's `STARTUP` directory. Upon reloading Word, you will see that the Forum group again exists on the Developer tab, as shown in Figure 16-21, and the file is now functional!

The last thing to check with this example is that it reacts as expected if the 2003 template is not available. Therefore, close Word and locate the `Forum_Launcher_v2003.dot` file. Either remove it from Word's `STARTUP` directory or rename the file. Upon launching Word 2007 again, you should receive the error message shown in Figure 16-22.

As you can see, the process for converting a Word 2003 template to function as the back end for a Word 2007 global template is much less work than converting the Excel version.

Figure 16-22: Error message regarding the missing 2003 template

Access Deployment Techniques

Having completed our detailed coverage of deploying Excel and Word customizations, we now shift our focus to Access. Deployment techniques for Access applications can vary depending on the environment, primarily due to the version and the type of installations of both Microsoft Access and Office. This section looks at deployment procedures geared toward two specific environments: those with the full version of Access and those using the Access Runtime edition.

In previous chapters we focused strictly on customizing the Ribbon. If you went through all the examples, then you've done everything from simply modifying built-in controls to literally starting from scratch. Those exercises focused on creating the customizations, so they didn't delve into many of the issues associated with efficiently deploying in multi-user environments or using Access Runtime installations.

Before we get into the details of specific scenarios, however, we need to cover several fundamental issues that are common to most deployments.

General Information Concerning Database Deployment

A major consideration when deploying Access applications is preventing general users from breaking into the design mode of the database and messing with your object designs and supporting code. Ribbon customization is one of many steps that you can take to protect your intellectual property and the application's integrity. This is not the place to discuss actual object or user-level security, but we will look at some common practices to lock down the design mode of the database file.

Preparing the Files for Multi-User Environments

One of the most important things to remember is that a multi-user environment demands special deployment and set-up techniques. It is not enough to just move an ACCDB file to a shared drive or server directory and have multiple users work with the single file, as this would eventually lead to performance issues and corruption problems.

To organize large amounts of data effectively, and avoid running into problems with the 2GB file size limit, you can split an Access database into two separate files. Indeed, some might argue that splitting an Access database is critical to a successful multi-user implementation.

NOTE **An added bonus of implementing a split application is the ease of deploying future updates. Separating the frontend objects from the data components enables us to simply deploy new and updated front ends to users by overwriting their existing ones and relinking to the backend data file.**

Splitting the application will result in a frontend file housing `Form`, `Query`, and `Report` objects as well as VBA code; and a backend file holding all the data tables. The frontend file uses table links to communicate with one or more backend files, which can be located on a shared drive. During deployment, each user will receive a copy of the frontend file, and restore the links to the backend file(s). This is demonstrated in an example a little later.

The built-in Database Splitter can establish the whole setup within seconds, and it makes the splitting process a fairly simple affair. In Access 2007, the Database Splitter can be found as an Access Back-End button under the Move Data group on the Database Tools tab, as shown in Figure 16-23.

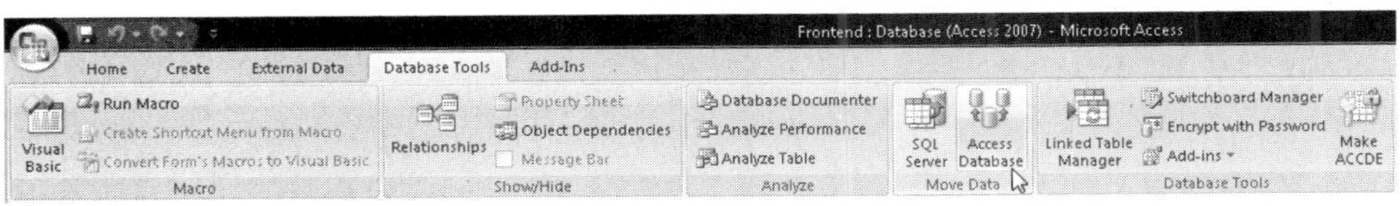

Figure 16-23: Use the built-in Database Splitter to divide an application

Another method of splitting an application would be the manual process of duplicating the Access file, deleting the tables from what will become the front-end file and all but the tables from the other file, and then creating table links in the front-end file. The External Data tab on the Ribbon provides tools for creating links to Access databases and other file types.

When working with external data files, the Linked Table Manager can be a very helpful tool for organizing and changing table links. It can also be found on the Database Tools tab. Open it by right-clicking on an existing linked table in the Navigation Pane.

NOTE **Linked tables can be identified by the blue arrow in front of the object name.**

In addition to creating new links, the Linked Table Manager can be used to refresh links to existing tables. This is necessary if the path to the data tables has changed. For example, when you deploy a customization, you will likely need to incorporate a process to refresh the links to the data files unless your development environment reflects the directory configuration of the user environment.

Since it is a good practice to avoid exposing the user to this complete process, we prefer to programmatically execute a procedure that will take care of relinking the tables. This is especially important when deploying the application to remote locations to which you do not have personal access. There are several ways to refresh table links using VBA.

For example, when deploying a replacement frontend, you would want the links to be refreshed at startup, so you could use a function to update links in the `RunCode` action of an AutoExec macro or behind the `OnLoad` event of a startup form.

Rather than have you type all the code for this by hand, we have included a split database in the chapter downloads. It illustrates not only using code to refresh the table links, but also further automates the process by implementing a browse utility. This extra touch allows the user to browse to the back-end location and dynamically pass the path of the selected file to the function used to refresh the links, thus relieving users of the need to type the folder paths.

To follow along, download the `Frontend.accdb` and `Backend.accdb` files from the chapter downloads. Open `Frontend.accdb` and confirm that the tables are linked by trying to launch one of the linked tables from the Navigation Pane. If the backend file is not in the right location anymore (which it won't be, as you have saved it somewhere we couldn't anticipate), Access should complain that it can't find the file.

Close the error message and click the Refresh Table Links button on the `frmRefreshTableLinks` form. Browse to the location where you stored the `Backend.accdb` file and select it. Your tables will now be relinked, as you can see if you try to open one.

Now let's add some security measures to the two component parts. Since every user of the back-end data requires full read, write, and delete permissions for the directory in which the file is housed on the server, it is common practice to prevent direct access to the backend.

To encrypt a database application with a password, it needs to be open in exclusive mode. Use the `Open` command of the main Office button drop-down menu. This will bring up the default Open dialog. Browse to the `Backend.accdb` file and select it. Now, instead of just pressing the Open button, use the little drop-down arrow next to it to specifically open the application in exclusive mode, as shown in Figure 16-24.

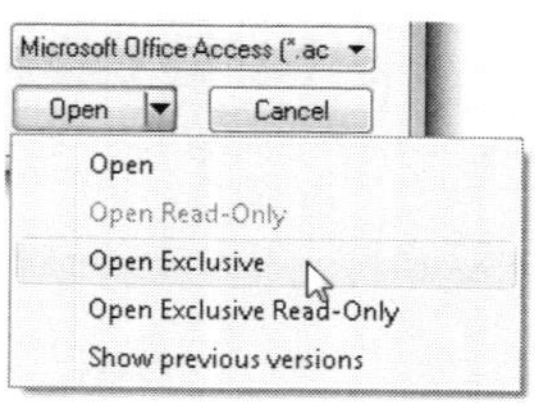

Figure 16-24: Opening the database in exclusive mode

Now that the database is open, go to Database Tools ➪ Encrypt with Password. Make sure you remember the database password you specify, as it is needed to individually open the back-end file by itself or to link to it.

NOTE **The main result of the work done in regard to security in Access 2007 was the database password feature. Access 2007 combines the old encryption feature of earlier versions with top-of-the-line encryption algorithms and the database password feature to make it much harder to get to your data and/or objects.**

After setting the database password for the back-end file, you need to open the front-end application and delete all established table link connections to the back-end; as the file now has a password, the previous links will no longer work. You then re-create the links using the Import Access Database button on the Import group of the External Data tab, shown in Figure 16-25.

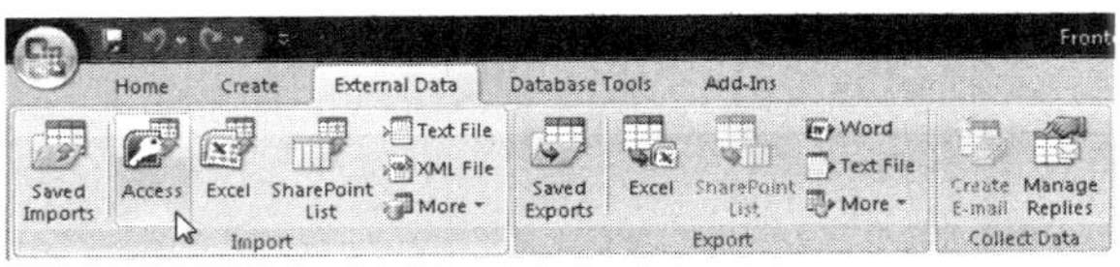

Figure 16-25: Relink Access front-end file to tables in the back-end file

The Get External Data wizard enables you to create linked tables by selecting "Link to the data source by creating a linked table." Next, you are prompted for the password for the backend file, and finally for the tables you wish to link. Behind the scenes, the password is stored internally with the link, eliminating the need for any further user interaction. To take this one step further, the encrypted data file can be used in conjunction with an ACCDE front-end file, discussed earlier.

Managing Access Startup Options

The majority of startup property settings can be accessed through the Current Database page of the Access Options dialog, which we explore in more detail shortly. Another approach in utilizing startup procedures at application opening is the AutoExec macro. Giving a macro the name "AutoExec" ensures that whatever actions it houses will execute every time your database launches. For example, you could utilize a `RunCode` action within the macro to call a public function that executes specific startup code. We will point out possible uses of an AutoExec macro throughout this section.

Leveraging the startFromScratch Attribute

Setting the `startFromScratch` attribute within your XML markup to `True` will completely hide the Ribbon and remove certain commands from the Office drop-down, as well as the QAT, if you do not specify any further actions.

CROSS-REFERENCE **The `startFromScratch` attribute is covered in Chapter 13, in the discussion of how to override and even repurpose built-in controls.**

Adjusting Access Options for Your Users

Additional limitations that you might want to set for your user's environment can be adjusted through the Current Database page of the Access Options dialog. Some of these settings include, but are not limited to, the ability to hide the Navigation Pane (Display Navigation Pane), hide the status bar (Display Status Bar), and disable Access special keys (Use Access Special Keys).

NOTE **Unless you have customized the Navigation Pane for user access, it is rarely a good idea to leave it visible to users.**

Although there is a manual setting to hide the Navigation Pane, many prefer to use code and hide it at run-time. One approach to do this is to put the selected code into a function and then call a `RunCode` action from the AutoExec macro. Just be aware that if you do hide the Navigation Pane, you may want to give users a way to show it again.

The following example demonstrates using a `toggleButton` to hide or show the Navigation Pane. As you'll see, coupling this ability with the `startFromScratch` attribute can quickly lock down the environment for your users. To follow along, download the `NavPane-Base.accdb` file from the chapter examples, which already contains the XML code for the `toggleButton` to show or hide the Navigation Pane. Open the database (ignoring the error about the missing callback), launch the VBA editor (Alt+F11), create a new code module through the Insert menu command, and paste in the following two callbacks:

```
Sub rxtglNavPane_getPressed(control As IRibbonControl, _
    ByRef returnedVal)
    DoCmd.RunCommand acCmdWindowHide
End Sub

Sub rxtglNavPane_click(control As IRibbonControl, pressed As Boolean)
    If pressed = True Then
        'show the Navigation Pane
        DoCmd.SelectObject acTable, "USysRibbons", True
    Else
        'hide the Navigation Pane
        DoCmd.SelectObject acTable, "USysRibbons", True
        DoCmd.RunCommand acCmdWindowHide
    End If
End Sub
```

TIP **Don't forget to set the reference to the Microsoft Office 12.0 Object Library, as discussed in Chapter 5, or your callbacks won't compile or run. You should also remember to follow the best practice of setting Option Explicit.**

Once you have compiled the code and saved the module, test the results by restarting the database. When it opens, you'll notice that the user has limited methods to get into design mode. Using the `getPressed` routine, which is called when the XML is evaluated, we hid the Navigation Pane. To display it again, just press the toggle button (see Figure 16-26).

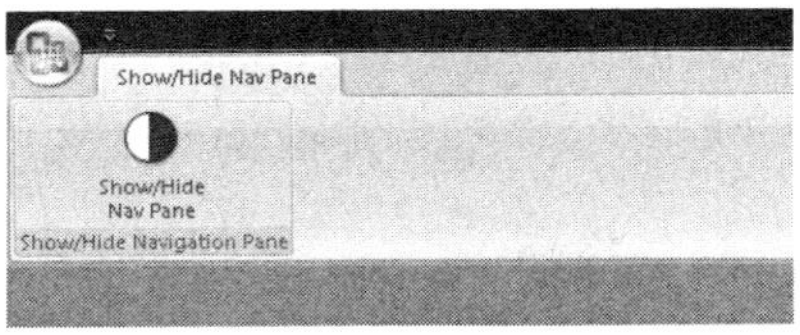

Figure 16-26: Limited user interface with hidden Navigation Pane

This is great, but keep in mind that holding down the Shift key during application startup will bypass all interface customizations. This means that the Ribbon customizations will not be deployed, so it seems prudent to implement code to prevent such actions. You can do that using the `CreateProperty` method, which is supported by the DAO object library. Use the following function to set the `AllowBypassKey` property to eliminate the Shift bypass feature:

CAUTION **If this is relatively new to you or you are working with an actual deployment file, then it is wise to create a backup before making changes that might lock you out of the Navigation Pane, the code, or even the ability to get into Design View. We highly encourage you to do this now!**

TIP **The DAO object library is set by default as the "Microsoft Office 2007 Access database engine Object Library" in the new ACCDB file format. Knowing this, you can count on being able to reference DAO objects and having them universally available with Access 2007 installations.**

To add this functionality, open the module in which you stored the Navigation Pane code and add the following VBA code:

```
Public Function SetAllowBypassKeyFalse(onOff As Boolean)
    'Setup Error Handler
    On Error GoTo Err_SetAllowBypassKeyFalse

    'Dimension (Variable Declaration)
    Dim db As DAO.Database, prp As DAO.Property

    'Set AllowBypassKey property if it exists
    Set db = CurrentDb
    db.Properties("AllowBypassKey") = onOff
    Set db = Nothing

'Exit Label
Exit_SetAllowBypassKeyFalse:
    Exit Function

'Error Handler
Err_SetAllowBypassKeyFalse:
```

```
'Property not found error
'Create property if it does not yet exist
    If Err = 3270 Then
      Set prp = db.CreateProperty("AllowBypassKey", dbBoolean, onOff)
      db.Properties.Append prp
      Resume Next
    Else
      'some unspecified error occurred
      MsgBox "SetAllowBypassKeyFalse", Err.Number, Err.Description
      Resume Exit_SetAllowBypassKeyFalse
    End If
End Function
```

You merely need to run the code one time for the property change to take effect and for it to be saved in the database. Activate the Immediate window by pressing Ctrl+G, type the following inside, and press Enter:

```
SetAllowBypassKeyFalse(False)
```

Since you don't want to lock yourself out of the application for future development, implement a reverse call to the function — before closing the database. One way to implement a hidden method of enabling and disabling the `AllowBypassKey` property would be to utilize two small command buttons on a form. Just set their `on_click` properties to call the function and pass in the appropriate Boolean value (`True` or `False`). You can set their `Transparent` property to `yes` to conceal your implementation from the user, as shown in Figure 16-27.

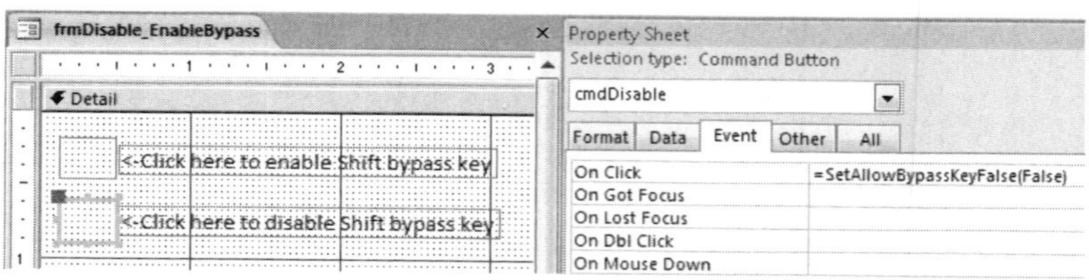

Figure 16-27: Transparent command button calling function

Creating an ACCDE File

Note that all of the preceding "security" precautions can typically be broken by experienced Access users. One very effective alternative method of quickly securing your database file, locking down the forms, reports, and code, is to convert it from an ACCDB format to the ACCDE format. Deploying an ACCDE file is a simple methodology that is popular with Access developers.

Before you actually trigger the process, it is advisable to manually compile your VBA code first by selecting the Compile command from the VBE's Debug menu, as this can help prevent errors in the conversion process. After you have done that, the Make ACCDE option button can be found on the Database Tools tab, as shown in Figure 16-28.

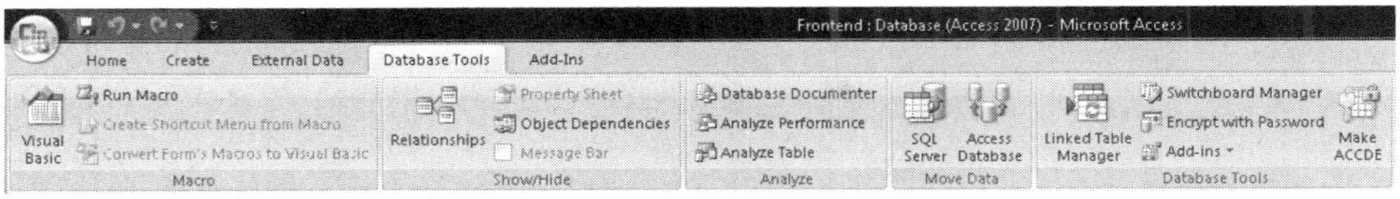

Figure 16-28: Make ACCDE command

CAUTION **Always be sure to keep a backup of the original ACCDB file in a secure location. The ACCDE file is locked down and not modifiable, so you need the ACCDB file in order to make any changes.**

TIP **For practice purposes you can use any of the database files provided for this book and just apply the "Make ACCDE" action. After successful compilation, you can open the new ACCDE file and try to access your code or try to make design changes to forms and reports. In addition, because developers tend to be a bit skeptical, it's a good time to review the host file folder and confirm that the original file is still there (with the** `.accdb` **file extension).**

Since we are discussing different file extension names, we can also quickly mention the ACCDR extension. When preparing an application for deployment with the packaging wizard that is part of the Access Developer Extensions (ADE) and specifying specific options, the ACCDB file format is automatically renamed to an ACCDR. If you are familiar with earlier Access versions, you might remember the `/runtime` command-line switch, which simulated the behavior of running your database in the Access Runtime environment.

Renaming the database file with an ACCDR extension has a similar effect on the application by enabling 2007 Runtime support. You do not need to utilize the packaging wizard to achieve that outcome. You can just rename the extension of the file itself. The result is a locked version of your application, which affects the user interface as well. We provide a little more detail about this when discussing the deployment of databases for a Runtime environment.

Loading the customUI from an External Source

In all the examples that we have shown so far, the XML code is stored within the application, and therefore already included when the files are deployed to users. There is another approach to deploying Ribbon customizations, however, which is to utilize the built-in VBA `LoadCustomUI` method of the Access application object. This enables you to store the actual XML markup code outside of the database application in a separate file, which can be beneficial in several situations. Following are just some of the reasons why you may wish to consider this approach:

- You need to deploy several application files with common navigation customization.
- You are utilizing a large number of customizations. These might be hard to operate within a Ribbon table field and would unnecessarily consume application space.
- You want use a single database to hold the XML code for multiple UIs, allowing several specialized databases to contact one local store for the correct UI.

Now that you have learned about possible implementation scenarios for the `LoadCustomUI` method, we'll look at the syntax, which is as follows:

```
LoadCustomUI(CustomUIName As String, CustomUIXML As String)
```

As you can see, the method is fairly straightforward and only takes two string parameters, which represent the name and XML of your customization. All you have to do to call it is retrieve the XML from an external file and pass it along as a string.

Let's walk through a sample implementation of this feature. If you want to see the final result, you can download the completed `LoadCustomUI.accdb` with the accompanying `LoadCustomUI.XML` file, or you can follow along and create the files on-the-fly.

Before starting Microsoft Access, create an external XML file to store the XML markup that will be loaded into the database at run-time. Open any regular text editor (such as Notepad) and paste the following XML into a new file:

```
<customUI xmlns="http://schemas.microsoft.com/office/2006/01/customui">
   <ribbon startFromScratch="true">
   </ribbon>
</customUI>
```

Save the file as `LoadCustomUI.XML`. Now you are ready to start Access and create a blank new database named `LoadCustomUI.accdb`. Save it in the same folder as your `LoadCustomUI.XML` file.

To use the `LoadCustomUI` method, you need to append the XML saved in the external file to a string variable. In order to retrieve the XML, you have the choice of using the `FileSystemObject`'s `OpenTextFile` method or sequential file access. Our example uses the `FileSystemObject` to demonstrate a small function that utilizes the `LoadCustomUI` method. Although sequential file access could be used just as easily, we chose the `FileSystemObject` to highlight its flexibility for use in other scenarios. Place the following code into a new standard module within your `LoadCustomUI.accdb` file:

```
Public Function LoadUIFromFile()
    Dim oFilesys, oTxtStream As Object
    Dim txtCustomUIPath, txtXML As String
```

```
    'assume file exists in same directory as application
    txtCustomUIPath = CurrentProject.Path & "\LoadCustomUI.XML"

    Set oFilesys = CreateObject("Scripting.FileSystemObject")

    'check if file exists
    If oFilesys.FileExists(txtCustomUIPath) = True Then

        'open file ForReading (constant = 1) and ReadAll
        Set oTxtStream = oFilesys.OpenTextFile(txtCustomUIPath, 1)
        txtXML = oTxtStream.ReadAll

        oTxtStream.Close
        Set oTxtStream = Nothing

        'load custom UI passing XML string
        Application.LoadCustomUI "YourCustomRibbon", txtXML
    End If

    Set oFilesys = Nothing

End Function
```

Because you stored the `LoadCustomUI.XML` file in the same directory as the database application file, you can dynamically construct the full path to it utilizing the `CurrentProject.Path` property. Then the code creates a `FileSystemObject` and ensures that the file actually does exist in the path specified. If the file exists, the function will continue and open a `TextStream` object, which allows you to retrieve all content within the file and append it to a string variable. Once the variable holds the complete contents of the `LoadCustomUI.XML` file, you can call the `LoadCustomUI` method and pass it along as the second parameter. You can manually add the first parameter to identify the custom markup that is being loaded.

NOTE Checking for the existence of the file is a good practice, as it helps to prevent errors that would be caused by attempting to access an external file that does not exist.

To call this function, set the `onLoad` property of a form to an event procedure that executes the following `on load` event. Open the form in Layout or Design View and open the property sheet. From the Event Tab, select On Load, select Event Procedure, and click the ellipses to open the VBE to that procedure. Modify the code to read as follows:

```
Private Sub Form_Load()
    Call LoadUIFromFile
    Me.RibbonName = "YourCustomRibbon"
End Sub
```

When you launch this form, you will notice that the default Access Ribbon is gone. This is the effect of only setting the aforementioned `startFromScratch` attribute within your external XML markup. Closing the form will return the regular Ribbon setup. If you specify this form to be the application's startup form in Access Options ➪ Current Database ➪ Display Form, you can ensure that your Ribbon customization will be launched when your database opens.

Another approach to loading the Ribbon customization into the application would be to use a RunCode macro action that calls the function within an AutoExec macro. This also ensures that the XML markup will be loaded at application startup. You can refer to it again at run-time when opening specific Form or Report objects.

Clearly, the `LoadCustomUI` method allows for great flexibility when working with run-time customizations and application deployment. The XML markup can be loaded from an internal table, straight from within code, or, as illustrated, from an external file.

Deploying Solutions to Users with Full-Access Installations

There are several different approaches you can take when deploying your application to users who have the full version of Microsoft Access installed. Ultimately, deciding which deployment implementation to use is up to you. As the developer, you can meld your preferences with the conditions of the target environment.

Deploying Customizations with Full Versions of Access

We can now look at the actual deployment of the application. Depending on your clients and their environment, there are several approaches to choose from.

One way to deploy application files is to compress them using your favorite compression utility and then send them to users via snail mail on read-only memory or through e-mail or Web downloads. Keep in mind that the zip file must include all external files (if there are any) in the appropriate hierarchy. For example, if you utilized the `LoadCustomUI` method, you would need to include the external XML file. If you have computer-savvy users and provide them with good installation instructions and documentations, this is a relatively trivial method of deployment.

A step up from this is to use a self-extracting zip file that literally places the files in pre-designated folders. In addition, if the required folders do not already exist, then they will be created during the process. One popular tool for this purpose is the WinZip Self Extractor.

TIP **The self-extracting zip file can be placed in an online file folder, and a link e-mailed to the intended recipients. Then, when the recipients click on the link in the e-mail, they are given the option to save or run the file. If they click Run, the contents of the zip file are extracted and saved in the specified locations. If they choose Save, they can run the extraction process another time from their computer.**

Another approach is to utilize the Access Developer Extensions (ADE) add-in mentioned earlier. This utility is provided free of charge by Microsoft for Access 2007 and can be downloaded from the Microsoft download page at `www.microsoft.com/downloads/details.aspx?familyid=d96a8358-ece4-4bee-a844-f81856dceb67&displaylang=en`.

After you download and install the add-in, restart Access. The new options will be available from the Developer menu, as shown in Figure 16-29.

Figure 16-29: The Access Developer Extensions add-in installed

NOTE **If you have multiple versions of Microsoft Access installed and switch between them, the ADE COM Add-in will become inactive. After relaunching Access 2007, you need to manually enable it through the Add-ins page of the Access Options dialog.**

The Access Developer Extensions add-in enables us to package our applications for easier installation. The packaging wizard options are somewhat self-explanatory, but we'll highlight some key features.

The first page of the Package Solution Wizard explains its purpose and allows you to indicate an output location for the installation package, including all files that the wizard will be creating. Click the Browse button and specify the location where you want the wizard to output the files. This directory has no effect on the target user's environment, and only reflects the installation files generated by the wizard, which you can then burn to a CD-ROM.

We can now proceed with the installation package. Press Next to be presented with details about installation, as well as shortcut options. Select the file to be packaged, which is your database file. In a split application environment this would be the front-end file. Afterward, you can pick the root installation folder for the application. The wizard gives you several options; it is up to you which one to pick. Because this will be handled as a separate software installation, you might want to utilize the Program Files directory. You can then denote the subfolder in which your application will be installed. For confirmation purposes, the wizard shows you the full installation path after settings these options.

NOTE **Do not use illegal file/folder name characters when denoting the subfolder directory. If you do, then Access will display an error when trying to create the package at the end.**

Because we are currently working under the premise that users have the full version of Access 2007 installed, you can leave this as the default setting for the pre-installation requirements.

In the Shortcut Options section of this wizard page, you can allocate a shortcut to the actual application file and specify whether it should be listed under the Windows Start menu, on the desktop, or both. Additional settings are optional, such as a custom shortcut icon or utilizing a startup macro, which uses the `/x macro` command-line switch in combination with the shortcut, if you are familiar with this feature.

Proceeding to the next wizard screen, you can work with external files and Registry entries. In the Additional Files section of the wizard, you can include additional external files to be incorporated into the installation package. This could be the back-end file if you are implementing a split application, an external XML file if you are loading your Ribbon customization markup from exterior sources, as well as other files and folders required for the particular project.

CAUTION **Always use caution when editing the Windows Registry manually or programmatically. In addition, before appending the trusted location to the Registry, you might want to use the `RegRead` method of the `WshShell` object to determine whether the folder is already listed as a trusted location. Although it won't generate an error if you try to add a location that exists, it is cleaner to not attempt to add a location if it isn't necessary.**

Since you do not want to expose users to disabled applications and security warnings, you can also work with the Additional Registry Keys section of the packaging wizard. This section enables you to implement a new trusted location on the target machine. You can pass along the following values for the Registry key:

```
Root: Current User
Key: Software\Microsoft\Office\12.0\Access\Security\Trusted↵
Locations\Value
Name: path
Value: c:\DirectoryOfYourApplication
```

NOTE **A trailing backslash is not required for the path in the Value field.**

The result might look as shown in Figure 16-30.

Figure 16-30: New trusted location for the target machine

CROSS-REFERENCE **We've mentioned trusted locations and enabling files throughout the book, and you can find a more detailed explanation in Chapter 17.**

An alternative method of adding a new trusted location is to implement code in the startup procedure of the application itself. You can utilize the `RegWrite` method of the `WshShell` object to add the Registry value at run-time and enable the application for future usage. The following function demonstrates such a procedure:

```
Public Function addTrustedLocation()
    Dim oWshShell As Object
    Dim txtPath As String
    Set oWshShell = CreateObject("WScript.Shell")
    oWshShell.RegWrite "HKEY_CURRENT_USER\Software\Microsoft\" & _
         "Office\12.0\Access\Security\Trusted Locations\" & _
         "YourLocation\Path", CurrentProject.Path
End Function
```

The preceding code will be particularly beneficial if you do not want to deploy your application with an installation package created by the packaging wizard. You should execute the code before trying to launch any other code within the application, and your users will need to follow instructions to enable the application the first time it is launched. After the trusted location is established through the function call, the database can be opened without any further security notices or additional user interaction. After including additional files and Registry keys, you can move on to the final page of the Package Solution Wizard. This page deals with information the user will see during installation, and program information displayed in the Windows Add/Remove Programs dialog. The required information to be specified includes Product Name, Feature Title, and Description, as well as a title for the installer package. You can include further personal information if you want to include legal and support information for the end user's benefit.

After you have finished any other options in the Package Solution Wizard, press OK to complete the packaging process. Before the package is created, the wizard will ask you if you want to save the changes made. Make your selection and wait for the process to complete. After the wizard has finished the package creation, it should open the setup files in the root directory specified in the first page of the wizard, under the output option's destination folder argument. You might see something similar to what is shown in Figure 16-31.

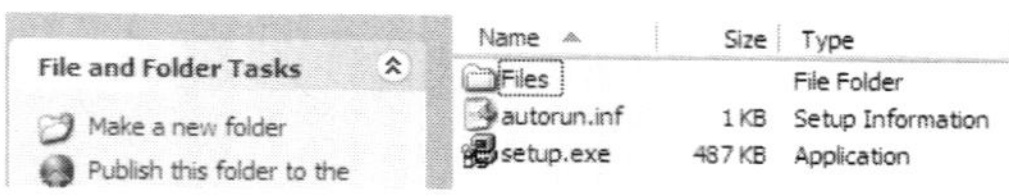

Figure 16-31: Result of the Package Solution Wizard

Deploying the solution can be as simple as burning the files created by the wizard to a blank CD-ROM and then handing the CD over to your users.

TIP **Before handing over the application to your client or users, it is always advisable to test the installation to ensure that everything functions as expected.**

Deploying Solutions to Users with the Access Runtime Version

The Access Runtime edition is a stripped-down version of the full Access installation. It allows users who do not have a full version of Access installed to use your database. As an added bonus — from a developer's perspective — it allows people to work with the user interface that is provided, but precludes any possibility of editing the design or code. Keep in mind that once the run-time is installed on a machine, it can also be used to open other Access files, not just those provided in your deployment package.

After you have downloaded the `AccessRuntime.exe` executable file, you can freely redistribute it with your application. Developers and clients will both appreciate this cost-effective approach, particularly because the 2007 Access Runtime edition, like the Access Developer Extensions, is a free download from the Microsoft download site. The Runtime can be obtained from the following page:

```
www.microsoft.com/downloads/details.aspx?familyid=
d9ae78d9-9dc6-4b38-9fa6-2c745a175aed&displaylang=en
```

This section describes how to include the Access Runtime files in the deployment package that was created with the Access Developer Extensions add-in. If you haven't already downloaded `AccessRuntime.exe`, we recommend that you do so now.

This scenario is based on the premise that Access 2007 is not installed on the user's computer, and so we will use the pre-installation requirements to include installing Access 2007 Runtime as part of the application deployment CD.

Again, you need to launch the Package Solution Wizard. Because you'll be following essentially the same steps described earlier, we won't repeat the entire process here. However, this time, we will use the pre-installation requirements to include the installation of the Access Runtime executable files. Therefore, click on the pre-installation requirements and browse to the downloaded Runtime executable file. After that, the remaining options of the wizard are comparable to those described in the previous section, so you can refer to that for guidance on other files that should be included in order for your database to function correctly, such as other external files or Registry keys.

NOTE **Installing the Runtime edition requires administrative privileges, so be sure to collaborate with your users about this.**

Furthermore, with Runtime installations, it is imperative that your application implements good error handling. The limited environment provided by the Runtime does not allow code debugging, and the program will literally quit when it encounters an unhandled error.

As briefly mentioned before, the packaging wizard automatically renames the database file extension to an ACCDR file. You should take advantage of that and check how your application will act with the Runtime support enabled. Specific components might not function within an individual Runtime edition installation (e.g., the spell checker or the `FileDialog` object), so testing the installation package in the Runtime environment to ensure optimal functionality is an important aspect of the deployment preparations.

CAUTION **The ACCDR extension will disable certain design capabilities, but if your users have a full retail version of Microsoft Access installed and rename the file back to an ACCDB format, they can view and/or modify any components of the database. If you want to avoid this behavior, then implement one of the aforementioned methods of locking down the application file, e.g., converting to an ACCDE.**

NOTE **Unlike prior versions, the Access 2007 and 2003 Runtime editions are automatically updated through Microsoft Updates, so even if they are the only Office component in the target environment, the Runtime should stay current when Microsoft releases program updates.**

Conclusion

Throughout this book, the customizations were contained in a workbook, a database, or a document. These structures work well for keeping custom tools with the appropriate files, as they are unloaded as soon as the user switches to another file — even within the same application. This is an improvement over the common effect in previous UIs, as many of us have encountered rather disastrous results when a developer failed to properly clean up the customizations and then those customizations inadvertently overwrote the default UI. However, as important as it is to contain your customizations, there are also many times when you need them to be available across all files in the program.

This chapter looked at several ways to share customizations. In addition to demonstrating how to implement and share customizations across different versions of Office, we also discussed the pros and cons and even the similarities between applications.

Whereas workbook and document-level deployments work well for creating a fully packaged solution, they also break the best practice rule about separating data from code. This can cause issues if you ever need to update the code, and it puts the data at risk if you make an error in the process. In addition, code deployed within a file could be a nightmare to update in full, as there is a tendency to end up with multiple versions of a file.

Templates centralize code a little more, and they resolve some of the maintenance issues. To change the code, you simply update the template, and all new workbooks or documents created from the templates are automatically based on the new standard. One thing that you need to be very aware of, however, is that any XML customizations in the templates are included with files based on the templates. While this could be a good thing, it can also cause issues, as any required macros may not be included when the file is updated. This is because the default setting is for all new files to be saved in a macro-free format. Therefore, if users don't change the file format to accept macros before they save the file, they may end up with a customization but lack any callbacks required to use it.

The final techniques introduced in the deployment section started by focusing on creating and deploying add-ins for Excel, and then covered global templates in Word. These files allow Ribbon customizations to be shared across all files open in the programs, yet they do not attach their customizations to any of the files created while they are loaded. This is an ideal situation if you are trying to add global toolsets.

After examining the individual deployment techniques, we explored our final RibbonX attribute: `idQ`. This attribute is specifically geared toward sharing tab and group elements across files, enabling a developer to load and unload Ribbon customizations from a central source. Again, you saw both Excel and Word examples.

Next we looked at issues that concern users who work in an environment where versions of Office prior to 2007 may also still be in play. We showed how legacy CommandBar code is placed within the Ribbon, and discussed different ways to work in a mixed environment. From creating add-ins and global templates specific to each application version, to using 2003 files as the back end for a RibbonX face, we looked at the techniques that allow users to share common functionality among the application versions.

We then turned our attention to the techniques required to deploy Ribbon customizations in Microsoft Access, and how they work. First we went through general deployment preparations that ensure the integrity of your database application in the target environment. This included practices to lock down the design environment with

XML markup, use of ACCDE file types, execute code with the AutoExec macro, and use VBA callbacks and VBA code to create and adjust the AllowBypassKey property.

Afterward, we looked at a method of loading XML markup from an external source file, which can be very beneficial in application deployment. We then moved on to actual deployment techniques, such as regular file sharing of the application files or creating installation packages. We explained how to use the Package Solution Wizard of the free Access Developer Extensions add-in to create specific installation settings, such as incorporating additional Registry keys to avoid security warnings. We also covered a methodology utilizing VBA code to attain a similar goal.

Packaging an application can be valuable for target environments that have the full version of Access installed, as well for those that do not include an Access installation. Last but not least, we wrapped up this chapter with deployment scenarios for inclusion of the Access Runtime edition.

In the final Chapter of the book, we explore security in Office, and how it affects the development and deployment of your customizations.

CHAPTER 17

Security In Microsoft Office

Reality dictates that while most programmers use their power and knowledge for good, there are also those who work with a far darker intent. Because of this, security has always been a big concern to educated Office users. Many safeguards have therefore been implemented to both complement and protect against the great amount of power that has been put at the fingertips of developers in the form of VBA.

The benefits of VBA are incredible, as it provides us with tremendous flexibility when working with a user's system, but VBA also affords the same capability to those with nefarious intent. While we can craft routines that automate entire business intelligence applications and span thousands of lines of code, it only takes a single line of correctly crafted code to render a system unusable. Not wanting to completely remove the functionality and benefits of automation, Microsoft has been left the difficult task of balancing the two sides of this coin: giving developers the access they need while protecting users from those with ill intentions. It is a difficult balance to strike, to be sure.

Fortunately, Office 2007 provides several enhancements to the security model that are targeted at both protecting the end user and making the life of the developer easier. Since every dynamic customization that we create requires using a VBA callback, it is imperative that we understand and master the concepts of security in the Office environment. This chapter discusses each of the concepts behind Office security, both old and new. Our goal is that by the end of this chapter, not only will you understand the concepts, you'll also feel comfortable and confident with the protections that they provide.

Security Prior to Office 2007

Since Office 97, Microsoft has constantly been working on and incorporating ways to improve security in the Office document field. When Office 97 was released, users were given the option to enable macros or not, and that was pretty much the extent of the choices. Because many users wanted macros for legitimate functionality, they would turn off the Macro Security flag, thereby leaving their computers vulnerable to a proliferation of macro viruses that made their way around the world on the backs of e-mails.

In Office 2000, we saw the introduction of *digital certificates*, which enable users to actually sign their code. As this tool is still valid for security today, it is discussed in much more detail later in the chapter; but the basic premise of the digital certificate is that if the code is modified on another machine, then the signature is discarded. If a specific signature is trusted on the user's machine, then the code will run without notification as long as the digital signature is intact.

Along with the digital certificate were three complementary settings of great importance. While these settings have been slightly modified in Office 2007, from Office 2000 through 2003, the user was able to set three security modes:

- High would grant execution rights only to code signed with a trusted certificate, and disable all others.
- Medium would grant execution rights to code signed by a trusted certificate and prompt the user for acceptance of any unsigned documents.
- Low would enable all macros, signed or not, to run without any notification.

Office XP (also known as Office 2002) added yet another wrinkle to the security model, which is still present in Office 2007. By default, each Office installation disables access to programmatically manipulate the Visual Basic Editor itself, as well as modules and userforms that may hold VBA code. While this can cause frustration for programmers who need to set options related to these components, it does add a level of protection by locking down some key areas of the computer system so that malicious code will not have the ability to run amok.

Office 2003 added one additional element to the security model, which was the ability to "Trust all installed add-ins and templates" as if they were digitally signed. This may seem like a minor enhancement, but was an important one for developers, as it allowed them to push out add-ins and global templates without the need to walk the user through installing a self-created or commercially purchased digital certificate. This setting was modified in Office 2007, as you'll see later in this chapter.

Macro-Enabled and Macro-Free File Formats

The first of Office 2007's security enhancements was specifically targeted to help the end user. Since Microsoft revamped the file formats for Word and Excel documents to use the openXML format, they were also able to split files into two distinct subformats: macro-enabled (`xlsm`, `docm`) files and macro-free (`xlsx`, `docx`) files. These two main file formats also have distinct differences in their icons, as shown in Figure 17-1. There are additional file types for each application, but those are not discussed in this chapter.

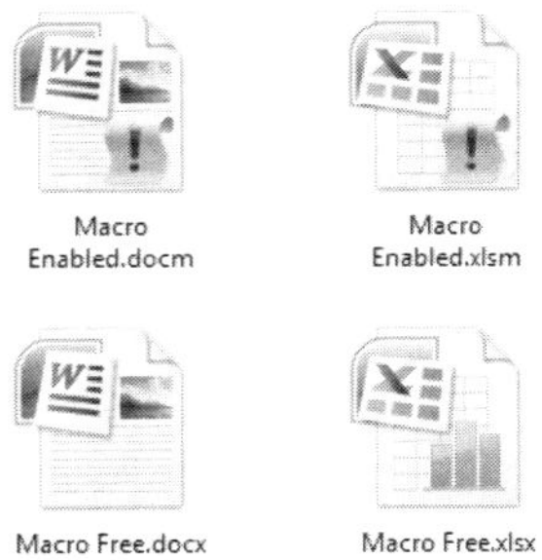

Figure 17-1: Word and Excel file icons

Notice that both of the macro-enabled file formats now bear an exclamation mark, signifying that they (most likely) hold macro code. This distinction provides a very obvious cue to the user that there may be more to the macro-enabled files than meets the eye. A user can take solace in the fact that if the file is saved in a `docx` or `xlsx` file format, it cannot contain any macros, as all VBA code will be stripped from the file when it is saved.

NOTE **When working with Word and Excel, keep in mind that macros and VBA are synonymous. Unlike Access macros, all Word and Excel macros are written in VBA.**

NOTE **Remember that files stored in a binary format, despite the fact that they don't have separate file formats for a macro-enabled and macro-free distinction, can still hold VBA code. The binary file format is used by Office 97–2003 and all Access files.**

While it's nice that there is a visual cue to differentiate between files that may hold code and those that don't, we all know that many users will either be ignorant of the symbol and its meaning, or will become so conditioned to cautions that they ignore this warning. This is why the file format should be considered only the first line of defense.

The Trust Center

In addition to the file structure split, there are also other enhancements to the Office 2007 core that affect both end users and developers alike.

Microsoft regrouped all of the security settings and put them into a central place called the "Trust Center." This new collection provides us with a central location for accessing and managing all the security settings related to how Office reacts to files that use potentially dangerous controls. This is important for developers; it is both a "one-stop shop" to configure the end users machine, and it enables developers to configure a specific setting in order to make their own development life a bit easier.

Throughout this section are many references to digital certificates and digital signatures, as many of the security settings reference this particular tool. The full discussion of digital certificates, including their creation, is covered later in this chapter.

The Trust Center can be accessed by clicking the Office button, selecting the application's Options button, and choosing Trust Center from the list on the left. Upon doing so, you are greeted by a screen containing some hyperlinks for learning more about security and privacy. The part that is of most interest to us is the Trust Center Settings. Go ahead and click that button, and you'll be taken to the interface shown in Figure 17-2.

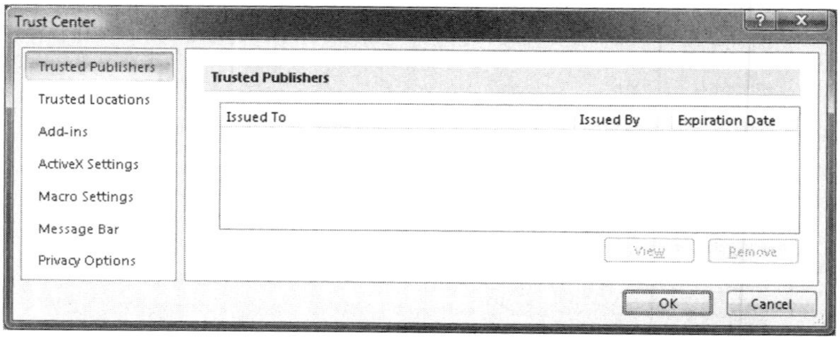

Figure 17-2: The Trust Center in Word

It appears that there are a lot of options here, so let's take a brief look at each one.

NOTE **Excel actually has one additional item in the Trust Center: External Content. As this is a setting specific to Excel functionality, it is not covered in this book.**

Trusted Publishers

The Trusted Publishers tab, highlighted in Figure 17-2, gives you a list of all of the digital certificates that you have trusted on your system. It is quite common for this list to be empty, but you may see items here if you have ever installed an add-in. Adobe's PDF Writer is a commonly used add-in that will install a digital certificate. Later in this chapter you will learn how certificates are added to this list (see the section "Trusting Digital Certificates").

Trusted Locations

Many of the options that are accessible in the Trust Center were available in prior versions of Office, albeit with some minor changes. There are also a few new features, and from a developer's perspective, the biggest enhancement is most likely the ability to trust locations. Both developers and users will have an instant affinity for the convenience that this setting affords. The interface for establishing Trusted Locations is shown in Figure 17-3.

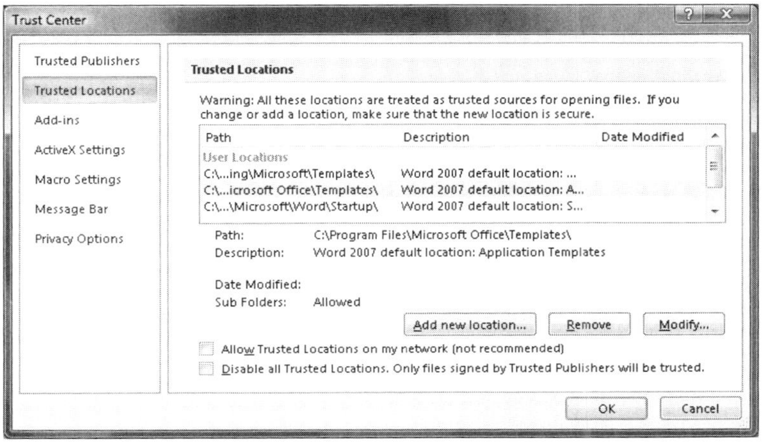

Figure 17-3: The default Trusted Locations tab in Word

To put it simply, the Trusted Locations tab is an interface that enables you to designate certain folders as "safe." This is a fantastic concept and one of the best enhancements to the Office security model for developers.

Trusting your development folders means that you can avoid all security messages as you load and unload files, without having to go through the extra steps of adding a digital certificate to each project. For those of us who create test files on a regular basis, this can truly save some time. It also means that we only actually need to worry about handling the files that we will distribute to others at the end of the development process.

The basic theory behind the Trusted Locations model is, of course, that you will only store in these trusted folders files that you are absolutely certain contain safe code. The instant that you violate that idea, you expose your system to any malicious code that resides in the file, and may as well be running without macro security.

CAUTION **Any file in a trusted folder has full rights to run on the user's system, including VBA macros, data connections, and ActiveX controls. Make sure that you only trust folders that you have control over and know are safe! It is strongly recommended that you *not* trust a location that would be a target of automatic downloads, such as your Documents folder or desktop.**

NOTE **As a means of protecting users from themselves and from malicious script, Microsoft has prevented certain locations from becoming a Trusted Location. The folders include the root of the C:\ drive, as well as the Temporary Internet Files folder.**

Adding, Modifying, or Removing Trusted Locations

To add, modify, or remove folders from the Trusted Locations tab, simply click the appropriate button and follow the prompts. Be aware that when you add or modify a folder, you will see a checkbox asking if you'd like to trust the subfolders as well, as shown in Figure 17-4.

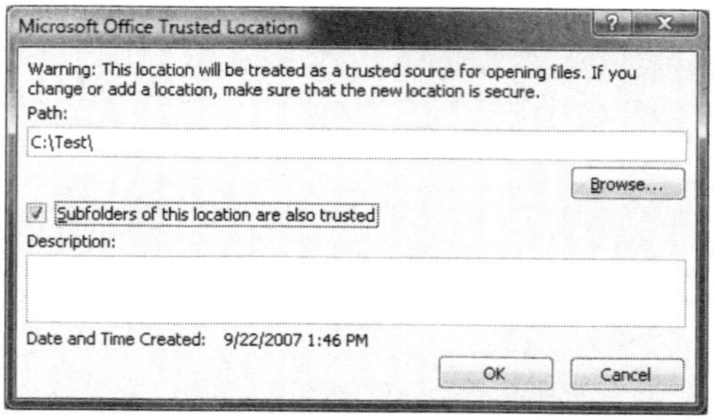

Figure 17-4: Trusting a new location, including its subfolders

Why not try giving it a test? Create a new folder on your C:\ drive (or use an existing folder if you prefer), and add it to your trusted folders. Create a new Word or Excel file with the following code in a standard module:

```
Sub Test()
    MsgBox "Hello World"
End Sub
```

Save the file (in the macro-enabled format) on your desktop. Close and reopen it; note that you are given the warning about macros in the file.

NOTE **If you do not get a macro warning, check the Macro Settings tab of the Trust Center and make sure that you have selected "Disable all macros with notification." You'll learn more about the Macro Settings tab momentarily.**

Now close the file and move it into the folder that you trusted. Upon reopening the file, no macro warnings will be present!

NOTE **Trusted locations are application specific. What you set for Excel needs to be set again in Word or Access if you wish to trust the location in all applications.**

Trusting Network Locations

There are two other settings on the Trusted Locations tab, the first of which is Allow Trusted Locations on my network (not recommended). As you'd expect, checking this option allows the user to set trusted locations on a network drive.

CAUTION **Chances are fairly good that you do not have control over what is or is not placed in folders elsewhere on the network, so trusting network locations can present a serious security risk!**

NOTE **You can trust locations on a USB thumb drive, but not at the root level. Instead, you must trust a folder on the USB drive. While this can be very handy if you like to carry code from one location to another, it also exposes you to the risk that someone else will have the same folder hierarchy that you have trusted. If that happens, their folder will also be trusted and they will be able to run code unguarded on your system.**

Disabling Trusted Locations

If you are a systems administrator or a user who is concerned about malicious code, then this setting is for you. You can check the box to "Disable all Trusted Locations. Only files signed by Trusted Publishers will be trusted" and stop any project dead in its tracks unless it has a digital signature. (Experiences will vary depending on the settings on the Macro Settings and ActiveX tabs.)

Add-ins

The security settings on the Add-ins tab are specifically designed for treatment of the Add-in file formats that you learned to build in Chapter 16 (including Word's global templates). Unlike the Office 2003 model, which required you to check a box in the security settings in order to trust all installed add-ins and templates, in Office 2007 these files are trusted by default. After all, it typically takes an intentional act to incorporate an add-in. However, there are a few options that allow you to override this setting, as shown in Figure 17-5.

In looking at this pane, it appears that you only have three options: all add-ins will run (the default), only add-ins signed by a trusted publisher will run, or no add-ins will run. However, as you'll soon learn, there are additional settings that provide more flexibility, particularly with the first option.

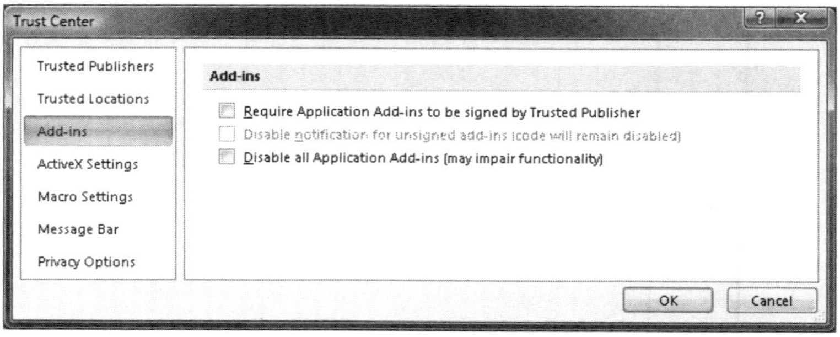

Figure 17-5: The Add-ins tab of the Trust Center

Requiring Add-ins to Be Signed

The first checkbox on this tab will prevent any add-in from executing code unless it is signed with a trusted digital certificate. If you select this option, then each add-in is checked for a trusted signature at load time. If a trusted signature is not present, then the add-in is not loaded, and a notification is displayed to the user.

NOTE **The user may still enable the unsigned add-in(s) based on your choice for the next setting.**

A word of caution should be issued here as well: Excel, in particular, gets a lot of its additional functionality through add-ins, including the Analysis Toolpak add-in, which is (finally) installed by default. This brings up a very important point: The term "add-in" includes tools that you create, as well as those created by Microsoft and third parties. Note also that even Microsoft is not a trusted publisher by default, so if this checkbox is set, users will be prompted with the message shown in Figure 17-6 upon restarting Excel. Of course, this add-in file is perfectly safe, but the message could be rather disconcerting and irritating to end users!

Naturally, checking "Enable all code published by this publisher" will trust Microsoft permanently and avoid this issue in the future.

The message for add-ins with no digital signature is quite similar. It includes the first two options shown in Figure 17-6, but does not offer the option to enable all code published by the publisher. The reason for this should be obvious, as no publisher is associated with the file.

Disabling Notification for Unsigned Add-ins

The "Disable notification for unsigned add-ins" checkbox only becomes active if the Trust Center is set to require add-ins to have signatures. By activating this checkbox, users will not receive a notification when an unsigned add-in is stopped.

That means users will not even receive a notification to give them the option of trusting an unsigned add-in. However, add-ins that are digitally signed but have not yet been trusted on the system will still generate a security notification.

Figure 17-6: Security settings triggered by allowing only signed add-ins

Disabling All Add-ins

The "Disable all Application Add-ins" setting rightfully carries a warning that you may lose functionality. This setting should only be used in the tightest of security environments.

NOTE **As a very interesting point, note that while setting this checkbox will disable all the VBA code in an add-in from running, the add-in still seems to load. This is demonstrated by the fact that disabling all add-ins does *not* block any RibbonX customizations that exist in those files. In other words, your add-in will still load and create new tabs and groups, and it will still move icons around. In addition, if all of your customizations were based on built-in controls alone, they would still function as designed.**

ActiveX Settings

This section of the Trust Center (not available in Access) is also new in Office 2007. It establishes how ActiveX controls will be treated from a security standpoint. As ActiveX controls are outside the scope of this book, these settings are not explored. However, it might be reassuring to know that the settings contain similar notations and guidance about the options and their effects.

NOTE **For those who have never used ActiveX controls, these are the controls that are added to documents and workbooks. They are found on the Developer tab.**

Macro Settings

The macro security settings are slightly different from those offered in prior versions of Office. This was to align them with the new Trusted Locations concept. The available settings are shown in Figure 17-7.

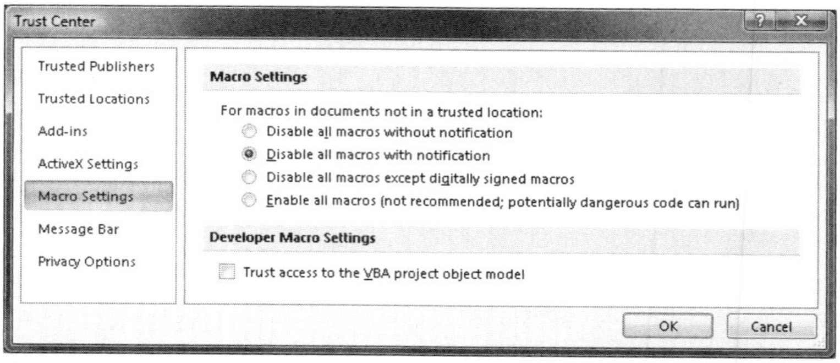

Figure 17-7: Macro settings in Office 2007

As you will immediately notice, the settings in the first section of this window (under the heading Macro Settings) are only applicable to files that are not in trusted folders. For reference, trusted folders run with the effective permission of "Enable all macros."

You'll also notice that the option most relevant to developers conveniently stands out with its own heading. That's because it is critical to trust the VBA project object model if you plan to use VBA to manipulate VBE components or code. The following sections explain these setting options.

Setting Macro Options

While the most secure setting is to automatically disable all macros without even notifying the user, this obviously obliterates the benefits of VBA code. As a person who would read this book, it is highly unlikely that you would want to do that.

The default setting for macro security is to disable all macros with notification. This is probably the nicest way to strike a balance between security and functionality, as users have the option to enable macros if they'd like.

The option to "Disable all macros except digitally signed" does exactly that, without any notification. If this setting is chosen, users do not have the option to enable the macro content for an unsigned macro.

NOTE **If a file is in a trusted location, the preceding setting is ignored when the file is opened. Therefore, it opens with macros enabled and without prompting, as we would expect with any file in a trusted location.**

Of course, "Enable all macros" is the most wide open setting, as it allows everything and anything to run. This setting is rarely recommended. A much better approach is to place applicable files in a trusted location, rather than effectively using a blanket switch to turn security off.

Trusting VBA Project Access

The last setting on this pane enables you to trust access to the VBA Project object model. In short, this setting allows you to successfully run code that can manipulate the VBA project components and structure, instead of just targeting the layer of the file that is seen in the user interface. This type of access allows code that can actually write, modify, or delete code, meaning that the code itself could even add or remove entire code modules.

Based on this simple explanation alone, you can see the power that someone would have if you allow and trust access to the VBA project. As a general rule, you would most likely never want to set this on a user's workstation. This is a global setting and it affects files both inside and outside the trusted location folders.

Message Bar

The message bar settings, shown in Figure 17-8, control how the application reacts when macro content has been disabled.

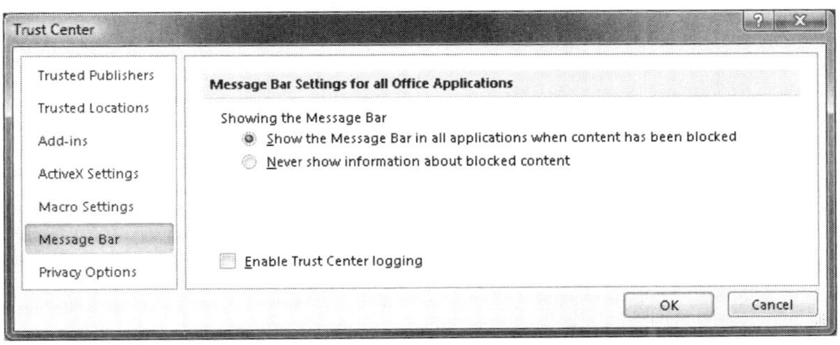

Figure 17-8: Message bar settings

By default, the message bar is shown when content is blocked, and appears as shown in Figure 17-9. Changing the setting to "Never show . . ." will, of course, stop the system from prompting the user when macro content has been disabled.

Removing this message also removes the convenient option that allows the user to enable macros associated with the file.

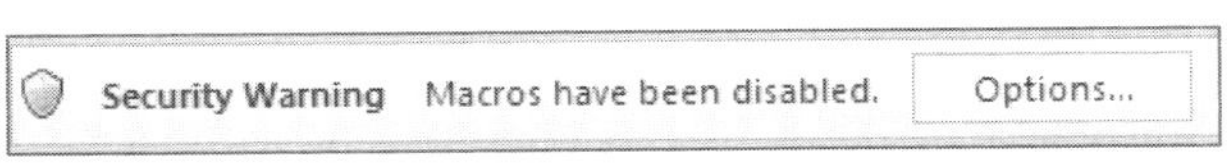

Figure 17-9: Message bar warning of disabled content

NOTE **The message bar is used to display warnings about what could be malicious data connections, as well as code. These warnings can also be triggered in Word when using the mail-merge feature.**

Privacy Options

As we are primarily concerned with exploring security, the privacy options are not covered in this book. This tab provides relatively clear options and guidance to help users customize their settings.

Digital Certificates

As mentioned at the outset of this chapter, digital certificates are an integral part of deploying a macro-enabled solution. In the past, digital certification used to be the only real security method for trusting files, but now this process is most applicable to files that lie outside the Trust Center's trusted folders.

While you may be able to avoid the digital certificate process if you are developing files only for your own use, their value quickly becomes apparent when you deploy applications to other users. Just imagine having to tell each user to set up the appropriate trusted folders for your files! Not only does this expose the client to unacceptable risk (as someone could dump a malicious file in there as well), but it appears unprofessional. Using a digital certificate can avoid these types of issues.

How Digital Certificates Work

To keep things simple, let's run through a scenario. Consider a developer who wants to secure his code. He goes to the "locksmith" and asks for two keys.

The first key, known as the *private key,* is a master key and is unique. The developer knows that the locksmith will never issue the same private key to anyone else, and that the locksmith has recorded his name next to it in a log book. Using this key will lock the code in the file and let everyone know that he wrote and secured it.

The second key, known as the *public key,* is almost identical to the first, but has a few less teeth. This key will unlock the code in the file so that the code is readable but not editable. Unlike the private key, which the locksmith marked with a "Do Not Copy" stamp, this key comes in sets that the developer will freely hand out to anyone who wants to use his work.

The developer takes his private key and turns it in the lock, thereby setting the security on the code in his application. It is this process that is known as digitally signing a file. He then sends the file out to his clients, along with a copy of the public key.

When the digitally signed file is opened by the client, the system recognizes that there is a lock on the file, and matches it with the appropriate key. The system looks up the developer in its list of trustworthy developers, and not finding him there, takes the actions dictated by the Macro Security Settings tab of the Trust Center. Assuming that the settings specify prompting the user, the system then asks the user whether they would like to run the code, and then offers the option to trust the developer permanently.

Assuming that the user agrees to trust the developer, the system adds his name to the list of trusted developers, uses the key to unlock the code, and puts the key in safekeeping until the next time. Thereafter, any file that is signed with the identical signature will be unlocked with the stored public key and the code will be allowed to execute. Keep in mind that several things had to happen to make this possible, including the user specifically stating that they trust the developer. It also requires that the code is still digitally signed. We're about to discuss some nuances to that.

NOTE **While the digital certificate proves who signed the code, it makes absolutely no guarantee that the code within the file is safe. It is completely up to users if they want to trust the issuer of the certificate on their system.**

Where the digital certificate proves its worth is in the mandate that the private key must sign the code. Any modifications made to code in a digitally signed file forces a validation of the digital certificate. Failing to get validated, the code in the file will no longer have a digital certificate.

Assume that in the preceding case, one of the developer's clients decided to modify the code. As they begin to make modifications, the lock pops open completely. Unlike most padlocks, however, which can be relocked simply by closing the hasp, this lock requires the private key to relock the file. Since the private key resides on the developer's computer, and not on the client's, the file cannot be relocked and the digital certificate evaporates. Unfortunately for the client, the developer's locksmith will not issue him a copy of the private key, so he is left with an unsigned file. Any attempts to open the file in future will then be treated as unsigned code and reacted to with the security permissions set in the Trust Center's Macro Settings area.

As you can see, the digital certificate offers assurance to both the developer and the client. The client can be assured that the code was delivered as intended by the developer, and the developer can be assured that the client has not changed the code in any way (or, if the code has been changed, it no longer carries the developer's digital certificate). This can be quite useful for the developer from a liability standpoint if any destruction is caused and blamed on his file. If the digital certificate is gone, it indicates someone has tampered with the code.

NOTE **While the preceding anecdote explains how a digital certificate works, a far more technical explanation can be found on Microsoft's Technet site at the following URL:** `www.microsoft.com/technet/security/guidance/cryptographyetc/certs.mspx`.

Acquiring a Digital Certificate

While digital code signing certificates can be purchased from a third-party vendor, they can also be created without cost using a self-certification program that is installed with Microsoft Office: `SELFCERT.exe`.

At first glance, you might think it is a no-brainer to simply use `SELFCERT.exe` to create a free certificate, rather than pay for a commercial version. As with most things, however, each approach has both benefits and drawbacks, the biggest of which are cost, verification, and acceptance.

As mentioned, the self-certification route carries a significant cost advantage over purchasing a digital certificate from a third-party issuer. Commercially purchased certificates can range in cost from $200–$500 on a yearly basis, depending upon the vendor that you choose.

Conversely, anyone can generate a certificate with the self-certification utility, so what does it really tell you about the developer? The signature could be published under any name, real or fictitious, and while it can't necessarily be forged, it could certainly be masquerading under someone else's name.

Part of what you pay for when you get a certificate from a commercial outfit is third-party entity identification. The cost of the certificate helps cover the staff time and resource costs for verifying the existence of the person or company who has requested the certificate. As the entire point of having a certificate is to add security, it only makes sense that we should also try to show that the developer actually exists!

A variety of third-party certificate authorities are currently doing business on the Internet. Microsoft's MSDN website carries a list of such businesses: `http://msdn2.microsoft.com/en-us/library/ms995347.aspx`.

TIP **If you are interested in purchasing a digital certificate from one of the commercial certificate authorities, make sure that you purchase a *code signing certificate,* rather than one of the other kinds.**

Using SELFCERT.exe to Create a Digital Signature

Because many of you will at least want to experiment with the self-certification tool, we will now look at the process.

To launch the self-certification program, go to the Windows Menu (or Start Menu in Windows XP) and choose All Programs ➪ Microsoft Office ➪ Microsoft Office Tools ➪ Digital Certificate for VBA Projects. This will launch the program, displaying the dialog shown in Figure 17-10.

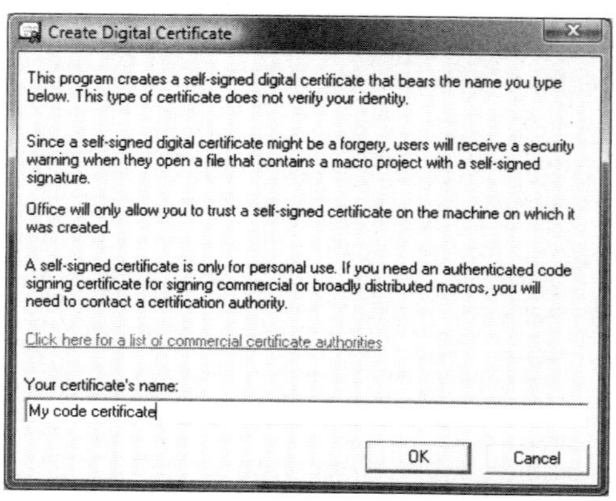

Figure 17-10: Creating a digital certificate with SELFCERT.exe

NOTE **Despite the warnings shown in Figure 17-10, you can actually trust the public key of a self-signed certificate on another computer. This is of critical importance to developers who want deploy solutions.**

To create your own digital certificate, all you need to do is enter a name and press OK. You will instantly receive notification that your certificate has been created.

Adding a Digital Certificate to a Project

After you have acquired a code signing certificate, either via self-certification or through a commercial certificate authority, you need to assign it to your project. Fortunately, this is also very easy to do.

Open your favorite macro-laden file (all applications use the same process) and enter the VBE. From the Tools menu, choose Digital Signature. You will find yourself at the screen shown in Figure 17-11.

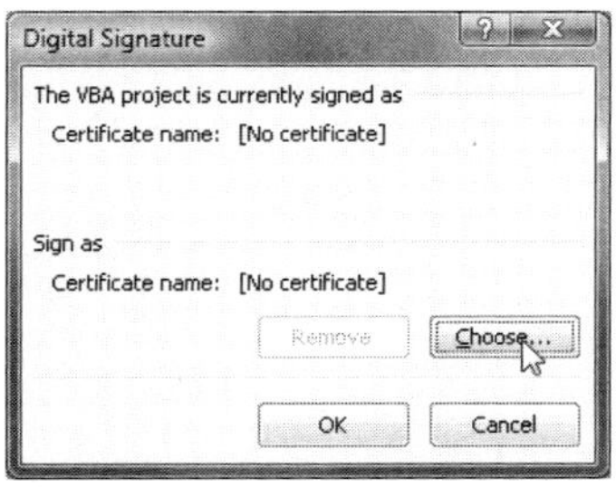

Figure 17-11: Selecting a digital signature

Notice that at this point, there is neither a signature associated with the project, nor a default certificate showing in the Sign As field.

NOTE **After you have signed your first project, the Sign As area will be prefilled with the name of the last certificate you applied. Clicking OK at that point will apply the certificate in the Sign As field to your active project.**

Click the Choose button to be shown a list of the existing digital certificates that are available for signing the code (see Figure 17-12).

As you can see, the certificate that you just created, My Code Certificate, is on the list. With that selected, click OK, and you will be returned to the digital certificate interface. At this point, the project is signed and the certificate name is listed in the Sign As area for easy application to other projects, as shown in Figure 17-13.

Upon clicking OK and saving the file, the project is signed and ready for distribution.

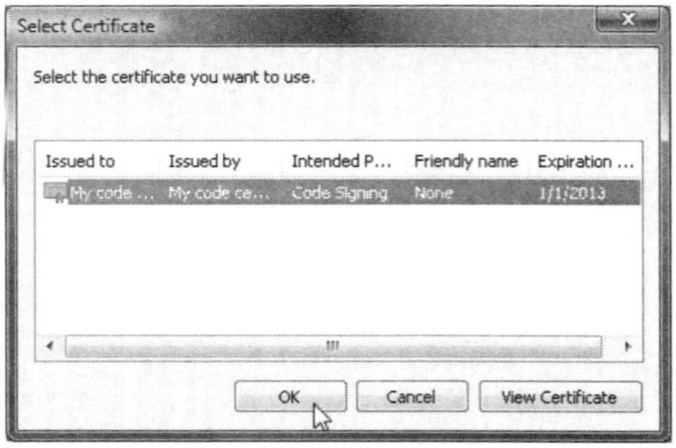

Figure 17-12: Selecting a digital certificate

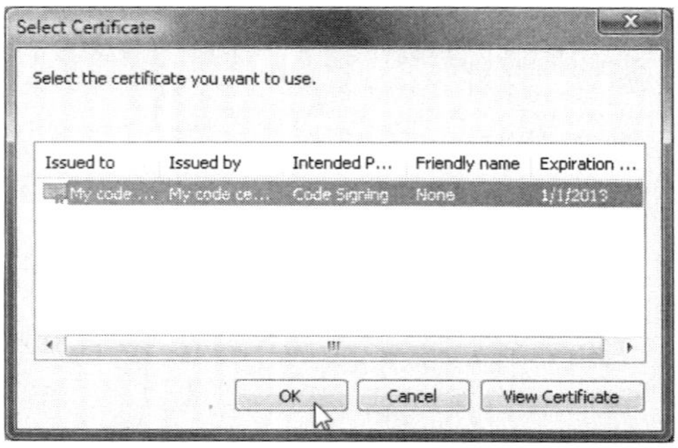

Figure 17-13: The digital certificate interface, showing the project is signed

Trusting a Digital Certificate on Another Machine

The process of trusting a digital certificate on a client's machine can seem cumbersome. Remember that this is in the end user's best interest, as it avoids unnecessary exposure to risks; and once your signature has been trusted, users will not have to repeat the process with future signed applications.

To begin the process, users must open a file that contains your digital signature. When prompted that macros are disabled, they click the Options box to be taken to the screen shown in Figure 17-14.

NOTE **If no macro warning is seen, check whether the Trust Center's Macro Settings are set to disable macros with notification. You may also want to check whether the file has been placed in a trusted location.**

Figure 17-14: Macro security alert details

NOTE **Figure 17-14 shows another difference between self-certified code and code signed by a commercial certificate. In Figure 17-6, where the code was signed by a Microsoft certificate, users had the option to trust it immediately; however, a self-signed certificate requires additional steps.**

At this point, the user must click the Show Signature Details link to be taken to the details of the digital signature file, as shown in Figure 17-15.

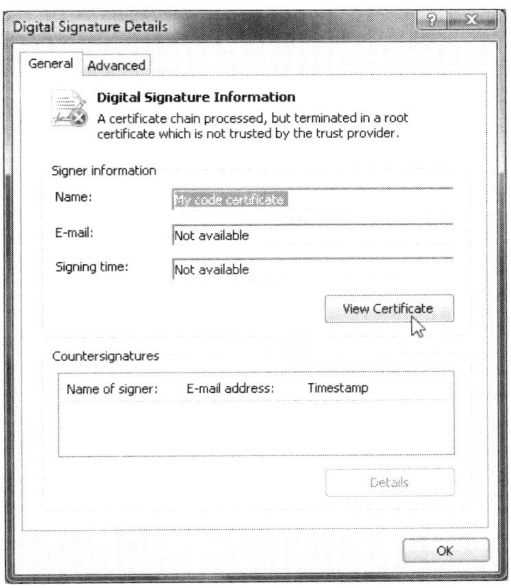

Figure 17-15: Digital Signature Details

Next, they need to click View Certificate, and then click Install Certificate. This will launch the Certificate Import Wizard.

At the Certificate Import Wizard's welcome screen, the user must click Next to be taken to the Certificate Store page. After selecting the "Place all certificates in the following store" radio button, the user would click Browse, and select Trusted Publishers from the list. The Certificate Store options would then appear, as shown in Figure 17-16.

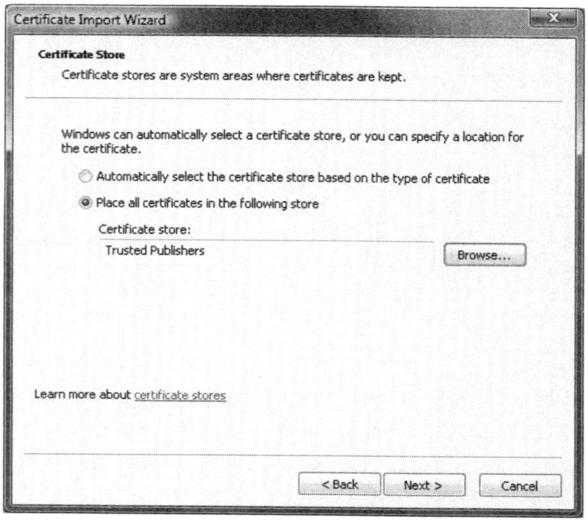

Figure 17-16: Certificate Store settings

The user then clicks Next, and then Finish, to complete the process of importing the digital certificate, finally clicking OK when notified of success. They need to keep clicking OK until they are returned to the original Macro Security warning message.

Finally, the user should click the "Enable this content" button and again click OK to finish loading the file.

This may seem like a lot of work, but try closing and reopening the file. Not a single warning in sight! Even better, if you sign another file and send it to this same PC, it will open like a breeze; the user won't need to repeat this lengthy process.

As a final comment on certificate installation, it is also worth noting that the trusted certificate now shows on the Trusted Publishers tab of the Trust Center, as shown in Figure 17-17.

Therefore, just by self-certifying, you can have your certificate listed with the likes of Microsoft, Adobe, and other major entities.

Deleting a Digital Certificate from Your Machine

While it is fairly straightforward to remove a digital certificate from the Trusted Publishers store (highlight it and click Remove in the Trust Center) or to remove a digital signature from a project (click Remove in the screen where you would apply it), what would you do if you actually wanted to delete the private key for some reason, effectively destroying the certificate?

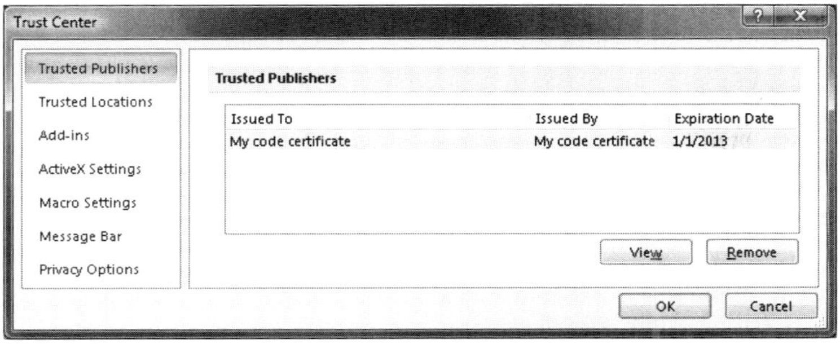

Figure 17-17: The digital certificate listed in the Trust Center

One way to remove the certificate and its private key is to locate the certificate file on your computer and delete it. This can be done by going into the VBE and choosing Tools ➪ Digital Signatures ➪ Choose. Select the certificate that you wish to delete and click View Certificate ➪ Details. Scroll down the list of items until you find Thumbprint, as shown in Figure 17-18.

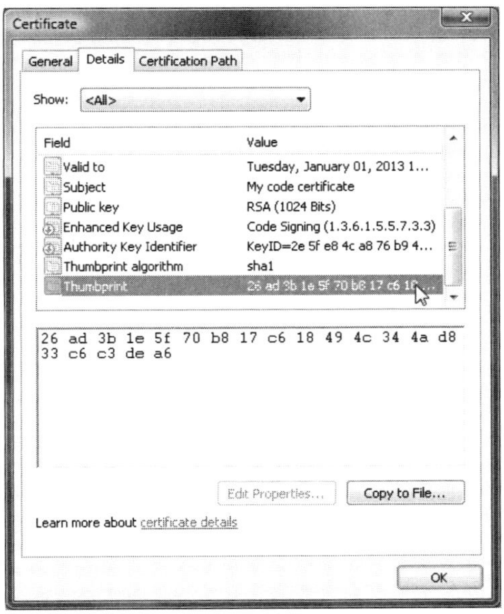

Figure 17-18: Locating a digital signature's thumbprint

Now, based on your version of Windows, browse your computer to locate the following folder:

- Windows Vista:

```
C:\Users\UserName\AppData\Roaming\Microsoft\SystemCertficates\My\
Certificates
```

- Windows XP:

```
C:\Documents and Settings\UserName\Application
Data\Microsoft\SystemCertificates\My\Certificates
```

As shown in Figure 17-19, there is a file with a very similar name. In fact, the filename is the same as the thumbprint value except for the spaces!

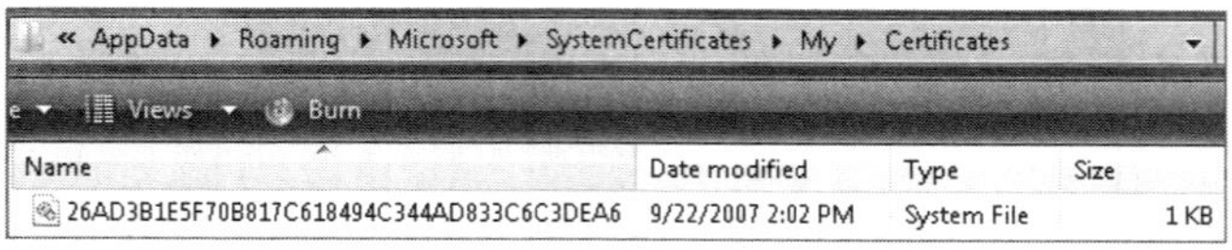

Figure 17-19: The digital signature file in the Certificates folder

The similarity between the file name and the thumbprint name is obviously no coincidence. This is the private key for the digital signature that you want to remove. To do so, first close all the digital signature windows in the VBE. Then, simply delete the file from the Windows Explorer window.

CAUTION **Before you remove a private key from your machine, be absolutely sure that you have the correct one, and that you really want to do this. Once the key has been deleted, *it can never be re-created,* as the keys have randomly generated hidden components. Creating a new key with the same name will not create a key identical to the one you deleted!**

In addition, keep in mind that *other* files may also rely on this key. In fact, all files that are certified by this developer (or other entity) will likely rely on that specific private key.

TIP **The ability to delete a certificate can come in handy if you need documentation to instruct end users about how to install a certificate. Simply create a (bogus) signature, apply it to a file, and then delete the certificate as explained. Upon launching the file, you will be prompted to install the unknown certificate. That way, you can go through the process and can take as many screen shots as you need!**

Conclusion

Microsoft has expended a fair amount of effort to improve the security features in Office 2007 for the benefit of both end users and developers.

For end users, splitting the file formats between macro-free versions and macro-enabled versions provides an obvious clue as to what kind of file they may be dealing with. The Trust Center also allows more security configuration options than were offered in prior versions, such as how to manage macro-laden files and ActiveX controls.

The major changes in Office 2007's security model, however, truly benefit developers. In the past, we could only avoid the nagging macro prompts by turning off our macro security settings or by digitally signing every project we started. The creation of the Trusted Folder in Office 2007 makes it easy to eliminate these annoying hassles. With the ability to designate entire directories as safe havens, developers can create and test files locally without needing to worry about the security settings.

After completing the local development and testing process, developers still have the ability to digitally sign the code before deployment. Using digital signatures, even self-signed certificates, is encouraged; and with the proper settings, end users can configure their machines to run trusted code without taking a carte blanche approach and disabling everything.

APPENDIX

A

Tables of RibbonX Tags

This appendix contains the tables of all elements required to build custom Ribbon solutions.

The appendix is divided into two main sections: RibbonX Container elements and Ribbon Control elements. The former includes all of the elements from the `CustomUI` element to the `group` element, and the latter includes detailed tables of the specific controls with which the user would interact.

Each element's table lists all of the static and dynamic attributes that may be assigned to a Ribbon element, including the VBA callback signatures for the dynamic elements. In addition, each attribute is marked with its allowed and default values.

You'll also appreciate that the files are available in the companion files for this book. These can be downloaded from the book's website at `www.wiley.com/go/ribbonx`.

How to Use This Appendix

Each of the tables within this appendix has a column labeled REQ to indicate which of the attributes are required when using an element. Some of the attributes are required, some are not, and in some cases only one of several attributes can be used, so we have devised Table A-1 to help you interpret this column in the tables.

Similar to the way in which they were covered in the chapters, the attributes are first grouped and then ordered by required attributes, then insert attributes, then all optional attributes.

NOTE **The # symbol in the Marking column is used to indicate a numeric value, and it should not be interpreted as part of the marking (i.e., R1, R2, etc.).**

Table A-1: Legend of Attribute Markings Used in Subsequent Tables

MARKING	INTERPRET AS
R	A required attribute
R#	One, and only one, of the required attributes with the specified number may be included in the RibbonX tag. However, other items denoted as required and attributes with other numbers may also be included.
O	An optional attribute
O#	Only one of the optional attributes specified with this number may be included in the RibbonX tag. However, other items denoted as optional, as well as attributes with different numbers, may also be included.
OR	A recommended (yet still optional) attribute
*	Characters followed by a * have a note about the element at the bottom of the table.

Ribbon Container Elements

This section of the appendix contains all of the container controls that are used to construct the Ribbon interface.

customUI Element

Table A-2 lists all of the static and dynamic attributes specific to the `customUI` element, as well as their allowed values, defaults, and callback signatures.

CROSS-REFERENCE **There is a detailed discussion of the `customUI` element in Chapter 3.**

Table A-2: Table of customUI Attributes

STATIC ATTRIBUTE	DYNAMIC ATTRIBUTE	REQ	ALLOWED VALUES	DEFAULT VALUE	VBA CALLBACK SIGNATURE
xmlns	(none)	R	`http://schemas.microsoft.com/office/2006/01/customui`	(none)	(none)
xmlns:Q	(none)	O	1 to 1024 characters	(none)	(none)
(none)	onLoad	O*	1 to 1024 characters	(none)	Sub onLoad (ribbon as IRibbonUI)
(none)	loadImage	O	1 to 1024 characters	(none)	Sub loadImage (imageID as String, ByRef returnedVal)

* The `onLoad` attribute is required in order to invalidate the `RibbonUI` object via a VBA callback

ribbon Element

Table A-3 lists all of the static and dynamic attributes specific to the `ribbon` element, as well as their allowed values, defaults, and callback signatures.

CROSS-REFERENCE **There is a detailed discussion of the `ribbon` element in Chapter 3.**

Table A-3: Table of ribbon Attributes

STATIC ATTRIBUTE	DYNAMIC ATTRIBUTE	REQ	ALLOWED VALUES	DEFAULT VALUE	VBA CALLBACK SIGNATURE
startFromScratch	(none)	O	true, false, 1, 0	false	(none)

contextualTabs Element

The `contextualTabs` element does not have any attributes, either required or optional.

tabSet Element

Table A-4 lists all of the static and dynamic attributes specific to the `tabSet` element, as well as their allowed values, defaults, and callback signatures.

CROSS-REFERENCE **There is a detailed discussion of the `tabSet` element in Chapter 3.**

Table A-4: Table of tabSet Attributes

STATIC ATTRIBUTE	DYNAMIC ATTRIBUTE	REQ	ALLOWED VALUES	DEFAULT VALUE	VBA CALLBACK SIGNATURE
idMso	(none)	R	Valid Mso tabSet name	(none)	(none)
visible	getVisible	O	true, false, 1, 0	true	Sub GetVisible (control As IRibbonControl, ByRef returnedVal)

qat Element

Table A-5 lists all of the static and dynamic attributes specific to the Quick Access Toolbar (`QAT`) element, as well as their allowed values, defaults, and callback signatures.

CROSS-REFERENCE **There is a detailed discussion of the `QAT` element in Chapter 14.**

Table A-5: Table of QAT Attributes

STATIC ATTRIBUTE	DYNAMIC ATTRIBUTE	REQ	ALLOWED VALUES	DEFAULT VALUE	VBA CALLBACK SIGNATURE
documentControls	(none)	O	Control specific to document	(none)	(none)
sharedControls	(none)	O	Control shared across documents	(none)	(none)

NOTE **The `QAT` element can only be adjusted if the `ribbon` element's `startFromScratch` attribute is set to `true`.**

sharedControls Element

The `sharedControls` element does not have any attributes, either required or optional.

documentControls Element

The `documentControls` element does not have any attributes, either required or optional.

officeMenu Element

The `officeMenu` element does not have any attributes, either required or optional.

CROSS-REFERENCE **There is a detailed discussion of the `officeMenu` element in Chapter 14.**

tabs Element

The `tabs` element does not have any attributes, either required or optional.

CROSS-REFERENCE **There is a detailed discussion of the `tabs` element in Chapter 3.**

tab Element

Table A-6 lists all of the static and dynamic attributes specific to the `tab` element, as well as their allowed values, defaults, and callback signatures.

CROSS-REFERENCE **There is a detailed discussion of the `tab` element in Chapter 3.**

Table A-6: Table of tab Attributes

STATIC ATTRIBUTE	DYNAMIC ATTRIBUTE	REQ	ALLOWED VALUES	DEFAULT VALUE	VBA CALLBACK SIGNATURE
id	(none)	R1	Unique text string	(none)	(none)
idMso	(none)	R1	Valid Mso tab name	(none)	(none)
idQ	(none)	R1	Unique tab idQ	(none)	(none)
insertAfterMso	(none)	O1	Valid Mso tab name	(none)	(none)
insertBeforeMso	(none)	O1	Valid Mso tab name	(none)	(none)
insertAfterQ	(none)	O1	Valid tab idQ	(none)	(none)
insertBeforeQ	(none)	O1	Valid tab idQ	(none)	(none)
keytip	getKeytip	O	1 to 3 characters	(none)	Sub GetKeytip (control As IRibbonControl, ByRef returnedVal)

Table A-6 *(continued)*

STATIC ATTRIBUTE	DYNAMIC ATTRIBUTE	REQ	ALLOWED VALUES	DEFAULT VALUE	VBA CALLBACK SIGNATURE
label	getLabel	OR	1 to 1024 characters	(none)	Sub GetLabel (control As IRibbonControl, ByRef returnedVal)
tag	(none)	O	1 to 1024 characters	(none)	(none)
visible	getVisible	O	true, false, 1, 0	true	Sub GetVisible (control As IRibbonControl, ByRef returnedVal)

group Element

Table A-7 lists all of the static and dynamic attributes specific to the `group` element, as well as their allowed values, defaults, and callback signatures.

CROSS-REFERENCE There is a detailed discussion of the `group` element in Chapter 3.

Table A-7: Table of group Attributes

STATIC ATTRIBUTE	DYNAMIC ATTRIBUTE	REQ	ALLOWED VALUES	DEFAULT VALUE	VBA CALLBACK SIGNATURE
id	(none)	R1	Unique text string	(none)	(none)
idMso	(none)	R1	Valid Mso tab name	(none)	(none)
idQ	(none)	R1	Unique group idQ	(none)	(none)
insertAfterMso	(none)	O1	Valid Mso group name	(none)	(none)
insertBeforeMso	(none)	O1	Valid Mso group name	(none)	(none)

Continued

Table A-7 *(continued)*

STATIC ATTRIBUTE	DYNAMIC ATTRIBUTE	REQ	ALLOWED VALUES	DEFAULT VALUE	VBA CALLBACK SIGNATURE
insertAfterQ	(none)	O1	Valid group idQ	(none)	(none)
insertBeforeQ	(none)	O1	Valid group idQ	(none)	(none)
image	getImage	O	1 to 1024 characters	(none)	Sub GetImage (control As IRibbonControl, ByRef returnedVal)
imageMso	getImage	O	1 to 1024 characters	(none)	Same as above
keytip	getKeytip	O	1 to 3 characters	(none)	Sub GetKeytip (control As IRibbonControl, ByRef returnedVal)
label	getLabel	OR	1 to 1024 characters	(none)	Sub GetLabel (control As IRibbonControl, ByRef returnedVal)
tag	(none)	O	1 to 1024 characters	(none)	(none)
visible	getVisible	O	true, false, 1, 0	true	Sub GetVisible (control As IRibbonControl, ByRef returnedVal)

Ribbon Control Elements

This section of the appendix contains all of the controls placed within Ribbon groups that the users will interact with.

box Element

Table A-8 lists all of the static and dynamic attributes specific to the box element, as well as their allowed values, defaults, and callback signatures.

CROSS-REFERENCE **There is a detailed discussion of the box element in Chapter 10.**

Table A-8: Table of box Attributes

STATIC ATTRIBUTE	DYNAMIC ATTRIBUTE	REQ	ALLOWED VALUES	DEFAULT VALUE	VBA CALLBACK SIGNATURE
id	(none)	R1	Unique text string	(none)	(none)
idQ	(none)	R1	Unique control idQ	(none)	(none)
insertAfterMso	(none)	O1	Valid Mso control name	(none)	(none)
insertBeforeMso	(none)	O1	Valid Mso control name	(none)	(none)
insertAfterQ	(none)	O1	Valid control idQ	(none)	(none)
insertBeforeQ	(none)	O1	Valid control idQ	(none)	(none)
boxStyle	(none)	O	horizontal, vertical	horizontal	(none)
visible	getVisible	O	true, false, 1, 0	true	Sub GetVisible (control As IRibbonControl, ByRef returnedVal)

button Element

Table A-9 lists all of the static and dynamic attributes specific to the button element, as well as their allowed values, defaults, and callback signatures.

CROSS-REFERENCE **There is a detailed discussion of the button element in Chapter 6.**

Table A-9: Table of button Attributes

STATIC ATTRIBUTE	DYNAMIC ATTRIBUTE	REQ	ALLOWED VALUES	DEFAULT VALUE	VBA CALLBACK SIGNATURE
id	(none)	R1	Unique text string	(none)	(none)
idMso	(none)	R1	Valid Mso control name	(none)	(none)
idQ	(none)	R1	Unique control idQ	(none)	(none)
onAction	(Standard)	R2	1 to 4096 characters	(none)	Sub OnAction (control As IRibbonControl)
onAction	(Repurpose)	R2	1 to 4096 characters	(none)	Sub OnAction (control As IRibbonControl, ByRef returnedVal)
insertAfterMso	(none)	O1	Valid Mso control name	(none)	(none)
insertBeforeMso	(none)	O1	Valid Mso control name	(none)	(none)
insertAfterQ	(none)	O1	Valid control idQ	(none)	(none)
insertBeforeQ	(none)	O1	Valid control idQ	(none)	(none)
description	getDescription	O	1 to 4096 characters	(none)	Sub GetDescription (control As IRibbonControl, ByRef returnedVal)
enabled	getEnabled	O	true, false, 1, 0	true	Sub GetEnabled (control As IRibbonControl, ByRef returnedVal)
image	getImage	O	1 to 1024 characters	(none)	Sub GetImage (control As IRibbonControl, ByRef returnedVal)

Table A-9 *(continued)*

STATIC ATTRIBUTE	DYNAMIC ATTRIBUTE	REQ	ALLOWED VALUES	DEFAULT VALUE	VBA CALLBACK SIGNATURE
imageMso	getImage	O	1 to 1024 characters	(none)	Same as above
keytip	getKeytip	O	1 to 3 characters	(none)	Sub GetKeytip (control As IRibbonControl, ByRef returnedVal)
label	getLabel	OR	1 to 1024 characters	(none)	Sub GetLabel (control As IRibbonControl, ByRef returnedVal)
screentip	getScreentip	O	1 to 1024 characters	(none)	Sub GetScreentip (control As IRibbonControl, ByRef returnedVal)
showImage	getShow↲ Image	O	true, false, 1, 0	true	Sub GetShowImage (control As IRibbonControl, ByRef returnedVal)
showLabel	getShowLabel	O	true, false, 1, 0	true	Sub GetShowLabel (control As IRibbonControl, ByRef returnedVal)
size	getSize	O	normal, large	normal	Sub GetSize (control As IRibbonControl, ByRef returnedVal)
supertip	getSupertip	O	1 to 1024 characters	(none)	Sub GetSupertip (control As IRibbonControl, ByRef returnedVal)

Continued

Table A-9 *(continued)*

STATIC ATTRIBUTE	DYNAMIC ATTRIBUTE	REQ	ALLOWED VALUES	DEFAULT VALUE	VBA CALLBACK SIGNATURE
tag	(none)	O	1 to 1024 characters	(none)	(none)
visible	getVisible	O	true, false, 1, 0	true	Sub GetVisible (control As IRibbonControl, ByRef returnedVal)

buttonGroup Element

Table A-10 lists all of the static and dynamic attributes specific to the `buttonGroup` element, as well as their allowed values, defaults, and callback signatures.

CROSS-REFERENCE **There is a detailed discussion of the** `buttonGroup` **element in Chapter 10.**

Table A-10: Table of buttonGroup Attributes

STATIC ATTRIBUTE	DYNAMIC ATTRIBUTE	REQ	ALLOWED VALUES	DEFAULT VALUE	VBA CALLBACK SIGNATURE
id	(none)	R1	Unique text string	(none)	(none)
idQ	(none)	R1	Unique control idQ	(none)	(none)
insertAfterMso	(none)	O1	Valid Mso control name	(none)	(none)
insertBeforeMso	(none)	O1	Valid Mso control name	(none)	(none)
insertAfterQ	(none)	O1	Unique control idQ	(none)	(none)
insertBeforeQ	(none)	O1	Unique control idQ	(none)	(none)
visible	getVisible	O	true, false, 1, 0	true	Sub GetVisible (control As IRibbonControl, ByRef returnedVal)

checkBox Element

Table A-11 lists all of the static and dynamic attributes specific to the `checkBox` element, as well as their allowed values, defaults, and callback signatures.

CROSS-REFERENCE **There is a detailed discussion of the** `checkBox` **element in Chapter 6.**

Table A-11: Table of checkBox Attributes

STATIC ATTRIBUTE	DYNAMIC ATTRIBUTE	REQ	ALLOWED VALUES	DEFAULT VALUE	VBA CALLBACK SIGNATURE
id	(none)	R1	Unique text string	(none)	(none)
idMso	(none)	R1	Valid Mso control name	(none)	(none)
idQ	(none)	R1	Unique control idQ	(none)	(none)
(none)	onAction	OR	1 to 4096 characters	(none)	Sub OnAction (control As IRibbonControl, pressed as Boolean)
insertAfterMso	(none)	O1	Valid Mso control name	(none)	(none)
insertBeforeMso	(none)	O1	Valid Mso control name	(none)	(none)
insertAfterQ	(none)	O1	Valid control idQ	(none)	(none)
insertBeforeQ	(none)	O1	Valid control idQ	(none)	(none)
description	getDescription	O	1 to 4096 characters	(none)	Sub GetDescription (control As IRibbonControl, ByRef returnedVal)
enabled	getEnabled	O	true, false, 1, 0	true	Sub GetEnabled (control As IRibbonControl, ByRef returnedVal)

Continued

Table A-11 *(continued)*

STATIC ATTRIBUTE	DYNAMIC ATTRIBUTE	REQ	ALLOWED VALUES	DEFAULT VALUE	VBA CALLBACK SIGNATURE
keytip	getKeytip	O	1 to 3 characters	(none)	Sub GetKeytip (control As IRibbonControl, ByRef returnedVal)
label	getLabel	OR	1 to 1024 characters	(none)	Sub GetLabel (control As IRibbonControl, ByRef returnedVal)
(none)	getPressed	O	true, false, 1, 0	false	Sub GetPressed (control As IRibbonControl, ByRef returnedVal)
screentip	getScreentip	O	1 to 1024 characters	(none)	Sub GetScreentip (control As IRibbonControl, ByRef returnedVal)
supertip	getSupertip	O	1 to 1024 characters	(none)	Sub GetSupertip (control As IRibbonControl, ByRef returnedVal)
tag	(none)	O	1 to 1024 characters	(none)	(none)
visible	getVisible	O	true, false, 1, 0	true	Sub GetVisible (control As IRibbonControl, ByRef returnedVal)

comboBox Element

Table A-12 lists all of the static and dynamic attributes specific to the `comboBox` element, as well as their allowed values, defaults, and callback signatures.

CROSS-REFERENCE **There is a detailed discussion of the** `comboBox` **element in Chapter 7.**

Table A-12: Table of comboBox Attributes

STATIC ATTRIBUTE	DYNAMIC ATTRIBUTE	REQ	ALLOWED VALUES	DEFAULT VALUE	VBA CALLBACK SIGNATURE
id	(none)	R1	Unique text string	(none)	(none)
idMso	(none)	R1	Valid Mso control name	(none)	(none)
idQ	(none)	R1	Unique control idQ	(none)	(none)
(none)	onChange	OR	1 to 4096 characters	(none)	Sub OnChange (control As IRibbonControl, text As String)
insertAfterMso	(none)	O1	Valid Mso control name	(none)	(none)
insertBeforeMso	(none)	O1	Valid Mso control name	(none)	(none)
insertAfterQ	(none)	O1	Valid control idQ	(none)	(none)
insertBeforeQ	(none)	O1	Valid control idQ	(none)	(none)
enabled	getEnabled	O	true, false, 1, 0	true	Sub GetEnabled (control As IRibbonControl, ByRef returnedVal)
image	getImage	O	1 to 1024 characters	(none)	Sub GetImage (control As IRibbonControl, ByRef returnedVal)
imageMso	getImage	O	1 to 1024 characters	(none)	Same as above
(none)	getItemCount	O	1 to 1024 characters	(none)	Sub GetItemCount (control As IRibbonControl, ByRef returnedVal)

Continued

Table A-12 *(continued)*

STATIC ATTRIBUTE	DYNAMIC ATTRIBUTE	REQ	ALLOWED VALUES	DEFAULT VALUE	VBA CALLBACK SIGNATURE
(none)	getItemID	O	1 to 1024 characters	(none)	Sub GetItemID (control As IRibbonControl, index As Integer, ByRef id)
(none)	getItemImage	O	1 to 1024 characters	(none)	Sub GetItemImage (control As IRibbonControl, index As Integer, ByRef returnedVal)
(none)	getItemLabel	O	1 to 1024 characters	(none)	Sub GetItemLabel (control As IRibbonControl, index As Integer, ByRef returnedVal)
(none)	getItem↵ Screentip	O	1 to 1024 characters	(none)	Sub GetItemScreenTip (control As IRibbonControl, index As Integer, ByRef returnedVal)
(none)	getItem↵ Supertip	O	1 to 1024 characters	(none)	Sub GetItemSuperTip (control As IRibbonControl, index As Integer, ByRef returnedVal)
keytip	getKeytip	O	1 to 3 characters	(none)	Sub GetKeytip (control As IRibbonControl, ByRef returnedVal)
label	getLabel	OR	1 to 1024 characters	(none)	Sub GetLabel (control As IRibbonControl, ByRef returnedVal)

Table A-12 *(continued)*

STATIC ATTRIBUTE	DYNAMIC ATTRIBUTE	REQ	ALLOWED VALUES	DEFAULT VALUE	VBA CALLBACK SIGNATURE
maxLength	(none)	O	1 to 1024 characters	1024	(none)
screentip	getScreentip	O	1 to 1024 characters	(none)	Sub GetScreentip (control As IRibbonControl, ByRef returnedVal)
showImage	getShow↵ Image	O	true, false, 1, 0	true	Sub GetShowImage (control As IRibbonControl, ByRef returnedVal)
showItem↵ Attribute	(none)	O	true, false, 1, 0	true	(none)
showItem↵ Image	(none)	O	true, false, 1, 0	true	(none)
showLabel	getShowLabel	O	true, false, 1, 0	true	Sub GetShowLabel (control As IRibbonControl, ByRef returnedVal)
sizeString	(none)	O*	1 to 1024 characters	12	(none)
supertip	getSupertip	O	1 to 1024 characters	(none)	Sub GetSupertip (control As IRibbonControl, ByRef returnedVal)
tag	(none)	O	1 to 1024 characters	(none)	(none)
(none)	getText	O	1 to 1024 characters	(none)	Sub GetText (control As IRibbonControl, ByRef returnedVal)

Continued

Table A-12 *(continued)*

STATIC ATTRIBUTE	DYNAMIC ATTRIBUTE	REQ	ALLOWED VALUES	DEFAULT VALUE	VBA CALLBACK SIGNATURE
visible	getVisible	O	true, false, 1, 0	true	Sub GetVisible (control As IRibbonControl, ByRef returnedVal)

* The default value for the `sizeString` attribute (if the attribute is not declared at all) is approximately 12, but this varies depending on the characters used and the system font.

dialogBoxLauncher Element

The `dialogBoxLauncher` element does not have any attributes, either required or optional.

CROSS-REFERENCE **There is a detailed discussion of the** `dialogBoxLauncher` **element in Chapter 11.**

dropDown Element

Table A-13 lists all of the static and dynamic attributes specific to the `dropDown` element, as well as their allowed values, defaults, and callback signatures.

CROSS-REFERENCE **There is a detailed discussion of the** `dropDown` **element in Chapter 7.**

Table A-13: Table of dropDown Attributes

STATIC ATTRIBUTE	DYNAMIC ATTRIBUTE	REQ	ALLOWED VALUES	DEFAULT VALUE	VBA CALLBACK SIGNATURE
id	(none)	R1	Unique text string	(none)	(none)
idMso	(none)	R1	Valid Mso control name	(none)	(none)
idQ	(none)	R1	Unique control idQ	(none)	(none)

Table A-13 *(continued)*

STATIC ATTRIBUTE	DYNAMIC ATTRIBUTE	REQ	ALLOWED VALUES	DEFAULT VALUE	VBA CALLBACK SIGNATURE
(none)	onAction	OR	1 to 4096 characters	(none)	Sub OnAction (control As IRibbonControl, Id As String, Index As Integer)
insertAfterMso	(none)	O1	Valid Mso control name	(none)	(none)
insertBeforeMso	(none)	O1	Valid Mso control name	(none)	(none)
insertAfterQ	(none)	O1	Valid control idQ	(none)	(none)
insertBeforeQ	(none)	O1	Valid control idQ	(none)	(none)
enabled	getEnabled	O	true, false, 1, 0	true	Sub GetEnabled (control As IRibbonControl, ByRef returnedVal)
image	getImage	O	1 to 1024 characters	(none)	Sub GetImage (control As IRibbonControl, ByRef returnedVal)
imageMso	getImage	O	1 to 1024 characters	(none)	Same as above
(none)	getItemCount	O	1 to 1024 characters	(none)	Sub GetItemCount (control As IRibbonControl, ByRef returnedVal)
(none)	getItemID	O	1 to 1024 characters	(none)	Sub GetItemID (control As IRibbonControl, index As Integer, ByRef id)

Continued

Table A-13 *(continued)*

STATIC ATTRIBUTE	DYNAMIC ATTRIBUTE	REQ	ALLOWED VALUES	DEFAULT VALUE	VBA CALLBACK SIGNATURE
(none)	getItemImage	O	1 to 1024 characters	(none)	Sub GetItemImage (control As IRibbonControl, index As Integer, ByRef returnedVal)
(none)	getItemLabel	O	1 to 1024 characters	(none)	Sub GetItemLabel (control As IRibbonControl, index As Integer, ByRef returnedVal)
(none)	getItem↵ Screentip	O	1 to 1024 characters	(none)	Sub GetItemScreenTip (control As IRibbonControl, index As Integer, ByRef returnedVal)
(none)	getItem↵ Supertip	O	1 to 1024 characters	(none)	Sub GetItemSuperTip (control As IRibbonControl, index As Integer, ByRef returnedVal)
keytip	getKeytip	O	1 to 3 characters	(none)	Sub GetKeytip (control As IRibbonControl, ByRef returnedVal)
label	getLabel	OR	1 to 1024 characters	(none)	Sub GetLabel (control As IRibbonControl, ByRef returnedVal)
screentip	getScreentip	O	1 to 1024 characters	(none)	Sub GetScreentip (control As IRibbonControl, ByRef returnedVal)

Table A-13 *(continued)*

STATIC ATTRIBUTE	DYNAMIC ATTRIBUTE	REQ	ALLOWED VALUES	DEFAULT VALUE	VBA CALLBACK SIGNATURE
(none)	getSelected↵ItemID	O	1 to 1024 characters	(none)	Sub GetSelectedItem↵ID (control As IRibbonControl, ByRef index)
(none)	getSelected↵ItemIndex	O	true, false, 1, 0	(none)	Sub GetSelectedItem↵Index (control As IRibbonControl, ByRef returnedVal)
showImage	getShow↵Image	O	true, false, 1, 0	true	Sub GetShowImage (control As IRibbonControl, ByRef returnedVal)
showItem↵Image	(none)	O	true, false, 1, 0	true	(none)
showItem↵Label	(none)	O	true, false, 1, 0	true	(none)
showLabel	getShow↵Label	O	true, false, 1, 0	true	Sub GetShowLabel (control As IRibbonControl, ByRef returnedVal)
sizeString	(none)	O*	1 to 1024 characters	12	(none)
supertip	getSupertip	O	1 to 1024 characters	(none)	Sub GetSupertip (control As IRibbonControl, ByRef returnedVal)
tag	(none)	O	1 to 1024 characters	(none)	(none)

Continued

Table A-13 *(continued)*

STATIC ATTRIBUTE	DYNAMIC ATTRIBUTE	REQ	ALLOWED VALUES	DEFAULT VALUE	VBA CALLBACK SIGNATURE
visible	getVisible	O	1 to 1024 characters	true	Sub GetVisible (control As IRibbonControl, ByRef returnedVal)

* The default value for the `sizeString` attribute (if the attribute is not declared at all) is approximately 12, but this varies depending on the characters used and the system font.

dynamicMenu Element

Table A-14 lists all of the static and dynamic attributes specific to the `dynamicMenu` element, as well as their allowed values, defaults, and callback signatures.

CROSS-REFERENCE **There is a detailed discussion of the** `dynamicMenu` **element in Chapter 9.**

Table A-14: Table of dynamicMenu Attributes

STATIC ATTRIBUTE	DYNAMIC ATTRIBUTE	REQ	ALLOWED VALUES	DEFAULT VALUE	VBA CALLBACK SIGNATURE
id	(none)	R1	Unique text string	(none)	(none)
idMso	(none)	R1	Valid Mso control name	(none)	(none)
idQ	(none)	R1	Unique control idQ	(none)	(none)
insertAfterMso	(none)	O1	Valid Mso control name	(none)	(none)
insertBeforeMso	(none)	O1	Valid Mso control name	(none)	(none)
insertAfterQ	(none)	O1	Valid control idQ	(none)	(none)
insertBeforeQ	(none)	O1	Valid control idQ	(none)	(none)

Table A-14 *(continued)*

STATIC ATTRIBUTE	DYNAMIC ATTRIBUTE	REQ	ALLOWED VALUES	DEFAULT VALUE	VBA CALLBACK SIGNATURE
(none)	getContent	R	1 to 4096 characters	(none)	Sub GetContent (control As IRibbonControl, ByRef returnedVal)
description	getDescription	O	1 to 4096 characters	(none)	Sub GetDescription (control As IRibbonControl, ByRef returnedVal)
enabled	getEnabled	O	true, false, 1, 0	true	Sub GetEnabled (control As IRibbonControl, ByRef returnedVal)
image	getImage	O	1 to 1024 characters	(none)	Sub GetImage (control As IRibbonControl, ByRef returnedVal)
imageMso	getImage	O	1 to 1024 characters	(none)	Same as above
keytip	getKeytip	O	1 to 3 characters	(none)	Sub GetKeytip (control As IRibbonControl, ByRef returnedVal)
label	getLabel	OR	1 to 1024 characters	(none)	Sub GetLabel (control As IRibbonControl, ByRef returnedVal)
screentip	getScreentip	O	1 to 1024 characters	(none)	Sub GetScreentip (control As IRibbonControl, ByRef returnedVal)

Continued

Table A-14: *(continued)*

STATIC ATTRIBUTE	DYNAMIC ATTRIBUTE	REQ	ALLOWED VALUES	DEFAULT VALUE	VBA CALLBACK SIGNATURE
showImage	getShow↵ Image	O	true, false, 1, 0	true	Sub GetShowImage (control As IRibbonControl, ByRef returnedVal)
showLabel	getShowLabel	O	true, false, 1, 0	true	Sub GetShowLabel (control As IRibbonControl, ByRef returnedVal)
size	getSize	O	normal, large	normal	Sub GetSize (control As IRibbonControl, ByRef returnedVal)
supertip	getSupertip	O	1 to 1024 characters	(none)	Sub GetSupertip (control As IRibbonControl, ByRef returnedVal)
tag	(none)	O	1 to 1024 characters	(none)	(none)
visible	getVisible	O	true, false, 1, 0	true	Sub GetVisible (control As IRibbonControl, ByRef returnedVal)

editBox Element

Table A-15 lists all of the static and dynamic attributes specific to the `editBox` element, as well as their allowed values, defaults, and callback signatures.

CROSS-REFERENCE **There is a detailed discussion of the `editBox` element in Chapter 7.**

Table A-15: Table of editBox Attributes

STATIC ATTRIBUTE	DYNAMIC ATTRIBUTE	REQ	ALLOWED VALUES	DEFAULT VALUE	VBA CALLBACK SIGNATURE
id	(none)	R1	Unique text string	(none)	(none)
idMso	(none)	R1	Valid Mso control name	(none)	(none)
idQ	(none)	R1	Unique control idQ	(none)	(none)
(none)	onChange	OR	1 to 4096 characters	(none)	Sub OnChange (control As IRibbonControl, text As String)
insertAfterMso	(none)	O1	Valid Mso control name	(none)	(none)
insertBeforeMso	(none)	O1	Valid Mso control name	(none)	(none)
insertAfterQ	(none)	O1	Valid control idQ	(none)	(none)
insertBeforeQ	(none)	O1	Valid control idQ	(none)	(none)
enabled	getEnabled	O	true, false, 1, 0	true	Sub GetEnabled (control As IRibbonControl, ByRef returnedVal)
image	getImage	O	1 to 1024 characters	(none)	Sub GetImage (control As IRibbonControl, ByRef returnedVal)
imageMso	getImage	O	1 to 1024 characters	(none)	Same as above
keytip	getKeytip	O	1 to 3 characters	(none)	Sub GetKeytip (control As IRibbonControl, ByRef returnedVal)

Continued

Table A-15 *(continued)*

STATIC ATTRIBUTE	DYNAMIC ATTRIBUTE	REQ	ALLOWED VALUES	DEFAULT VALUE	VBA CALLBACK SIGNATURE
label	getLabel	OR	1 to 1024 characters	(none)	Sub GetLabel (control As IRibbonControl, ByRef returnedVal)
maxLength	(none)	O	1 to 1024 characters	1024	(none)
screentip	getScreentip	O	1 to 1024 characters	(none)	Sub GetScreentip (control As IRibbonControl, ByRef returnedVal)
showImage	getShow↵ Image	O	true, false, 1, 0	true	Sub GetShowImage (control As IRibbonControl, ByRef returnedVal)
showLabel	getShowLabel	O	true, false, 1, 0	true	Sub GetShowLabel (control As IRibbonControl, ByRef returnedVal)
sizeString	(none)	O*	1 to 1024 characters	12	(none)
supertip	getSupertip	O	1 to 1024 characters	(none)	Sub GetSupertip (control As IRibbonControl, ByRef returnedVal)
tag	(none)	O	1 to 1024 characters	(none)	(none)
(none)	getText	O	1 to 1024 characters	(none)	Sub GetText (control As IRibbonControl, ByRef returnedVal)

Table A-15 *(continued)*

STATIC ATTRIBUTE	DYNAMIC ATTRIBUTE	REQ	ALLOWED VALUES	DEFAULT VALUE	VBA CALLBACK SIGNATURE
visible	getVisible	O	1 to 1024 characters	true	Sub GetVisible (control As IRibbonControl, ByRef returnedVal)

* The default value for the `sizeString` attribute (if the attribute is not declared at all) is approximately 12, but this varies depending based on the characters used and the system font.

gallery Element

Table A-16 lists all of the static and dynamic attributes specific to the `gallery` element, as well as their allowed values, defaults, and callback signatures.

CROSS-REFERENCE **There is a detailed discussion of the `gallery` element in Chapter 8.**

Table A-16: Table of gallery Attributes

STATIC ATTRIBUTE	DYNAMIC ATTRIBUTE	REQ	ALLOWED VALUES	DEFAULT VALUE	VBA CALLBACK SIGNATURE
id	(none)	R1	Unique text string	(none)	(none)
idMso	(none)	R1	Valid Mso control name	(none)	(none)
idQ	(none)	R1	Unique control idQ	(none)	(none)
(none)	onAction	R	1 to 4096 characters	(none)	Sub OnAction (control As IRibbonControl, selectedId As String, selectedIndex As Integer)
insertAfterMso	(none)	O1	Valid Mso control name	(none)	(none)

Continued

Table A-16 *(continued)*

STATIC ATTRIBUTE	DYNAMIC ATTRIBUTE	REQ	ALLOWED VALUES	DEFAULT VALUE	VBA CALLBACK SIGNATURE
insertBeforeMso	(none)	O1	Valid Mso control name	(none)	(none)
insertAfterQ	(none)	O1	Valid control idQ	(none)	(none)
insertBeforeQ	(none)	O1	Valid control idQ	(none)	(none)
columns	(none)	O	1 to 1024 characters	1	(none)
enabled	getEnabled	O	true, false, 1, 0	true	Sub GetEnabled (control As IRibbonControl, ByRef returnedVal)
image	getImage	O	1 to 1024 characters	(none)	Sub GetImage (control As IRibbonControl, ByRef returnedVal)
imageMso	getImage	O	1 to 1024 characters	(none)	Same as above
(none)	getItemCount	O	0 to 1000	(none)	Sub GetItemCount (control As IRibbonControl, ByRef returnedVal)
itemHeight	getItemHeight	O	1 to 4096	150	Sub getItemHeight (control As IRibbonControl, ByRef returnedVal)
(none)	getItemID	O	Unique text string	(none)	Sub GetItemID (control As IRibbonControl, index As Integer, ByRef id)

Table A-16 *(continued)*

STATIC ATTRIBUTE	DYNAMIC ATTRIBUTE	REQ	ALLOWED VALUES	DEFAULT VALUE	VBA CALLBACK SIGNATURE
(none)	getItemImage	O	1 to 4096 characters	(none)	Sub GetItemImage (control As IRibbonControl, index As Integer, ByRef returnedVal)
(none)	getItemLabel	O	1 to 4096 characters	(none)	Sub GetItemLabel (control As IRibbonControl, index As Integer, ByRef returnedVal)
(none)	getItem↵ Screentip	O	1 to 4096 characters	(none)	Sub GetItemScreenTip (control As IRibbonControl, index As Integer, ByRef returnedVal)
(none)	getItem↵ Supertip	O	1 to 4096 characters	(none)	Sub GetItemSuperTip (control As IRibbonControl, index As Integer, ByRef returnedVal)
itemWidth	getItemWidth	O	1 to 4096	200	Sub getItemWidth (control As IRibbonControl, ByRef returnedVal)
keytip	getKeytip	O	1 to 3 characters	(none)	Sub GetKeytip (control As IRibbonControl, ByRef returnedVal)
label	getLabel	OR	1 to 1024 characters	(none)	Sub GetLabel (control As IRibbonControl, ByRef returnedVal)

Continued

Table A-16 *(continued)*

STATIC ATTRIBUTE	DYNAMIC ATTRIBUTE	REQ	ALLOWED VALUES	DEFAULT VALUE	VBA CALLBACK SIGNATURE
rows	(none)	O	1 to 1024 characters	1	(none)
screentip	getScreentip	O	1 to 1024 characters	(none)	Sub GetScreentip (control As IRibbonControl, ByRef returnedVal)
(none)	getSelected↵ ItemID	O	1 to 1024 s characters	(none)	Sub GetSelected ItemID (control As IRibbonControl, ByRef index)
(none)	getSelected↵ ItemIndex	O	1 to 1024 characters	(none)	Sub GetSelected ItemIndex (control As IRibbonControl, ByRef returnedVal)
showImage	getShow↵ Image	O	true, false, 1, 0	true	Sub GetShowImage (control As IRibbonControl, ByRef returnedVal)
showItemImage	(none)	O	true, false, 1, 0	true	(none)
showItemLabel	(none)	O	true, false, 1, 0	true	(none)
showLabel	getShowLabel	O	true, false, 1, 0	true	Sub GetShowLabel (control As IRibbonControl, ByRef returnedVal)
sizeString	(none)	O*	1 to 1024 characters	12	(none)
supertip	getSupertip	O	1 to 1024 characters	(none)	Sub GetSupertip (control As IRibbonControl, ByRef returnedVal)

Table A-16 *(continued)*

STATIC ATTRIBUTE	DYNAMIC ATTRIBUTE	REQ	ALLOWED VALUES	DEFAULT VALUE	VBA CALLBACK SIGNATURE
tag	(none)	O	1 to 1024 characters	(none)	(none)
visible	getVisible	O	1 to 1024 characters	true	Sub GetVisible (control As IRibbonControl, ByRef returnedVal)

* The default value for the `sizeString` attribute (if the attribute is not declared at all) is approximately 12, but this varies depending on the characters used and the system font.

item Element

Table A-17 lists all of the static and dynamic attributes specific to the `item` element, as well as their allowed values, defaults, and callback signatures.

CROSS-REFERENCE **There is a detailed discussion of the `item` element in Chapter 7.**

Table A-17: Table of item Attributes

STATIC ATTRIBUTE	DYNAMIC ATTRIBUTE	REQ	ALLOWED VALUES	DEFAULT VALUE	VBA CALLBACK SIGNATURE
id	(none)	R	Unique text string	(none)	(none)
image	(none)	O	1 to 1024 characters	(none)	(none)
imageMso	(none)	O	1 to 1024 characters	(none)	(none)
label	(none)	OR	1 to 1024 characters	(none)	(none)
screentip	(none)	O	1 to 1024 characters	(none)	(none)
supertip	(none)	O	1 to 1024 characters	(none)	(none)

labelControl Element

Table A-18 lists all of the static and dynamic attributes specific to the `labelControl` element, as well as their allowed values, defaults, and callback signatures.

CROSS-REFERENCE **There is a detailed discussion of the** `labelControl` **element in Chapter 10.**

Table A-18: Table of labelControl Attributes

STATIC ATTRIBUTE	DYNAMIC ATTRIBUTE	REQ	ALLOWED VALUES	DEFAULT VALUE	VBA CALLBACK SIGNATURE
id	(none)	R1	Unique text string	(none)	(none)
idMso	(none)	R1	Valid Mso control name	(none)	(none)
idQ	(none)	R1	Unique control idQ	(none)	(none)
insertAfterMso	(none)	O1	Valid Mso control name	(none)	(none)
insertBeforeMso	(none)	O1	Valid Mso control name	(none)	(none)
insertAfterQ	(none)	O1	Valid control idQ	(none)	(none)
insertBeforeQ	(none)	O1	Valid control idQ	(none)	(none)
enabled	getEnabled	O	true, false, 1, 0	true	Sub GetEnabled (control As IRibbonControl, ByRef returnedVal)
label	getLabel	OR	1 to 1024 characters	(none)	Sub GetLabel (control As IRibbonControl, ByRef returnedVal)
screentip	getScreentip	O	1 to 1024 characters	(none)	Sub GetScreentip (control As IRibbonControl, ByRef returnedVal)

Table A-18 *(continued)*

STATIC ATTRIBUTE	DYNAMIC ATTRIBUTE	REQ	ALLOWED VALUES	DEFAULT VALUE	VBA CALLBACK SIGNATURE
showLabel	getShowLabel	O	true, false, 1, 0	true	Sub GetShowLabel (control As IRibbonControl, ByRef returnedVal)
supertip	getSupertip	O	1 to 1024 characters	(none)	Sub GetSupertip (control As IRibbonControl, ByRef returnedVal)
tag	(none)	O	1 to 1024 characters	(none)	(none)
visible	getVisible	O	true, false, 1, 0	true	Sub GetVisible (control As IRibbonControl, ByRef returnedVal)

menu Element

Table A-19 lists all of the static and dynamic attributes specific to the menu element, as well as their allowed values, defaults, and callback signatures.

CROSS-REFERENCE **There is a detailed discussion of the menu element in Chapter 9.**

Table A-19: Table of menu Attributes

STATIC ATTRIBUTE	DYNAMIC ATTRIBUTE	REQ	ALLOWED VALUES	DEFAULT VALUE	VBA CALLBACK SIGNATURE
id	(none)	R1	Unique text string	(none)	(none)
idMso	(none)	R1	Valid Mso control name	(none)	(none)
idQ	(none)	R1	Unique control idQ	(none)	(none)

Continued

Table A-19 *(continued)*

STATIC ATTRIBUTE	DYNAMIC ATTRIBUTE	REQ	ALLOWED VALUES	DEFAULT VALUE	VBA CALLBACK SIGNATURE
insertAfterMso	(none)	O1	Valid Mso control name	(none)	(none)
insertBeforeMso	(none)	O1	Valid Mso control name	(none)	(none)
insertAfterQ	(none)	O1	Valid control idQ	(none)	(none)
insertBeforeQ	(none)	O1	Valid control idQ	(none)	(none)
description	getDescription	O	1 to 4096 characters	(none)	Sub GetDescription (control As IRibbonControl, ByRef returnedVal)
enabled	getEnabled	O	true, false, 1, 0	true	Sub GetEnabled (control As IRibbonControl, ByRef returnedVal)
image	getImage	O	1 to 1024 characters	(none)	Sub GetImage (control As IRibbonControl, ByRef returnedVal)
imageMso	getImage	O	1 to 1024 characters	(none)	Same as above
itemSize	(none)	O	normal, large	normal	(none)
keytip	getKeytip	O	1 to 3 characters	(none)	Sub GetKeytip (control As IRibbonControl, ByRef returnedVal)
label	getLabel	OR	1 to 1024 characters	(none)	Sub GetLabel (control As IRibbonControl, ByRef returnedVal)

Table A-19 *(continued)*

STATIC ATTRIBUTE	DYNAMIC ATTRIBUTE	REQ	ALLOWED VALUES	DEFAULT VALUE	VBA CALLBACK SIGNATURE
screentip	getScreentip	O	1 to 1024 characters	(none)	Sub GetScreentip (control As IRibbonControl, ByRef returnedVal)
showImage	getShow↵ Image	O	true, false, 1, 0	true	Sub GetShowImage (control As IRibbonControl, ByRef returnedVal)
showLabel	getShowLabel	O	true, false, 1, 0	true	Sub GetShowLabel (control As IRibbonControl, ByRef returnedVal)
size	getSize	O	normal, large	normal	Sub GetSize (control As IRibbonControl, ByRef returnedVal)
supertip	getSupertip	O	1 to 1024 characters	(none)	Sub GetSupertip (control As IRibbonControl, ByRef returnedVal)
tag	(none)	O	1 to 1024 characters	(none)	(none)
visible	getVisible	O	true, false, 1, 0	true	Sub GetVisible (control As IRibbonControl, ByRef returnedVal)

menuSeparator Element

Table A-20 lists all of the static and dynamic attributes specific to the `menuSeparator` element, as well as their allowed values, defaults, and callback signatures.

CROSS-REFERENCE **There is a detailed discussion of the** `menuSeparator` **element in Chapter 10.**

Table A-20: Table of menuSeparator Attributes

STATIC ATTRIBUTE	DYNAMIC ATTRIBUTE	REQ	ALLOWED VALUES	DEFAULT VALUE	VBA CALLBACK SIGNATURE
id	(none)	R1	Unique text string	(none)	(none)
idQ	(none)	R1	Unique control idQ	(none)	(none)
insertAfterMso	(none)	O1	Valid Mso control name	(none)	(none)
insertBeforeMso	(none)	O1	Valid Mso control name	(none)	(none)
insertAfterQ	(none)	O1	Valid control idQ	(none)	(none)
insertBeforeQ	(none)	O1	Valid control idQ	(none)	(none)
title	getTitle	O	1 to 1024 characters	line	Sub GetTitle (control As IRibbonControl, ByRef returnedVal)

separator Element

Table A-21 lists all of the static and dynamic attributes specific to the `separator` element, as well as their allowed values, defaults, and callback signatures.

CROSS-REFERENCE **There is a detailed discussion of the** `separator` **element in Chapter 10.**

Table A-21: Table of separator Attributes

STATIC ATTRIBUTE	DYNAMIC ATTRIBUTE	REQ	ALLOWED VALUES	DEFAULT VALUE	VBA CALLBACK SIGNATURE
id	(none)	R1	Unique text string	(none)	(none)

Table A-21 *(continued)*

STATIC ATTRIBUTE	DYNAMIC ATTRIBUTE	REQ	ALLOWED VALUES	DEFAULT VALUE	VBA CALLBACK SIGNATURE
idQ	(none)	R1	Unique control idQ	(none)	(none)
insertAfterMso	(none)	O1	Valid Mso control name	(none)	(none)
insertBeforeMso	(none)	O1	Valid Mso control name	(none)	(none)
insertAfterQ	(none)	O1	Valid control idQ	(none)	(none)
insertBeforeQ	(none)	O1	Valid control idQ	(none)	(none)
visible	getVisible	O	true, false, 1, 0	true	Sub GetVisible (control As IRibbonControl, ByRef returnedVal)

splitButton Element

Table A-22 lists all of the static and dynamic attributes specific to the `splitButton` element, as well as their allowed values, defaults, and callback signatures.

CROSS-REFERENCE **There is a detailed discussion of the** `splitButton` **element in Chapter 9.**

Table A-22: Table of splitButton Attributes

STATIC ATTRIBUTE	DYNAMIC ATTRIBUTE	REQ	ALLOWED VALUES	DEFAULT VALUE	VBA CALLBACK SIGNATURE
id	(none)	R1	Unique text string	(none)	(none)
idMso	(none)	R1	Valid Mso control name	(none)	(none)
idQ	(none)	R1	Unique control idQ	(none)	(none)

Continued

Table A-22 *(continued)*

STATIC ATTRIBUTE	DYNAMIC ATTRIBUTE	REQ	ALLOWED VALUES	DEFAULT VALUE	VBA CALLBACK SIGNATURE
insertAfterMso	(none)	O1	Valid Mso control name	(none)	(none)
insertBeforeMso	(none)	O1	Valid Mso control name	(none)	(none)
insertAfterQ	(none)	O1	Valid control idQ	(none)	(none)
insertBeforeQ	(none)	O1	Valid control idQ	(none)	(none)
enabled	getEnabled	O	true, false, 1, 0	true	Sub GetEnabled (control As IRibbonControl, ByRef returnedVal)
keytip	getKeytip	O	1 to 3 characters	(none)	Sub GetKeytip (control As IRibbonControl, ByRef returnedVal)
showLabel	getShowLabel	O	true, false, 1, 0	true	Sub GetShowLabel (control As IRibbonControl, ByRef returnedVal)
tag	(none)	O	1 to 1024 characters	(none)	(none)
visible	getVisible	O	true, false, 1, 0	true	Sub GetVisible (control As IRibbonControl, ByRef returnedVal)

toggleButton Element

Table A-23 lists all of the static and dynamic attributes specific to the `toggleButton` element, as well as their allowed values, defaults, and callback signatures.

CROSS-REFERENCE **There is a detailed discussion of the** `toggleButton` **element in Chapter 6.**

Table A-23: Table of toggleButton Attributes

STATIC ATTRIBUTE	DYNAMIC ATTRIBUTE	REQ	ALLOWED VALUES	DEFAULT VALUE	VBA CALLBACK SIGNATURE
id	(none)	R1	Unique text string	(none)	(none)
idMso	(none)	R1	Valid Mso control name	(none)	(none)
idQ	(none)	R1	Unique control idQ	(none)	(none)
(none)	onAction	OR	1 to 4096 characters	(none)	Sub OnAction (control As IRibbonControl, selectedId As String, selectedIndex As Integer)
insertAfterMso	(none)	O1	Valid Mso control name	(none)	(none)
insertBeforeMso	(none)	O1	Valid Mso control name	(none)	(none)
insertAfterQ	(none)	O1	Valid control idQ	(none)	(none)
insertBeforeQ	(none)	O1	Valid control idQ	(none)	(none)
description	getDescription	O	1 to 4096 characters	(none)	Sub GetDescription (control As IRibbonControl, ByRef returnedVal)
enabled	getEnabled	O	true, false, 1, 0	true	Sub GetEnabled (control As IRibbonControl, ByRef returnedVal)
image	getImage	O	1 to 1024 characters	(none)	Sub GetImage (control As IRibbonControl, ByRef returnedVal)

Continued

Table A-23 *(continued)*

STATIC ATTRIBUTE	DYNAMIC ATTRIBUTE	REQ	ALLOWED VALUES	DEFAULT VALUE	VBA CALLBACK SIGNATURE
imageMso	getImage	O	1 to 1024 characters	(none)	Same as above
keytip	getKeytip	O	1 to 3 characters	(none)	Sub GetKeytip (control As IRibbonControl, ByRef returnedVal)
label	getLabel	OR	1 to 1024 characters	(none)	Sub GetLabel (control As IRibbonControl, ByRef returnedVal)
(none)	getPressed	O	true, false, 1, 0	false	Sub GetPressed (control As IRibbonControl, ByRef returnedVal)
screentip	getScreentip	O	1 to 1024 characters	(none)	Sub GetScreentip (control As IRibbonControl, ByRef returnedVal)
showImage	getShow↵ Image	O	true, false, 1, 0	true	Sub GetShowImage (control As IRibbonControl, ByRef returnedVal)
showLabel	getShowLabel	O	true, false, 1, 0	true	Sub GetShowLabel (control As IRibbonControl, ByRef returnedVal)
size	getSize	O	normal, large	normal	Sub GetSize (control As IRibbonControl, ByRef returnedVal)

Table A-23 *(continued)*

STATIC ATTRIBUTE	DYNAMIC ATTRIBUTE	REQ	ALLOWED VALUES	DEFAULT VALUE	VBA CALLBACK SIGNATURE
supertip	getSupertip	O	1 to 1024 characters	(none)	Sub GetSupertip (control As IRibbonControl, ByRef returnedVal)
tag	(none)	O	1 to 1024 characters	(none)	(none)
visible	getVisible	O	true, false, 1, 0	true	Sub GetVisible (control As IRibbonControl, ByRef returnedVal)

APPENDIX

B

Tables of Tab and Group idMso Names

This appendix is divided into three main sections covering tab elements, contextual tabs, and built-in groups. The first provides a table of the idMso identifiers for the built-in `tab` elements that are common across all three applications.

The second section of this appendix contains lists of the idMso identifiers for each of the contextual tabs, and is broken down by specific application. It might be helpful to note that the terms may differ by application.

The third and final section holds tables of the idMso identifiers for Microsoft's built-in groups that are available in each application. These tables contain the individual group names and their default tab. This will be an invaluable reference, providing a fast and easy way to locate the idMso you need.

As an added bonus, we've included these tables in the chapter download, so that you can easily search, copy, and paste the names to avoid typos. This file (`idMsoGuide_TabAndGroupElements.xlsx`) can be downloaded from the book's website at `www.wiley.com/go/ribbonx`.

Common Tab idMso Identifiers

Table B-1 lists all of the idMso identifiers for the built-in tabs that are present in Excel, Access, and Word. The applications are listed in columns, making it easy to identify whether the tab name changes between applications.

Table B-1: idMso Identifiers for Common Built-in tab Elements

TAB NAME	EXCEL	ACCESS	WORD
Home	TabHome	TabHomeAccess	TabHome
Insert	TabInsert	(none)	TabInsert
Create	(none)	TabCreate	(none)
Page Layout	TabPageLayoutExcel	(none)	TabPageLayoutWord
Formulas	TabFormulas	(none)	(none)
Data	TabData	(none)	(none)
References	(none)	(none)	TabReferences
Mailings	(none)	(none)	TabMailings
External Data	(none)	TabExternalData	(none)
Database Tools	(none)	TabDatabaseTools	(none)
Review	TabReview	(none)	TabReviewWord
View	TabView	(none)	TabView
Developer	TabDeveloper	(none)	TabDeveloper
AddIns	TabAddIns	TabAddIns	TabAddIns

Contextual Tab idMso Identifiers

This section of the appendix lists the idMso identifiers for the contextual tabs specific to each application.

Contextual Tab idMso Identifiers for Excel

The idMso identifiers for Excel's contextual tabs are as follows:

- `TabChartToolsDesign`
- `TabChartToolsFormat`
- `TabChartToolsLayout`
- `TabDrawingToolsFormat`
- `TabHeaderAndFooterToolsDesign`
- `TabInkToolsPens`
- `TabPictureToolsFormat`
- `TabPivotChartToolsAnalyze`

- TabPivotChartToolsDesign
- TabPivotChartToolsFormat
- TabPivotChartToolsLayout
- TabPivotTableToolsDesign
- TabPivotTableToolsOptions
- TabPrintPreview
- TabSmartArtToolsDesign
- TabSmartArtToolsFormat
- TabTableToolsDesignExcel

Contextual Tab idMso Identifiers for Access

The idMso identifiers for Access's contextual tabs are as follows:

- TabAdpDiagramDesign
- TabAdpFunctionAndViewToolsDesign
- TabAdpSqlStatementDesign
- TabAdpStoredProcedureToolsDesign
- TabControlLayout
- TabFormToolsDesign
- TabFormToolsFormatting
- TabFormToolsLayout
- TabMacroToolsDesign
- TabPivotChartDesign
- TabPivotTableDesign
- TabPrintPreviewAccess
- TabQueryToolsDesign
- TabRelationshipToolsDesign
- TabReportToolsAlignment
- TabReportToolsDesign
- TabReportToolsFormatting
- TabReportToolsLayout
- TabReportToolsPageSetupDesign
- TabReportToolsPageSetupLayout
- TabSourceControl
- TabTableToolsDatasheet
- TabTableToolsDesignAccess

Contextual Tab idMso Identifiers for Word

The idMso identifiers for Word's contextual tabs are as follows:

- `TabBlogInsert`
- `TabBlogPost`
- `TabChartToolsDesign`
- `TabChartToolsFormat`
- `TabChartToolsLayout`
- `TabDiagramToolsFormatClassic`
- `TabDrawingToolsFormatClassic`
- `TabEquationToolsDesign`
- `TabHeaderAndFooterToolsDesign`
- `TabInkToolsPens`
- `TabOrganizationChartToolsFormat`
- `TabOutlining`
- `TabPictureToolsFormat`
- `TabPictureToolsFormatClassic`
- `TabPrintPreview`
- `TabSmartArtToolsDesign`
- `TabSmartArtToolsFormat`
- `TabTableToolsDesign`
- `TabTableToolsLayout`
- `TabTextBoxToolsFormat`
- `TabWordArtToolsFormat`

Group idMso Identifiers

Like the contextual tab identifiers, this section is broken down by application to provide a listing for the group idMso identifiers. To make it easier to search these tables, we have listed the groups with their tab, in the order that the tabs appear on the Ribbon. Simply look up the tab name in the first column, and you'll find the name of the applicable group elements listed in the second column. Again, the items are in the order in which they appear, rather than alphabetical. You will also see a few groups repeated, as some groups appear on multiple tabs.

Excel's Group idMso Identifiers

Table B-2 lists all of the group idMso identifiers for Microsoft Excel, along with the tabs on which the group can be found.

Table B-2: Group idMso Identifiers for Microsoft Excel

TAB idMso	GROUP idMso
TabHome	GroupClipboard
TabHome	GroupFont
TabHome	GroupAlignmentExcel
TabHome	GroupNumber
TabHome	GroupStyles
TabHome	GroupCells
TabHome	GroupEditingExcel
TabInsert	GroupInsertTablesExcel
TabInsert	GroupInsertIllustrations
TabInsert	GroupInsertChartsExcel
TabInsert	GroupInsertLinks
TabInsert	GroupInsertText
TabInsert	GroupInsertBarcode
TabPageLayoutExcel	GroupThemesExcel
TabPageLayoutExcel	GroupPageSetup
TabPageLayoutExcel	GroupPageLayoutScaleToFit
TabPageLayoutExcel	GroupPageLayoutSheetOptions
TabPageLayoutExcel	GroupArrange
TabFormulas	GroupFunctionLibrary
TabFormulas	GroupNamedCells
TabFormulas	GroupFormulaAuditing
TabFormulas	GroupCalculation
TabData	GroupGetExternalData
TabData	GroupConnections
TabData	GroupSortFilter
TabData	GroupDataTools
TabData	GroupOutline
TabReview	GroupProofing
TabReview	GroupComments

Continued

Table B-2 *(continued)*

TAB idMso	GROUP idMso
TabReview	GroupChangesExcel
TabReview	GroupInk
TabView	GroupWorkbookViews
TabView	GroupViewShowHide
TabView	GroupZoom
TabView	GroupWindow
TabView	GroupMacros
TabDeveloper	GroupCode
TabDeveloper	GroupControls
TabDeveloper	GroupXml
TabDeveloper	GroupModify
TabAddIns	GroupAddInsMenuCommands
TabAddIns	GroupAddInsToolbarCommands
TabAddIns	GroupAddInsCustomToolbars
TabPrintPreview	GroupPrintPreviewPrint
TabPrintPreview	GroupPrintPreviewZoom
TabPrintPreview	GroupPrintPreviewPreview
TabSmartArtToolsDesign	GroupSmartArtCreateGraphic
TabSmartArtToolsDesign	GroupSmartArtLayouts
TabSmartArtToolsDesign	GroupSmartArtQuickStyles
TabSmartArtToolsDesign	GroupSmartArtReset
TabSmartArtToolsFormat	GroupSmartArtShapes
TabSmartArtToolsFormat	GroupShapeStyles
TabSmartArtToolsFormat	GroupWordArtStyles
TabSmartArtToolsFormat	GroupArrange
TabSmartArtToolsFormat	GroupSmartArtSize
TabChartToolsDesign	GroupChartType
TabChartToolsDesign	GroupChartData
TabChartToolsDesign	GroupChartLayouts

Table B-2 *(continued)*

TAB idMso	GROUP idMso
TabChartToolsDesign	GroupChartStyles
TabChartToolsDesign	GroupChartLocation
TabChartToolsLayout	GroupChartCurrentSelection
TabChartToolsLayout	GroupChartShapes
TabChartToolsLayout	GroupChartLabels
TabChartToolsLayout	GroupChartAxes
TabChartToolsLayout	GroupChartBackground
TabChartToolsLayout	GroupChartAnalysis
TabChartToolsLayout	GroupChartProperties
TabChartToolsFormat	GroupChartCurrentSelection
TabChartToolsFormat	GroupShapeStyles
TabChartToolsFormat	GroupWordArtStyles
TabChartToolsFormat	GroupArrange
TabChartToolsFormat	GroupSize
TabDrawingToolsFormat	GroupShapes
TabDrawingToolsFormat	GroupShapeStyles
TabDrawingToolsFormat	GroupWordArtStyles
TabDrawingToolsFormat	GroupArrange
TabDrawingToolsFormat	GroupSize
TabPictureToolsFormat	GroupPictureTools
TabPictureToolsFormat	GroupPictureStyles
TabPictureToolsFormat	GroupArrange
TabPictureToolsFormat	GroupPictureSize
TabPivotTableToolsOptions	GroupPivotTableOptions
TabPivotTableToolsOptions	GroupPivotTableActiveField
TabPivotTableToolsOptions	GroupPivotTableGroup
TabPivotTableToolsOptions	GroupPivotTableSort
TabPivotTableToolsOptions	GroupPivotTableData
TabPivotTableToolsOptions	GroupPivotActions

Continued

Table B-2 *(continued)*

TAB idMso	GROUP idMso
TabPivotTableToolsOptions	GroupPivotTableTools
TabPivotTableToolsOptions	GroupPivotTableShowHide
TabPivotTableToolsDesign	GroupPivotTableLayout
TabPivotTableToolsDesign	GroupPivotTableStyleOptions
TabPivotTableToolsDesign	GroupPivotTableStyles
TabHeaderAndFooterToolsDesign	GroupHeaderFooter
TabHeaderAndFooterToolsDesign	GroupHeaderFooterElements
TabHeaderAndFooterToolsDesign	GroupHeaderFooterNavigation
TabHeaderAndFooterToolsDesign	GroupHeaderFooterOptions
TabTableToolsDesignExcel	GroupTableProperties
TabTableToolsDesignExcel	GroupTableTools
TabTableToolsDesignExcel	GroupTableExternalData
TabTableToolsDesignExcel	GroupTableStyleOptions
TabTableToolsDesignExcel	GroupTableStylesExcel
TabPivotChartToolsDesign	GroupChartType
TabPivotChartToolsDesign	GroupChartData
TabPivotChartToolsDesign	GroupChartLayouts
TabPivotChartToolsDesign	GroupChartStyles
TabPivotChartToolsDesign	GroupChartLocation
TabPivotChartToolsLayout	GroupChartCurrentSelection
TabPivotChartToolsLayout	GroupChartShapes
TabPivotChartToolsLayout	GroupChartLabels
TabPivotChartToolsLayout	GroupChartAxes
TabPivotChartToolsLayout	GroupChartBackground
TabPivotChartToolsLayout	GroupChartAnalysis
TabPivotChartToolsLayout	GroupChartProperties
TabPivotChartToolsFormat	GroupChartCurrentSelection
TabPivotChartToolsFormat	GroupShapeStyles
TabPivotChartToolsFormat	GroupWordArtStyles

Table B-2 *(continued)*

TAB idMso	GROUP idMso
TabPivotChartToolsFormat	GroupArrange
TabPivotChartToolsFormat	GroupSize
TabPivotChartToolsAnalyze	GroupPivotChartActiveField
TabPivotChartToolsAnalyze	GroupPivotChartData
TabPivotChartToolsAnalyze	GroupPivotChartShowOrHide
TabInkToolsPens	GroupInkSelect
TabInkToolsPens	GroupInkPens
TabInkToolsPens	GroupInkFormat
TabInkToolsPens	GroupInkClose
None (Not in the Ribbon)	Group3DEffects
None (Not in the Ribbon)	GroupShadowEffects
None (Not in the Ribbon)	GroupDrawBorders

Access's Group idMso Identifiers

Table B-3 lists all of the group idMso identifiers for Microsoft Access, along with the tab on which the group can be found.

Table B-3: Group idMso Identifiers for Microsoft Access

TAB idMso	GROUP idMso
TabPrintPreviewAccess	GroupPrintPreviewPrintAccess
TabPrintPreviewAccess	GroupPageLayoutAccess
TabPrintPreviewAccess	GroupZoom
TabPrintPreviewAccess	GroupPrintPreviewData
TabPrintPreviewAccess	GroupPrintPreviewClosePreview
TabHomeAccess	GroupViews
TabHomeAccess	GroupClipboard
TabHomeAccess	GroupTextFormatting
TabHomeAccess	GroupRichText

Continued

Table B-3 *(continued)*

TAB idMso	GROUP idMso
TabHomeAccess	GroupRecords
TabHomeAccess	GroupSortAndFilter
TabHomeAccess	GroupWindowAccess
TabHomeAccess	GroupFindAccess
TabCreate	GroupCreateTables
TabCreate	GroupCreateForms
TabCreate	GroupCreateReports
TabCreate	GroupCreateOther
TabExternalData	GroupImport
TabExternalData	GroupExport
TabExternalData	GroupCollectData
TabExternalData	GroupSharepointLists
TabDatabaseTools	GroupMacro
TabDatabaseTools	GroupViewsShowHide
TabDatabaseTools	GroupAnalyze
TabDatabaseTools	GroupMoveData
TabDatabaseTools	GroupDatabaseTools
TabDatabaseTools	GroupAdminister
TabSourceControl	GroupDatabaseSourceControl
TabSourceControl	GroupSourceControlShow
TabSourceControl	GroupSourceControlManage
TabAddIns	GroupAddInsMenuCommands
TabAddIns	GroupAddInsToolbarCommands
TabAddIns	GroupAddInsCustomToolbars
TabFormToolsFormatting	GroupViews
TabFormToolsFormatting	GroupFontAccess
TabFormToolsFormatting	GroupFormatting
TabFormToolsFormatting	GroupFormattingGridlines
TabFormToolsFormatting	GroupFormattingControls

Table B-3 *(continued)*

TAB idMso	GROUP idMso
TabFormToolsFormatting	GroupAutoFormatAccess
TabControlLayout	GroupMarginsAndPaddingControlLayout
TabControlLayout	GroupControlAlignmentLayout
TabControlLayout	GroupControlPositionLayout
TabControlLayout	GroupFieldsTools
TabFormToolsDesign	GroupViews
TabFormToolsDesign	GroupFontAccess
TabFormToolsDesign	GroupDesignGridlines
TabFormToolsDesign	GroupControlsAccess
TabFormToolsDesign	GroupToolsAccess
TabFormToolsLayout	GroupAutoFormatAccess
TabFormToolsLayout	GroupMarginsAndPadding
TabFormToolsLayout	GroupControlAlignment
TabFormToolsLayout	GroupSizeAndPosition
TabFormToolsLayout	GroupPosition
TabFormToolsLayout	GroupLayoutShowHide
TabReportToolsFormatting	GroupViews
TabReportToolsFormatting	GroupFontAccess
TabReportToolsFormatting	GroupFormatting
TabReportToolsFormatting	GroupGroupingAndTotals
TabReportToolsFormatting	GroupFormattingGridlines
TabReportToolsFormatting	GroupFormattingControls
TabReportToolsFormatting	GroupAutoFormatAccess
TabReportToolsLayout	GroupMarginsAndPaddingControlLayout
TabReportToolsLayout	GroupControlAlignmentLayout
TabReportToolsLayout	GroupPositionLayout
TabReportToolsLayout	GroupFieldsTools
TabReportToolsPageSetupLayout	GroupPageLayoutAccess
TabReportToolsDesign	GroupViews

Continued

Table B-3 *(continued)*

TAB idMso	GROUP idMso
TabReportToolsDesign	GroupFontAccess
TabReportToolsDesign	GroupGroupingAndTotals
TabReportToolsDesign	GroupDesignGridlines
TabReportToolsDesign	GroupControlsAccess
TabReportToolsDesign	GroupToolsAccess
TabReportToolsAlignment	GroupAutoFormatAccess
TabReportToolsAlignment	GroupMarginsAndPadding
TabReportToolsAlignment	GroupControlAlignment
TabReportToolsAlignment	GroupPosition
TabReportToolsAlignment	GroupControlSize
TabReportToolsAlignment	GroupLayoutShowHide
TabReportToolsPageSetupDesign	GroupPageLayoutAccess
TabRelationshipToolsDesign	GroupRelationshipsTools
TabRelationshipToolsDesign	GroupRelationships
TabQueryToolsDesign	GroupQueryResults
TabQueryToolsDesign	GroupQueryType
TabQueryToolsDesign	GroupQuerySetup
TabQueryToolsDesign	GroupQueryShowHide
TabQueryToolsDesign	GroupQueryClose
TabMacroToolsDesign	GroupMacroTools
TabMacroToolsDesign	GroupMacroRows
TabMacroToolsDesign	GroupMacroShowHide
TabMacroToolsDesign	GroupMacroClose
TabPivotTableDesign	GroupViews
TabPivotTableDesign	GroupPivotTableShowHideAccess
TabPivotTableDesign	GroupPivotTableSelections
TabPivotTableDesign	GroupPivotTableFilterAndSort
TabPivotTableDesign	GroupPivotTableDataAccess
TabPivotTableDesign	GroupPivotTableActiveFieldAccess
TabPivotTableDesign	GroupPivotTableToolsAccess

Table B-3 *(continued)*

TAB idMso	GROUP idMso
TabPivotChartDesign	GroupViews
TabPivotChartDesign	GroupPivotChartShowHide
TabPivotChartDesign	GroupPivotChartFilterAndSort
TabPivotChartDesign	GroupPivotChartDataAccess
TabPivotChartDesign	GroupPivotChartActiveFieldAccess
TabPivotChartDesign	GroupPivotChartType
TabPivotChartDesign	GroupPivotChartTools
TabTableToolsDatasheet	GroupViews
TabTableToolsDatasheet	GroupFieldsAndColumns
TabTableToolsDatasheet	GroupDataTypeAndFormatting
TabTableToolsDatasheet	GroupDatasheetRelationships
TabTableToolsDatasheet	GroupSharePointList
TabTableToolsDesignAccess	GroupViews
TabTableToolsDesignAccess	GroupTableDesignTools
TabTableToolsDesignAccess	GroupTableDesignShowHide
TabTableToolsDesignAccess	GroupSharePointList
TabAdpFunctionAndViewToolsDesign	GroupViews
TabAdpFunctionAndViewToolsDesign	GroupAdpQueryTools
TabAdpFunctionAndViewToolsDesign	GroupAdpOutputOperations
TabAdpStoredProcedureToolsDesign	GroupViews
TabAdpStoredProcedureToolsDesign	GroupAdpQueryTools
TabAdpStoredProcedureToolsDesign	GroupAdpOutputOperations
TabAdpStoredProcedureToolsDesign	GroupAdpQueryType
TabAdpSqlStatementDesign	GroupViews
TabAdpSqlStatementDesign	GroupAdpSqlStatementDesignTools
TabAdpDiagramDesign	GroupViews
TabAdpDiagramDesign	GroupSchemaTools
TabAdpDiagramDesign	GroupAdpDiagramShowHide
TabAdpDiagramDesign	GroupAdpDiagramLayout

Word's Group idMso Identifiers

Table B-4 lists all of the group idMso identifiers for Microsoft Word, along with the tab on which the group can be found.

Table B-4: Group idMso Identifiers for Microsoft Word

TAB idMso	GROUP idMso
TabHome	GroupClipboard
TabHome	GroupFont
TabHome	GroupParagraph
TabHome	GroupStyles
TabHome	GroupEditing
TabInsert	GroupInsertPages
TabInsert	GroupInsertTables
TabInsert	GroupInsertIllustrations
TabInsert	GroupInsertLinks
TabInsert	GroupHeaderFooter
TabInsert	GroupInsertText
TabInsert	GroupInsertSymbols
TabInsert	GroupInsertBarcode
TabPageLayoutWord	GroupThemesWord
TabPageLayoutWord	GroupPageLayoutSetup
TabPageLayoutWord	GroupPageBackground
TabPageLayoutWord	GroupParagraphLayout
TabPageLayoutWord	GroupArrange
TabReferences	GroupTableOfContents
TabReferences	GroupFootnotes
TabReferences	GroupCitationsAndBibliography
TabReferences	GroupCaptions
TabReferences	GroupIndex
TabReferences	GroupTableOfAuthorities
TabMailings	GroupEnvelopeLabelCreate

Table B-4 *(continued)*

TAB idMso	GROUP idMso
TabMailings	GroupMailMergeStart
TabMailings	GroupMailMergeWriteInsertFields
TabMailings	GroupMailMergePreviewResults
TabMailings	GroupMailMergeFinish
TabReviewWord	GroupProofing
TabReviewWord	GroupChineseTranslation
TabReviewWord	GroupComments
TabReviewWord	GroupChangesTracking
TabReviewWord	GroupChanges
TabReviewWord	GroupCompare
TabReviewWord	GroupProtect
TabReviewWord	GroupInk
TabView	GroupDocumentViews
TabView	GroupViewShowHide
TabView	GroupZoom
TabView	GroupWindow
TabView	GroupMacros
TabDeveloper	GroupCode
TabDeveloper	GroupControls
TabDeveloper	GroupXml
TabDeveloper	GroupProtect
TabDeveloper	GroupTemplates
TabAddIns	GroupAddInsMenuCommands
TabAddIns	GroupAddInsToolbarCommands
TabAddIns	GroupAddInsCustomToolbars
TabOutlining	GroupOutliningTools
TabOutlining	GroupMasterDocument
TabOutlining	GroupOutliningClose
TabPrintPreview	GroupPrintPreviewPrint

Continued

Table B-4 *(continued)*

TAB idMso	GROUP idMso
TabPrintPreview	GroupPrintPreviewPageSetup
TabPrintPreview	GroupZoom
TabPrintPreview	GroupPrintPreviewPreview
TabBlogInsert	GroupInsertTables
TabBlogInsert	GroupInsertIllustrations
TabBlogInsert	GroupBlogInsertLinks
TabBlogInsert	GroupBlogInsertText
TabBlogInsert	GroupBlogSymbols
TabBlogPost	GroupBlogPublish
TabBlogPost	GroupClipboard
TabBlogPost	GroupBlogBasicText
TabBlogPost	GroupBlogStyles
TabBlogPost	GroupBlogProofing
TabSmartArtToolsDesign	GroupSmartArtCreateGraphic
TabSmartArtToolsDesign	GroupSmartArtLayouts
TabSmartArtToolsDesign	GroupSmartArtQuickStyles
TabSmartArtToolsDesign	GroupSmartArtReset
TabSmartArtToolsFormat	GroupSmartArtShapes
TabSmartArtToolsFormat	GroupShapeStyles
TabSmartArtToolsFormat	GroupWordArtStyles
TabSmartArtToolsFormat	GroupArrange
TabSmartArtToolsFormat	GroupSmartArtSize
TabChartToolsDesign	GroupChartType
TabChartToolsDesign	GroupChartData
TabChartToolsDesign	GroupChartLayouts
TabChartToolsDesign	GroupChartStyles
TabChartToolsLayout	GroupChartCurrentSelection
TabChartToolsLayout	GroupChartShapes
TabChartToolsLayout	GroupChartLabels

Table B-4 *(continued)*

TAB idMso	GROUP idMso
TabChartToolsLayout	GroupChartAxes
TabChartToolsLayout	GroupChartBackground
TabChartToolsLayout	GroupChartAnalysis
TabChartToolsFormat	GroupChartCurrentSelection
TabChartToolsFormat	GroupShapeStyles
TabChartToolsFormat	GroupWordArtStyles
TabChartToolsFormat	GroupArrange
TabChartToolsFormat	GroupSize
TabPictureToolsFormat	GroupPictureTools
TabPictureToolsFormat	GroupPictureStyles
TabPictureToolsFormat	GroupArrange
TabPictureToolsFormat	GroupPictureSize
TabDrawingToolsFormatClassic	GroupShapesClassic
TabDrawingToolsFormatClassic	GroupShapeStylesClassic
TabDrawingToolsFormatClassic	GroupShadowEffects
TabDrawingToolsFormatClassic	Group3DEffects
TabDrawingToolsFormatClassic	GroupArrange
TabDrawingToolsFormatClassic	GroupSizeClassic
TabWordArtToolsFormat	GroupWordArtText
TabWordArtToolsFormat	GroupWordArtStylesClassic
TabWordArtToolsFormat	GroupShadowEffects
TabWordArtToolsFormat	Group3DEffects
TabWordArtToolsFormat	GroupArrange
TabWordArtToolsFormat	GroupSizeClassic
TabDiagramToolsFormatClassic	GroupDiagramLayoutClassic
TabDiagramToolsFormatClassic	GroupDiagramStylesClassic
TabDiagramToolsFormatClassic	GroupShadowEffects
TabDiagramToolsFormatClassic	Group3DEffects
TabDiagramToolsFormatClassic	GroupDiagramArrangeClassic

Continued

Table B-4 *(continued)*

TAB idMso	GROUP idMso
TabDiagramToolsFormatClassic	GroupSizeClassic
TabOrganizationChartToolsFormat	GroupOrganizationChartShapeInsert
TabOrganizationChartToolsFormat	GroupOrganizationChartLayoutClassic
TabOrganizationChartToolsFormat	GroupOrganizationChartStyleClassic
TabOrganizationChartToolsFormat	GroupOrganizationChartSelect
TabOrganizationChartToolsFormat	GroupShadowEffects
TabOrganizationChartToolsFormat	Group3DEffects
TabOrganizationChartToolsFormat	GroupDiagramArrangeClassic
TabOrganizationChartToolsFormat	GroupSizeClassic
TabTextBoxToolsFormat	GroupTextBoxText
TabTextBoxToolsFormat	GroupTextBoxStyles
TabTextBoxToolsFormat	GroupShadowEffects
TabTextBoxToolsFormat	Group3DEffects
TabTextBoxToolsFormat	GroupTextBoxArrange
TabTextBoxToolsFormat	GroupSizeClassic
TabTableToolsDesign	GroupTableLayout
TabTableToolsDesign	GroupTableStylesWord
TabTableToolsDesign	GroupTableDrawBorders
TabTableToolsLayout	GroupTable
TabTableToolsLayout	GroupTableRowsAndColumns
TabTableToolsLayout	GroupTableMerge
TabTableToolsLayout	GroupTableCellSize
TabTableToolsLayout	GroupTableAlignment
TabTableToolsLayout	GroupTableData
TabHeaderAndFooterToolsDesign	GroupHeaderFooter
TabHeaderAndFooterToolsDesign	GroupHeaderFooterInsert
TabHeaderAndFooterToolsDesign	GroupHeaderFooterNavigation
TabHeaderAndFooterToolsDesign	GroupHeaderFooterOptions
TabHeaderAndFooterToolsDesign	GroupHeaderFooterPosition

Table B-4 *(continued)*

TAB idMso	GROUP idMso
TabHeaderAndFooterToolsDesign	GroupHeaderFooterClose
TabEquationToolsDesign	GroupEquationTools
TabEquationToolsDesign	GroupEquationSymbols
TabEquationToolsDesign	GroupEquationStructures
TabPictureToolsFormatClassic	GroupPictureToolsClassic
TabPictureToolsFormatClassic	GroupShadowEffects
TabPictureToolsFormatClassic	GroupBorder
TabPictureToolsFormatClassic	GroupArrange
TabPictureToolsFormatClassic	GroupPictureSizeClassic
TabInkToolsPens	GroupInkSelect
TabInkToolsPens	GroupInkPens
TabInkToolsPens	GroupInkFormat
TabInkToolsPens	GroupInkClose

APPENDIX

C

imageMso Reference Guide

This appendix contains a reference guide to `imageMso` and three tools (one for each application discussed in the book) that you can use to find the `imageMso` reference for the majority of controls available in the Ribbon. Keep in mind that although the lists provided in these tools are extensive, they are by no means exhaustive, and we can always hope that more controls are added.

We start by arming you with a method for manually obtaining the `imageMso` reference. It's a good thing to know and it fortifies your understanding of how things work. After covering those basic steps, however, we promptly move on to providing you with three handy tools that you can use to quickly scan through the images, grab the reference needed for a specific image, and then place the XML code for the button in the clipboard.

You'll also appreciate that the files are available in the companion files for this book. These can be downloaded from the book's website at `www.wiley.com/go/ribbonx`.

How to Get Your Own imageMso References

Let's begin with a trick to find the reference for an `imageMso`. Start by opening the Application Options window and clicking the Customize option. Then, from the Choose Commands From drop-down list, you can choose one of the built-in tabs (or show all commands) and then simply point to and hover over the icon of your choice. After a second or two, a help tip will appear, indicating the `imageMso` for that icon. Figure C-1 shows how this is done.

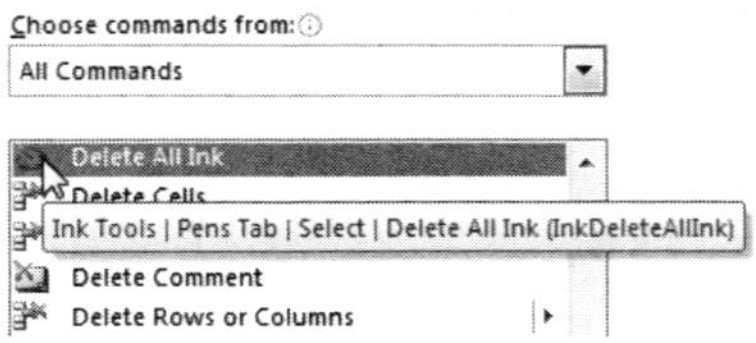

Figure C-1: Finding your `imageMso` reference

As shown in Figure C-1, by pointing to the Delete All Ink icon, you can determine that the `imageMso` for it is `InkDeleteAllInk`.

That is really all you have to do in order to get the reference you need.

The process is the same regardless of the application that you are using. The next section presents you with handy tools that list the `imageMso` references.

Your Own Reference Tool

In the previous topic, you learned how to manually look up the `imageMso`. Knowing where to go is definitely the way to go (if you forgive us the pun). Not only will you have a current and more accurate listing, but this enables you to be independent — you will no longer be reliant on Internet searches or someone else's tables to find out about some obscure `imageMso` that you so desperately want to use in your project.

However, if you'd like a simpler approach that provides most of the references with just a few clicks, you can use the handy tools that we've created and are generously providing to you in this book! It puts the `imageMso`s into galleries, which are grouped by a range of letters from A to Z, such as A–E, F–M, and so on.

Figure C-2 shows a sample of the reference for Excel. Files for Excel, Word, and Access are available with the download for this appendix. All you need to do is open the file (using Office 2007, of course) and it will display the icon images. Then, just click on the image and the XML code will be generated for that button.

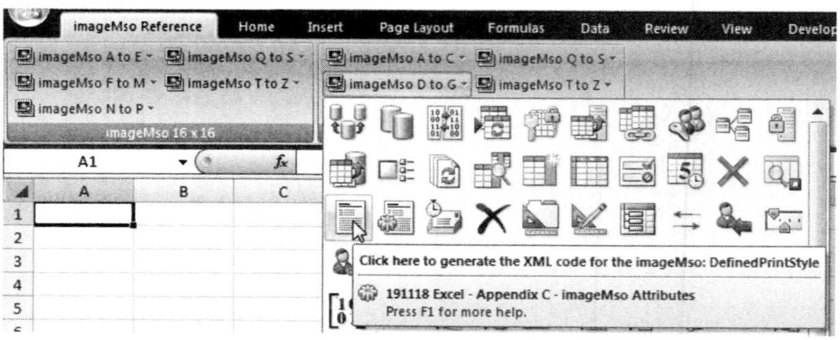

Figure C-2: imageMso reference workbook

Upon clicking the image of the `imageMso` you want, a message will be shown indicating that the XML code has been copied onto the clipboard, as shown in Figure C-3.

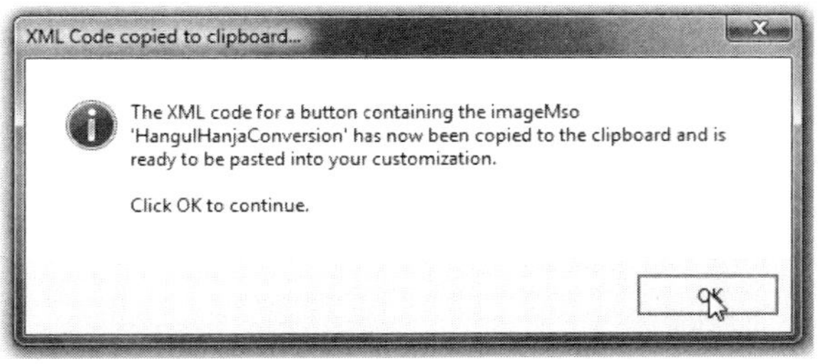

Figure C-3: Message box indicating that XML code has been copied to the clipboard

Once you click OK, the code will be in the clipboard ready for pasting. In this particular case, our tool will generate the following XML for a button whose `imageMso` is the `rxHangulHanjaConversion`. The code is as follows:

```
<button id="1_rxHangulHanjaConversion" label="rxHangulHanjaConversion"
imageMso="HangulHanjaConversion"/>
```

The XML code for our little tools is very long, running into tens of pages, so we will not display it here. However, the constructs are essentially the same as what we've been using. In addition, you can review the code to your heart's content after you download the files for this appendix. In fact, for Access, the XML code for the appendix tool is stored in a Word file, so you can open and inspect it directly without using Access and the VBE.

You'll notice and appreciate that we even added a shared callback to the buttons, which, when clicked, generate the XML code for the specific button. We even took that a step further, adding the code to the clipboard. Talk about going the extra mile! But that's what this book is all about; we want to make it as easy as possible for you to create Ribbon customizations.

NOTE **The Access tool loads the UI from the online download files this appendix. This is necessary because the Memo field cannot store all the data required to create the UI. Make sure this file is in the same location as the Access file; otherwise, the UI will fail to load.**

CAUTION **Because all three tools provided here use VBA code, you must place these sample files in a trusted location. If you don't, you must explicitly grant execution privileges to the tools so that they can perform their magic.**

APPENDIX

D

Keytips and Accelerator keys

The keyboard is probably the quickest way to perform an action in just about any application. This is mainly because you do not need to take your hands away from the keyboard to reach for the mouse in order to actually execute a command — you just keep on typing and never lose the positioning of your fingers.

This appendix provides a list of common keytips and accelerator key combinations that you can use to open some common dialog boxes, such as the Format Cells dialog box in Excel or the Font dialog box in Word.

You call either a keytip or an accelerator by pressing the Alt key or the F10 function key followed by the letters that make up the sequence. This is different from the shortcut key, which must be pressed simultaneously to get the desired result. Keytips and accelerator keys require that the keys be pressed in sequence, one after the other.

Keytips and Accelerator Keys for Excel

Using the keyboard instead of the mouse often represents a gain in terms of speed when performing an action. If you are someone who prefers to use the keyboard instead of the mouse, then you should be happy to learn that the Ribbon offers even more possibilities to quickly perform tasks without ever reaching for the mouse.

The list in this appendix is not exhaustive, but it gives you a sense of what is possible with accelerator keys (a legacy from previous versions of Office).

TIP **To remove the keytips or accelerator sequence displays, press either Alt, F10, or Esc.**

The Office 2007 keytips are covered in Chapter 11, and since they can easily be displayed, there's no need for a list. Accelerator keys, however, don't have a convenient display mechanism, so Table E-1 provides a list of command actions that can be accomplished using accelerator keys. As you review the list, you'll notice that many accelerator key combinations require more keystrokes than the corresponding shortcut combination. Keep in mind that shortcuts require all keys to be pressed at the same time, which can present a challenge for many users. Using keys in a sequence can be a welcome alternative.

Table D-1: Accelerator Keys for Excel/Access/Word 2003 Applicable to Version 2007

ACCELERATOR KEY	WHAT IT DOES	APPLIES TO
Alt → E → B	Opens the Office clipboard	Excel, Word, and Access
Alt → E → C	Copies the selection (same effect as Ctrl+C shortcut)	Excel, Word, and Access
Alt → E → E	Replaces (same effect as Ctrl+H shortcut)	Excel, Word, and Access
Alt → E → F	Finds (same effect as Ctrl+F shortcut)	Excel, Word, and Access
Alt → E → P	Pastes clipboard content over the current selection (same effect as Ctrl+V shortcut)	Excel, Word, and Access
Alt → E → R	Repeats an action (same effect as Ctrl+Y shortcut)	Excel and Word
Alt → E → R	Deletes a record (same effect as Del)	Access
Alt → E → T	Cuts the selection (same effect as Ctrl+X shortcut)	Excel, Word, and Access
Alt → E → U	Undoes an action (same effect as Ctrl+Z shortcut)	Excel, Word, and Access
Alt → F → C	Closes the open window	Excel, Word, and Access
Alt → F → A	Opens the Save As dialog box	Excel, Word, and Access
Alt → F → D → M	Sends to mail recipient	Excel, Word, and Access
Alt → F → I	Application options (previously workbook/document properties)	Excel, Word, and Access

Table D-1 *(continued)*

ACCELERATOR KEY	WHAT IT DOES	APPLIES TO
Alt → F → S	Saves	Excel, Word, and Access
Alt → I → M	Inserts a comment	Excel and Word
Alt → I → N → D	Opens the Name Manager dialog box	Excel
Alt → O → E	Opens the Format Cells dialog box	Excel
Alt → O → F	Opens the Font dialog box	Word
Alt → O → P	Shows the Paragraph dialog box	Word
Alt → T → I	Opens the Add-In Manager	Excel and Word
Alt → T → I → A	Opens the Add-In Manager	Access
Alt → T → L → T	Thesaurus (same effect as Shift+F7 shortcut)	Word (use shortcut in Excel)
Alt → T → M → V	Opens the VBE window (same effect as Alt+F11)	Excel, Word, and Access
Alt → T → O	Opens the Options dialog box	Excel, Word, and Access
Alt → T → S	Spelling grammar (compare with F7)	Excel, Word, and Access
Alt → V → P	View in Print Layout View in Page Break View object properties	Word Excel Access (in Layout or Design mode)
Alt →F → P	Opens the Print dialog box (same effect as the Ctrl+P shortcut)	Excel, Word, and Access

It is important to recognize that this list applies only to English versions of Office. If you are using a localized version of Office, you must use the localized accelerator sequence as well as the localized shortcut key combination. A shortcut key combination or accelerator sequence for English may perform a totally different action in another language.

APPENDIX

E

RibbonX Naming Conventions

To help you avoid confusion when writing callbacks in a VBA project, we devised an easy-to-follow naming convention for your RibbonX objects. When naming objects, you can, of course, follow your own whims — but when other people need to interpret your code, following a standard style can make life a whole lot easier for everyone. Additionally, naming conventions can minimize conflicts when sharing customizations or moving them to additional projects. Moreover, you'll definitely appreciate having used naming conventions when you later have to interpret and modify code that you wrote months or years before.

We do not expect you to blindly follow the recommendations laid out here. Rather, we are sharing our advice with the hope that it guides you to make prudent choices that not only make it easier to create customizations, but also avoid conflicts and make it a lot easier and less frustrating when it comes time to interpret and share your customizations.

How Our Naming System Works

The naming convention we devised is based on the Reddick naming convention.

NOTE **A description of the Reddick convention (RVBA) can be found at** `www.xoc.net/standards/rvbanc.asp`.

Our convention also includes parts from VBA and throws in the naming of attributes from the XML Schema for the Ribbon. Therefore, our naming convention includes an identifier for the Ribbon, the control, and the action to be invoked.

Thus, you when you have a button control and want to use the `onAction` attribute to define a callback, you would have something like this:

```
rxbtnDemo_click
```

This example consists of the following parts:

- **Prefix:** We have adopted the `rx` prefix to clearly identify code provided for Ribbon customizations and to differentiate it from all other code in the project.
- **Tag:** We have adopted the RVBA tagging system to tag Ribbon controls. The tag is very important because it tells users what the control/object really is. For example, a `checkBox` control in VBA would have the `chk` tag. When we translate this into our Ribbon naming convention, we add the `rx` so it becomes `rxchk`. In doing so, the VBA code clearly indicates that this checkbox comes from the Ribbon and not from a `checkBox` control within your VBA project (such as on a form).

CROSS-REFERENCE **Chapter 4 provides additional information about the Reddick VBA naming convention, including a link to the website.**

- **BaseName:** This is the description of the control itself. For example, you could have a Ribbon button and define its prefix and tag as `rxbtn`, but what does this button do? If it were a demo button you could name it `rxbtnDemo`, thereby conveying a clear meaning with the name.
- **Event suffix:** You already have a button, but what will happen when a user clicks it? This is VBA, so an event is triggered — specifically, the click event. In order to make life easier, we use the common VBA event suffixes to describe such actions. For example, if you have an `onAction` attribute attached to the previously mentioned demo button, the procedure should be named `rxbtnDemo_click`.
- **Shared event:** In the previous example, we have a click for the demo button. However, what if you wanted to share this event with other buttons? Or with other controls that have the `onAction` attribute? In this case, you would not be able to add the tag used for an individual event suffix; instead, you'd use a generic tag to indicate that the `onAction` attribute is shared among many different controls — for example, `rxshared_click`. This clearly indicates that the click is shared by many other controls that have an `onAction` attribute. However, the click event can perform different actions depending on the control that called it (as discussed in Chapter 5).
- **Repurpose suffix:** We mentioned earlier that we use event suffixes to match the VBA events. However, when you use a built-in control, you may want to repurpose its action using the `onAction` attribute. The `onAction` attribute returns a

`Click` suffix, so it would not be clear to a reader of your code (or maybe even to yourself after some time away from the project) that this is a built-in control being repurposed. In such cases, you use the `idMso` as the prefix and then the base name, followed by an underscore and the word `Repurpose` to make it clear that the built-in control is being repurposed. For example, `rxFileSave_Repurpose` means that the built-in `FileSave` control has been repurposed to perform some other action.

CROSS-REFERENCE **For a list of `idMso` names, see Appendix B.**

The naming convention that we adopted for the Ribbon and used in this book is certainly not an *International Treaty on Naming Conventions*. However, it is very appropriate for the scope of the book, and it provides you with an excellent jump-start on implementing a naming convention for the Ribbon XML code and callbacks handled in VBA or, for that matter, whatever language you decide to use for programming the Ribbon.

Naming Samples

Now that we've reviewed how the naming convention works, we'll provide a list of the common naming conventions and terms that you will come across while creating customizations

Table E-1 shows prefixes and tags for common RibbonX controls.

Table E-1: Prefixes and Tags for RibbonX Common Controls

PREFIX AND TAG	CONTROL REFERRED TO
rxbox	box
rxbtn	button
rxbgrp	buttonGroup
rxcbo	comboBox
rxchk	checkBox
rxcmd	command
rxctl	control
rxdd	dropDown
rxdmnu	dynamicMenu
rxgal	gallery
rxgrp	group
rxitem	item

Continued

Table E-1 *(continued)*

PREFIX AND TAG	CONTROL REFERRED TO
rxlctl	labelControl
rxmnu	menu
rxmsep	menuSeparator
rxrib	RibbonX
rxsbtn	splitButton
rxsep	separator
rxtab	tab
rxtgl	toggleButton
rxtxt	editBox

Table E-1 gives you the prefixes and tags for common controls. You also need to name callbacks to be handled through the use of common attributes in the Ribbon. Table E-2 follows our naming conventions and provides names for common callback base signatures, and explains where they are used. We do not include the base name, as you will determine the base name depending on what the control will actually do (something you decide when programming the Ribbon).

As you are reviewing the table, keep in mind that most of the events are available to multiple controls and objects. To provide familiar examples, we've incorporated the base name for common controls, such as `btn` and `tgl`, into the list of signatures. As explained in the second column, you merely replace `btn` with the appropriate base, so for the `onAction` event of a `comboBox`, you would write `rxcbo_Click`.

Table E-2: Naming Convention for Common RibbonX Callback Attributes

CALLBACK BASE SIGNATURE	RIBBONX ATTRIBUTE REFERRED TO
rxbtn_click	Refers to the `onAction` attribute of a button. Change "`btn`" for the other control prefixes to refer to them.
rxbtn_getEnabled	Refers to the `getEnabled` attribute of a button. Change "`btn`" for the other control prefixes to refer to them.
rxbtn_getImage	Refers to the `getImage` attribute of a button. Change "`btn`" for the other control prefixes to refer to them.

Table E-2 *(continued)*

CALLBACK BASE SIGNATURE	RIBBONX ATTRIBUTE REFERRED TO
rxbtn_getKeytip	Refers to the `getKeytip` attribute of a button. Change "`btn`" for the other control prefixes to refer to them.
rxbtn_getLabel	Refers to the `getLabel` attribute of a button. Change "`btn`" for the other control prefixes to refer to them.
rxbtn_getScreentip	Refers to the `getScreentip` attribute of a button. Change "`btn`" for the other control prefixes to refer to them.
rxbtn_getSupertip	Refers to the `getSupertip` attribute of a button. Change "`btn`" for the other control prefixes to refer to them.
rxbtn_getVisible	Refers to the `getVisible` attribute of a button. Change "`btn`" for the other control prefixes to refer to them.
rxFileSave_repurpose	Refers to repurposing a built-in control using the `onAction` attribute. In this case, we're repurposing the `FileSave` command.
rxIRibbonUI_onLoad	Refers to the `onLoad` event for setting the `Ribbon` object
rxMacroName.ObjectName	Refers to the use of macros in MS Access to add functionality to controls
rxshared_getLabel	Refers to a shared callback among any control that has a `getLabel` attribute. This is expanded to other objects – for example, `rxshared_click`.
rxtgl_getPressed	Refers to the `getPressed` attribute for a pressable `toggleButton`. Change "`tgl`" for the other control prefixes to refer to them, such as a `checkBox`.

Finally, Table E-3 shows the last set of naming conventions for the Ribbon. It lists the names for shared namespaces.

Table E-3: Naming Convention for Shared Namespaces and Shared Controls

SHARED NAMESPACES	REFERS TO
nsQa	Refers to the local name in a shared namespace environment and is incremental. Thus, `nsQa` refers to the first local name; `nsQb` refers to the second, and so on.
nsQaShared	Refers to the actual namespace being shared and is also incremental along the `nsQ` prefix
rxbtnnsQaShared_Click	Refers to a shared click in a shared namespace environment. Note that the callback can be placed within whichever AddIn shares the same namespace.

APPENDIX

F

Where to Find Help

One of the biggest challenges confronting anyone attempting to learn a new skill is what to do once you have worked through all of the material in the course or book. While we have attempted to make this text as complete as possible, we recognize that you may want to do things which were not covered here.

This appendix is dedicated to giving you additional resources to help further your development. The resources contained in these pages are all free, and many are hosted by volunteers and MVPs. Keep in mind that the lists are essentially snapshots, so some will disappear or become lost in the multitudes as new sites emerge; and although we cannot vouch for the content of the sites, we are confident enough to recommend them for reference material — at this time.

Websites with RibbonX Information

While websites offering help with VBA are too numerous to cover, the number of sites with RibbonX-related information is just beginning to burgeon. Table F-1 lists a few of the sites that are currently recognized as providing credible information.

Table F-1: Selected Websites with RibbonX-related Information

TARGET APPLICATION	SITE NAME	URL
All	MSDN Ribbon Developer Portal	http://msdn2.microsoft.com/en-us/office/aa905530.aspx
All	PSchmid.Net	http://pschmid.net/index.php
All	Office UI Overview	http://office.microsoft.com/en-us/help/HA101679411033.aspx
Excel	Excel Team Blog	http://blogs.msdn.com/jensenh/default.aspx
Excel	ExcelGuru.ca	www.excelguru.ca/blog/2006/12/01/ribbon-example-table-of-contents/
Excel	Ron deBruin (Ribbon)	www.rondebruin.nl/ribbon.htm
Excel	Ron deBruin (QAT)	www.rondebruin.nl/qat.htm
Access	Access Ribbon Customizations	http://office.microsoft.com/en-us/access/HA102114151033.aspx
Access	Access Team Blog	http://blogs.msdn.com/access/archive/2006/07/13/664757.aspx
Access	Access Freak	www.access-freak.com/tutorials.html#Tutorial05
Access	Avenius Gunter	www.accessribbon.com

Websites Maintained by the Authoring and Tech Edit Team

In addition to the RibbonX sites listed in Table F-1, one or more websites are maintained by each of the authors and technical editors who worked on this book. Although these sites are not necessarily RibbonX-specific, they offer a wealth of useful information, tips, tricks, and programming techniques. The team members' sites are listed in Table F-2.

Table F-2: Websites of the Authoring and Tech Edit Team

TEAM MEMBER NAME	SITE STYLE	ADDRESS
Robert Martin	Site	`www.msofficegurus.com`
Ken Puls	Site	`www.excelguru.ca`
Ken Puls	Blog	`www.excelguru.ca/blog`
Teresa Hennig	Site	`www.datadynamicsnw.com`
Teresa Hennig	Site	`www.SeattleAccess.org`
Oliver Stohr	Site	`www.access-freak.com`
Nick Hodge	Site	`www.nickhodge.cc.uk`
Nick Hodge	Blog	`www.nickhodge.co.uk/blog`
Jeff Boyce	Site	`http://informationfutures.net`

Newsgroups

Microsoft provides a user community in the form of Microsoft newsgroups. The newsgroups are heavily supported by MVPs, and are also visited from time to time by Microsoft staff as well, so this can be a great place to get answers right from the source, and from recognized experts. The Office-specific newsgroups can be accessed in a number of ways:

- Through Microsoft's Community website at `www.microsoft.com/office/community/en-us/default.mspx`
- Through Google's Groups interface, located at `http://groups.google.com`
- Using an NNTP newsreader such at Outlook Express

The most popular way to access Microsoft's busy newsgroups is to use an NNTP newsreader. Complete instructions for setting up Outlook Express to communicate with the newsgroups can be found at the following URL:

```
www.microsoft.com/windows/ie/community/columns/newsgroups101.mspx
```

TIP **Note an issue that arises when using Outlook Express as your NNTP newsreader if you attempt to use multiple computers. Because Outlook Express is installed locally and runs separate instances on each machine, you must sync two copies of the program in order to have the files on more than one computer. This issue can be avoided by using Mozilla's Thunderbird Portable client, which can be installed on, and run from, a USB flash drive. This essentially enables you to have your newsgroup client (complete with all the files) on any computer — even a public or shared system. Thunderbird Portable can be downloaded from the following URL:**

`http://portableapps.com/apps/internet/thunderbird_portable`.

Web Forums

Web forums are an alternative to newsgroups. They tend to have much richer formatting than the text-based interface of the newsgroups. Many sites also provide instant e-mail notification when someone replies to your questions, and some sites allow posters to upload full files to demonstrate the issue that they are trying to solve. A list of some Web forums is contained in Table F-3.

Table F-3: A Selection of Popular Web Forums

FORUM FOCUS	FORUM NAME	URL
RibbonX	Patrick Schmid's Office UI Forum	`http://pschmid.net/office2007/forums/index.php`
VBA	VBAExpress.com	`www.vbaexpress.com`
Excel	JMT Q&A Board	`www.puremis.net/excel/cgi-bin/yabb/YaBB.pl`
Excel	Mr Excel.com	`www.mrexcel.com/board2/`
Office	Office Experts	`www.theofficeexperts.com/forum/`
Access	UtterAccess.com	`www.utteraccess.com`

Index

Index

A

E

F

H

I

J

N

O

P

Q

S

U

V